HISTORY OF THE TANTRIC RELIGION

History of the Tantric Religion

An Historical, Ritualistic and Philosophical Study

N.N. BHATTACHARYYA

MANOHAR
2026

First published 1982
Second revised edition 1999
Reprinted 2025, 2026
First eBook edition 2025

ISBN 978-81-7304-025-2 (hardbound)
ISBN 978-93-6080-893-8 (eBook)

Published by
Ajay Kumar Jain for
Manohar Publishers & Distributors
4753/23 Ansari Road, Daryaganj
New Delhi 110 002

Printed and bound in India

Preface to the Second Edition

That the first edition of this work, published in 1982, was able to evoke the interest of the readers has been attested by the publication of its several reprints. In the present revised volume the formulations made in the earlier edition have been critically examined. Some of them have been discarded because the author feels that they were based on scanty evidence. But the basic conclusions have been retained and substantiated by fresh evidence. A few sections have been omitted and new ones added. The bibliography has been made upto date. In preparing the second edition the author was assisted by his daughter Dr. Parnasabari Bhattacharyya and his students, Sri Amartya Ghosh and Sri Ardhendu Roy. The author acknowledges his indebtedness to them. At the same time he wants to put on record his profound grief at the sudden demise of his esteemed friend Prof. Debiprasad Chattopadhyaya who was his constant source of inspiration behind this work. The author also thanks Sri Ramesh Jain of Manohar Publishers & Distributors for the interest he has taken in the printing and publication of this edition.

NARENDRA NATH BHATTACHARYYA

Joraghat
Chinsurah 712101
W. Bengal

Preface to the First Edition

The present work, as its name implies, proposes to present, in an historical outline, the genesis, development and structural analysis of what is known as the Tantric tradition of India. Its main purpose is to determine the exact place of Tantrism in Indian religious and philosophical systems and to find out the social and functional significance of certain Tantric ideas and their derivatives which have not as yet been absolutely obscured in the efflux of time.

Tantrism with its vast literature containing intricate ritualistic and theoretical details occupies a significant place in the religious and social life of India. But the subject is still an enigma to us, notwithstanding numerous works in this field, scholarly as well as amateurish. This has been due to the fact that there has hitherto been no attempt to interpret the essentials of Tantrism by detecting and analysing, in a historical sequence, the origins and development of the components by which it is constituted.

Earlier scholars relegated Tantra to a class of black magic, unworthy of study by a man of good taste, while the advocates of Tantra like John Woodroffe, Sibchandra Vidyārṇava, Panchanan Tarkaratna, Gopinath Kaviraj and others equated it with the totality of Hinduism and declared it to be the essence of the Vedas. (They were, however, inclined to think that for the purpose of interpreting Tantrism it was sufficient to remain confined to those thoughts and ideas which were in fact superimposed on its original contents). Most of the modern writers on this subject insist solely on its sexual elements, minimal though they are, compared to the vastness of the subject, and purport to popularise certain modern ideas pertaining to sex problems in the name of Tantra.

Thus the historical study of Tantrism has been handicapped, complicated and conditioned by the preoccupations of the writers in this field. It is perhaps inevitable, because the vision of the historian is always circumscribed by the dominant outlook of his own age. As Mircea Eliade had rightly observed:

> When one approaches an exotic principality, one understands principally what one is predestined to understand by one's own vocation, by one's own cultural orientation and that of the historical moment to which one belongs. This truism is of general application.

As a result, in the field of Tantric studies, we find the emergence of various theoretical approaches, each claiming to have explained all the intricacies of the subject in its own way. Among these, the traditional Indian approach finds no difficulty in equating the essentials of Tantrism with the Vedantic interpretation of the contents of the major Śaiva-Śākta schools. So far as the modern approaches are concerned, the principal one seeks to find certain norms in Tantrism with a pragmatic anticipation of the peculiar and manifold mental, emotional and spiritual problems of our times, as if these are intended to explore the obscure zones of the unconscious to which are attributed the problems of man's physiological, social, cultural and religious conditioning.

Scholasticism belonging to the former category, despite its inherent contradictions caused by the conscious and surreptitious, but often unsuccessful, attempts of the medieval commentators and their modern counterparts to convert Tantra into a kind of Vedānta, is however, intelligible. Followers of this line have a *locus standi.* Because of their complete dependence on the texts, saturated and overburdened though they are by superimposed elements, they have some sort of objectivity in their approach. And they are apparently justified when they equate Tantrism with the totality of Hinduism beacuse Tantric ideas are so inextricably blended with different aspects of the Hindu way of life and with the doctrines of various religious sects and communities that it becomes a matter of proverbial difficulty to separate the Tantric elements from the huge conglomeration of materials accrued in space and time.

The psychological approach, outlined above, seeking to explore the obscure zone of the unconscious with the Tantric key, has eventually resulted in the study of the so-called sexual elements found in the Tantras which have been interpreted by the traditionalists as 'purely symbolical' and by the others as 'appliedly symbolical'. According to H.V. Guenther, the sexual aspects of the Tantras are nothing but the corrective against the one-sided intellectualism and rationalism which is unable to cope with the problems of every day life. The symbolic *yuganaddha* points to the unique harmony and interpenetration of masculinity and femineity. Bi-sexuality is inherent in all beings and this aspect has to be exercised in order to understand the truth of one's own nature. Sexual partnership is therefore the best expression for the most intimate relation between the two opposites. For the man, woman is the material object of concentration, a goddess for meditation and a symbolic truth for comprehension.

Such rationalizations of Tantric sexual elements are basically subjective, the interpretations being in all cases largely conditioned by their author's outlook and approach. Anyone working on Tantrism cannot ignore the sexual elements, but difficulty arises when the entire Tantric tradition is superimposed on these elements, even by scholars of the rank of Giuseppe Tucci or Agehananda Bharati. Sole emphasis on things sexual has resulted in the publication of numerous books on Tantra containing glimpses of modern sexual psychology and burdened with erotic photographs of Konarak-Khajuraho tradition; in the development of the queer conception of modern Tantric art depicting varieties of copulative acrobatics; in the production of pornographic fictions sanctified with Tantric quotation; and in the emergence of a class of recent godmen or *gurus* giving spiritual sanction to all forms of vulgar and gross sensualities of their moneyed clientele. All this is due to the insistence on a 'misplaced reality' in Tantric studies, which even the most qualified scholars could not avoid.

Historically one has to admit that certain Tantric ideas and practices are evidently rooted in primitive sex rites based on the magical association of natural and human fertility. One should not fail to recall in this connection that such primitive sex rites contributed everywhere to the development of religious ideas and, in a broad sense, to the evolution of human thought as a whole. However, with the advent and popularity of the new religious doctrines like Zoroastrianism, Judaism, Christianity or Islam preached by distinguished individuals the Tantric or near-Tantric rites associated with earlier existing religious systems sank into oblivion. In India, however, under diverse historical conditions, these primitive elements survived and were given new forms and interpretations in accordance with the changing demands of time and taste.

In connection with the sexual elements of Tantrism, Debiprasad Chattopadhyaya has raised two important questions. What could be the ultimate material basis of Tantric *dehavāda* or body theory and the practices related to it and what was the course of development that this archaic outlook eventually underwent? He argues that the *dehavāda* and the cosmogony of Tantrism are but elabroations of the corollaries of a most primitive belief and that the Sāṅkhya philosophy was originally a development of the primitive proto-materialism which formed the substratum of Tantrism itself. The primitive empirical and analogical belief in the equation of earth and woman, of natural and human fertility, forming the infrastructure of numerous agricultural rites, revealing the mode of securing the material means of subsistence, invariably connects the mystery of nature with that of the human body, from which it transpires that the birth of the universe is the result of the same or similar process as the birth of the human beings.

The Tantric sex rites might have something to do with the Phrygian mysteries associated with the cult of Kubele or Cybele, the Eleusian mysteries observed in Greece and in the Hellenistic colonies, and those associated with the rituals of the Egyptian Isis and Osiris. Ideas similar to the primitive Tantric cosmogony may also be traced to the myths of the vegetative cycles current in Western Asia and the Mediterranean and Aegean region which were clustered around a great goddess and her young subordinate male partner—the Devī and her Bhairava of the Tantric tradition. The psychophysical personality of the goddess was perhaps attributed to the woman of flesh and blood whose energy was thought of, as it were, to be transmited into the psychic centres or planes of consciousness of the aspirant impersonating her male partner, thus calling forth a new orientation to the earlier concept of Indian Yoga. Primitive cosmogonic myths connected with the equally primitive Mother Goddesses found legendary and literary expressions in works like Kālidāsa's *Kumārasambhava* and subsequently in the Devī oriented Purāṇas.

But the ideas of immaculate conception, the goddess creating out of her own self Brahmā, Viṣṇu and Śiva and dividing herself in parts bringing forth the world through union with them and such other legends were hardly found suitable for an advanced Tantric understanding of cosmogonical problems. Most of the schools of Indian philosophy hold that every real entity is a cause and also an effect, but the first cause as an effect has no cause, and as such it is no effect. The Buddhists, Jains, Sāṅkhyas and Mīmāṃsakas were basically atheistic. They held that if God might be regarded as a free agent he could not have the desire to create, and if taken as an agent under bondage he could not have the capacity to create. On the other hand the non-theistic Vedānta schools held that the cause alone was real and its apparent transformation in the form of the effect was only an illusion. It was thus extremely difficult for the ancient and medieval exponents of Tantrism to lead the pattern of progress from crude unconnected notions to more refined ideas and broader views demonstrating the process of a steady but multifarious advance from a concrete physical principle to the abstract, ritualistic, theistic, atheistic, physiological and psychological world views variously upheld by different schools and sects.

In primitive Tantric cosmogony woman as the mother of the race was considered essentially to be the life producer. Her organs and attributes had been the life-giving symbols *par excellence.* The concept of *yonī* i.e. female organ or female womb, as the first principle (cf. the list of cosmogonical theories in the *Śvetāśvatara Upaniṣad*) found its best theoretical expression in the Sāṅkhya concept of Prakṛti or Pradhāna, the material as well as the female principle of creation, the substratum of the earlier Tantras. But under diverse historical conditions Tantrism eventually came under the Vedantic fold. The Buddhist Tantras, owing to their affiliation with the philosophical tenets of Śūnyavāda and Vijñānavāda, upheld certain world views, which were akin to the Vedantic formulations. Secondly, with the progress of time the Sāṅkhya, which provided the substratum of the earlier Tantras, lost much of its original contents which were replaced by purely Vedantic accretions.

The Vedantic orientation of later Tantric cosmogony gave rise to numerous anomalies and contradictions by which the medieval Tantric texts and commentaries are pronouncedly characterized. The purely illusory position of the world, as suggested by the absolute non-dualistic form of Vedānta on the basis of the queer logic that the cause alone is real and that its apparent transformation in the form of effect is only an illusion, created much confusion among the Tantrics who believed in an organic psycho-physical process of creation in which qualities as were common to the cause and its effects were stressed. It was also anomalous to establish the Tantric dogma of the static and vibrating aspects of Śakti in terms either of the transformation (*pariṇāma*) or of the transfiguration (*vivarta*) of *brahman.*

Indian philosophical tradition in the language of Eliade, speaks of the 'conditionings' of man in space and time resulting from his temporality. It is categorically stated that man is a fettered being and that his purpose in life is to get rid of all fetters and attain *mokṣa* or liberation. In accordance with the established norms followed by different schools of thought, the Tantric schools also speak about the problem of human bondage and suggest various means of liberation. According to W.V. Evans-Wentz, the Buddhist Tantras represent 'a philosophy of knowledge, a system of meditation which will produce the power of concentrating the mind upon anything whatsoever and an art of living which will enable one to utilise each activity (of body, speech and mind) as an aid of the path of liberation.' The same is also said in regard to the Hindu Tantras by eminent authorities.

But Tantrism was not basically a *mokṣa-śāstra* or science of the liberation of soul, notwithstanding conscious and deliberate attempts to convert it into the same. Tantrism was in fact an attitude towards life, a distinct outlook or viewpoint, that had permeated all forms or mental, intellectual and cultural activities of the peoples of India throughout the ages, and as such its association with different religious and philosophical ideas was natural. But it was more than a mere religious system or stream or undercurrent. Its intimate association with the practical aspects of life is proved by the emphasis it attached to the arts of agriculture, metallurgy, manual and technical labour, chemical sciences, physiology, embryolgy and medicine. The sociological viewpoints expressed in the Tantras were in virtual opposition to those upheld by the Smārta -Puranic tradition. It was a form of knowledge pertaining to different walks of human activities, functioning as a parallel tradition with that of the dominant and sophisticated class and standing in reciprocal relation with the latter by way of influencing and getting influenced.

The intimate connection of Tantrism with different forms of Indian religious systems makes it imperative that the study of the subject should be made in terms of and with reference to the systems to which it is involved. Thus the history of Tantrism should also be in one sense the history of Indian religious systems. There are two sets of religious beliefs and ideas in India, one represented by the dominant class and the other by the masses. To the former category belong the so-called higher religions, viz., Brahmanism, Buddhism and Jainism. These are basically atheistic and share in common absolute dependence on the doctrine of *karma* and rebirth. To characterise Brahmanism as atheistic may appear to be a bizarre conclusion, but it appears to be justified in view of the fact that all the major Brahmanical philosophical systems, with the exception of the later Nyāya-Vaiśeṣikas, hold that the concept of God is an illusion, a subjective error, given the status of objective truth. This anti-theism is doubly substantiated by the sole insistence on *karma* and rebirth on which God can have no control logically.

Such an approach cannot, however, inspire the imagination of the common people who need a personal god, supposed to look after them, help them in their struggle for existence, ignore their lapses and bestow grace when it is needed. This popular sentiment gave rise to the cult of *bhakti* or devotion to a personal god. This cult of *bhakti* found expression through innumerable local and tribal deities, no question whether crude or refined. In course of time, these deities were grouped according to their nature and temperament and became either identified or associated with the supreme beings of what came to be known later as *pañcopāsanā* or the five major forms of devotional religious systems, and also made their way into Buddhism and Jainism. A large number of such deities from the said systems and also from Mahāyāna Buddhism had a reorientation in Tantrism.

The purpose of the present work has already been stated above. Here the contents of Tantrism have been enumerated and ayalysed with a sense of historical enquiry. I do not claim to throw any new light on Tantrism or to suggest any new interpretation or to give any wider dimension to its study. I have only sought to help my readers to get acquained with different aspects of Tantrism, its vastness and intricacies, its heterogenous and contradictory elements, and to outline the historical processes through which this conglomeration has been accumulated in space and time. Any historical study of Tantrism, as a I have pointed out earlier, is not possible by ignoring the general background of the Indian religious systems with which it is inextricably blended. The readers of this book are therefore expected also to be acquainted with the major aspects of various religious systems which have characterized the history of India throughout the ages.

This unusually big preface should be taken not as the summary of the contents of this book, but as a reflection of my own impression resulting from the study of Tantrism and allied systems. Pedantic terms could not have always been avoided, but a very useful glossary of Tantric technical terms with reference to the texts and commentaries has been added. I crave the indulgence of my sympathetic readers for the mistakes and blemishes that must have crept into this work. I express my deep feeling of gratitude to the memory of the late Kālikānanda Avadhūta of Chinsurah, a well known Tantric teacher, though very much unusually critical and sceptic in regard to his own creed, from whom I was able to clarify many difficult points, especially those pertaining to the so-called Tantric secret rituals. My thanks are also due to Prof. Pranab Roy who has helped me in many ways, to Mrs. J. Mansingh of Delhi who has gone through every page of the typescript and suggested various improvements, to Sri Amalesh Majumdar who has prepared the index, to the University Grants Commission for giving some financial assistance and finally to Ramesh Jain of Manohar Publishers & Distributors for the sincere interest he has taken in publishing this work.

Dept. of Ancient Indian History and Culture
Calcutta University
51/12 Hazra Road
Calcutta 700019

NARENDRA NATH BHATTACHARYYA

Contents

1

Introduction

What is Tantra?

Kullukabhaṭṭa in his commentary on Manu II. 1. divided traditional knowledge into Vedic and Tantric, and this division was not baseless. Like the Veda, Tantra was primarily the way or means to understand the mysteries of life and universe, somewhat akin to the old Pythagorean concept of 'philosophy' which was 'contemplation, study and knowledge of nature'. At the earlier stage of history, Tantra arose as the sum total of man's knowledge of the objective world around him. It was a way of life that sought the significance of knowledge, not in the realisation of an illusory absolute, but in the day-to-day activities of men, in the simple facts of life like agriculture, cattlebreeding, distillation, iron-smelting, etc., and in experimental sciences like alchemy, medicine, embryology, physiology and so forth, with a deliberate theoretical orientation that the structures of the microcosm and the macrocosm are identical and that the key to the knowledge of nature is to be found in the body.

Etymological interpretations of the word Tantra, as found in the ancient texts, clearly and conclusively point out that originally Tantra had no special religious or metaphysical significance. In the Vedic texts the word Tantra occurs in the sense of a loom.[1] The Śrautasūtras use the word in the sense of a process of work containing many parts and in that of an act serving the purpose of many other acts.[2] The latter interpretation is confirmed in the Mīmāṃsā tradition[3] according to which Tantra is an act-process—a method of doing or making something. In the *Mahābhāṣya*[4] the word Tantra signifies a branch of knowledge, while the writers of the sciences of polity and medicine used the word *Tantraniryukti* to mean 'canons', 'propositions', 'principles', 'expositions', etc.[5] The scientific treatises composed in India are generally known as Tantras; their sections and subsections also bear the same title. Any system or thought-structure was also known as Tantra. Śaṅkara used the term *Kapilasya-tantra* to denote the system expounded by Kapila, i.e. the Sāṅkhya philosophy and *Vaināśika-tantra* to denote the Buddhist philosophy of momentary existence.[6] Later writers too sometimes followed the tradition of Śaṅkara and treated the word as denoting a special branch of knowledge. Bhāskara-rāya referred to the Mīmāṃsā philosophy as *Jaimini-tantra* in his commentary on the *Devīmāhātmya.* Bhaṭṭoji in his *Tantrādhikārinirṇaya* had used the terms *pūrva-tantra* and *uttara-tantra* to denote the Pūrvamīmāṃsā and Uttaramīmāṃsā systems respectively. The word Tantra is derived from the root *tan* (meaning, to spread or propagate) the significance of which will be discussed later.

The etymological interpretations point to the fact that Tantra was a general term for any system serving as the guiding principle of any work and that the use of the word in a strictly religious sense was a later growth. In the religious sense Tantra first came to mean 'the scripture by which knowledge is spread' (*tanyate vistāryate jñānam anena iti tantram*). In the next stage it was defined as a class of texts 'which promulgates profound matters concerning *tattva* (theory, which later came to mean "pure knowledge") and *mantra* (practical means, which later came to denote "mystic sound")' and was therefore looked upon as a technical branch of spiritual knowledge (*tanoti vipulānarthān tattvamantra samanvitān*). Thus Tantra came to mean the essentials of any religious system and, subsequently, special doctrines and rituals found only in certain forms of various religious systems. This change in the meaning, significance, and character of the word Tantra is quite striking and is likely to reveal many hitherto unnoticed elements that have characterised the social fabric of India through the ages.

Veda and Tantra

It is to be noticed that although later Tantric writers wanted to base their doctrines on the Vedas, the orthodox followers of the Vedic tradition invariably referred to Tantra in a spirit of denunciation stressing its anti-Vedic character.

In the *Āgamaprāmaṇya* of Yāmunācārya it is stated that the Vedas do not support Tantric rites and that the Tantras are much in vogue among the low class people. In works like the *Deśopadeśa* and *Narmamālā* of Kṣemendra and in the *Bharatakadvātrimiśka* of the Jains Tantric rites are depicted as ridiculous and most detestable. The *Siddhānta-tantras* of the South are considered to be anti-Vedic in the *Vāyusaṃhitā* as quoted by Appaya Dikṣita in his *Śivārkamaṇidīpikā*. According to the *Varāhapurāṇa* (LXX.41; LXX.9, 53-5; cf. LX. 35-8) the Tantras were compiled to delude people fallen from the Vedic path. The *Kūrmapurāṇa* (Pūrva XII. 255-9; Upari XVI) also says the same thing and suggests that one should not speak to the Pāñcarātras and and Pāśupatas. According to the *Sāmbapurāṇa* (as quoted in *Vīramitrodaya*, Vol. I, p. 24) the Tantras are for the persons fallen from Vedic rites and afraid of Vedic penances. Aparārka has quoted passages from Smṛti texts to show that the followers of the Tantric way should be socially ostracised and that any act of social intercourse with them should be followed by expiatory rites (Com. on *Yājñavalkya*, pp.12-18). Several verses of Manu have been interpreted as referring to Tantric rites in a disparaging manner. Śaṅkara in his commentary on the *Brahmasūtras*, Puruṣottama in his *Bhāṣyaprakāśa* on Vallabha's *Anubhāṣya*, and Appaya Dikṣita in his *Vedāntakalpatarupārimala* have all sought to prove the unauthoritativeness of the Tantras on account of their anti-Vedic character.[8]

What is the need of Tantra when there is Veda? What is the need of Veda when there is Tantra ? Such questions are frequently found in the polemical writings of both the traditions and they are not without significance. Although later authors of the Tantric texts, and commentators on these texts sought to base their doctrines and commentaries on the Vedas, Tantra remained a separate branch of knowledge quite outside the pale of Vedic tradition. This was due to the fact that in the ideological conflict between the two traditions, the Vedic and the Tantric, the latter held its own, although many of its theoreticians, mostly Brāhmaṇas—those belonging to the elite class—surreptitiously or openly supported the Vedic tradition and fabricated Tantra in the Vedic line. In spite of all these, Tantra received a wide denotation and functioned as a parallel tradition incorporating within itself most of the living creeds from a certain period of Indian history. One of the causes of its survival as a parallel tradition was the adherence of the so called lower people to the Tantric way of life.

The Vedas, like the Tantras, consist of heterogeneous elements contributing to all forms of primitive knowledge, from the brewing of wine to the highest cosmogonical speculations. Subsequently, however, the Vedic language became obscure, the real meaning and significance of the original passages were forgotten, artifical and imaginary interpretations were invented and the basic contents overlooked. Eventually the Vedas came to be looked upon as a symbol of spiritual knowledge, a very sacred and unchallengable tradition not to be approached lightly, and a strong taboo for the ordinary people. Its study and interpretation were monopolised by persons belonging to the dominant class who denied the existence of any empirical knowledge in them, highlighted the illusions and stamped out the realities. It reached the extent that if a Śūdra ventured to go through the Vedas to acquire knowledge of his own profession he was liable to receive punishment.

The lacuna thus created in the field of material knowledge, the utility of which was denied in the Vedic tradition, was naturally filled by the Tantras which appeared as a parallel tradition. To the working people Tantra meant something more than a mere religious system. To them knowledge meant worldly knowledge, that which guided them in their multifarious practical and productive works, and the repository of these was the Tantras which supplied them the materials for achieving professional success and satisfaction.

But in the course of time, as we shall see later, Tantra also became class-oriented. Owing to the increasing rigidity of the hierarchial system and social exploitation the toiling masses became poorer and poorer and the number of literate persons belonging to the lower strata reached a marginal point. The texts were soon beyond their reach. Thus, they could not develop their professional skill and knowledge by going through the texts, because they had gradually been led to become illiterate. At the same time, and for the same reason, they could not record the results of their professional experiences which, in turn, prevented the formation of new scientific Tantras.

The Parallel Tradition

In the quest for the foundations and early development of Tantrism, we have to depend more on the parallel tradition itself as manifested in numerous non-Brahmanical and heterodox, scientific and technological treatises, regional, tribal, proletarian, and popular cults, beliefs, and practices and on the broad background of the history of Indian thought in general, rather than on surviving Tantric texts themselves which, valuable though they are in many respects, are in their present form burdened with superimposed elements and thus bear only a parochial and limited significance.

In spite of all sorts of Brahmanical interpolations, grafting and handling, Tantra clearly rejects the *varṇa* system and patriarchy and, in the field of religion, all external formalities in regard to spiritual quest. These viewpoints are in virtual opposition to those upheld in the Smārta-Purāṇic tradition, and that is why the followers of this system have been condemned and various attempts have been made to blacken the Tantric ideals. The tradition of *varṇāśrama* was always patronised by the ruling class, even by the Buddhist, Muslim and British rulers who were theoretically opposed to it. A critical student of religious history cannot fail to observe that certain forms of religious systems, especially those which uphold and justify a social system based on the principles of inequality and oppression, have been given massive support by the ruling class in all ages.

But the religion of the dominant class which created a pantheon in each system, in terms of the existing social hierarchy with its supreme being as the acknowledged overlord and allied deities as subordinates, substantiated also by a philosophy of illusion, had little to do with the greater section of the masses who subscribed to a different tradition: a tradition consisting of popular beliefs, cults, and rituals; liberal social ideals; and an ethics and philosophy that gave a real meaning to life. This tradition was enriched by a host of teachers and religious leaders in different ages and sometimes created new forms of religion which were basically protestant and liberal. It also happened that some of these systems became class-oriented in later times as we find in the case of Buddhism—the tribal, low-born (*vṛṣala*) Buddha, in time, became a Kṣatriya, a *cakravartin*, a universal monarch.

The five great Tantric teachers, regarded in the Nātha tradition as Ādi-siddhas, came from the lower section of society. Mīnanātha, also known as Matsyendranātha—identified by the Buddhists with Avalokiteśvara and by the Muslims with Machandali or Mochrā Pīr—was a fisherman. Gorakṣanātha, with whom such Tantric works as *Gorakṣasaṃhitā*, *Gorakṣasiddhāntasaṃgraha*, etc., are connected, was either a fisherman, or a *keotiya* or Kaivarta. Hāḍipā, or Jālandharī-pa, was a Hāḍi (or a net-holder according to another tradition) who served as a stable-sweep in the palace of queen Maināmatī of Pāṭikā. Of the traditional eighty-four Siddhācāryas, mentioned in the Tibetan texts, Lui-pa, Kaṅkāli-pa, Khaḍaga-pa, Kaṇha-pa, Thagana-pa, Kṣatra-pa, Tanti-pa, Kūsūli-pa, Māhila-pa, Rāhula-pa, Celuk-pa, Nirguṇa-pa, Bhikhana-pa, Kalakala-pa, Dhahuri-pa, Kambala-pa,

Sarvabhakṣa-pa, Putuli-pa and Anaṅga-pa were Śūdras, Ajogī-pa, Meko-pa, Bhali-pa and Udhari-pa came from the trading class, Mīna-pa and Gorakṣa-pa were fishermen, Camāri-pa was a leather-worker, Dhombhi-pa was a washerman, Acinti-pa was a wood-cutter, Kampari-pa was a blacksmith, Jogi-pa was a Ḍoma, Gundari-pa or Gorur-pa was a fowler, Carpari-pa was a Kahar, Kanthāli-pa was a tailor and Pancha-pa was a shoe maker. Yoginī Maṇibhadrā was a Gṛhadāsī or maid-servant.[9]

Many of these eighty-four Siddhas were reputed authors of Tantric treatises. The names of their works are recorded, and a few of the works have come to light. One of the most striking features of their teaching is that they asked their fellowmen to follow their own crafts honestly and sincerely and asserted that this would lead them to liberation. The upholders of the Sant tradition also came mostly from the non-privileged social strata. They preached their own ideas among the toiling masses and in doing so they were actively opposed by the upholders of the Brahmanical tradition. The existing religious systems, approved and upheld by the Purāṇas, and the severity of the social laws enumerated in the Smṛti texts, had no appeal to the toiling masses. This accounts for the rise of new cults and disciplines outlined by men of their *own* social standing or class. The main features of this new wave were the revival of primitive beliefs and practices, of course not in their original forms, a simpler and less formal approach to the personal deity, orientation of life by the instructions of the *guru* or preceptor, a liberal and respectful attitude towards women, and denial of the caste system.

From the earliest period to the end of the medieval age, Indian literature shows a set of ideas, and corresponding practices, different from the officially acknowledged norm, which have found expression in the beliefs and rituals of the Auls, Bauls, Sahajiyās, Kāpālikas, Nāthas, Lokāyatas and various other sects. All these come within the purview of Tantra. In all these systems, besides the aforesaid ethical and social values, supreme importance is attributed to the body (*deha, kāya*) because the clue to the mysteries of the universe is to be sought in those of the body. The Tantric maxim is : That which is not in the body is not in the universe. There are reasons to believe that the earlier Tantric view of life did not encourage such beliefs as the existence of the soul apart from the body, etc. The liberation of the soul was not conceived as *puruṣārtha* or the aim of life. Rather, we have the concept of *jīvanmukti* or liberation within the span of life in the form of the attainment of immortality.

On the basis of a description of Lokāyatikas, as found in the *Tarkarahasyadīpikā* of Guṇaratna (14th-15th century), Haraprasad Sastri has pointed out the intimate relation that existed between the Lokāyatikas, and the Kāpālikas, Sahajiyās, etc., of the Tantric tradition. Expounding the Lokāyata doctrine Guṇaratna said:

> At first the doctrine of the atheists is being stated. Many among the Brāhmaṇas and the low-born Yogins and Kāpālikas, who smear their bodies with ashes, are atheists. They do not believe in soul, virtues, etc. According to them the world is composed of four elements. Some Cārvākas consider space as the fifth element. According to them consciousness is produced, like the intoxicating power produced by the mixture of the components of wine, from matter (*bhūta*). Soul is like the bubbles of water. Body endowed with consciousness is the human being. They (the atheists) eat meat and drink wine, and, what is more, indulge in illicit sexual union even with mother. On a certain day in every year they assemble together and have sexual union with women.[10]

The last line is evidently suggestive of a collective sexual ritual reminding us of the Tantric *cakra* or *maṇḍala*. Sastri's remark in this connection is worth-noting:

> The influence of the Lokāyatikas and of the Kāpālikas is still strong in India. There is a sect and a numerous one too, the followers of which believe that *deha* or the material human body is all that should be cared for, and their religious practices are concerned with the union of men and women and their success (*siddhi*) varies-according to the duration of union. They call themselves Vaiṣṇavas, but they do not believe in Viṣṇu or Kṛṣṇa or his incarnations. They believe in *deha*. They have another name *sahaja* which is the name of a sect of Buddhists which arose from Mahāyāna in the last four centuries of their existence in India.[11]

In fact every religious system in India maintains a parallel tradition different from and opposed to the one supported and patronised by the dominant class. All known forms of Indian religion have Tantras and Tantric rites which prove that in spite of all that was said against it this parallel tradition had a special potency which was able to influence the contents of the major religious systems of India and even to create new religious systems like Śāktism under Hinduism and Vajrayāna under Buddhism. Certain sects of the Pāñcarātras, Gāṇapatyas, Pāśupatas were direct creations of this parallel tradition, as we shall see later.

Because of its original association with the simpler peoples, popular cults and rituals became an integral part of the Tantric way of life. This brought the cult of the Mother Goddess and the fertility rites associated with its original conception into close relationship with Tantra. The magical rites performed to obtain greater fertility of land, which really underlay elaborate Tantric rituals, were not the creations of fancy or the fruit of leisure. Rather they served as a guide to action, as an illusory technique complementary to the deficiencies of real techniques. By this illusory technique, which consisted of the miming of an incident, or symbolical representation of a coveted object, primitive man thought he could secure the actual occurrence of what he desired. This was the basis not only of magico-religious art, but also of ancient drama, thematic songs and dances, rituals indicative of the efficacy of sound and symbolism of words, and so on—all that had characterised the earlier ingredients of Tantra.

'Pure Knowledge' versus Empirical Knowledge

The parallel Tantric tradition which was evolving since time immemorial as the philosophy of the masses, had a great metamorphosis when elements of the dominant section were imposed on it. It was distorted and its principles were remodelled so that they would conform to the philosophy of illusion. The scientific and materialistic traditions were relegated to background, and all references to technical and manual labour, observation and experiment, were divested of importance in the texts. This contempt for worldly knowledge was possible only because one section of the community lived on the surplus produced by another and withdrew itself from the responsibility of labour and hence from the obligtion of acknowledging the reality of the material world. It created the illusion of 'pure knowledge'—a form of transcedental wisdom in which world and worldly action had no place—and rejected everything that went against it.

This happened not only in India but in other parts of the world as well. In Greece, with the growth of the elaborate institution of slavery, the illusion of 'pure knowledge' became the driving force of philosophical speculation. Empirical knowledge on which Heraklitos laid so much emphasis and which was regarded by Demokritos as the power of man to achieve mastery over nature, was relegated by Plato to a kind of limbo, as the bastard knowledge of a slave. To Plato wisdom meant a knowledge not of nature but of a super-nature constituted only by ideas.[12]

In the *Laws* Plato organises society on the basis of slavery and, having done so, puts a momentous question: 'We have now made excellent arrangements to free our citizens from the necessity of manual labour; the business of the arts and crafts have been passed on to others; agriculture has been handed over to slaves on condition of their granting us a sufficient return to live in a fit and seemly fashion; how now shall we organise our lives?' A still more pertinent question would have been: How will our new way of life reorganise our thoughts? For the new way of life did bring a new way of thinking, and one that proved inimical to science. It was henceforth difficult to hold to the view that true knowledge could be arrived at by interrogating nature, for all the implements and processes by which nature is made to obey man's will had become, if not in fact yet in the political philosophy of Plato and Aristotle, the province of a slave.[13]

We do not know when and how this contemptuous attitude towards worldly knowledge began to gain ground in India. The genuinely earlier portions of the *Ṛgveda* knew neither caste-distinction nor contempt for empirical knowledge and its functioning in different spheres of life. Far from being looked down upon with contempt, arts and crafts were originally considered so important that Tvaṣṭṛ, the craftsman, was raised to the status of a powerful deity. The making of the world was conceived in terms of woodcraft, done as if by a carpenter's or joiner's skill.[14] In a Ṛgvedic verse the poet does not hesitate to proclaim that his father is a leech, mother a grinder and he himself a bard, and that they all jointly strive for cattle.[15]

But with the disintegration of undifferentiated tribal life and with the growth of the class or caste-divided society, this attitude began to change. This is illustrated by the fate of the Aśvins, the master-physicians. Their position was lowered and even their right of drinking *soma* in the assembly of gods was denied, probably due to their professional association with the so called lower peoples. In fact the work of physicians entails their association with all sorts of people, from a Brāhmaṇa to a Caṇḍāla, and it was not possible for them to follow the way of *varṇāśrama* which was introduced in the post-Ṛgvedic age and enforced in social life by the kings and the administration. This is why men of the medical profession were not given due recognition in the Smṛtis. The science of healing, to which a number of Tantras were devoted, was relegated to the class of *avidyā* or false knowledge. What is the need of medicine when disease is caused by the *karma* of the past life? This was the argument put forward by the upholders of 'pure knowledge'. Not only medicine but other branches of practical knowledge were looked down upon. According to the Dharmasūtras, the Vedas and agriculture are destructive of each other.[16] Manu says that even when compelled to follow the profession of Vaiśya, the third caste, the Brāhmaṇas and Kṣatriyas must avoid agriculture, because it is slavish and involves injury.[17]

The *Chāndogya Upaniṣad* contains an interesting story which, incidentally, throws light on the conflict between material knowledge and 'pure knowledge.[18] Śvetaketu, son of (Uddālaka) Āruṇi, being commanded by his father, repaired to a tutor and returned home after twelve years, quite confident of his knowledge of the Vedas. Then his father asked: 'Have you, O Śvetaketu, enquired of your tutor about the subject which makes the unheard of heard, the unconsidered considered and the unsettled settled?' In other words, he wanted to know whether his son had acquired any knowledge about the new-fangled concept of *brahman*, the aim of the so called pure knowledge. Śvetaketu's frank answer was: '*Verily my learned teachers knew it not. Had they known it, why should they have omitted to impart it to me?*' Evidently, the tutors of Śvetaketu meant empirical knowledge by the Vedas which they had imparted to their pupil.

Although from the Upaniṣadic period we come across the insistence on 'pure knowledge', as opposed to worldly empirical knowledge, by the intellectuals belonging to the upper strata of society, but since the country was vast and its development uneven, the cult of 'pure knowledge' had to face challenge from many quarters—from the adherents of the Lokāyata, Sāṅkhya, Nyāya-Vaiśeṣika, Mīmāṃsā, Jain and other schools. The Nyāya-Vaiśeṣikas developed the atomic structure of the universe which was regarded as the composite of eternal unalterable, causeless atoms and they reduced all composite objects to four kinds of the atoms—of earth, water, fire and air. The basic texts of this system, the *Nyāya* and *Vaiśeṣika Sūtras*, did not accept the existence of God. It was not until a subsequent period that the doctrines of the Nyāya-Vaiśeṣikas were changed into theism.[19] The Buddhists belonging to the Sarvāstivāda school—the Vaibhāṣikas and Sautrāntikas—who also accepted the atomic theory had challenged the doctrine of 'pure knowledge' upheld by the

Mādhyamika and Yogācāra schools, the foster parents of Vedānta.[20] The Mīmāṃsā school, which had a popular basis and which wanted to revert to the primitive undifferentiated way of life where the *Yajñas* could revive their original significance, challenged the Vedāntic view of 'pure knowledge' with the argument that if the world is produced from *brahman* which is free from all defects, then the world should also be defectless. Likewise *māyā* cannot be at the root of creation because there was no entity other than *brahman* on the eve of creation. This cannot be said that *brahman*, the only reality, has induced the unreal dreamlike *māyā* to create.[21] The Jains also postulated the atomic concept of the universe and with their 'unsettling logic' proved that the material world was eternal, without any beginning or end.[22] Most vital, however, was the challenge that came from the Sāṅkhya which, as the precondition of any philosophical enquiry, put forward a formidable law of causation according to which the effect was the real modification of the cause. The same thing which is explicit in the effect is implicit in the cause, and hence the cause of the material world is obviously nothing but matter.

Eventually, however, the champions of 'pure knowledge' succeeded in imposing their views upon other systems. They did this in several ways, the most effective of which was the fabrication of the texts. The process is clearly visible in the case of the Sāṅkhya. Because of its basic materialism the Sāṅkhya had become the most dangerous adversary of the champions of 'pure knowledge'. Śaṅkara declared the Sāṅkhya to be his enemy number one (*pradhāna malla*) and said that 'Kapila's doctrine not only contradicts the Vedas but also the sayings of those persons like Manu who follow the Vedic way' (*kapilasya tantrasya veda viruddhatvaṃ vedānusārī manuvacana viruddhatvañca*) and that 'in order to establish the sayings of Vedānta, systems like the Sāṅkhya and others are to be eradicated' (*vedānta-vākyāni vācakṣānaiḥ samyagdarśanapratipakṣabhūtāni sāṅkhyādi-darśanāni nirākaraṇiyānīti*).[23] That is why there was a conscious attempt to revise and recast the Sāṅkhya in the light of Vedānta. Vijnānabhikṣu, the confirmed Vedāntist, in his introduction to the *Sāṅkhyasūtra,* frankly declared that his purpose was to fabricate Sāṅkhya (*kālārkabhakṣitaṃ sāṅkhyaśāstraṃ jñānasudhākaram, kalāvaśiṣṭaṃ bhūyo'api purāyiṣye vaco'amṛtaiḥ*) and he actually did it by burdening the Sāṅkhya with Vedāntic elements. In order to reduce the Sāṅkhya into a form of Vedānta, Gauḍapāda, in his commentary on the *Sāṅkhyakārikā*, tried to establish that *puruṣa* was one and not many (*anekaṃ vyaktamekavyaktaṃ tathā pumānapyekaḥ*) evidently with a view to bringing the concept in relation to the Vedāntic idea of *brahman*.[24] The final triumph of 'pure knowledge' found its culmination through the Mahāyāna Buddhist logicians and the Vedāntists who proclaimed absolute idealism and considered the whole world of experience as completely unreal, an appearance, a mere network of unintelligible relations. They argued that things which were produced by concurrent causes were not produced by themselves and hence did not exist in themselves. They denied all possible sources of empirical knowledge and had only dreams and sense illusions to fall back upon.

The materialistic world-view of Tantra, in the same way, was rejected in favour of *a priori* principles smuggled into it. Although Tantra in its earlier stage opposed the Vedāntic philosophy of illusion and admitted the reality of the world and its evolution out of a material primal principle, the *prakṛti* of the Sāṅkhyas, the superimposed elements brought it into line with Vedānta. Thus Tantra came to mean the way of realising the true nature of *brahman*, and was conceived as a *mokṣa-śāstra*, i.e. a scripture meant for liberation from wordly fetters. Not only the followers of Tantra, but those of other quasi-materialistic systems as well—like the Jains, the Sāṅkhyas, the Mīmāṃsakas, the Nyāya-Vaiśeṣikas, etc., which came more or less close to a mechanistic conception of nature—could not free themselves from the influence of this concept of *mokṣa*. The aim of even medical science was thus directed towards the ideal of liberating individual souls from the bondage of physical existence.

Such ideas which sought their justification in intuitional knowledge instead of direct material knowledge about the nature of things, and which were utilised for the realisation of self and considered to be conducive to liberation or *mokṣa*, were inherent in Upaniṣadic idealism. These ideas easily penetrated the so called Brahmanical systems. In the case of the non-Brahmanical systems the infiltration was probably due to the Brāhmaṇa converts who came with certain preconceived ideas which they did not discard but further developed within the framework of their adopted system. But there were other factors also. We should not forget that within the general thought-structure of a given system itself there exists a distinct possibility of ideas developing according to their own peculiar qualities. This process of change may culminate in a final qualitative transformation of the original ideas.

Tantra and Science

In view of what has been stated above while dealing with the scientific contents of the Tantras, it should be remembered that, just as in Greece after Aristotle, the term metaphysics lost its original meaning and its subject matter came to be identified with speculative philosophy as against the pre-Socratic naturalism of the Ionian physicists, so also most of the Indian systems when they received a good deal of sophistication at the hands of the educated elite class, especially the Brāhmaṇas, they set themselves the impossible task of explaining the concrete realities of existence by establishing a standard of judgement, the very existence of which was not proved and could not be proved.

The Tantric maxim that the body is the epitome of the universe is the basis of Indian medical science; it rests on the assumption that the elements forming the body cannot be dissociated from environmental elements and that by applying the laws which govern the latter, the former may be brought to order. This environmental matter, which is not different from bodily matter, is called Prakṛti in the Sāṅkhya and conceived here as the Female Principle from which everything in the world is produced. Prakṛti is characterised by three qualities which influence and attract a number of forces of varying qualities and properties. These forces are conceived as Puruṣas or Male Principles, and it is only by the union of Prakṛti with the Male Principles that creation starts in different spheres. Prakṛti is in a constant process of evolution and is subject to the law of cause and effect. The whole cosmos exists in a subtle form in Prakṛti and becomes manifest in creation, which is only the unmanifest becoming manifest, the *avyakta* becoming *vyakta*.

This dualism is accepted in principle in the scientific tradition of Tantra, although here the properties and attributes of the Male and Female Principles are somewhat changed. This was probably due to the monistic influence of Vedānta. The Tantric concepts appear to be more akin to the Chinese principles of Yang and Yin, symbolising the positive and negative forces, the Male and Female Principles, which have found diverse applications in elaborating the theoretical principles of Chinese medicine, chemistry, music, etc. In the Tantric *rasa* school of alchemy the basic ingredients to be mixed or combined are conceived as having properties of the Female Principle while the process which produces the effect, or the essence of the effect itself, as having those of the Male. This brings to mind the ancient Lokāyata idea of consciousness, conceived as the Male Principle in the Sāṅkhya, and produced in the same way as the intoxicating power of liquor is created by the combination of various ingredients in different proportions. The Male and Female Principles again symbolise the Tantric physiology in which thirty-two subtle glands are viewed in terms of the former and the nervous system in terms of the latter which is revealed in such feminine names attributed to the nerves as *iḍā, piṅgalā, susumnā, gandhārī, hastijihvā, puṣā, yaśasvinī, alambūṣā, śaṅkhinī,* etc.

One should not fail to notice, especially in the field of medicine, that Tantric drugs are still used. In India there is even today a flourishing trade of medieval chemical products with Tantric labels. Indian almanacs liberally advertise Tantric drugs. It is, of course, purely a commercial business, the main capital of which is the exploitation of the goodwill and reputation which Tantric drugs once enjoyed in the past. Indian medical science as revealed in the *Carakasaṃhitā* and *Susrutasaṃhitā* is basically Tantric. Although in the present form of these texts *a priori* ideas have been grafted, and these accretions are spiritual in nature, the basic structure of scientific reasoning still prevails in these works. The medical tradition of India lays the greatest emphasis on a cause-effect relation; and it is interesting that the Buddha himself based his doctrine of suffering on the medical tradition. The Four Noble Truths proclaimed by the Buddha remind us of the similar maxims concerning diseases as found in the *Carakasaṃhitā* which, although in its present form belongs to the beginning of the Christian era, contains much of the earlier Tantric medical tradition. The earlier logicians, the followers of the Nyāya school, wanted to base their argument on the authority of the science of Mantra and Āyurveda,[25] which means that they wanted to follow the same method of reasoning as was followed by the Tantrics and men of the medical profession. Tantra is also known as Mantraśāstra.

Although we come across the names of many Tantric treatises on scientific subjects, there are very few texts extant. All the medical texts are lost but a few of the texts on alchemy still survive. In the religious texts, which are mostly rewritten fabricated versions of the lost originals, we have some scientific information but they are mostly saturated with abstract religious and metaphysical ideas. In these religious texts knowledge about the human body is presented under the following categories: *śarīrotpattikramaḥ* (the process by which the body is formed), *śarīrasthānādinirṇayaḥ* (location of nerves, etc., within the body), *bhūtaguṇāḥ* (qualities of matter by which body is formed), *śarīrasthavāyu nirṇayaḥ* (identification of the element of air in the body) and *śarīrakoṣavarṇanam* (description of the muscles of the body).[26] The knowledge has necessarily, many limitations if judged by modern standards. But some forms of observation and experiment were involved in their understanding because dissection for anatomical purposes was known. A class of Tantra was dedicated to the science of surgery and dissection of the body. We have not enough material in hand, but there are reasons to hold that the original purpose of the Tantric *śavasādhanā* was dissection. However, the difficulty with these religious texts is that though they begin with a purely scientific approach to the question of the formation of the body (their description of the origin and development of the foetus in the womb is basically correct even if judged by modern standards) ultimately the approach is given a religious and metaphysical orientation in accordance with the demand of the philosophy of *karma* and *mokṣa*.

From the evidence in the extant medical texts we come to know that eight forms of Tantric texts were current as treatises on the science of healing which formed the basis of the eight main divisions of Āyurveda. These were *Śalyatantra* (healing of wounds and diseases of the lower limbs through surgery, ointments and medicine), *Śālakyatantra* (healing of the wounds and diseases of the upper limbs), *Kāyacikitsātantra* (healing of all external and internal diseases of general types), *Bhūtavidyātantra* (dealing with mental diseases), *Kaumārabhṛtyatantra* (dealing with diseases of children), *Agadatantra* (science of toxicology), *Vājīkaraṇatantra* (prescription for enhancing sexual vigour, etc.) and *Rasāyanatantra* (science of chemical preparations needed for medicinal and other purposes). Of these eight sciences, only a few texts dealing with *rasāyana* still survive. Of the rest we have only a few names of the writers of some of the lost texts belonging to the aforesaid groups in the extant medical treatises. Aupadhenava, Aurabhra, Pauṣkalāvata and others wrote treatises on *Śalyatantra*, and Janaka, Nimi, Kāṅkāyana, Kṛṣṇatreya, etc., wrote on *Śālakyatantra*, as is known from different sources, but their works are all lost. The name *Kaumārabhṛtyatantra* was evidently connected with Jīvaka Kumārabhṛtya who was the physician of the Buddha and a renowned child specialist. A special type of Tantric treatment of diseases was known as *Avadhaūtikā cikitsā*, and its practitioners are found in India even today.

The Tantric physicians who depended mostly on chemical drugs were known as Rasavaidyas and formed a sect of their own. They used mainly drugs produced from mercury, sulphur, iron, mica, gold, and silver. In the field of mercurial drugs specially the Rasa sect made wonderful progress. On the one hand they devised a philosophy of body in terms of its chemical reactions, known as *Raseśvara-darśana* or *Kāyatattva* and on the other made numerous preparations out of mercury. We have the names of their chief exponents: Mahādeva, Ādinātha, Nityanātha, Candrasena, Gorakṣanātha, Kapāli and others. The Siddha sect of the South also depended on mercurial drugs and the method of their treatment was known as *Siddhacikitsā*. Also called Māheśvara Siddhas of the Śuddamārga, they had as the founder of one of their seven subsects a Chinese Taoist named Bhoga who possessed wonderful knowledge of alchemy. The Nātha Siddhas were closely allied with the Raseśvara Siddhas. Each of the nine Nātha Siddhas was generally held to stand at the head of a community of expert alchemists who were masters in the preparation of antidotes against old age, diseases, and poisons.

Tantric Texts on Chemical Sciences

Earlier scholars relegated the Tantras to a class of black magic, full of obscene and repulsive elements, unfit for a man of good taste to study. Those who had faith in the Tantras considered them, on the other hand, to be the way and means for spiritual quest and exercise, having nothing to do with worldly affairs. It was Acharya Prafulla Chandra Ray (1861-1944), the renowned chemical scientist, who was the first to proclaim boldly that Indian chemistry had very largely derived its colour, flavour, and nourishment from the Tantras which were repositories of a great amount of chemical information and many alchemical recipes. In fact, his celebrated *History of Hindu Chemistry* was mainly based on Tantric treatises.[27] In this work he not only gave copious quotations from the extant Tantric texts but also reproduced extracts and relevant portions of the texts in the appendices.

As we have already stated, the Tantras deal with medicinal preparations consisting mostly of mercury. In the *Kubjikātantra* belonging to the Kubjikāmata school, a manuscript of which is found in Gupta characters, we come across a passage in which Śiva himself speaks of *pārada* or mercury as his generative principle, and eulogises its efficacy when 'killed' six times. In this work we also find allusions to the transmutation of copper into gold with the aid of mercury, as also to other chemical processes. In the well-known *Rudrayāmalatantra* we have a section called *Rasakalpa* which deals with metals, minerals and the process of 'killing' them.[28] Methods for the extraction of the essence of copper pyrites and those of zinc from calamine have also been recorded. It should be noted in this connection that there is a work called *Dhātukriyā* (operation of metals) or *Dhātumañjarī* which pretends to be a part of the *Rudrayāmalatantra.*[29] This work cannot be placed earlier than 16th century A.D. and it contains much Arabic influence. Here we come across a term called *dahajala* meant to denote sulphuric acid. The work deals mainly with metals and their alloys.

Nāgārjuna's *Rasaratnākara* is a celebrated Tantric treatise on alchemy.[30] This Nāgārjuna, who was also the reputed author of *Kakṣapūṭatantra* and *Ārogyamañjarī* and the redactor of the *Suśrutasaṃhiṭā,* is dated to 8th century A.D. and was different from the famous exponent of the Mādyamika system who was also Buddhist and his *Rasaratnākara* bears the stamp of Mahāyāna Buddhism. Two other treatises by Nāgārjuna have also been recorded in the Nepal collection of manuscripts.[31] One is *Yogasāra* which contains recipes for improving the physical body, and the other is known as *Yogāṣṭaka* which contains recipes for cosmetics and for the cure of diseases of the hair. The *Rasaratnākara,* with which we are concerned at present, contains methods for the purification of important minerals—crude copper by means of 'poling', extractions of the essence of minerals, liquefaction of mica, fixation of mercury, a recipe for Aethiops mineral, 'killing' of mercury, and also description of the nature of the apparatuses. There is another work called *Rasaratnākara* composed by Siddha Nityanātha which deals mainly with the tests for 'killing' mercury.[32]

Rasārṇava, a Śaiva Tantric work of the 12th century,[33] is mainly based upon the aforesaid celebrated work of the alchemist Nāgārjuna. It gives a list of the apparatuses used for chemical purposes and treats of crucibles and the colour of flames. It also deals with the alkalis, colouring and 'killing' of metals, purfication of quicksilver, ex-traction of zinc and copper and a variety of other chemical subjects. Here mercury is said to have been composed of five elements representing Śiva himself. Three other Tantric texts, of Buddhist origin, should also be noted. They are Bhikṣu Govinda's *Rasahṛdaya*,[34] Somadeva's *Rasendracuḍāmaṇi*,[35] and Yaśodhara's *Rasaprakāśa-sudhākara*.[36] These texts were composed between the 11th and 13th century A.D. and drew heavily upon from Nāgārjuna. But Yaśodhara made some substantial contribution to the metallurgy of zinc. The *Rasacintāmaṇi* of Madanāntadeva describes the processes of the preparation of calomel, the fabrication of gold and silver, extraction of zinc from calamine, copper from blue vitriol, etc.[37] The *Kākacaṇḍeśvarīmata-tantra* mainly deals with mercurial preparation, copper, and liquefaction of mica.[38] It also gives a method for the transmutation of iron into gold, but the process is not very clear.

Of the works on medicinal chemistry, the most important is the *Rasaratnasamuccaya*[39] which deals exhaustively with minerals having medical properties and classes them under the four categories of *rasa, uparasa, ratna* and *loha. Rasa* was almost exclusively applied to the employment of mercury and metal in medicine. *Abhra* (mica), *vaikrānta, makṣika* (pyrites), *vimala, adrija* (bitumen), *sasyaka, capala* and *rasaka* were the eight principal *rasas*. Sulphur, red-ochre, vitriol, alum, orpiment, realgar, *añjana* and *kamkuṣṭha* were the eight *uparasas* useful in the operation of mercury. *Ratna* or gems were also regarded as agencies which would help the fixation or coagulation of mercury. So also were *lohāni* or metal like gold, silver, iron, tin, brass, bell-metal, etc. Elaborate rules are also laid down in this text for initiation through Tantric rites into the secrets of mercurial lore. The text also deals with the practical questions of laboratory, technical terms, apparatus, etc. Emphasis is laid upon the ingredients for crucibles, and the purification, fixation, and incineration of mercury, and so on.

Other texts on medicinal chemistry are cast in the same mould as *Rasaratnasamuccaya*. Of these texts, the *Rasarājalakṣmī*[40] of Viṣṇudeva, which gives an account of common *rasas* and *uparasas*, is of some importance because it contains references to previous Tantric works on this subject and to their writers. The *Rasanakṣatramālikā*[41] of Mathanasiṃha and *Rasendracintāmaṇi*, the authorship of which is disputed, are general texts. The *Rasasāra* of Govindācārya deals with eighteen operations of mercury. It is interesting to note that the author describes his indebtedness to the Buddhists of Tibet for the knowledge of certain processes. *Dhāturatnamālā*[42] is devoted exclusively to short processes of 'killing' metal and minerals. The use of opium as a drug which finds mention in these texts was probably due to foreign influence, since the term *ahiphena*, which was coined for denoting opium, is not found in the early Sanskrit lexicons. Chinese drugs are also mentioned in texts of this kind. *Phiraṅgaroga*, or the disease of the Portuguese, suggestive of veneral disease, and its treatment with calomel (*rasakarpura*) and china-root (*chobcini*, Smilax-China) are mentioned in such texts as *Rasapradīpa*, *Rasendracuḍāmaṇi*,[43] etc.

Of the other texts belonging to the late medieval period, the *Sāraṅgadhara-saṃgraha* is based upon the *Carakasaṃhitā* on the one hand and Tantric chemical treatises on the other. The author dates this work in Saṃvat 1420 or A.D. 1363. *Rasendrasārasaṃgraha* of Gopāla Kṛṣṇa is a compilation from the earlier chemical Tantras. Likewise the *Rasendrakalpadruma* is mainly based upon the *Rasārṇava*. Other late medieval compilations are the *Rasakaumudī*; *Bhāvaprakāśa*, *Arkaprakāśa*, Śālinātha's *Rasamañjarī*, *Rasarañjana*, *Rasārṇava* (distinct from the standard alchemical work bearing the same title), *Rasaratnākara* (different from two other works bearing the same title) and *Suvarṇatantra*.

A great many names of Tantric alchemical texts and their authors are scattered throughout the mass of chemical and medical literature. We have the names of such authors as Balabhadra, Brahmajyoti, Gahanāndanātha, Manthanabhairava, Svacchandabhairava, Vyādi, etc., whose works are not mentioned, and also such works as *Bandhasarvasva*, *Raseśvarasiddhānta*, etc., whose authors are not mentioned. But there are also a good number of cases where the texts are mentioned along with the names of their authors. Such texts are Ānandānubhava's *Rasadīpikā*, Bhojadeva's *Rasarājamṛgāṅka*, Candrasena's *Rasacandrodaya*, Carpaṭa's *Carpaṭasiddhānta*, Cuḍāmaṇi Miśra's *Rasakāmadhenu*, Dhanapati's *Divyarasendrasāra*, Garuḍadattasiddha's *Rasaratnāvalī*, Gorakṣanātha's *Gorakṣasiddhānta*, Harihara's *Rasaviśvadarpaṇa*, Kaṅkālī's *Rasakaṅkālī*, Kapāli's *Rasarājamahodadhi*, Keśavadeva's *Yogaratnākara*, Mallari's *Rasakautuka*, Narahari's *Rasayogamuktāvalī*, Rāmarāja's *Rasaratnapradīpa*, Siddha Bhāskara's *Rasendrabhāskara*, Siddha Prāṇanātha's *Rasadīpa*, Srinātha's *Rasaratna*, Trimallabhaṭṭa's *Rasadarpaṇa*, Vaidyarāja's *Rasa-kaṣāyavaidyaka*, Bandimiśra's *Yogasudhānidhi* and Vāsudeva's *Rasasarveśvara*. These works, however, are yet to be found.

In the Tibetan Tanjur and Kanjur collections we have a number of Tantric treatises on alchemy and medicine, very few of which have as yet been deciphered. In 1932 MM. Vidhusekhar Sastri referred to four Sanskrit treatises on alchemy as translated into Tibetan which were *Rasasiddhiśāstra*, *Dhātuvādaśāstra* or *Dhātu vādaśāstroddhṛti*, *Sarveśvararasāyana*, and *Dhātuvāda*. The first work is lost—only its name occurs in the Tibetan catalogue. The work was composed by Vyādipāda and was translated into Tibetan by Narendrabhadra and Ratnaśrī. The second work formed part of the first one, and is to be found in the Xylographs of the Tanjur manuscripts belonging to the libraries of the Asiatic Society of Bengal and Calcutta University. The third and fouth works were recovered from the Xylographs of the Tanjur manuscripts of Narthang edition belonging to Viśvabhāratī University. They have been translated into English and published along with the original Tibetan texts (reproduced in Ray's book which also contains the text and translation of another Tibetan treatise called *Rasāyanaśāstroddhṛti* by S.K. Pathak) in Roman script by Vidhusekhar Sastri.[44]

In the preceding section we have already had occasion to refer to the South Indian Tantric Siddhas (Sittar in Tamil) who were zealous adepts in alchemy. On their works and views the following may be stated:

> The works of the *Sittars* deal either with alchemy by itself, alchemy and *yoga*, alchemy and medicine or medicine pure and simple. They are written in verse, using easy, colloquial and ungrammatical words and often hiding the names of the herbs or minerals in big phrases and metaphors. Detailed instructions are given for the apparatus and processes. There are many *nigantus* or lexicons of these works, which give the names of herbs and minerals which are synonymous. They recognise Śiva for their God and reject everything in the Śaiva cult which is inconsistent with pure theism. Many recipes containing minerals, metals, herbs and salts are mentioned in these works.[45]

It should be observed in this connection that many of the Sittars reveal a strong antagonism to Śaṅkarācārya's doctrine of pure illusion,[46] which is suggestive of their original genuine scientific approach which admits of the reality of the world. The very concept of an illusory world, the existence of which is as false as the cognition of snake in rope, goes against the spirit of scientific enquiry. But, as had happened in the case of all other systems, the Sittars also could not retain the pristine purity of their approach and they had to allow alien or even hostile thoughts to be grafted on to their original system. Although according to Tamil tradition the origin of the

Sittars is traced to the mythical Agastya, they actually belong to the 10th century A.D. and after. We have already referred to Bhoga (Bogar in Tamil) who was a Chinese Taoist and became the founder of one of the seven subsects of the Sittars. It is said that he came to India in the 3rd century A.D. (the date is doubtful), visited Arabia, and got some of his pupils initiated in Chinese mechanical and alchemical arts by sending them to China. It is said that he himself went to China with them. Tamil works mention Bogar's name and also that of his disciple Pulipani who came with him and settled in South India. Quite a large number of works were left by the Tamil Sittars but only a few are now in print.[47]

Tantric Alchemy and the Concept of Revitalising the Body

In the medieval Tantric chemical texts *a priori* spiritual ideas are often blended with scientific matter from diverse sources. In some cases it is found that, owing to the technological backwardness of a given age, basically scientific concepts have to be justified in terms of theistic arguments which eventually transform the case into its opposite. This happened in the case of the Nyāya-Vaiśeṣikas who had to incorporate the idea of God into their system in order to rationalise their purely scientific doctrine of atomism, and eventually they had to defend the idea of God with all possible arguments thus shifting their subject from the realm of science to that of pure theism. A similar process must have been at work in the case of the scientific Tantras, but here the situation was very complicated because at a certain stage of its development Tantra had incorporated within itself elements from all known forms of Indian thought, allowing each of them to work in its own way with the result that there was a shifting tension among the conflicting ideas. That is why the Tantric theistic position could not be uniform and absolute.

In spite of Vedāntic and other idealistic influence Tantra as a whole could not establish absolute theism because of its heterogeneous constituents. Tantra could not accept idolatory because according to the very nature of its principles a deity could be adored only by one becoming the deity oneself. The idea of a separate far-seeing God, the creator who rules the universe from heaven, is absent in Tantra because according to the Tantric view, the body of the *sādhaka* is the universe which is the abode of the desired (*iṣṭa*) and the goal to be sought (*sādhya*). The unfolding of the self-power (*ātmaśakti*) is to be brought about by self-realisation (*ātmadarśana*) which is the aim of *sādhanā*. Śakti or power, conceived as the Female Principle, is in the individual, and it is only for this Śakti that the existence of the individual is justified. This Śakti is conceived as existing like butter in milk, or the power of burning in fire throughout the created world of moving and unmoving things, through the conscious and unconscious, through the gross and the subtle. The repository of this Śakti is regarded as a static principle conceived as the Male Principle, which is symbolised by the name of the god of any system. The human body is the abode of both these principles, the static Male and the dynamic Female, and the purpose of Tantric *sādhanā* is to get these two principles in non-dual and absolute union within the body. Therefore to a Tantric aspirant there is nothing apart from the body, the functioning of which is considered to belong to the same order as cosmic functioning.

To what extent such ideas derived their main impulses from the popular cults and beliefs in which the human body was regarded as the source of all spiritual experience will be discussed later, but it should be noticed here that the idea of the body as the microcosm of the universe thus received a spiritual denotation as against the purely physical denotation of the earlier tradition. Under this changed view the idea of rendering, by varied physico-chemical processes, the human body deathless and also the spiritual liberation of man by his monadic transfiguration began to gain ground. It was believed that preservation of the body might be achieved by the use of mercury, medicaments and breathing exercises. Reverberating, cleansing, stimulating and projecting the body with the help of a special *elixir vitae* were considered to be essential preconditions for emancipation within the span of life. The use of mercurial drugs was one step in the process of overcoming death—it aimed at the purifying and curing of the cells, tissues, and organs of the body.

The idea of revitalising the body was not inconsistent with the basic approach to life, but when this idea was carried to its extreme form, the transfiguration of the material body came to denote something entirely different. It was believed that the material body was made up of impure *māyā* and that the change in bodily structure and function should mean the elimination of such ingredients at the first stage and then complete dematerialisation of the body at the second. In the scheme calculated to make the body undecaying and immortal, the scientific tradition of the Tantras, as manifested in alchemy and medicine, was first utilised, but subsequently it was discarded because the original premise on which the doctrine of revitalising the body stood was itself given up. The concept of a celestial substance, as against the material substance, forming the body was invented which became the basis of a new theory of transmutation insisting on *divya-tanu* or divine and non-material body, and the whole question thus came under the domain of subjective speculation.

The Apathy Towards Tantra

In the 19th century Western scholars of Indian religious systems regarded Tantra as a degraded form of Hinduism which consisted of the most barbarous, repulsive, and obnoxious elements.[48] It has been said:

> The use of animal food and spirituous liquors, indulged to in excess, is the rule of these strange ceremonies, in which Śakti is worshipped in the persons of a naked woman, and the proceedings terminate with the carnal copulation of the initiated, each couple representing Bhairava and Bhairavī (Śiva and Devī), and becoming thus for the moment identified with them. This is *śrīcakra*, 'the holy circle' or the *purṇābhiṣeka*, 'the complete consecration', the essential act or rather fore-estate of salvation, the highest rite of this delirious mysticism. . . . In fact a Śākta of the left hand is almost always a hypocrite and a superstitious debauchee.[49]

Indian scholars also believed that obscenity was the soul of this cult which demanded every excess that liquor and lust could prompt. The great Bengali writer and Hindu revivalist, Bankim Chandra Chatterjee, viewed Tantra as a misguiding principle which offered only wine and woman in the name of religion. R.L. Mitra did not hesitate to state that in Tantra

> theories are indulged in and practices enjoined which are at once the most revolting and horrible that human depravity could think of and compared to which the words and specimens of Holiwell street literature would appear absolutely pure.[50]

This aversion continued even in the first half of the 20th century. Insisting on its so called vulgar aspects, Benoytosh Bhattacharyya, who was one of the pioneers in the field of Vajrayanic studies, frankly observed that

> if at any time in the history of India the mind of the nation as a whole has been

diseased, it was in the Tantric age, or the period immediately preceding the Muhammedan conquest of India. The story related in the pages of numerous Tantric works is supposed to be so repugnant that, excepting a few, all respectable scholars have condemned them wholesale and left the field of study severely alone. In spite of what the great historians of Sanskrit literature have said against Tantrism and Tantric literature, no one should forget that the Hindu population of India as a whole is even today in the grip of this very Tantra in its daily life, customs and usages, and is suffering from the same disease which originated 1300 years ago and consumed its vitality slowly but surely during these long centuries. Some one should therefore take up the study comprising the diagnosis, aetiology, pathology and prognosis of the disease so that more capable men may take up its treatment and eradication in the future.[51]

The reality appeared to him as a *disease* to be cured. This may be called a moralist's approach to a historical problem. But the problem remains. As Debiprasad Chattopadhyaya rightly observed:

> We cannot look at Tantrism as mere perversion without at the same time looking at ourselves as a nation of perverts. . . . In all likelihood, therefore, there must have been some original significance attributed to these particular beliefs and practices, which we are apt to miss if we allow ourselves to be carried away by a spirit of sheer moral repugnance. The *vāmācāra* of Tantrism, since our ancestors were so serious about it, could not have meant mere perversion, though they are manifestly so if practised in the context of our developed knowledge and moral values. And it is necessary to know why our ancestors had such absurd beliefs in order to understand how we have become what we are today.[52]

The Other Side

Despite its primitive legacies and its 'cruel', 'barbarous' and 'immoral' rites, Tantra has a special appeal for millions of Indians. A.S. Geden refers to the view of an eminent exponent of Tantra who asserts that 'two-thirds of our religious rites are Tantric and almost half our medicine'. He also refers to a passage, quoted by H.H. Wilson from one of the principal Tantras, which claims that most of the major religious sects have secret followers of Tantra.[53] Tantric saints have a place of honour in Indian society. Moreover, Tantra is committed to certain moral values, the excellence of which even the critics of this system are forced to admit. According to Sir Charles Elliot,

> apart from the ceremonial which they inculcate, the general principles of

Tantra breathe a liberal and intelligent spirit. Caste-restrictions are minimized; travelling is permitted; women are honoured; they can act as teachers; the burning of widows is forbidden; girl widows may remarry and the murder of a woman in peculiarly heinous. Prostitution is denounced. Whereas Christianity is sometimes accused of restricting its higher code to Church and Sundays, the opposite may be said of Tantrism. Outside the temple its morality is excellent.[54]

One of the main causes of the apathy towards Tantra was the baseless Aryan bias. Earlier scholars equated Tantra with the so called degraded forms of Hinduism supposed to be the legacies of uncivilized aboriginal cultures. It is true that Tantra contains much of a primitive way of life and many repulsive rites. But to judge them simply on the ground of the morality of a given age, ignoring their real social basis, goes against all canons of historical criticism. To those learned Western scholars, just as the Englishmen came to India with a 'civilizing mission' to bear the 'white man's burden', so also in the past aboriginal Indians were 'civilized' by the Aryans who came from outside. To them, whatever is noble and praiseworthy in Hinduism is found in this so called Aryan tradition, i.e. the Vedic texts and Brahmanical literature, and all the barbarous and degraded aspects attributed to Tantra are derived from the uncivilized non-Aryans. This idea was also shared by the learned Indians who belonged mostly, if not exclusively, to the upper strata of society and took pride in thinking of themselves as direct descendants of the great Aryan race. Though the myth of Aryanism has now been exploded its residue is still at work creating a bar to the proper understanding of Tantra.

The all-pervading influence of Tantra in Indian life and its misinterpretation by the leading scholars did not escape the notice of the upholders of the neo-Tantric movement, launched in the beginning of this century, who depended on the scholastic writings on Tantra. They equated Tantra with the totality of Hinduism and declared it to be the essence of the Vedas. In a letter addressed to Sir John Woodroffe, Śivacandra Vidyārṇava wrote:

At the present time the general public are ignorant of the principles of the Tantra śāstra. The cause of this ignorance is the fact the Tantra-śāstra is a Sādhana-śāstra, the greater part of which becomes intelligible only by Sādhanā. For this reason the Śāstra and its teachers prohibit their general promulgation. So long as the Śāstra was learnt from Gurus only, the golden rule was of immease good. In course of time the old Sādhanā has become almost extinct, and along with it, the knowledge of the deep and mighty principles of the Śāstra is almost lost. Nevertheless some faint shadowings of these principles have been put before the public partly with a view to preserve Śāstric knowledge from destruction, and partly for commercial reasons. When I commenced to write *Tantratattva* some 25 years ago, Bengali society was in a perilous state, owing to the influx of other religions, want of faith and a spirit of disputation. Shortly before this a number of English books had appeared on the Tantra-śāstra which, whilist ignorant of Dharma, Sādhanā and Siddhi, contained some hideous and outrageous pictures, drawn by the Bengali historians and novelists ignorant of, and unfaithful to, Śāstric principles. The English books by English writers contained merely a reflection of what English-educated Bengalis of those days had written. Both are even today equally ignorant of the Tantra-śāstra.[55]

The approach is basically correct, but the difficulty with these great Tantric scholars and preachers is that they are inclined to think that for the purpose of interpreting Tantrism it is sufficient to confine themselves to those thoughts and ideas which were in fact superimposed on original Tantra. They fail to notice that external theological and philosophical speculations derived from all known forms of Indian thought, and also that Brahmanical social ideals were superimposed on the original Tantra to such a fantastic extent that the real contents are completely obscured. They feel comfortable, however, with these grafted elements because they are in agreement with their own preoccupations. They try to explain the conflicting and contradictory elements by imaginary interpretations and when they are not able to, they simply ignore them.

As a matter of fact, external superimpositions are so common in the religious and philosophical history of India that without a critical identification and examination of these any historical study on the religious or philosophical systems of India is bound to be futile. To take the example of Buddhism, its Brāhmaṇa converts, when they got a lead in the organisation due to their traditional association with learning, introduced their own philosophical terms and concepts into the framework of Buddhism and eventually made it a totally different system, one far from what the Buddha had actually preached. In the case of philosophical speculations the process of superimposition has already been exemplified with reference to the Sāṅkhya. Evidence that the medieval Tantric texts are burdened with extraneous elements is abundant. For example, Tantra according to its very nature has nothing to do with the caste system but in the later Tantras caste elements are pronounced. This is due to the fact that although many of our known Tantric teachers were non-Brāhmaṇas, rather belonging to the lower ranks of society, almost all of the known authors of the Tantric treatises were Brāhmaṇas who could not give up their caste prejudices notwithstanding their conversion to Tantrism.

Tantrism and the Hindu Religion

In view of what has been said in the preceding sections it is quite clear that Tantra is a very wide subject which has a rich tradition of human endeavour and wisdom. However, it is impossible to present this rich tradition in its *entirety* owing to the paucity of material. It is only the religious elements of Tantra which can be worked out from an historical viewpoint.

The popular belief that Tantra is the same as Śāktism is evidently wrong. This misunderstanding is due to the fact that Tantra attaches supreme importance to the doctrine of Śakti, but this doctrine is not the feature of Śāktism alone. It is shared by all known forms of the Hindu religion. Besides the popular religious beliefs and cults and also the elements derived from Buddhism and other non-Vedic philosophical systems, the most important constituents of the Hindu religion are the five systems (collectively known as *pañcopāsanā*) which are devoted to the worship of Viṣṇu, Śiva, Śakti, Gaṇapati and Sūrya respectively. *Pañcopāsanā,* too, has Tantric rituals. Even today there are two distinct modes of worship in each of these religious systems, the Vedic and the Tantric.

Each of these systems has a general form patronised by the adherents of *varṇāśrama* and approved by the Smṛtis and Purāṇas. But side by side there is a special form, known as *atimārgika,* which is followed by the adherents of the Tantric tradition. This stream was naturally in conflict with that represented by the former and was condemned in the Purāṇas and other Brahmanical texts. We have already commented on how the followers of Tantra were denounced for their anti-Vedic attitude. A few more examples may be cited here. In the *Devībhāgavata* it is stated that the scriptures which are opposed to the Śruti (Vedas) and Smṛti (Brahmanical legal texts) belong to the *tāmasa* category. The Āgamas of the Vāmas, Kāpālikas, Kaulakas, and Bhairavas were created by Śiva for rectification and for no other purpose. It was for rescuing the Brāhmaṇas who were driven out from the Vedic path owing to the curses of Dakṣa, Bhṛgu or Dadhīci that step by step the Āgamas of the Śaivas, Vaiṣṇavas, Sauras, Śāktas and Gāṇapatyas were created by Śaṅkara (Śiva).[56]

The *Devībhāgavata* is a late Purāṇa with a professedly Śākta character, but its Brāhmaṇa writer could not eschew his belief in the infallibility of Śruti and Smṛti and did not hesitate to note that the five main forms of the Hindu religion were non-Vedic. In the same Purāṇa[57] another story is related according to which the great sage Gautama cursed a group of Brāhmaṇas as a result of which they rejected the Vedas and neglected Vedic sacrifices. They lost faith in the Śrauta and Smārta code of conduct, and became the worst sort of Brāhmaṇas using the symbols of conch, disc, etc. (emblems of Viṣṇu), followers of Kāpālika, Buddhist and Pāṣaṇḍa rites and believers in Pāñcarātra, Kāmaśāstra, Kāpālikism and Buddhism. They were reborn in the Kali age as *vedabāhya*, i.e. outside the pale of Veda, having no faith in the Sandhyās, Gāyatrī, Agnihotra, etc., and were known as Pāṣaṇḍas. Some of them were marked with symbols made by hot iron (probably the Gāṇapatyas were meant) and others indulged in sexual rites. They became Kāpālikas, Kaulikas, Buddhists and Jains and founders of all ugly practices.

The legend of Gautama's curse is also found in the *Kūrmapurāṇa* in which it is stated that after having fallen from the Vedic path, owing to the curse, these peoples began to propitiate Śiva and Viṣṇu with *popular* hymns.[58] Therefore Śiva requested Viṣṇu to reformulate a religious system so that those who had fallen from Vedic way might be saved. At this Viṣṇu replied:

> O Śaṅkara, there can be no trace of virtue in a person who is outside the Veda. It is due to the fact, O Great God, that the Laws spring from the Veda. In spite of this, O Maheśvara, for the sake of affection to our devotees, though they are on the way to hell, we ought to protect all of them. Therefore, O Vṛṣadhvaja, for the purpose of protecting those who are outside the Veda and also for that of rectifying the sinners, we shall introduce scriptures.
>
> Having thus been addressed by Murāri Mādhava Rudra, and having been sent by Śiva, Keśava composed the scriptures of the Kapālas, Nākulas, Vāmas, Bhairavas (eastern and western), Pāñcarātras, Pāśupatas and others.[59]

Here it is also categorically said that the Pāñcarātra and Pāśupata systems had originally nothing to do with the Vedas. This tradition is found in other texts as well. In the *Sūtasaṃhitā* it is said that Gautama cursed some Brāhmaṇas with the following words:

Be you all worst of the Brāhmaṇas, having got yourselves initiated into the Pāñcarātra, Kāpālika, Kālāmukha and Śākta doctrines. Be you all worst of the Brāhmaṇas, having got yourselves initiated into Bauddha, Arhat, Pāśupata and Sāmbhava doctrines. Be you all worst of Brāhmaṇas, having got yourselves initiated into other similar non-Vedic (*aśrauta*) Pāṣaṇḍa doctrines.[60]

All the known forms of Hindu religion are non-Vedic according to this tradition. This is surprising. It is even more interesting to note that the Tantrics also used the same Gautama legend against their opponents. Evidently Tantra was *Vedabāhya,* i.e. outside of the realm of the Vedas. But as we have already observed, later Tantric writers wanted to base their doctrines on the Vedas. Their target was, however, the followers of Advaita Vedānta who claimed the sole monopoly of the Vedic tradition. The Tantric writers argued that those who were the victims of Gautama's curse were not the Pāñca-rātras or Pāśupatas or Śāktas, rather they were those who based their religious doctrines on Advaita Vedānta. According to the *Maheśvaratantra* Gautama cursed them with the following words:

Owing to your deeds you all will become fallen from the Vedic way and ungrateful. In the Kali age you all will become fools by denouncing the Veda, Brāhmaṇa, Go (cow) and Mantra and by accepting the Brahmavāda. Wicked at heart and apparently clean in appearance, you will give up works of religious merit because of the arrogance caused by the study *hetuvidyā* (logic) and the knowledge of *brahman. Brahman* is true; world is false. When the world is false what is the need of doing meritorious acts?[61]

When all the forms of the surviving Hindu religion are treated as non-Vedic, how is it that they have been accepted by orthodox tradition? The fact is that religious systems like Pāñcarātra, Pāśupata, Śākta, Gāṇapatya, etc., were exclusively Tantric, originally having nothing to do with the Vedas. These forms of religion were extremely popular among the masses, and hence the followers of the Vedic tradition had to give them Vedic sanction. Slowly but steadily Vedic elements were infused into these systems which resulted in the separation of the original elements stamped *atimārgika.* The grafted elements were given publicity and patronised by the ruling class and the elite, while the *atimārgika* elements were blackened and severely condemned. But these elements could not be stamped out, completely and their followers, though isolated, did not become totally extinct.

NOTES

1. *Ṛgveda*; X.71.9; *Atharvaveda*, X.7.42; *Taittirīya Brāhmaṇa*, II.5.5.3. Pāṇini derived the word *tantraka* (V.2.70), meaning a cloth taken away from the loom, from Tantra.
2. *Āpastamba*, I.15.1; *Śāṅkhyāyana*, I.16.6.
3. Śabara on Jaimini XI.I.I.
4. On Pāṇini IV. 2.60.
5. Kauṭilya XV; Caraka, *Siddhisthāna*, XII.40-5; Suśruta, *Uttaratantra* LXV.
6. *On Brahmasūtra* II.2.32; cf. *Ahirbudhnya Saṃhitā*, XII.18ff.
7. J. Woodroffe, *Śakti and Śākta*, 8th edn, Madras, 1975 (rpt), p. 34.
8. C. Chakravarti, *The Tantras: Studies on their Religion and Literature*, Calcutta, 1963, pp. 29-37, summary quoted. See section 10.
9. B.N. Sharma, *Social Life in Northern India*, Delhi, 1966, pp. 351-2. My friend Dr. Alaka Chattopadhyaya has recently worked on the 84 Siddhas mentioned in the Tibetan texts. In some texts their pictures are given in all of which they carry their professional implements.
10. *Tarkarahasyadīpikā*, Calcutta, 1905, p. 300.
11. H.P. Sastri, *Lokāyata*, Dacca University Bulletin No. 1 (1925), p. 6.
12. B. Farrington in *Philosophy for the Future*, New York, 1949, pp. 4-5.
13. B. Farrington, *Greek Science*, London, 1944, Vol. I, pp. 105-6.
14. X. 31.7; X. 72.2, X. 81. 2-4.
15. *Ṛgveda*, IX. 112.3.
16. Cf. *Baudhāyana Dharmasūtra*, I.5.101.
17. Manu, X. 83-4.
18. VI.I.
19. See my *History of Indian Cosmogonical Ideas*, New Delhi, 1971, pp. 63-6.
20. Ibid., pp. 79-81.
21. Ibid., pp. 66-8.
22. See my *Jain Philosophy: Historical Outline*, New Delhi, 1976, pp. 138-40.
23. *Śārīrakabhāṣya*, II. 1.1.
24. *Sāṅkhyakārikābhāṣya*, XI.
25. *Nyāyasūtra*, II. 1. 68; mantrāyurveda prāmāṇya vacca, tat prāmāṇya māptaprāmānyāt.
26. Cf. *Śāktānandataraṅgiṇī*, I. 6ff. Ed. P. Sastri, Āgama Anusandhāna Samiti, Calcutta, 1349 B.E., pp. 5ff.
27. Vol. I, 1902; Vol. II, 1908; now incorporated in to the nicely edited *History of Chemistry in Ancient and Medieval India* (ed. Priyadaranjan Ray), Calcutta, 1956.
28. Ibid., pp. 156-7, 366-70.
29. Ibid., pp. 197-9, 414-42.
30. Ibid., pp. 129-34, 311-20.

31. H.P. Sastri, *A Catalogue of Palmleaf and Selected Paper Mss. belonging to the Durbar Libaray Nepal* (hereafter *Nepal Catalogue*), Vol. I, Calcutta, 1905, p. 135, Vol. II, Calcutta, 1915, p. 75.
32. Ray, op. cit., pp. 196, 407-8.
33. Ibid., pp. 135-40, 321-29.
34. Ibid., pp. 147-9, 330-44.
35. Ibid., pp. 151-2, 351-4.
36. Ibid., pp. 153-4, 355-62.
37. Ibid., pp. 155, 363-5.
38. Ibid., pp. 150, 345-50.
39. Ibid., pp. 165-95, 371-403.
40. Ibid., pp. 404-5.
41. Ibid., pp. 406-7.
42. Ibid., pp. 409-10.
43. Ibid., pp. 411-13.
44. Vidhusekhar Bhattacharya (Sastri), 'Sanskrit Treatises on Alchemy' in *Acharya Ray Volume*, Calcutta, 1932, pp. 121ff.
45. K.C. Viraraghava in ibid., p. 460.
46. Ibid.
47. Most of the works are scattered as manuscripts which are to be found in Madras Oriental Manuscript Library, Sarabhoji Maharaja's Library at Tanjore, Aduthurai Matha at Tanjore and at various South Indian Maṭhas. In 1951, D.V. Subha Reddy published a list of 27 works indicating the nature of their contents, originally prepared by W. Ainslie in *Madras Medical Journal*, Vol. II, No. 2 adding an extra list of 38 Tamil books composed by the Sittars.
48. H.H. Wilson, *Essays and Lectures on the Religion of the Hindus*, London, 1862, Vol. I, pp. 248-57; M. Monier-Williams, *Indian Wisdom*, London, 1875, pp. 501ff; *Brahmanism and Buddhism*, London, 1891, pp. 191ff; E.W. Hopkins, *Religions of India*, Boston, 1885, pp. 489-92; etc.
49. A. Barth, *Religions of India*, London, 1882, p. 205.
50. Quoted in H.P. Sastri's *Bauddha Dharma*, in Bengali, p. 82.
51. B.T. Bhattacharyya, *An Introduction to Buddhist Esoterism*, Oxford 1932, Preface.
52. D.P. Chattopadhayaya, *Lokāyata*, Delhi 1959, pp. 65-6.
53. *Encyclopaedia of Religion and Ethics*, Vol. XII, p. 193.
54. C. Elliot, *Hinduism and Buddhism*, London, 1921, rpt 1957, Vol. II, p. 285.
55. J. Woodroffe, *Śakti and Śākta*, 8th edn, Madras, 1975, pp. 9-10. A free translation of Vidyārṇava's *Tantratattva* was published by Woodroffe in 1914 under the title *Principles of Tantra*, 2nd edn, Calcutta, 1916, rpt Madras, 1952. The Bengali original has recently been reprined.
56. *Devībhāgavata*, VII. 39. 26. 2-30.
57. XII. 9. 56ff.

58. *Astuvan laukikaiḥ stotrairucehiṣṭiriva sarvagaiḥ*, *Kūrmapurāṇa*, I.16, III-12.
59. Ibid., I. 16. 115-19.
60. *Sutasaṃhitā*, IV (I). 32. 39-41.
61. *Maheśvaratantra*, 18th *Paṭala*.

2

Tantric Literature

The Traditional Classification, Nature, Date, etc.

According to the tradition found in the Tantric texts themselves, Tantras are innumerable.[1] The *Nityaṣoḍaśikārṇava*[2] says that Tantras are endless in number but records only sixty-four Kaula Tantras. The *Saundaryalaharī*, attributed by some to Śaṅkarācārya, refers to sixty-four Tantras.[3] The *Tantrāloka* of Abhinavagupta[4] states that there are three groups of ten, eighteen and sixty-four Śaiva Tantras. The *Śaktisaṅgamatantra*[5] refers to the Tantric sects and treatises of the Vaiṣṇavas, Gāṇapatyas, Śaivas, Svāyambhūvas, Candras, Pāśupatas, Cīnas, Jainas, Kālāmukhas and Vaidikas. The *Sammoha* or *Sammohana-tantra* knows the existence of 402 Śaiva Tantras, 339 Vaiṣṇava Tantras, 180 Saura Tantras, 122 Gāṇapatya Tantras and 39 Bauddha Tantras. The numbers are fictitious, but they show that the author of the said Tantra had a vague idea of the sects and their texts. The same Tantra states that China possesses 100 principal Tantras and 7 subsidiary ones, Draviḍa 20 principal and 20 subsidiary ones, and Gauḍa 27 principal and 16 subsidiary ones.

A classification of the Tantric texts according to the mythological periods of time like Varāhakalpa, Kālakalpa, etc., is found in the Tantric tradition, but more well known is the classification according to the geographical divisions. In the *Mahāsiddhasāratantra* India and its adjoining regions are divided into three *krāntās* or divisions, viz., Viṣṇukrāntā (the land east of the Vindhya hills extending right upto Java), Rathakrāntā north of the Vindhya hills including Mahācīna) and Aśvakrāntā (the rest of the country), Each of these *krāntās*, it is said, has 64 Tantras.[7] A number of Tantric texts speak of nine or six *āmnāyas* or regions—eastern, western, northern, southern, upper and lower—each containing its distinctive texts, cults and rituals.[8] From a more realistic geographical point of view Tantras are divided into four classes, viz., Kerala, Kāśmira, Gauḍa and Vilāsa. The Kerala class is said to prevail in all countries from Aṅga to Mālava, the

Kāśmīra class from Madra to Nepāla, the Gauḍa class from Śilahaṭṭa to Sindhu while the Vilāsa class is found in all countries.

A classification of Tantric texts on the basis of the three currents of Tantric tradition—*dakṣina*, *vāma* and *madhyama*—is also found each of which is again subdivided into two classes, inner (*hārda*) and outer (*bāhya*).[9] This division is also made in terms of *divya*, *kaula* and *vāma*. The *āmnāya* divisions, six or nine, of the regions are often brought under two general categories—Kādimata and Hādimata.[10] There is also a tradition of classifying Tantras into *aṣṭaka*, *mangala*, *cakra* and *śikhā*.[11] Tantric texts are known by such names as Tantra, Upatantra, Āgama, Saṃhitā, Yāmala, Ḍāmara, Tattva, Kalpa, Arṇava (ka), Uḍḍāla, Uḍḍīśa, Upasaṃkhyā, Cuḍāmaṇī, Vimarśiṇī, Cintāmaṇi, Purāṇa, Upasajñā, Kakṣapuṭi. Kalpadruma, Kāmadhenu, Sabhāva, Avataraṇaka, Sukta, Amṛta (tarpaṇa), Darpaṇa, Sāgara, etc.

The terms Tantra, Āgama and Saṃhitā are very often used in the same sense, each of which denotes any type of religious text. According to *Piṅgalāmata* Āgama is that by which the objects around are known. The name is also explained as that class of Tantra which is addressed to Pārvatī by Śiva. It is said that the word is formed by the first letters of *āgata* (that which comes from Śiva), *gata* (that which goes to Pārvatī) and *mata* (that which is established). It is called Āgama because knowledge proceeds from it, Śāstra because everything is controlled and protected by it, Jñāna because everything can be known through it, and Tantra because everything is preserved and perpetuated by it. According to the *Vārāhītantra*,[12] Āgama deals with seven topics, viz., cosmology, destruction, worship of god, *sādhanā*, *puraścaraṇa*, six forms of rites and four forms of meditation. The number of Āgamas of the Pāñcarātra school is generally stated to be 108, but on comparison with different lists their number appears to be more than 200. The basic Śaiva Āgamas are 18 in number according to one tradition, and 28 according to another. Other sects have their own Āgamas also.

The *Vārāhītantra* gives a list of twelve special Āgamas which are *Muktaka*, *Prapañca*, *Śāradā*, *Nārada*, *Mahārṇava*, *Kapila*, *Yoga*, *Kalpa*, *Kapiñjala*, *Amṛtaśuddhi*, *Vira* and *Siddhasamvaraṇa*. Another class of Tantric literature is called Ḍāmara which traditionally consists of six texts known as *Śiva*, *Yoga*, *Durgā*, *Sārasvata*, *Brahmā* and *Gandharva*. *Yāmala* is a special class of Tantric literature, the principal ones being eight in number: *Rudra*, *Skanda*, *Brahma*, *Viṣṇu*, *Yama*, *Vāyu*, *Kubera* and *Indra*. Two other old texts—*Piṅgalāmata* and *Jayadratha*—belong to the Yāmala group. Besides there are other Yāmalas like *Āditya* and *Gaṇeśa*.

An ordinary Tantra has a form somewhat similar to that of a Purāṇa, since it theoretically discusses in order the same five subjects (*pañcalakṣaṇa*): the creation and dissolution of the universe, the worship of gods, the attainment of supernatural power, and union with the supreme being. But here the mythological elements are absent. Instead we find details of ritual acts and practices which remind us of the contents of Brāhmaṇa literature. We have Tantric parallels of all Smārta and Purāṇic rites. A fourfold division of Tantra topics into *Vidyā, Kriyā, Yoga* and *Caryā* is indicated in many texts. In some cases *Yoga* and *Caryā* are indicated in many texts. In some cases *Yoga* and *Caryā* have been substituted by *Upāya* and *Siddhi*. There is also a twofold division into *Kriyātantra* and *Yogatantra*.

In a good number of Purāṇic texts Tantric subjects have been incorporated. Aparārka quotes a passage from the *Devīpurāṇa* wherein the qualification of a Sthāpaka, i.e. one who performs the installation of God, is considered in terms of his ability in Tantric rituals.[13] The *Kālikāpurāṇa* devotes many chapters to the description of *mantras, mudrās, kavacas, nyāsas,* etc. The *Agnipurāṇa*[14] states that the worship of Viṣṇu and other gods should follow the Vaidikī, Tāntrikī or Miśra way, the first and third being for the higher varṇas and the second or Tantrikī for the Śūdras. The *Bhāgavatapurāṇa*[15] mentions Tantric cults of Viṣṇu, Vaidikī and Tāntrikī *dīkṣā,* Tantric methods of *aṅgas, upāṅgas, āyudhas,* etc. Many Tantric elements are found in the medieval Nibandhas.

Tantric texts in their present form mostly belong to the medieval and late-medieval period. However, manuscripts of several Tantric texts have been found in Gupta characters,[16] the most important being that of *Kubjikāmata,* now in the Asiatic Society of Bengal. The Śaiva Āgamas of the South are mentioned in a 6th century Kailāsanātha temple inscription of Rajāsiṃhavarman.[17] Epigraphic references to a number of Tantric texts which were introduced in Cambodia as early as the beginning of the 9th century exist.[18] Buddhist Dhāraṇīs are fairly old, a good many of which may be assigned to 4th century A.D. The Horiuzi palm-leaf manuscripts of Japan contain a few old Tantric works. Many early Buddhist Tantric texts are to be found in Chinese translations. Lāmā Tāranātha has supplied us a lot of information regarding the formation of Buddhist Tantric texts and their regional distribution.

Of all the available Tantric texts, the majority are still in manuscript form and are as yet unpublished. The published materials on the other hand are in many cases anonymous because the existence of different works under the same title is not unknown. For example, a manuscript of the *Kulārṇavatantra*, complete in twelve chapters, is found which differs substantially from the printed work of the same name which has seventeen chapters.[19] Similar repetitions of titles are also found in other cases. The number of exegetical works written on Tantra is by no means small. Moreover, there are the digests which occupy a very important place in the literature of the Tantras and also the individual works of Tantric teachers.

The Pāñcarātra Saṃhitās

The term Pāñcarātra is difficult to define. It appears that once this term, like that of the Bhāgavata, had a wider denotation since the Pāñcarātra works were associated with the names of deities like Śiva, Devī, Gaṇeśa, Brahmā and Mahākāla.[20] The *Nāradapāñcarātra*[21] enumerates seven kinds of Pāñcarātra of which three are connected with the names of Brahmā, Śiva and Kumāra. The *Agnipurāṇa*[22] refers to Saptarātra along with Pāñcarātra and some scholars are of the opinion that the former was associated with the cult of Brahmā and that the latter was its offshoot which came to be connected with Viṣṇu. But these are only speculations. Accroding to the *Pādmatantra*,[23] the Pāñcarātra was so-called because the existing five Śāstras or systems became dark in its presence. A Pāñcarātra text known as *Puruṣottamasaṃhitā* says that any system which lays supreme emphasis on Bhakti or devotion may be called Pāñcarātra which is also known as Ekāyanaveda, Mūlaveda, Sātvata, Tantra and Āgama. It is a *rahasya-āmnāya* or mysterious area of knowledge taught by Viṣṇu to Brahmā who had learnt it in five nights—literally Pāñcarātra—and since it is the only way to salvation, it is called Ekāyana. The doctrines and rituals for divine attainment contained in it make it a form of Āgama. Because it serves the purpose of Veda it is called Mūlaveda. And it is called Tantra because it spreads (*tanoti*) real knowledge and saves man from the ocean of suffering.[24] The *Nāradapāñcarātra*[25] interprets the term Pāñcarātra as a Śāstra which expounds five types of knowledge. In any case, Pāñcarātra came finally to be connected with Vaiṣṇavism and became an integral part of it. In the *Īśvarasaṃhitā*[26] it is held that Pāñcarātra is *svāttvika* in nature and that it is superior to Vaikhānasa which is *tāmasika* in nature.

According to tradition there are 108 Pāñcarātra Saṃhitās. But we actually have the names of more than 200 texts. Schrader compiled a list of 224 Pāñcarātra texts variously classed as Saṃhitās, Tantras and Āgamas on the basis of the names given in the *Kapiñjala, Pādma, Viṣṇu* and *Hayasīrṣa* Saṃhitās and the *Agnipurāṇa.*[27] According to the *Nārada Pāñcarātra* the texts are said to be of seven types.[28] The *Agnipurāṇa* also divides them into seven types and gives their number as 25.[29] In the *Māheśvaratantra* it is also stated that these Pāñcarātra Saṃhitās are 25 in number. It is quite likely that originally there were 25 basic texts upon which subsequent teatises were written. Schrader groups the bulk of the Pāñcarātra literature under three classes: (1) the original Saṃhitās to which belong most of the extant works; (2) the much smaller South Indian class comprising the legitimate descendants of the first group; and (3) the still smaller class, North and South Indian, of apocryphal or spurious Saṃhitās.[30] He fixed the tentative order of some of the texts in this way. 1 *Pauṣkara, Varāha, Brahmā*; 2 *Sātvata*; 3 *Jaya*; 4 *Ahirbudhnya*; 5 *Parameśvara*; 6 *Sanatkumāra, Parama, Padmodbhava, Mahendra, Kāṇva*; 7 *Pādma*; 8 *Īśvara.* All these are supposed to have been composed before A.D. 800. Utpala, the Kashmirian writer of the 10th century, mentioned by name such early Pāñcarātra texts as *Jayākhya* (*Śrījaya, Jaya*), *Haṃsaparameśvara, Vaihāyasa* and *Śrīkālaparā* in his *Spandapradīpikā.*

Regarding the nature of the Pāñcarātra Āgamas Sanjukta Gupta states:[31]

> The Pāñcarātra Āgamas are classed under four headings: Āgama-siddhānta, Mantra-siddhānta, Tantra-siddhānta and Tantrāntara-siddhānta. The term Siddhānta is apparently a synonym for Āgama. The classification is made according to the deity on whom the text focuses attention. When attention centres on the four *vyūhas* the text falls within the category of Āgama-siddhānta. When nine of twelve forms of Viṣṇu are worshipped, the text is classified as Mantra-siddhānta. When a single form of Viṣṇu is the chief object of worship, the text is classified as Tantra-siddhānta, and when worship centres on a non-anthropomorphic form of Viṣṇu (e.g. the man-lion incarnation) the text is classified as Tantrāntara-siddhānta. The *Sāttvata Saṃhitā*, the *Pauṣkara Saṃhitā*, the *Jayākhya Saṃhitā* and the *Hayagrīva Saṃhitā* respectively, are examples of these four types of Āgamas. It is very important that the initiate should be careful not to confuse the different modes of worship prescribed in the various types of texts.[32]

Like other Tantras of different religious sects, the Pāñcarātra texts deal with four principal topics—*jñāna* (knowledge), *yoga* (concentration), *kriyā* (making), and *caryā* (conduct or doing). In Tamil these are known as *ñānam, yokam, kirikai* and *sarithai.* The ideology of pure creation preceding the intermediate creation is the starting point of Pāñcarātra cosmology. The eternally existing supreme being, Viṣṇu, has the germs of all creation nascent in him in the time of *pralaya* or dissolution. He does not take any active part in the beginning of creation, but projects his will or *icchā* (efficient cause) to his Śakti, the Female Principle of creation, often personified as Śrī-Lakṣmī, in whom rest the aspects of *kriyā* (acting, instrumental cause) and *bhūti* (becoming, material cause), and the combination of these three Śaktis is responsible for *śuddhasṛṣṭi* or pure creation from which other forms of creation take place by stages.

The theological and ritualistic aspects of the Pāñcarātra system have attracted many scholars and a number of texts have been edited and published.[33] Of these the *Sātvata saṃhitā* which describes the system as *rahasyāmnāya*, or a secret method of *sādhanā*, gives a mystic arrangement of letters and formula, the meditations on them, and the special modes of worship by means of *mantras* or various dispositions, and states that this śāstra is fruitful to any person irrespective of caste and colour who has resorted to self-surrender. According to this text, pure creation consists of six *guṇas* the first three of which—*jñāna* (knowledge), *aiśvarya* (lordship), and *śakti* (potency)—form the group of *viśrāmabhūmayaḥ* or stages of rest, while the last three—*bala* (strength), *vīrya* (virility), and *tejas* (splendour)—make up the group of *śramabhūmayaḥ* or stages of action. Each of the three *guṇas* of one group has an innate propensity to pair with one of the other, and the pairing off of the *guṇas* of the opposite groups is at the root of the conception of Vyūha. The three pairs of ideal *guṇas* symbolised by three divine entities—Śaṅkarṣaṇa, Pradyumna and Aniruddha—have Para Vāsudeva as their fountainhead. These conceptions are again brought into relation with the existing Sāṅkhya-Tantric process of cosmic evolution. The combination of Saṅkarṣaṇa with Prakṛti, the primordial substance, yields Manas or Buddhi, the principle of intelligence; that of Pradyumna with Manas yields Ahaṃkāra, the principle of egoity; that of Aniruddha with Ahaṃkāra yields the five Mahābhūtas, the elements with their qualities.

Such texts as *Jayākhya, Pauṣkara, Parama, Ahirbudhnya,* etc., were probably composed before and during the Gupta period. Of these the *Jayākhyasaṃhitā,*[34] which may be assigned to *c.* 5th century, is an important work which contains, besides metaphysical and cosmological speculations, such typically Tantric topics as *yakṣiṇī-sādhanā, cakra-yantra-sādhanā, stambhana*, etc. It deals with *puraścaraṇa* initiation and syllables as also *nyāsas* of various kinds, indicative of its Tantric affiliation, and emphasises that *mantras* must be employed in *homa*, in rites for manes, in destructive activities, and also for securing *mokṣa*. It also serves as the model for a number of later Pāñcarātra texts, such as the *Lakṣmītantra*. The *Paramasaṃhitā* is an important Pāñcarātra Tantra.[35] Its main contribution is to a new interpretation of the Vyūha doctrine. Here it is stated that all gods and worldly objects are the Śaktis of the supereme being, and hence the Śaktis are numerous. Of these, Brahmā, Go or Śiva and Viṣṇu are the main ones. They are conceived as Puruṣas or male principles. Of these principles Viṣṇu is evidently superior since he is endowed with Sattva qualities and functions as the preserver. Owing to the differences of qualities and actions he is variouly known as Puruṣottama, Nārāyaṇa, Vāsava, Vāsudeva, Hari, etc. He resides in all the world as four Vyūhas, each representing the four qualities of *dharma, jñāna, vairāgya* and *aiśvarya*, the four Vedas, the four Varṇas, the four Āsramas and the four directions. The speciality of this doctrine lies in the fact that here a Śakti of the supreme being, not the supreme being itself, is the fountainhead of the Vyūhas and that the Śaktis are regarded as male principles.[36] The *Pauṣkarasaṃhitā*, as we have seen above, falls in the Mantra-siddhānta group of Pāñcarātra works in which different forms of Viṣṇu have been dealt with in addition to the four well known topics of discussion, viz., *jñāna, yoga, kriyā* and *caryā*. Here it is said that Brahmā received the Pāñcarātra scriptures from Aniruddha. It makes a clear distinction between the *para* and *vyūha* aspects of the supreme being.[37] Surprisingly though, the *Pauṣkarasaṃhitā* refers to five *vyūhas* instead of four.[38] Details of *Ahirbudhnya Saṃhitā* and *Lakṣmītantra* will be given in subsequent sections.

The earlier Pāñcarātra works were probably composed in the Kashmir region—because many images have been found of Viṣṇu showing external traits of the Vyūha doctrine. Saṃhitās like *Īśvara, Upendra, Bṛhadbrahma*, etc., were probably composed in the southern region of India. The *Īśvarasaṃhitā* mentions Saṭkopa and Rāmānuja which proves that it was written not earlier than 12th century A.D. According to this text, the main Pāñcarātra texts are *Pauṣkara, Sātvata* and *Jayākhya* while *Parameśvara, Īśvara* and *Pādma* are their developments. The *Sātvatasaṃhitā*[40] on the other hand mentions *Pauṣkara, Vārāha* and *Prājāpatya* or *Brāhma* as did the earlier texts, but in *Pauṣkarasaṃhitā, Sātvata* is mentioned. According to the *Pauṣkara,*[41] the *Parameśvarāgama,* is the root of all Pāñcarātra texts. The *Jayākhyasaṃhitā*[42] mentions Saṃhitā texts in general, but no one in particular. The *Ahirbudhnya Saṃhitā* mentions *Sātvata* and *Jayākhya* as earlier works.[43] According to the *Pādmasaṃhitā,* six texts may be regarded as the six gems of Mantrasiddhānta, and these texts are *Pādmasaṃhitā, Sanatkumārasaṃhitā, Paramasaṃhitā, Pādmodbhavasaṃhitā, Mahendrasaṃhitā* and *Kāṇvasaṃhitā.*[44] Accroding to the *Viṣṇutantra,* quoted in other works, the Mantrasiddhānta is constituted by nine gems which are *Pādmatantra, Viṣṇutantra, Kapiñjalasaṃhitā, Brahmasaṃhitā,*[45] *Mārkaṇḍeyasaṃhitā, Śrīdhara-saṃhitā, Paramasaṃhitā, Bhāradvāja* or *Parāsarasaṃhitā* and *Nārāyaṇatantra.* It is impossible to determine the relative priority and chronology of the Pancaratra texts because of the baffiing references in the texts themselves. On the basis of internal evidence, B.T. Bhattacharyya wanted to assign the *Jayākhyasaṃhitā* to *c.* 5th century A.D.[46] but since it is mentioned in the *Ahirbudhnya saṃhitā* as an earlier work, the latter may be assigned to a somewhat later date. Regarding other texts, nothing can be said with certainty.

The Vaikhānasa Āgamas are pro-Vedic, according to the Vaikhānasa tradition itself, while the Bhāgavata belongs to the pure Tantric and Pāñcarātra to the mixed Tantric categories.[47] According to the *Śāṇḍilyasaṃhitā,*[48] the worship of Viṣṇu is of six types—Vedic, Tantric, Smārta, Mixed, Purāṇic and Devotional. Of these the Tantric method is two fold, Vaikhānasa and Pāñcarātra. The former was created by Brahmā and the latter by Nārada. According to the Vaikhānasa tradition, Atri composed four Tantras (*Pūrva, Ātreya, Viṣṇu,* and *Uttara*), Bhṛgu thirteen Adhikāras (*Khila, Purātantra, Vāsa, Citra, Māna, Kriyā, Arcā, Yajña, Varṇa, Prakīrṇa, Pratigṛhya, Nirukta* and *Khilādhikāra*), Kaśyapa three Kāṇḍas (*Satya, Tarka* and *Jñāna*), and Marici eight Saṃhitās (*Jaya, Ānanda, Saṃjñāna, Vīra, Vijaya, Vijita, Vimala* and *Jñāna*). The prose recension of the original *Vaikhānasāgama* belongs to the older category of Viṣṇuite Āgamas. Its metrical version, belongs to a later period.

The Ahirbudhnya Saṃhitā

Of the Pāñcarātra Saṃhitās, the *Ahirbudhnya* is the most impotant.[49] According to this text there was originally an undifferentiated scriptural complex which for the requirement of the times was divided and freshly moulded by Apāntaratapā, Kapila, Hiraṇyagarbha, Śiva-Paśupati and Viṣṇu.[50] The Pāñcarātra scriptures were originally divided into ten Saṃhitās: *Bhagavat, Karma, Vidyā, Kāla, Kartavya, Vaiśeṣikī-kriyā, Saṃyama, Cintā, Mārga* and *Mokṣa*.[51] That these texts might have actually been in vogue is proved by Madhva's references to passages of the *Kāla* and *Karma Saṃhitās*.[52] The *Ahirbudhnya Saṃhitā* deals elaborately with the Vyūha doctrine and traces the origin and development of the Vyūha representatives like Saṅkarṣaṇa, etc., from Vāsudeva, the embodiment of six qualities (*ṣāḍguṇya-vigrahadeva*), surprisingly in a mythical chronological set up.[53] It also enumerates thirty-nine Avatāras of Viṣṇu.[54] Besides typical matters characteristic of Vaiṣṇavism, it deals with systems like the Sānkhya, Yoga, etc. The Sāṅkhya is here called Sāṅkhya-tantra, sixty topics of which are mentioned but these differ from those mentioned in other texts.[55] It is stated that the doctrines of Kapila's Sāṅkhya-tantra were originally divdided into *maṇḍalas*, called Prākrta and Vaikṛta, and these two had thirty-two and twenty-eight topics respectively.[56] Regarding *Yoga* it says that Hiraṇyagarbha was the first to propound two Yogasaṃhitās, of which one was called Nirodha-yoga having twelve subdivisions, and the other was called Karma-yoga.[57] The significance of typical Vaiṣṇava symbols, like those of the Sudarśana-cakra, etc., are described.[58] *Ahirbudhnya Saṃhitā* also lays down rules about the places where the *puraścaraṇa* of a *mantra* may be practised.[59] Such places are river banks, caves, mountain tops, grounds near *tīrtha*, confluences of rivers, holy forests, parks, etc.[60] It deals elaborately with linguistic occultism,[61] and holds that *mantras* have three senses, and provides a procedure of Mahābhiṣeka as a remedy against diseases, for destroying all enemies, and for the attainments of all desired objects.[62]

The Lakṣmītantra

For the study of Tantric Vaiṣṇavism the most useful work is *Lakṣmītantra* which is a Pāñcarātra text with definite Śākta orientation.[63] Because of its exclusive treatment of Lakṣmī as Śakti of Viṣṇu, later Śākta philosophers and commentators like Bhāskara-raya, Nagesa-bhaṭṭa, Appaya-dikṣita and others have not only mentioned it but also cited it as an authoritative work for the understanding of Śāktism. It was composed some time between the 9th and 12th centuries A.D. It deals mainly with the Pāñcarātra philosophy and cosmogony and with *mantraśāstra.* Moreover, it alludes to the peculiar *sādhanā* of the left-handed Tantras that requires a female partner.[64] It has two objectives in view—to establish the supermacy of Lakṣmī as a philosophical principle, ranking if not higher than Viṣṇu then at least equal to him, and to set down a full record of exclusive Śākta-Upāsanā within the framework of the Pāñcarātra religion.[65] Here the Vyūha doctrine is explained in terms of Lakṣmī as the supreme being. Lakṣmī says in this Tantra:

> As the brilliance of a diamond shines forth in all directions, so does my pure course (of creative energy) diffuse its rays in every direction. Pure creation issues from my form of concentrated (absolute) knowledge, whose (tranquility) resembles a cloudless sky or a still ocean. Devoid of all activity, ever blissful, pure, all-embracing and supreme, the primal *jñāna* (knowledge), becomes manifest and is called Śaṅkarṣaṇa. Aiśvarya (the divine attribute) is my sovereign power to create the universe without dependence on any factor outside myself. That is my (form) Pradyumna, the excellent person. My *śakti* that is immanent, irresistible and which pervades the whole of this variegated universe is known as my Aniruddha form. These resplendent, blue lotus-eyed Puruṣas (Pradyumna, Aniruddha and Śaṅkarṣaṇa) are my forms manifesting (the divine attributes), *vijñāna, aiśvarya* and *śakti* (*kriyā*). Pradyumna, Aniruddha and Śankarṣaṇa are respectively responsible for the creation, maintenance and dissolution of creation. My primordial form when the urge to create (the universe) first stirs in me is Vāsudeva who may be compared to an absolutely waveless ocean or to a cloudless sky. The manifestation (all six of my divine attributes), *jñāna, śakti, bala, aiśvarya, vīrya* and *tejas* in equal proportion is called Vāsudeva.[66]

Lakṣmītantra is divided into forty-nine chapters. Pure creation is traced in this work to Lakṣmī, the embodiment of six ideal attributes. Then the text goes on to describe the transformation of the ideal attributes into the phenomenal attributes contributing to the emergence of a material creation. Characteristics of the four *vyūhas* are described in terms of Lakṣmī. Emanations of Mahāśrī, Mahāvidyā and Mahāmāyā from Mahālakṣmi are dealt with. Evolution of the material world from Prakṛti has been traced in terms of the Sāṅkhya categories. The six *koṣas* of Śakti have been described. Other topics include the *tattvas* and the *jīva* as the object and subject of knowledge; the avatāras of Lakṣmī in the six sheaths; the exclusive incarnations of Śakti; the three types of avatāras of God; Viśākhayūpa and the Vibhava incarnations; the five-fold divine functions; the true form the *jīva*; the true nature of Śakti (Lakṣmī); various methods of attaining ultimate truth; elaboration of the said methods; the secret method of self-surrender; the course of *mantras* and their characteristics; the origin of letters; explanation of the *mātṛkas*; analysis of the structure of a *mantra* and the qualities looked for in a preceptor and in a disciple; description of Lakṣmī's *mantra*-form; description of *mātṛkā*; the structure of *tāraka* with its parts and the method of initiation in the practice of meditation; Tārā and Anutārā *mantras*; elucidation of the seven *vidyās*, viz., Tārā-Tārā, Anutārā, Vāgbhava, Kāma, Sarasvatī and Mahālakṣmi bījas; duties of an adept; different aspects of Śakti; Tārikā in the three stages of existence; hand postures; purification of body; images; external sacrifice and worship; initiation; *puraścaraṇa*; secret Tārikā *mantras*; revelation of Lakṣmī's various manifestations; and cultic characteristics, etc.

The Śaiva Āgamas

It was Śaivism that probably supplied a better ground for the development of the Tantras. The commentators on Śaṅkarācārya's works speak of four Śaiva schools—Śaiva, Pāśupata, Kārukasiddhāntin and Kāpālika. The third has been named Kāruṇikasiddhāntin by Vācaspati, while both Rāmānuja and Keśava Kaśmīrī, in the course of enumerating the same four schools, describe the third as Kālāmukha which is also referred to by Śrīnivāsa in the *Vedāntakaustubha* and Vedottama in his *Pāñcarātraprāmāṇya*. Some comparatively late Purāṇas, like the *Śivapurāṇa*[67] qualifies the Śaiva schools as following the Siddhāntamārga and mentions the Kālāmukha Śaivas as Mahāvratadharas. The *Tantrādhikārinirṇaya*[68] attributes to *Liṅgapurāṇa* a verse which refers to the sects variously as Vāma, Pāśupata, Soma, Lāṅgala, Kāpāla Bhairava, and Nākula. Nākula and Lāṅgala evidently refer to the Lakulīśa-Pāśupatas. The Kāpālas or Kāpālikas appear to have been closely related to the Somas, Saumas or Somasiddhāntins.[69] A number of their subsects like Bharaṭa, Bhakta, Laiṅgika, etc., have been mentioned by Guṇaratna.[70] The Mattamāyūraka sect that flourished in the 9th and 10th centuries in Madhya Pradesh had a number of temples and some scriptural works. The *Vīrāgama*[71] refers to four schools of Śaivas as Sāmānya-Śaiva, Pūrva-Śaiva, Miśra-Śaiva, and Śuddha-Śaiva. Of the subsequent Śaiva schools, the Pratyabhijñā school of Kashmir, the followers of the Siddhāntāgamas of the South, and the Vīraśaiva of the Kannaḍa-speaking areas are each well-known for their large following and a rich literature of their philosophy and rituals.

The Pāśupata was the oldest form of Śaivism prevalent in North India. The *Mahābhārata* says that the Pāśupata doctrines were first preached by Śiva Śrīkaṇṭha who was probably a human teacher.[72] Lakulīśa was probably his disciple. Facts about Lakulīśa, the great exponent of the Pāśupata sect, are found in an inscription dated A.D. 380-1 (G.E. 61), belonging to the reign of Chandragupta II from which it appears that he flourished about the 2nd century in the Kathiawar region.[73] He had four disciples—Kuśika, Garga, Mitra and Karuṣya. Variants of the last three names are found in the Purāṇas. The earliest text dealing with the principal tenets of the Pāśupata system is known as the *Pāśupatasūtra*.[74] The name of its author is not known but it was commented by Rāśīkara Kauṇḍinya who flourished in the Gupta age. It is divided into five chapters each dealing respectively with *kārya, kāraṇa, yoga, vidhi* and *duhkhānta*, the five fundamentals of the Pāśupata system. The Pāśupata system as described in Mādhava's *Sarvadarśanasaṃgraha* totally corresponds to that found in the aforesaid work.

One of the important streams of the ancient Pāśupata system later culminated in what may be called Āgamānta Śaivism. This school possessed a considerable literature called Āgamas, a number of which are preserved in manuscripts of the 8th and 9th centuries, numbering eighteen according to one tradition and twenty-eight according to another.[75] The eighteen Āgamas, which are also called Śiva Tantras, are *Vijaya, Niśvāsa, Svāyambhūva Vātula, Vīrabhadra, Raurava, Mākuṭa, Vireśa, Candrahāsa, Jñāna, Mukhabimba, Prodgīta, Lalita, Siddha, Santāna, Sarvodgīta, Kiraṇa* and *Parameśvara*.[76] A list has also been found which mentions ten more Śiva Tantras: *Kāmika, Yogada, Divya, Karaṇa, Ajita, Dīpta, Sukṣma, Sahasra, Aṣṭa* and *Aṃśubheda*. According to the tradition twenty-eight Āgamas were produced from the five mouths of Śiva. From the mouth known as Sadyojāta came the five beginning with the *Kāmika*, from that known as Vāmadeva came the five beginning with *Surprabheda*, form that known as Aghora came the six beginning with *Vijaya*, from that known as Tatpuruṣa came the six beginning with *Raurava*, and from that known as Īśāna came the six beginning with *Kiraṇa*. It should be remembered that these traditional twenty-eight Śaiva Āgamas are regarded as authoritative by all Śaiva sects, even by the later social reformistic Vīraśaivas. The Āgamānta Śaivas appear to have contributed to the development of Tantric ideas in Tamil Śaivism. Rājendra Cola, during his expeditions in northern India, came in touch with some teachers of this school and brought them to his own country. Of these teachers Aghora-Śivācārya of the 12th century composed a valuable treatise known as *Kriyā-Karmadyotinī*. This was followed by Trilocana's *Siddhāntasārāvalī* and Nigama Jñānadeva's *Jīrṇoddhāra-daśakam*.

The Kāpālikas and Kālāmukhas, as we have stated above, were the two extreme offshoots of the Pāśupata system. They were known as Atimārgikas. Their literature is lost but the tenets of their beliefs and practices may be gleaned from other literary sources. Incidentally it may be noted that the name of the teachers belonging to the Atimārgika schools almost invariably end in such suffixes as *rāśi*, *śakti* and *jīya*. Another sect that flourished in the medieval age was the Mattamāyura referred to in some inscriptions in the Cedi country of Central India. This sect also had its centre in Kāśi and Bengal. The names of the Mattamāyura teachers almost invariably ended either in *śambhu* or in *śiva*. They have their own literature. Somaśambhu, an *ācāryā* of the Golakimaṭha, wrote the work *Somasambhupaddhati* in which a comprehensive account of the Śaiva Āgamas is given.[77] Īśānaśivagurudevamiśra's *Īśānaśivagurudevapaddhati* is a Tantra of this sect and was composed about A.D.1100 or a little later.[78] It is in four parts—Sāmānyapāda, Mantrapāda, Kriyāpāda and Yogapāda—and contains 18,000 ślokas. It expounds the six categories of Śaivism—*paśu, pāśa, pati, śakti, vicāra* and *kriyācāra*.

The Kashmir school of Śaivism was sponsored by Vasugupta of the 9th century who is said to have derived his spiritual impulses from Śiva-Śrīkaṇṭha known as the founder of the Āgama literature and the author of *Śivasūtra*.[79] It is said that the Śivasūtras were revealed to him through the divine inspiration of Śiva, the purpose of which was to identify Śiva Śrīkaṇṭha with the great god so that the authoritativeness and importance of these *sūtras* could be established beyond any question. The texts of Kashmir Śaivism are divided into Āgamaśāstra, Spandaśāstra and Pratyabhijñāśāstra. Among the Āgamas on which this school banks, the chief ones are *Mālinīvijaya, Svacchanda, Vijñānabhairava, Ucchuṣmabhairava, Ānandabhairava, Mṛgendra, Netra, Naiśvāsa, Svāyambhūva* and *Rudrayāmala*. Of the Spandaśāstra, the first and foremost is the *Śpandasūtra* or *Spandakārikā*, a compendium (*saṃgraha-grantha*) attributed to Vasugupta himself. His disciple Kallaṭa wrote a *vṛtti* on this *sūtra* and the two together are called *Spandasarvasva*. On the *Spandakārikā* we have such commentaries as the *Spandanirṇaya* and *Spandasandoha* by Kṣemarāja (who also wrote commentaries on the *Śivasūtra* and on *Svacchanda* and other Tantras), the *Spandavivṛti* by Rāmakaṇṭha and the *Pradīpikā* by Utpala Vaiṣṇava. These commentators belonged to the 11th and 12th centuries. Somāṇanda, a disciple of Vasugupta, who flourished about the end of the 9th century and became celebrated as the exponent of the Pratyabhijñā school, wrote a book called *Śivadṛṣṭi*. The *Īśvarapratyabhijñā* or the *Pratyabhijñā sūtra* by Utpala, a pupil of Somānanda, is an interpretation of the former work. Commentaries on it are the *vṛtti* by Utpala himself and the *Pratyabhijñāvimarśinī* [*Laghu-vṛtti*] and the *Pratyabhijñāvivṛtti-vimarśinī* (*Bṛhad-vṛtti*) by Abhinavagupta who also composed the *Tantrāloka* and *Tantraśāra* and also commentaries on *Pañcatriṃśika-tantra*, etc. The *Bhāskarī* is a lucid and very helpful *ṭīkā* on Abhinavagupta's commentaries.[80] His *Tantrāloka*, with Jayaratha's commentary,[81] is a veritable encyclopaedia of the system. His *Paramārthasāra*[82] with Yogarāja's commentary, and *Tantraśāra*[83] and also Kṣemarāja's *Pratyabhijñāhṛdaya*[84] are three small but important works of this school.

The Vīraśaiva school, which flourished in the Kannaḍa-speaking areas, came into existence as a revolutionary social reform movement about the middle of the 12th century under the dynamic leadership of Vasava. The philosophy of this school is directly inspired by the twenty-eight Śaiva Āgamas. In the Kannaḍa language, the *Vacanas* of Vasava, and works like *Vasavapurāṇa*, *Channavasavapurāṇa*, etc., contain much information on this school. Some tenets of Vīraśaiva doctrines are found in the *Sutasaṃhitā* of the *Skandapurāṇa*, the *Kāmikāgama* and the *Vātulatantra*, but the doctrines are elaborated and systematised in such works as Reṇukācārya's *Siddhāntaśikhāmaṇī*, *Prabhuliṅgalīlā*, Māyīdeva's *Anubhavasūtra* and others. In Vīraśaiva system greater importance is laid upon the doctrine of Śakti and that is why it is also called *Śaktiviśiṣṭādvaitavāda*. Vasava freed Śaivism from the chains of *varṇāśrama*; his insistence on physical labour, the social supremacy of women, the importance of science and technology must have been inspired by the Tantras of the earlier tradition.

The Śaiva Siddhānta or Tamil Śaivism is also based upon the twenty-eight Śaiva Āgamas, the most authoritative of which, according to this school, is *Kāmikāgama*. The devotional songs of the Śaiva saints who were known as Nāyanmars, laid the basis of Tamil Śaivism as an organised religio-philosophical entity. The canonical literature of this system owes its present arrangement to Nambi Āṇḍar Nambi who flourished about the beginning of the 11th century. The *Śivajñānabodham* of Meykaṇḍār written in the first half of the 13th century is the first attempt at a systematic statement of the tenets of Tamil Śaivism.[85]

This is a short treatise of a dozen of aphorisms (*sūtras*) which seem to have been translated from a Sanskrit original. The author has added *vārttikas* of his own which explain and illustrate the argument of each of the *sūtras*. Śiva-jñāna-munivar, the commentator on the *sūtras* says that they form part of the *Raurava-āgama*. The next work of importance is Arunandi's *Śivajñānasiddhiyār*.[86] Mānavāśagangaḍandār's *Uṇmai-vilakkam* is a catechism which claims to reveal the essence of all Āgamas. Umāpati-Śivācārya was the author of eight works of which the *Śivappirākāsam, Śaṅkarpa-nirākaranam,* and *Uṇmai-neri-vilakkam* are the most important.[87]

The Niśvāsatattva Saṃhitā

The second text in the list of the Śaiva Āgamas, the *Niśvāsa*, seems to be same as the *Niśvāsatattva Saṃhitā*, a manuscript of which written in Gupta characters was found by H.P. Sastri in the Nepal Darbar library.[88] The manuscript consists of 114 palm-leaves and belongs to the 8th century A.D. Its contents have been summarised by P.C. Bagchi:

> The importance of the text lies in the fact that it mentions a large number of Tantric texts which existed at the time of its compilation. The text consists of five *sūtras* and though they form a complete whole, each of them may be taken independently of others. The five *sūtras* are (i) *Laukikadharma*, (ii) *Mūlasūtra*, (iii) *Uttarasūtra*, (iv) *Nayasūtra*, and (v) *Guhyasūtra*. The last is more extensive than the four others taken together. According to a verse occurring on fol. 23b the section of *Laukikadharma* is left out and the next four sections are said to form the main body of the text. . . . On fol. 41b it is said that the text is called a *saṃhitā* because five texts have been put together. They represent five currents of literary traditions communicated by mouth and hence they are called *Niśvāsa* . . . In the first section (*Mulāsūtra*) the Devī says that she has learnt the doctrines of the Vedānta and twenty-five Sāṅkhyas, and now desires to learn the Śivatattva. The first chapter deals with initiation and the initiated; the second chapter with sacrifice and the mode of worshipping Śiva; the third chapter with *muktimaṇḍalam*; the fourth with *muktidīkṣā* and the fifth with the nature of the *mantras*. The subject matter of the last three chapters is not well arranged. In the second section (*Uttarasūtra*) there are five chapters, the first

two dealing with *Śivālaya-sthāpana*, *Mātṛkā* and *Homa*; the third and the fourth with *abhiṣeka* and *dikṣā* and the fifth with *jñānayoga*. A number of holy places and rivers is mentioned on fol. 9b and 42. . . . In the same chapter five kinds of Liṅgas are spoken of. . . . On fol. 24a and 24b there is a description of the Śivatantras.[89]

Śaiva Tantras in the Far East

There are reasons to believe that among the five or four texts of the *Niśvāsatattva Saṃhitā* the *Uttara* and *Nayasūtras* formed part of the Cambodian Tantric text *Nayottara*. The inscription of Sdok-kak-Thom[90] mentions the introduction of the mystic cult of Devarāja (phallic representation of Śiva) along with some Tantric texts in Kambuja during the reign of Jayavarman II (beginning of the 9th century A.D.) and also the initiation of the king's high priest Śivakaivalya by a Brāhmaṇa called Hiraṇyadāma into the secret cult upheld by such scriptures as the *Śiraścheda*. *Vināśika*, *Sammoha* and *Nayottara* supposed to have been issued from the four faces of Tumburu (emanation of Śiva). On these four texts B.R. Chatterji observes:

> There were three regions each with its special Tantras and that among the Tantras of Viṣṇukrāntā region (which includes Bengal and extends to Chittagong) the names of the *Sammohana* and the *Niruttara* Tantras approach very closely to the titles of the two (out of four) of the Tantras (*Sammoha* and *Nayottara*) taught by Hiraṇyadāma. The Tantras *Muṇḍamālā* and *Chinnamastā* mean (as far as the names go) almost the same thing as *Śiraścheda*—the third text taught to the Kambuja priest. The word Tumburu (of which according to the inscriptions, the four texts constitute the four faces) is the name of a Gandharva, and there is a *Gandharva Tantra* in the Viṣṇukrāntā group.[91]

Bagchi has correctly identified Tumburu with Śiva.[92] The tradition that the scriptures were revealed from the four mouths of Tumburu is simply a Cambodian borrowing of the idea that the Tantras were originally issued from the four mouths (*vaktras*) of Śiva. So far as the geographical distribution of the Tantras are concerned, Bagchi wants to depend more on the *srota* (current) divisions than on the *krāntā* divisions. A passage of the *Brahmayāmala* distinctly says that three texts known as *Sammoha*, *Nayottara* and *Śiraścheda* issued from the left current. The first is not difficult to identify while the second has been proved to be combination of the *Naya* and *Uttara-sūtras* of the *Niśvāsatattva Saṃhitā*. According to Bagchi, *Śiraścheda* was no other than the *Jayadrathayāmala*. The latter text itself (*Ṣaṭka* III, fol. 215a, Darbar Library Mss) clearly speaks of it. The *Vaināśika* seems to have been a supplement of *Jayadrathayāmala* connected with the Vaināśika-Bhairavas.[93]

Other inscriptions from Cambodia also refer to the Śaiva Tantras.[94] They mention the *Śivaśāstra, Śaivāgama, Sarvāgama* and *Śaiva-vyākaraṇa*. These were connected with the Āgamānta form of Śaivism. In an Angkorvat inscription we find reference to a well-known Tantric text, the *Parameśvaratantra*, also called *Parameśvaramatatantra*, which is one of the eighteen traditional Śaiva Āgamas. It is also included in the later lists of twenty-eight Āgamas.[95] The influence of the Āgamas can be amply traced to the Śaivite cults practised in Kambuja and Campā.

Some Śaiva Tantras of the Nepal Collection

We have seen that four Tantric texts mentioned in a Cambodian inscription of A.D. 802, of the reign of Jayavarman II, are partly preserved in old manuscripts in the Nepal Darbar Library. Of these the *Sammohatantra* is found in a late Newari manuscript. It consists of sixty-seven pages divided into ten *paṭalas*. The palm-leaf manuscript of the *Brahmayāmala* is dated 172 Nepal Samvat (A.D. 1052). The writing is old hooked Newari. It seems to have been copied from an earlier manuscript. The palm-leaf manuscript of the *Piṅgalāmata* is dated 294 Nepal Samvat (A.D. 1174). The *Jayadrathayāmala* is a very big work divided into four parts or *Ṣaṭkas*, each containing six thousand verses. The manuscript of the fourth part belongs to the 12th century A.D. while those of the other parts belong to a much later date. The second part is incomplete.[96]

The *Sammohatantra* begins with the enumeration of the nine tradition of *mantras* according to the *Kalikāmata* and the twenty divisions of the Śāmbhavas in terms of their holy places, literary traditions, and script and language used. Then it deals with various kinds of Pīṭhas and countries in which the *Kādi* and *Hādi* modes of practice were prevalent. In Chapter 5 there is an enumeration of various Tantric sects, their distribution and the account of Tantric literature prevalent in various countries. The followers of the *Kādi* and *Hādi* modes are distributed into nine *āmnāyas* or divisions. The four general divisions—Kerala, Kāśmīra, Gauḍa, and Vilāsa—and three main types of rites—Divya, Kaula and Vāma—are mentioned along with the number of principal and subsidiary Tantras in different countries. In chapter 6 there is a detailed enumeration of the literature of various sects, while in Chapter 7 there is a sixfold classification of Tantric *sādhanā* from various points of view.

The *Brahmayāmala* relates how the original knowledge was communicated in 125,000 verses to Śrīkaṇṭha who imparted it to others in amplified versions in different countries. Its main emphasis is on *Srotanirṇaya,* i.e. classification of the Tantric sects according to the three currents of *dakṣiṇa* (right), *vāma* (left) and *madhyama* (middle), details of which are given in terms of their deities, modes of wor-ship, holy places, and sacred texts. A list of the gods and sages who divulged the knowledge of Śiva is given. In enumerating the *dakṣiṇa* current special importance is given to the Bhairavas of the *Vidyāpītha* and *Mantrapītha.* To the former category belong Svacchanda, Krodha, Unmatta, Ugra, Kapāli, Jhaṅkāra, Śekhara and Vijaya and to the latter Canda, Guḍakā, Vīra, Mahā, and Mahā-vīreśa.

The *Piṅgalāmata* is narrated in the form of a conversation between the goddess Piṅgalā and Bhairava. It begins with explanations of such words as Āgama, Śāstra, Jñāna, Tantra, etc., and the purpose of the communication of Tantric knowledge to others. The *Piṅgalāmata* belongs to the Kalpārtha subdivision of the *Kriyāsūtra* which is described in the text as one of the seven classes of Tantras. The *Praśna-prakaraṇa* section of this text deals with the definition of a Liṅga and gives a list of the Ācāryas who are competent to worship it. Then follows a distinction between the general and special types of worship. The materials for making the Liṅgas and the places fit for their installation are mentioned. It claims that it belongs to the uncommon or *asādhāraṇa* type of Tantra, seeks to explain the denomination (*abhidhāna*), cause (*nimitta*), maker (*kartā*) and extent (*pariṇāma*) by which things are conditioned.

The *Jayadrathayāmala* contains much important material for the history of Tantric literature; this is dealt with in Chapter 35 of the first part which is known as Sambandhāvatāra. The next chapter called Sūtranirṇaya contains an enumeration of the Tantras of various tradition. Chapter 41 deals with the Yāmala, Maṅgala, Aṣṭaka and the lineage of the sages who promulgated the Tantras. The second part, divided into forty-one chapters (not all have been found), deals with the deities and their rituals. The third and fourth parts have also similar contents, in which *mantras* and *maṇḍalas, dhyānas,* description of the deities, and various modes of initiation have been described.[97]

The Buddhist Tantras

In one type of texts efforts are made to expound Tantra within the general structure of Buddhist philosophy. At the first stage in the history of Buddhist research, such texts, mainly found in Nepal and Tibet where Tantrism flourished, were studied by European scholars, especially by those belonging to the Russian school. Tibetan studies were initiated by Alexander Csoma de Koros in 1834 and aspects of Tibetan Buddhism began to come to light through the works of C.F. Köppen, V.P. Vasilev (W. Wassiljew), E. Schlaginweit, W. Rockhill, A. Waddell and others. In Tibet Sarat Chandra Das collected a great deal of material from the ancient libraries of Sākya and Sam-ye monasteries of Lhasa. The travels of Das in Tibet and the publication of some texts by him aroused considerable interest among Indian scholars, as a result of which the Buddhist Text Society was established in Calcutta in 1892.

In Tibet, the collection of translations of Indian texts numbers more than 4,556 which are divided into two groups, viz., Bkaḥ-ḥgyur (Kanjur) consisting of 1,108 texts, and Bstan-ḥgyur (Tanjur) consisting of 3,458 texts. The Kanjur is divided into seven parts—Vinaya, Prajñāpāramitā, Buddhāvataṃsaka, Ratnakūṭa, Sūtra, Nirvāṇa and Tantra—while the Tanjur is divided into two—Tantra and Sūtra.[98] Historical works on Buddhism, mainly preserved in the Tibetan collections, are also of immense help in the study of Tantric Buddhism. Of such works, Vasumitra's *Samayabhedaparacanacakra*, Bhāvaviveka's *Nikāyabhedavibhaṅgavyākhyāna*, and Vinītadeva's *Samayabhedaparacanacakre-Nikāyabhedapradarśnasṃgraha*, all dealing with the history of the transformations of the Buddhist sects, are important.[99] The *Biography of Dharmasvāmin* is of greater importance since it deals with the so called decadent phase of Buddhism which was characterised by its Vajrayāna or Tantric form.[100] Bu-ston's work on the history of Buddhism, *Chos-byung*, is also very helpful for the study of Buddhist Tantra,[101] but the most important is Lāmā Tāranātha's history, r*Gya-gar-chos '-byuṅ.*[102] Sumpa Mkhan Po's *Pag-sam-jon-Zang* is another important work for the study of Vajrayāna Buddhism, its doctrines, literature, and succession of teachers.[103]

Tantric elements are found in the *Dhāraṇīs* which constitute a large and important part of the *Mahāyāna* literature. We have a Tibetan version of a group of *Sūtras* with Tantric affiliations, collected as early as the 4th century A.D. under the title *Mahāsannipāta.* The first *Sūtra* in this collection, known as *Ratnaketudhāraṇī*[104] which was translated into Chinese in the 5th century A.D., presupposes the Tantric trend by which other texts like *Bhaiṣajyaguru, Ekādaśamukha, Hayagrīvavidyā, Sarvatathāgatādhiṣṭhāna vyūha*, etc., were also characterised.[105] S. Levi suggested that the *Mahāmāyuri-sūtra*, one of the five *pañcarakṣā* or protective spells, other being *Mahāpratisarā, Mahāsāhsrapramardinī, Mahāśitāveti* and *Mahārakṣāmantrānusāriṇī*, was composed about third-fiourth century A.D. The Tibetan Kanjur contains, among works of Dhāraṇī type, *Vajravidāraṇānāma-dhāraṇī* which belongs to fourth-fifth century. The *Prajñāparamitā-sūtras* also throw much light on Tantric Buddhism.[106] They contain all the paraphernalia of worship which is to be found in Tantra. The *Sūtras, Hṛdayasūtras, Dhāraṇīs* and *Mantras* contained in them presuppose the Tantric cults of Vajrayāna Buddhism. Of the earlier Tantras which were composed before and about the 8th century A.D. reference should be made to the *Guhyasamāja*,[107] *Mahāvairocana*,[108] *Sarvatathāgatatattva saṃgraha* (found both in Tibetan and Sanskrit Mss.),[109] *Vajraśikhara* (a version of the preceding one), *Vajrabhairava* (found both in Tibetan and Sanskrit Mss.), *Cakrasaṃvara* (also known as *Saṃvara* and *Ḍākinījāla* and having various recensions in Tibetan) and *Mañjuśrīmūlakalpa*.[110]

The composition of the *Mañjuśrīmūlakalpa* and the *Guhyasamāja* must have taken place sometime after the *Kāraṇḍavyūha* and the *Mahāpratyaṅgirā-dharāṇi*, i.e. about the 5th or 6th century A.D. There was some controversy over the date of the composition of the *Mañjuśrīmūlakalpa* between B.T. Bhattacharyya and M. Winternitz, the former holding the opinion that the original form of this text was much shorter and was composed about the 2nd century A.D. while the latter was inclined to the view that its composition should be placed in the 6th or 7th century A.D.[111] In its present form, however, the work belongs to the 8th century A.D. since it gives an account of king Gopāla's accession to the throne but does not refer to the activities of Dharmapāla and Devapāla. The *Guhyasamāja* is mentioned by Śāntideva (7th century A.D.) in his *Śikśāsamuccaya* and by Indrabhūti in his *Jñānasiddhi*. Details about these texts will be given in a subsequent section.

Of the Tantras composed between the 8th and 11th centuries we may refer to such works as *Hevajra*,[112] *Rakta-Yamāri, Ārāli, Buddhakapāla, Mahāmāyā* (Sanskrit Mss. available), *Tilaka* or *Mahāmudrātilaka, Kṛṣṇayamāri. Sampuṭa* or *Caturyoginīsampuṭa* (Sanskrit Mss. available), *Yoginīsamcaryā, Vajrāmṛta* (Sanskrit Mss. available), and *Kālacakra* (Sanskrit Mss. available). Most of these texts and their authors are mentioned by Lāmā Tāranātha. According to him the *Hevajratantra* was introduced by Padmavajra and Kambala. Padmavajra is mentioned in the list of teachers given in the *Pag-Sam-Jon-Zang* and translations of his works are preserved in the Tibetan Tanjur. Tārānātha makes him a contemporary of Indrabhūti, Lalitavajra and Kukkuripā. This Lalitavajra is said to have introduced the three divisions of the *Kṛṣṇayamāri-tantra,* while Kukkuripā is believed to have introduced into Vajrayāna the *Mahāmāyā-tantra.* Besides the *Hevajratantra,* Padmavajra had another work called *Guhyasiddhi*[113] written in twilight language or *sandhyābhāṣā.* He was also the author of the *Utpattikramasādhanā* and a few other works. According to Tāranātha, Saraha introduced the *Buddhakapāla-tantra,* Luipa the *Yoginīsaṃcaryā,* Kṛṣṇācārya the *Sampuṭatilaka,* Gambhīravajra the *Vajrāmṛta tantra* and Pito the *Kālācakra-tantra.*

Tāranātha wrote that at the time of Dharmakīrti there were three *Ācāryās* headed by Saraha and his disciple Luipā. In the Tibetan catalogue Luipā is mentioned as the author of *Śrībhagavadabhisamaya, Vajrasattvasādhanā, Abhisamayavibhaṅga* and *Buddhodaya.* He was probably different from his namesake who was the composer of the *Dohās.* Kambala, who collaborated with Padmavajra in introducing the *Hevajratantra,* wrote *Prajñāpāramitā-navaśloka-piṇḍārtha* and *Svasaṃvedanaprākṛtaśāstra.* Anaṅgavajra who succeeded Padmavajra, wrote a number of works of which only the *Prajñopāya-viniścaya-siddhi* is available in the original Sanskrit. Indrabhūti, who succeeded Anaṅgavajra, was the author of the *Jñānasiddhi.*[114] He composed another work called *Sahajasiddhi.* Indrabhūti's sister Lakṣmīṃkarā was the celebrated writer of *Advayasiddhi,* the original Sanskrit manuscript of which is extant.

Some other Tantric texts in the Tibetan collections should also be mentioned. These are *Guhyagarbha, Dhyānottarapaṭala, Ekavīra* (Sanskrit Mss. available), *Śuddhikara, Mahāmāyūrī* (Sanskrit Mss. available), *Mahāpratisarā* (Sanskrit Mss. available), *Krodhavijaya, Amoghapāśa* (Sanskrit mss. available), *Vajraḍāka* and *Dākārṇava* (Tibetan and Apabhraṃśa).[115] The *Guhyagarbha* in which the Bodhisattva Samantabhadra is extolled was composed about the sixth century A.D. The *Vairocanābhisambodhi* is associated with the cult of Vajrapāṇi. There is another text called *Mañjuśrīnāmasaṃgīti,* formerly a Yoga Tantra, later attached to the *Kālacakra,* of which we have Tibetan and Sanskrit versions. According to Alex Wayman, the

Mañjuśrīnāmāsaṃgīti has a character like the *Tattvasaṁgraha* which is the type of a compendium condensing numerous topics. The *Sādhanamālā* is a collection of very short Tantric texts dealing with the conceptual forms of the deities of Vajrayāna and hence very important for iconographical studies.[116] Of the commentaries the earlier ones of Virūpa, Saraha, Kukkurī and others are missing. Of the works known to be extant in Sanskrit, reference may be made to Saroruha or Padmavajra's *Padminī* and Kṛṣṇācārya's *Yogaratnamālā*, commentaries on the *Hevajra*; Nāgārjuna's *Pañcakrama*,[117] which is an extract of the *Guhyasamāja*; the commentary of Āryadeva on *Dākinījāla*, that of Bhadrapāda on *Saṃvara*, that of Dharmādāsa on *Kṛṣṇayamāri*, and that of Kumāradāsa on *Vajrabhairava*. Besides, there are other works like the *Vimalaprabhā* commentary on the *Kalācakra* and Nāḍapāda's *Sekoddeśaṭikā*.[118] The *Advayavajrasaṃgraha*, a collection of twenty short Tantric texts ascribed to Advayavajra,[119] and Abhayākaragupta's *Niṣpannayogāvālī*,[120] which deals with the doctrine of *maṇḍala*, are important works on Vajrayāna Buddhism.

The Guhyasamāja Tantra

The *Guhyasamāja*[121] is one of the earliest extant Buddhist Tantras which was composed evidently before the 7th century A.D. According to Wayman it was composed about the fourth century A.D. Later works like the *Guhyasiddhi* of Padmavajra and the *Jñānasiddhi* of Indrabhūti acknowledge *Guhyasamāja* as the highest authority. *Guhyasamāja* means a secret society, which, it is believed was the organisation which first introduced tenets of Vajrayāna into Buddhism. They are said to have been introduced in an assembly of the faithful by Lord Buddha who is called here Sarva-Tathāgata-Kāya-Vāk-Citta.

The *Guhyasamāja* deals mainly with *yoga* and *anuttarayoga* and incidentally with *maṇḍalas*. Its chief aim is to explain the *tathāgataguhya*, i.e. the unknowable reality, the source of all Tathāgatas as also of the phenomenal world, and how to realise it. According to this text, the truth is *vajra* or the oneness of the universe in which there is no distinction between a man and a woman, or even between a wife or sister or mother. *Kāya* or body, *vāk* or speech, and *citta* or mind are called *tri-vajra*.[122] It puts forward a quick and short method for realising Buddhahood and for the attainment of miraculous powers such as killing an enemy with magical rites, causing rainfall in a drought, etc.,[123] and methods for the attainment of *siddhi*, which is of two kinds, ordinary (*sāmānya*) and extraordinary (*uttama*).[124] It sets forth six *aṅgas* of Yoga, omitting the first three of Patañjali and adding *anusmṛti*.

Besides, the *Guhyasamāja* knows of six black acts (*ṣaṭkarmāṇi*)—*śānti* (for averting diseases), *vaśīkaraṇa* (for bewitching) *stambhana* (stopping the movements of others), *vidveṣana* (creating bad blood), *ucāṭana* (driving away persons) and *māraṇa* (killing).[125] It permits the use of several kinds of flesh[126] and allows the killing of animals, speaking untruth; intercourse with women including even incest with mother, sister and daughter.[127]

The Mañjuśrīmūlakalpa

The *Mañjuśrīmūlakalpa*[128] is also an earlier extensive work on Tantric Buddhism, which has been published in the Trivandrum Sanskrit Series in three volumes edited by T. Ganapati Sastri. Like the *Guhyasamāja* it is written in the Saṅgīti style in prose and verse in mixed Sanskrit. It is interesting to note that though basically a work of the Vajrayāna tradition the *Mañjuśrīmūlakalpa* does not refer specially to the doctrine of five Dhyānī Buddhas, or even their names, *mudrās*, *mantras*, families, Śaktis, colour, and directions. There are endless *mantras*, *maṇḍalas*, and *mudrās* scattered here and there without any systematisation; their correlation with the Vajrayāna pantheon is totally absent.

The *Mañjuśrīmūlakalpa* is included in the Tibetan Kanjur. It has now fifty-five chapters but a Chinese translation of the 10th century exists which has only twenty-eight chapters. It deals with the legendary biography of Buddha up to his *nirvāṇa*, gives some historical information and teaches that the observances of moral precepts, austerities, offering of oblations. Muttering of prayers and meditation are the prerequisites for success in the *mantra* cult, and are to be performed under the guidance of a mantrācārya who gives the initiation and then imparts the *mantra*. It names and defines 108 *mudrās* and holds that the combination of *mantras* and *mudrās* bring success in all actions and that calendrical observances of vows and fasts are of no use.

A section of the *Mañjuśrīmūlakalpa* is devoted to *paṭavidhāna*, i.e. directions for drawing pictures of different Buddhas, Bodhisattvas, Tārā and other goddesses as also of the Krodharājas, Yamāntakas,

Yakṣas and Yakṣiṇīs. It is interesting to note that the Bengali artists called Paṭuyās still maintain the art traditions set forth in this text. The drawing of *maṇḍalas* is another important feature of this work, each of which is associated with certain rites and ceremonies for worshipping deities. Modes of painting abstract ideas are also described. Apart from all these, the text furnishes us with a list of holy places for quick success in the *mantra* cult.

Despite many references to later conditions by which the present text is burdened, it may reasonably be held that the *Mañjuśrīmūlakalpa* belongs to the earlier Buddhist Tantric tradition. The special expression Vajrayāna is absent in this text. Instead, we find the term Mantrayāna which points to the fact that the text was originally composed when Tantric Buddhism was yet to be characterised by its most popular name.

The Sādhanamālā *and the* Niṣpannayogāvālī

The *Sādhanamālā* is a collection of numerous *sādhanas*, i.e. conceptual descriptions, meditative forms, and ritualistic aspects of Buddhist deities intended for the attainment of *siddhi* which is miraculous power or self-realisation. These *sādhanas* were written, both in prose and in verse, in Sanskrit and were translated into Tibetan. The Tibetan versions are now preserved in the Tanjur collection. In other Tantric texts also a good number of *sādhanas* are available. These were collected and given the names of *Sādhanamālā* and *Sādhanasamuccaya*, and a critical edition of all available *sādhanas* was published in two volumes by B.T. Bhattacharyya. This edition is comprised of 312 *sādhanas* and contains description of numerous Buddhist deities. The *Sādhanamālā* not only gives valuable details regarding the deities, but a study of this work reveals much information on the Tantric tradition, its philosophy and psychic exercises, and also of the Tantric authors, Siddhas, *mantras, maṇḍalas* and various other matters of historical and cultural interest. The *sādhanas* of which the text is constituted reveal on the one hand the nature of Buddhist Tantric worship and on the other help to differentiate the Buddhist deities from those of the Hindus and Jains, thus proving themselves to be the most valuable and important aids to the study of Buddhist iconography. A *sādhana* is prescribed for the realisation of a particular god or goddess according to a fixed procedure laid therein. The worshipper is asked to identify himself with the deity. It is said that the gods have no independent, real existence apart from that in the mind of the worshipper and the manner of worship. They possess no external form but represent purely the mental conceptions of the aspirant. The *Sādhanamālā* refers to four great centres of Tantric cults—Uḍḍiyāna, Pūrṇagiri, Kāmarūpa and Śrīhaṭṭa.

The *Niṣpannayogāvālī* was written by Abhayākara Gupta of the Vikramaśilā monastery who flourished during the reign of the Pāla king Rāmapāla (A.D. 1084-1130). It is a work on *maṇḍalas* describing numerous deities of Tantric Buddhism. It contains in all twenty-six *maṇḍalas* in as many chapters. Many of the deities described in this work are not mentioned elsewhere and as such a large number of its descriptions are absolutely original, highly interesting and informative specially in relation to iconographical studies. The religious and philosophical contents of this work are also of great value, as we shall see while dealing with the history of Vajrayāna Buddhism.[129]

The Prajñopāya *and the* Hevajratantra

The *Prajñopāya-viniścaya-siddhi*[130] was composed about A.D. 705 by Anaṅgavajra, one of the eighty-four Siddhas venerated in Tibet. It is a text on the Vajrayāna system dealing mainly with the concepts of Prajñā and Upāya, the two basic entities conceived as the Female and Male Principles. The state of perfection, according to this text is neither duality nor non-duality. Wisdom, conceived as the Female Principle, and the means of its attainment through the male, are to be combined in one's own self for the purpose of liberation which is perfect enlightenment through the practical experience of the Female Principle. Prajñā or wisdom is linked with a state of intense emotion called *sukha* or *mahāsukha* (great bliss) which is conducive to complete enlightenment. Prajñā is often definitely identified with flesh-and-blood woman, and the concept of *mahāsukha* is sought to be explained in terms of sexual symbolism, which is in general agreement with the common Tantric tradition.

The *Hevajratantra*[131] is a basic work of Tantric Buddhism which has been edited and translated by D. Snellgrove in two parts. The second part contains Sanskrit and Tibetan texts based on a Nepalese manuscript and a commentary called *Yogaratnamālā* which has been included from an old Bengali manuscript, while the first part consists of an introduction, English translation, contents, diagrams, glossary, etc. It may be a work of *c.* 8th century A.D. since, as the editor has shown, the *Advayavajrasaṃgraha* and the *Sekoddesaṭīka* have drawn heavily from it. There are several manuscripts of the *Hevajratantra.* The Sanskrit manuscripts of the text are divided into two *kalpas*, of ten chapters each. In the Chinese translation, however, the numbering of the chapters is continuous. Hevajra is the technical name for the Buddhist supreme being in the non-dual state. In particular Hevajra is Heruka-in-union-with-his-Śakti, in *yuganaddha* position. There is also another work called *Heruka-tantra.* The *Hevajra-tantra* deals with various topics, the most important of which is the process of attaining enlightenment through union with women. The term Śakti does not occur in this work. Its place is taken by Prajñā. The text describes how the followei s of Tantra have sexual experiences with women called *mudrās* and how thereby they attain *siddhi.* It also deals with the *kāyasādhanā* and holds that there are thirty-two *nāḍīs* in the body which carry the Bodhicitta upwards, ultimately pouring into the place of great bliss (*mahāsukhasthana*). Three amongst the *nāḍīs* are principal and they are called *lalanā, rasanā* and *avadhūtī.* The first one is characterised by Prajñā and the second one by Upāya. The third one known as *avadhūtī* is suggestive of absolute non-duality which is conceived as beyond the reach of 'the taken' and 'the taker' (*grāhya-grāhaka*). The same idea is found also in the *Herukatantra.* In one chapter the *Hevajra-tantra* deals with *sandhyā-bhāṣā* which is characterised as the *mahāsamaya* of the Yogis and also as great language (*mahābhāṣā*) full of meaningful significance. The term *mahāsamaya* denotes the doctrine of the school represented by the *Hevajra.* Of other things of interest to be found in the *Hevjratantra,* mention may be made of the cult-centres like Jālandhara, Oḍḍiyāna, Pūrṇagiri and Kāmarūpa which later become celebrated Śākta Piṭhas.

The Śākta Tantras

The range of the Śākta Tantras is wide and seeks to include, besides the works belonging to its own category, works of other Tantric schools, especially those of the Śaivas. According to the traditional Śākta-Tantric viewpoint, Śakti is inherent in Śiva as the power of burning is in fire. The supposed five faces of Śiva—Īśana, Tatpuruṣa, Sadyojāta, Vāmadeva and Aghora—symbolise the functioning of Śakti in the spheres of consciousness (*cit*), bliss (*ānanda*), will (*icchā*), knowledge (*jñāna*), and action (*kriyā*) respectively. The five mouths had produced intially ten Āgamas: *Kāmika, Yogaja, Cintya, Mukuṭa, Aṃśumān, Dīpta, Ajita, Sukṣma, Sahasra* and *Suprabheda.*[132] These were the precursors of eighteen Raudra Āgamas: *Vijaya, Niśvāsa, Madgīta, Pārameśvara, Mukhavimba, Siddha, Santāna, Narasiṃha, Candrāṃśu, Vīrabhadra, Āgneya, Svayambhū, Visara, Raurava, Vimala, Kiraṇa, Lalita* and *Saumeya.*[133] All these together constitute the twenty-eight Śaiva Āgamas.

According to another tradition the southern face of Śiva represent the principal of non-duality and is called Yoginīvaktra. The remaining four faces represent four conditions—denotative, denoted, extinguishing and extinguished. The products from each of these combine to form the sixty-four Bhairva Āgamas, classed under the category of eight Aṣṭaka listed below:

1. Bhairavāṣṭaka: *Svachhanda, Bhairava, Caṇḍa, Krodha, Unmatta, Asitāṅga, Mahocchūṣma* and *Kaṅkālīśa.*
2. Yāmalāṣṭaka: *Brahmā, Viṣṇu, Rudra, Ātharvan, Ruru, Vetāla, Indra* and *Svacchanda.*
3. Matākhyāṣṭaka: *Raktākhya, Lampaṭākhya, Lakṣmī, Matta, Cālikā, Piṅgala, Utphullaka* and *Viśvādyā.*
4. Maṅgalāṣṭaka: *Bhairavī, Picu, Samudbhava, Brāhmīkalā, Candrākhyā, Maṅgalā, Vijayā,* and *Sarvamaṅgalā.*
5. Cakrāṣṭaka: *Mantra, Varṇa, Śakti, Kalā, Kāla, Vindu, Nāda* and *Guhya.*
6. Śikhāṣṭaka: *Bhairavī, Vīṇā, Viṇāmaṇī, Sammoha, Ḍamaru, Ātharvaka, Kavandha* and *Śiraścheda.*
7. Bahurūpāṣṭaka: *Andhaka, Rurubheda, Ajākhyā, Malasaṅgaka, Varṇakaṇṭha, Vibhaṅga, Jvālina* and *Mātṛrodana.*
8. Vāgīśāṣṭaka: *Bhairavī, Cihikā, Haṃsākhya, Kādambikā, Hṛllekhā, Candralekhā, Viddyullekhā* and *Vidyunmāla.*

Some of the works mentioned above are found in extant Tantric literature; it is probable that other names are not imaginary. A more realistic list is, however, given in the *Vārāhī-tantra* which refers to twenty Śākta Tantric texts: *Nīlapatākā, Vāmakeśvara, Mṛtyunjaya, Yogārṇava, Māyā* or *Mahā, Dakṣiṇāmūrti, Kālikā, Kāmeśvarī, Haragaurī, Kubjikā, Kātyāyanī, Pratyaṅgirā, Mahālakṣmī, Tripurārṇava, Sarasvatī, Yoginī, Vārāhī, Gavākṣī, Nārāyaṇīya,* and *Mṛḍaṇī.* Other similar lists are found in different Tantric texts but there is no need to enumerate each of them. A good number of texts occurring in the lists are found in manuscript form, and a few of them have been published, but these manuscripts belong to a much later date. For example, the *Yoginītantra*, which appears to be an old work if the lists are to be belived, is in its present form not older than the late medieval period.[134] It seems that the texts mentioned in the lists had an earlier existence but in the course of time they were lost. Subsequently they were written again in the medieval and late-medieval period on the basis of the oral tradition preserved by a succession of teachers. This may be exemplified with reference to the *Kubjikātantra* which is mentioned as a *mahātantra* (great tantra) in the *Vārāhī* list quoted above. H.P. Sastri has shown that the *Kubjikāmata* (so called in the list) belonged to a distinct school in which were also included different branches like Kulālikāmnāya, Śrīmata, Kādimata, Vidyāpīṭha, etc. It had a few supplements like *Śrīmatottara* or *Manthānabhairava, Kubjikāmatottara*, etc. The original *Kubjikā* literature consisted of four *ṣaṭkas* each comprising 6,000 verses.[135] We have already referred to a *Kubjikā* manuscript in the collection of the Asiatic Society of Bengal, Calcutta, written in Gupta characters. Abhinavagupta in his *Triṃśikā* refers to the *Kubjikāmata*. From the 12th century onwards works of this tradition ceased to be produced. There were many such earlier works which were lost and often sometimes revived after a lapse of few centuries.

Apart from the lists mentioned in the Tantras like the *Vārāhī*, a good number of texts are quoted in the Tantric digests and commentarial literature. A few of them are *Bhūtaḍāmara, Jayadrathayāmala, Grahayāmala, Deviyāmala, Nityā, Niruttara, Guptasādhana, Cāmuṇḍā, Muṇḍamālā, Mālinīvijaya, Bhūtaśuddhi, Mantramahodadhi, Tripurāsāra, Tripurārahasya, Kulārṇava, Jñānārṇava, Mahākaulajñānavinirṇaya, Prapañcasāra, Śāradātilaka, Matsyasūkta, Mahānirvāṇa*, etc. The original *Vāmakeśvara-tantra* is probably lost, but a part of it survives under the tittle *Nityaṣoḍaśikārṇava*.[136] Its commentary, known as *Setubandha* was written by the celebrated Śākta scholar Bhāskararāya. The last three chapters of *Nityaṣoḍaśikārṇava* form a different Tantra known as *Yoginīhṛdaya*, the *Dīpikā* commentary on which was composed by Amṛtānandanātha, disciple of Puṇyānandanātha.[137] *Tantarājatantra*, which was probably associated with the earlier forms of *Yoginī* and *Mṛdānī* Tantras, is an important text dealing with Kādimata in thirty-six chapters.[138] It has a few well-known commentaries of which *Manoramā* by Subhagānandanātha deserves mention. Another commentary also on it was written by Prāṇamāñjarī, wife of the famous Tantric author

Premanidhi Pantha.[139] Reference to the *Kulārṇavatantra* has been made elsewhere. The *Jñānarṇava* is also a very important work containing 26 *paṭalas* and 2,300 verses.[140] The *Rudrayāmalatantra*, although portions of it belong to a later period, is regarded as an authoritative work by the writers of the digests and commentaries. It has more than 6,000 ślokas in *anuṣṭubh* metre divided into sixty-six chapters.[141] The *Śaktisaṅgamatantra* is an earlier work which mentions different Tantric sects including the Chinese one. It is divided into four parts, Kālī, Tārā, Sundarī and Chinnamastā, each devoted respectively to the said deities.[142] The *Pārānandasūtra*[143] is another Tantric text, composed some time after A.D. 900 while the *Paraśurāmakalpasūtra*[144] is earlier than A.D. 1300. Of the later Tantras mention should be made of *Tārātantra*, in 6 *paṭalas* and 150 verses, which refers to the Tārā Vaśiṣṭha legend and Buddha as a Tantric teacher. It also mentions nine Kaula *gurus* whose names end in Nātha and quotes the *Mahācīnākhyātantra*.[145] To this category belong *Kulacuḍāmaṇitantra*[146] which is in 7 *paṭalas* and 430 verses, the *Kālivilāsatantra*[147] which deals with the Five Ms. and was probably composed in Eastern Bengal and Assam, the *Tantrābhidhāna*,[148] the *Dakṣiṇamūrtisaṃhitā*[149] the *Pādukāpañcaka*,[150] the *Maheśvara-tantra*,[151] and so on. Of the most recent Tantras, the *Merutantra* is an extensive work in 35 chapters and 16,000 verses.[152] It refers to the English people and the city of London. The *Mahānirvāṇatantra* is a late but important work containing much of the earlier tradition. The work was first published by the Ādi Brahmo Samāj. The preface stated that three manuscripts were consulted to prepare the edition—one belonging to the library of the Samāj, the second supplied by Śrī Durgadas Chaudhuri, and the third taken from the library of Raja Rammohun Roy.[153] The *Mahānirvāṇa* represents the best of the sophisticated Tantric tradition.

Many Tantric works have been attributed to Śaṅkarācārya, of which the *Prapañcasāra* is regarded as an authoritative work in the Śākta tradition.[154] It is written in thirty-six *paṭalas* and its commentary, known as *Vivaraṇa*, is attributed to Padmapāda. *Saundaryalaharī*, a hymn to the Divine Mother, is also attributed to Śaṅkara.[155] It has numerous commentaries of which those of Gaṅgahari and Lakṣmīdhara contain much information on different aspects of the cult of Śakti. Śaṅkara is also said to have commented on a few Tantric works like the *Śrīvidyāratnasūtra* attributed to Gauḍapāḍa.[156] Puṇyānandanātha's *Kāmakalāvilāsa* is a well-known Tantric treatise.

Its commentary known as *Cidvallī* was written by Natanānandanātha. One of the most important Tantric digests is the *Śāradātilaka* of Lakṣmaṇa Deśika which was composed about 11th century A.D.[157] This celebrated work has several commentaries, the most learned and lucid of which is the *Padārthādarśa* of Rāghava Bhaṭṭa composed about the end of the 15th century.[158]

The *Matsyasūkta* designated as a *mahātantra* was composed by Halāyudha Miśra who was a courtier of king Lakṣmaṇasena. It is a big work in sixty-four *paṭalas* and is frequently quoted in subsequent Tantric literature. Mahīdhara's *Mantramahodadhi*,[159] composed in A.D. 1589 is a very popular work which gives *mantras* of various deities. Pūrṇānanda of the 16th century compiled several Tantra works. Of these, the *Śyāmārahasya* deals with various rites in connection with the worship of the goddess Śyāmā or Kālī and consists of sixteen chapters.[160] His *Śrītattvacintāmaṇi* deals with the Tantra rites in general with special reference to cult of Śrīvidyā.[161] Another work in eighty-five verses is also ascribed to him entitled *Ṣaṭcakranirūpaṇa*.[162] Brahmānandagiri, who was the teacher of Pūrṇānanda, composed *Śāktānandataraṅgiṇī*[163] in eighteen chapters—it deals with various rites to be performed in connection with the worship of Śakti—and *Tārārahasya* in four sections dealing with in worship of Tārā in her various forms.[164] Narasiṃha Ṭhakkura's *Tārābhaktisudhārṇava* is a late text composed about the end of the seventeenth century.[165] It is a large work in eleven *taraṅgas* in which the Buddhist character of Tārā finds no mention. Of the other works of individual authors, the *Kaulāvalinirṇaya* of Jñānasiddhi,[166] the *Cidgaganacandrikā* attributed to Kālidāsa,[167] the *Tripurarahasya* of Haritāyana with the commentary called *Tātparyadīpīka* of Śrīnivasa,[168] the *Tripurasārasamuccaya* of Nāgabhaṭṭa with the commentary of Govindācārya,[169] and the *Mātṛkācakraviveka* of Svatantrānandanātha with the commentary of Śivānanda deserve mention.[170]

The *Tantrasāra* of Kṛṣṇānanda Āgamavāgīsa is the most comprehensive and popular of the numerous digests known in India.[171] The commentaries of Bhāskararaya, one of the greatest Indian scholars and thinkers who flourished in the first half of the 18th century, should be especially noted, the outstanding ones being the *Setubandha*[172] on the *Nityaṣoḍaśikārṇava* section of the *Vāmakeśvaratantra*; the *Saubhāgyabhāskara*[173] on the *Lalitāsahasranāma* section of the *Brahmāṇḍapurāṇa*; the *Guptavatī*[174] on the *Devīmahātmya* section of the *Mārkaṇḍeyapurāṇa*, and the *Varivasyārahasya* which is an independent treatise elucidating different aspects of Śaktism.[175] Among his disciples Umānandanātha composed the *Nityostava*[176] which is a supplement to *Paraśurāmakalpasūtra*. Nīlakaṇṭha, who flourished in the middle of the 18th century, is famous for his commentary on the *Devībhāgavata* which is very important for the understanding of Śākta-Tantric ideals. Of the more recent works, the *Prāṇatoṣaṇī*,[177] compiled by Ramātoṣana Vidyālaṅkāra in 1743 Ś.E. at the instance of Prankrishna Biswas, a landlord of Khardaha near Calcutta, has been printed several times and is very popular with the followers of Tantra. It is a huge compilation consisting of more than 1,000 pages. Another rich landlord of the Tagore family of Calcutta, Harakumar, compiled several works pertaining to different aspects of Tantra under the titles *Haratattvadidhiti* and *Puraścaraṇabodhinī*.[178]

The Pārānandasūtra

The *Pārānandasūtra* is an earlier Tantric work which was composed about A.D. 900.[179] It is a work on Kauladharma which is described as the cream of the Vedas.[180] It holds that the supreme being is one and refers to seven sectarian deities—Brahmā, Viṣṇu, Śiva, Gaṇeśa, Surya, Śakti, and Bhairava. According to this text, of the three ways of *sādhanā* the Dakṣiṇamārga is sanctioned by the Vedas, the Smṛtis, and Purāṇas; the Vāmamārga by the Vedas and the Āgamas, and the Uttaramārga only by the words of the *guru* or preceptor. Each succeeding one is superior to each preceding one. Vāmamārga is of two kinds; that which insists on the *Pañca-tattva* is the better one.[181] The *Pārānandasūtra* prescribes that the disciple has to undergo *dīkṣā* or initiation from a qualified *guru*, who should preferably be *jīvan-mukta*, i.e. one who is liberated and is not tainted in any way.[182] The preceptor should collect the materials of the five *makāras* and hand over to the disciple a bowl for drinking wine, *mudrā* (fried cereal), and a women (generally a courtesan). It is stated that young women, even a courtesan, is *brahman*. She is Śakti incarnate. Always and in all conditions she is the purest entity. Details of Kauladharma are given in this text.[183] It describes the procedure of Tantric festivals,[184] the efficacies of *mantras* and *mudrās*, names of teachers ending in Ānanda,[185] and details of sexual techniques[186] which may appear repulsive and vulgar to many of us.

The Kulārṇavatantra

The *Kulārṇava* is one of the most important Tantric works. We have already had occasion to mention it because of some of its textual problems. It is said to be Tantra of *Urdhva-āmnāya* and part of a lost mammoth work of one and a quarter lakh verses. In its present form it is in seventeen *ullāsas* or chapters and contains over two thousands verses. It is a celebrated work quoted in numerous Tantric digests and commentaries. It was composed probably before A.D. 1000.[187] According to the *Kulārṇava*, the Kauladharma is the essence of the Vedas. One who has studied the Vedas but is ignorant of Kauladharma is inferior to a Caṇḍala, while a Caṇḍala who knows it is superior to a Brāhmaṇa.[188] Śiva is called Akula and Śakti Kula. Those who contemplate on Kula and Akula and know that *mokṣa* is secured through an understanding of these two principles are known as Kaulikas. The *Kulārṇava* says that every woman is born in the *kula* of the Great Mother and hence she must be regarded as an object of veneration.[189] To follow the path of *kula* is more diffcult than walking on the edge of a sword; if by merely drinking wine or eating meat or indulging in sexual intercourse a man were to attain *siddhi*, then all drunkards and debauchees might have attained it.[190] Two chapters of the *Kulārṇava* are devoted to the qualifications and greatness of the *guru*.[191] It warns against false *gurus* who pretend to know the truth and give instruction motivated by a greed for money.[192] It emphasises that the order of the succession of *gurus*, the Āgamas, Āmnāya, *mantra* and practices when learnt from the lips of the right *guru* become fruitful and not otherwise.[193] The *Kulārṇava* recommends the drinking of wine, sexual intercourse with woman, eating of flesh, etc., to the followers of Kaula doctrine, but at the same time it also endeavours to give an esoteric meaning to the five *makāras*. Thus wine is equated with the nectar oozing from the *sahasrārapadma*, i.e. the lotus in the crown of the head where the Kulakuṇḍalinī Śakti rising from *mulādhāra* meets its source. Meat is the symbol of the flesh of ego cut with the sword of knowledge. Sexual union is suggestive of the union of the highest Śakti with the self.[194] It states that *puraścaraṇa* is so called because of its five constituents.[195] It lays down rules where *puraścaraṇa* of a *mantra* is to be practised and says that mantras confer the highest spiritual and supernatural power. It deals with *dīkṣā, nyāsa, yantras* and other Trantric symbols and concepts. It refers to eighteen Śākta Piṭhas: Uddīyāna, Devīkoṭṭa, Hiṅgulā, Koṭimudrā, Jālandhara, Vārāṇasī, Antarvedī, Prayāga, Mithilā,

Magadha, Mekala, Aṅga, Vaṅga, Kaliṅga, Siṃhala, Strīrājya, Rāḍha and Gauḍa.

The Śāradātilaka

The *Śāradātilaka* of Lakṣmaṇa-deśikendra is another famous work on Tantra which was composed about the 11th century A.D. It has several commentaries, of which the most important is Rāghavabhaṭṭa's *Padārthādarśa* composed about A.D. 1493-4. The *Śāradātilaka* is divided into 25 *paṭalas* and contains more than 4,500 verses.

According to this text, Śiva is both *nirguṇa* and *saguṇa*, the two aspects being conceived in terms of difference from and identity with Prakṛti. When Śiva is identical with Śakti or Prakṛti, he is *saguṇa.* From Śakti or Prakṛti evolves *nādā* (apara) and from this *nādā* arises *bindu*. The latter is divided into *bindu* (apara), *bīja* and *nāda* (apara). The first is again identified with Śiva, the second with Śakti and third with both in identical relation. Śakti, also called Parā-śakti and Parā-devatā, is conceived as Śabda-brahma that flashes like lightning in the *ādhāra-cakra* and assumes the form of Kuṇḍalinī in the human body. From Śiva in the form of the said bindu of the apara category come out in succession Sadāśiva, Īśā, Rudra, Viṣṇu and Brahmā. The Sāṅkhya categories also are traced to the *bindu*. The all-pervading and at the same time the most subtle Śakti remains coiled like a serpent in her Kulakuṇḍalinī form and becomes manifest in the form of the fifty letters of the Sanskrit alphabet.[196]

Besides the theory of Kulakuṇḍalinī, which will be discussed in detail in a subsequent chapter, the *Śāradātilaka* deals especially with the *mantras*. It divides the *mantras* into masculine (those ending in *hum* and *phaṭ*), feminine (those ending in *svāhā*), and neuter (those ending in *namaḥ*) and brings them in relation to the letters. *Mantras* devoted to such deities as Durgā, Tripurā, Gaṇapati, Candramas, Sarasvatī, Lakṣmī, Bhuvaneśvarī, Tvaritā and others are given in abundance.[197] Although it does not deal with sexual practices, or the use of wine or flesh, etc., it contains *mantras* for magical purposes such as bringing women under control,[198] bringing about the destruction of the enemy[199] and prescribes the drawing of *yantras* for wicked purposes. *Dīkṣā*, *nyāsa* and *puraścaraṇa* have been dealt with elaborately in this work.[200] Rāghavabhaṭṭa in his commentary is very exhaustive on the details of *puraścaraṇa* that are common to all *mantras*.[201] The *mantras* of infusing life, as is found in the *Śāradātilaka*,[202] has been quoted in the late medieval digests on the Dharmaśāstras such as the *Devapratiṣṭhā-tattva, Divya-tattva, Vyavaharā-mayukha, Nirṇayasindhu*, etc.

The Mahānirvāṇatantra

The *Mahānirvāṇatantra* has been regarded by scholars as a 'refined' work. The present form of the text is not much earliar than the 18th century and it is burdened with Vedantic elements, but there are reasons to believe that the text had an older form. Its very name suggests that its earlier versions were utilised by the Buddhists. Subsequently Vedantic ideas were interpolated, pure Tantric ritualistic aspects were modified, and it was fashioned in such a way that it would appeal to the Hindu taste in general.

It puts forward the Vedantic conception that the supreme being is one, without a second. He is *brahman* who is beyond the three *guṇas—sat, cit,* and *ānanda.*[203] Those who worship the highest *brahman* do not require any other means to achieve salvation. The best *mantra* is *om saccidekam brahma.*[204] Side by side, the *Mahānirvāṇa* upholds a Śākta monotheism with Durgā as the highest *prakṛti* who is also known by the names of Mahāvidyā goddesses and equated with Lakṣmī, Sarasvatī and Śakti. She assumes various forms for the sake of her devotees and also for the destruction of demons. She is spoken of as the primordial Śakti; all gods, including Śiva himself, derive their power from her.[205] The Sāṅkhya *tattvas* like Prakṛti, Mahat, Ahaṃkāra, etc., and Vedic *mantras* have also been grafted in the body of the text.

The *Mahānirvāṇa* frankly states that the Vedas, Purāṇas and Śāstras are hardly of any use in the *kaliyuga,*[206] that perfection cannot be attained without following the Kula practices and that the rituals of Five Ms are necessary. But it prescribes a milder form of such rituals. It says that a *sādhaka* should drink a limited quantity of wine so that he should not feel intoxicated and that women should simply smell it. The *sādhaka* should confine himself to the woman he chooses as his Śakti.[207] Wife may also act as Śakti in the case of the householders. It refers to *bhairavī-cakra* and *tattva-cakra* and says that no one has the right to engage himself in the performance of *cakra* rituals unless he is qualified to do so. In the *cakra* rituals the Five Ms or *tattvas* like wine, etc., should be collected and placed in front of the goddess and then properly performed.

Chapter 8 of the *Mahānirvaṇa* deals with the duties of *varṇas* and *āśramas*, the duties of the king and his officers and so on. Persons should observe caste restrictions in regard to marriage, dining and so on, but the caste restrictions are not valid in the case of those who have undertaken Tantric initiation. Chapter 9 describes the ten *saṃskāras* from *garbhādhāna* to marriage.[208] It prescribes a special form of marriage known as the Śaiva marriage in which there is no question of caste, creed or age. Chapters 10 to 12 of the *Mahānirvāṇa* deal respectively with *śrāddhas, prāyaścittas* and *vyavahāra*. Dikṣā, nyāsa, puraścaraṇa, efficacy of *mantras* and other common features of Tantric texts have also been elaborately dealt with in this work.

A Few Other Śākta Tantras

The *Paraśurāmakalpasūtra* is an earlier work composed about A.D. 1300.[209] Its commentary is known as *Saubhāgyodaya* written by Rāmeśvara. The special features of this work are the *āmnāya* classifications, insistence on the secrecy of the knowledge conveyed by the preceptor and worship of the five *makāras*, thirty-six *tattvas* including those of the Sāṅkhya system, *āsana, maṇḍapa, kuṇḍa, maṇḍala, dikṣā,* etc. It provides that after the initiation the preceptor is to give a name to the disciple which should end in Ānandanātha. Rameśvara, the commentator of the *Paraśurāmakalpasūtra*, says that one who has not conquered his senses has no right to follow the Kaula path. The efficacy of *mantras* is very much stressed in this work and it is held that the *sādhaka* should come to feel that the *guru, mantra*, deity and his own self are all one.

The *Jñānārṇava-tantra* emphasises the functioning of the *cakras* or nerve plexuses within the body and the wonderful power of the *mantras*.[210] It states that at the time of initiation the *guru* has to instruct the disciple as regard the six *cakras*, together with the number of petals in each, the colour of each, and the letter with the alphabet assigned to each.[211] It names over thirty *mudrās*.[212] It also holds that *maṇḍala* and *cakra* are synonymous and lays down rules for making different kinds of *maṇḍalas*. It mentions eight important Śākta Pīthas: Kāmarūpa, Malaya, Kaulagiri, Kulāntaka, Cauhāra, Jālandhara, Uḍḍiyana, and Devīkoṭṭa. The *Jñārṇava* was evidently composed before the 16th century since it has been quoted amply by Brahmānanda and Pūrṇānanda, the celebrated medieval Tantric teachers. It contains 26 *paṭalas* and about 2,300 verses.

The *Kaulāvalinirṇaya* was composed by Jñānānandagiri in twenty-one *ullāsas.*[213] It gives a list of Tantric works including the Yāmalas and names eight Tantric *gurus.*[214] It deals mainly with the Kaulamārga with emphasis on the rituals of Five Ms.[215] Women are highly praised in this work as manifestations of the Great Mother.[216] It is interest-ing to note that the *Kaulāvalinirṇaya* offers various substitutes for the Five Ms.[217] It lays supreme empasis on sexual union.[218] It also describes in detail the *mantrasiddhi* or *śavasādhanā* in which the aspirant has to perform rituals with a corpse. Such practices will be described more fully in a subsequent chapter. The *Kulacuḍāmaṇitantra* and the *Tārābhaktisudhārṇava* also describe the *savasādhanā-vidhi.* The *Kālivilāsatantra* which is a late text and composed somewhere in eastern India, is similar to the *Kaulāvalinirṇaya.* It lays great emphasis on sexual intercourse and drinking wine. In this work we come across the idea of giving an upward motion to semen during sexual intercourse.

The *Rudrayāmala* is a very extensive work in 66 chapters and has over 6,000 verses. One of the important features of this work is that it contains a panegyric of *Atharvaveda* saying that all gods, all beings, all sages, Kāmavidyā and Mahāvidyā dwell in it. It deals with the mysterious Kuṇḍalinī, Yogic practices, and the six *cakras* in the body. It also prescribes sexual union and the use of wine; it states that a *vīra* should drink wine and use a beautiful woman who is capable of arousing sexual passion. This woman may be his own wife or another's. The *guru* or preceptor is regarded as the source of all spiritual efforts. 'If Śiva is angered, the Guru can save the pupil, but if Guru is angered, no one can save him.' The *Rudrayāmala* mentions Kāmarupa, Jālandhara, Uḍḍīyāna, Pūrṇagiri and a few other Śākta Pīṭhas. It states that the goddess appeared to the sage Vaśiṣṭha and asked him to go to Cīnadeśa where he was initiated into doctrine of the Five Ms by the Buddha himself.

The *Śaktisaṅgamatantra* holds that Kaulācarā in general is nothing but the cult of Śakti in any of her forms and aspects, but its particularity is a special form of worship done with wine, flesh, fish, cereals, and sexual union. The knowledge conveyed by the *guru* and the worship with five *makāras* should be kept secret.[219] It is interesting to note that the *Śaktisaṅgamatantra* states that the Devī manifests herself for the destruction of the Buddhist and other heretical sects, for the removal of the confusing admixture of different cults, and for the establishment of true religion.[220] Symbolic interpretations of the Five Ms have been given, according to which *madya, mudrā, maithuna,* etc., are not be used in the ordinary popular sense.[221] The text regards an eclipse of the sun or the moon as the best time for undergoing initiation.[222] The *Śaktisaṅgamatantra* is divided into four parts: Kālī, Tārā, Sundarī, and Chinnamastā. It was composed sometime between the 16th and 17th centuries A.D.

Tantras of Other Religious Sects

While dealing with the traditional classification of the Tantric texts we have had occasion to refer to the Tantras of the Gāṇapatyas, Sauras and other religious sects. In the Yāmala literature we have works dedicated to Skanda, Brahmā, Indra, Viṣṇu, Āditya, Yāma, Kubera, and others. A few Ḍāmaras are dedicated to Sarasvatī, Brahmā, and other deities. The Upatantra lists contain Tantras attributed to a bewildering variety of gods and goddesses. In fact, as we have seen above, every religious sect of India has some form of a Tantric cult.

An important sectarian Tantra is *Gaṇapatitattva,* found in an old Javanese collection, which refers to the march of the Kulakuṇḍalinī through the six *cakras* of the body by means of Kāyasādhanā, to the six Angas of Yoga, to the concepts of *vindu, nādā, mantra, vija* and so on.[223] Ānandagiri has referred to the Tantric sects of the Gāṇapatyas. Their theories and practices will be discussed elsewhere in this book. That the Tantric cult of Gaṇeśa spread as far as South East Asia is proved by the discovery of his images in Java and Cambodia. The image found at Bara in Java shows the god seated on human skulls clearly indicating his Tantric affiliation.

The *Kaulajñānanirṇaya*[224] is an important Tantric work belonging to the Nātha tradition, supposed to have been composed by Matsyendranātha who was the founder of one of the Kaula schools called Yoginī-kaula. The doctrines of this school, as may be gathered from this text, have something in common with the Buddhist Tantras of the Sahajiyā class. H.P. Sastri assigned the manuscript of this work to the 9th century A.D., but P.C. Bagchi placed it in the middle of the 11th century.

The *Gorakṣasiddhāntasaṃgraha*[225] is another important Tantric text which says that the Kaula Tantras were introduced on earth by the nine Nātha teachers. Both the Nātha cult and Vajrayāna had a fundamental unity in their esoteric aspects. Jālandharī, better known as Hāḍi-pā wrote some treatises in Sanskrit on Tantric cults, such as

Vajrayoginīsādhanā, *Śuddhivajrapradīpa* (a gloss on *Hevajrasādhanā*) *Śrīcakrasaṃvaragarbhatattva vidhi* and *Humkāra-cittavindu-bhāvana-krama*. These are mentioned in the Tanjur catalogue. From the same source we learn that Ācarya Cauraṅgī composed a Yogic work under the title *Vāyutattvopadeśa*. The present form of the *Gorakṣasaṃhitā* is a rather late compilation.

The followers of the Śuddhamārga depend for the whole of their disciplinal, sacramental, mystical, and dogmatic contents on the *Kāladahanatantra* of the *Kāmikāgama* and the *Mṛtyunāśakatantra* of the *Vijayāgama*. They seek for the liberation of man by his monadic transfiguration. Glimpses of their doctrine are available in Kumāradeva's *Śuddhasādhaka*, to which perhaps may be linked Rāvaṇārādhya's *Śivajñānadīpa* as a useful supplement.

NOTES

1. For a long list of Tantras see A. Avalon, *Principles of Tantra*, Calcutta, 1914, 1916, rpt. Madras, 1952, Vol. I, pp. 390-2.
2. I. 13-22.
3. Verse 31 which begins with *Catuṣṣaṣṭyā tantraiḥ*.
4. I. 18; Kashmir Sanskrit Series (hereafter *KSS*), Vol. XXII, p. 35.
5. V. 92-3.
6. P.C. Bagchi, *Studies in the Tantras*, Calcutta, 1939, p. 100.
7. A. Avalon, op. cit., 'Introduction', p. LXV.
8. Cf. *Kulārṇava*, III. 6-7, 41-4; *Paraśuramakalpasūtra*, I.2.
9. Cf. *Brahmayāmala*, Ch. XXXIX, srotanirṇaya section.
10. E.g. in *Sammohatantra*, 5th *paṭala*.
11. *Jayadrathayāmala*, I. 47.
12. As quoted in *Śabdakalpadruma* under the word Tantra.
13. Com. on *Yājñavalkya*, Ānandāśrama edn. (hereafter ANDS), pp. 16, 18.
14. CCCLXXII, 34.
15. XI. 11. 37; XII. 11.2, etc.
16. H.P.Sastri, *Nepal Catalogue*, Vol. I, pref. LXXVII, pp. 10, 85, 117.
17. E. Hultzsch, *South Indian Inscriptions*, Vol. I, Nos. 24-5.
18. P.C. Bagchi in *Indian Historical Quarterly* (*IHQ*),Vol. V, pp. 754ff; Vol. VI, pp. 97ff; also see his *Studies in the Tantras*, pp.1-26.
19. C. Chakravarti, '*Kulārṇava-tantra:* Its extent and contents'. *Annals of the Bhandarkar Oriental Research Institute* (hereafter *ABORI*), Vol. XII, pp. 206 -11.
20. *Kavīndracārya List*, Gaekwad's Oriental Series (hereafter *GOS*), p. 23
21. I.1. 56-7.

22. XXXIX. 1.
23. I.1. 69.
24. *Puruṣottamasaṃhitā*, I. 3-4; I. 5; I. 6. 2-7; I.10.2-11; I. 12-17
25. I. 1.44.
26. I. 62.
27. F.O. Schrader, *Introduction to the Pāñcarātra and the Ahirbudhnya Saṃhitā*, Adyar, Madras, 1916, pp. 6-12.
28. I. 1.56.
29. Ed. Krishnapriyacharya, Chowkhamba Sanskrit Series (hereafter *CSS*), Banaras, 1940, XXVI.16
30. F.O. Schrader, op. cit., p.19.
31. S. Gupta, *Lakṣmī-tantra*, Leiden, 1972, pref. XVIII.
32. Cf. Vedānta Deśika, *Śrī Pāñcarātra Rakṣā*, Adyar Library, 2nd edn., Madras, 1967, pp. 3-13.
33. For a detailed bibliography see K.K.A. Venkatachari, *Pāñcarātra Nūl Viḷakkam*, Madras, 1967.
34. Published in *GOS*, Baroda.
35. Eng. tr. in *GOS*, LXXVI.
36. II. 43; II. 94-104; IV. 29ff.
37. XXVI. 678-82.
38. XXXVIII. 209.
39. I. 64.
40. IX. 133.
41. XXXIX. 18. 1-2.
42. XVIII. 44.1.
43. V. 59.
44. IV. 33.202-3.
45. A text of this name is published, with Jīva Gosvāmin's commentary, in *Tantric Texts* (hereafter *TT*), Āgama Anusandhāna Samiti, Calcutta, Vol. XV.
46. See his foreword to the *Jayākhya Saṃhitā*, *GOS*, pp. 26-34.
47. *Prakīrṇādhikāra*, Kriyāpāda, XXX. 4; *Yajñadhikāra*, LI. 1-4.
48. *Bhaktikhaṇḍa*, I. 10. 33-6.
49. F.O. Schrader, op. cit.
50. Chs. XI-XII.
51. XII. 44.
52. *Bhāgavatatātparyanirṇaya*, XI. 3.6-7; XI. 16.8.9, etc.
53. IV. 59: V.2-5, 16-20, 26, 29, 34, 37, 45, etc.
54. V. 50-7.
55. XII. 20-9.
56. XII. 18-19.
57. XII. 32-3.
58. Ch. XXX.
59. XX. 52-3.

60. Cf. *Kulārṇava*, XV. 22.24; *Śāradātilaka*, II. 138-40.
61. LII. 2-85.
62. Ch. XXXIX.
63. Sanskrit edn. by Pandit V. Krishnamacharya and published in the Adyar Library Series, No. 87. Eng. edn. with translation, introduction and notes by Sanjukta Gupta, Leiden, 1972.
64. XXIIV. 44-7; XLII. 30-1.
65. S. Gupta, op. cit., Pref.
66. IV. 6-13; ibid., pp. 18-19.
67. Vāyavīya, II. 24-177.
68. Rajrajesvari Press Edn., Banaras, V.S. 1945, p. 2.
69. See C. Chakravarti, "The Soma or Sauma Sect of the Śaivas', *IHQ*, Vol. VIII, pp. 221-3.
70. *Ṣaḍdarśanasamuccaya*, Bibliotheca Indica, Calcutta, p. 51.
71. *Descriptive Catalogue of the Madras Government Oriental Mss. Library* (Madras 1901-37), XI, 5502; Ādau sāmānyaśaivaṃ tu pūrvaśaivaṃ dvitīyakam, miśraśaiva tṛtiyantu śuddhaśaivaṃ caturthakaṃ.
72. XII. 349. 64-8.
73. *Epigraphia Indica* (hereafter *EI*), Vol. XXI, pp.1-9.
74. Ed. with Rāśīkara Kauṇḍinya's com. by R. Anantakrishna Sastri, *TSS*, CXLIII, 1940.
75. P.C. Bagchi, op. cit., pp. 4, 95.
76. *Niśvāsa, Kiraṇa* and *Parameśvara* are still preserved in Nepal in mss. of 8th and 9th centuries. A copy of *Parameśvara*, the mss. being dated A.D. 859, is in the Cambridge collection.
77. IHQ, Vol. XXVI, 1950, pp. 15ff.
78. Published in *TSS*.
79. Published in Kashmir Sanskrit Series I with Kṣemarāja's commentary known as *Śivasūtravimarśinī*. The Śivasūtra is also called *Sivopaniṣad saṃgraha* and *Śivarahasyāgama-śāstrasaṃgraha*. Besides the com. of Kṣemarāja, there is a *Vṛtti* on it of doubtful authorship and a *Varttika* by Bhāskara.
80. For a detailed account of Abhinavagupta and his works see K.C. Pandey, 'Abhinavagupta: An Historical and Philosophical Study', *CSS*, Studies Vol. 1. Banaras, 1935.
81. Published in several volumes in Kashmir Sanskrit Series.
82. Ed. with Eng. tr. by L.D. Barnett in *Journal of the Royal Asiatic Society* (hereafter *JRAS*), 1910, pp. 707-47.
83. Published in *KSS*, 1918.
84. Tr. under the title *The Secret of Recognition* with notes by K.F. Leidecker, Adyar Library, Madras, 1938.
85. Tr. with intro. and com. by J.M. Nallasvami Pillai, Dharmapuram Adhinam, 1945.

86. Ibid., 1948.
87. Eng. tr. by Hoisington in *Journal of the American Oriental Society*, (hereafter *JAOS*), 1854.
88. H.P. Sastri, *Nepal Catalogue*, Vol. I, pp. LXXVII. 137.
89. P.C. Bagchi, op. cit., pp. 93-6.
90. *Bulletin de l'Ecole Francaise d' Extreme—Orient*, Vol. XV, pp. 70-1.
91. B.R. Chatterji, *Indian Cultural Influence in Cambodia*, Calcutta, 1928, pp. 273-4
92. P.C. Bagchi, op. cit., pp. 22ff.
93. Ibid., pp. 5ff.
94. Bergaigne, *Inscription de Campa et du Cambodge*, II. 157, 384, 389-92.
95. T.A. Gopinath Rao, *Elements of Hindu Iconography*, Vol. II, Pt. I.367-8.
96. H.P. Sastri, *Nepal Catalogue*, Vol. I, p. 175, Vol. II, pp. 1ff, 60, 183.
97. For details see Bagchi, op. cit., pp. 96-114.
98. It was P. Cordier who first published a catalogue of the Tanjur collection (1902-10), an index of which was published by M. Lalou (1933). Recently a project has been taken up by my friend Alaka Chattopadhyaya to present, in a re-arranged way the essential information contained in Cordier's and Lalou's works in three volumes along with a supplement containing the history of the formation of the Kanjur and Tanjur collections. The first volume which was published in 1971 is an alphabetically arranged catalogue numbers, authors, translations, places of translations, etc. The available Tibetan texts were originally prined at Peking between 1763 and 1795. This Peking edition was reprined by the Otani University under the editorship of Suzuki in 1957. Besides, there are other editions of the Tibetan Tripiṭaka, the best known one being Snar-than, or Nar-thang, originally printed in 1742. A good number of texts belonging to this edition are in the possession of the Academy of Sciences USSR, the Bibliotheque Nationale and Musee Guimet of France and other institutions.
99. Tr. into French by A. Bareau in *Journal Asiatique*, 1954, pp. 235ff; 1956, pp. 167ff, 192ff.
100. Eng. tr. by Roerich in collaboration with A.S. Altekar, published by the Jayaswal Research Institute, Patna, 1959.
101. Eng. tr. by E. Obermiller, 1931.
102. It was first translated into Russian in 1866 by Vasilev and published in 1869 along with its German rendering by A. Schiefner. Vasilev's Russian and Schiefner's German apart, the only complete translation of Tāranātha's *History* exists in Japanese which was done by Enga Teramoto in 1928. The great Indian linguist Harinath De started translating Tāranātha's *History*, and a few pages of his translation appeared in a journal called *The Herald* (January 1911). N. Dutta and

U.N. Ghosal translated into English portions of Schiefner's German translation, *IHQ*, Vol. III, pp. 60-8, 508-9, 803-7, Vol. IV, pp. 530-3; Vol. V, pp. 715-21; Vol, VI, pp. 334-44; Vol. VII, pp. 150-60; Vol. VIII, pp. 247-52, Vol. X, pp. 551-7, Vol. XII, pp. 41-50). Recently (1970), a translation has come out, made by Lama Chimpa and Alaka Chattopadhyaya. It is a better work, free from the errors made by Schiefner and Vasilev. It follows mainly the Potala edition of 1946, but has been thorougly checked from the first letter-press edition of St. Petersburg which was originally published by Schiefner in 1868.

103. Ed. by S.C. Das, Calcutta, 1908.
104. Ed. N. Dutt and S.N. Sharma in *Gilgit Manuscripts*, Vol. IV, Calcutta, 1959, pp. 114-16.
105. Ed. in ibid., Vol. I, Srinagar, 1939.
106. *Aṣṭasāhasrikā-Prajñāpāramitā*, Sanskrit ed. R.L. Mitra, Bib. Ind. Calcutta, 1888; *Prajñāp* 100,000, incomplete, ed. R. Ghosh, Bib. Ind. Calcutta, 1902-14; *Prajñāp* 25,000, ed. N. Dutt, Calcutta Oriental Series, 1934; *Prajñāp* 18,000, Sans. incomplete text, ed. E. Conze, Rome, 1962; *Prajñāp* 10,000, two chs. retranslated into Sans. by S. Know, Oslo, 1941; *Prajñāp* 25,00, Sans. edn. Hikata, Fukoka, 1958, reprinted in P.L. Vaidya's *Mahāyānasūtrasaṃgraha*, Buddhist Sanskrit Text Series (BST), Darbhanga; *Prajñāp* 700, Sans. ed. G. Tucci, Rome, 1923, J. Masuda, Tokyo, 1930, rpt. in BST; *Prajñāp* 300, Sans. ed. F. Max Müller, Oxford, 1881, rpt. in BST, tr. in *Sacred Books of the East*, by Max Müller, 1894. The *Prajñāp* literature has been specially studied by E. Conze.
107. Ed. B.T. Bhattacharyya in *GOS* No. LIII, Baroda, 1931.
108. Part tr. by Tajima in *Etude sur le Mahāvairocanasūtra*, Paris, Maisonneuve, 1936.
109. One Tibetan version of this text has been partially edited and translated by Kazi Dawa-Samdup as *Śricakra-sambhāratantra*, Calcutta, 1919.
110. Ed. T. Ganapati Sastri in Trivandrum Sanskrit Series (hereafter *TSS*) Nos. XXVI, LXX, 1920-22; see also J. *Przyluski in Bulletin de l'ecole Francaise d' Extreme Orient*, Vol. XXIII, 1923, pp. 301ff.
111. *IHQ*, Vol. IX, pp. 1ff.
112. Ed. and Eng. tr. D. Snellgrove, 2 Vols., London, 1959.
113. Mss. in Oriental Institute, Baroda. See *Sadhanamālā*, intro., XLVII.
114. Both *Prajñopāya-viniścaya-siddhi* and *Jñānasiddhi* were edited by B.T. Bhattacharyya in *GOS*, Vol. XLIV, Baroda, 1929.
115. Apabhraṃśa edn., N.N. Chaudhuri, Calcutta, 1935.
116. Sanskrit edn. B.T. Bhattacharyya, 2 Vols, XXVI, XLI, *GOS*, Baroda, 1925-28.
117. Ed. La Vallee Poussin, Gand, 1896.

118. Ed. M.E. Carelli, *GOS*, Baroda, 1941.
119. Ed. H.P. Sastri, *GOS*, Vol. XL, 1927.
120. Ed. B.T. Bhattacharyya, *GOS*, CIX Baroda, 1949.
121. B.T. Bhattacharyya, op. cit. See fn. 107.
122. Ibid., pp. 31, 35-6, 43.
123. Ibid., pp. 84, 96.
124. Ibid., p. 162. A. Wayman, *Yoga of the Guhyasamāja*, Delhi, 1977.
125. Ibid, pp. 81ff.
126. Ibid., p. 26.
127. Ibid., p. 120
128. See fn. 110.
129. B.T. Bhattacharyya, op. cit.
130. Ed. B.T. Bhattacharyya, *GOS*, XLIV, 1929.
131. D. Snellgrove, op. cit.
132. The *Kiraṇāgāma* substitutes *Kāraṇa* for *Mukuṭa*.
133. The *Kiraṇāgāma* substitutes *Prodgīta* for *Madgīta*, *Candrahāsa* for *Candrāṃśu*, *Bhadra* for *Vīrabhadra*, *Virakta* for *Visara*, *Kauravya* for *Raurava*, *Mukuṭa* for *Vimala* and *Para* for *Saumeya*.
134. Ed. J. Vidyasagara, Calcutta, 1897.
135. H.P. Sastri, *Nepal Catalogue*, Vol. I, pp. LXIVff.
136. Published in ANDS (1908, 1944) with *Setubandha* commentary.
137. Sarasvati Bhavana Texts (herefater *SBT*), No. 7, Banaras, 1923.
138. Ed. in *TT*. Vols. VIII, XII; rpt. Ganesh and Co., 1954.
139. An edition of the first chapter of this commentary was published by J.B. Chaudhuri, Calcutta, 1940.
140. Published in ANDS, Poona.
141. Ed. J. Vidyasagara, Calcutta, 1892.
142. Published in *GOS*, Baroda; cf *Poona Orientalist*, XXI, pp. 47-9.
143. Published in *GOS*, Baroda, 1931.
144. Published in ibid., 1923.
145. Ed. Girish Chandra, *Gauḍagranthamālā*, No. 1, 1913.
146. Ed. A. Avalon in *TT*, Vol. IV, 1915.
147. Ibid., Vol. VI, 1917.
148. Ibid., Vol. I.
149. Published in *SBT*.
150. Ed. A. Avalon in *TT*, Vol. II, 1913.
151. Published in *CSS*.
152. Published by Venkateswar Steam Press, Bombay, 1908.
153. See above and also the Intro. and Pref. to the tr. of the work by A. Avalon, Calcutta, 1913, Madras, 1928.
154. Published in *TT*, Vol. III and later in a new edition in Vols. XVIII-XIX, 1934; also in the *Memorial Edition of the Works of Saṅkara*, Vols. XIX-XX, Venivilas Press, Srirangam.

155. Ed. J. Woodroffe, Adyar, Madras, 1937; with three commentaries and Eng. tr. Ganesh and Co., Madras, 1957; ed. with Eng. tr. by Norman Brown, Harvard University Press, 1958.
156. Ed. Gopinath Kaviraj, STB, Banaras, 1924.
157. Published in KSS; tr. with notes by A. Avalon in *TT*, Vol. X; rpt. Ganesh and Co., Madras, 1953.
158. Published in *TT*, Vols. XVI, XVII. Lakṣmaṇa-Deśika might have been the author of the *Tārāpadīpa* written as a supplement to the *Śaradātilaka*. See *Indian Culture*, Vol. V, pp. 212-13. Hindi edn. and tr. of *ST* by C. Gautam, 1973.
159. Published by R. Chatterji in his *Vividhatantrasaṃgraha*, Calcutta, 1881-6; ed. J. Vidyasagara, Calcutta, 1893; Venkateswar Steam Press, Bombay, 1910. About Mahīdhara and his works see *ABORI*, Vol. XXI, pp. 248-61.
160. Ed. by P.C. Pal and Bros., Calcutta, 1948 V.S.; J. Vidyasagra, Calcutta, 1896.
161. *CSS*, No. 19.
162. *TT*, Vol. II.
163. First Published in Rasikmohan Chatterji's *Vividhatantrasaṃgraha*, Calcutta, 1881-6.
164. Ed. P.C. Pal and Bros, Calcutta, 1948 V.S.; J. Vidyasagara, Calcutta, 1896; P.K. Sastri, Calcutta, 1908.
165. Ed. Panchanan Bhattacharyya, in *TT*, Vol. XX, 1940.
166. Ed. A. Avalon in *TT*, Vol. XIV.
167. Ed. Trivikramatīrtha in ibid., Vol. XX.
168. Published in *SBT*.
169. Ed. J. Vidyasagara, Calcutta, 1897.
170. Published in *SBT*, 1934.
171. Editions in Bengali script by Rasikmohan Chatterji, Calcutta, 1880, Vaṅgavāsī Press, Calcutta, 1929, Vasumati Press, Calcutta, 1929; also published in *CSS*, Banaras.
172. Published in ANDS, Poona.
173. Published by the Nirnayasagar Press, Bombay, 4th edn., 1935.
174. Published by the Venkateswar Steam Press, Bombay, 1916.
175. Ed. with an Eng. tr. by S. Subrahmanya Sastri in the Adyar Library Series, Madras, 1934, 1941, 1948.
176. Published in *GOS*, Baroda, 1923.
177. First published in 1823; ed. J. Vidyasagara, Calcutta, 1898, Vasumati edn., Calcutta, 1929.
178. Published respectively by Harakumar's sons Saurindra Mohan Tagore, Calcutta, 1881 and Jatindra Mohan Tagore, Calcutta, 1885.
179. Published in *GOS*, 1931.
180. Ibid., p. 7
181. Ibid., pp. 1-3, 13.
182. Ibid., pp. 5-7.

183. Ibid., pp. 15-17.
184. Ibid., pp. 70-1.
185. Ibid., pp. 72, 91.
186. Ibid., pp. 80-3.
187. Published in *TT*, Vol. V, 1917.
188. Ibid., II. 11, 67.
189. Ibid., XI, 64-5.
190. Ibid., II. 116-19, 122.
191. Ibid., XII-XIII.
192. Ibid., XIII. 128.
193. Ibid., XI. 46, XIV. 3-4, 91, 97.
194. Ibid., V. 107-12.
195. Ibid., XVII. 87.
196. *Śaradātilaka*, I. 52ff.
197. Ibid., VII-XXIII.
198. Ibid., IX. 103-4, X. 76.
199. Ibid., XI. 601-24; XXI. 95; XXII. 1ff.
200. Ibid., VII. 58-9, XXIV. 17-21.
201. Ibid, XVI. 56.
202. Ibid., XXIII. 71ff.
203. *Mahānirvāṇa* IV. 34- 47.
204. Ibid., III. 14.
205. Ibid., IV. 10ff.
206. Ibid., II. 31.
207. Ibid., VI. 14.
208. Ibid., VIII. 150.
209. Published in *GOS*, 1923.
210. Published in ANDS.
211. Ibid., XXIV. 45-53.
212. Ibid., IV. 31-47, 51-6; XV. 47-68.
213. Ed. A. Avalon in *TT*, Vol. XIV.
214. Ibid., I. 2 14, 92-3.
215. Ibid., II. 101-05, IV. 24-8.
216. Ibid., X. 88.
217. Ibid., V. 113-23.
218. Ibid., IV. 15ff.
219. *Tārākhaṇḍa*, XXXVI. 24-5.
220. *Kālīkhaṇḍa*, I. 17-19.
221. *Tārākhaṇḍa*, XXXII. 13-15.
222. Ibid., XVII. 36-8.
223. Critically edited, annotated and trs. by Sudarsadevi Singhal, New Delhi, 1958.
224. Ed. P.C. Bagchi, in *CSS*, 1934.
225. Published in *SBT*, 1925.

3

External Influences and Interactions

Tantrism and the Universal Mother Goddess Cult

Although Tantrism as a way of life, and also as a religious undercurrent, is basically Indian, its primitive substratum was nourished by certain beliefs and rituals which had acquired a universal character owing to their prevalence among peoples widely separated from one another. Ancient religious systems of the world, specially those in which the cult of the Mother Goddess or the Female Principle was deep rooted, contained beliefs and rituals quite similar to those found in Indian Tantric cults. Examples are the *galli* of the Syrian Mother Goddess Astarte of Hierapolis, the Eleusinian and Phrygian mysteries, the Dionysian rites, the Marian secrets, and so on. Throughout Phrygia, Syria, Lydia, Cappadocia, Pontus and Galatia, where the Mother Goddess reigned supreme, orgiastic, ecstatic and secret forms of her worship recalling the Tantric modes were found prevalent.

The Greek Thesmophoria was celebrated in honour of the two *thesmophoroi*, i.e. the law-bringing goddesses, Demeter and Persephone. This festival was marked by indiscriminate sexual intercourse.[1] The ritual of the union of Cybele and Attis, like that of Aphrodite and Adonis, or Ishtar and Tammuz, was marked by sex festivals. The union of Demeter and Zeus was imitated by men and women in the sex rites at Eleusis in order to make the fields wave with yellow corns. Frazer marks these similarities and concludes:

> that a great Mother Goddess, the personification of all the reproductive energies of nature, was worshipped under different names but with substantial similarity of myth and ritual by many peoples of Western Asia; that associated with her was a lover, or rather a series of lovers, divine yet mortal, with whom

she mated year by year, their commerce being deemed essential to the propagation of animals and plants, each in their several kind; and further, the fabulous union of the divine pair was stimulated and, as it were, multiplied on earth by the real, though temporary, union of the human sexes at the sanctuary of the goddess for the sake of thereby ensuring the fruitfulness of the ground and the increase of men and beasts.[2]

In Asia Minor and around the shores of the Mediterranean are found many examples of a Mother Goddess with a young subordinate god by her side. Hogarth notes that:

In Punic Africa she is Tanit with her son; in Egypt, Isis with Horus; in Phoenicia, Ashtaroth and Tammuz (Adonis); in Asia Minor, Cybele with Attis; in Greece (and especially in the Greek Crete itself), Rhea with young Zeus. Everywhere she is *unwed*, but made the mother first of her companion by immaculate conception, and then of the gods and of all life by the embrace of her own son. In memory of these original facts her cult (especially the most esoteric mysteries of it) are marked by various practices and observances symbolic to the negation of true marriage and obliteration of sex.[3]

In 1916, before the dramatic discovery of Mohenjodaro, R.P. Chanda wrote:

For a conceptioon of the godhead analogous to that of the Śākta conception of the Devī we should travel beyond the countries dominated by the Vedic Aryans and the Avestic Iranians to Asia Minor, Syria, Egypt and other countries bordering on the Mediterranean. There is a strong resemblance between the Indian Śākta conception of Śakti and the Śākta ritual of the followers of Vāmācāra and Kulācāra, who practised ceremonial promiscuity on the one hand, and the Semitic conception of Astarte, the Egyptian conception of Isis and the Phrygian conception of Cybele on the other.[4]

Scholars on the Foreign Elements in Tantrism

It is against this background that we are to evaluate the view of M.M. Haraprasad Sastri and B.T. Bhattacharyya that Tantrism was of foreign origin. According to Sastri, Tantra really means the worship of Śakti which most probably came from Western Asia with the Magi priests of the Scythians.[5] He also quotes a significant stanza from the *Kubjikātantra* which says:

Go to India to establish yourself in the whole country and make manifold creations in the sacred places of primary and secondary importance.[6]

The view that Phrygia was the original centre of the Mother

Goddess cult from where it spread in different directions (a view that has no imprtance nowadays) was very popular in the last quarter of the 19th century and the first quarter of the 20th century. That is why B.T. Bhattacharyya unhesitatingly wrote:

> The introduction of the Śakti worship in religion is so un-Indian that we are constrained to admit it as an external or foreign influence.[7]

Sir John Woodroffe postulated a theory of Chaldean origin.[8] Probably he had in mind the goddess Nana-Nina-Nanaia-Inanna, the original city-goddess of Urk who was later identified with the mother of Attis and the Iranian Anahita and was able to extend her cult into India. Her name occurs on the coins of the Kuṣāṇa kings. Bibi Nani, the local name of the goddess of the Śākta Pīṭha at Hinglāj in Baluchistan, Naina Devi of the Kulu valley, Sirmur and Bilaspur, Naini Devi of Nainital, etc., were evidently linked with the goddesses of the Nana group. The region around ancient Chaldea appeared to him as Śākadvipa of the Indian tradition.

Such theories are hypothetical and coloured by the preoccupations of their formulators. But there are clear indication in Tantric literature which definitely point out that mystic practices of Chinese origin crept into the Indian Tantric theories and practices. In 1900, Haraprasad Sastri pointed out, using Sanskrit texts, the connection of the goddess Tārā with Tibet and China and of the Vāmācāra practices with those of China.[9] The story recorded in the *Tārātantra* describes how Vaśiṣṭha went to Mahācinā to get instruction from Buddha. He brought from there the cult known as *Mahācīnakramācāra* which prescribes the worship of Mahācīnatārā. There is some truth in the story. We shall see later that Taoist and Tantric principles have much in common and that Chinese Taoism and Indian Tantrism have a genetic and historical relation. In the establishment of this relationship, Buddhism evidently played a significant part.

Buddhism, Confucianism and Taoism: Background of Chinese Influence

There was no organised religion in China before the introduction of Buddhism in the 1st century A.D. Early Chinese religious life consisted of popular and tribal cults and rituals like those of the Mother Goddesses, spirits of ancestors, elemental spirits such as those of earth or wind or river, deities under the title 'Dragon-Woman',

Eastern Mother', 'Western Mother', 'Shang Ti', and so forth. Along with all these there also developed a rudimentary idea of the co-existence of two opposite principles, Yang and Yin, symbolising the positive and negative forces of nature, conceived of respectively as the Male and the Female Principles, which subsequently pervaded all forms of Chinese thought.

Buddhism was able to absorb the local religious elements by incorporating the existing deities into its own pantheon or by imposing its own deities upon the existing popular ones, but it had to face a great challenge from two opposing philosophical concepts—Confucianism and Taoism. The origin of these two schools may be traced to a very early period, around the 6th century B.C. The first school was developed through the efforts of its founder Kung-fu-tzu (Confucius) and its great exponents like Mo-tzu, Meng-tzu, Hsün-tzu and others. The rise of Taoism was traditionally connected with the name of Lao-tzu and its subsequent exponents were Yang-chu, Chuang-tzu, Chang tao-ling and Ko-hung. The works regarded as most important and ultimately incorporated in the so-called Confucian canon were the *Wu Chung* or Five Classics, probably brought together in the time of the Han dynasty (202 B.C.-A.D. 220) and the *Ssu-Shu* or the four Books, while the Taoist texts comprised *Tao-te-king* attributed to Lao-tzu, and the works of Chuang-tzu, Lieh-tzu (Lieh Yü k'ou), Ko-Hung and others.[10]

The attention of Confucius (551-479 B.C.) was mainly devoted to the problem of social organization in accordance with the ethical principles which he believed to have come down from an immemorial past. According to him the fate of a man is ordained by *heaven.* All men are unalterably either *noble* or *base.* The youth must humbly submit to their seniors, subordinates to their superiors. These principles were of course designed to serve the purpose of a feudalistic order. But since Confucianism was simply a school of thought and not a uniform doctrine, it was swayed by the preoccupations of its main advocates at various times. Thus, Mencius (372-289 B.C) emphasised the idea of the paramount role of the people and the subordinate role of the ruler, though he attributed social inequality to the *will of heaven* which he regarded as the highest guiding power. His philosophical theories were based upon idealism, since he denied the role of sensory perception as a process of cognition. Morality was traced to man's inborn qualities which he considered to be innately good.

In the 11th and 12th centuries, Chu-hsi and others introduced Neo-Confucianism which under the influence of Buddhism and Taoism turned to the elaboration of metaphysical problems by postulating the existence of the two fundamentals in the universe, Li and Chi. The former is a basic concept in Chinese philosophy signifying 'law', 'the order of things', 'form', 'code of conduct of various social groups' and so on. The Neo-Confucians interpret it as the spiritual immaterial creative principle in contrast to the material principle Chi. Originally Chi meant 'air', 'vapour', 'breath', but gradually it acquired a broader meaning—'primary matter', 'basic matter of nature', 'the vital force' and so on, and came to be associated with two other basic Chinese philosophical concepts, the positive Male Principle, Yang, and the negative Female Principle, Yin. According to Chu-hsi, the ideal substance Li is devoid of form and properties and is inaccessible to sensory perception. The Great Ultimate gives rise to the force of motion (Yang) and the force of rest (Yin). There is constant alternation of motion and rest, and in this process five material prime elements arise (cf. the Sāṅkhya and Tantric concept of Puruṣa and Prakṛti and the evolutes of the latter). Chu-hsi considered the ideal element Li as primary and the material element Chi as secondary. He deduced man's innate nature from the ideal element Li by which he justified the supremacy of the privileged classes. Subsequently Chu-hsi's doctrine was officially reorganised and became the basis of the traditional educational system of China.

Like Confucianism, Taoism was basically a school of thought and not an organised religion but it stood for a totally different set of principles. Taoism is the doctrine of *tao* or the way (of things) which maintains that all things originate and change due to their own way or *tao*. All things are mutable and turn into their opposite in the process of mutation. Man should adhere to the naturalness of things without striving or crying. *Tao* is one of the key categories in Chinese philosophy. Originally *tao* denoted 'the way' and was later used in philosophy to denote the 'path' of nature and the 'laws' governing it. *Tao* also denotes 'ethical standard', 'purpose of life', 'logic' reason and argument'. Lao-tzu, the founder of Taoism, considered *tao* as a materialistic principle symbolising the natural way of things and the law that governs them. This interpretation was followed by Hsün-tzu, Wang chung and others. Early Taoism, as expounded by Lao-tzu, insisted on man's adherence to the naturalness of things and it was opposed to the domination and oppression of the ruling class—its sole emphasis was on the return to the primitive community of the ancients. Yang-chu contended that by observing the natural laws of life (*tao*) man would 'preserve his nature intact', while Hsun-tsiang and Yin-wen believed that adherence to *tao* would yield every man wisdom and knowledge.

The materialistic tradition of early Taoism was adopted by the philosopher Wang-chung who in his *Animadversions* (Lun-heng) opposed mysticism and idealism and the doctrine of 'heaven'as the supreme guiding force that controls the origin and development of things and phenomena. According to him, everything in the world has its source in the basic material elements, the *Chi*. Man is part of nature and comes into being as a result of the concentration of Chi. But while the materialistic philosophers interpreted *tao* as the natural way of things, those belonging to the idealistic way of thinking tried to interpret *tao* in a different way. Thus, Chuang-tzu blended the materialistic world-view of Taoism with such idealistic propositions as 'non existence of objective truth', 'life being an illusion' and 'the true being springing from the eternal and independently existing *tao*'. In the writings of Wang-pi and others *tao* came to be regarded as 'the ideal principle', 'the true non-being', and so on. Tung-chung-shu regarded *tao* as the divine way and all these interpretations became the ideological embryo of Taoism as a religion as distinguished from philosophical Taoism.

The materialistic and rational tradition of Taoism led to the development of what may be called the physical sciences in China. It began with the quest of an 'elixir of immortality' which resulted in the study of and researches in alchemy. This reminds us of Indian Tantra. The philosophical basis of this scientific enquiry was the primitive Chinese concept of the primary sources, the five elements in nature, the combination of which was responsible for the diversity of material phenomena. Side by side, the principles of the doctrine of opposite and interconnected Yang (active) and Yin (passive) forces were regarded as the cause of motion and change in nature. Why and how Taoism was able to supply a theoretical basis of the scientific development of China is a subject of historical enquiry. L.C. Goodrich explains it as follows:

> Taoism organized into a complete whole the original primitive beliefs and customs, those that centred about the worship of nature, which was considered animate. . . . The *tao* or way was the road one travelled in order to obtain three ultimate aims; happiness, wealth and long life. The intellectuals could do

this by meditating on the writings of the masters and following their intellectual teachings and by consciously seeking longevity through studying alchemy and observing certain physical requirements such as selective diet, breathing exercises, calisthenics and sexual practices.[11]

Although Taoism began and expanded as a philosophical movement in the course of time it took the form of a distinct religion. This was probably due to the influence of Buddhism. From its very inception Taoism advocated certain esoteric rituals and practices derived from the ideals of primitive community life, a return to which was always urged by the earlier exponents of Taoism who were opposed to domination and oppression of all types, particularly social and political. However, with its growth as a specialised religion, Taoism developed an elaborate pantheon of its own. Some of the Taoist deities were nature and astral beings, others were adopted from Buddhism or invented by imagination. A few of them were deified human beings. Lao-tzu himself was elevated to the rank of a deity. At the head of the pantheon was the traid of Three Pure Ones, evidently formed in imitation of the three *Kāyas* of Buddha. They consisted of (i) Yuan Shih T'ien Tsun (or Yuan Shih Tien Wang, later merged with Yu Huang Shang Ti) the First Principle, (ii) Tao-Chen, the controller of the opposite principles of Yin and Yang, and (iii) Lao-tzu, who expounded the doctrine emanating from Honourable Tao.

The extent of the influence which Buddhism exerted on Taoism can be estimated if we take into account the following criticism of the Neo-Confucianist Chu-hsi (A.D. 1130-1202) offered against Buddhism and Taoism. Chu-hsi wrote:

> Taoism was at first confined to purity of life and to inaction. These were associated with long life and immortality, which by and by became the sole objects of the cult. Nowadays they have thought it advisable to adopt a system of magical incantations, and chiefly occupy themselves with exorcism and prayers for blessings. Thus, two radical changes have been made. The Taoists have the writings of Lao-tzu and Chuang-tzu. They neglected these, and the Buddhists stole them for their own purposes; whereupon the Taoists went off and imitated the Sūtras of Buddhism. This is just as the scions of some wealthy house should be robbed of all their valuables and then go off and gather up the old pots and pans belonging to the thieves. Buddhist books are full of what Buddha said and Taoist books are similarly full of what Tao said. Now Buddha was a man, but how does Tao manage to talk? This belief, however, has prevailed for eight or nine centuries past. Taoism began with Lao-tzu. Its Trinity of the Three Pure Ones is copied from the Trinity

of the three persons as taught by Buddhism. By their trinity the Buddhists mean (1) the spiritual body (of Buddha); (2) his joyful body (showing Buddha rewarded for his virtues); (3) his fleshly body under which Buddha appears on earth as a man. The modern schools of Buddhism have divided their Trinity under three images which are placed side by side, thus completely missing the true signification (which is Trinity in unity), and the adherents of Taoism wishing to imitate the Buddhists in this particular, worship Lao-tzu under (another version of) the Three Pure Ones, namely (1) as the original revered god, (2) the supreme ruler Tao, and (3) the supreme ruler Lao-tzu. Almighty God (T'ien) is ranked below these three, which is nothing sort of an outrageous usurpation. Moreover, the first two do not represent the spiritual and joyous bodies of Lao-tzu and the two images set up cannot form a unity with him; while the introduction of the third is an aggravated copy of the mistakes made by the Buddhists. Chuang-tzu has told us in plain language the death of Lao-tzu, who must now be a spirit; how then can he usurp the place of Almighty God?[12]

Taoism and Tantra

S.K. Chatterji observes:

> Just as certain schools of Buddhism like Dhyāna Buddhism of Bodhidharma became an important factor in Chinese Buddhist religious thought and practice, so it is belived that some later Taoist ideas and practices, which were partly religious, partly magical, partly scientific and partly also in the plane of an erotic or sexual ritualism with mystic and philosophical implications came to India from China. The sudden and widespread development of Tantric doctrines and practices, both among the Buddhists and the Brāhmanists, from the second half of the first millennium after Christ, is rather significant in India.[13]

Reference has already been made to the very ancient Chinese concept the Male and Female Principles—*Yang* or the male positive power of light and heat and *Yin* as the female negative power of darkness and cold—as working through everything in life and being. The proper harmonisation of these two opposite principles is regarded in Taoism as the aim for the purpose of making man transcend his physical limitations by acquiring supernatural powers and even immortality in his physical body. This harmonisation of the Male-Female Principle evidently leads us to the question of sexual rites and techniques inherent in practical Taoism. The achievement of material immortality is known as *Hsien* which can be attained through the discipline of certain techniques of living like (1) respiratory techniques, (2) heliotherapeutic techniques, (3) gymnastic techniques, (4) sexual techniques, (5) alchemical and pharmaceutical techniques and (6) dietary techniques.[14] The respiratory technique is analogous to the Indian *Prāṇāyāma.* The heliotherapeutic technique has its analogue in many a solar ritual of India. The gymnastic technique reminds us of Tantric *Haṭhayoga* and *Kāyasādhana.* The dietary technique also has an Indian parallel.

But more important are the two remaining techniques, the alchemical-pharmaceutical and the sexual. These two are also fundamentals of Indian Tantrism. We have already had occasion to deal elaborately with Tantric alchemy in the introductory portion of this work. As had happened in the case of the Indian Tantras, the idea of immortality was linked with the study of alchemy. The Taoist philosophers believed that immortality could be obtained by the use of certain foods and medicines and a great deal of effort was thereupon directed towards the preparation of mixtures which could prolong life and eventually produce immortality. Chang-tao-ling, who is said to have devoted his life to the study of alchemical and dietary procedures, was able to prepare a compound known as 'Blue Dragon and White Tiger' which could prolong life and revitalize fading youthfulness. It is not impossible that Taoist and Tantric alchemists maintained a close relation and interchanged the results of their researches. While dealing with the Rasasiddhas mention has already been made of Bhoga or Boger, a Chinese Taoist, who actually settled in India and headed a school of Indian alchemists.

As regards the Chinese sexual techniques and their impact on Tantra the following observation of K.H. Van Gulik, as presented to us by H. Goetz is important:

> This (sexual) practice, again, has been the starting point of a secret Tantric-Taoist ritual intended not only to increase the length of life but even to win immortality for the adepts. . . . This ritual sheds a most important light on certain obscure doctrines and practices of Indian and Tibetan mysticism, especially on Yoga, the Buddhist Siddācāryas and the Kaulacakra of the Vāmācara Śāktas.[15]

And Joseph Needham writes in this connection:

> It is then of great interest to find that just as ancient or early medieval Tantrism was deeply interested in the phenomena of sex, so also this was central to Taoism. The *vajra* (thunderbolt or lightning flash) was identified

with the male external generative organ, the *liṅgam* (*seng chih*), while the lotus, *padma* (*lien*)—so characteristic of Buddhist iconography—was identified with that of the female, the *yoni* (*nü ken*). Essentially the theological doctrine was that the mystical or divine energy of a god (or of a Buddha) resided in his female counterpart, from whom he received it in an eternal embrace. There had to be one of these *śakti*, therefore, for each god or Buddha. The logical conclusion followed that the earthly *Yogī* seeking for perfection must also embrace his *Yoginī*, in a sexual union (*maithuna*) prepared for and conducted with special rites and ceremonies (*cakra*). There followed also the worship of women (*strī pūjā*) as a preliminary to *maithuna*. The whole forms a remarkable parallel to early medieval Taoism, though Buddhism seems to have come a long way from its origin when we find the phrase *Buddhatvaṃ yoṣid-yonī samāśritam*.[16]

The ideas and beliefs behind the Chinese sex rites have been described by Needham with reference to practices like the *Kulacakras* of Indian Tantras.[17] One should not forget that Buddhist Sūtras containing the nucleus of Tantrism began to be translated as early as the 4th century A.D. The contributions to this field by Chu-fa-hu (Dharma-rakṣa) and others are well known. The Buddhist *Dhāraṇīs* contained methods of rain-making, getting water from rocks, finding springs and sources, stopping storms, etc. Buddhist Tantric ideas were popularised in China by three celebrated Indian monks—Śubhakara-siṃha (Shan-wu-wei A.D. 636-735) who came to China in A.D. 716, Vajra-bodhi (Chin-kang-chih, d. A.D. 732), and Amoghavajra (A-mon-ka or Pu-khung, d. A.D. 774). The Chinese also had celebrated Tantric teachers. Chih-thung wrote much on Tantrism. I-chiṇg translated a Tantric work under the title *Ta Khung Chhüeh Chou Wang Ching*. I-hsing (A.D. 673-713), the great Chinese astronomer and mathematician of his time, was also a reputed Tantric. It should also be noted that in A.D. 520 Song Yun, the Chinese traveller, during a short visit he paid to northern India, lectured on the *Tao-te-king* of Laotzu before the king of Udyāna in the north-western frontier of India. When the Chinese envoy Li Yi Piao was in India about A.D. 646, he went to Kāmarūpa where he talked with the king, Kumāra Bhāskara, about the *Tao-te-king*, and the Indian prince was eager to have this work translated into Sanskrit, and also wished to have an image of Lao-tzu. In view of all these Needham observes:

> At the first sight, then Tantrism appears to have been an Indian importation to China. But closer inspection of the dates leads to a consideration, at least, of the possibility that the whole thing was really Taoist. . . . We saw that Taoist

sexual theories and practices were flourshing between the second and the sixth centuries in China definitely before the rise of the cult in India, and its reimportation (if it was a reimportation) by the Buddhists. Bhattacharyya significantly tells us here that the principal localities associated with Buddhist Tantrism were in Assam. This reminds us that one of Pelliot's most remarkable memoirs concerned a Sanskrit translation of *Tao-te-king*. It was made for Bhāskara-Kumāra, king of Kamarūpa (Assam), who had asked Wang hsuan-tshe for it in 644. A very living account of the work being done, with all the difficulties which the translation involved, exists in the *Chi Ku Chin Fo Tao Lun Hêng* (Critical Collection of Discourses on Buddhist Doctrine in Various Ages), under date 647, Pelliot translated this. In Tantric literature, moreover, China (Mahācīna) occupies a very important place as being the seat of a cult *Cīna-caryā* which worshipped a goddess called *Mahācīna-tārā*. Sages such as Vaśiṣṭha were said to have travelled there to gain initiation into this cult, in which women played a very prominent part. Possibly, therefore, Tantrism was another instance of foreigners amiably instructing Chinese in matters with which the Chinese were already quite familiar. However, the sexual element in Indian religion had from ancient times been so marked that Buddhist Tantrism may actually well be considered a kind of hybrid of Buddhism and Hinduism. The *sakti* idea is certainly ancient.

In any case it is possible to find detailed parallels of much precision between Taoism and Tantrism. . . . Mention is made of Taoist practice of *huan ching*, " making the *ching* or seminal essence, return". In this method pressure was exerted on the urethra at the moment of ejaculation in such a way as to force the seminal discharge into the bladder, whence it was afterwards voided by the urine; the Taoists imagined, however, that it made its way up into the brain, which it nourished in some marvellous way. Now in Bose's book on the Post-Caitanya Vaiṣṇava (Hindu) Sahajiā cult of Bengal, still existing, we find that an exactly similar method is used. In this sect, where the rites of *maithuna* are a kind of elaborately stylized and ritualized physical love, whether of couples married (*svakīyā*) or otherwise (*parakīyā*), the semen is made to go upwards to the region of *paramātmā*. Though the physiological technique is not clearly described the correspondence is too close to be accidental. There is, moreover, an epithet, *ūrdhva-retas* (literally meaning 'upward semen'), which occurs commonly in the *Mahābhārata* and *Rāmāyaṇa* epics, and which has often been translated 'chaste' or 'continent', but which may well have reference to this technique.[18]

To this observation of Needham, Chatterji adds:

Buddhism brought to China certain new things, no doubt, and was welcomed by the deeper spirit of quest in the Chinese mind which sought to transcend life and nature. But the accceptance of Nature as such and the logical termination of the line of argument in which Nature, conceived as the result of the eternal play of *Yang* and *Yin* which were living forces, led Taoism to the idea of *Hsien*-ship and the possibility of its attainment, and this proved to be an attractive ideology and discipline for those who in their mental composition or temperament were, to speak in the Indian way, inclined towards the full and free play of the *pravṛtti* or natural inclination and did not feel happy with the spirit of *nivṛtti* which led to abstinence and asceticism. It was in this way that when they came close to the atmosphere of later Taoism from the early centuries of the Christian era, that some Buddhists from India also found in it an alluring doctrine, which was sublimated and philosophized in the Indian way. In place of the Chinese *Hsien* or immortal, in India we have the *Siddha* or *Avadhūta*, the adept with miraculous power (*siddhis*) which he can attain through Tantric practices, preferably of the *vāmācāra* school. This would appear to come to India with Tantric Buddhism sometime after the middle of the first millennium A.D. and then joined forces with Indian naturism and eroticism, mysticism and magic, and was established as *Vāmācāra* or the leftist way, as opposed to *Dakṣiṇācāra* or the rightist way. In Brahmanical Tantra, it associated itself with Śiva and Umā, and acquired a kind of spiritual or mythological *imprimatur* in later Hindu thought in general.[19]

Vaśiṣṭha and Cīnācāra

Mention has already been made of the observation of H.P. Sastri that many of the rituals of the goddess Tārā which were known as *Cīnācāra* were of Chinese origin. Sylvain Levi also holds, on the authority of the *Tārātantra* and other works described by Sastri, that the worship of Tārā and the Tantric Vāmācāra practices, involving the use of Five Ms came from China.[20] Sir John Woodroffe takes a similar view.[21]

As early as 1874 Rasik Mohan Chatterjee brought out a series of Hindu Tantric texts from Bengal Mss. and published them in the Bengali script. Among the works he brought out were Brahmānanda's *Tārārahasya*, the *Rudrayāmala* and the *Mahācinācārakrama*, all of which refer to the Vāmācāra practices connected with the worship of Tārā as being brought by the sage Vaśiṣṭha who was instructed by Buddha himself. The *Merutantra*[22] also mentions that the Vāmācāra rituals were of Chinese origin. The *Tārātantra*[23] opens with the following question of Devī Tārā or Mahānīla-Sarasvatī: ' Thou didst speak of the two Kula-Bhairavas, Buddha and Vaśiṣṭha. Tell me by what Mantra they become Siddha.' The same Tantra defines a Bhairava as follows:[24] 'He who purifies these five (Ms) and after offering the same (to the god) partakes thereof is a Bhairava. Buddha then is said to be a Kula-bhairava.'

A.K. Maitra, the editor of the *Tārātantra* gives quotations from both the *Rudrayāmala* and the *Brahmayāmala* which narrate the story of Vaśiṣṭha obtaining the Vāmācāra practices from China. According to the *Rudrayāmala*,[25] the sage Vaśiṣṭha practised for six thousand years severe austerities in a lonely spot, but the goddess did not appear to him. Thereupon he went to his father Brahmā and wanted a different *mantra* from him. Brahmā advised him to carry on austerities. Vaśiṣṭha did it once again, but this time when the goddess did not appear he became angry, and having sipped water uttered a terrible curse. Thereupon the goddess appeared to him and pointed out that he had not taken the right mode of *sādhanā*. She advised him to go to Mahācīna, the country of the Bauddhas. Vaśiṣṭha then went to China where Buddha was established (Buddhapratiṣṭha). Having repeatedly bowed to the ground he said to Buddha:

Protect me, O Mahādeva, the imperishable one, in the form of Buddha. I am humble Vaśiṣṭha, son of Brahmā. For my perturbed mind I have come here for the *sādhanā* of the Mahādevī. . . . But doubts assail my mind (*bhayāni santi me hṛdi*) having seen the methods (*ācāra*). Remove them and also the weakness of my mind which is inclined to the Vedic way (*vedagāminī*). O Lord, here I find rites which are outside Veda (*vedavahiṣkṛta*). How is that wine, meat, women are drunk, eaten and enjoyed by Siddhas who are naked (*digambara*), high (*vara*) and about to drink blood (*raktopānodyata*). They drink constantly and enjoy beautiful women (*muhurmuhu prapivanti ramayanti varāṅganām*). . . . They are beyond the Vedas (*vedasyāgocarāḥ*) and always indulged in wine and women (*madyastrisevane ratāḥ*). . . . How can inclinations to such things purify mind? How can there be *siddhi* without Vedic rites?

Buddha was not perturbed at these direct questions, but delivered a lecture on the duties of the Kaulas and explained to him their mysteries and utility, and acquainted him with the secret rites and practices connected therewith. Vaśiṣṭha was fully convinced and followed the way of Buddha and eventually attained final liberation by an unrestrained use of the five *makāras*.

Again, in the *Brahmyāmala*[26] the same story is repeated but with a slight modification. Here it is told that Vaśiṣṭha was practising austerities on the Blue Mountain (*Nīlācala*), the site of the celebrated goddess Kāmākhyā of Kāmarūpa, and that he was asked by the Devī to go to Mahācīna and get himself initiated into *Cīnācāra*. Vaśiṣṭha went there to see a land inhabited by great *sādhakas* and thousands of beautiful and youthful women, full of mirth by the inspiration of wine and doing sexploiting gestures. He was surprised to see Buddha with eyes drooping from wine. He asked himself: 'What is Viṣṇu doing in his Buddha form? This way (*ācāra*) is opposed to Veda (*vedavādaviruddha*). I do not approve of it.' At once he heard a voice coming from air telling him not to think in this way. Being afraid he sought refuge with Buddha who explanied to him the mysteries of the Tāriṇī (Tārā) cult which involved Five *Makāras*, known as Cinācāra. Buddha explained the principal features of this cult, namely, its freedom from the rules of ordinary worship, from bathing, purification, *japa*, etc. It was nothing but worship in the mind. There were no rules as to auspicious and inauspicious time, or as to what should be done by day and by night, what is pure and impure, and so on. The goddess should be worshipped even though the place and worshipper be unclean. Women should be considered as her manifestation and be worshipped for they are objects of veneration.

The peculiar features of these storeis to be noted are these: Vaśiṣṭha is described as basically a follower of the Vedic way. He is surprised to see *Cīnācāra* rites and disapproves of them at first sight. He speaks of them as 'outside Veda' (*vedavahiṣkṛta)* and even opposed to Veda (*vedāvādaviruddha*). It is also to be marked that Vaśiṣṭha had done penances and performed the Tārā rituals in Nīlācala, which is, even today, the seat of the goddess Kāmākhyā, the Hinduised form of the goddess Ka-me-khā of the matrilineal Khasi tribes worshipped in the form of a *yoni* or the female organ. There is still a place called Vaśiṣṭhāśrama near Gauhati where the shrine of Kāmākhyā is situated which is largely visited by pilgrims. So there is some geographical assignment to the Vaśiṣṭha legend, according to the Tantric tradition which cannot be brushed aside, and the tradition can thus be localised. It is also noteworthy that the flower of the Devī is *jabā*, the scarlet hibiscus or Chinese rose.

The Tārā Cult: Its Renovation, Migration and Influence

In the Vaśiṣṭha legend referred to above the cult of Tārā is a basic factor. The word *Tārā* denotes star. The name of this goddess has an apparent similarity with that of Astarte, or Ishtar or Ashtaroth, the celebrated Mother Goddesses of Western Asia. In the Indian tradition, the name is a modification of the word *tāra* signifying protection, and this tradition, is reflected in the conception of her as the saviour. In the Buddhist tradition she saves or protects her devotees from eight great fears (*aṣṭamahābhaya*). Her early history is not very clearly known to us but on the basis of Subandhu's *Vāsavadattā* it may be held that by the 6th century A.D. her cult became very popular in India. She made her way into the Buddhist religion and came to be conceived of as the Śakti or female counterpart or repository of energy of the Boddhisattva Avalokiteśvara.

Her cult passed from India to Tibet where she came to be known as Sgrol-ma or Dol-ma in the Tibetan translation of her name. Like her husband Avalokiteśvara she was also conceived of under numerous forms. The Tārā cult, with the goddess in her various forms, also went to China as the Śakti of Avalokiteśvara. But in China, Avalokiteśvara was already on the way to transformation from a god to a goddess through the influence of the pre-Buddhist (Taoist and Confucian) Mother Goddess Si Wang-Mu, the representative of Yin or the Female Principle. This happend in the 7th and 8th centuries A.D., when Tārā became absolutely merged with her husband, who became transformed into the goddess Kuan-yin in China. This double form of Tārā became very popular in China and brought about her connection with most of the existing beliefs and rituals, specially those belonging to Taoism. The Taoist rituals which thus came into the fold of the Tārā cult in China as well as Yinism or Exaltation of the Female Principle in Taoism, which developed in that system as a corollary of the aforesaid Chinese Buddhist cult of the Female Principle, were also able to exert counter-influence upon the development of the Indian Vāmācāra rites of both the Buddhist and non-Buddhist Tantras.[27]

P.C. Bagchi, on the basis of a *sādhāna* found in the *Sādhanamālā*,[28] has tried to establish the identity of Mahācīna-tārā with Ekajaṭā whose cult is said to have been recovered by Siddha Nāgārjuna from Tibet.[29] The *sādhanā* of the goddess Ekajāṭa was discovered by him in the country of Bhoṭa. The description of Ekajaṭā is found in six different *sādhanās*[30] and closely agrees with that of Mahācīnakramatārā as found in other *sādhanās*.[31] Corresponding to these goddesses we find in the Hindu pantheon Tārā, Ugratārā, Ekajaṭā and Mahā-Nīlasarasvatī. The *dhyānas* of these goddesses as found in the Hindu Tantras literally correspond to those found in the Buddhist *sādhānās*. According to the *Sammoha-tantra*, Nīlasarasvatī or Ugratārā was born in a lake called Cola on the western side of the Meru which was included in Cīna-deśa. Bagchi suggests that Cola is probably to be connected with the common word for lake *Kul* or *Col*, which is found with the names of so many lakes to the west and north of T'ịen-shan, that is to say the pure Mongolian zone.

A number of countries beyond India are enumerated and described in the *Sammohatantra* as the centres of Tantric culture. These are Bāhlika (Balkh), Kirāta (hill tribes of the Himalayan zone), Bhoṭa (Tibet), Cīna (China), Mahācīna (Mongolia?), Maida (Media?) Parśvakika (Pārasik, Persia?), Airāka (Iraq?), Kamboja, Hūṇa, Yavana, Gandhāra, and Nepāla. It is not impossible that some Tantric schools associated themselves with these countries either through tradition or through the community of some mystic beliefs, of which the history is not clearly known. The same Tantra holds that China alone possessed a hundred primary and seven subsidiary Tantras (*śatam tantrāṇī cīne tu upatantrāṇi sapta ca*). It should also be remembered that of the earlier Śakti Pīṭhās—Kāmārūpa, Pūrṇagiri, Oḍḍiyāna and Jālandhara—three were situated on the high roads leading to countries outside India. Oḍḍiyāna was situated on the high road that connected the upper valley of the Indus with Balkh, Samarkhand, etc., on the one hand and the Pamirs, Khotan, Kashgarh, etc., on the other by the Gilgit valley. Jālandhara was situated on another highway that connected Tibet with India through the Shipki pass and Kāmarūpa had to a great extent been the centre of activities of foreign people since very ancient times.[32]

NOTES

1. H. Licht, *Sexual Life in Ancient Greece*, London, 1963, pp. 110-11.
2. J.G. Frazer, *Adonis Attis Osiris*, London, 1907, pp. 34-5.
3. Hogarth in *Encyclopaedia of Religion and Ethics*, Vol. I, p. 147.
4. R.P. Chanda, *Indo Aryan Races*, Rajsahi, 1916, rpt. Calcutta, 1969, pp. 148-9.
5. See his Intro. to N.N. Vasu's *Modern Buddhism*, Calcutta, 1911, pp. 10-11.
6. *Nepal Catalogue*, p. LXXIX.
7. B.T. Bhattacharyya, *Buddhist Esoterism*, Oxford, 1932, p. 43.
8. A. Avalon, *Mahānirvāṇa Tantra*, Madras, 1953, 3rd edn., p. 560.
9. H.P. Sastri, *Notices of Sanskrit Mss.* second series, Vol. I, Calcutta, 1900, pref. XXXII, p. 152.
10. *The Wu Chung* or Five Classics are *I king* (Book of Changes), *Shu King* or *Shang Shu* (Book of History), *Shih King* (Book of poetry), *Li Ki*

(Ceremonial Records) and *K'un K'iu* (Spring and Autumn Annals). The *Ssu Shu* or Four Books are *Lun Yü* (Analects), *Ta Hsüch* (The Great Learning), *Kuang Yung* (Doctrine of the Mean, ascribed to Tzu Ssu, also called K'ung Chi, grandson of Confucious) and *Ku Hung Ming* (The Conduct of Life). English translation of these texts done mostly by J. Legge are to be found in the *Sacred Books of the East* (Vols. III, XXVII-XXVIII) and the *Chinese Classics Series* (Vols. I-V). The first translation of *Tao-te-king* in European language was in French made by S. Julien (1842). Eng. tr. J. Legge in *SBE*, Vol. XXXIX, pp. 45-124.

11. L.C. Goodrich, *Short History of the Chinese People*, New York, 1943, quoted in R.B. Blackney's *Translation of Lao-tzu* Mentor, 1955, intro.
12. Bruce, *Chu Hsi and His Masters*, pp. 237-9.
13. S.K. Chatterji in *Journal of the Asiatic Society* (hereafter *JAS*), Vol. I, 1959, p. 104.
14. J. Needham, *Science and Civilisation in China*, Vol. II, Cambridge, 1956, pp. 33-164.
15. A condensed account of Gulik's 'Erotic Colour-prints of the Ming Period, with an Essay on Chinese Sex Life from the Han to the Ch'ing Dynasty' has been given by Goetz in ABORI, Vol. XXXVI, 1955, pp. 133ff.
16. J. Needham, op. cit, pp. 425-6.
17. Ibid., pp. 149-51.
18. Ibid., pp. 427-8.
19. Chatterji in *JAS*, Vol. I, 1959, p. 113.
20. S. Levi, *Nepal*, Vol. I, Paris, 1905, p. 346.
21. J. Woodroffe, *Śakti and Śākta*, 8th edn., Madras, 1975, p. 123.
22. Venkateśvara Press edn. Bombay, 1908, I. 58ff.
23. Ed. A.K. Maitreya, Varendra Research Society, Rajsahi, 1913, I.2.
24. IV. 10.
25. Ch. XVII.
26. *Paṭala* I.
27. Chatterji in *JAS*, Vol. I, 1959, p. 118.
28. No. 127.
29. P.C. Bagchi, op.cit., pp. 42-4, 46.
30. *Sādhanamālā*, Nos. 123-8.
31. Ibid., Nos. 100, 101.
32. P.C. Bagchi, op. cit., pp. 47-9.

4

The Primitive Substratum

Vāmācāra and the Primitive Female-dominated Societies

Of the existing modes of Tantric worship the Vāmācāra is so important that the term has become a synonym of Tantra itself. The conception of Dakṣiṇācāra as opposed to Vāmācāra seems to be a later development, and it is possible that the first word of the expression Vāmācāra is not *vāma* or left, but *vāmā* or woman.

A main feature of the Tantras is the higher standard to which they have raised womanhood. Śakti is manifested in women. When they are approached with reverence, purity, and devotion they raise men to the standards of gods. In the *Devībhāgvata*[1] it is said that women, as manifestations of the great world cause, are entitled to respect and even to veneration. Whoever offends them incurs the warth of Prakṛti, mother of all, whilst he who propitiates them offers worship to Prakṛti herself. According to the *Pārānandasūtra*,[2] a woman is Śakti incarnate, and there is no doubt that she is *brahman*. She is to be worshipped with clothes, ornaments, and food. She is god, the very life-breath, and the most valuable of all living things. She should not be censured or angered. Women are also regarded as the manifestation of Śakti in the *Śaktisaṅgama-tantra*.[3] A half-verse *striyo devāḥ striaḥ prāṇāḥ striya eva hi bhuṣaṇam*, found in many Tantric texts,[4] also occurs there. According to the *Kulārṇavatantra*[5] every woman is born in the *kula* of the Great Mother and that is why they should be treated with the utmost consideration. Extravagant praise is bestowed upon women also in the *Kaulāvalinīrṇaya*.[6]

Though in modern times Tantra has become male-dominated, there is reason to believe that once it belonged to the females. R.G. Bhandarkar wrote:

> The ambition of every pious follower of the system is to become identical with Tripurasundarī, and one of his religious exercises is to habituate himself to think that God is a woman. Thus the followers of the Śakti school

justify their appellation by the belief that god is a woman and it ought to be the aim of all to become a woman.[7]

Similarly speaking of the Sahajiyās, M.M. Bose observed:

The Sahajiyās also believe that at a certain stage of spiritual culture the man should transform himself into a woman, and remember that he cannot have experience of true love so long as he cannot realise the nature of the woman in him.[8]

The *Ācārabhedatantra* prescribes that women should be worshipped with *Pañcatattva* (the Five Ms) and *Khapuṣpa* (menstrual blood and allied secretions), and that the Para-śakti (the supreme being) should be worshipped by the followers of Vāmācāra, *only by becoming a woman.*

Pañcatattvaṃ khapuṣpañca pūjayet Kulayoṣitam
Vāmācāro bhabettatra vāmā bhūtvā yajet parāṃ.[9]

It appears from a legend found in the *Devībhāgvata*[10] that Brahmā, Viṣṇu and Śiva were transformed into women before they were allowed to see the Devī in her highest form. These legends of sex transformation may have some bearing on the widespread custom according to which it is compulsory for the priest to use female robes during his priestly function. In a *caryā* song we find that the Yogin Kanha became effeminate.[11] Among the followers of Tantra, female shamanesses called Bhairavīs and Yoginīs still occupy an important place. The seven *padmas* or lotuses on the *susumnā* cord are nothing but the seven seats of femininity inherent in every human being, and the *śaktis* like Kulakuṇḍalinī, Vāruṇī, Lākinī, etc., residing in the lotuses are also conceived of as female. Even in the Vaiṣṇava Sahajiyā literature, the Kulakuṇḍalinī Śakti is conceived as Rādhā, i.e. the Female Priniciple of the Vaiṣṇavas. Dasgupta also observes:

In the Caryā songs we find frequent references to this female force variously called as Caṇḍālī, Ḍombī, Śabarī, Yoginī, Nairāmaṇī, Sahajasundarī, etc. and we also find frequent mention of the union of the Yogin with this personified female deity.[12]

According to Bagchi, the *Jayadratha-Yāmala*, while discussing the special doctrines of different Tantric schools, mentions the practices of the Lāmās (*Lāmāvarga*), Śakinis and Yoginīs. Lāmā here is not the commonly known Tibetan word, *Bla-ma* meaning 'scholar', but something different. According to the text mentioned above, the Lāmās were otherwise known as Rūpikā and Cumbikā. Association with them is conducive to spiritual success. They are called Rūpikā because they assume different shapes during their intercourse with others and Cumbikā because they kiss at the very first introduction. In the *Hevajratantra* the Lāmās are referred to in the company of the Ḍākinīs and called Khaṇḍarohā and Rūpinī (*Ḍakinī tu tathā lāmā Khaṇḍarohā tu Rūpinī*). The Lāmās therefore constituted a mystic group of adepts who had their own special practices.[13]

The Ḍākinīs, Rākinīs, Lākinīs, Kākinīs, Śākinīs and Hākinīs were also women of flesh and blood, later raised to the standard of divinity. In western Tibet there is a class of sorcerers and witches called Lha-k'a, from whom the Lākinīs derived their name. Similarly the shamanesses—priestesses or witches—distantly connected with the Dags (people of Dagistan) and with the Śaka or Śākas were probably refered to in the Tantras as Ḍakinīs and Śākinīs respectively. The *Jayadratha-yāmala* refers to twenty-four varieties of Lāmās—Yoginī, Rūpiṇī, Lāmā, Śākinī, Nalinī, Khāgī, Culī, Bilā, Trikhagagā, Pesinī, Dehinī, Jalā, Klevati, Bedhani, Luki, Paḍabhī, Raktinī, Hisā, Karoṭhī, Kaluśī, Bhadrā, Dundubhi, Mukharā, and Āturā.[14] The *Guhyasamāja* while describing the different ceremonies in connection with initiation mentions *prajñābhiṣeka* or initiation of the disciple with Prajñā or Śakti.[15] The preceptor takes the hand of Vidyā or Śakti, a beautiful woman, and placing it on the hand of the disciple says that as Buddhahood is impossible to attain by any other means this Vidyā should be accepted and never abandoned in life. The *Sammohatantra* gives a list of the Vidyās whose worship was current in different parts of India. Some of them are well-known names of the Buddhist and Brahmanical goddesses.[16] But if the original concept of Vidyā, as enumerated in the *Guhyasamāja*, be understood it is possible to believe that originally at least some of them were female human beings, later raised to the standard of divinity.

The leading part played by women in religious life, their identification with the Mother Goddess, the symbolism of various concepts and relations ascribed to women, extravagant praises showered on them, the insistence on the cult of sex and of the female organ as the sole seat of all happiness, the function of women as priestesses or shamanesses, the idea of the superiority of the goddess over the gods, the concept of the supreme being as a Female Principle, etc., must have a social basis. According to Starbuck:

> Female deities have often enjoyed the highest place among the gods. This depends upon the nature of social organisation and the respect in which

women are held. Clan life in which the mother is the head of the group is likely to lift the Mother Goddess into a supreme position.[17]

The superiority of the goddesses over the gods, and priestesses over the priests can reasonably be explained in terms of a social system in which maternity counts more than paternity, where descent is traced and property handed down through women rather than through men.

There is a large body of evidence to show that the Semites before their separation passed through a matriarchal form of society. All those traits which are the oldest and most permanent in the character of Ashtart-Ishtar are those which for other reasons we must predicate of the ancient Semitic tribal mother.[18]

Among the Semites of antiquity traces of an older system of mother-right appear to have long survived in the sphere of religion. Frazer supports this view:

In later times father-kin had certainly displaced mother-kin among the Semitic worshippers of Astarte, and probably the same change had taken place among the Phrygian worshippers of Cybele. Yet the older custom lingered in Lycia down to the historical period; and we may conjecture that in former times it was widely spread through Asia Minor.[19]

But father right elements gradually encroached upon matters of descent and property in these countries and this brought a significant change in the field of religion. For instance:

In old Arabian religion gods and goddesses occur in pairs, the goddess being the greater, so that the god cannot be her Baal, that the goddess is often a mother without being a wife, and the god her son, and that the progress of things was towards changing goddesses into gods or lowering them beneath the male deity.[20]

Frazer shows that in Egypt the archaic system of mother-right lasted down to Roman times.

The union of Osiris with his sister Isis was not a freak of the story-teller's fancy: it reflected a social custom which was itself based upon practical considerations of the most solid kind. When we reflect that this practice of mother-kin as opposed to father-kin survived down to the latest times of antiquity, not in an obscure or barbarous tribe, but in a nation whose immemorial civilisation was its glory and wonder of the world, we may, without being extravagant, suppose that a similar practice formerly prevailed in Syria and Phrygia, and that it accounts for a superiority of the goddess over the god in the divine partnership of Adonis and Astarte, of Attis and Cybele.[21]

We have seen that in the Śākta-Tantric scheme of cosmogonical process, the unmanifested Prakṛti alone existed before creation. The Sāṅkhya and Tantric principle of Prakṛti or Pradhāna was the basis of the concept of the all-pervading Female Principle. Essentially the Sāṅkhya is the doctrine of Prakṛti, but within this it has a place for the Puruṣa or the Male Principle and the place is highly anomalous. The origin of this anomalous position of the Puruṣa can presumably be traced to the same position of the males in a female-dominated society. In the present form of the Sāṅkhya, as well as in the Tantras, the term Prakṛti has acquired a purely metaphysical connotation, but basically it stood for the Mother Earth, the fruit-bearing soil. The Sāṅkhya preaches a law of causation according to which the effect is the real modification of the cause. The cause of the material world is thus nothing but matter, since Prakṛti is the primordial matter or substance. In the Sāṅkhya, this primordial matter is represented as the Female Principle. The relation between Puruṣa and Prakṛti is explained in terms of the relation between a man and a woman. Prakṛti charms Puruṣa just as a woman charms a man. The activities of Prakṛti are also conceived in terms of the emotional activities of a love-stricken damsel. Prakṛti is sometimes conceived as a blushing bride and sometimes as a beautiful dancing actress.

Just as a dancing girl, after showing performances desists from dancing, so does Prakṛti desist after exhibiting herself to Puruṣa.[22]
As the birth of a child proceeds from the union of the male and female, so the production of creation results from the union of Prakṛti and Puruṣa.[23]

But the same Sāṅkhya holds that Puruṣa is subordinate, inactive, and nothing but a passive spectator. Prakṛti is the chief principle. This has given rise to great confusion. Ancient as well as modern writers have been baffled in their attempts to rationalise the role of the Puruṣa in the Sāṅkhya system. If creation is made possible by the union of Puruṣa and Prakṛti, how is it that the role of Puruṣa is so insignificant? Or if Puruṣa is so insignificant and indifferent, how is it that he takes so important a part in the affair of creation? This contradiction was taken into account by Śaṅkara who asked: '*kathañcodāsīnaḥ puruṣaḥ pradhānaṃ pravartayet?*' Garbe comments:

What place, however, in a system which holds such views is to be found for the Puruṣa? Strangely enough, former scholars who made exhaustive investigations into the Sāṅkhya system did not succeed in answering the question. They regard the Puruṣa in this system as entirely superfluous, and hold that its founder would have shown himself much more logical if he had altogether eliminated it.[24]

The contradiction cannot be explained except by postulating a matriarchal origin for the system. In a female-dominated society there is always a problem regarding the position of the male or the husband, as we find among the Khasis of Meghalaya and other matrilineal tribes of India. Here the mother is the head and the only bond of union of the family. The father has no kinship with his children, who refer to him curtly as a begetter. The role of husband in a female-dominated society perhaps finds its expression in the Sāṅkhya philosophy. Just as in such a society the child has no real kinship with the father, so also the world, in spite of its production by the union of Puruṣa and Prakṛti, has no real relation with the former.

References to female-dominated societies in ancient India are found in the literary descriptions of the *Strī-rājyas* or Women's kingdoms.[25] These kingdoms were located mainly on the north eastern and north-western borders of India. Megasthenes and subsequently Arrian, Polyaenus and Solinus, referred to the queen-rulers of the Pāṇḍya country,[26] and it is interesting to note that in Kerala and adjoining regions corresponding to the ancient Pāṇḍya country vestiges of ancient mother-right are still found. Hiuen Tsang referred to the Suvarṇagotra (Su-fa-la-na-kin-ta-lo) country in the Kumaon-Garhwal region as the kingdom of women.[27] This country with its typical social system is mentioned in the *Garuḍapurāṇa*[28] and the *Vikramāṅkadevacarita.*[29] The statement of the Chinese pilgrim seems to be supported by the account of the Nu-wang tribe of Tibet, said to have been ruled by a woman who was called Pin-chin. The pepole in each successive reign chose a woman as their sovereign.[30] Hiuen Tsang also mentions another *Strī-rājya*, called by him Western Women's country, near Lāṅgala in the present Baluchistan region.[31] The same country seems to be located in Varāhamihira's *Bṛhat-saṃhitā*,[32] in the north-western part of India.

Apart from the various references in the ancient texts, if we look at the social organisations of the surviving Indian tribes we find that they still have many traces of a matriarchal system of social organisation. Matrilineal descent and inheritance and matrilocal marriage are found among the Khasis of Meghalaya. While reckoning descent only the mother counts. Only daughters are entitled to share the property which belongs to the mother, the youngest daughter usually getting the larger share. In the matter of religion the priest (*lyngdoh*) acts as the deputy of the priestess, and he has to vacate his office if he has no woman of a proper relationship to assist him in the performance of his sacred duties.[33] Among the Garos, all property is inherited through the women and the males are ineligible to inherit in their own right. The clans are divided into different houses called *maharis* or 'motherhoods'.[34] The Nayar joint family or *tarward* consists of a woman and her daughters, the children of those daughters, and so on. The son's children do not belong to that *tarwad* but are affiliated to the *tarwads* of their wives. The strength of this matrilineal joint family is mainly due to the typical form of matrilocal marriage current among them. Nayar women are entitled to keep more than one husband; and this is possible only in a matrilocal residence, where husbands are merely occasional visitors.[35]

Vātsyāyana connected the Strī-rājyas with the Vāhīkas with whom it had certain customs in common.[36] In the *Mahābhārata* it is said that among the Āraṭṭas and Vāhīkas the sister's son inherits the property of his maternal uncle.[37] The kings of Travancore followed *aliya-santāna* (from mother's brother to sister's son) inheritance. Matrilineal inheritance prevails among the Ambattan, Ampalavasi, Chakkyar, Kavati, Krishnavakkar, Kuduni, Kurava, Kurukal, Malayarayan, Maravan, Malayali, Paliyan, Panan, Paravan, Pattaria, Pushpakan, Parayan, Pulayan, Samantan, Ulladon, Variyar, Villas, Visavan, Agasa, Bedar, Bestha, Gudigara, Helava, Holeya, Kumbara, Madiga, Nattuvan, Vannan, Cheruman, Gauda, Kallan, Kalasi, Karaga, Kottai, Vellala, Kannuvan, Mali, Mannan, Mappila, Tiyan, Wyena, etc., of South India,[38] and also among the Bedias, Halabas, Kaikaris, Kurmis, Mangs, Rajjhars, etc., of Madhya Pradesh.[39] Matrilocal marriage and residence are also found among many of these peoples.[40]

Baron Omar Rolf Ehrenfels observed that mother-right elements in India were stronger, both in extent and in degree, than those in any other part of the world and that a violent overthrow of the ancient mother-right in this country had taken place in an abrupt and artificial way through 'three typically Indian institutions'—hypergamy, child marriage and *satī* (burning of widows). The special vigour needed to overthrow mother-right necessarily presumes, as

Ehrenfels rightly claims, a corresponding special vigour of mother-right prevalent in India since pre-Vedic days. But even then, as Ehrenfels himself has shown, the matriarchal culture elements could not be stamped out from lives of the masses.[41] These are revealed in the survivals of the social customs and institutions like matrilineal descent and inheritance, matrilocal marriage and residence, and other allied features so common in Indian tribal life, the cults and rituals of the Mother Goddess, and a female-oriented world view manifested in Śāktism and the Tantric forms of religious systems. In the field of the Tantric forms of religious systems matriarchal influence was so deep-rooted that in South-East Asia even priests of the Tantric cults followed a matrilineal system of succession. The Cambodian Sdok-kak-Thom inscription records that the succession of priests was determined according to the *mātṛvaṃśa*, i.e. maternal lineage (*tanmārtṛvaṃśe yatayas striyo vā jātā vidyā vidyā-vikrama-yuktabhavāḥ, tadyajakās syuḥ....*[42]

These are all vestiges of a very primitive way of life. According to E.O. James:

> Whether or not this reflects a primeval system of matriarchal social organization, as is by no means improbable, the fact remains that the goddess at first had precedence over the young god with whom she was associated as her son or husband or lover.... That an infant is the offspring of the mother could never be in doubt, however its origin and generation may have been explained, if indeed, there was any speculation on the subject in its physical aspects. The role of the father might be very obscure and even non-existent, but that of the mother was not open to question, being merely a matter of observation.... Woman with her inexplicable nature and unaccountable attributes and functions, such as menstruation, pregnancy, childbirth and lactation, has been a mysterious person, calling forth a numinous reaction and evaluation, permeated with religious sentiments, rendering her once sacred and tabu.[43]

Elsewhere we have referred to the virgin goddess with a young subordinate god by her side who was her son and consort born out of immaculate conception. Such virgin goddesses are relics of an age when the father had no significance at all, and of a society in which a man's contribution to the business of procreation was hardly recognised. Cults of a virgin goddess were known in India from remote antiquity. In later Vedic literature we come across the goddess Kanyākumārī whose shrine at the southernmost point of India was mentioned by the author of the *Periplus of the Erythrean Sea.*[44]

'Wherever gynaecocracy meets us,' said Bachofen, 'the mystery of religion is bound up with it and lends to motherhood an incorporation of some divinity'.[45] Herein lies the significance of *Kumārī-pūjā* or worship of the Great Mother in the person of a virgin to which the Tantras attach special importance.[46] Even today the Newars of Nepal believe that their country belongs to the *Kumārī*, a young girl elected from time to time and worshipped as the living form of Kālī or Durgā, so that the king has to take a fresh mandate from her every year to rule the land.

In the earlier phases of human history when paternity was a matter of inference as opposed to maternity which was a matter of observation, it was quite likely that society would be driven to base its rights upon the mother. The practice of counting descent through the mother's line must have originated at a time when no connection was known to exist between pregnancy and sexual intercourse. However, there were also economic causes as Thomson points out:

> In the pre-hunting stage there was no production, only simple appropriation of seeds, fruits and small animals, and therefore there can have been no division of labour at all. With the invention of the spear, however, hunting became the men's task, while the women continued the work of food gathering. This division is universal among hunting tribes, and it was doubtless dictated in the first instance by the relative immobility of mothers. Hunting led to the domestication of animals, and accordingly cattle-raising is normally man's work. On the other hand, the work of food gathering, maintained, as we have seen, by the women, led to the cultivation of seeds in the vicinity of the tribal settlement; and accordingly garden-tillage is almost universally women's work. Finally, when garden tillage had given place to field tillage and the hoe to the cattle-drawn plough, the work of agriculture was transferred to the men. These ever-shifting tensions between the sexes correspond to the gradual transition from matrilineal to patrilineal descent.[47]

According to Briffault:

> The development of agricultural civilization without any intervening pastoral phase enhanced the matriarchal position of women not only as owners and heiresses of the arable land but also through their traditional association with agricultural magic and religion, which assumed in archaic societies a momentous development in correlation with that of agricultural pursuits, the women retaining for a long period the character of priestess.[48]

The whole process may be summed up as follows: Originally the clan centred on women on whose responsibility rested the essential and vital function of rearing the young and of imparting to them whatever could be characterised as the human heritage of the primitive stage. With subsequent changes in the mode of food-gathering and food production male-domination began to be imposed step by step. The process began with hunting, probably with the invention of the spear, and in the post-hunting age, among those peoples that developed pastoral economy, male supremacy came to exercise even greater hold, because stock-raising is almost everywhere man's work. But where agriculture predominated over hunting in providing food, it accordingly raised the status of women, because agriculture was their invention and business, at least till the invention of the cattle-drawn plough. Thus, among the earlier agricultural peoples the primitive social superiority of the females was retained if not enhanced. But with the development of the higher forms of agriculture, more specially with introduction of the cattle-drawn plough, this *matria-potestas* was finally overthrown, its relics are still found among surviving tribal institutions like matrilocal marriage, avunculate, female oriented religion, and so on.

The following observation of Robert Briffault is also important.

> The differentiation of the man as the warrior and fighter is certainly not due to any constitutional indisposition or incapacity in primitive women, but to economic necessities. While women are frequently known to share in the active pursuits of men, the constructive occupations which have given rise to the development of material culture belong, in rudest societies, almost exclusively to the sphere of women's work, and the men take no share in them. All industries were at first home industries and developed therefore in the hands of women.

Among many surviving matrilineal peoples it is often found that the authority is held by specific males like brother, mother's brother and so on. It is due to the fact that these are largely of the nature of extant cases from one stage to another. It should also be taken into account that the growth of many primitive communities has been retarded by the economic problems of their habitats and that the more backward peoples have been continually subjected to the cultural influence of the more advanced.

Role of Women in Tantric Cults

We have seen that the initial stages of agricultural economy created the material conditions for the social supremacy of females and that mother-right in India was historically connected with the early agricultural economy. The peculiar tenacity with which the matriarchal elements have survived in the lives of Indian people, despite violent attempts to suppress them by the upholders of the Smārta-Purāṇic tradition, is due to the fact that the majority of them still remain the tillers of the soil among whom the cults and rituals of the Mother Goddess are deeply ingrained, those of the male deities having only a secondary place.

A predominant, if not the most conspicuous, feature of the female-dominated world view is Tantrism, with its supreme emphasis on the Female Principle. In matrilineal societies generally we come across the superiority of the priestess over the priest based on a corresponding superiority of the goddess over the god. Frazer says that at Rome the Fliamen Dialis was bound to vacate his priesthood on the death of his wife, the Flaminica. The latter had originally been the more important functionary of the two and the former held office only by virtue of his marriage with the latter. He and his wife represented an old line of priestly kings and queens, who played the part of Jupiter and Juno, or perhaps Dianus and Diana respectively. The custom which obliged him to resign his priesthood on the death of his wife seems to prove that of the two deities whom they personified the goddess was indeed the better half.

A similar process is found among the Khasis. The Khasi priest is usually called *Lyngdoh.* The nature of his work varies in different Siemships, but there is one point in which we find agreement everywhere. The *Lyngdoh* must be assisted at the time of performing sacrifices by a female priestess called *Ka-soh-blei, Ka-soh-sla* or simply *Ka-lyngdoh.* The priest merely acts as her deputy. The High Priestess of Nongkrem had not only many duties to perform, she was also the actual head of the state at the same time although she delegated her temporal powers to one of her sons or nephews. The *Siem-sad,* or priestess, at Mawsynram on the appointment of a new Siem or chief had to assist at certain sacrifices. At Khyrim, the *Lyngdoh* is assisted by a priestess called *Ka-soh-sla* who is his mother, or sister, niece or some other maternal relation. Among the Khasis, as at Rome a priest would clearly have had to vacate his office if he had no woman of proper relationship to assist him in the performance of his sacred duties.[49]

In the Tantric religious system a woman has the right of initiating persons into the secrets of the cult and acting as guru. The ancient, and evidently matriarchal, tradition of the priestesses is maintained in the Tantras in which women are conversant with religious exercises as *uttarasādhikās*. *Mudrā*, one of the five *makāras*, basically means a woman. Although the term later came to mean cereals and bodily poses in the Hindu Tantras, the Buddhist Tantras consistently refer to this term in the sense of a woman.[50] *Maithuna* or sexual union with women is the most important feature of Tantric rituals. According to the *Mahānirvāṇatantra*,[51] God Śaṅkara declared five *tattvas*—wine, flesh, fish, mudrā (cereals, hand or finger poses or the woman-helper of the aspirant), and sexual intercourse—as the means for the attainment of the position of *vīra*. A person therefore should be devoted to the Kaula practices through all these. The woman with whom sexual intercourse is to be had is called *Śakti* or *Prakṛti* or *Latā* and this special ritual is called *Latāsādhanā*.[52]

According to the *Kaulāvalinīrṇaya*,[53] sexual intercourse is the only means by which the aspirant can bacome a *siddha*. Every woman is fit for intercourse, except the wife of the Guru or of one who has attained the status of *vīra*. Adultery and incestuous intercourse are valid, as it is also stated in *Kālivilāsa-tantra*.[54] The *Pārānandasūtra*[55] presents various repulsive descriptions of the sexual union of the Tantric partners. The most significant Tantric sex rites is *cakrapūjā*, i.e. worship in a circle. According to a description of it found in the *Kaulāvalinīrnaya*,[56] an equal number of men and women, without distinction of caste and even of blood-relation secretly meet at night and sit in a circle. The goddess is represented by a *yantra* or diagram. The women cast their bodices in a receptacle and each of the assembled men finds a female companion for that night by taking a bodice out of those contained in the receptacle.

Such sex rites baffled many of the ancient and medieval writers. Excesses in these rites alarmed even some followers of the Tantric way. That is why in the *Mahānirvāṇa* attempts have been made to convey the idea that these are all symbolic and that the passages of sexuality are designed to denote the union of the male-female elements within one's own entity. In Rājaśekhara's *Karpuramañjari*[57] Tantric rituals involving women are ridiculed. The *Yaśastilaka-campū* and the *Mattavilāsa* quote a verse ascribed to Bhāsa in which the Tantric practices of drinking wine and union with woman are treated with contempt. The same attitude is found in Kṣemendra's *Daśāvatāracarita* where the concept of liberation achieved through the drinking of wine from the same pot with washermen, weavers, workers in hide, the Kāpālikas and through the procedure of *cakrapūjā* and dalliance with women is described contemptuously.[58]

These sex rites obviously require some explanation. Whatever their original purpose may have been, there is no doubt that they were used as a means for satisfying the perverted sexual instincts of wealthy persons in the name of religion. In Kalhaṇa's *Rājataraṅgiṇī* we come across the fact that king Kalasa (A.D. 1063-89) indulged in such repulsive rites under the inspiration of his guru, Pramadakaṇṭha, who himself committed incestuous intercourse with his own daughter.[59] This tradition was maintained all through. Dewan Jarmani Das in one of his books on the private lives of the Indian princes of the native states has given a vivid description of such a Tantric rite held in the court of a prince of the Punjab. After the independence of India, though the native states are no more, such practices have received greater encouragement and patronage among the wealthier sections of the people, and the number of Tantric *gurus* wearing silken ochre robes and flanked by aristocratic female companions is everyday increasing.

However, we are not concerned here with such perversions. Since the Tantric texts are so serious about the sex rites and the role of woman in the field of religion, we must accept the premise that the original purpose of all these rites was different. We must enquire why so much emphasis was laid upon the cult of sex.

Maithuna: Social Significance of the Sex Rites

One of the principal features of the Aśvamedha or horse sacrifice, which later came to be looked upon as the only touchstone for the might of the kings, was the union of the chief queen with a horse. In one of the Cārvāka polemics against Brahmanism and Brahmanical rituals, quoted from the so-called sūtras of Bṛhaspati by Mādhava in his *Sarvadarśanasaṃgraha* it is stated that *aśvasyātra hi śiśnaṃ tu patnīgrāhyaṃ prakīrtitaṃ* which means that the wife or the queen had to take the generative organ of the horse. In the Śrautasūtras[60] this ritual has been elaborately described. The horse is praised by uttering the verse from *Ṛgveda*, I. 163. Then a piece of cloth is spread over the grass. Thereon a mantle is spread and a gold piece placed on it. The horse is taken on to the mantle and killed. The four wives of the king go round the dead body of the horse thrice from left to right and thrice from right to left uttering verses from the *Vajasaneyī*

Saṃhitā, XXIII. 19. They fan the dead horse with their garments and enact a ceremonial mourning. The crowned queen then lies down by the side of the dead horse. The *adhvaryu* (priest) covers them with the same mantle on which the horse lies, and the queen unites with it. The *hotṛ* (another priest) abuses the crowned queen in obscene language and she returns the obscenities helped by her attendant princesses. Other priests (*brahman* and *udgātṛ*) and queens also take part in an obscence dialogue in which verses from the *Vājasaneyī Saṃhitā* XXIII. 22-31 are recited.

Clearly it is miming of a very ancient ritual. Even in the Vedic period the Aśvamedha in its real form was a thing of past. The *Taittirīya Saṃhitā*[61] and the *Śatapatha Brāhmaṇa*[62] state that the Aśvamedha sacrifice was then *utsanna*, i.e., gone out of vogue. Most of the Vedic hymns were meant to be chanted by one or more priests, but the dialogue-hymns were of more importance since they were meant to be performed or mimed before a group of persons assembled for certain purpose. The dialogue of the priests and the queens, as is found in the *Vājasaneyī Saṃhitā*. XXIII. 22-31, was likewise meant to be a part of an older ritual act in which a man, evidently a priest, had to unite with the queen—the part played by the horse here—and after his ceremonial sexual union he was put to death.

The *Vājasaneyī* verses mentioned above tell us that the queen and the priest are to be raised up high by a few persons and in that position they are required by the ritual to have sexual intercourse. In Uvaṭa's commentary on the *Vāj. Saṃ*, this rite is explained in greater detail. *Śatapatha Brāhmaṇa*[64] also refers to the queen's union with the priest. This ritual was later transformed into the Aśvamedha sacrifice in which a horse was used as a substitute for the priest. But the question is: why sexual intercourse?

Those who shiver at the thought of Tantric *maithuna* rites will perhaps be surprised to learn that in the Vedic texts sexual union is identified with *yajña* or sacrifice. Numerous passages of the *Śatapatha Brāhmaṇa*[65] equate sexual union with *yajña*. In the *Chāndogya Upaniṣad* we have the following passage:

> One summons; that is a *hiṃkāra*. He makes request; that is a *prastāva*. Together with the woman he lies down; that is an *udgītha*. He lies upon the woman; that is a *pratihāra*. He comes to an end; that is a *nidhāna*. He comes to a finsh; that is a *nidhāna*. This is the Vāmadevya Sāman as woven upon copulation. He who thus knows this Vāmadevya Sāman as woven upon

copulation, comes to copulation, procreates himself from every copulation, reaches a full length of life, lives long, becomes great in offspring and cattle, great in fame. One should never abstain from any woman. That is his rule.[66]

In many scattered passages of the Upaniṣads, the woman is conceived of as the sacrificial fire, her lower portion as the sacrificial wood, the genital region as the flame, the penetration as the carbon and the copulation as the spark.[67] The *Bṛhadāraṇyaka Upaniṣad* states that the lower portion of a woman (*upastha*) is to be conceived as the sacrificial altar (*vedi*), the pubic hair (*lomāni*) as the sacrificial grass, the outer skin (*bahiścarman*) as the floor for pressing of the *soma* plants (*adhiṣavana*), and the two labia of the vulva (*muṣkau*) as the inmost fire. He who remembers this during copulation reaps the reward of the Vājapeya sacrifice. The same text goes on to state that if a woman refuses sexual union she must be forced to do so.[68]

When it is said that through sexual union one can expect the reward of the Vājapeya sacrifice, there is no difficulty in arriving at the conclusion that originally the sacrifices were simple rituals, magical rather than propitiatory, and that there is a gulf of difference between the original and later forms of the sacrifices. Referring to the sacrifices as described in the Brāhmaṇa literature, Keith observed:

In the vast majority of these cases the nature of the ritual can be solved at once by the application of the concept of sympathetic magic and this is one of the most obvious and undeniable facts in the whole of the Vedic sacrifice: it is from the beginning to the end full of magic elements.[69]

Similar views were also held by Weber, Bergaigne, Geldner, Winternitz and others. Macdonell wrote:

It is thus impossible to suppose that the sacrificial priests of the *Ṛgveda*, the composers of the old hymns, should have occupied an isolated position, untouched by magical practices derived from a much earlier age and afterwards continued throughout the priestly literature of later times. In fact, a close examination of the hymns of the *Ṛgveda* actually affords the evidence that even in them the belief in magical powers independently of the gods is to be found ..... Every page of the *Brāhmaṇas* and of the *Sūtras* shows that the whole sacrificial ceremonial was overgrown with the notion that the sacrifice exercised power over the gods and, going beyond them, could directly influence things and events without their intervention.[70]

The original purpose for which magic was used was economic. It was directly connected with food-gathering or food-production.

Thomson's analysis is that:

> primitive magic is founded on the notion that by creating the illusion that you control reality, you can actually control it. It is an illusory technique complementary to the deficiencies of the real technique. Owing to the low level of production the subject is as yet imperfectly conscious of the objectivity of the external world, and consequently the performance of the preliminary rite appears as the cause of success in the real task; but at the same time, as a guide to action magic embodies the valuable truth that the external world can, in fact, be changed by man's subjective attitude towards it.[71]

Again referring to the potato-dance of the Maori, Thomson observes: 'It is not possible that the potatoes will be influenced by the dance, but the dance may influence the dancers theselves. At least they believe that their dance has something to do with the growth of plants, and when they tend the plants with this belief, their capacity and self-reliance obviously increase. Thus, though primitive and insufficient, magic was a valuable productive technique. This finds support in the Vedic sacrificial tradition. The collective *satra-yāgas* belong to the oldest category of the Vedic *yajñas*. One of the most significant rituals of this category is *Mahāvrata* which means *anna* or food.[72] The Vājapeya also means 'food and drink'.[73] Though in subsequent ages its purpose was changed, it was originally an agricultural ritual, as Keith has poined out rightly.[74] So it appears that the original purpose of sacrifice does not differ fundamentally from that of magic. With the change in the technique of production the pre-class tribal societies disintegrated, but magical practices did not die entirely. Their purpose began to change. In class societies primitive magic transformed itself into the esoteric art of the ruling or privileged class. It survived as a part of religion in its changed and distorted form.[75]

Since the *Bṛhadāraṇyaka Upaniṣad* states that by copulation, according to the rules prescribed, one gets the result of the Vājapeya sacrifice and since Vājapeya means 'food and drink', there is no difficulty in supposing that by sexual union one is entitled to get food and drink. In other words sexual union is regarded here as a means, or rather a technique, of food-production. The ritual intercourse of the priest and the queen referred to above, has significantly been shown as a parallel to the act of sowing in the field in Uvaṭa's commentary on *Vājasaneyī Saṃhitā* XXIII.27: *yathā kṛṣivalaḥ dhānyaṃ śuddham kurvan grahaṇa mokṣau jhaṭiti karoti.* It is due to the fact that the magical or religious rites intended to secure the fertility of the fields were thought of as belonging to the special competence of women who were the first cultivators of the soil and whose power of child-bearing was believed to have a sympathetic effect on the growth of the plants. The identification of earth with woman was once universal.[76] In the law book of Manu, man is identified with seed (*vīja*) while woman with field (*kṣetra*).[77] E.O. James observed:

> So intimate appeared to be the relation between the process of birth and generation and those of fertility in general that the two aspects of the same 'mystery' found very similar modes of ritual expression under prehistoric conditions.[78]

Peoples of the past instinctively projected their own experiences into the objects around them and associated various ideas in order to constitute a practical philosophy of life, making unconscious use of the only principle available to them—the principle of anology. Thus, they came to the conclusion that natural productivity should be viewed in terms of human productivity, Earth-Mother in terms of human mother. This is why the ritual association of sexual union with agriculture is universal. Pages may be filled with examples from India and elsewhere showing how sexual union has been used as a means to promote the fruitfulness of the earth.[79] Referring to such customs Briffault says:

> The belief that sexual act assists the promotion of abundant harvest of the earth's fruits and is indeed indispensable to secure it, is universal in the lower phases of culture.[80]

According to Frazer:

> At the present day it might perhaps be vain to look at civilized Europe for customs of this sort observed for the explicit purpose for promoting the growth of vegetation. But ruder races in other parts of the world have consciously employed the intercourse of the sexes as a means to ensure the fruitfulness of the earth; and some rites which are still, or were till lately, kept in Europe can be reasonably explained only as stunted relic of a similar practice.... It was an important social duty in default of which it was not lawful to sow the seeds.[81]

The Phallic cult, or the worship of human generative organ, which was once widespread among primitive peoples and the relics of which are still found all over the world, was evidently inspired by the same belief. Various phallic symbols representing the goddess and her consort have been found in the ancient tracts of the Aegean, in Egypt and the land of the Semites. At Mohenjodaro we come across the models of *liṅga* and *yoni* which were probably used as life-bestowing amulets,[82] while at Harappa a number of conical *liṅgas*, representing the male organ and large undulating rings of stone, thought to symbolise the Female Principle, have been recorded.[83] The beginning of the Tantric cult of Śrīcakra, which is nothing but the representation of the female generative organ,[84] can thus be historically traced to the ruins of the Harappa culture. Primarily the *liṅga* was the symbol of the act of cultivation while the *yoni* represented Mother Earth. This finds support in a statement of Manu: *iyam bhūmirhi bhūtānāṃ śāśvatī yoniruccate.*[85] It should be remembered that the primitive hoe was designed to resemble the male organ, and the word *lāṅgala* (plough) is philologically associated with *liṅga.*[86] Later on, when metaphysical values were attributed to them, the principles of the cult of *liṅga* and *yoni* came to be interpreted in terms of a dualistic philosophical outlook.

In Tantra special importance is attached to the rituals centering round the female genital organ and these rituals are called *Bhaga-yāga* or *Latāsādhanā*. From the earliest time the word *bhaga* has been used in Sanskrit in different senses; and in subsequent ages its meaning underwent several changes. In the Vedas, we have references to a god called Bhaga who is said to have been a son of Aditi.[87] The word also connoted a certain quality, the exact nature of which should be clarified. It is said that all men, rich and poor, desire *bhaga* from the god of the same name and also from other gods like Indra, Savitṛ, Soma, Pṛthivī and Bṛhaspati.[88] Now what is the quality or thing that was called *bhaga*? The answer is obviously connected with the original meaning of the word, which is the female sexual organ. In this sense the word occurs at least once in the *Ṛgveda.*[89] Later on, *bhaga* was looked upon as the sum total of all the six forms of material prosperity, called *ṣaḍaiśvarya*. This is how the word denoting the female organ came to mean the source of all material wealth.

The religious prostitution practised in various parts of the ancient world was likewise a custom based upon some objective understanding, a custom quite in accordance with the primitive belief in the identical relation of earth and woman. In Babylon every woman was bound, at least once in her life, to dedicate her body to a stranger in the temple of the goddess Mylitta. This custom was also prevalent in

Cyprus at Heliopolis or Baalbee in Syria, in the temple of Aphrodite at Corinth, in Lydia and in many parts of Western Asia.[90] Among the Armenians the goddess Anaitis was worshipped with sacred prostitution.[91] The goddess Ishtar had a following of unchaste women and harlots, and as a goddess of prostitution the epithet 'consecrated' was applied to her.[92] Lactantius says that Aphrodite or Venus instituted the art of courtesanship and taught the women of Cyprus to seek gain by prostitution, which she commanded so that she alone might not appear unchaste.[93] Prostitution has something to do with the goddess cults in India. Even today the 'sacred earth' of a harlotry is required in Durgā worship. In Southern India religious prostitution in the temples was legally abolished only a few years ago. In the Tantric worship of Jagannātha at Puri the dance of Devadāsī was a substitute for an actual *maithuna* ritual. In Tantric cults, female partners were very often recruited from prostitutes and fallen women.

Incestuous sexual relations, as we have already seen, are also prescribed in the Tantras. Guenther treats the problem from a psychological viewpoint,[94] but it appears that this was a relic of a very old custom. In the *Vājasaneyī Saṃhitā*[95] we find that Ambikā was originally the sister of Rudra, just as Hera was the sister of Zeus, and Isis the sister of Osiris. According to the *Ambaṭṭha Sutta*[96] and *Mahāvastu*[97] the Śākyas used to marry their sisters. The commentary of the *Suttanipāta* refers to the Śākyas who were rebuked by the Koliyans for cohabiting like dogs with their own sisters.[98] In the *Dasaratha Jātaka*, Sītā is represented as the sister as well as the wife of Rāma. According to the Ceylonese *Mahāvaṃsa* Sīhavāhu, king of Vaṅga, and Rāḍhā, married his sister Sihasīvalī.[99] The Jain *Āvaśyaka-curṇi* states that king Uṣabha married his own sister, that king Pupphaketu allowed his son to marry his own sister and that this kind of marriage was prevalent in the country of Golla.[100] Relics of sister-marriage are found in many places, but it was in ancient Egypt that the system of sister-marriage was developed to its fullest extent. Earlier scholars wanted to explain this custom in terms of matrilineal inheritance. When property passes from mother to daughter only two alternatives are left open to the sons of the family. Either they marry the real heiresses, that is, their sisters, or they leave their homes and reside with their wives' families. The former custom was evidently the earlier and when it came to be looked down upon the latter gained ground. Personally I find no fault in this argument, although there are many who do not subscribe to this view. However, the fact remains that incestuous sexual relation, as is suggested by the evidence of sister-marriage, was a social reality.

All the same, such incestuous affairs must also have had some ritual significance. In the *Ṛgveda*[101] we come across the incestuous dialogue of Yama and Yamī in which the sister, in passionate words, glowing with desire, draws the brother on to love. Yama is reluctant, but Yamī persists. This dialogue-hymn apparently reflects the conflict of two sets of moral values, but there are grounds to suppose that the whole episode is basically ritualistic, as we find in the case of another dialogue-hymn between Urvaśī and Purūravas.[102] In the *Śatapathā Brāhmaṇa*, too, we come across the legend of Prajapati's incestuous sexual relation with his own daughter.[103] It is stated thus:

> Prajāpati conceived a passion for his own daughter—either the Sky or the Dawn. 'May I pair with her', thus (thinking) he united with her. This assuredly was a sin in the eyes of the gods. 'He who acts thus, towards his own daughter, our sister, (commits a sin),' they thought. The gods then said to this god who rules over the beasts (Rudra): 'This one surely commits a sin who, acts thus towards his own daughter, our sister. Pierce him.' Rudra, taking it, pierced him. Half of the seed fell to the ground. And thus it came to pass. Accordingly it has been said by the Ṛsi with reference to that (incident): 'When the father embraced his daughter, uniting with her, he dropped his seed on the earth.' This (became) the chant (*uktha*) called *Agnimaruta*; in (connection with) this it is set forth how the gods caused the seed to spring. When the anger of the gods subsided, they cured Prajāpati and cut out that dart of this (Rudra); for Prajāpati doubtless is this sacrifice.[104]

According to the version of the legend given in the *Aitareya Brāhmaṇa*,[105] Prajāpati transformed himself into a roe-buck (*ṛṣya*) and approached his own daughter who assumed the shape of a doe (*rohita*). Out of their most fearful forms the gods then fashioned a divine being called Bhūtavat (i.e. Rudra) in order to punish Prajāpati for his incestuous deed. The latter was accordingly pierced by Bhūtavat's arrow and bounded up in to the sky, where he became the constellation Mṛga, while his daughter became the star Rohinī. This legend is also found in the *Pañcaviṃśa Brāhmaṇa*.[106]

In both versions of this legend we find that the woman with whom Prajāpati had sexual union was his own daughter. The whole affair was regarded as a case of incest and the killing of Prajāpati was interpreted as an act of punishment. But the subsequent stages of the legend show that this interpretation is oversimplified. It is stated that disgusted at the vile act of Prajāpati, Rudra discharged an arrow at him, whereupon Prajāpati was pierced and the semen (*retas*) fell upon the ground. Why is there reference to the semen of Prajāpati? Then it is stated that the semen was seen by Bhaga and at once he became blind. Why was it seen by him and why did he become blind? Again it is stated that the semen was tasted by Puṣan as a result of which he lost his teeth. Why did such things happen? Had it been a simple case of incest the matter would have ended with the punishment of Prajāpati. Why, then, did Bhaga and Puṣan have to suffer?

According to the *Aitareya* version of the story, the daughter, before her union with Prajāpati assumed the shape of a *rohita* (*rohitaṃ bhūtam*). The word *rohita* has been translated as *doe*, but according to Sāyana it means menstruation: *rohitaṃ lohitaḥ bhūtā prāptā ṛtumatī jātetyarthaḥ.* This reminds us of the menstrual rites associated with vegetation and fertility current in different parts of the world.[107] In Tantra special importance is attached to *khapuṣpa* or menstrual blood, as we shall see below. So it appears that the legend refers to a very old ritual, the significance of which was not understood even in the Brāhmaṇa literature. Now, the same legend is also found in the *Ṛgveda* in which Rudra is described as playing the part of Prajāpati. There it is stated that Rudra had sexual union with his daughter Uṣā, but this was not regarded as incestuous. It was simply regarded as a ritualistic affair.

The semen, capable of producing heroic children, increased and was about to overflow. He then, for the welfare of being, discharged that. He infused that semen into the body of his own beautiful daughter; when the father conceived such passion for his own youthful daughter, he united with her and she extracted much semen from the copulation. That semen was infused into a lofty frame, the container of good deeds. When the father made sexual intercourse with his own daughter *he did that with the earth* and infused semen therein. The intelligent gods made the *brahman* out of it and created Vāstospati, the protector of rites.[108]

Kha-puṣpa or Menstrual Blood

The identification of earth with woman which, as we have seen above, gave rise to sexual rites and practices in relation to agricultural operations and other practical aspects of life, basically implies that the functions of the earth and those of women are alike and that the same preconditions which fertilise women are thought to fertilise Mother-Earth. Here we may refer to the fertility ritual called *ambuvācī* which is observed by Bengali women on and from the seventh day of the third month of the Hindu calendar. It is believed that during the four days of the said ritual Mother Earth menstruates in order to prepare herself for her fertilistic work. During this period, there is an entire cessation of all ploughing, sowing and other farm work. Widows have to undergo a number of taboos since procreation is forbidden to them.

Aristotle, Pliny, and other naturalists believed that the embryo is formed from the blood retained in the uterus after the stoppage of menstruation. The same belief is also found in numerous scattered passages of the *Mahābhārata* and the Purāṇas. Since earth is identified with woman, the concept of the menstruating earth-goddesses is quite natural. In the Punjab, Mother Earth sleeps for a week in each month.[109] In the Deccan, after the *Navarātrā* her temple is closed from the tenth day to the day of the full moon while she rests and refreshes herself.[110] A similar rite of purification is done in the case of the goddess Bhagavatī of Kerala.[111] In Malabar Mother Earth rests during the hot weather until she gets the first shower of rain.[112] In many parts of India great importance is attached to the menstruation of Pārvatī.[113] The temple of Kāmākhyā of Assam is kept closed for some time in a year because it is believed that for that period she remains unclean because of her menstruation. A red liquid, prepared artificially, is sold to the devotees as her blood. Thomson says:

> It is important to observe that the magic of human fecundity attaches to the process, not to the result.... to the lochial discharge, not to the child itself, and consequently all fluxes of blood, menstrual as well as lochial, are treated alike as manifestation of the life-giving power inherent in the female sex. In primitive thought, menstruation was regarded, quite correctly, as a process of the same nature as childbirth.[114]

Before the Bhils begin sowing they set up a stone in the field and smear it with vermilion.[115] As vermilion stands for menstrual blood, the act of smearing it on the stone implies the infusion of productive energy into the earth. Most of the figures of the Mother Goddess from Mohenjodaro are painted over with a red slip or wash. The oldest extant figurines of the Mother Goddess, such as the Venus of Willendrof, are painted red. Some of the Egyptian, Maltese, Cypriot and Danubian figurines are also found ruddled.[116] The relation between vermilion or red ochre and the productive aspects of nature has been shown by Robert Briffault with copious illustrations.[117] Thomson writes:

It is worldwide custom for menstruating or pregnant women to daub their bodies with red ochre, which serves at once to warn the men away and to enhance their fertility. In many marriage ceremonies the bride's forehead is painted red ... a sign that she is forbidden to all men save her husband and guarantee that she will bear him children.... Red is the renewal of life. That is why the bones from the upper palaeolithic and neolithic interments are painted red. The symbolism becomes quite clear when we find, as we commonly do, that the skeleton has been laid in contracted or uterine posture. Smeared with the colour of life, curled up like a babe in the womb... what more could the primitive man do to ensure that the soul of the departed would be born again?[118]

The sign of blood had the double effect of forbidding contact and of imparting vital energy. Thus, one of the common methods of placing persons or things under a taboo was to mark them with blood or the colour of blood. At the same time blood or the colour of blood was regarded sacred and employed on cult objects for sanctifying purposes. There developed evidently a spirit of ambivalence in regard to this blood of life. On the one hand we come across the concept of menstruating goddesses, their supposed blood being regarded as most holy and efficacious, and on the other we also come across a deeply ingrained dread of impurity and unholiness attributed to menstruating women.[119] According to the combined evidence of the Vedic Gṛhyasūtras,[120] Purāṇas, and the Smṛtis:[121]

A student must not see a woman in her courses. After the *samāvartana* he must be careful at least for three days so that he may not come across a menstruating woman. He must not talk or play with girls in their menses. When a woman is in this state of impurity, scriptures must not be recited before her; she should not be seen or touched by one who has retired from family life or by a Brāhmaṇa engaged in dinner. If any one takes water from her, he has to perform *cāndrāyana* rite in order to purify himself. The menstruating woman must not touch any man or woman or animal belonging to any class, not even the utensils of copper, brass and steel. On the first day of her courses she must be treated as a *caṇḍālī*, on the second day as a *brahmaghātinī* and on the third day as a *rajakī*. The first and third terms are denotative of women who belong to lowest castes while the second is of one who has killed a Brāhmaṇa. When a woman in this state of impurity dies, her body should not be burnt immediately.[122]

Menstrual blood is also dreaded in the Mosaic Law Book of the Holy Bible[123] as well as in the *Koran*.[124] Pliny's account of the effect produced by a menstruating woman expresses substantially the beliefs found in the religious and legal texts of India and elsewhere:

But to come again to women hardly can there be found a thing more monstrous than is that flux and course of theirs. For if during the time of this their sickness they happen to approach or go over a vessel of wine, be it never so new, it will presently sour: if they touch any standing corn in the field, it will wither and come to no good. Also, let them in this estate handle any grasses, they will die upon it; the herbs and young buds in a garden, if they do but pass by, will catch a blast, and burn away to nothing. Sit they upon or under trees while they are in the case, the fruit which hangeth upon them will fall. Do they but see themselves in a looking glass, the clear brightness thereof turneth into dimness, upon their very sight.[125]

The deeply ingrained dread of impurity and unholiness and the terror attached to the taboo on menstruating women is not to be found in the primitive and original form of the concept. There are instances specially those of the bleeding goddesses in which menstrual blood had developed a sanctifying and purifying influence as manifestations of the life-giving power inherent in the female sex. This explains why in the Tantras menstrual blood has been regarded as so sacred that it is prescribed as an offering to the great god Śiva and his consort Devī.

In the Tantras the menstrual blood of a virgin is the most desired object for worship.

Harasamparkahīnāyāḥ latāyāḥ kāmamandire/
Jātam kusumamādau yanmahādevyai nivedayet//
Svayambhūkusumaṃ devi raktacandanasañjñitam//
Tathā triśulapuṣpañca vajrapuṣpaṃ varānane//
Anukalpaṃ lohitākṣacandanaṃ haravallabham//[126]

It means that the flower or blood (*kusuma*), which comes out from the generative organ of a girl (*latā*) who has not had sexual intercourse with a male (*hara*), is known as *sayambhūkusuma* or *raktacandana.* If it is not avilable she should be offered *triśūlapuṣpa* or *vajrapuṣpa,* i.e. the menstrual blood of a Caṇḍālī. It is to be noted that all women belonging to the socalled lower caste are regarded in the Tantras as natually initiated.[127] If the blood of a Caṇḍālī is not available, red sandalwood paste may be used as a substitute. The blood of a woman whose husband is alive is known as *kuṇḍodbhava* while that of a widow *golodbhava.*

Jīvadbhartṛkanāriṇām paṅkamañceva kārayet/
Tasyā bhagasya yaddravyaṃ tatkuṇḍodbhavamucyate //
Mṛtabhartṛkanāriṇām paṅkamañceva kārayet/
Tasyā bhagasya yaddravyaṃ tadgolodbhavamuccate //[128]

Śavasādhanā: Concept of Death and Resurrection: Fertility Beliefs

One of the strangest Tantric practices is *śavasādhanā* or the ritual of the corpse. On a selected new-moon night the aspirant has to secure the dead body of a robust person belonging to a lower caste, preferably a Caṇḍāla. The corpse should be undiseased, of one who has died of an accident. But how is it possible that a Caṇḍāla will, conveniently for the aspirant, have an accidental death on a fixed day of the calendar and at the right moment? The common practice might have been, therefore, to tempt a yọuthful Caṇḍāla, to get him drunk and finally kill him. This is, however, nothing but an inference. Then the body is to be anointed and used for the purpose of *sādhanā*. According to the *Kaulāvalinīrṇaya*, on a fixed new-moon night the aspirant should go to a cemetery, or some other lonely spot, after one watch of the night and secure the corpse of a Caṇḍāla, or one who has been killed by someone with a sword; or one bitten by a snake, or a young handsome warrior dying in a battle. He should wash the corpse, offer worship to it and utter *durge durge rakṣaṇī svāhā*. He will then have to experience terrifying sights and sounds, and if he is not frightened by all these, he will have *mantrasiddhi*—that is command over every aspect of life.[129] Details of this ritual and the very long procedure involved in it are mentioned in many other Tantras,[130] but there is no need to go into them here. The essence is that after proper anointation—according to some Tantras the corpse will be enlivened by such acts—the aspirant should sit on it, close all doors of his sensory organs and contemplate the figure of the great goddess. His inner perception will then begin to function. At the first state of his meditation he will have the vision of temptation in the form of wealth, beautiful damsels, etc., and if he is moved by all these, his efforts will be lost, and he may become insane. At the second stage he will have fearful experiences, too terrible to bear. If he is successful in enduring these the goddess will come to him, generally in the form of a little girl, and reward him for his efforts.

Such ideas are evidently baseless, although it is possible that in a secluded and fearful place, in the dead of night, a lonely person sitting on a corpse may have some sort of hallucinations, and since his mind is conditioned by certain preconceived notions relaing to his expectations, he may interpret his hallucinations in terms of some spiritual achievement. I am acquainted personally with a Tantric teacher who claims to have undergone the rites of *śavasādhanā*, but this did not give him any supernatural power. His name is Kalikananda Mukhopadhyaya and he has his hermitage at Joraghat in Chinsurah, the place where I live. He claims to be a *Baṭuka-siddha* and also an *Avadhuta*; the latter term he uses as his pseudonym, since he is also a writer in Bengali and has earned some reputation by recording his experiences in three autobiographical works. In *Marutīrtha Hiṅglāj* he describes his experiences as a pilgrim to the shrine of the goddesss Hiṅglājeśvarī, locally known as Bibi Nānī, at Hinglaj in Baluchistan. In *Vaśikarāṇa* he deals with the way of life of the half-naked ascetics found all over India, and in *Uddhāraṇpurer Ghāṭ* he describes his experiences as an aspirant to become a *siddha* in the great cremation ground at Uddhāraṇpur in Bardwan district. But this intelligent, educated and very reasonable gentleman has frankly confessed that despite all his serious efforts the *śavasādhanā* gave him nothing, no miraculous power. He is also wise enough to admit that although such rites are part of the faith and are to be conducted in the prescribed manner, the purpose is quite unknown. They are merely a mechanical continuation of rites practised in the past.

This observation of a well known Tantric teacher is significant. Some forms of *śavasādhanā* are still performed at the Tārāpīṭha in Birbhum district of West Bengal, but the performers themselves do not know the purpose of all these. It is quite possible that the writers of the medieval and late-medieval Tantras were also unaware of the purpose of *śavasādhanā*. They give a procedure of this *sādhanā* which is impossible to practice. The purpose is described as *mantrasiddhi* by which is understood command over everything through spells. But it has not been explained in the texts how the items of such rites are connected with the attainment of *siddhi*. In fact, the writers of these Tantras unquestioningly recorded a stock of relics of some rituals of hoary antiquity which had been fabricated through the ages and overlaid with external superimpositions.

It appears that the Tantric *śavasādhanā* was a typical and clumsy overgrowth of the primitive beliefs and rituals connected with fertility, death and revival. At a subsequent stage, when Tantra was basically concerned with material knowledge, in all probability corpses were handled for the purely scientific purpose of dissection. However, no verse from the extant Tantric literature in favour of this hypothesis can be cited and we can only depend on indirect and circumstantial evidence. Firstly, in the chapters on dissection as found in the extant medical treatises the nature and condition of the corpses needed for surgical training are almost the same as those of the corpses required for Tantric *sādhanā*. Secondly, as we have noted above, several Tantric sects laid supreme emhasis upon the revitalisation and renovation of the body through drugs and other chemical processes. It is, therefore, not unlikely that these people required corpses for their experiments.

But more significant is the association of Tantric *śavasādhanā* with primitive beliefs clustering around death, revival, and fertility. Many fertility rituals were developed from a primitive concept of death and rebirth. This concept owed its origin probably to the observation of the functioning of plant life, its death and revival. The idea of life after death was the natural conclusion of this observation. The rites of the annual decay and revival of plant life undoubtedly gave rise to the myths of Osiris and Isis in Egypt, Attis and Cybele in Phrygia, Tammuz and Ishtar in Syria and Babylon and Adonis and Aphrodite in Cyprus and Greece.[131] Among the ancients, every significant turning point of life was equated with death, as we find in the case of *upanayana* which sanctions a rebirth to the initiated one. Among primitive tribes, the person to be initiated has usually to pretend that he is dead.[132] Likewise when a man becomes a recluse, he has to change his name and make his own funeral rites. Evidently, the idea of death and rebirth at every turning point of an individual's life contributed to the growth of the concepts of *karma*, transmigration of soul, metempsychosis, and so on.

The primitive female figurines in many cases are grim embodiments of the Mother or Earth Goddess who is also the guardian of the dead—'an underworld deity connected alike with the corpse and seed-corn buried beneath the earth'.[133] The present forms of the Holi and Dewali festivals contain relics of primitive rituals connected with the concepts of fertility, death, and renewal of life.[134] In different parts of India, specially in many districts of Uttar Pradesh, Bihar, and Orissa, fire festivals are held during the celebration of Holi, and the ashes thus produced from the kindling of the fire are sprinkled on the ground for the multiplication of crops and fruits. Prof. N.K. Bose connects the origin of the fire-rites of Holi with such tribal rites as the Meria-killing of the Khonds. It was a human sacrifice for increasing the productivity of the fields. They believe that Mother Earth bestows the power of life through harvest and that the power of life can be returned to her by offering life, i.e. by a human sacrifice. Accordingly, the body of the victim was burnt and the ashes were sprinkled on the earth. This rite was also characterised by heavy consumption of wine and indiscriminate sexual intercourse and this explains the relation between Holi and sex rites, relics of which are still found in the sexual gestures and obscene types of mockfights, dances, songs and jokes forming essential features of the festival in different parts of the country. Human sacrifice for enhancing fertility of the fields, which survived till lately among the wild tribes like the Khonds, was once widely current among the peoples of India but with the spread of relatively advanced ideas which were evolved under different historical conditions, it went out of vogue. Its relics are not completely stamped out and still survive in such practices as stepping on the fire, burning of animals, burning of artificial human bodies, imitation of the act of killing, etc.[135]

The death and resurrection theme also finds expression in the ritual of an actual dead body which is connected with the popular *gājana* and *caḍaka* festivals of Dharma. In this ritual a game is played with the head of a dead person. The *bāṇavrata* of Śiva is another ritual connected with a corpse in which a human skull anointed with vermilion and oil becomes the occasion for a collective dance in which the priests and devotees are the participants. The phallus of Śiva which is kept for a whole year under water in a pond is recovered and worshipped. The head priest gives a show of the supernatural power he has acquired through such rituals by perforating his tongue and by other feats of physical endurance.[136] It is also interesting to note that the concluding function of the *caḍaka* ritual is the resuscitation of the dead. The chief devotee cooks a *sol* fish, roasting it in embers. Some parboiled and husked rice is also cooked and rice-wine is poured on the fish and the rice, which are placed in an earthen pot. These are taken at midday to a tree standing in some lonely meadow, and the food is placed on a plantain leaf for the ghosts to devour. This offering is sometimes made in the meadow where the village dead are cremated. Thus, even in the popular festivals relics of very primitive death-rites can be observed, while a specially channelised form of such primitive rites finds expression in Tantric cults.

Madya: The Efficacy of Wine

Like other ingredients of the Tantric *pañca-makāra*, the ritual use of wine was also a very primitive practice, originally connected with fertility and funeral rites, which made its way under different historical conditions into the religious life of the people. The Tantras lay special emphasis on the dirnking of wine as a means to attain liberation. According to the *Mahānirvāṇatantra*,[137] wine is the goddess Tārā in the form of fluid substance. As the mother or producer of *bhoga* and *mokṣa* and as the remover of diseases and misfortunes wine serves a very important purpose. Tantric works such as the *Pārānandasūtra*, *Kaulāvalinīrṇaya* and others make wine an essential precondition for the attainment of perfection. The *Kulārṇavatantra*[138] refers to the preparation of different kinds of wine and describes the procedure of its ritual use.

Scholars who have tried to justify or rationalise the Tantric rituals of wine, sexual intercourse, etc., resort to a mystic interpretation of such rituals. D.N. Bose, for example, suggests that the real significance of the five *makāras* has been deliberately perverted. According to him wine is the nectar-stream that issues from the highest cerebral region. Likewise fish symbolises 'suppression of vital airs', meat a 'vow of silence', and sexual intercourse 'meditation on the acts of creation and destruction'.[139] Likewise Sir John Woodroffe offered a symbolic explanation of the word 'drinking' used in the *Pārānandasūtra*. The verse is as follows:

Jīvanmuktaḥ pivedevamanyathā patito bhavediti/
Punaḥ pītvā punaḥ pītvā patitvā dharaṇītale/
Utthāya ca punaḥ pītvā punarjanma na vidyate//[140]

The verse suggests that an individual may escape from rebirth by dringking again and again, by falling upon the ground and rising up again owing to the state of intoxication. Similar verses are found in many other Tantras.[141] According to Woodroffe, the verse really refers to the movement of the *kuṇḍalinī*, its ascent and descent being symbolised by the drunkard's falling on the ground and getting up again:

Being thus awakened Kuṇḍalinī enters the great road to liberation (*mukti*), that is Susumnā nerve, and penetrating the centres one by one, ascends to the Sahasrāra, and there coming in blissful communion with the Lord of Lords again descends down to the same passage to the Mūlādhāra-cakra. Nectar is said to flow from such communion. The Sādhaka drinks it and becomes supremely happy. This is the wine called *kulāmṛta*, which the Sādhaka of the spiritual plane drinks. . . . In reference to a Sādhaka of the spiritual (*ādhyātmika*) class the Tantra says '*pītvā, pītvā. . . . vidyate*'. During the first stageof Saṭ-cakra-sādhanā the Sādhaka cannot suppress his breath for a sufficiently long time at a stretch to enable him to practise concentration and meditation in each centre of power. He cannot, therfore, detain Kuṇḍalinī within the Susumnā longer than his power of *kumbhaka* permits. He must consequently come down upon the earth, i.e. the Mūladhārā, which is the centre of the element earth, after having drunk of the heavenly ambrosia. The Sādhaka must practise this again and again and by constant practice, the cause of rebirth, i.e. *vāsanā* (desire) is removed.[142]

Surprisingly enough, attempts to give such imaginary interpretations are found even in some Tantric texts. It appears that their writers also sought to justify or rationalise the apparently repulsive rites with some preconceived ideas. The *Mahānirvāṇa* and *Tantrarāja* state that to drink wine without *śuddhi* is like swallowing poison. Any person doing that will suffer from diseases and die prematurely. Even the *Kulārṇava*[143] says that wine should be drunk only by those who have attained some stages of perfection. It should be consumed only to reach an ecstatic state. Drinking beyond this state is bound to make the aspirant a sinner. Some texts prescribe substitutes for the five *makāras.* Thus, *madya* may mean coconut water or any other liquid or even intoxicating knowledge. The *Mahānirvāṇatantra*[144] says that *madhura-traya* may be substituted for wine. The *Kaulāvalīnirṇaya*[145] substitutes hemp (*bhāṅg* or *vijayā*) for wine and states that if a man after partaking of *bhāṅg* engages in meditation he will directly visualise the goddess. In the *Kaulajñānanirṇaya*[146] and also in Bhāskararāya's writings[147] it is stated that when *kuṇḍalinī* is roused it reaches the thousand-petalled *cakra* known as *sahasrāra* from which drops nectar which is figuratively spoken of as *madya* or wine.

But wine is simply wine. Its use in religious purposes is universal. Drinking was an essential feature of Vedic sacrifices. The first important ritual of the Vājapeya is that of collective drinking in which the sacrificer offers five Vājapeya (food and drink) cups to Indra uttering the verses of *Vājasaneyī Saṃhitā,* IX. 2-4 and also seventeen cups of Soma and seventeen cups of Surā to thirty-four gods (the traditional thirty-three and Prajāpati as the thirty-fourth) deposited on earth mounds situated in front of or behind the axle. This is a type of Ekāha sacrifice consisting of three services or pressings (*savana*) at each of which certain cups of liquor are drawn, to be ultimately consumed by the priest and the sacrificer after libations to respective deities.[148] The common form of wine used by the Vedic peoples was called Soma which occupied a very important place in Vedic literature, being considered as a means through which men could overcome death and attain immortality.[149] Soma was also a Vedic god and the important rituals centering round this god (*Soma-yāgas*) are quite well known. Two other kinds of wine, Surā and Pariśrut, were used specially in the Vājapeya sacrifice.

According to Keith the use of wine in Vājapeya sacrifice was connected with ancient beliefs and rituals of fertility.[150] William Crooke has shown that liquor as the vehicle of magical power lies at the root of the tribal rituals all over India.[151] For example, the Oraons before the transplanting of rice-seedlings make a libation of wine on the ground. The Bagias before cultivation scatter a line of wine along the boundary of the cultivable land. This is due to the fact that in primitive thought wine was regarded as a life-giving principle. Debiprasad Chattopadhyaya has furnished two sets of examples to show that liquor is resorted to for the purpose of overcoming death and that the use of liquor is designed to ensure birth.[152] That wine overcomes the contamination of death (cf. the Ṛgvedic passage: 'We have drunk Soma and have become immortal') is evidenced from the funeral rites among backward people in different parts of the world.

> The Irish wake is a familiar example of the practice of drinking to celebrate death. In West Africa the Tshi people drink heavily during the feast which follows a death. . . . The same is the case among the Yorubas. . . . At funerals among the Woolwa Indians there is much drinking of *mishla*. . . . As soon as a Bangla man dies, the family gets in large supplies of sugarcane wine....The Guinea Indians drink and dance at the funeral feast.... Among the Tshinyai of the Zambesi the native beer, *pombe*, plays a considerable part in post-funeral rites....[153]

A similar use of wine in funeral rites is not at all uncommon in India. One of the commonest names for locally made wine is *mṛtasañjīvanī*, that which restores life, a name also very frequently used in Tantric and Āyuredic (medical) traditions. The same belief probably explains the use of wine in the puberty rites, the essence of which is death and rebirth. Wine also plays an important part in the marriage rituals all over the world as an agent of procreation.[154] One of the best known examples of the belief that wine induces the reproductive urge in the human being is retained in the creation legend of the Santals.[155] So in primitive thought wine is the agent that helps man not only to overcome death but also to create new life, and it is here that the ritual use of wine for enhancing the fertility of the earth is to be sought.

The magical use of wine, so common in fertility and funeral rites, also finds expression in popular religious festivals like the *Gājana* of Dharma and other deities. A gigantic vessel of wine called *bhāṇḍāl* is brought in front of the deity along with other smaller vessels. Dances are held around the principal vessel and the participants become quite senseless; this is caused sometimes by mere pretence and sometimes by the actual intoxicating effect of the liquor. In many places mock or actual fights are held among the participants for the possession of the vessel. In some villages of Birbhum district the Dharma-stone is carried in procession to the house of a Śuṇḍi (one belonging to the wine-making caste) who anoints it with oil and wine. In other places the actual task of brewing is performed before the god.[156]

Dīkṣā *or Initiation*

The Tantras categorically assert that without proper *dīkṣā* or initiation all efforts are bound to be futile.[157] This subject has been treated elaborately in all Tantric works.[158] The word *dīkṣā* is derived from the root *dā* (to give) and *kṣi* (to destroy), and hence, according to the Tantric tradition, *dīkṣā* confers divine knowledge and destroys sin. Most of the Tantric works provide that the knowledge conveyed by the *guru* must be kept secret.[159] In the Tantras, any qualifed person, irrespective of caste or sex, can act as *guru* but he must be careful in selecting disciples, and for this purpose he may have to wait for years.[160] The *Śāradātilaka*[161] sets out the qualification of the Tantric *guru* and also of the disciple. The *guru* must know the essence of the Āgamas and other scriptures. His words should be convincing and authoritative. He must possess a quiet mind. The disciple should rely solely on him and be ready to surrender everything to the *guru*. Two *ullāsas* of the *Kulārṇava* are devoted to the qualifications and greatness of *guru*.[162] The Buddhist Tantras also have the highest praise for the *guru*.[163] But there are also false *gurus* —those who pretend to know the truth and give false instruction—motivated by a greed for money. Warning against such *gurus* has also been given.[164]

According to *Mahānirvāṇatantra*, persons belonging to sects like Śākta, Saura, Śaiva, Vaiṣṇava, and Gāṇapatya may have sectarian *gurus*, but in order to become a Kaula initiation from a proper Kaula teacher is necessary.[165] The *Śaktisaṅgamatantra* regards an eclipse of the sun or the moon (particularly of the moon) as the best time for initiation (the reason will be given later).[166] The *Kālivilāsatantra* suggests the fifth lunar day of the dark half of the month of Phālguna as the most suitable day for initiation, and if on that day the Svātī star can be found it is extremely auspicious. A *dīkṣā* is of four kinds—Kriyāvatī,[167] Varṇamayī, Kalāvatī and Vedhamayī. There is a difference between *dīkṣā* and *upadeśa*. While the former includes *abhiṣeka* or complete consecration, the latter means communication of *mantra* in a solar or lunar eclipse, at a *tīrtha*, or a *siddhakṣetra*, or in a temple. The *Mahānirvāṇa*[168] lays down an elaborate procedure for complete *abhiṣeka*. One day prior to the function worship is to be offered to Gaṇeśa, the eight Śaktis, the Lokapālas, and others. On the day of initiation the novice, after a bath, is to offer gold, or its substitute, to the *guru* for the removal of his sins. Then the *guru* draws a *sarvatobhadramaṇḍala* on an altar, sanctifies the five *makāras* or *tattvas*, places an auspicious jar and fills it with wine. The *guru* consecrates the novice by sprinkling holy water and uttering *mantras* invoking the deities, and then gives a new name to him as a symbol of his new life.

This system of initiation is quite in accordance with the entirety of the Indian tradition of initiation in which the idea of death and rebirth is the driving force. In the Brahmānical *Upanayana*, the concept of *dvijatva* also stands for the same belief that at initiation the individual dies and is born again. Herein lies the significance of giving the initiated person a new name. The rebirth of the initiate is often represented dramatically by a magical representation of the act of dying and being born from the womb.[169] Here is an example from the *Aitareya Brāhmaṇa:*

> "Him whom they consecrate the priests make into an embryo again." He should be bathed in water (equated with *retas*), anointed with *navanīta* or clarified butter (symbol of embryo according to the text), and purifed with *darbha* or *kuśa* grass. Then collyrium is to be put in his eyes, just as it is in the eyes of the new-born. After this, the candidate will have to enter and stay in a hut shaped like a female organ (*yoni*). He should not come out of the hut and must not see the sun. He is to be covered at first with a cloth (symbol of the *ulva* or the placenta) and then with the skin of a black antelope (*kṛṣṇājina*, symbol of the uterus). So long as he stays in the hut, he will have to keep his hands clasped (*muṣṭi*), just as a child remains in the womb. When all this is done, he will have to come out of the hut still covering the body with that piece of cloth symbolising the *ulva* because the body comes out of the mother's womb under the coating of the placenta.[170]

The idea of death and rebirth in Tantric initiation is not only indicated by the new name given to the candidate, but also by the time selected for this purpose. The time of eclipse, preferably the lunar, is regarded as the best time. Since the moon, in primitive thought, was regarded as the source of magical powers and the cause of conception and generation, it is evident that the ideas of generation and rebirth and the rituals connected with them have some logical bearing on the phases of the moon.[174] The concept of rebirth is conspicuously associated with the moon, particularly with its eclipses—symbolising death and revival. That is why during the eclipse men usually follow the customs which are traditionally connected with the event of a man's death in a family. Old utensils are given away and a ceremonial bath is taken. The regular course of the moon itself suggests the death and revival theme. The periodical death and revival of the moon is responsible for the observance of various local rites throughout India which are mainly characterised by a ceremonial bath and fasting.

Many features of the Vedic *upanayana* and Tantric *dīkṣā* are sophisticated developments of the primitive tribal rites of initiation. Among the primitive tribes the members of a community are found graded according to age—as children, adults, and elders—the transition from one grade to another being effected by the rites of initiation. The most important of these marks the transition from puberty to adulthood—it is an introduction to full tribal status and a precondition for marriage or sex-life. For example, among certain tribes of Central India, one who has not undergone the prescribed puberty rites is treated as a *bhūta* or devil and is not subject to tribal restrictions as to food, etc.[172] In Fiji, uncircumcised youths are regarded as unclean, and as such they are not admitted to the group of elders.[173] The same holds good in the case of the Central Australian tribes.[174] Among the South-East Australian tribes uninitiated persons, however old they may be in age, are regarded as stupid, unworthy of receiving the honours of tribal ceremonies.[175]

The importance of initiation at puberty becomes quite evident when we look at the primitive secret societies headed by tribal elders. These societies bear distinctive totems, traditions and rituals, and in many cases they have magico-religious functions to perform. Admissibility into such groups is restricted to those who have undergone the appropriate rites and customs. The novices must undergo trials of strength or tests of endurance; failure in these means disqualification or disgrace.[176] The motive for the severity of these ordeals is perhaps purification. Just as application of heat is necessary to bend a piece of iron to give it a new shape, so also purification through a prolonged and painful test of endurance is necessary for a renewal of life. Finally, the novice receives instruction in the customs and traditions of the tribe as well as in sexual behaviour.[177] The whole ceremony is secret, performed at a distance from the settlement, and often preceded by a probationary period of seclusion. When the novices return to the settlement they are strictly forbidden to reveal to the uninitiated anything that they have done or heard or seen.

This idea of primitive secret societies reminds us of the Buddhist Guhya Samāja—the name itself has the same meaning. Tantric converts to early Buddhism, although they professed a belief in the Buddha, Sangha and Dharma, did not give up the traditional beliefs and rituals which they used to practise in secret. The secret conclaves which thus grew within the monastic order developed, in the course of time, into organisations known as the Guhya Samājas. Their teachings and practices were not sanctioned in early Buddhism, but they were not slow to find means of obtaining this sanction. They tried to introduce their doctrines into Buddhism by the composition of a new *saṅgīti* or collection of verses which came to be known as the *Guhyasamājatantra*, and attributing these doctrines to the Buddha they were able to secure many followers within the Buddhist church.[178] The development of Tantric Buddhism will be dealt with in a subsequent chapter. Here it is emphasised that in the history of Tantric Buddhism we come across the existence of such organisations which may be regarded as a developed and sophisticated form of the primitive secret societies. It should also be noted that the general system of Buddhist initiation was directly borrowed from that of the tribal initiation.[179]

The So-called Black Acts and Miraculous Powers

The *Ahirbudhnya-saṃhita*,[180] referred to in the preceding pages, provides a procedure of *mahābhiṣeka* by which diseases may be cured, enemies destroyed, and all desired objects attained. The origin of such beliefs in the wonder-working power of spells and rites can reasonably be traced to primitive magical beliefs and practices. Even in the Buddhist Tantras it is claimed that the attainment of various objects—from success in love affairs to liberation—can be secured by *mantras*. We have already had occasion to refer to the contents of the *Guhyasamājatantra* which deals with all these. The *Sādhanāmālā* asserts that everything, even Buddhahood, can be accomplised by *mantras*. It mentions eight *siddhis: khaḍga* (a sword sanctified by spells for success in the battle field), *añjana* (collyrium which when applied to the eyes enables one to see buried things), *pādalepa* (ointment applied to the feet enabling one to move anywhere unnoticed), *antardhāna* (to be invisible), *rasarasāyana* (transforming baser metal into gold and preparing the drug of immortality), *khecara* (to fly in the sky), *bhūcara* (going swiftly anywhere), and *pātālasiddhi* (diving undereath the earth).[181] The text also states that by means of certain *mantras* the wealth of Kubera can be appropriated[182] and that gods like Hari, India, Brahmā and others, and also *apsarās* or heavenly damsels, can be utilised as servants.[183] Even for defeating opponents in public discussions the *mantras* are efficacious.[184]

The concept of the eight *siddhis* or miraculous powers is very ancient. The earliest mention of it is found in the *Āpastamba Dharmasūtra*.[185] The *Prapañcasāra*[186] also enumerates eight *siddhis*—*aṇimā* (atomisation), *laghimā* (levitation), *mahimā* (magnification), *garimā* (greatness), *prāpti* (power of getting any thing), *prākāmya* (non-obstruction of desire), *vaśitva* (power of charming) and *iśitva* (sovereignty over all things)—and states that one who is endowed with these eight *siddhis* is a liberated soul. The *Kalpataru*[187] quotes a long passage from the ancient writer Devala and illustrates the eight *siddhis* or *vibhutis* substituting *yatra-kāmāvasā yitva* (the power of determinīng things according to one's will) for *garimā*, and this is mentioned in the commentaries on the *Yogasūtra*.[188]

Besides the *siddhis* there are six special rites which have been characterised as black acts. These are *māraṇa* (destruction), *ucāṭana* (driving away), *vaśīkaraṇa* (bringing under control), *stambhana* (arresting), *videṣana* (causing antagonism), and *svastyayana* (rites of welfare). The *Prapañcasāra*[189] contains a *mantra* called *trailokyamohana* for these six rites. It also describes a diagram (*yantra*) with the help of which one can smite a woman with passion.[190] These rites are elaborated in other Tantras.[191] According to the *Śaradātilaka* there are six methods through which the six rites are to be practised, and these are *granthana, vidarbha, sampuṭa, rodhana, yoga*, and *pallava*.[192]

These rites continue the primitive magical tradition. Traces of some of the Ṣaṭkarmas are found in Vedic literature. Two hymns of the *Ṛgveda*[193] clearly refer to the practice of removing co-wives and thereby controlling the husband. These two hymns have been explained in clearer terms in the *Āpastamba Gṛhyasūtra*.[194] Another hymn of the *Ṛgveda* purports to drive away diseases.[195] There are also some passages in the *Ṛgveda* dealing with destructive rites reminiscent of the Tantric *māraṇa*.[196] Such practices are also mentioned in the *Vājasaneyī Saṃhitā*,[197] *Kātyāyana Śrautasūtra*[198] and *Taittirīya Āraṇyaka*.[199] The *Taittirīya Saṃhitā*[200] prescribes a sacrifice called *saṃgrāhanī* by which persons can be won over. The *Taittirīya Brāhmaṇa*[201] relates how Sītā, daughter of Prajāpati, resorted to magical practices to win the love of Soma. These practices are similar to the *vaśīkaraṇa* of the Tantras. The original name of *Atharvaveda* is *Atharvāṅgirasa* which is a combination of two terms denoting beneficial and destructive magical rituals. The *abhicāra, strīkarma, sāmmanasya, pauṣṭika* and other magical rites of the *Atharvaveda* have their analogues in the Tantras. Likewise, the Purāṇas also contain the Tantric tradition of magical acts for good and evil purposes. The *Agnipurāṇa* devotes a complete chapter to this subject.[202] The *Matsyapurāṇa* refers to rituals for the purpose of bringing a woman under control, and that of driving someone away (*ucāṭana*). It also suggests a pure Tantric rite for the purpose of creating bad blood and also for killing.[203] This rite is for the purpose of *vidveṣaṇa* and *abhicāra*. One should prepare a triangular *kuṇḍa* on which *homa* should be offered by the priests wearing red flowers, red sandalwood paste, sacred thread in the *nivīta* way, red turbans and red garments. The fuel should be smeared with the blood of crows collected in three vessels and offered with the left hand holding the bones of a hawk. With hair untied the priest should desire the destruction of the enemy and utter *durmitrīyās-tasmai santu* along with the syllables *hrim* and *phaṭ*. The *mantra* which is used in the *syenayāga* should be recited over a razor. Then the high priest should cut an effigy of the enemy into pieces with that razor and throw the pieces into the fire. This is a clear instance of imitative magic practised in different parts of the primitive world. Such practices are common even today among many surviving backward tribes and also among peoples belonging to higher grades of culture. In Bengal villages it is commonly known as *bān-mārā*. An effigy of the person to be killed is prepared and the conductor of the rite, known as *guṇin*, meaning 'competent person' or 'one who has supernatural power', utters some *mantras* and finally pierces the effigy with a sharp instrument, and it is believed that the person concerned is bound to die as a result of this act. The common

Indian practice of burning the *kuśaputtalikā* or effigies made of straw of political leaders is inspired by the same primitive belief in imitative magic.

NOTES

1. IX 1, 137-45.
2. 64-5, 74-76, 80-81, op. cit., pp. 16-17.
3. Kālīkhaṇḍa III. 142-4, Tārākhaṇḍa XIII. 43-50.
4. Tārākhaṇḍa XXIII. 30.
5. XI. 64-5.
6. X. 66-9, 88.
7. R.G. Bhandarkar, *Collected Works,* Poona, 1936, Vol. IV, p. 208.
8. M.M. Bose, *Post-Caitanya Sahajiyā Cults of Bengal,* Calcutta, 1930 p.42.
9. N.N. Vasu, *Viśvakoṣa,* Vol. VII, p. 512.
10. III. 4, 6-10.
11. S.B. Dasgupta, *Obscure Religious Cults as Background of Bengali Literature,* Calcutta, 1946, pp. 105, 116-17.
12. Ibid., p. 116.
13. P.C. Bagchi, op. cit., pp. 49-50.
14. Ibid., pp. 51-2.
15. *Guhyasamāja,* p. 161.
16. P.C. Bagchi, op. cit., pp. 100-1.
17. *Encyclopaedia of Religion and Ethics,* Vol. V, p. 828.
18. Ibid., Vol. II, p. 15.
19. J.G. Frazer, *Adonis Attis Osiris,* London, 1907, pp. 394-5.
20. W. Robertson Smith, *Kinship and Marriage in Early Arabia,* London, 1903, p. 306.
21. J.G. Frazer, op.cit., p. 398.
22. *Sāṅkhyasūtra,* III, 68.
23. *Sāṅkhyakārikā,* XXI.
24. *Encyclopaedia of Religion and Ethics,* Vol. XI, p. 191.
25. *Jaiminībhārata,* Ch. XXII; *Skandapurāṇa,* Maheśvara, Kumārikā XXXIX. 27ff.; *Jayamaṅgalā* com. on *Kāmasūtra* (GOS) I. 249; *Rājataraṅginī,* IV. 173, 185, 587, 666; *Mārkaṇḍeyapurāṇa,* LVIII. 39; *Mahābhārata,* III. 51, XII.4; *Rāmāyaṇa,* IV. 43.20.
26. R.C. Majumdar, *Classical Accounts of India,* Calcutta, 1960, pp. 222-3, 456-8.
27. T. Watters, *On Yuan Chwang's Travels in India,* London, 1904, p. 330.
28. Ch. IV.
29. XVIII. 57.
30. C.A. Sherring, *Western Tibet,* London, 1906, p. 338.
31. T. Watters, op. cit., II, p. 257.

32. XIV. 22.
33. P.R.T. Gurdon, *The Khasis*, London, 1907, pp. 62ff.
34. A. Playfair, *The Garos*, London, 1909, pp. 80ff.
35. E. Thurston, *Castes and Tribes of Southern India*, Madras, 1909. Vol. V, pp. 294, 323; L.K.A.K. Iyer, *Cochin Tribes and Castes*, Madras, 1909, Vol. II, p. 49; K.M. Kapadia, *Marriage and Family in India*, Oxford, 196, pp. 336ff.
36. *Kāmasūtra*, ed. P. Tarkaratna, Vangabasi edn., p. 385.
37. VIII. 45. 13.
38. Iyer, op. cit., Vol. I, pp. 28-9, 76, 98; E. Thurston, op. cit., Vol. II; pp. 66, 296, Vol. III, pp. 33, 73, 268, 424; Vol. IV, pp. 119, 350, 440, 455, Vol. VII, p. 163; H.V. Nanjundayya and L.K.A.K. Iyer, *Mysore Tribes and Castes*, Mysore, 1928-35, Vol. II, pp. 3, 7, 108; Vol. III, pp. 149, 247, 315, 332, 433; Vol. IV, pp. 10, 138, 422.
39. R.V. Russell, *Tribes and Castes of the Central Provinces of India*, London, 1916, Vol. II, p. 224; Vol. III, pp. 139, 299, 394; Vol. IV, 65, 187, 408.
40. For details about the matrilineal societies in India see my *Indian Mother Goddess*, 1st edn. 1971, pp. 65-97, 2nd edn. 1977, pp. 253-77; also O.R. Ehrenfels, *Mother-right in India*, Hyderabad, 1941.
41. Ehrenfels, op. cit., pp. 18ff., 121-9, 201-4.
42. *BEFEO*, 1915, P. 62.
43. E.O. James, *Cult of the Mother Goddess*, pp. 228-9.
44. Cf. *Taittirīya Āranyaka*, X. 1.7.
45. J. J Bachofen, *Das Mutterrecht*, Stuttgart, 1861, p. XV.
46. *Tantrasāra*, Vasumati edn., pp. 642ff.; *Devībhāgavata*, III. 26-7.
47. G. Thomson, *Aeschylus and Athens*, London, 1950, pp. 15-16.
48. R. Briffault, *The Mothers*, London, 1952, Vol. II, p. 251.
49. P.R.T. Gurdon, op. cit., pp. 120-24.
50. *Prajñopāya* (GOS), V. 24; *Sekoddeśaṭīkā*, ed. M.E. Carelli (GOS), p. 56.
51. I. 57. cf., *Kaulāvalīnirṇaya*, II. 101. 105; IV. 24-8.
52. *Mahānirvāṇa*, I. 52; VI. 18 20; *Kulārṇava*, VII. 39 43.
53. IV. 15ff., VIII. 223-5.
54. X. 20-1.
55. Ibid., pp. 76-81.
56. VII.76.
57. I. 22ff.
58. *Daśāvatāracarita*, p. 162.
59. *Rājataraṅgiṇī*, VII. 278.
60. *Āśvalāyana*, X.8. 1ff.; Āpastamba, XX, XXII; *Kātyāyana*, XX., etc.
61. V. 4.12.3.
62. XIII.3.3.6.
63. For details see my *Ancient Indian Rituals and Their Social Contents*, New Delhi and London 1975, pp. 1-24.

64. XIII. 2.7-9; see also J. Eggeling's, tr. in *SBE*, Vol. XLIV, pp. 316ff.
65. I. 9.2.7; I. 9.2. 11; VI. 4.3.7; VI. 6.2.8; VI. 6.1.11, etc.
66. II.1.3., Hume's tr.
67. Cf. *Chāndogya*, V.8. 1-2; *Bṛhadāraṇyaka*, VI.2.13.
68. VI. 4.
69. A.B. Keith, *Religion and Philosophy of the Veda*, Harvard Oriental Series, 1925, pp. 258-9.
70. *Encylopaedia of Religion and Ethics*, Vol. VIII, p. 312.
71. G. Thomson, *Aeschylus and Athens*, pp. 13-14.
72. *Śatapatha Brāhmaṇa*, IV.6.42; *Tāṇḍyamāhabrāhmaṇa*, IV. 10.2.
73. For details about the Vājapeya see my *Ancient Indian Rituals*, pp. 48-69.
74. A.B. Keith, *The Veda of the Black Yajus School*, Harvard Oriental Series, 1914, pp. CX-CXI.
75. G. Thomson, *Religion*, London, 1956, p. 9.
76. R. Briffault, *The Mothers*, Vol. II, pp. 251-2, Vol. III, p. 56f.
77. Manu IX. 33.
78. E.O. James, *Prehistoric Religion*, New York, 1957, p. 172.
79. See my *Indian Mother Goddess*, 1st edn. 1971, p. 34; 2nd edn. 1977, pp. 6ff.
80. Briffault, op. cit., III, p. 207.
81. J.G. Frazer, *The Golden Bough*, abridged edn., pp. 135-6.
82. J. Marshall, *Mohenjodaro and the Indus Civilization*, London, 1931, pls. XIII.I, 7; XIV. 2,4, etc.
83. M.S. Vats, *Excavations at Harappa*, Delhi, 1950, pp. 51, 53, 55ff.,140.
84. R.G Bhandarkar, *Collected Works*, Vol. IV, p. 209.
85. Manu IX. 37.
86. P.C Bagchi, *Pre-Dravidian and Pre-Aryan in India*, Calcutta, 1929, pp. 10, 14.
87. *Ṛgveda*, VII. 41; *Vāj. Saṃ.*, XXXIV. 35f; *Atharvaveda*, III. 16.
88. *Ṛgveda* II. 17.7, III. 30; III. 62.II; VI. 41.2; *Vāj. Saṃ.* V.7; *Atharvaveda*, XII.1,5; XIX. 4 3.
89. X.11.6; cf. *Nirukta*, III. 16.
90. For details see my *Indian Mother Goddess*, 1971 edn., pp. 37ff.
91. Strabo, XI, 14, 16.
92. N.K. Sanders, *Epic of Gilgamesh*, Pelican, pp. 83ff.
93. *Divinae Institutiones*, I.7.
94. H.V. Guenther, *Yuganaddha*, Banaras 1952, pp. 106-12.
95. II.59.
96. *Dīgha Nīkāya*, III. 14; S. Beal, *A Catena of Buddhist Scriptures*, London, 1871, p. 126.
97. J.J. Jones, *The Mahāvastu*, London, 1949, I, p. 296.
98. I. 357; also *Kunāla Jatāka* (No. 536), p. 412.
99. W. Geiger, *Mahāvaṃsa*, Colombo, 1950, p. 53.

100. II. 81.178.
101. X.10.
102. X. 95; D.D. Kosambi, *Myth and Reality*, Bombay, 1952, pp. 42ff.
103. I. 7. 4.1-8; cf. II. 1.2.9 (Mādh); II.7.2.1-8; I.1.2., 5-6(Kān).
104. *Sacred Books of the East*, Vol. XII, pp. 208-10.
105. II. 33-4.
106. VIII. 2.20.
107. See my *Indian Puberty Rites*, Calcutta, 1968, pp. 5ff.
108. *Ṛgveda*, X. 61.5-7.
109. *North Indian Notes and Queries*, Vol. II, p. 172.
110. M.M. Underhill, *The Hindu Religious Year*, Calcutta, 1921, p. 34.
111. V. Nagam Aiya, *Travancore State Manual*, Trivandrum, 1906, Vol. II, pp. 89ff.
112. L.K.A.K. Iyer, *Cohin Tribes and Castes*, Madras, 1909, Vol. II, p. 78.
113. *Indian Antiquary*, Vol. XVIII, pp. 155ff.
114. G. Thomson, *Studies in Ancient Greek Society*, Vol. I, London, 1949, p. 25.
115. W. Crooke, *Religion and Folklore in North India*, Oxford, 1926, p. 250.
116. E. Mackay, *Further Excavations at Mohenjodaro*, London, 1937, Vol. I, p. 259.
117. R. Briffault, *The Mothers*, London, 1952, Vol. II, pp. 412ff.
118. G. Thomson, op. cit., pp. 209-10.
119. *Śāṅkhyāyana*, II. 12.10; IV. 7.48; IV.11.6; VI. 1.3; *Pāraskara*, IV. 7.48; *Khadira* III. 1.36; *Gobhila*, III. 5.6., etc.
120. Viṣṇu III. 8; *Garuḍa Pūrva*, XCV. 20; *Vāyu*, VII. 42; VIII. 84-5; *Brahmāṇḍa*, VII. 82-4; *Vāmana*, XIV.40; Śiva, *Sanatkumāra* XXIII. 34; *Kūrma*, Upari, XVI. 36, XCII. 30; *Agni*, CLV. 25; CLXX. 34.42; *Varāha*, CXLII, etc.
121. *Manu*, III. 239; IV. 40-2; *Āpastamba*, VII. 4-21; *Viṣṇu* XXII. 71-2; XXXVI. 7; LXXXI. 6; *Parāśara*, VII. 13-20; *Dālavya*, 146-54; *Bṛhad-parāśara*, VII. 226-36; *Bṛhad-yama*, V. 7; *Laghuyama*, 12-17, *Atri*, V. 49-69; *Aṅgiras*, 35-9; *Vaśiṣṭha*, I. 35; *Bṛddha-hārīta*, VIII. 203; *Vādhula*, 44-8; *Vyāsa*, II. 27-39; etc.
122. N.N. Bhattacharya, *Indian Puberty Rites*, Calcutta, 1968, pp. 8-11.
123. *Leviticus*, XV.
124. I. 122; II. 228.
125. *Historia Naturalis*, VII. 64f.; XVII. 226; XXVIII. 38ff. (Philemon Holland's Old Eng. tr.); also see Columella's *De re Rustica*, X. 358ff; XI. 3, 38ff; Cassinus Bassu's *Geoponica*, I. 15; X. 2.ff; XVI. 2.10; Porphyry's *De abstinentia*, III. 3; Dioscorides' *Materia Medica*, II. 99.
126. *Muṇḍamālā*, Paṭala II.
127. Cf. *Niruttaratantra*, Paṭala XI.
128. *Samayācāra-tantra*, Paṭala II.

129. *Kaulāvalinirṇaya*, XIV. 75-207.
130. Cf. *Tārābhaktisudhārṇava*, IX, pp. 345ff.; *Kulacuḍāmaṇitantra* (TT, Vol. IV), VI. 19-28; etc.
131. J.G. Frazer, *Adonis Attis Osiris*, pp. 182-93, 219-34, 269-77.
132. For an ancient Indian parallel see *Aitareya Brāhmaṇa*, I.3.
133. S. Piggott, *Prehistoric India*, London 1950, p. 127.
134. N.N. Bhattacharyya, *Ancient Indian Rituals*, New Delhi 1975, pp. 114-129.
135. N.K. Bose, *Hindu Samājer Gaḍan*, in Bengali, Viśvabhārati, p. 71-77.
136. H.K. Mukherjee, *Birbhum Bibarani*, in Bengali, Vol. II, pp. 5-9.
137. XI. 5ff.
138. II. 126, V.15ff., XI.22-35.
139. D.N. Bose, *Tantras, Their Philosophy and Occult Secrets*, Calcutta, p.11.
140. 81-2, p.17.
141. Cf. *Kulārṇava*, VII. 100; *Kaulāvalītantra*, VIII. 164ff.; *Kālivilāsatantra*, V. 25, etc.
142. J. Woodroffe (A. Avalon), *Principles of Tantra*, Part II, pp. CVII-CVIII.
143. VII. 97-8.
144. VIII. 170, 173.
145. III. 111.
146. VI. 18-19, p. 16.
147. *Saubhāgyabhāskara* com. on *Lalitāsahasranāma*, 87-91.
148. *Śatapatha Brāhamaṇa*, X.I.2ff; N.N. Bhattacharyya, *Ancient Indian Rituals*, pp. 50-1.
149. *Ṛgveda*, IV. 48.3.
150. A.B. Keith, *Religion and Philosophy of the Vedas* (HOS, 32), Cambridge Mass, 1925, p. 91.
151. W. Crooke, *Religion and Folklore of Northern India*, Oxford, 1926, pp. 100ff.
152. Chattopadhyaya, *Lokayāta*, pp. 309ff.
153. *Enyclopaedia of Religion and Ethics*, Vol. V, pp. 79-80.
154. Ibid.
155. *Journal of the Asiatic Society of Bengal* (Science), Vol. XIX, pp. 12-14.
156. N.N. Bhattacharyya, *Ancient Indian Rituals*, pp. 153-4.
157. Cf. *Kulārṇava*, XIV. 3-4, 91, 97.
158. *Kulārṇava*, XIV; 39ff.; *Prapañcasāra*, V-VI; *Śāradātilaka*, IV; *Jñānārṇava*, XXIV; *Viṣṇusaṃhitā*, X; *Mahānirvāṇa*, X. 112-119, etc.
159. *Parasurāmakalpasūtra*, I.12. *Śaktisaṅgama*, *Tārākhaṇḍa* XXXVI. 24-25.
160. Cf. *Tantrarājatantra*, II. 37-8.
161. II. 142-4; III. 145-52.
162. XII-XIII.
163. Cf. *Jñānasiddhi*, XIII. 9-12; *Prajñopāya-Viniscaya-Siddhi*, III. 9-16, etc.
164. Cf. *Kulārṇava*, XIII.128.
165. X. 201-2.

166. *Tārākhaṇḍa,* XVII. 36-8.
167. VI. 3-4.
168. X. 113-93.
169. H. Webster, *Primitive Secret Societies,* New York, 1932, pp. 38ff.
170. I. 3.
171. For illustrations see my *Ancient Indian Rituals,* pp. 122-5.
172. W. Crooke in *Journal of the Anthropological Institute,* Vol. XXVII, p. 246.
173. B. Thomson, *The Fizians,* London, 1908, p. 16.
174. B. Spencer and F. Gillen, *Native Tribes of Central Australia,* London, 1899, p. 401.
175. A.W. Howitt, *Native Tribes of South East Australia,* London, 1904, p. 530.
176. H. Webster, op. cit., pp. 34-5, 49-66.
177. Ibid., pp. 49-50.
178. B.T. Bhattacharyya, *Guhyasamājatantra* (GOS No. LIII), intro. pp. XXXIIff.
179. For details see Chattopadhyaya, *Lokāyata,* pp. 485ff; N.N. Bhattacharayya, *Ancient Indian Rituals,* pp. 79-80.
180. Ch. XXXIX.
181. *Sādhanamālā,* No. 172, p. 350.
182. Ibid., No. 296, p. 580.
183. Ibid., No. 260, pp. 509-10.
184. Ibid., Nos. 151, 155, 256.
185. IL. 9.23. 6-7.
186. XIX. 62-3.
187. *Mokṣakāṇḍa,* pp. 216-17.
188. *On Yogasūtra,* III. 44; IV.1.
189. XXIII. 5.
190. XXXIV. 33.
191. *Śaradātilaka,* XXIII. 121-35; *Śaktisaṅgama, Kālikhaṇḍa,* VIII. 102-6; *Mantromahodadhi,* XXV.
192. XXIII. 137-41.
193. X. 145; X.159.
194. IX. 5-9.
195. X. 162,
196. I. 191; VI. 52; VII. 50; VII. 104; etc.
197. VII. 3.
198. IX. 4.39.
199. IV. 27.
200. II. 3.10.
201. II. 3.1.
202. Ch. CXXXVIII.
203. XCIII. 139-56.

5

Tantrism and the Earlier Forms of Indian Religious Systems

Tantrism in Pre-Vedic Religion

The Zhob and Kulli sites in northern and southern Baluchistan, belonging to *c.* fourth millennium B.C., have furnished a fair number of terracotta figurines in which we recognise the earliest embodiment of the primitive Mother Goddess. The Kulli figurines finish at the waist on a splayed pedestal, arms bent with hands on the hips, breast usually shown, eyes fashioned from small stones, hair elaborately dressed, ornamented by oval pendants resembling cowrie shells and bangles on arms and wrists. In the cultures to the north and north-east of Quetta grouped around the Zhob river, a number of identical terracotta figurines have been found at sites of Dabarkot, Periano Ghundai, Surjangal and Mughal Ghundai. They are of Kulli type, with necklaces, large beak-like noses, hooded heads, exaggerated breasts, circular eye-holes and slit mouths. That they had a fertility significance is shown by the representation of the cowrie shells and by that of a phallus carved in stone at the mound of Mughal Ghundai near the left bank of the Zhob river and at the neighbouring mound of Periano Ghundai on the right bank of the river where a *yoni* is depicted with great prominence.

To some extent, the Zhob and Kulli cultures appear to coincide with each other in certain phases of development and to overlap in their latest phases with the Harappan culture of the Indus valley. The Mother Goddesses of Harappa and Mohenjodaro are significantly nude save for a very short skirt round the waist secured by a girdle. The figurines, as a rule, are burdened with jewellery consisting of elaborate neck collars, long chains, armlets, bangles, anklets, earrings, etc. The Harappan figurines do not represent mere busts as the Zhob and Kulli figures do but are modelled with legs and hands showing a variety of positions. The goddesses wear a distinctive head-dress which rises from the back of the head, in some cases directly from the head, while in others it forms part of the coiffure. Black stains on the pannier-like side projections of the head-dress were probably produced from smoke caused by lamp offerings to the goddess.

The Mother Goddess figurines, scenes on seals and ritual objects, notably large stone *liṅgas* and *yonis*, give glimpses of Tantric survivals of magic fertility rites that formed the basis of primitive Tantrism, and of the deities arising out of them. In Tantra, as also in popular Hinduism *liṅga* and *yoni* (male and female organs) stand for Śiva and Devī, and the prototype of the former is found in seals unearthed at Harappa and Mohenjodaro. Provided with horns on the head, and in one instance surrounded by animals, the three-faced male God, who is seated in the posture of a Yogin on several seals, may rightly be regarded as the prototype of the Indian God Śiva, the consort of the Mother Goddess.[1]

The existence of a Male Principle is not inconsistent with the cult of the Female Principle. In the later Śākta-Tantric system, we find that the Male Principle has some part to play although it is described as the connotative of static existence and dissociated from Śakti or the Female Principle, it is no better than a corpse.[2] Also in the Sāṅkhya, *Prakṛti* is all in all, *Puruṣa* or the Male Principle being nothing but a passive spectator. We have already seen that the anomalous position of the Male Principle in the Sāṅkhya can be explained in terms of the position of males in a female-dominated society. The concept of a material *Prakṛti* evolved from that of a material Earth Mother supposed to represent the forces that stimulate the generative powers of nature. Magical fertility rites, originally performed by women, to ensure the process of nature, were invariably associated with such a concept of the material Earth Mother as was found in the Harappa culture. These rites survived through the ages in popular beliefs and customs and were conserved and crystallised in the Tantras.

The specimens of the *liṅga* and *yoni* cults found at Harappa prove the extent of the influence of magical fertility rites upon the basically agricultural Harappan society. The predominantly pastoral Ṛgvedic tribes did not patronise such cults and that is why Indra is depicted in the *Ṛgveda* as crushing and exterminating the Śiśnadevas or phallic worshippers.[3] Female deities play practically no part in the pastoral and purely patriarchal religion of the early Vedic tribes.[4] But this religion could not deny the existence of two female deities—Aditi and Uṣas—probably because they belonged to a very old tradition. Aditi is the mother of the gods, but in spite of this her position in the *Ṛgveda* is unimportant. Although Uṣas is mentioned in twenty separate hymns, and her name occurs in the *Ṛgveda* more than 300 times, the Ṛgvedic poets were pleased to find her raped and crushed by Indra.[5]

Reference has already been made to the Harappan seals depicting a god in yogic posture. Also there are some broken statuettes, commenting on which R.P. Chanda wrote:

> The only part of the statuettes that is in a fair state of preservation, the bust, is characterised by a stiff erect posture of the head, the neck and the chest, and the half-shut eyes looking fixedly at the tip of the nose. This posture is not met with in the figure sculptures whether prehistoric or historic, of any people outside India; but this is very conspicuous in the images worshipped by all Indian sects including the Jainas and the Buddhists, and is known as the posture of the Yogin or one engaged in practising concentration.[6]

The non-Vedic and pre-Vedic origin of Yoga has been pointed out by many eminent scholars.[7] It appears that this practice was looked down upon in the early Vedic religion. In the *Kauṣītaki Upaniṣad* Indra says: '*Triśīrṣāṇāṃ tvāṣṭram ahanaṃ aruṇmukhān yatīn sālāvṛkevyaḥ prāyaccham*' which means that he has killed the three-headed son of Tvāṣṭṛ and thrown the *Yatis* to the wolves.[8] Who were these *Yatis*? According to R.P. Chanda:

> The only possible answer to this question is that the *Yatis* were not original priests of the Vedic cult like the Bhṛgus and Kaṇvas, but of non-Vedic rites practised by the indigenous pre-Aryan population of the Indus valley. In the legend of the slaughter of the *Yatis* by Indra, we probably hear an echo of the conflict between the native priesthood and the intruding *Ṛṣis* of the protohistoric period. If this interpretation of the legend is correct, it may be asked what was the religious or magico-religious practice of the *Yatis*? In classical Sanskrit *Yati* denotes an ascetic. The term is derived from the root *yat*, to strive, to exert oneself, and is also connected with the root *yam*, to restrain, to subdue, to control. As applied to the priest, etymologically *Yati* can only mean a person engaged in religious exercise such as *tapas*, austerities and *yoga*. The marble statue of Mohenjodaro with head, neck and body quiet erect and half-shut eyes fixed on the tip of the nose has the exact posture of one enaged in practising Yoga. I therefore propose to recognise in these statuettes the images of the *Yatis* of the protohistoric and prehistoric Indus valley.[9]

References to the slaughter of the *Yatis* by Indra are found in many passages of Vedic literature.[10] From the circumstantial evidence it therfore appears that the pre-Vedic religion of India consisted of the cult of Mother Goddess, worship of *liṅga* and *yoni*, sexual dualism, i.e. the concept of *Puruṣa* and *Prakṛti* as the Male and Female Principles of creation, and the practice of Yoga in which the human body was conceived of as the abode of all mysteries of the universe. All these principles stood in reciprocal relation, being components of an undifferentiated religous and ritualistic complex, which subsequently came to be known as the Tantric tradition.

Tantric Elements in the Vedic Religion

There was evidently a Vedic age in Indian history which was characterised by a special type of civilization that flourised in north-western and northern India and extended its influence over other regions after the fall of the Harappan civilization. On the basis of the internal evidence of the Vedic texts it may be assumed that a civilization mainly based on pastoral economy, patriarchal social organisation, natural gods and sacrificial cults has a vigorous existence in the Indus and Gangetic region from *c.* 12th century B.C. onwards, although this civilization could not for long retain its original character. A critical examination of the Vedic texts reveals the existence of a number of material cultures of different grade under a common tradition and ideology. Unfortunately, we have no archaeological evidence of Vedic civilization, although attempts have been made, with little or no success, to connect the post-Harappan archaeological findings, specially those of the painted grey ware cultures, with different aspects of Vedic civilization.

The earlier Vedic tribes were predominantly, if not exclusively pastoral. Out of 10,462 verses of the *Ṛgveda*, only 25 refer to agriculture, and significantly enough, 22 of the said 25 verses belong to the later portions of the *Ṛgveda*.[11] This purely pastoral economy of the early Vedic tribes eventually declined but the patriarchal social organisation and patrilinear inheritance were retained by their heirs. These traits are historical realities which can be traced, identified, and documented and as an undifferentiated cultural complex originally stood in opposition to the female-dominated Tantric outlook inhrerited from the pre-Vedic way of life. Ultimately, out of conflict a synthesis emerged when the Tantric elements gradually worked their way into the practices of the dominant class.

Many of these elements were successfully absorbed while others were never *legitimised* by the sacred texts in spite of their wide prevalence.

Goddesses like Ambikā, Umā, Durgā, Kālī, etc., were popular Tantric deities who made their way into the Vedic texts. The different names of these Mother Goddesses appear to have originally indicated different local or tribal deities who were afterwards identified with the wife of Śiva-Paśupati, the pre-Vedic god, supposed to have been worshipped by the Mohenjodaro peoples. Ambikā is called Rudra's sister in the *Vājasaneyī Saṃhitā*,[12] while the *Taittirīya Āraṇyaka* describes her as his spouse.[13] The latter work also refers to such goddesses as Vairocanī, Durgī, Kātyāyanī and Kanyākumārī.[14] Umā, the daughter of Himavat, is mentioned in the *Kenopaniṣad.* It is perhaps due to her Upaniṣadic epithet Haimavatī that in later works she has been identified with Pārvatī or Durgā. The names of these goddesses emphasise their relation with inaccessible mountain regions. Kālī, Karāli, Bhadrakālī and similar Tantric deities were also included in the Vedic scriptures.[15]

The revival of the pre-Vedic Mother Goddess cult in the post-Ṛgvedic age was evidently due to the extension of agricultural economy. Numerous rituals designed to secure the fertility of fields, mainly sexual in character, found their way into the Vedic texts and became the visible portions of the Tantric iceberg. In the preceding chapter we have referred to passages from the Vedic texts in which sexual union is associated with sacrifice. Subsequently, however, ingenious explanations were devised in order to account for these practices. Even then, the evidences relating to sexual rituals and their connection with agriculture and the cult of the Mother Goddess could not be completely brushed aside and it is interesting to note that in almost every period Vedic literature shows traces of sexual rituals and a pattern of sexual behaviour different from the officially accepted norm.

Besides the sex rites, we have seen that traces of the *ṣaṭ-karmas* of the Tantras like *māraṇa, vaśīkaraṇa,* etc., are distinctly mentioned in different parts of Vedic literature. Many of the Atharvanic practices of witchcraft are almost identical with similar practices of the Tantras. Reference has also been made to the use of wine in Vedic rites. Traces of monosyllabic and seemingly unmeaning *mantras*—on the importance of which the Tantras lay much emphasis—are also found in Vedic literature. But more important is the fact that a considerable section of the upholders of Tantra, especially those who could not give up their Brahmanical prejudices despite their conversion to Tantrism, went to the extent of attempting to demonstrate the Vedic origin of Tantra and so they often twisted Vedic passages to suit their purpose.

According to the *Rudrayāmala*[16] the supreme goddess is of the Atharvavedic group (*Atharvaveda-śākhinī*). The *Kulārṇava* also emphasises the Vedic origin of Trantra. Here *Kula-śāstra* is described as *vedātmaka*, i.e., Vedic in spirit.[17] Bhāskararāya considers the Tantras to be supplements of the Upaniṣads.[18] Natanānandanātha, in his commentary on the *Kāmakalāvilāsā*,[19] has attemped to trace the origin of the Tantric *mantras* to the Vedas. Lakṣmīdhara has quoted extacts from the *Taittirīya Saṃhitā* and *Brāhmaṇa* and explained them as having reference to Śrīvidyā.[20] The most interesting development is the utilisation of the Vedic *mantras* in the Tantric practice of the Five Ms. The *Tantrasāra* refers to *mantras* as *RV* I.154.2 to be used in connection with meat, *RV* VII 59.12 with fish, *RV* I.22.20-1 with *mudrā*, *RV* IV 40.5 with wine, and *RV* X184.1-2 for sexual intercourse. The *Paraśurāmakalpasūtra* mentions all these *mantras* from the *Ṛgveda*.[21] It also prescribes an additional *mantrà* from the *Taittirīya Āraṇyaka* for the rituals of wine.[22] We also come across Tantric adaptations of the Vedic *Gāyatrī-mantra* for invocation of differen deities.

Modern writers also, like the medieval and late-medieval Tantric writers, want to find a Vedic origin of the Trantras. Even great scholars like Gopinath Kaviraj and Sir John Woodroffe belong to this category. They have carefully gone through the pages of Vedic literature looking for the word Śakti, and also ideas and rituals similar to those found in the Trantric texts, and they have been partly successful.[23] It is a fact that the Vedic texts contain many Tantric ideas and practices. Even the principles underlying the Vedic sacrifcial cult are not basically different from those of the Tantras. But the Vedic texts and the Vedic tradition are two different things. This we have seen in the introductory portion of this work. In spite of the wide prevalence of Tantric elements, the Vedic tradition does not acknowledge them as an integral part of it. For the various reasons discussed above, the Tantric tradition continued to have independent existence.

We have already stated that the principles underlying the Vedic sacrificial cult were not basically different from those of Tantra. Although much has been written on Vedic sacrifice it is still not very clear to us. Most of the Indologists hold that the elaborate sacrificial system, as seen in the Vedic texts, was created by the priestly class mainly for their self-interest. According to B.K. Ghosh:

> It is clear that the intellect and mentality revealed by the extensive Brāhmaṇa texts was the monopoly of the cabalistic priests of the later Vedic age *and not a characteristic of the enlightened section of the peoples.* As literature, the Brāhmaṇas, digressive portions apart, may prove to be of interest only to the students of abnormal psychology. At the risk of a little exaggeration it may perhaps be maintained that all that is noble and beautiful in Hinduism was foreshadowed already by the *Ṛgveda* and all that is filthy and repulsive in it by the Brāhmaṇas.[24]

The same is also said about the Tantras, and this is the view of all the great Mahāmahopādhyāyas. But this is surely an oversimplified and unhistorical approach. The critical scholar cannot fail to notice that sacrifice is the soul of the Vedic religion. In the *Ṛgveda* we come across two types of sacrifices, individual and collective. How the latter was performed in the age of the *Ṛgveda* can be demonstrated with reference to the Aśvamedha. There is a gulf of difference between the Ṛgvedic Aśvamedha and that of the later period. In the *Ṛgveda* it is stated why and how the horse is to be killed. The horse is identified with Āditya, Trita, and Yama, and it is desired that it will go straight to heaven after it is eaten. The horse is anointed with *svaru* and then cut to pieces. The flesh is cooked and a small piece is offered to the fire. Then the assembled persons eat that flesh amidst joyous sounds like *āghu, yājyā,* and *vaṣaṭkārā.*[25]

Clearly this is an instance of the collective eating ritual of the tribes who lived on hunting. Although in Ṛgvedic mythological conceptions nature gods predominated, but in the case of rituals the legacies of the pre-pastoral hunting stage of the Vedic tribes prevailed. Subsequently, even when sacrifice became sophisticated and complicated, the custom of animal-killing was continued with undiminished vigour. Although in later times when sacrifice came into the grip of the privileged class and became very expensive, the sacrificer still had to observe the collective tradition of the past. Many persons were required to be invited and satisfied with food and drink. The collective eating and drinking was a relic, or rather a miming, of the collective life of the past. The cruelty underlying animal killing has been remarked by historians, but they did not care to understand that the persons assembled for the sacrifice were to be fed, even if only as a courtesy, and for that purpose the slaughter of animals was necessary.

Vedic sacrifices were basically magical performances, and this is the view of all critical Vedic scholars.[26] We have previously stated that magic was an illusory technique to control nature, complementary to the deficiencies of real techniques. Its significance can be understood only against the background of primitive, undifferentiated, collective life. It is a fact that the original and sophisticated forms of Vedic sacrifices are not the same, and that in the post-Ṛgvedic age sacrifices became extremely complicated. Their purpose too changed. The history of a stupendous social transformation—from pre-class undifferentiated life to the class-divided society of later times—can be understood if the history of the evolution of sacrifice is critically studied. The earlier *satra-yāgas* were basically collectrive in which the sacrificers were many; the sacrificers themselves performed the functions of priests.[27] The word *yajamāna* stands for sacrificer. Monier-Williams defines the word as follows:

> The person paying the cost of a sacrifice, the institutor of sacrifice (who, to perform it, employs a priest or priests, who are often hereditary functionaries in a family), any patron, host, rich man, head of a family or tribe.[28]

In later times evidently *yajamāna* denoted such persons but originally the word stood for a different purpose. The word is derived from the root *yaj* to which the suffix *sānac* is added. According to Pāṇini the suffix *sānac* can be added to the root when it is indicated that a man is getting the result of his own action.[29] From this viewpoint *yajamāna* is a man who makes a sacrifice for his own interest. In the subsequent age, *yajamāna* is the enjoyer of the fruit of sacrifice, but he does not do it personally. The priests perform the act against remuneration. But from the evidence of the *Ṛgveda*[30] it is quite clear that there was once a time when the *yajamānas* themselves performed the functions of the priests in sacrifices and that many *yajamānas* used to assemble together to perform sacrifices collectively. Reference should be made in this connection to the ancient *satra-yāgas* which remind us of the primitive collective way of life. This did not escape the notice of eminent Indologists like Oldenberg and Keith.[31] Ganganath Jha frankly referred to the *satra-yāgas* as 'communistic sacrifice'.[32]

In later times with the growth of the class-divided society there was an end to the ancient collective way of life. The *yajamānas* were not now collective entities. They were wealthy peoples, and in most of the cases, Kṣatriyas. They were not to perform the sacrifice themselves. It was to be done by professional priests on their behalf. From a legend found in the *Aitareya Brāhmaṇa* it is known that once Sacrifice deserted the gods.[33] The Kṣatriyas and Brāhmaṇas followed him to bring him back. The Kṣatriyas who symbolised ruling power, could not get hold of him through their weapons. But the Brāhmaṇas could, because Sacrifice, being obstructed by them, saw in them his own power. So he agreed to return to the Brāhmaṇas and said that he was ready to oblige the Kṣatriyas provided that they would depend on the Brāhmaṇas. Very significantly this story throws light on the *entente* between the ruling and priestly classes.

The 19th century scholars were directly or indirectly influenced by the reformist movements of their time. Most of the non-Indian writers were monotheistic Christians. Indian writers were also attracted to monotheism which they justified by the Upaniṣadic concept of *brahman*, and as such did not favour the ritualistic elements like sacrifice, etc., of the Vedic texts. They tried to show that Hinduism was basically monotheistic. Their line of argument was as follows: The gods of the *Ṛgveda* represented different aspects of nature. Gradually the Vedic peoples felt that the root of these diverse aspects of nature was one, which could be no other than the *brahman* of the Upaniṣads. This *brahman* subsequently became identified with the chief deities of the sectarian religions, like Viṣṇu of Vaiṣṇavism or Śiva of Śaivism. This line of argument still prevails.

But the difficulty is that the Vedic texts, including the earlier Upaniṣads, are basically ritualistic and full of sacrificial technicalities. How can this be ignored? By labelling it simply as the 'wickedness of the Brāhmaṇas' or as the 'degrading aspects of Hinduism', great scholars from Max Müller to Radhakrishnan wanted to avoid this unpalatable constituent of the Vedic religion. The fact is that there was a philosophical system in ancient India, the Pūrvamīmāṃsā, which held that sacrifice alone was real while the concept of God was false. The anti-theistic arguments of Kumārila, the most well-known exponent of the Pūrvamīmāṃsā philosophy, may be summarised as follows:

> If anyone says, God alone exised before creation, he may be asked where, when, how and why that God exised, whether he was with or without a body. If he had no body he could not have any desire to create, and if he had a body, he himself was not evidently the maker of the body. So another God was

required to create him, another to create this new one, and thus even by importing millions of gods the problem cannot be solved. The next question is in regard to the materials. If the materials of creation exised before the commencement of creation, whence did they come, who was their maker? If these materials were produced from a source other than the God, then God must be regarded as an agent under bondage and as such he cannot be regarded as God. If it is said that God has produced the materials of creation out of his own body, just as a spider makes its cobweb, then God must have a body. This again calls forth the problem already stated. The next question is in regard to purpose. Why should God create this world? What is his gain in creating a world of misery and imperfection? If it is said that he had created the world, being guided by compassion, the question is, compassion for whom? Why then is the world unhappy and cruel? If he had created the world without any purpose, he was worse than a fool, because even a fool works with certain purpose. And if he had created the world with some purpose, it proves that he is not perfect. If the world was made for his sport, he must be called irresponsible.[34]

Kumārila's target was Nyāya-Vaiśeṣika theism. Here we will not deal with the technical and sophisticated portions of his arguments but the Mīmāṃsakas were able to shatter the very plinth on which theism rested. At the same time, they also refuted idealism, the philosophical views of Buddhist Mādhyamika and Yogācāra schools, and also Śaṅkara's Advaita-Vedānta, which treat the material world as an illusion. Kumārila, before refuting idealism, states the idealistic position thus: The perceptibility of pillar, etc., is false, because they are perceptible, and whatever is open to perception is false, e.g. dream. Whatever is seen in dream is false no doubt, but that can be understood only by waking. In other words, the falseness of dream can only be proved by the perception of the waking state. Kumārila refutes the view of the idealists thus: The knowledge of external objects is true because there is no knowledge which can reject it, just as the experience of the waking state, which rejects that of the dream, is perfectly true. The Vedantic conception of *brahman* has also been rejected by the Mīmāṃsakas. Keith says:

> Kumārila, however, does not contend himself with refuting the Nyāya-Vaiśeṣika doctrine. He attacks equally the Vedānta on the simple ground that if the absolute is, as is asserted to be, absolutely pure, the world itself should be absolutely pure. In Kumārila's own way of putting the point, an impure world cannot be viewed as the outcome of the pure *brāhman*. Moreover, there could be no creation, for nescience (*avidyā* or *māyā*) is impossible in such an absolute. If, however, we assume that some other cause

starts nescience to activity, then the unity of the absolute disappears. Again, if nescience is natural it is impossible to remove it, for that would be accomplished only by knowledge of the self which, on the theory of the natural character of the nescience, is out of question.[35]

Scholars who considered monotheism and devotional religion as belonging to a superior quality of human thought did not care to recollect that the basis of their arguments had been negated long ago by the Mīmāṃsakas. But why, despite their sharp arguments and scientific approach, did the Mīmāṃsakas become staunch supporters of the Vedic sacrifical cults? Their sole emphasis on this subject indicates that there must be something wrong in our understanding of such things.

What do we really unsderstand by *yajña* or sacrifice? Modern scholars hold that at the root of sacrifice is a kind of reciprocal arrangement. I offer something to please God, and in return God is expected to give me what I want. In the Bible it is stated that Abraham was prepared to sacrifice his own son in order to please God. This wrong conception also prevailed among many of the ancient Indians. The Mīmāṃsakas hold that their opponents utterly misunderstood the significance of *yajña*, in believing that *yajña* is a means to please the gods, because in reality there are no gods. According to the Mīmāṃsakas *yajña* is for the sake of *yajña* only, and not for that of the gods. Ritual is the first and last word, the performance of which yields *apūrva*, 'that which was not before'. It means that what did not exist before can be produced by ritual as an effect of performing it. Śabara says that, according to the Vedas, the cause of producing effect is sacrifice and not the gods, because the effect is *puruṣārtha* which is achieved through human efforts and not through the agency of God. If it be said that sacrifice is to be offered to the gods, then the gods must necessarily possess a shape and eat the food offered to them at the sacrifice, but neither is possible. If it is hoped that being satisfied God will grant the desired object, this cannot be an argument because god's ownership of worldly objects is not proved. So the question of appeasing the gods cannot arise.[36] Therefore *yajña* is not prayer or propitiation. It simply consists of some definite rituals for the fulfilment of worldly desires, and these rituals are effective by themselves.

It therfore appears that the main principles of the Mīmāṃsaka defnition of srcrifice are quite in accordance with those of primitive magic rituals. We have repeatedly said that the real significance of magic can be understood only in the context of primitive, undifferentiated, collective life. A question then naturally arises: When in this country the method of philosophical argument reached an advanced stage of development and when the Mīmāṃsakas themselves displayed much skill in sophisticated arguments by which they mercilessly refuted the concept of God and allied idealistic philosophcial viewpoints, why did they themselves want to resort to the magical rites of the primitive age?

In reply to this question it may be pointed out that the growth of any particular religious or philosophical doctrine is always conditioned by the demands of contemporary social life. This can be clearly demonstrated with reference to Buddhism and Jainism. Both the Buddha and Mahāvira wanted to revive the ethical values of the past as a way out of the crisis of their own age: Said the Buddha in a *suttānta*:

> I behold the rich in this world, of the goods which they have acquired, in their folly they give nothing to others; they eagerly heap riches together and further and still further they go in their pursuit of enjoyment. The king, although he may have conquered the kingdoms of the earth, although he may be ruler of all land this side the sea, up to the ocean's shore would still be insatiate, covet that which is beyond the sea.... The princes, who rule kingdoms, rich in treasures and wealth, turn their greed against one another, pandering insatiably their desires. If these acts are thus restlessly, swimming in the stream of impermanence, carried along by greed and carnal desire, who then can walk on earth in peace?[37]

The Mīmāṃsakas also were not silent spectators. They saw the stupendous social transformation, the new power equations with all their ugliness, the rise of autocracy as an organisation of plundering and oppressing the people, and the ruthless extermination of the ancient moral values. In their own way they tried to offer a solution to overcome the great social and moral crisis which occurred as an inevitable process of history. They wanted to bring back the ancient golden days of equality and urged a return to that primitive unsophisticated way of life in which the Vedas would regain their original significance. It was only in such an undifferentiated society, in the primitive collective way of life, that the *yajñas* could be really efficacious, being restored in their original form and content. The metamorphosis of the concept of sacrifice was a symbol. It was found that the gods who had previously been created beacuse of the needs of sacrifice had now gained ascendency over it, in exactly the same way as the ruling or privileged class came to power, and a considerable number of people began to view sacrifice in terms of pleasing the gods in the same way as they had become accustomed to flatter their overlords.

In the preceding chapter we have dealt with the nature of Vedic sacrifices and the sexual and other Tantric rites involved therein. In Brāhmaṇa literature sexual union is not only regarded as the means of achieving spiritual happiness, but it is identified with sacrifice itself. The tasks of maintaining Agnihotra, performing consecration, constructing altars, and even composing verses, are conceived in terms of sexual symbolism.[38] In the Upaniṣads and Sūtras, and also in the commentarial works, observance and performance of sexual union as a religious rite, or a part of religious rite, are prescribed.[39] The Vedic texts prescribe Somayajñas and Haviryajñas which included the Śautrāmaṇi using libations and drinks of intoxicating liquor. According to the *Śatapatha Brāhmaṇa* wine is always pure and hence purifies the sacrificer. It is *paramāhuti*, the nectar of immortality. The same work prescribes the measure and number of drinks to be offered or taken at a sacrifice.[40] The *cakra*-sitting of the Tantras has unmistakable similarity with the Vājapeya and Sautrāmaṇi. Even the Tantric castelessness is foreshadowed in a passage of the *Aitareya Brāhmaṇa* which states that when performing *yajña* in company, the members of the company become Brāhmaṇas and there is no distinction of castes.[41] The Tantric practices of *ācamana*, which is a form of ablution in which certain parts of the body are touched with water, are found in the Vedic texts.[42] The ritual of purifying the body by uttering some *mantras* as *bījas* while contemplating the deities on certain parts of their bodies and touching such parts as found in the Vedic texts,[43] corresponds to Tantric *nyāsa*. The use of mystic sounds like *khaṭ*, *phaṭ*, *huṃ*, etc., are also found in Vedic texts.[44]

It is apparent from the evidence of the Vedic sources that the principles and even the contents of the rituals of the later Tantric texts were not basically different from the Vedic sacrificial cults and that they were already foreshadowed in the Vedas. Therefore, it is surprising that the Vedic *yajñas*, which contain similar 'repulsive' rites as those found in the Tantras, have been held in high esteem by the followers of the Vedic tradition while the Tantric rituals have been treated otherwise and regarded as being outside the pale of the Vedas. Later Tantric writers who wanted to base their doctrines on the Vedas and sought a Vedic sanction of Tantrism depended mainly on the Vedic sacrificial tradition, as did their modern counterparts like John Woodroffe or Gopinath Kaviraj. But in spite of all their attempts to prove the Vedic origin of the Tantric rites, they failed to explain why, notwithstanding similarities in form and content, a different treatment was accorded to Tantra. Why Tantra with its cults, ideas, practices and institutions has been regarded as *Vedabāhya*, i.e. outside the Vedic tradition, and belonging to an inferior level? Why were the Vedic forms of *Pañcopāsana* (pertaining to the five major Hindu cults of Viṣṇu, Śiva, Śakti, Gaṇapati and Sūrya) praised and its Tantric forms condemned?

This point is vital and calls for a historical explanation which invariably leads us to the question of the class-orientation of Tantras. It has already been shown why and how Tantra, from a given point of time, began to function as an independent and parallel tradition with special reference to its followers, the non-privileged masses, and their way of life and position in society. Unless this parallel tradition as manifested in the material culture and social institutions of the simpler peoples and also in numerous popular cults and beliefs—some which are recorded in non-Vedic and non-Brahmanical sources and even in a few Brahmanical ones—is worked out, it will not be possible to have a comprehensive view of the functional role of Tantra in Indian social and religious life.

Tantra in Post-Vedic Thought

In the *Śvetāśvatara Upaniṣad*, composed about the 5th or 4th century B.C. we come across eight views regarding the origin of life and the universe. These are Īśvara, Kāla, Svabhāva, Niyati, Yadṛcchā, Bhūta, Yoni and Puruṣa.[45] This list with some modification also occurs in the *Suśurutasaṃhitā*,[46] composed about the 4th century A.D., i.e. eight hundred years after the *Śvetāśvatara*, in which Puruṣa is omitted and Bhūta and Yoni have been combined into Prakṛti. In the Buddhist *Aṅguttara Nikāya* (*c.* 3rd century B.C.) and in *Mahāniddesa* and *Cullaniddesa* (*c.* 1st century B.C.) we come across religious sects like Ājīvika, Nirgrantha, Jaṭilaka, Parivrājaka, Aviruddhaka, Muṇḍa-śravaka, Māgaṇḍika, Traidaṇḍika, and Devadharmika along with the cults of elephant, horse, cow, dog, crow, Vāsudeva, Balabhadra, Pūrṇabhadra, Maṇibhadra, Yakṣa, Nāga, Asura, Gandharva, Mahārāja, Agni, Candra, Indra, Brahmā, Deva, and Dik. In the Buddhist *Dīgha* and *Majjhima* Nikāyas and in Jain *Suyagaḍa*, *Uttarādhyayana*, etc., we come across the views of the contemporaries of the Buddha and Mahāvīra. The Buddhist texts mention sixty-two philosophical views, grouped under two categories—Purvānta Kalpika and Aparānta Kalpika. The Jain texts mention more than three hundred doctrines classed under four categories—Kriyāvāda, Akriyāvāda, Ajñānavāda and Vinayavāda. The contemporaries of the Buddha and Mahāvīra, whose views have been quoted in the texts mentioned above, were Puraṇa Kassapa, Pakudha Kaccāyana, Ajita Keśakambali, Sañjaya Belaṭṭhiputta and Gośāla Maṅkhaliputta.

Elements of Tantrism are to be found in all these systems. The *Śvetāśvatara* list begins with Īśvaravāda or absolute theism to which later followers of Tantra, at least a considerable section of them, are found to contribute. The *Śvetāśvatara* postulates a monotheistic concept of Rudra or Śiva who is equated with *brahman*. Each of the five major Hindu cults of the later period readily accepted the spirit of *Śvetāśvatara* and each organised itself into a monotheistic system with its chief God as Viṣṇu or Śiva, or Śakti, or Gaṇapati, or Sūrya, as the Supreme Being. The doctrine of *bhakti* or devotion and self-surrender popularised by the *Bhagavadgītā* quickened the process. But absolute theism was not able to have a solid basis because there is no proof of God's existence and it is impossible to establish that the world is God's creation. The arguments of the Mīmāṃsakas and of Kumārila in this respect have already been mentioned. The Sāṅkhya does nat believe in theism. The Buddhists, Jains and Cārvākas also do not subscribe to such a conception. It is only the Nyāya-Vaiśeṣikas that tried to establish theism on the basis of reason. Being confronted with the question how the unintelligent atoms would combine themselves, the Nyāya-Vaiśeṣikas held that just as a potter makes a pot with the help of the material cause, clay, so also God as an intelligent agent combines the atoms to fashion worldly objects. But this God of the Nyāya-Vaiśeṣikas is no better than a potter because he is an agent under bondage. He requires a frame or body for himself, the materials of creation, and the will and capacity to create. All these go against the conception of God's perfection and hence, as an agent under bondage, he really ceases to be a God. This was the argument put forward by the Mīmāṃsakas, Buddhists, Jains and even a group of Vedāntists. Nyāya-Vaiśeṣika theism was soundly and absolutely refuted by the Jains logician Guṇaratna.[47]

The doctrine of time or Kāla is very ancient in Indian philosophy. In the *Atharvaveda* Kāla has been described as the cosmogonic agent and as the lord of everything.[48] The *Śvetāśvatara* also reviews the concept of time as the cause of the universe.[49] According to Nīlakaṇṭha, Kāla is the conductor of the knowledge of things.[50] In the Buddhist doctrine of Kṣaṇikavāda time has some importance. It is also one of the nine *tattvas* of Jain philosophy which has been viewed as *anastikāya*, i.e. without any form. Time forms a part of the nine Nyāya-Vaiśeṣika categories of substances. In spite of all these, the doctrine of time was not able to exert much influence on Indian thought in general. In the Tantras, however, the concept of time is given prominence; it contributed to the idea of such goddesses as Kālī, Mahākālī, Kālarātri, etc.

The doctrine of Niyati, or destiny, was not very influential either. It was Gośāla Maṅkhaliputta who raised the doctrine of destiny to a philosophical level and was able to found a religious sect which came to be known as the Ājīvakas. The doctrine of destiny has been described in detail in a Prakrit work called *Gommaṭasāra*. In the Śaiva Āgamas, Kāla and Niyati have been described as the evolutes of Aśuddha Māyā. Though the Tantras in no way subscribe to the doctrine of destiny some Ājīvika rituals have crept into its fold as we shall see later.

According to the Svabhāvavāda, with which Tantric ideas have much in common, everything in the world is the product of natural laws. The universe is law-governed and guided by cause-effect relations in which there is no room for the supernatural. The sharpness of thorns, the attitude of birds and beasts, the sweetness of sugarcane—everything is due to Svabhāva—the inherent nature of things. According to this nature of things the basic elements combine to form the worldly objects. But whereas the doctrine of Svabhāva has a scientific basis in the form of cause-effect relation, the doctrine of Yadṛcchā, also found in the *Svetāśvatara*, holds that everything is accidental. According to Guṇaratna the followers of the doctrine of Svabhāva believe that the transformation of a thing takes place owing to its inherent nature.[51] A particular cause can produce a particular effect. Cotton cannot produce a pot, and clay cannot produce cloth. This natural law is absent in the doctrine of Yadṛcchā which maintains that the world is a chaos and ascribes whatever order is seen in it to mere chance. Unfortunately, in the religious and philosophical literature of India Svabhāvavāda has been presented in a distorted way mainly because the texts of this school are lost. In the *Laṅkāvatāra-sūtra*[52], the *Buddhacarita*[53] and the *Mahābhārata*[54] we have a few glimpses of Svabhāvavāda which prove that the followers of this system had an ethic of their own and that they were basically materialist so far as their world-view was concerned (*svabhāvaṃ bhūtacintakāḥ*). In Indian tradition Svabhāvavāda is often equated with the Bārhaspatya, Cārvāka and Lokāyata doctrines.

In the *Śvetāśvatara* list the doctrines of Bhūta, Yoni and Puruṣa are mentioned. In the *Suśruta,* it will be remembered, Puruṣa is omitted and the term Prakṛti is used as a substitute for Bhūta and Yoni. These four concepts denote the earlier stages of the evolution of the Sāṅkhya and Tantric ideas. Reference has already been made to the concept of Yoni and the cults that clustered around it. We have tried to assert that in olden days the process of the creation of the world was viewed in terms of human procreation and that is why supreme emphasis was laid upon the concept of Prakṛti or the Female Principle of creation. Subsequently, however, with the recognition of the role of the male in the process of procreation, we come across the development of the concept of Puruṣa or Male Principle, but this male element was still inactive and passive.

The Sāṅkhya is essentially a materialistic philosophy which holds that everything is produced through the evolution of Prakṛti. This doctrine is not palatable to those who do not like to see the existence of materialism in this 'spiritual' country. The Puruṣa element of the Sāṅkhya has, however, been used by them to argue that although Prakṛti is primordial matter, Puruṣa can be no other than the principle of consciousness. This attempt is by no means modern. Commentators like Vijñānabhikṣu tried to equate the Sāṅkhya concept of Puruṣa with the Vedantic concept of *brahman.* In doing so they denied the plurality of Puruṣa and thus distorted Sāṅkhya to the extreme. In the Sāṅkhya sole emphasis is laid upon the cause-effect relation which reminds us of Svabhāvavāda.[55] According to Nīlakaṇṭha, *svabhāva iti pariṇāmavādināṃ sāṅkhyānāṃ.*[56] Thus, he frankly equates Sāṅkhya with Svabhāvavāda. Gauḍapāda says, *Sāṅkhyānāṃ svabhāvo nāma kaścit kāraṇamasti.*[57] Śaṅkara also categorically states that the Sāṅkhya was the other name of Svabhāvavāda. This explains why the Sāṅkhya is basically atheistic.

The doctrine of Bhūta, as mentioned in the *Śvetāśvatara,* suggests that everything in the world is created by the combination of four or five material elements. These elements are earth, water, fire, air and space. These are called the five *Mahābhūtas* in the Sāṅkhya and pertain to all forms of Indian thought including Tantra. The *Ṛgveda* acknowledges a single element as the primal material cause of creation—water, which reminds us of the view of the Greek philosopher Thales. The Svabhāvavādins believe in the existence of four material elements. They are not inclined to count space as the fifth element. In the Sāṅkhya all the five elements are described as the evolutes of Prakṛti. The doctrine of elements is also acknowledged in the Nyāya-Vaiśeṣika and Mīmāṃsā traditions. The first four have colour and touchability while the fifth, i.e. space, is the container of sound. In the *Vaiśeṣika-sūtras*[58] it is stated that every element as cause can produce effect, and this production of effect is conditional. For example, water can produce vapour and also ice. Earth is by nature hard, but under some given conditions it can be reduced into atoms. Earth and water have motion and weight but the latter quality is absent in fire and air. Matter of wider dimension can hold that of smaller, and finally, that which is all pervading, i.e. space, can hold everything. These ideas which are reflections of scientific reasoning were able to make their way into Svabhāvavāda, Sāṅkhya, Tantra and other forms of Indian thought. Under different historical conditions although this materialistic outlook was suppressed, it could not be totally excluded from the frame work of idealistic philosophical systems.

In the Buddhist texts the two important philosophical contents—Purvānta Kalpika and Aparānta Kalpika—are mainly concerned with the validity of the concept of soul and its functioning after death. Some of these sixty-two schools remind us of the Western sceptic and agnostic approaches. The Jain texts likewise mention 363 schools of thought grouped under four general categories of Kriyāvāda, Akriyāvāda, Ajñānavāda, and Vinayavāda. From the combined evidence of the Buddhist and Jain sources we come across the names and views of five great teachers who were contemporaries of Buddha and Mahāvīra. These teachers basically belonged to the Akriyāvāda school according to which all human actions and endeavours are fruitless. They believed in the doctrine of elements and held that after death the elements of which the human body is formed revert to their respective sources. They were basically pessimists and the cause of their pessimism can easily be traced to the changing socio-political condition of the age in which they lived.[59]

Of these teachers, Gośāla Maṅkhaliputta (called Makkhali Gośāla in the Buddhist texts) is the most important, being the founder of a religious sect which came to be known as the Ājīvikas. The Jain texts mention two former teachers of this sect whose names are Nanda Vacca and Kisa Samkicca. Two other contemporaries of the Buddha and Mahāvira—Puraṇa Kassapa and Pakudha Kaccāyana—might have been the followers of the Ājīvika creed.[60] The most important part of Gośāla's doctrine is his insistence solely on causelessness, non-action, and fate. Side by side he also laid emphasis on the tribal way of life which was facing extermination during his time. On his death bed he urged a revival of the golden days of the past; he was haunted by the thought of the dangerous consequences of Ajātaśatru's campaign against the Vajjians. The Ājīvikas maintained tribal traditions and rituals, as prescribed by Gośāla, for a long time. Subsequently, however, they could not maintain their independent entity and eventually came under the fold of Pāśupata Śaivism. Many of the Pāśupata rites that became an integral part of the later Tantric way of life are of Ājīvika origin, as we shall see while dealing with the Pāśupata sect.

The followers of Tantra are often branded as Nāstika by the upholders of the Vedic tradition. The term Nāstika does not denote an atheist. It is applied only to those who do not believe in the Vedas. The Sāṅkhyas and Mīmāṃsakas do not believe in God, but they believe in the Vedas and hence they are not Nāstikas. The Buddhists, Jains and Cārvākas do not believe in the Vedas; hence they are Nāstikas. Manu said, *nāstiko vedanindakaḥ.*[61] Pāṇini understood the words Āstika and Nāstika in terms of a simple affirmation and negation of the existence of things.[62] Subsequently it was said that the concepts of affirmation and negation should be used only in connection with the belief in the existence of the other world. In a later period the term Nāstika was used for mutual slandering. For example, in order to abuse the Śaivas it was said, *liṅgārcana parāḥ śaivā nāstikāḥ parikīrtitāḥ*, which means that 'the phallus-worshipping Śaivas are Nāstikas'. The same holds good also in the case of the term Pāṣaṇḍa which was frequently attributed to the Buddhists, Jains, Cārvākas, and Tantrics.

In Indian tradition the terms Lokāyata and Cārvāka are often used in the same sense although they have functional differences. The Cārvāka philosophy rests on five basic principles: (1) Bhūtavāda, according to which the four material elements—earth, water, fire, and air—are the only real entities by the combination of which everything is formed; (2) Dehātmyavāda, which means that the concept of soul apart from the body is baseless; (3) Pratyakṣaprāmāṇyāvāda, which means that of all the sources of valid knowledge, perception alone is acceptable; (4) Svabhāvavāda, which recognises that things are as their nature makes them; and (5) Paraloka-vilopavāda, which holds that there can be so such thing as the other world. All these principles influenced Tantrism profoundly. The idea that there is no soul apart from the body contributed to a great extent to the Tantric *dehatattva* according to which the body is the microcosm of the universe. Likewise the Cārvāka belief in the non-existence of the next life and the other world has something to do with the Tantric idea of the attainment of immortality and also that of *jīvanmukti*, i.e. liberation within the span of life. Apart from the Bhūtavāda, or doctrine of the material elements, by which Tantra is basically characterised, the influence of the doctrine of Svabhāva is also conspicuous, and that is why the earlier writers did not hesitate to label Tantra as a brand of Svabhāvavāda.

Doctrines similar to those of Cārvākas are undoubtedly ancient. A few sects of the Akriyāvādins mentioned in Jain literature, like Sāyavāda, Samucchedavāda, Na-santi-paralokavāda, etc., and also the Adhityasamutpannika, Ucchedavāda, Dṛṣṭadharmanirvāṇavāda, etc., found in the Buddhist works, have much in common with the Cārvākas. The doctrine of Ajita Keśakambali as found in the Sāmaññaphalasutta of the *Dīgha Nikāya* contains some important Cārvāka views. The Cārvāka doctrine, often under the general name of Lokāyata, is directly mentioned in Haribhadra Suri's *Ṣaḍ darśanasamuccaya*, Śāntarakṣita's *Tattvasaṃgraha*, Kṛṣṇamiśra's *Prabodhacandrodaya*, Sadānanda Yati's *Advaitabrahmasiddhi*, and Mādhava's *Sarvadarśanasaṃgraha*. Unfortunately no Cārvāka text has yet been found. In the works mentioned above the Cārvāka doctrine has been used as *pūrvapakṣa* or the view of the opponent. The general Indian custom is that if a logician wants to establish his own view, he has to refute the views of others. The fundamentals of the view to be refuted should, therfore,be recorded as *pūrvapakṣa* or the view of the opponent. Needles to say, in such cases the view of the opponent is presented in a very distored form. Cārvāka philosophy has been the worst victim of this process.

Although ancient writers sometimes understood Cārvāka and Lokāyata in the same sense, the scope of the latter is much wider. More accurately, the Cārvāka doctrine reveals only one aspect of a way of life called Lokāyata. There is some evidence available pertaining to Lokāyata, apart from the Cārvāka doctrine, in Indian literature of different ages. According to this evidence, Lokāyata does not denote any pure philosophical doctrine; it only indicates a special way of life which was in vogue since remote antiquity. As we have sated in the introduction, this way of life survived among the Āuls, Bāuls, Sahajiyās, Tantrics, etc., although not in its original form. Since the term Lokāyata may be subject to some misunderstanding it is better to use the general term *tantra* to denote this particular way of life. By this *tantra* we do not mean the existing Hindu and Buddhist Tantric texts, for we have already seen that Tantra is very ancient and the vast mass of Tantric texts were composed in later times. Although many features of the early Tantric way of life are preserved in these texts, it is emphasised again that these texts contain numerous superimposed elements. There fore, without denying the importance of the surviving Tantric texts, for a bettter understanding of the Tantric tradition in its entirety, we should look beyond their present contents, explore their implications, take into account all forms of Indian thought in general—even if they are found in sources which do not appear to have any formal bearing on Tantra—their structural developments and also their functional influence on society and life.

Tantric Influence on Early Buddhism and Jainism

The origin of Buddhism and Jainism cannot be ascribed to a single cause, though the material milieu of their growth can be understood. The real cause of their rise evidently lay in the conflicts—political, economic, social, religious,and intellectual—which characterised the pre-Buddhist and pre-Jain history of India. What the exact nature of such conflicts was, the ultimate culmination of which was manifested in Jainism and Buddhism in the form of a great qualitative change, is not definitely known. But from circumstantial evidence it appears that the conflict was between tribal disintegration and the rise of the state power.

The Buddha and Mahāvīra were born in an age when the *janapadas* (tribal settlements) were developing into *mahā-janapadas* (bigger confederacies) leading to the rise of organised states. Already four *mahā-janapadas* became distinguishable as powerful states and the forces behind the subsequent Magadhan imperialism could be seen. Mahāvīra was from Vaiśālī,[63] a tribal settlement belonging to a confederation of tribes collectively known by the name of the Vajjis. His maternal uncle Ceṭaka was the leader of the confederacy. The rise of Magadhan state power was really a natural threat to the survival of the Vajjian confederacy of tribes. The growth of Magadhan state power required annihilation of many a tribal settlement. Bimbisāra, the first powerful Magadhan king who was a senior contemporary of the Buddha and Mahāvīra did not hesitate to annex the settlements of the Aṅgas and the Kāsis, while his son and successor, Ajātaśatru launched a vigorous invasion against the Vajjian confederacy. Ceṭaka, the maternal uncle of Mahāvīra, committed suicide because of this invasion. The tremendous bloodshed and massacre caused by the campaign of Ajātaśatru had a great impact on the Buddha and Mahāvīra. The Sākya tribe, to which the Buddha himself belonged was annihilated by the Kosalan prince Viḍuḍabha and the Buddha was witness to it.

The contemporaries of the Buddha and Mahāvīra were also greatly perturbed by the drastic social transformation of the age, the collapse of the tribal institutions, the rise of new values ushered in by the state power and the new forces of injustice and untruth and they tried to understand the problems in their own way. Overwhelmed by bloodshed and massacre, Puraṇa and Pakudha thought that there was no difference between merit and demerit, between violence and non-violence. Ajita could not distinguish between the fool and the wise, for both were doomed to death, and Sañjaya preferred to stay silent since the deeply ingrained faith behind the ideas was up-rooted. Gośāla, the leader of the Ājīvikas, became a fatalist who was forced to believe that human activity could do nothing to change the course of events. Everything appeared to him to have been determined by the forces of fate or destiny. He became mad and died of despair.

The impact of the changing turbulent modes is reflected in the doctrines of Buddhism and Jainism. At this critical stage of Indian history when the free tribes were being ruthlessly exterminated by the expanding state powers, both the Buddha and Mahāvīra tried to model their *saṃghas* on the basic principles of tribal society in order to provide the people at least with an *illusion* of a reality which was fast disappearing. The *saṃgha* or 'community of brethren' was evidently modelled on the pattern of tribal democracies and was meant to be the ideal substitute for a vanished way of life. How thoroughly the tribal model was imitated can be understood if we take into account the Buddhist and Jain rules relating to the procedure of entry into the order, the internal administration of the order, and the rules for personal or private property within the order. Both of these enlightened teachers took great care to see that the members of the *saṃgha* would live a perfectly detached life, i.e. detached from the great historic transformation going on in the society at large, *the course of which was obviously beyond their power to change.*

But, at the same time the Buddha and Mahāvīra had to face the *dual requirements* of their age, and this alone explains why a considerable number of contemporary aristocrats formed their front rank associates. That is why Buddhism and Jainism gave moral support to the interests of the trading class and accepted the new social requirements. On the one hand, in the new class society they offered the oppressed people a suitable illusion of ancient tribal communism which was being trampled and undermined in reality, and on the other, they boosted some of the progressive features of the already established class society in public life and also rescued some of the beneficial aspects of tribal life.

Evidently the doctrines propounded by the Buddha and Mahāvīra were concerned with the social and moral problems of their times. How is it that in such atheistic, intellectual, and strictly ethical systems Tantric ideas and practices were able to make their way? From a critical study of the growth of Indian religio-philosophical ideas it may be held that outside the pale of Vedic culture and religion, specially in eastern India. pre-Vedic and non-Vedic ideas still survived and flourished, that there were persons (among whom the earlier Tīrthaṃkaras and the predecessors of the Buddha might have belonged) and institutions fighting for the cause of their survival and development and that some of the pre-Vedic ideas and practices had to be revived by the Buddha and Mahāvīra for practical reason's.

In 1934, R.P. Chanda drew the attention of scholars to the pre-Vedic elements revived by the Buddha and Mahāvīra in their own religious systems. In many of his works he pointed out that the practices of meditation and disciplining of the body and mind, by which Buddhism and Jainism are characterised and which later became the basis of Yoga, are basically non-Vedic in character. As one of sources of this understanding he has referred to the famous statuette from Mohenjodaro depicting the Yogic posture with half-shut eyes and also to the seals indicating the same practice. Long before Chanda, H. Jacobi came to the conclusion that the interest of Jainism to the student of religion consists in the fact that it goes back to a very early period, and to primitive currents of religious and metaphysical speculation which gave rise to the oldest Indian philosophies—Sāṅkhya and Yoga—and to Buddhism.[64]

More interesting however, is the evidence furnished by the elaborate mythology of the Buddhists and the Jains. While most of the Vedic gods figure in the Buddhist and Jain pantheon, it is interesting to note that the 'lower' and folk deities of the Vedic cults, such as the Yakṣas, Rakṣas, Nāga, etc., have been accorded a special position in Buddhism and Jainism.[65] Buddhism in India was always in a state of flux. Like its doctrine of momentariness it was constantly in the process of transformation. Originally it was a way of life meant exclusively for the monks. Subsequently its role was pronounced as a 'thought-complex', the crucible for generating many a system, than an institutionalised religion. That is why, as we shall see later, it became a natural receptacle for containing various Tantric ideas and practices, especially after the advent of its Mahāyanic forms.

The cult of the primitive Mother Goddess was also revived in the Buddhist and Jain pantheon.[66] The popularity of this goddess among various agricultural peoples and that of the rituals by which it was characterised—the primitive Tantric undercurrents—was responsible for making their way into the disintegrating phase of the Vedic religion and also what is known as Puraṇic Hinduism. The Buddhist Tārādevīs and other female divinities, the Jain Mātṛkās, Vidyādevīs, Śāsanadevatās, Yoginīs, etc., all came from a primitive Tantric complex marked by the popular cult of the Female Principle. Although basically early Buddhism or Jainism had nothing to do with the cult of the Female Principle, the reason for its acceptance by the Buddhists and Jains evidently lay in its functional role in the religious history of India.

So far as other Tantric rituals are concerned, B.T. Bhattacharyya has correctly observed that these were continued because some converts to the creed who were previously accustomed to such practices could not give up their traditional habits despite their conversion to Buddhism. It was among these people that Tantric rites were secretly maintained. Subsequently they made serect conclaves (*guhyasamāja*) within the *saṃgha*, composed their scriptures and got these sanctioned by the name of the Buddha.[67] It should also be observed that although the Buddha was definitely against such practices, at least from his theoretical point of view, he himself had often to resort to them for practical reasons. Whatever the original purpose of the primitive collective magical performances might have been, subsequently these became the esoteric art of a class of people who made exorcism and sorcery a means of their livelihood, taking advantage of the superstitious beliefs of the innocents. Even for honest purposes very often such practices were used to attract ordinary people. The performance of miracles by simple tricks is still employed by religious teachers to attract devotees and patrons.

The Jain texts refer to Tantric practices current among certain contemporary sects.[68] Tantrism in the form of the Mother Goddess cult, magical rites like the *ṣaṭ-karmas*, curative spells, incantations, efficacy of *mantra*, etc., are also met with in Jainism.[69] Mahāvīra is also said to have performed numerous miracles. This Tantric element in Jainism came about the same way it did in the case of Buddhism. But owing to its very rigid nature the Jain religion was able to escape fundamental changes in the course of its development, and that is why the influence of Tantric ideas and practices is not deep-roooted in it. The success of Jainism in India is solely due to its lay converts whose way of life was completely restricted by detailed rules which could only be disobeyed at the cost of excommunication. This rigidity prevented the 'influx' of Tantric ideas. Except the cult of the Mother Goddess and the concept of the efficacy of the *mantras* Tantrism could produce no other permanent effect on the Jain religion.

Tantric ideas and practices were, however, able to exert a greater influence on early Buddhism. The Buddhist texts record that the Buddha himself performed many miracles; despite his aversion to magical practices he could not aviod them. The *Mahāpadāna Sutta* which contains legends of the Buddha is full of miracles.[70] The *Pāṭika Sutta* describes the Buddha not only as taking part in the competition of making miracles but also as boasting of his miraculous powers.[71] The stories of his transforming a dragon into an insect, of sending fire to the cold-stricken mendicants, of his walking on rivers, of his miracles at Sāṅkāsya and Śrāvasti, his conversion of Nanda by showing him heavenly nymphs, etc., may be recalled in this connection. His celebrated disciple Moggalāna was also reputed to be famous for magical powers.

To us, however, it appears that these miracles had nothing to do with Tantrism and that such stories were invented in later times to glorify the Master, although it is possible that the Buddha did something which appeared to the ordinary person as miraculous. There are numerous passages in early Buddhist literature which show that the Buddha personally did not like such things. In the *Brahmājala-Sutta*[72] we come across an interesting list of arts which the Buddha condemned as *tiracchānavijjā, micchā* and *ājiva.* He asked not only his disciples but all good men not to encourage such things. The aspirant for *arhat*-hood attains some supernatural power called *ṛddhi* (*iddhi* in Pali), and the Buddha is said to have repeatedly warned his disciples not to utilise this power. The false declaration of this power was a serious offence. In the *Vinaya Piṭaka*[73] it is stated that a monk doing this is guilty of a *dukkaṭa* offence.

But there are other passages in the early Buddhist texts which are suggestive of Tantric influence. In the *Lalitavistara* it is stated that the Buddha himself practised *āsphānaka-yoga.*[74] The first teacher of the Buddha was Ālāda Kālāma who was an exponent of the Sāṅkhya philosophy. In the *Majjhima Nikāya* it is stated that the Buddha himself in his early days had stayed in a cemetery with bones as his pillow.[75] In the *Dīgha Nikāya* the Buddha mentions *pañca-kāma-guṇa-diṭṭha-dhamma nibbāṇa-vāda*—a philosophical view according to which the soul attains *nirvāṇa* through the full indulgence of the pleasures of the five senses. This is, however, the view of a philosophical school which was contemporary with the Buddha. Likewise the *Majjhima Nikāya* mentions the view of a class of Śramaṇas and Brāhmaṇas according to which sexual intercourse with youthful female ascetics is a way to achieve salvation.[76] Such views, although they reveal the existence of Tantric ideas and practices, are not directly concerned with the theories and practices of early Buddhism. A passage of the *Kathāvatthu* clearly refers to *maithuna* or sexual union as a means of salvation, but this also pertains to a different sect.[77]

It is quite possible that persons belonging to these sects were later converted to Buddhism and that this class of people was responsible for smuggling Tantric ideas and practices into the Buddhist order. The use of skulls as alms bowls by the Buddhist monks, referred to in the *Cullavagga*[78] was evidently due to Tantric influence. This also holds good in the case of the Buddhist belief in the efficacy of *mantra.* In the *Cullavagga* a *mantra* or charm is mentioned as being prescribed by the Buddha to be used as a means of warding off the fear of snake bite.[79] The *Ratnana Sutta* of the *Khuddaka Nikāya* prescribes the recital of *triratna* to ward off all calamities and to bring prosperity. We learn from the *Tivijja Sutta* that there were some Śramaṇas and Brāhmaṇas who lived by teaching spells for preserving the body, for procuring prosperity, for causing adversity, for removing sterility, and so on, which reminds us of the Tantric *ṣaṭ-karmas*.[80] This Tantric infiltration eventually succeeded in transforming Buddhism beyond recognition, as we shall see in a subsequent chapter.

Tantra and Early Vaiṣṇavism

While dealing with the Pāñcarātra Saṃhitās or Āgamas we have seen how Tantra was able to exert a great influence upon Vaiṣṇavism. Pāñcarātra Āgamas such as the *Lakṣmītantra* are regarded as authoritative even by the followers of the Śākta school. We have already had occasion to note that all the five major systems by which present Hinduism is constituted have two forms, Vedic and Tantric. Vaiṣṇavism is no exception.

Vaiṣṇavism is a composite religion with a long history of evolution. Originally it was known as the Bhāgavata religion of which it is really an offshoot. The most important constituent of this composite cult is the Vedic sun-god Viṣṇu. Of the other constituents, the tribal cult of the Vṛṣṇi heroes, especially those of Vāsudeva and Saṅkarṣaṇa, the cult of Nārāyaṇa and that of a Female Principle associated with all these deities under different names and chatacteristics, should also be noted.

Vaiṣṇavism is monotheistic and its principal deities are equated with the supreme being Viṣṇu. This monotheism was the fulfilment of a process that began as early as the days of tribal disintegration. The idea of a supreme God ruling over the universe was based solely upon the new-fangled principle of absolute monarchy. In pre-class societies, as we have seen, men had control over the gods. They believed that they could bring the forces of nature under their control by collective rituals and other performances. In subsequent stages of social evolution, these ancient beliefs ceased to function; the gods represented the ruling class, to be pleased only by propitiation and devotion and monotheism was the logical culmination of this process. The quest for the divine prototype of a human monarch was satisfied by the resuscitation of the Vedic God Viṣṇu and the pre-Vedic God who later came to be known as Śiva. But it was not until the 3rd century B.C. that Vaiṣṇavism as a distinct religious system became popular. Śaivism achieved prominence at a somewhat later date.

It is in one of the later section of the *Mahābhārata* that we come across the term Vaiṣṇava in the sense of a religious creed.[81] But

Pāṇini's reference to the worshippers of Vāsudeva and Arjuna proves the antiquity of the cult of the Vṛṣṇi hero.[82] Arjuna also appears to have been defied along with Vāsudeva. The *Mahābhārata* preserves the tradition about the existence of the worshippers of Arjuna and it states that the two heroes, Vāsudeva and Arjuna, were really two ancient deities known by the names of Nara and Nārāyaṇa.[83] One Kṛṣṇa-Devakiputra is mentioned in the *Chāndogya Upaniṣad*[84] and there is no reason to differentiate him from the Vāsudeva-Kṛṣṇa of the *Mahābhārata*. The Buddhist *Niddesa* commentary, belonging to the pre-Christian period, mentions the cult of Vāsudeva.[85] The *Ghaṭa Jātaka* mentions some of the anecdotes of Kṛṣṇa's life.[86] The Jain *Uttarādhyayana Sūtra* mentions Vāsudeva as Keśava, and describes him as a contemporary of Ariṣṭanemi, the twenty-second Tīrthaṃkara.[87] Megasthenes mentions Vāsudeva Kṛṣṇa as Herakles, his worshippers the Sātvatas as Saurasenoi, the two cities where his cult flourished as Methora and Kleisobora and the river flowing between them as Jobares.[88] Other classical writers, who based their works on Megasthenes, also identified Kṛṣṇa with Herakles and Śiva with Dionysos.

One of the earliest archaeological evidences regarding the worship of Vāsudeva Kṛṣṇa in northern India is the Besnagar pillar inscription of Heliodoros, written in Brahmī characters of the 2nd century B.C. which records that a *Garuḍadhvaja* was erected in honour of Devadeva Vāsudeva, by one *Bhāgavata* Heliodoros, son of Dion, originally an inhabitant of Taxila and a Yavana, sent as an ambassador of the local Indo-Greek king Antialkidas to the court of king Kāsiputra Bhāgabhadra of Vidiśā.[90] Another inscription of about the same time found at Ghosundi, not far from Nagari near Chitor records that 'one (king) Pārāśarīputra Gajānana who had performed an Aśvamedha sacrifice, but was a devotee of Bhagavān (Vāsudeva) caused to be made a *pūjā*-stone wall Nārāyaṇavātikā for the divinities Saṅkarṣaṇa and Vāsudeva who are unconquered and lords of all'.[90] Evidence of the Mathura inscriptions suggests that the cult of Vāsudeva was very much in vogue in the locality during the time of the Śaka Satraps of northern India. A fragmentary inscription found in a well at Mora, a village near Mathura, indicates the popularity of the cult of the Vṛṣṇi heroes in that region.[91]

The early form of the Bhāgavata or Vaiṣṇava religion was based solely upon the doctrine of *bhakti*, i.e. devotion to a personal God. In Vaiṣṇavism this God is Vāsudeva Kṛṣṇa, and sometimes Nārāyaṇa, identified with the Vedic God Viṣṇu. In the Pāñcarātra works like the *Pādmatantra*[92] it is said that *Sūri, Suhṛit, Bhāgavata, Sātvata, Pāñcakalāvit, Ekāntika, Tanmaya,* and *Pāñcarātra* are different designation of the *bhakti* cult. In this list the term Vaiṣṇava is conspicuously absent. Varāhamihira did not use the word Vaiṣṇava. Instead he used the term Bhāgavata to denote this system. Utpala preferred the term Pāñcarātra. Although the name Parama-Vaiṣṇava occurs in some inscription of the Gupta period, the Gupta kings described themselves as Paramabhāgavatas. We prefer to maintain the term Vaiṣṇava because all forms of this *bhakti* cult have Viṣṇu, or one of his forms, as the supreme being.

The doctrine of devotion so much stressed in the *Bhagavadgītā* cannot, however, cover all the aspects of this composite system. Of all the names of this system the term Pāñcarātra has a separate denotation. Reference to a vast mass of Pāñcarātra literature has already been made. Firstly, the Pāñcarātra texts deal with four principal topics which are discussed in four parts (*pādas*). These are *jñāna* (knowledge), *yoga* (concentration), *kriyā* (action) and *caryā* (way of doing). Such a division of categories is absent in the *Bhagavadgītā,* but it accords very well with the scheme laid down in the Śaiva Āgamas and the Śākta Tantras. Secondly, the Pāñcarātras used to worship the supreme being in terms of five forms—Para, Vyūha, Vibhāva, Antaryāmī and Arcā. Of these forms, the concept of Para or supreme being, that of Antaryāmī as the all-knower and that of Vibhāva as Avatāra or incarnation, may be traced in the *Bhagavadgītā* but there is no mention of Vyūha and Arcā. The doctrine of Vyūha has no place in the *Bhagavadgītā,* and this also holds good in the case of Arcā, i.e. cult-image. There is reason to believe that these two concepts came from a different source.

The doctrine of Vyūha is connected with an early form of Sāṅkhya, and here the element of *Prakṛti* or the Female Principle is very conspicuous. How is it that where the God is one and the only one the concept of a Female Principle should become so prominent? Again, in this Vyūha doctrine Vāsudeva is not the only reality. Other Vṛṣṇi heroes are incorporated within the frame of the Vyūha doctrine. It appears that the Vyūha doctrine was a development of a localised tribal cult of the five Vṛṣṇi heroes; the scheme of this doctrine itself is suggestive of the fact that there was a popular reluctance as regards the question of the merger of these tribal deities into one entity. Even one of its constituents, the Sāmbaelement, was withdrawn because the cult-character upheld by it was basically different. The Vyūha doctrine found in most of the Pāñcarātra Saṃhitās may be summarised as follows:

The Bhagavat Vāsudeva in the act of creation produces from himself, not only *Prakṛti*, the indiscreet primal matter of the Sāṅkhyas, but also a *Vyūha* or phase of conditioned spirit called Saṅkarṣaṇa. From the combination of Saṅkarṣaṇa and *Prakṛti* spring *Manas* corresponding to the Sāṅkhya *Buddhi* or intelligence, and also a secondary phase of conditioned spirit called Pradyumna. From the association of Pradyumna with *Manas* spring the Sāṅkhya *Ahaṃkāra* or consciousness, and also a tertiary phase of conditioned spirit known as Aniruddha. From the association of Aniruddha with *Ahaṃkāra* spring the Sāṅkhya *Mahābhūtas* or elements with their qualities.[93]

This basic theme of the Vyūha doctrine has been grossly expanded in the Pāñcarātra Saṃhitās. The four principal characters have been multiplied by six *guṇas* or qualities (*jñāna* or knowledge, *aiśvarya* or lordship, *śakti* or potency, *bala* or strength, *vīrya* or virility, and *tejas* or splendour) as a result of which we have twenty-four emanatory forms. To this totality are added other deities evolved in the emanatory process. But the point which deserves our special attention is the association of the Vyūha emanation with the Sāṅkhya categories, the evolutes of Prakṛti. This association evidently refers to a non-Vedic origin of the Vyūha doctrine.

Elsewhere we have stated, on the evidence of the *Kūrmapurāṇa, Devīpurāṇa, Devībhāgavata, Skandapurāṇa, Sutasaṃhitā, Maheśvara-tantra, Āgamaprāmaṇya, Śivārkamaṇidīpikā* and other texts, that the Pāñcarātra system has been regarded as *Vedabāhya*, i.e. outside the pale of Vedic tradition. This is also the view of the *Mahābhārata*. Its insistence on the Sāṅkhya might have been one of the reasons for its exclusion from the Vedic domain. The anti-Vedic character of the Sāṅkhya system did not escape the notice of Śaṅkara who held categorically that *Kapilasya tantrasya vedaviruddhatvaṃ vedānusārimanuvacana viruddhatvañca*, i.e. Kapila's doctrine contradicts not only the Vedas but also the sayings of people like Manu who follow the Vedic way. It should also be pointed out here that in the subsequent stages of the development of the Vaiṣṇava ideas we come across a marked departure from the Sāṅkhya line and a close clinging to that of the Vedānta. In fact the later Vaiṣṇava theoreticians, as we shall persently see, wanted to base their doctrines upon the Vedānta, which is traditionally regarded as the essence of the Vedas, in order to obtain a Vedic sanction for their system.

The conception of Arcā or cult image may also be traced to a non-Vedic source. In the Vedic sacrificial tradition there is no room for cult images. In the pre-Vedic religion of India, of which we have a definite idea on the basis of the material remains of the Harappa civilization, cult images and emblems of the Mother Goddess and her male partner were very much in vogue. Literary and archaeological evidences of the early historic period leave no doubt that the non-Vedic deities like the Yakṣas, Nāgas, etc., were worshipped by the common peoples—we have actual inscribed images of Yakṣas, Yakṣiṇīs, Nagās and divinities of the centuries immediately preceding the Christian era. These deities were able to make their way into the anti-Vedic religious systems like Buddhism and Jainism which account for the bas-reliefs on the railings and gateways of Bharhut and Sanchi. A large stone image of Yakṣa Maṇibhadra belonging to *c.* 1st century B.C. has been found at Pol or Padam Pawaya in Gwalior with an inscription referring to its installation. Such images served as models for the icons of later cults, as has been demonstrated by distinguished art historians.

Tantric elements began to make their way into Vaiṣṇavism through the existing cults of the Mother Goddesses who later came to be identified with the consorts of Viṣṇu. Of these goddesses Śrī or Lakṣmī was able to predominate. Originally Śrī and Lakṣmī, regarded as two different personalities, were described as the two wives of Āditya. Later tradition made Śrī and Mahāśvetā the two wives of Sūrya, one on either side of the sun image. This was followed by the still later concept of Lakṣmī, identified with Śrī, and Sarasvatī as the two wives of Viṣṇu. The cult of Śrī-Lakṣmī of which we have sufficient numismatic evidence, besides the well known Gajalakṣmī type, was popular even before the beginning of the Christian era. In the *Mahābhārata*, the goddess who is brought into the closest connection with Viṣṇu is Bhū or Pṛthivī, i.e. Mother Earth. In the Durgāstotras (hymns addressed to the goddess) of the *Mahābhārata* although the great goddess is described as the 'younger sister of Kṛṣṇa', 'eldest-born in the family of the cowhered Nanda', 'the consort of Narayaṇa', etc., her Vaiṣṇavite association does not prove strong. In the Gupta period, of all the female deities associated with Viṣṇu, the concept of Lakṣmī or Śrī as his wife was finally established. This is confirmed by literary, numismatic, epigraphic, and sculptural evidences. Besides the Sanskrit poetical works, Lakṣmī as the divine consort of Viṣṇu, and also as the eternal Female Principle, is mentioned in the writings of the Tamil Āḷvārs. It is interesting to note that the Gopī element in Vaiṣṇavism, which is the forerunner of the later conception of Rādhā as the eternal Female Principle associated with the supreme being Kṛṣṇa, is met with in the devotional songs of the Āḷvārs. Āṇḍal or Kodai, daughter of Periyāḷvār, saw herself as one Kṛṣṇa's *gopīs,* and approached the God, her beloved, in that spirit.[94]

In the *Viṣṇupurāṇa* (4th century A.D.) the Female Principle is regarded as Mahālakṣmī who is the consort of Viṣṇu. Also, there are passages in the *Mārkaṇḍeya Purāṇa* which describe the goddess as Viṣṇumāyā, the *śakti* or energy of Viṣṇu, and Nārayaṇī, the wife of Nārāyaṇa. The Mātṛkās have also been connected with Vaiṣṇavism and we have the concept of the goddess Vaiṣṇavi as one of the seven or eight Divine Mothers. The concept of the Tantric goddess Vārāhī may also be mentioned in this connection. These are all glimpses of Tantrism in typically Vaiṣṇavite cults and rituals, but in the present state of our knowledge we are not in a position to state precisely the functional aspects of these Tantric elements. It is only the *Lakṣmītantra,* a Pāñcarātra text, compiled in 9-11th centuries, that we come across a distinct *atimārgika* form of the Vaiṣṇava cults in which the principles of left-handed Tantrism are found clearly operating. It is evidently a continuation of the left-handed Tantric tradition in Vaiṣṇavism, the origin and early stages of which, however, cannot be logically and systematically traced in earlier Vaiṣṇava sources. We have only one evidence in a fragmentary inscription dated in the Mālava year 480 (A.D. 423-4) found at Gangdhar in Malwa. The inscription records that one Mayurākṣa, a minister of Viśvavarman, the father of Kumāragupta I's feudatory Bhānuvarman 'caused to be built for the sake of his religious merit this very terrible abode ... filled full of female ghouls, of the Divine Mothers, who utter loud and tremendous shouts in joy (and) who stir up the (very) oceans with the mighty wind rising from the magic rites of the religion'.[95]

The above is Fleet's English rendering in which the words *tantra* and *ḍākinī,* have been translated as 'magic rites of religion' and 'female ghouls'. The original passage is: *Mātrīṇāñca pramudita-ghanātyartha-nihrādinīṇāṃ tantrodbhūtaprabalapavanodvarttit-āmbhonidhināṃ .... gatamidaṃ ḍāhinī samprakīrṇam veśmat-yugraṃ nṛpatisacivo' kārayat puṇyahetoḥ.* Here the word *tantra* evidently stands for Tantric rites and *ḍākinī* for the Ḍākinī cult. But the most interesting point is that this Mayurākṣa who is responsible for the erection of the temple was a devout Vaiṣṇava as is mentioned in the said inscription itself: *Viṣṇoḥ sthānamakārayat Bhāgavatas-Śrīmānā-Mayurākṣ-kaḥ.* This evidence by itself is not sufficient, however, to prove that the Tantric rites of terrible nature (*veśmatyugra)* involving the cults of the Ḍākinīs and the Mātṛkas were an integral part of the Vaiṣṇava faith to which Mayurākṣā belonged. But the evidence of the *Lakṣmītantra,* which was composed a few centuries later, clearly demonstrates that there were Vāmācāra elements in Vaiṣṇavism and that these elements are to be found even in the earlier Vaiṣṇava tradition. The inscription under review is suggestive in this respect.

From the 8th century onwards the concept of Śakti and also the inclusion of Tantric ideas and practices became more prominent in Vaiṣṇavism, the history of which will be dealt with in a subsequent chapter.

Tantra and Pāśupata Śaivism

The pre-Vedic God who, under different historical conditions, came to be regarded as Śiva was closely associated with the Mother Goddess cult of the Harappan religion. From about the 3rd century B.C. Śaivism appeared in India as a distinct sectarian religion. By nature Śaivism was a religion of the masses, specially of the lower orders of society; hence it had the greatest potentiality of absorbing the Tantric elements. And, it was in Śaivism that the Tantric ideas found a ground most favourable for their expansion.

J.N. Banerjea is of the opinion that many of the seals or seal-amulets of steatite, faience, etc., and other objects unearthed in the Harappan sites bear unmistakable traces of Tantrism and that some of the composite figures engraved on the seals remind us of the hybrid figures of Pramathas and Gaṇas, attendants of Śiva.[96] He has also referred to the Keśi-sūkta of the *Ṛgveda*[97] in which Keśi is described as belonging to an order of ascetics who are half naked—wearing short brown-coloured garments soiled with dust. He is said to have been a friend of the winds, inspired by gods, frenzied by the performance of austerities, travelling on the oceans, and so on, all of which remind us of the *atimārgika* followers of the Pāśupata creed.

In the *Ṛgveda* there are many hymns dedicated to Rudra. In most of them he symbolises the dreadful and destructive forces of nature.[98] The Śatarudrīya verses of the *Yajurveda*[99] contain one hundred names of Rudra, some of which allude to his terrific and others to his auspicious forms. This dual aspect is maintained in the post-Ṛgvedic texts, and the word Śiva which was previously used as an adjective to denote his pacific aspect became a proper name added to that of Rudra. In the *Śvetāśvatara Upaniṣad* Śiva is raised to the status of the supreme being, and in the *Atharvāśiras Upaniṣad*, which is a late work, he is the head of a sectarian religion. Pāṇini, who may be assigned to *c.* 5th century B.C., records several names of Rudra such as Bhava, Sarva, Rudra and Mṛḍa in one of his *sūtras.*[100] He also mentions a word *Śivādibhyon* probably to convey the idea that the words like *Śaivan*, derived by the application of the suffix *an* to such words as Śiva, etc., denote the descendants of them. Patañjali makes clearer references to Rudra and Śiva, and also to the exclusive worshippers of Śiva as Śiva-Bhāgavata. This is the earliest certain reference to Śaiva sect. The Greek writers found in Śiva a parallel of their own God Dionysos.

On some coins from Ujjayinī, belonging to *c.* 3rd-2nd century B.C. we come across the figure of three-faced Śiva carrying a *daṇḍa* and *kamaṇḍalu.* Two-armed Śiva is shown with a trident and knotted club on the Sirkap inscribed bronze seal of Śivarakṣita, on some copper coins of Maues and Gondophares, on a few coins of the Audumbara chief Dharaghoṣa and on Kuṣāṇa coins. Wema Kadphises was undoubtedly a sectarian Śaiva which is proved not only by the trident bearer God on his coins, but also the attributive epithet *maheśvara* in his coin-legend.[102] Śiva in his phallic form is also represented on coins. Phallism in the Śiva cult is perhaps a continuation of the Harappan tradition. Although in the Vedic texts the Śiśnadevas or phallic worshippers were condemned, the cult was popular among the masses. Its popularity in the beginning of the Christian era is amply testified by the celebrated Gudimallam phallus found near Renigunta in Andhra Pradesh.

That Rudra-Śiva was outside the pale of Vedic gods and Vedism (*vedabāhya*) is clear from the Dakṣa-Yajña[103] story of the *Mahābhārata* which indicates that the orthodox followers of the Vedic religion did not include Śiva and Devī in their pantheon. According to the *Mahābhārata*, Dakṣa arranged for a horse sacrifice at Hardwar which was attended by all the gods. The sage Dadhīci happened to notice that Maheśvara (Rudra Śiva), the consort of Pārvatī was not present in the assembly, and when he asked Dakṣa the reason for Śiva's absence, the latter replied that there were eleven Rudras with matted hair, each holding a spear, but he did not know who among them was Maheśvara. The insult made Pārvatī angry, and in order to please her

Śiva created Vīrabhadra. Mahākālī, also called Bhadrakālī, born of Devī's wrath, followed Vīrabhadra to the place of Dakṣa's sacrifice and they destroyed the sacrificial materials. The destruction of his sacrifice brought Dakṣa to his senses, and he was advised by Vīrabhadra to propitiate Śiva. Dakṣa prayed to Śiva, and Śiva, having been moved by his fervent appeal, appeared on the spot and consoled Dakṣa delivering a brief lecture on his own religious view. Chanda remarks:

> It should be noticed that the Śiva whom Dakṣa ignored in his sacrifice was not the Vedic Rudra but the Śiva worshipped by the Pāśupatas. The legend of Dakṣa's sacrifice indicates that the Pāśupata conception of Rudra or Śiva arose outside the pale of Vedism and the orthodox followers of the Veda could not persuade themselves to acknowledge them readily. No share of sacrificial food is claimed on behalf of Śiva's consort, Durgā.[104]

In the *Bhāgavata Purāṇa*[105] we have an elaborate version of this story which shows how Śiva was viewed by the followers of the other religious sects. The author, a devout Vaiṣṇava, made Dakṣa describe Śiva as monkey-eyed, roaming in the burning ground with his attendants, the ghosts and the goblins, impure and riteless, naked with matted locks on his head, wandering here and there like a mad man, sometimes laughing and at other times crying, smeared with ashes of funeral pyres, wearing bones and a garland of skulls as ornaments, inauspicious though his name speaks otherwise, mad and beloved of the insane, endowed with ugly qualities, and so on. Just as Dadhīci was the supporter of Śiva in the *Mahābhārata*, so also we find in Nandīśvara of *Bhāgavata* a supporter of Śiva vehemently criticising the Vedic way of life. Although some of the characteristics of the Vedic Rudra were infused into the Śiva of later times, his basic features were composed of anti-Vedic elements. His popular character and association with the lower order is also indicated in the *Rāmāyaṇa*.[106]

It has been pointed out that the earliest reference to a class of exclusive Śiva-worshippers is found in Patañjali's *Mahābhāṣya*.[107] Commenting on another *sūtra* of Pāṇini,[108] he says that the suffixes *ṭhak* and *ṭhañ*, if added to the words *āyaḥśūla* and *daṇḍājina*, should denote such persons as want to achieve their ends by means of a spear or trident made of iron (*lauhaśūla*), staff (*daṇḍa*) and animal-skin (*ajina*). Further he explains that the Śivabhāgavatas are indeed *āyaḥśūlika*, i.e. users of the iron trident. Wandering ascetics, with a bamboo staff in their hands, are mentioned by Pāṇini in his *sūtra: maskara-maskariṇau veṇuparivrājakayoḥ*.[109] This has been commented on by Patañjali in terms of the wandering ascetics who used to teach the doctrine of non-action. Such groups of ascetics, preaching *akriyā*, have been very frequently mentioned in Buddhist and Jain literature, as we have already noted.

Of these wandering ascetics, the Ājīvikas later came into prominence owing to the efforts of Gośāla Maṅkhaliputta who was a contemporary of the Buddha and Mahāvīra. Goṣāla was not, however founder of this sect. We know the names of at least two of his predecessors, Nanda Vacca and Kisa Saṃkiccha. Jarl Charpentier remarks that the Ājīvikas were an older sect to which Goṣāla belonged.[110] Basham also, on the basis of South Indian materials came to the conclusion that two other contemporaries of Buddha, viz., Puraṇa Kassapa and Pakudha Kaccāyana, were followers of the Ājīvika creed. Although, Ājīvikism, a distorted account of which is found in the Buddhist and Jain texts, is supposed to uphold a doctrine of non-action and fate, some of its rituals bear a close similarity with those of the Pāśupaṭas. Basham has located a number of Ājīvika terms and concepts from the Buddhist and Jain texts and their commentaries.[111] Some of these terms and concepts hold good also in the case of the Pāśupata doctrines and rituals. The concept of nudity common among the Jains and the Pāśupatas was probably due to Ājīvika influence. The Ājīvikas smeared their bodies with dust and ashes and did such things as 'eating the ordure of a calf', 'squatting painfully on the heels', 'swinging in the air like bats', 'reclining on thorns', and 'scorching themselves with five fires'.[112] These are found even today in the *Caḍaka* and *Gājana* rituals of Śiva, mainly performed by the lower orders of society.

The Nārāyaṇīya section of the *Mahābhārata* names the Pāśupata school as one of the five systems—Sāṅkhya, Yoga, Pāñcarātra, Veda and Pāśupata. According to this classification Veda and Pāśupata are distinct and independent of each other. This is one of the earliest clear references to the Pāśupata sect. The *Atharvāśiras Upaniṣad* refers to Pāśupata-vrata, the main feature of which is the ceremonial touching of the different limbs with ashes in the pattern of the Tantric *nyāsa*. In the *Mahābhārata*[113] it is stated that the Sāṅkhya was propounded by the great sage Kapila, Yoga by Hiraṇyagarbha, Veda by the great teacher Āpantaratamā who was also known by the name Prācīnagarbha, Pāñcarātra by the God (Kṛṣṇa) himself and Pāśupata by Śiva Śrīkaṇṭha, the consort of Umā, the lord of spirits and the son of Brahmadeva (*Umāpatirbhūtapatiḥ Śrīkaṇṭho Brāhmaṇaḥ sutaḥ, uktavānidamavyagro jñānam Pāśuptam Śivaḥ*). A similar opinion is found in the Pāñcarātra Saṃhitās.

R.G. Bhandarkar expressed his doubts very logically regarding the historicity of Śiva-Śrikaṇṭha as the divine founder of the Pāśupata sect, but he tried to prove, on the basis of the *Vāyu*, *Kūrma* and *Liṅga Purāṇas* and on that of a few inscriptions that the real founder of the Pāśupata system was, nevertheless, a historical personality. According to the Puranic legends when Vāsudeva Kṛṣṇa, the best of the Yadu family, appeared on the earth at the time of the twenty-eighth repetition of the *Yugas*, Maheśvara also incarnated himself as a Brahmācārin with the name of Lakulin.[114] This he did by entering into a corspe at a place called Kāyāvatāra on Kāyāvarohana (Karvan in Kathiawar). He had four disciples whose names were Kuśika, Mitra, Garga and Karusya. They smeared their bodies with ashes and went to Rudraloka after their death by following Maheśvara-yoga. D.R. Bhandarkar, the son of R.G. Bhandarkar, subsequently proved on the basis of textual and epigraphic data that the Pāśupata system was founded by one Lakulīśa who was regarded as the twenty-eighth or last incarnation of Śiva.[115] An early medieval inscription in the temple of Nātha near that of Ekaliṅgaji, about fourteen miles to the north of Udaipur, mentions as the founder of Pāśupata Yoga system a Brahmācārin with *laguḍa* or club in his hand, who flourished in Bhṛgukaccha and had four disciples whose names have been mentioned above. Another inscription from the Somnath temple, known as *Cintra-praśtasti*, for it was taken to Cintra in Portugal, which belongs to the second half of the 13th century, tells the same thing, but gives the names of his disciples slightly differently: Kuśika, Gārgya, Kauruṣa and Maitreya. In an inscription dated A.D. 943 found at Hemavati in Mysore it is stated that Lakulīśa was reborn as Muninātha Cilluka, The Lakulīśa tradition is maintained in Mādhava's *Sarvadarśanasaṃgraha* in which his name is mentioned as Nakulīśa.

Earlier scholars, especially the senior Bhandarkar, were inclined to place Lakulīśa about the middle of the the second century B.C. and to consider him as the founder of that religious order which was mentioned by Patañjali as the Śivabhāgavatas. But the Mathura stone pillar inscription of the time of Candragupta II, dated Gupta year 61, mentions one Uditācārya who is described as the tenth in the spiritual succession from Kuśika, one of the four immediate disciples of Lakulīśa.[116] Allotting twenty-five years to each of the ten predecessors of Uditācārya, Lakulīsa thus can be placed in the 2nd century

A.D., and if this dating be accepted we can assume that the Pāśupata system existed before the days of Lakulīśa and that the latter only revitalised the creed. Nothing very definite is known about the career of Lakulīśa. Mādhava in his *Sarvadarśanasaṃgraha* has described him as the author of a text known by the name of *Pañcādhyāyī* or *Pañcārthavidyā.*

The earliest known work of the Pāśupata sect is the *Pāśupata sūtra.*[117] Nothing about its authorship is known. It was commented on by Rāśīkara Kauṇḍinya of the Gupta period. But it appears that this learned commentator did not do full justice to this work, probably owing to his Brahmanical preoccupations. It is quite certain that Mādhavācārya of the 14th century depended on this commentary for his systematic exposition of the Pāśupata system in his *Sarvadarśanasaṃgraha.* The contents of the *Pāśupatasūtra* and its commentary deal with the five main tenets of the system which are *kārya, kāraṇa, yoga, vidhi* and *duḥkhānta.* This arrangement of the contents of the Pāśupata doctrine reminds us of the arrangements found in the Buddhist and medical treatises. In fact these five categories are the same as the four Ārya-satyas preached by the Buddha. The concepts of suffering and its extinction, and of the cause-effect relation, etc., however, reveal a different line of thinking.

The first category of the Pāśupata doctrine is known as *kārya,* or effect, by which is meant all the problems and conditions of worldly existence. These are effects because they are all produced by certain causes. The problems and conditions of wordly existence are concerned mainly with the man or individual who is also an effect. In the Pāśupata system this man or individual is known as *paśu.* His organs are known as *kalā* while the qualities are known as *vidyā.* According to the Paśupata system the evolution of *kārya* and its production from *kāraṇa* follow the Sāṅkhya pattern. What is seen as the effect, or *kārya,* which is manifested in the material world and worldly beings is formed by the combination of the five *mahābhūtas* or material elements (earth, water, fire, air and space) and five *tānmātras* or subtle elements. Other *tattvas* of the Sāṅkhya like the five sense organs, five physical organs, mind, intellect and the principle of egoity are regarded as the subsrata on which the production of the effect rests. So long as the *paśu* or individual is conditioned by all these elements he remains fettered.

The second category is known as *kārana.* Existence and suffering are produced by concurrent causes. This idea is shared equally by the Buddhists and the Pāśupatas. But while the Buddhists trace the cause of suffering to *avidyā* or false knowledge, the same view is put forward by the Pāśupatas in a different way. They ascrible the cause of suffering to the faliure to recognise Śiva as the creator, preserver and destroyer at one and the same time. The ultimate cause is Śiva, in their own terminology *pati* or Lord, who is omnipotent and almighty. The world, or individual, or *paśu*, fails to recognise him owing to *pāśa* or fetters. Since the individual is a conditioned entity it is not always possible for him to break all fetters to meet his source which is Śiva. This takes us to the third category which is called *yoga*, or union or connection. The term *yoga* has been used here in its simplest sense. The union or *yoga* of *paśu* and *pati* is to be achieved through mental action or the conceptual faculty which is called *citta* in Pāśupata terminology. This mental action may be of two kinds *sātmaka*, or active, and *nirātmaka*, or passive. The former consists of actions such as muttering of *mantras, japa, dhyāna*, worship, etc., and the latter insists on attaining the union through intense feeling which is known as *samvid*.

This union leads to the fifth category which is called *duḥkhānta* which is the extermination of suffering. This category clearly reveals the influence of Buddhist doctrines on the Pāśupatas. The *Pāśupata-sūtra* states that suffering will be ended only for one who is free from all sorts of illusion by the grace of God (*apramādī gacchet duḥkhānāṃ antan īśāprasādāt.*[118] Rāśīkara Kauṇḍinya in his commentary says that suffering is of three kinds. The *ādhyātmika* which is mental or physical suffering of the *paśu* caused by anger, lust, fear, sorrow, jealousy, malice, etc., and bodily ailments like diseases. The *ādhibhautika* is of five types which are 'living in mother's womb in the foetal stage', 'getting physical birth', ignorance', 'old age', and 'death'. This reminds us of the Buddhist *pratītyasamutpāda*. The *ādhidaivika* suffering consists of 'fear appertaining to worldly life', 'fear concerning the next world', 'association with evil', 'separation from virtue', and 'unfulfilment of one's desire'. It is only by the realisation of the supreme being that a Pāśupata can become free from all types of suffering. This freedom is *anātmaka-mokṣa*. But mere extinction of suffering is not his only aim. Side by side he wants to achieve supernatural power which is possible by five kinds of supramental knowledge and three kinds of divine power. The former consists of the power of visualising (*dūrdarśana*), hearing (*śravaṇa*), and knowing its three forms (*manana, vijñāna* and *sarva-jñatā*), while the latter consists of the power of doing anything which arises in mind (*manojavita*), of assuming any form (*kāmarūpitva*), and of holding the ability in all conditions (*vikaraṇadharmitva*).[119] There are other miraculous powers which also can be achieved.

The fourth category is known as *vidhi* or means to achieve the end. The important *vidhis* are known as *caryās,* which are again subdivided into *vrata* (vows) and *dvāra* (door). The main features of the *vrata* consists of smearing the body with ashes, lying on ashes, laughing, singing, dancing, making *huḍukkāra* (peculiar sounds), prostration, muttering *mantras,* etc. The main features of *dvāra* consist of *krāthana* (feigning sleep when really awake), *spandana* (shaking limbs), *maṇḍana* (loose walking), *śṛṅgāraṇa* (sexual gestures), *avitatkaraṇa* (acting as though insane), and *avitadbhāṣana* (speaking absurd words).[120] The Pāśupata should travel among people as if he is a mad man.[121] The commentator Kauṇḍinya, whose Brahmānical bias has already been indicated, describes these rites as anti-Brahmānical (*avyakta pretonmattādyaṃ brāhmaṇakarmaviruddhaṃ kramaṃ*). With reference to the Pāśupatas in his commentary on the *Bṛhatsaṃhitā* Bhaṭṭa Utpala says that their scripture is known as *Vātulatantra* which means the *tantra* of the lunatics.[122] In this connection it should be noted that there is actually a Śaiva Āgama by the same name.

It is not claimed that because of such unusual rites the Pāśupata system is Tantric. Its anti-Brahmānical character, however, invites an enquiry into the reason why it has been regarded as *Vedabāhya.* The essence of the Pāśupata doctrine has nothing to do with the Vedic tradition because in the latter, world and worldly existence have never been conceived of in terms of suffering and its extinction. In character it is, thus, more akin to Buddhism, though it insists on pure theism. Another aspect which should be noticed in this connection is that in the early Pāśupata system the concept of the Female Principle, or the Śakti of Śiva by which later Śaivism is dominated, has not been crystallised.

Evolution of the Concept of Śakti

In its present form Śāktism is essentially a medieval religion, but it is a direct offshoot of the primitive Mother Goddess cult which was so prominent a feature of the religion of the agricultural peoples. We have seen that the origin of the anomalous position of the Male

Principle in the Śākta religion can reasonably be traced to a similar position of males in a female-dominated society; that rituals based upon fertility magic must have played a very significant part in the development of the concept of Mother Goddess which is as varied as the degrees of culture attained by separate communities of mankind; and that this can be seen in various types of the goddess cult prevailing in different regions and among diverse peoples.

In the religious history of India, Mother Goddess never ceased to be an important cult of the people. Reference has already been made to the figurines of the goddess found in the pre-Harappan and Harappan sites, and also to the emblematic ring stones and seals found therein which testify the popularity of this cult in pre-Vedic India. A good number of goddesses occur in the *Ṛgveda*, but their position is very insignificant evidently due to the patriarchal outlook which resuled from a purely pastoral economy. In the post-Ṛgvedic literature we come across new goddesses like Ambikā, Umā, Durgā, Kālī, etc., who may be regarded as the prototypes of the Śākta goddess of a later period. The names of these goddesses appear originally to indicate different tribal deities who were afterwards identified with the wife of Śiva Paśupati, the pre-Vedic God known to have been worshipped by the Mohenjodaro peoples. The revival of the pre-Vedic Mother Goddess cult in the post -Ṛgvedic age was evidently due to the initiation of the Vedic tribes into the agricultural way of life. With this they also adopted numerous rituals, mainly sexual in character, designed to secure the fertility of the fields, which must have played a very significant part among the neighbouring agricultural societies.

The tradition of the Harappan ring stones associated with the Mother Goddess cult, found continuation in almost similar, but much more decorated, flat stone discs belonging to the early historical periods unearthed from such old sites as Taxila, Kosam, Rajghat, Patna, etc. One such object of the Maurya-Śuṅga period was found by Marshall at Hathial near Taxila. It is three and one-fourth inches in diameter and has the centre perforated. There are four nude female figures alternating with honey-suckle design engraved in relief around the central hole. The nude figures probably represent the Mother Goddess.[123] Likewise the tradition of the Harappan seals had also a continuation. An oblong seal from Harappa shows on the right side of its obverse face a nude female, upside down with legs wide apart, and a plant issuing from her womb. A similar seal was found at Bhita in which the goddess is shown with her legs in much the same position with a lotus issuing from her womb.[124] According to Banerjea these seals reveal the Śākambharī aspect of the goddess expressed in a passage of the Devīmāhātmya section of the *Mārkaṇḍeya Purāṇa* in which the Devī says that during the time of drought she will nourish the world by the life-sustaining vegetables growing from her body.[125] The continuation of the Harappan iconic tradition is found in the post-Vedic Mother Goddess figurines from Inamgaon, Vadgaon, Bhinmal, Lauriya Nandangarh and Piprahwa and also in the terracotta pieces of the Maurya and Śuṅga period found at various sites in Uttar Pradesh, Bihar, Maharashtra and Andhra.[126]

In the time between the Maurya and the Gupta period an extensive cult of the Mother Goddess flourised. Besides a vast mass of terracotta figurines of the goddess collected from such widely separated sites as Sarnath, Basarh, Bulandibagh, Kumrahar, Bhita, Nagri, Samkisa, Kosam, Taxila, and other places we have her representations in sculptures and reliefs and also on coins. The Gajalakṣmī type, the goddess of wealth being anointed with water by two elephants standing on either side of her, became popular even among the Buddhists and Jains. This type appears on the coins issued about the beginning of the Christian era by the local rulers of Ayodhya, Kausambi, Ujjayini and other places and also in the reliefs of Bharhut, Anantagumpha and many other sites. Apart from Gajalakṣmī, other goddesses, standing or seated, identified or unidentified, indigenous or even foreign, occur on coins. The Kuṣāṇa coins contain a variety of types. This evidence from coins and sculptures is corroborated by literary evidence. The two Durgāstotaras of the *Mahābhārata*[127] and the Ārya-stava of *Harivaṃśa*[128] leave no doubt that by the time they were composed a great deal of development had taken place in the worship of the goddess and many elements had merged to give it a definite shape.

The currency of the cult of the Female Principle in South India in the early centuries of the Christian era is amply indicated in early Tamil literature, the Saṅgam classics, in which occur such goddesses as Amarī, Kumārī, Gaurī, Samarī, Śūlī, Nīlī, Aiyai, Sayyaval, Karravai, Nallāī, Kaṇṇı, Śankarı, etc. Of these goddesses, Kumāri, the Virgin Goddess Kanyākumārī of the *Taittirīya Āraṅyaka* who gave her name to the southern-most point of India, is mentioned in the *Periplus*. The story of the deification of a human being called Kaṇṇaki into Paṭṭanikaḍavul, the goddess of chastity, is met with in the great Tamil epic *Śilappadikāram* (2nd century A.D.). The Bhagavatī temple of Cranganore in Kerala, dedicated to Bhadrakālī, whose wrath is supposed to be the cause of all epidemic diseases, is said to have been founded between the yeas A.D. 115-25 by Senguttuvan Perumal to commemorate the tragic end of Kaṇṇaki, the heroine of the *Śilappadikāram.*[129] How and when the Kannṇaki cult was assimilated into the Kālī or Bhagavatī cult cannot be said in our present state of knowledge. In the *Śilappadikāram* also occur such goddesses as Aryāṇī, Aiyai Kumārī, Āpya, Antari, Barati, Pitari, Māyaval, etc. The idea that Lakṣmī, Sarasvatī, Pārvatī, etc., represent different aspects of the same power is evident from the *venba* in Canto XXII of the *Śilappadikāram.* The cult of Durgā is found in the Vettuvavari of the same epic. The worship of Maṇimekalai, the chief guardian deity of the sea, is mentioned in the *Maṇimekalai,*the second Tamil epic, in which she acted as the guide of the heroine who is her namesake. Two other important goddesses of the epic are Cintā and Kāḍamarśelvi.

The new social and economic set up of the Gupta age radically changed the whole religious outlook of India. The ceremonial worship of the image of Viṣṇu, Śiva, Buddhist and Jain deities, along with their consorts, installed in numerous temples of magnificent proportions, became a very important feature of religious life, the installation of such temples and image being due to the social surplus introduced by the new economic conditions. Buddhism changed qualitatively from the pristine simplicity of an austere moral code to the most complex system of Mahāyāna. In the case of other religions the change was still quantitative. The progress of Jainism was slow in the process of transformation, while Vaiṣṇavism and Śaivism moved closer to each other as evidenced by the attempts to establish the unity of Viṣṇu and Śiva and to combine in a single iconographic motif the attributes of different Vaiṣṇavite and Śaivite deities. To Viṣṇu and Śiva was added Brahmā of the older pantheon, and they formed the official trinity. Also a qualitative change took place in the cult of the Female Principle. The mass strength behind it placed goddesses by the side of gods of all religions, but even by doing so the entire emotion centering round the Female Principle could not be channelised. So the need was felt for a new religion, entirely female-dominated, a religion in which even the great gods like Viṣṇu or Śiva would remain subordinated to the goddess. This new religion came to be known as Śāktism. The Śākta principles find expression in the Devīmāhātmya section of the *Mārkaṇḍeya Purāṇa* in which the goddess is invoked thus:

Thou art the cause of all the worlds. Though characterised by three qualities, even by Hari, Hara and other gods thou art incomprehensible. Thou art the resort of all; thou art this entire world which is composed of parts. Thou verily art the sublime original nature untransformed.... Thou art Medhā, O Goddess; thou hast comprehended the essence of all scriptures. Thou art Durgā, the boat to cross the ocean of existence, devoid of attachments. Thou art Śrī who has her dominion in the heart of the enemy of Kaiṭabha. Thou indeed art Gaurī who has fixed her dwelling in that of the moon-crested God.[130]

The Śākta Devī in her developed form absorbed with herself innumerable goddesses representing different streams. The foregoing invocation mentions a few goddesses who stand by themselves as independent deities, though the poet knew them only as forms of the great goddess unto whom they were absorbed. In the concluding portion of the Devīmāhātmya section of the *Mārkaṇḍeya Purāṇa* the Devī assures the gods by granting them the boon that she will always become incarnate and deliver the whole world whenever it is oppressed by the demons.[131] Of her incarnatory and other forms, Gaurī, Śatākṣī, Śākambharī, Annapūrṇa, etc., were undoubtedly the developed forms of the rudimentary Earth and Corn Mothers. The second stream leading to monotheistic Śāktism was represented by the Umā-Pārvatī group which developed under the garb of Śaivism. Umā of the *Kena Upaniṣad* and that of the *Kumārasambhāva* or the Purāṇas are not the same. The epithet Haimavatī (daughter of Himavat) was responsible for her identification with Pārvatī and Durgā. The latter was associated with inaccessible regions, and it is also possible that she was originally conceived of as the protectress of forts (*durga*). However, fanciful explanation of Durgā was invented on etymological ground by associating her with the slaying of a demon called Durgama. Whether a demon-slayer or saviour, Durgā is equipped with many arms, a feature which is totally absent in the concept of Pārvatī -Umā who is extremely homely as the daughter of Himavat, wife of Śiva, mother of Kumāra.

Most of the Purāṇas do not insist upon the demon-slaying conception of the goddess and her terrible forms. It is in the *Mārkaṇḍeya, Vāmana,* and the later Devī-oriented Purāṇas that we have her terrible demon-slayer form represented by Raktadantikā, Bhimā, Bhrāmarī, Caṇḍikā or Kauśikī, Kālī, Cāmuṇḍā, etc. These goddesses were evidently adopted in the Śākta pantheon from the surviving tribal divinities. Kālī in the Kālañjara mountain, Caṇḍikā in Makarandaka, and Vindhyavāsinī in the Vindhyas are mentioned in the *Matsya Purāṇa*[132] as the different manifestations of the supreme goddess. Her particular interest in wine and meat is found in the *Viṣṇupurāṇa.*[133] In Bāṇabhaṭṭa's *Kādambarī* and in Vākpati's *Gauḍavaho* we have references to the goddess cult of the wild Śabaras and their cruel rites. In Subandhu's *Vāsavadattā* the blood-thirsty goddess Kātyāyanī or Bhagavatī of Kusumapura is mentioned. In the *Mārkaṇḍeya* and other Devī-oriented Purāṇas the Devī is conceived of mainly as the war goddess. The Mātṛkās or Divine Mothers also play a very important role in the Devī legends. Of all the major achievements of Devī, the story of her fight with Mahiṣāsura became most popular as is proved by numerous Mahiṣamardinī sculptures. The Mahiṣāsura episode of the Devīmāhātmya section of the *Mārkaṇḍeya Puraṇa* suggests in itself a nice outline of the Śākta conception of Devī as the embodiment of an all-pervading power. The gods being defeated, humiliated and oppressed by Mahiṣāsura went for protection to Viṣṇu and Śiva. Having heard their grievances, Viṣṇu, Śiva and other gods emitted flames of anger from their eyes. These were transformed into a mass of intense energy which, shortly afterwards, took the shape of an exquisite lady, called Caṇḍikā, whose face was made by Śiva's energy, hair by Yama's, arms by Viṣṇu's, breasts by moon's, waist by Indra's, legs by Varuṇa's, hips by the earth's, feet by Brahmā's. toes by sun's, hands and fingers by the Vasu's, nose by Kuvera's, teeth by Prajāpati's, eyes by Agni's and ears by Vāyu's energy. This conception of the goddess—her creation from the energy of all gods—became popular and was further elaborated in the later Puraṇas.

The idea of Śakti became so deep-rooted in the Indian mind that even in sectarian religions like Vaiṣṇavism, Śaivism, etc., the Female Principle had to be given a prominent position. Nor could the basically atheistic religions like Buddhism and Jainism avoid this popular influence. Later Buddhism is in fact, nothing but a disguised Tantric cult of the Female Principle. The cause of this popularity was evidently connected with the changing social pattern arising out the new economic conditions resulting from changes in the mode of production and distribution, expansion of internal and external trade, administrative norms, and the growth of urbanism. The agriculturists and other professionals, apart from the priestly, warrior and trading classes, formed the majority of the population, and it was the religion of this majority, the Mother Goddess of the agriculturists, that found its way into the higher levels of society. The higher religions, in order to gain popularity among the masses and wider acceptance had to compromise with the existing cults and beliefs, and this was one of the processes through which the female divinities of the lower strata of society broke into the strongholds of the male-dominated cults. Goddesses and rituals connected with them are also found in considerable numbers, among the tribal peoples who, unable to maintain themselves by their traditional mode of production, had to come in contact with the advanced peoples and were graded socially on the basis of the quality of the services they offered. The popularity of the concept of the goddess slaying the demons had also a clear social significance. It offered a cathartic dream to the toiling masses of all ages, the illusion of a cherished reality of the ultimate triumph of the good over the evil, of truth and justice over tyranny and social oppression.

NOTES

1. For pre-Harappan and Harappan religion see my *History of the Śākta Religion*, New Delhi, 1974, pp. 11-18, *Indian Mother Goddess*, 2nd edn., New Delhi, 1977, pp. 146-52.
2. Cf. *Saundaryalaharī*, I.
3. VII. 27.5; X. 99.3, etc.
4. A. Macdonell, *Vedic Mythology*, Strassburg, 1897, p. 124.
5. *Ṛgveda*, II. 15.6; IV. 30. 8-11; 73.6; X. 138.5.
6. R.P. Chanda, *Survivals of the Prehistoric Civilization of the Indus Valley*, Memoirs of the Archaeological Survey of India (hereafter MASI) No. 41, Delhi, 1929, p. 25.
7. Cf. R. Garbe in *Encylopaedia of Religion and Ethics*, Vol. XII, p. 833.
8. III. 1.
9. R.P. Chanda, op. cit., p. 33.
10. *Taittirīya Saṃhitā*, III. 3.7.3; II. 5.1.1; *Aitarya Brāhmaṇa*, VII. 28; *Śatapatha Brāhmaṇa*, I.2.3.2; XII. 7.1.1; *Pañcaviṃśa Brāhmaṇa*, XIV. 11.28, etc.
11. In the older portions of the *RV* we have only three words of agricultural significance: *udara* (II.14.11), *dhānya* (V. 53.13) and *vapanti* (VI. 4.6). *RV.* IV. 57.1-8 are also proved to be later interpolation. See Hopkins in *Journal of American Oriental Society*, Vol. XVII, p. 85n.
12. III. 57; cf. *Taittirīya Br.*, I. 6. 10.4-5.

13. X. 18.
14. X. 1.7.
15. *Muṇḍaka Upaniṣad,* 1.2.4; *Sāṅkhyāyana G.S.*, II. 15.14.
16. Ch. XVII.
17. *Kulārṇava* II. 10; II. 85; II. 140-1.
18. *Setubandha,* ANDS, p. 5.
19. See A. Avalon's edn., p. 13.
20. Com. on *Saundaryalaharī* 32.
21. III. 30.
22. X. 1.15.
23. For Tantric elements in the Vedic texts and their references see Woodroffe, *Śakti and Śākta,* pp. 44-71.
24. *The Vedic Age,* Bharatiya Vidya Bhawan, Bombay (1971 rpt.), p. 422.
25. *Ṛgveda,* I.162-3.
26. M. Winternitz, *History of Indian Literature,* Vol. I, p, 181; A.B. Keith, *Religion and Philosophy of the Veda,* HOS, 1925, pp. 258-9, etc.
27. *Kātyāyana Śrautasūtra,* I. 6.14; *Jaiminisūtra* (with Śabara's com.), VI. 2.1; VI. 6.16.23; X 2.34-8; X. 6.45-9.
28. M. Monier-Williams, *Sanskrit English Dictionary,* Oxford, 1899, p. 839.
29. I. 3.72.
30. I. 27.11; I. 51.8; I. 81.2; I. 83.3; I. 92.3; I. 127.2; I. 138.4; IV. 17.15; X. 17.19; X. 45.11; 122.8; X. 151.4.
31. Cf. A.B. Keith, op. cit., p. 290.
32. G. Jha, *Pūrvamīmāṃsā and Its Sources,* Banaras, 1942, pp. 318f.
33. VII. 19.
34. Cf. *Ślokavārtika,* 43-113.
35. A.B. Keith, *The Karma Mīmāṃsā,* London, 1921, pp. 63-4.
36. See Śabara's com. on *Mīmāṃsāsūtra* II. 1.5; VI. 1.2; VII. 1.34; X. 4.23.
37. H. Oldenberg, *Buddha,* Eng. tr., London, 1927, p. 64.
38. Cf. *Śatapatha,* III. 2.1.2; IV. 6.7.9-10; VI. 5.3.5; XI. 6.2.10; *Aitareya,* II. 5.3; III 5.4; V. 3.1; VI. 5.10.
39. *Lāṭyāyana S.S.* IV. 3.17; *Kātyāyana S.S.* XIII. 42; *Taittirīya Āraṇyaka,* IV. 7.50; X. 62.7; *Aitareya Āraṇyaka,* I. 2.4. 10; V. 1.5. 13; *Gobhila G.S.*, II. 5.69-10; *Sāṅkhyāyana G.S.*, I. 19.2-6; *Hiraṇyakeśī G.S.*, I. 24.3; *Āpastamba S.S.* V. 25.11; etc.
40. V. 1.2.9; V. 5.4.27; VI. 6.3.7; XII. 8.1.16; cf. *Aitareya,* III. 1.5; VI. 3.1; VIII. 5.7.
41. VIII. 1.4.
42. *Taittirīya Āraṇyaka,* II. 11; *Gobhila G.S.*, I. 2.5.
43. *Aitareya Āraṇyaka,* III. 2; *Ṛgvidhāna* II. 16.
44. Cf. *Taittirīya Āraṇyaka,* IV. 27.
45. *Śvetāśvatara,* I. 1-2.

46. *Śārīrasthāna*, I. 11.
47. *Tarkarahasyadīpikā*, 115-24.
48. XIX. 44.
49. VI. 6.
50. Com. on *Mbh.* XIII. 232.21.
51. *Tarkarahasyadīpikā*, 13-15.
52. Kyoto edn. 1923, p. 184.
53. IX. 52.
54. XII. 179, 222, 224, 232, etc.
55. Cf. R.E. Hume, *Thirteen Principal Upaniṣads*, London, 1921, p. 8.
56. Com. on *Mbh*, XII. 232.21.
57. Com. on *Sāṅkhyakārikā*, XXVII.
58. Com. on *Brahmasūtra* II. 2.3-5.
59. II. 1. 6-7; V. 1.17-18; V.2.13, etc.
60. For details see N.N. Bhattacharyya, *Jain Philosophy: Historical Outline*, New Delhi, 1976, pp. 64-80.
61. A.L. Basham, *History and Doctrine of the Ājīvikas*, London, 1951, pp. 80ff.
62. II.11.
63. IV. 4.30.
64. *Uttarādhyayana Sūtra*, VI. 17.
65. *Encyclopaedia of Religion and Ethics*, Vol. VII, p. 465.
66. For the pre-Vedic character see A.K. Coomaraswamy, *Yakṣas*, rpt., New Delhi, 1971.
67. See my *History of the Śākta Religion*, pp. 38-42, 45-7, 65-8, 90-2, 104.
68. B.T. Bhattacharyya, *Buddhist Esoterism*, London, 1932, pp. 22ff.
69. *Sūyagaḍa*, II.2; *Ṭhāna*, IV. 4.
70. For details see M.B. Jhaveri, *Comparative and Critical Study of Mantraśāstra* (with special treatment of Jain Mantravāda) Ahmedabad, 1944; U.P. Shah, 'A Peep into the Early History of Tantra in Jain Literature' in *Bhārata Kaumudi*, II, Allahabad, 1947, pp. 839ff.
71. *Dīgha Nikāya*, XIV.
72. Ibid., XXIV.
73. Ibid., I.
74. *Cullavagga*, VIII. 2.
75. Ed. R.L. Mitra, *Bib. Ind.*, p.315.
76. I. 79; Chalmers, *Further Dialogues of the Buddha* (PTS), Vol. I, p. 35.
77. Culladhammasamādāna Sutta, *Majjhima* (PTS), Vol. I, p. 305.
78. XXIII. 1-2.
79. V. 10.2; *SBE*, Vol. XX, p. 89.
80. V.6.
81. *Buddhist Suttas*, tr. T.W. Rhys-Davids in *SBE*, Vol. XI, pp. 196, 199-200.
82. XVIII. 6.97.
83. Pāṇini, IV. 3.98.

84. V. 49.19.
85. III. 17.6.
86. R.G. Bhandarkar, *Vaiṣṇavism, Śaivism and Minor Religious Systems* Strassburg, 1913, p. 3.
87. Ibid., p. 38.
88. J. Charpentier's ed., pp. 164-9; *SBE*, Vol. XIV, pp. 122-9.
89. Bhandarkar, op. cit., p. 9.
90. D.C. Sircar, *Select Inscriptions*, 90-1.
91. *Epigraphia Indica*, Vol. XXII, p. 204.
92. Ibid., Vol. XXIV, pp. 194ff.
93. IV. 2.88.
94. Grierson in *Indian Antiquary*, 1908, p. 261.
95. J.F. Fleet, *Corpus Inscriptionum Indicarum*, Vol. III, pp. 76-8.
96. J.N. Banerjea, *Development of Hindu Iconography*, Calcutta, 1956, pp. 161ff.
97. X. 136.
98. For references see Bhandarkar, op. cit., p. 103.
99. *Taittirīya Saṃhitā*, XV. 5; *Vājasaneyi Saṃhitā*, XVI.
100. IV. 1.49.
101. IV. 1.112.
102. J.N. Baanerjea, op. cit., pp. 117ff. and Plates.
103. XII. 282-3.
104. R.P. Chanda, *Indo Aryan Races*, p. 129.
105. IV. 2-7.
106. V. 89.6ff.
107. Com. on Pāṇini IV. 1.112.
108. V. 2.76; *ayaḥśūladaṇḍājinābhyāṃ ṭhakṭhañau.*
109. VI. 1.154.
110. *Journal of the Royal Asiatic Society* (hereafter *JRAS*), 1913, pp. 669-74.
111. A.L. Basham, *History and Doctrine of the Ājīvikas*, London, 1951, pp. 240ff.
112. *Jātakas*, Nos. 390, 493.
113. XII. 349. 64-8.
114. *Vāyu*, XXIII; *Liṅga*, XXIV; *Kūrma*, LIII; *Śiva*, V.
115. *Archaeological Survey of India: Annual Report for 1906-7*, pp. 190-1; *Journal of the Bombay Branch of the Royal Asiatic Society*, Vol. XXII, pp. 151-3.
116. *Epigraphia Indica*, Vol. XXI, pp. 1-9.
117. Edited with Kauṇḍinya's commentary by R. Ananthakrishna Sastri in TSS, No. CXLIII.
118. IV. 49,
119. *Pāśupatasūtra*, I. 21ff.
120. Ibid., I. 2ff; III. 11ff.
121. Ibid., IV. 6; IV. 8.

122. Com. on *Bṛhatsaṃhitā* (ed. S. Dvivedi), LIX. 29.
123. *Archaeological Survey of India: Annual Report for 1927-28*, p. 66.
124. J. Marshall, *Mohenjodaro and the Indus Civilization*, Vol. I, p. 52.
125. J.N. Banerjea, op. cit., pp. 489-90.
126. N.N Bhattacharyya, *Indian Mother Goddess*, 2nd edn. 1977, pp. 152ff.
127. IV. 6; VI. 23.
128. *Viṣṇuparva*, Ch. III.
129. *IHQ*, Vol. II, pp. 621-2.
130. Pargiter's tr.
131. Cf. *Vāmana Purāṇa*, LVI. 67-70.
132. XIII. 32ff.
133. V. 2.84.

6

Development of Tantric Buddhism

Tantric Background of the Buddhist Doctrine of Elements

Practically nothing or very little is known about what the Buddha had actually preached, because there was a long time-gap between the days of the Buddha and the formation of the canonical literature. Rhys-Davids, Oldenberg, Kern, etc., believed that the Pali sources must have preserved the 'original', 'pure' and 'true' forms of Buddhism and that it was redundant to look for anything else as original Buddhism beyond the normal suggestivity of the Pali sources. Some scholars again hold that Sanskrit sources are as important as the Pali sources and that both these sources were derived from a lost original which was composed in some Māgadhi dialect. But there are others who hold that the Buddhist texts and their commentaries were mainly composed by the Brāhmaṇas, since they were the scholarly class throughout the ages, and that they employed their traditional terminologies and conceptions in interpreting the essentials of Buddhism. There may also have been conscious or unconscious attempts to fabricate the one in the light of the other, for instance while mixing milk with mango juice, the mango-seed, which was original Buddhism, was probably thrown aside.

Another group of scholars devoted themselves to the study of the scholastic literature of Buddhism which they believed to be nearer the original doctrine. Of these scholars, Stcherbatsky insisted on the exact meaning of the Buddhist technical terms which had so far been translated just anyhow, either on the basis of etymology or of common sense. Stcherbatsky's methodology was to depend on what the Buddhist materials themselves had to say on the terms and concepts. His chief source was not the Pali canon, but a later work, the *Abhidharmakośa,* which he believed to be systematic exposition of a much earlier work.

Stcherbatsky holds that the *dharma* theory is the basis of all forms of Buddhism and the starting point of all later developments. By *dharma* is meant a fundamental principle, for instance the idea that existence is an interplay of a plurality of subtle, ultimate, and not further analysable elements of matter, mind and forces. We do not know of any form of Buddhism without this doctrine and its corollary classifications of elements into *skandha, āyatana* and *dhātu*, and the laws of their interconnection (*pratītya-samutpāda*). This doctrine of elements was current in the pre-Buddhistic systems too but in Buddhism it acquired a changed significance. Just as Mahāvira was not the first to proclaim Jainism, so also the Buddha might have adopted and spread a doctrine which he found in the philosophical traditions of India. He, indeed, is reported to have emphatically disowned the authorship of a new teaching, but claimed to be the follower of a doctrine established long ago by former Buddhas.

According to Stcherbatsky, the idea of a self or soul as a psycho-physical entity, arising out of the rudimentary doctrine of elements was not unknown in the earlier traditions. But the idea of an immortal soul was quite unknown to the Vedas and the older Upaniṣads. The new conception of the immortal soul, called *ātmavāda* by the Buddhists, was accepted by all the subsequent philosophical systems—except the Buddhists, the materialists, and the Lokāyatas of the Tantric tradition whose sole emphasis was on the older tradition of *dehātmavāda*—but with considerable amendments. By the *anātmavāda* of the Buddhists we understand a plurality of separate elements without real unity, a concept which must have been in existence in pre-Buddhist tradition.[1] We have seen that in the Sāmaññaphalasutta and Brahmajālasutta of the *Dīgha Nikāya* mention is made of philosophical schools and individual teachers upholding the doctrine of *dehātmavāda* in which the existence of soul apart from the body is not recognsied. In fact this is the continuation of a primitive Tantric tradition from which these philosophical schools and teachers and also Buddhism have drawn heavily. Although in later Tantric texts the doctrine of soul independent of body found a place owing to the influx of Brahmanical ideas, it is basically inconsistent with the main spirit of Tantra which only recognises the human body as the source of all spiritual experience, the revitalisation of which, through certain physical processes, has been regarded as the object of salvation. The main source of the Buddhist concept of *anātma* evidently lies in this Lokāyata-Tantric tradition.

The Mahāyāna: Its Tantric Association

The Tibetans do not differentiate between Mahāyāna and Vajrayāna; they equate the Mahāyāna Sūtras (*mDo*) with Tantra (*rGyud*).[2] They are basically correct because there is no difficulty in establishing that Mahāyāna Buddhism contains a lot of Tantric elements.

Mahāyāna brought a significant change in the history of Buddhism. According to Hīnayāna, the Buddha was a man who pondered upon human suffering and suggested effective means for its extinction. This human character of Buddha is denied in Mahāyāna; he is regarded here as a superhuman entity, a god, and eventually the highest god, who resides in heaven and exercises control over a host of gods and goddesses. The concept of suffering by which early Buddhism was characterised is denied in Mahāyāna by denying the existence of the world itself. It is said that the understanding of the doctrine of vacuity (*śūnya*), i.e. world is merely an illusion and not a reality, will lead the way to Nirvāṇa. Hīnayāna Buddhism upholds the doctrine of Arhathood. An Arhat is an ideal person who is free from all worldly fetters. This perfection is to be attained by individuals who are desirous of it. The concept of Arhathood is negated in Mahāyāna and is substituted by that of Bodhisattvahood. A Bodhisattva may be a god, a householder, a recluse and even a non-human being. His function is to help man to achieve salvation. For this salvation there is no need to take up the difficult eightfold path; some good actions (*pāramitās*) will do. The purpose of Mahāyāna is mass- salvation, and that is why it claims itself to be the great (*mahā*) vehicle.

The cause of the rise of Mahāyāna lay in the attempt to take Buddhism to the masses. In the religion preached by the Buddha there was no room for householders. It was a purely monastic religion meant for those who had given up all worldly connections and taken refuge in the *Saṅgha*. Lay people could utter the *triśaraṇa*, offer flowers and candles to the *stūpas*, and give alms to the monks. However, no definite way of life was prescribed for them by the Buddha. Since it was impossible for ordinary householders to follow the most difficult eightfold path Mahāyāna insisted on the cultivation of easy virtues (*pāramitās*). Outside the Buddhist church and discipline the Bhakti cult was very influential specially among the Śaivas and Vaiṣṇavas. Thinking of this particular popular emotion Mahāyāna also introduced a typical cult of the Buddha by making him the highest god and allowing his worship in images. In all forms of religion there is an intermediate group between the gods and their devotees; the Bodhisattvas belong to this class. In order to reach the masses Mahāyāna also had to make a compromise with the local cults and rituals, just as Christianity had in Europe by conferring sainthood upon Pagan deities. Once this process is started it multiplies, and this happened in the case of Mahāyāna.

In reality, however, two contradictory sets of elements were amalgamated in Mahāyāna. One was the set of popular elements which was directly concerned with the religious demands of the greater section of the people; and the other was the idealistic viewpoint, an acute form of idealism, which regarded the world as a false or void entity. The growth of idealistic thinking, was facilitated by the Mādhyamika (Śūnyavāda) and Yogācāra (Vijñānavāda) systems of Mahāyāna and their theoretical offshoot the Brahmanical Advaita Vedānta. But the diffculty with Mahāyāna was that the two sets of elements—popular religious ideas and the doctrine of extreme idealism—of which it was composed, could not be properly mixed, very much like water and oil.

While the central doctrine of Buddhism—that of *anātma*—is conceived in Hīnayāna as the conglomeration of five elements (*skandhas*) which are constantly changing (*anitya*) and momentary (*kṣaṇika*), in Mahāyāna they are regarded as actually non-existent (*śūnya*). For example, it may be said that the Hinayānist does not recognise the existence of any eternal inner reality or self of an earthen pot because it may also be given the shape of a horse; but the existence of the element, that is clay, of which the earthen pot or horse is made, is not denied. But the Mahāyānist denies even the existence of clay; just as the pothood or horsehood of clay is false, so also the clay itself. The first is *pudgalaśūnyatā* and the second *dharmaśūnyatā*. The essence of Mahāyāna teaching is that the worldly person travels in the world of false notions. These false notions are created by six imperfect sense-organs. He has his Nirvāṇa, or perfect knowledge, when he comes to understand that everything is *śūnya*—as false as a dream.

According to the Mahāyānic Yogācāra or Vijñānavāda, pure consciousness or *vijñāna* is self-effective and the ultimate reality beyond which nothing exists. This consciousness constitutes the world of apparent existence. The Advaita Vedānta system of subsequent Indian philosophy has its main source in this Yogācāra. The followers of Yogācāra divide the basic ingredients of existence into two categories—constituted and unconstituted. These ingredients are not *rūpa* or matter; they are produced from *citta* or mind. External objects have no real existence, because we can have no medium outside consciousness which can distinguish between the knower and the knowledge. An apparently visible pillar is nothing but a mental form. While the Yogācāra thus declares everything to be the creation of mind and rejects the reality of all external objects, the Mādhyamika goes a step further and declares that even what is called consciousness is false. Nāgārjuna, the best exponent of the Mādhyamika system, says that world of experience is nothing but an appearance, a network of some unintelligible relations. The ingredients of the so-called constituted objects which have origin, existence, and destruction are really false because origin, existence, and destruction cannot coexist in a single entity. Existence or non-existence cannot be proved as the basic entity of an object. An object is known by its qualities and in that sense we understand earth, water, and other elements, but the qualities cannot be self-existent. Colour cannot exist without eye, and that is why the relative existence of the qualities are really void existence, and hence the objects which are regarded as the container of the qualities have also no real existence. Therefore, there is no effect and no cause, a thing is not created by itself or from anything else. Objects are neither momentary nor eternal, neither produced nor destroyed, neither composite nor separate. What is produced by concurrent causes is not produced by itself and hence does not exist in itself.

In brief the above is the Mahāyānic idealistic standpoint with which popular cults and rituals have been curiously blended. A pure devotional religion with the Buddha as the highest god who is eternal, without any origin and decay, and ultimate reality which is beyond any sort of description, was grafted into the frame of the *Śūnya* doctrine of Mahāyāna. This Buddha was also regarded as the head of a pantheon, the members of which came from a variety of sources with their typical cults and rituals. It is in this way that specific Tantric cults and deities came into the fold of Mahāyāna. The Buddha was conceived of as having three *kāyas* or bodies—*dharma, sambhoga,* and *nirmāṇa* or *rūpa.* The *dharma-kāya* is the real body of the Buddha which is all pervading, formless and eternal. This body can not be seen, but for the sake of devotees of exceptional merit the Buddha sometimes appears in the form of a god which is his *sambhoga-kāya.* For the welfare of mankind the Buddha sometimes assumes human form which is subject to birth and death. This is his material body (*rūpa-kāya*) or created body (*nirmāṇa-kāya*): Gautama Buddha was thus the human form of the original Buddha and was born in the world (*sahā-lokadhātu*) where we live. Other human Buddhas were also born in different worlds. Side by side with this *tri-kāya* concept arose that of the incarnations of the human Buddha, the Buddhās of the past, present, and future. Legendary careers and achievements were ascribed to each of these Buddhās. Five Dhyānī Buddhās were also conceived, each symbolising one of the five *skandhas* or elements. They were known as Vairocana, Akṣobhya, Ratnasambhava, Amitābha, and Amoghasiddhi supposed to have sprung from one Ādi Buddha. Each of these Buddhas had a Bodhi-sattva and a goddess as female consort.

One of the main characteristics of Mahāyāna is the concept of Bodhisattva. Originally Bodhisattvahood was an ideal, as opposed to Arhathood. One who actively endeavours for the development and upliftment of intellect and mind (bodhi-*citta*) with the purpose of the attainment of Buddahood is a Bodhisattva. Thus from a theoretical viewpoint every Mahāyānist is a potential Bodhisattva. Although in the beginning the ideal of Bodhisattvahood was man-oriented, i.e. it was argued that every human being should strive for Bodhisattvahood, in a later period a class of gods was created that came to be known as Bodhisattvas. They were powerful deities who could grant desired effects to their worshippers. Of such Bodhisattvas the important ones are Avalokiteśvara, Mañjuśrī, Vajrapāṇi, Samantabhadra, Ākāśagarbha, Mahāsthānaprāpta, Bhaiṣajyarāja, and Maitreya. Avalokiteśvara is the god of compassion whose female consort Tārā represents *prajñā* or wisdom. She is the saviour of mankind in distress. Mañjuśrī is ever young. He is also the god of knowledge and the teacher of the future Buddha Maitreya.

A class of Mahayānic literature, which was composed between the 4th and 8th centuries A.D., is known as *Dhāraṇī* which refers to *mantra, mudrā, maṇḍala, kriyā, caryā,* etc., by which the Tantric cults are characterised. Occasional references to this kind of literature are found in early Mahāyāna texts.[3] The Gilgit manuscripts of the 5th and 6th centuries A.D. contain many *mantras* and *dhāraṇīs*. A good number of the Mahāyāna Sūtras, especially the shorter Prajñāpāramitā Sūtras, are of the *Dhāraṇī* type. Of the extant *Dhāraṇis* having purely Tantric contents, reference should be made to the *Mahāmāyurī-Vidyārajñī*, translated into Chinese by Śrīmitra (beginning of the 4th century A.D) and Kumārajīva (beginning of the 5th century A.D);

Ekādaśamukha, translated into Chinese by Yaśogupta (6th century A.D.); *Nīlakaṇṭhadhāraṇī* discovered in Central Asia; and *Mahāpratyaṅgirā*, etc. Śāntideva has quoted a good number of *dhāraṇīs* in his *Śikṣāsamuccaya.*[4]

The spell *om maṇipadme hum* occurs in the *Divyāvadāna.*[5] The *Bodhisattvabhūmi* also contains numerous spells and deals with the mystic aspect of the syllables.[6] The Prajñāpāramitā Sūtras lay greater emphasis on the cult of the Female Principle. In these texts, the goddess Prajñāpāramitā is conceived of as the supreme being and the mother of all Tathāgatas. This cult, along with the sex rites associated with it, was probably popularised by the Andhra Vaitulyakas, as is hinted in a passage of the *Kathāvatthu.*[7] The *Kāraṇḍavyūha-sūtra*, an earlier Mahāyāna text, contains not only Tantric terminology and rituals as well as the concept of the Female Principle, but also some eminent Puranic deities who later became the chief objects of the Hindu Tantric cult. Its prose version refers to a rudimentary concept of Avalokiteśvara as emanating from an Ādi Buddha-like entity.[8] The same holds good in the case of the *Suvarṇaprabhāsasūtra* which is to a great extent Tantric in its contents, formulae, and rites.[9] It mentions four Dhyānī Buddhas, a few Bodhisattvas and goddesses associated with the cult of the Female Principle. The *Bhaiṣajyaguru-vaidurya praharāja* also shows remarkable Tantric influence. It specially mentions rituals of *ugra* or dreadful types.[10] The *Dharmasaṃgraha*, attributed to Nāgārjuna, knows of the five Dhyānī Buddhas and their female consorts and also of the eighteen *lokapālas*, six *yoginīs* and eight Bodhisattvas.[11] A rudimentary form of the doctrine of Ādi Buddha is indicated in the *Mahāyānasūtrālaṅkāra.*[12] In Śāntideva's *Śikṣāsamuccaya* mention is made of a number of deities who became prominent figures in the Vajrayāna. Texts such as the *Saddharmapuṇḍarīka*, *Sukhāvatīvyūha*, etc., contain many elements which foreshadow various Vajrayānic concepts.

We have asserted that the Tibetan tradition makes no distinction between Mahāyānism and Tantrism. The great exponents of Mahāyānism have been described in the Tibetan tradition also as experts in Tantric lore. According to this tradition Nāgārjuna, the great Mādhyamika theoretician, was a great *siddha* who promulgated esoteric teachings, medical sciences, and alchemy. We have already seen that there was more than one Nāgārjuna; there is no doubt that the Tibetan historians have caused confusion. Likewise, teachers like Asaṅga and Maitreyanātha have also been connected with Tantric ideas and practices. Bu-ston attributes to Maitreyanātha a work called *Mahāyānottāra-tantra*, a text in which the concept of the *Sahajakāya* is present. According to Hiuen Tsang, Asaṅga was gifted with certain mystic powers. It is possible that because these great theoreticians enjoyed great fame and prestige, the Tibetan writers wanted to associate Tantrism with them. At the same time it is not impossible that these teachers may have also contributed in some way or other to the growth of certain ideas and practices from which existing forms of Tantrism drew much inspiration.

Tenets of Tantric Buddhism

We have previously remarked that Mahāyāna Buddhism, in order to popularise itself among the masses, made a compromise with the existing local cults and rituals as a result of which numerous local, regional, and tribal deities were incorporated in the Buddhist religion. In the agrarian societies of India the cults and rituals of the Mother Goddess were a very powerful force. This female-oriented religious phenomenon assumed a distinct shape later in the Śākta religion. The cult of the Female Principle and the sexual rites involved therein have already been explained in terms of primitive Tantrism which was neither Hindu nor Buddhist. It was a very ancient way of life, an undercurrent which influenced all forms of Indian religious systems in some way or other. The concept of the primitive Mother Goddess of the agricultural societies contributed to the growth of that of Prakṛti as the embodiment of all the reproductive forces of nature, and subsequently to that of Śakti as the only principle responsible for the functioning of these forces. In Vaiṣṇavism this Śakti has been defined as Lakṣmī the consort of Viṣṇu, or Rādhā the consort of Kṛṣṇa; in Śaivism this Śakti is Devī, consort of Śiva; and in Buddhism it is conceived of in the forms of different goddesses associated with the Buddhas and the Bodhisattvas and at the philosophical level it has been conceived of as Prajñā or Śūnyatā.

Thus, with the influence of the concept of Śakti, the primitive Tantric rituals, basically sexual in character, the origin of which we have already discussed, made their way, as the highly technical and sophisticated culture of the Five Ms or *pañca-makāra*, into different kinds of religious systems. The Buddhists could not remain impervious to this trend; thus woman, flesh, and sexual intercourse came to be regarded as essential preconditions for the attainment of liberation. The idea of *yuganaddha*, i.e. god-in-sexual-union-with-the-goddess, an iconological form by which the Buddhas and Bodhisattvas were frequently represented, shows to what a great extent the Buddhists were influenced by the Tantric way of life. In Anangavajra's *Prajñopāya-Viniścayasiddhi* it is stated that for the experience of *mahāmudrā* the aspirant has to indulge in indiscriminate sexual intercourse. It is also stated that in order to achieve perfection he has to have sexual intercourse even with his mother and sister. The efficacy of wine, flesh, women, and sexual intercourse amounting even to incest is also stressed in the *Guhyasamāja* and other works on Tantric Buddhism.[13] Ideas similar to the Śākta *kāyasādhana* are also to be found in the Buddhist Tantras.

While the master logicians like Śāntideva, Diṅnāga or Dharmakīrti were devising hair-splitting arguments to interpret the world as a void entity, how Tantric ideas captured the heart of Buddhism through the backdoor, makes a very interesting historical topic. We have seen that already in the *Dhāraṇī* literature, which was composed about 4th-8th centuries A.D., references to *mantra, mudrā, kriyā, maṇḍala* and *caryā* are frequently found. In the *Mañjuśrīmūlakalpa*[14] we come across the goddess Tārā with the epithet Vidyārajñī and her various forms like Locanā, Māmakī, Pāṇḍarā, Bhṛkutī, Śvetā, Sutārā, etc. The *Guhyasamāja*[15] describes Locanā, Māmakī, Pāṇḍarā, and Śyāmatārā as emanations of the original Buddha Vairocana. The concept of Tārā as the highest goddess is found in the *Mahā-pratyaṅgirādhāraṇī* in which she has been described as having a white complexion, carrying thunderbolt in her hand, and as having the effigy of Vairocana on the crown. By the 8th century A.D. the cult of Tārā had become immensely popular. Many hymns in her praise were composed; the best one was the *Sragdharā-stotra* by the Kashmiri poet Sarvajñamitra.

The central theme of the two basic works on Tantric Buddhism—the *Mañjuśrīmūlakalpa* and the *Guhyasamāja*—deals with the *mudrās* and *maṇḍalas* connected with goddesses and spiritually-oriented women who can come from any class of people. The aspirant has to understand that woman, or her generative organ, is the source of existence and that sexual functioning is the imitation of the process of creation. By this process, from Ādi Buddha and his Śakti emanated the goddesses Locanā, Māmakī, Pāṇḍarā and Śyāmatāra who represent respectively form, sound, smell and touch—*dveśarati, moharati, rāgarati* and *vajrarati*; the four elements—earth, water, fire, and air; and four *skandhas—vedanā, saṃskāra, saṃjña,* and *vijñāna.* Locanā is earth, Māmakī water, Pāṇḍarā fire, and Tārā air.

According to the Tantric view, the act of creation is due to the union of the Female and Male Principles, the former being the more important functionary. In Buddhist Tantras these two principles are known as Prajñā and Upāya or as Śūnyatā and Karuṇā respectively. The union of Prajñā and Upāya is *yuganaddha* or *samarasa.* One who can unite these two principles in oneself can have the highest knowledge and supreme bliss and become free from the fetters of birth and death. This is real Buddhahood. In order to have this spiritual experience man and woman should first realise that they are representatives of Upāya and Prajñā respectively and that their physical, mental, and intellectual union alone can bring the experience of the highest truth. Accordingly men and women should jointly strive for this secret knowledge and culture. Prajñā is the Female Principle and as such she is Bhagavatī or the goddess herself. She is also known as Vajrakanyā and Yuvatī. The woman who is to impersonate Prajñā should preferably be a beautiful maiden of sixteen years. Prajñā also denotes the female sexual organ which is the seat of all happiness. Upāya, the Male Principle, is also known as Vajra, which means male generative organ. The union of man and woman, of Upāya and Prajñā, brings the maximum pleasure in which all mental action is lost and the world around forgotten; only a pleasing experience of non-duality prevails. This is known as Mahāsukha, the greatest pleasure, or Nirvāṇa, the *summum bonum,* and the real manifestation of Bodhicitta.

According to the Mahāyāna, Śūnyatā and Karuṇā, being combined, develop Bodhicitta (etymologically intellectual and mental faculties) which helps an individual to obtain *bodhi* or the highest knowledge. This Bodhicitta is achieved through ten stages or *bhūmis.* The highest stage is known as Dharmamegha where the striving individual becomes a Bodhisattva. In Tantric Buddhism the concept of Bodhicitta acquired a changed significance; its function here is to create Mahāsukha or Nirvāṇa through sexual union between man and woman. The motivating force behind this sole emphasis upon the physical union of man and woman is the ancient Tantric maxim: 'That which is not in the body, is not in the world'. The human body is the abode of all truth and therefore all the mysteries of the world should be explained in terms of those of the human body.

This ancient belief is at the root of the concept of *kāyasādhana*, so much emphasised in the Śākta and the Buddhist Tantras. According to the Śākta scheme there are six nerve cycles (*ṣaṭcakras*) within the human body and these are in the *mūlādhāra* (rectal region), *svādhiṣṭhāna* (the region around the generative organ), *maṇipura* (the region of the navel), *anāhata* (region around the heart), *viśuddha* (the region connecting the spinal cord and the lower portion of the medulla oblongata), and *ājñā* (the region between the brows). The highest cerebral region is known as *sahasrāra*. The *Kuṇḍalinī Śakti*, i.e., Śakti as serpent-power, remains latent in the *mūlādhara*. By Yogic exercises this *Kuṇḍalini Śakti* has to be pushed up through the two main nerves, *iḍā* and *piṅgalā*, so that it may reach the *sahasrāra* or the highest cerebral region where it should meet its source.

The Buddhist Tantras speak of three nerve-cycles symbolising the three bodies of the Buddha—*dharma, sambhoga* and *rūpa* or *nirmāṇa*. They also speak of an additional nerve-cycle which is *uṣṇīṣa-kamala* in the central cerebral region which is the symbol of the Buddha's *vajra-kāya* or *sahaja-kāya* and which corresponds to the Śākta concept of *sahasrāra*. Below this, around the neck is *sambhogacakra*, near the heart *dharmacakra*, and near the navel *nirmāṇacakra*. There are innumerable nerves within the body, of which thirty-two are vital. Of these, three are the most important—the two symbolising Prajñā and Upāya are on either side of the spinal cord and, in between them, into which both these are combined, is one which is known as *sahaja* or *avadhutī*. Like the *Kuṇḍalinī Śakti* of the Śākta Tantras, the Buddhist Tantras speak of a female energy having the force of fire which resides in the *nirmāṇacakra* and is known as Caṇḍālī. This Caṇḍālī, being accelerated, kindles the *dharma* and *sambhoga cakras* and ultimately reaches the *uṣṇisā-kamala*, the highest cerebral region, and then returns to its own place.[16]

Bodhicitta, Prajñā and Upāya

In Tantric Buddhism the Mahāyānic idea of Śūnyatā has been transformed into that of Vajra.[17] To the word *vajra*, which means thunderbolt and denotes the real nature of things which is Śūnyatā, is added the term *sattva* implying pure knowledge,[18] and the combination of these two principles has been crystallised in the form of a personal god, the supreme being, Lord Vajrasattva or Vajradhara, regarded as the essence of Śūnyatā—transcending all imagination, omniscient, embodiment of pure wisdom, abode of all merits, and so on.[19] The Mahāyānic idea of the three *kāyas* of Buddha seems to have contributed to the idea of *Vajra kāya* or *Sahajakāya* as the fourth *kāya* of Buddha in Tantric Buddhism. With the development of the idea of Vajrasattva or Vajradhara as the supreme being and also as the Ādi Buddha or the Primal Enlightened One, there evolved a new pantheon in the Vajrayāna—five Dhyānī Buddhās emanating from him and representing the five *skandhas*, namely, *rūpa* (material element), *vedanā* (feeling), *saṃjñā* (conceptual knowledge), *saṃskāra* (mental states) and *vijñāna* (consciousness). Details of this pantheon will be given in a subsequent section.

The supreme being of Vajrayāna is often equated with Bodhicitta. In Mahāyāna, as we have already seen, *bodhi* is pure knowledge and *citta* is the mind bent on attaining perfect enlightenment. It is in the latter that a perfect harmony of Śūnyatā and Karuṇā takes place. This view is maintained in Vajrayāna and in other schools of Tantric Buddhism which hold that Bodhicitta is a state of supreme realisation transcending both *bhava* (existence) and *nirvāṇa* (extinction); it is without beginning or end, quiescent, immutable in existence and also in non-existence, the non-duality of Śūnyatā and Karuṇā.[20] In Tantric Buddhism the terms Śūnyatā and Karuṇā are substituted by Prajñā and Upāya respectively, and in addition to their original connotation they are regarded as the Female and the Male Principles. In the *Hevajratantra*, Prajñā is conceived of as *mudrā* or woman and Upāya as the *yogin*, and their union is supposed to produce Bodhicitta as the embodiment of Śūnyatā and Karuṇā.[21] The union of Prajñā and Upāya is like a mixture of water and milk in a state of non-duality.[22]

We have seen that in the Buddhist Tantras Prajñā is variously designated as a goddess (Bhagavati),[23] a woman to be adopted for *sādhanā* (Mudrā, Mahāmudrā, Vajrakanyā), a young woman (Yuvatī),[24] and sometimes as the female organ.[25] In the *Hevajratantra* Prajñā is called Jananī (mother), Bhaginī (sister), Rajakī (washer-woman), Nartakī (dancing girl), Duhitā (daughter), Ḍombī (Ḍoma girl), etc. She is also the female organ, which is the seat of great pleasure (*mahāsukha*).[26] Prajñā and Upāya are also called Lalanā and Rasanā which are also names of the two nerves *iḍā* and *piṅgalā* which are said to carry seed and ovum respectively.[27] Prajñā and Upāya, as Lalanā and Rasanā respectively, have also been associated with the moon and the sun (*lalanā rasanā raviśaśī tuḍia veṇṇa vi pāse*). In some Buddhist Tantras such as the *Nirṇāda* or *Ucchuṣma*, Prajñā and Upāya have been identified with Śakti and Śiva.[29]

The principle of the union of Prajñā and Upāya is also known as Yuganaddha. In the *Pañcakrama*, Yuganaddha is technically defined as a state of absolute non-duality marked by the absence of notions like *saṃsāra* (worldly process) and *nivṛtti* (cessation of the process), *saṃkleśa* (adherence) and *vyavadhāna* (distinction), *grāhya* (perceivable) and *grāhaka* (perceiver), etc.[30] In the *Sādhanamālā*, Yuganaddha is also described as the non-dual state and identified with the Bodhicitta.[31] In other texts this principle is equated with the *dharma-kāya* of the Buddha.[32] In the Vajrayāna pantheon this principle is represented by the deity embracing his consort closely in the act of sexual union.[33] In the *Sādhanamālā* we find descriptions of the major deities, including the Dhyānī Buddhas, who are to be meditated on, as being in union with their female consorts.[34] In the *Herukatantra*,[35] Heruka is represented in sexual union with Vajravairocanī, a depiction of which is frequently found in sculptures.

The union of Prajñā and Upāya through the principle of Yuganaddha for the purpose of the realisation of the non-dual state, symbolised by the physical union of the adept and his female partner, brings in succession *rāga* and *mahārāga* (emotion and intense emotion, evidently transcendental, resulting from a genuine feeling of compassion), *samarasa* (oneness of emotion in which there is no cognition of Prajñā and Upāya), and finally the *mahāsukha* or great bliss leading to Nirvāṇa. This *mahāsukha* or great bliss is of the nature of the absolute unity of Prajñā and Upāya, the non-dual quintessence of all the entities, without which perfect wisdom is never possible.[36]

Buddhist and Hindu Tantras: Similarities in Modus Operandi

We have seen that originally Upāya was called Karuṇā, or the principle of compassion, and that subsequently it came to denote the Male Principle. For compassion another term was devised which was called Kṛpā. At a still later stage the original meaning of the term Upāya (the way or means) became more popular. The ultimate reality of Tantric Buddhism came to be regarded as the unity of Prajñā (wisdom) and Upāya (means). In the *Guhyasamāja*, Upāya is described as Vajrayoga or the way for obtaining *bodhi* or enlightenment. It is fourfold: *upasādhana, sādhana, mahāsādhana* and *sevā*. In Tantric Buddhism the word *sādhana* is especially used to mean the invocation of deity by meditating on his or her form or symbol, and the prefixes *upa* and *mahā* are suggestive of its degree and extent. *Sevā* is of two kinds, *sāmanya* and *uttama*, the former consisting of the four *vajra* practices—the feeling of vacuity (*śūnyata*), its transformation in the form of a seed (*bīja*), conception of the seed in the form of a deity (*vimba*), and the feeling of the deity in different parts of the body (*nyāsa*)—and the latter of the six Yogic practices—control of sense organs (*pratyāhāra*), meditation (*dhyāna*), breath-control (*prāṇāyāma*), concentration on *mantra* (*dhāraṇa*), remembrance (*anusmṛti*) and obtaining perfect wisdom (*samādhi*).[37] These practices are the same as those found in the non-Buddhist Tantras.

The Buddhist Tantras, like the non-Buddhist ones, lay much emphasis upon the importance of the *guru* or-preceptor. The *guru* is expected to have complete grasp over the mystic and confidential doctrines and practices; he should be reverenced even as the Lord. Without his guidance salvation is impossible to achieve and hence he should never be offended.[38] Even after the attainment of liberation the disciple should still cling to his teacher.[39] As in the Hindu Tantras, great importance is also attached to the *mantras* or spells. A *mantra* is a syllable or series of syllables of the same frequency, unmeaningful outwardly but having esoteric significance. In Chinese it is denoted by such terms as *chou* (incantations), *chen-yen* (true words) and *shen-chow* (divine spell) and in Tibetan by *gsan-sNags* (secret spells). The *mantra* tradition continues from the Vedic period. In fact Nāro-pa and Advayavajra were inclined to use the term Mantranaya to designate Tantric Buddhism.[40] It is said in the Buddhist Tantras that if the *mantras* are applied according to the proper rules anything can be performed; their power and efficacy are beyond dispute. They can even confer Buddhahood on the aspirant.[41] The concept of *maṇḍala* is also the same in the Hindu and Buddhist Tantras; it is described as the essence of all doctrines and is equated with Bodhicitta and Mahāsukha.[42]

The Vajrayāna Pantheon

In the *Tattvaratnāvalī*, collected in the *Advayavajrasaṃgraha*, Mahāyāna is subdivided into two schools—Pāramitānaya and

Mantranaya. The latter is claimed to be a distinctly superior way and is to be adopted only by those who are free from delusions and are of high intellectual calibre.[43] This Mantranaya or Mantrayāna is the precursor of Vajrayāna and its offshoots, Kālacakrayāna and Sahajayāna. Vajrayāna has no clear-cut definition in the Buddhist texts. In the *Guhyasamāja* it is described as the cult of five *kulas* or families of the Bodhisattvas, each representing a distinct mental state of the aspirant.[44] In the *Sādhanamālā* it is described as a path of transcendental perfect enlightenment, to be achieved through different rites and ceremonies, *mantras,* and meditations.[45] Elsewhere Vajrayāna is compared to a raft on which one can cross the ocean of existence.[46]

In practice Vajrayāna introduced the theory of five Dhyānī Buddhas as embodiments of the five *skandhas* or cosmic elements, formulated the theory of their *kulas* or families and also that of their emanat ions, the male and female deities. It also introduced the cult of Prajñā or Śakti. Vajrayāna considers Śūnya or vacuity as the ultimate reality and innumerable gods and goddesses as its manifestations. The gods have no real existence; they are born of the mind, issuing from the *bījamantras* uttered by the worshipper. The Śūnya takes the form of a divinity in accordance with the germ-syllable uttered and exists only as a positive idea in the mind of the aspirant. It takes different forms according to the different functions it has to discharge, for instance, the form of Siṃhanāda when a disease is to be cured, that of Jānguli when there is snakebite, that of Kurukullā when there is a love affair, and so on. The number of gods and goddesses increases when Śūnya manifests itself in different forms; since the inspirations of these manifestations are innumerable, the deities can also be innumerable.

But all thesse are creations of mind and basically symbolical. The cosmic concept of Śūnya or vacuity is thus naturally equated with Bodhicitta which has been defined as the mind bent on attaining perfect enlightenment. The weapons and emblems by which the deities of Vajrayāna are characterised are nothing but the weapons needed by the Bodhicitta to fight against the elements obstructing the path of knowledge. For instance, when the darkness of ignorance is to be dispelled the Bodhicitta becomes a sword, when the heart of the wicked is to be pierced it becomes the *aṅkuśa* or goad, when a bad element is to be cut away it becomes a *kartari* or knife, and so on. The *mudrās* also serve the same purpose. When protection is needed the Bodhicitta becomes *abhaya*; when a boon is desired it becomes *varada*; when instruction is required it becomes *dharmacakra*.[48]

The five cosmic elements, as we have seen, are deified in the Vajrayāna as the five Dhyānī Buddhas, emanating from the highest being Vajradhara or Vajrasattva (often conceived of as the sixth Dhyānī Buddha) who is identified with Śūnya and Ādi Buddha. Each of the Dhyānī Buddhas has a Śakti, a Bodhisattva and a number of emanations, male and female. By far the most ancient among the Dhyānī Buddhas is Amitābha who resides in the Sukhāvati heaven in peaceful meditation. The colour associated with him is red, originating from the red syllable *hrīḥ*. He belongs to the lotus family and is of the nature of the cosmic element called *saṃjñā*. He is an embodiment of attachment and stands for the vital fluid. He has a lotus as his symbol and he exhibits the *samādhi mudrā* in two hands. He presides over a group of letters beginning with *ṭa* (cerebrals). His consort or Śakti is Pāṇḍarā or Pāṇḍaravāsinī and his Bodhisattva Padmapāṇi who later became celebrated as Avalokiteśvara. Pāṇḍarā is conceived of as also originating from the red syllable *pāṃ*. She is the embodiment of the element of fire and also has the lotus as her symbol.

Akṣobhya originates from the blue syllable *huṃ* and represents the cosmic element *vijñāna* of consciousness. He belongs to the Vajra family and presides over a group of letters beginning with *ca* (palatal). He is two-armed and one-faced, exhibits the *bhūśparśa* (earth-touching) *mudrā* and sits in the *vajraparyaṅka* pose. His consort is Māmakī or Māmakā and Bodhisattva Vajrapāṇi. Māmakī's colour is also blue and she has all the symbols of Akṣobhya. She is the embodiment of the element water. Vajrapāṇi, when represented, either stands or sits, and carries usually a lotus on which is placed the family symbol of *vajra*. Sometimes he holds the *vajra* in one hand against his chest.

Vairocana originates from the white syllable *oṃ* and represents the cosmic element *rūpa* (form). He belongs to the family of Tathāgata and presides over a group of letters beginning with *ka* (guttural). He exhibits the *dharmacakra mudrā*. His symbol is a white discus, his vehicle a dragon. He also has a four-faced and eight-handed form. His consort is Locanā and Bodhisattva Samantabhadra. Locanā's colour is white and she has all the symbols of Vairocana. She is the embodiment of the cosmic element earth. The Bodhisattva Samantabhadra is also white in colour. He usually holds a stem of lotus on which the family symbol, *cakra* or discus, is shown.

Amoghasiddhi originates from the green syllable *khaṃ* and represents the cosmic element of *saṃskāra* (conformation). He belongs to the family of Karma and presides over a group of letters beginning with *pa* (labial). He is green and exhibits the *abhaya* (protection) posture. His symbol is double-thunder or *viśvavajra* and vehicle Garuḍa. His consort is Tārā, who was destined to play a greater role in subsequent religious history, and Bodhisattva Viśvapāṇi. Tārā's colour is green and she has all the symbols of Amoghasiddhi. She is the embodiment of the element of air. Viśvapāṇi is also green and has the symbol of *viśvavajra* or double thunderbolt.

Ratnasambhava originates from the yellow syllable *trāṃ* and represents the cosmic element of *vedanā* (sensation). He belongs to the family of Ratna and presides over a group of letters beginning with *ta* (dental). He is yellow and has a jewel as his symbol. His left hand rests on the lap with open plam, and the right exhibits the *varadamudrā.* His vehicle is a pair of lions. His consort is Vajradhātvīśvarī and Bodhisattva Ratanpāṇi. Vajradhātvīśvarī too is yellow and has all the symbols of Ratnasambhava. Ratnapāṇi is also yellow and has the symbol of the jewel.

Vajrasattva, who is sometimes considered as the sixth Dhyānī Buddha originates from the syllable *huṃ* and is white. He is two-armed and one-faced and holds in his hands the *vajra* and *ghaṇṭā* (bell). His worship is always performed in secret and is not open to those who are not initiated into the mysteries of Vajrayāna. Unlike the other Dhyānī Buddhas he wears all ornaments, also a rich dress and a crown. He is represented in two forms, single and *yuganaddha* (*yab-yum*). When represented in *yab-yum,* he is shown in close embrace with his Śakti who is generally known as Vajrasattvātmikā, carries the *kartari* (knife) in the right hand and *kapāla* (skull) in the left. The Bodhisattva of Vajrasattva is Ghaṇṭapāṇi whose colour is white and symbol *ghaṇṭā* (bell).[47]

Besides the five major Bodhisattvas deriving their origin from the five Dhyānī Buddhas there are others representing different aspects of life and universe. The *Niṣpannayogāvalī* mentions three lists each containing a set of sixteen Bodhisattvas. From these lists we have twenty-five names: Samantabhadra, Akṣayamati, Kṣitigarbha, Ākāśagarbha, Gaganagañja, Ratnapāṇi, Sāgaramati, Vajragarbha, Avalokiteśvara, Mahāsthāmaprāpta, Candraprabha, Jālinīprabha, Amitaprabha, Pratibhānakūṭa, Sarvaśokatamonirghātamati, Sarvanivāraṇaviṣkambhin, Maitreya, Mañjuśrī, Gandhahastī,

Jñānaketu, Bhadrapāla, Sarvāpāyanjaha, Amoghadarśin, Suraṅgama and Vajrapāṇi.[48]

Of these Bodhisattvas, Avalokiteśvara and Mañjuśrī became most popular. In the *Mahāvastu* we come across Avalokita Bodhisattva whose duty was to instruct new adherents. In the *Kāraṇḍavyūha* he is said to manifest himself in countless forms of godhead for the welfare of mankind. This explains why his forms have been multiplied. No less than 108 forms have been attributed to him which include almost all the Bodhisattvas and other Buddhist gods as Lokeśvaras. 'He soon became the most popular of the northern Buddhist gods, being looked upon as a representative of the Buddha, the guardian of the Buddhist faith until Maitreya should appear on earth as Mānuṣī Buddha.'[49] He is the embodiment of universal compassion. We come across at least thirty-eight *sādhanas* which describe a variety of his forms. Of all these forms, Padmapāṇi is the most common—generally one-faced and two-armed, and represented as displaying the *varada* pose with the right hand and holding a lotus stem with the left. Other important forms of Avalokiteśvara are Ṣaḍakṣarī Lokeśvara, Siṃhanāda, Khaṣarpaṇa, Lokanātha, Hālāhala, Padmanartteśvara, Harihariharivāhana, Trailokyavaśaṅkara, Rakta-Lokeśvara, Māyājalakrama, Nīlakaṇṭha, Sugatisandarśana, Pretasantarpita, Sukhāvati Lokeśvara, Vajradharma, etc. Many of these deities are well represented in sculpture.

Mañjuśrī is mentioned in the Buddhist texts as one of the greatest Bodhisattvas who confers upon his devotees wisdom, retentive memory, intelligence, and eloquence. According to the Nepalese tradition, as preserved in the *Svayambhū Purāṇa,* he was originally a human being who performed many pious deeds and subsequently came to be deified as a Bodhisattva. The *Āryamañjuśrīmūlakalpa*[50] contains the earliest conceptual description of Mañjuśrī. Forty-one *sādhanas* are ascribed to him in the *Sādhanamālā*. According to the *Niṣpannayogāvalī* he is three-faced and six-armed. In his three right hands he has the *Prajñāpāramitā* manuscript, a blue lotus, and a bow; and in the three left hands he has a sword, *varada-mudrā,* and arrow.[51] In sculptural representation he is generally one-faced and carries a sword in his right hand for dispelling ignorance and a manuscript in his left hand for transcendental wisdom. These symbols are often placed on lotuses. Of the different forms of Mañjuśrī described in the texts and represented in sculptures mention may be made of Vajrarāga, Dharmadhātu, Mañjughoṣa, Siddhaikavīra, Vajrānaṅga,

Nāmasaṅgīti, Vāgīśvara, Mañjuvara, Arapacana, Sthiracakra, Vādirāt, etc.

Each of the Dhyānī Buddhas has a number of emanations, gods and goddesses. Of the gods emanating from Amitābha mention may be made of Mahāvala and Saptaśatika Hayagrīva. Both of these deities bear the colour and effigy of Amitābha. Mahāvala is clad in a tiger-skin and wears ornaments of snakes. Saptaśatika Hayagrīva is also terribly awe-inspiring with three eyes, brown beard, protruding belly, garland of skulls, *vajra* and staff.[52] The female divinities that emanate from Amitābha are three in number, the most important and popular among them being Kurukullā, to whose worship no less than fourteen *sādhanas* are devoted in the *Sādhanamālā*. She is said to confer success in the Tantric rite of *vaśīkaraṇa* or the rite of enchanting persons. Her *mantra* is *Oṃ Kurukullā huṃ hriḥ svāhā* which, if uttered ten thousand times, is capable of bewitching any person, even if he be a king. When two-armed, she is called Śukla Kurukullā, and when four-armed she is called Tārodbhava Kurukullā, Uḍḍiyana Kurukullā, Hevajra-Krama Kurukullā and Kalpokta Kurukullā. Bhṛkutī is a companion of Avalokiteśvara as a minor goddess. She is four-armed, one-faced, three eyed, and blooming with youth. Mahāśitavatī is four-armed, one-faced and shown as being red.

The number of deities emanating from the Dhyānī Buddha Akṣobhya is quite large. The blue colour of Akṣobhya is associated with terrible deities. In fact, with the exception of Jambhala, all the male emanations of Akṣobhya have a terrible appearance—distorted face, bare fangs, three blood-shot eyes, protruding tongues, garlands of severed heads and skulls, tiger skin and ornaments of snakes. Of these deities Caṇḍaroṣaṇa is the most important figure in the celebrated *Caṇḍamahāroṣana tantra* dedicated to his cult. His worship is always to be performed in secret. His *dhyāna* is silent about his Śakti, but in paintings he is represented in *yab-yum* with his female consort. Heruka is one of the most popular deities of Tantric Buddhism to whose worship the *Herukatantra* is devoted. He stands on a corpse in the *ardhaparyaṅka* attitude, is clad in human skin with a *vajra* in his right hand and a *kapāla*, full of blood, in the left. From his left shoulder hangs a *khaṭvāṅga* in a flowing banner. Decked with ornaments of bones, his head is decorated with five skulls.

Nairātmā is the Śakti or Prajñā, i.e. the female consort of Heruka. When in embrace with this Śakti, Heruka is known as Hevajra. When represented singly, Nairātmā is conceptualised as dancing in *ardhaparyaṅka* on the breast of a corpse; he has two hands, the right holding *kartari* and left *kapāla* with *khatvāṅga*. Hevajra in *yuganaddha* form is popular in Tibet. To him is dedicated the *Hevajratantra*. He is also blue, one or three or eight-faced, two or four or sixteen-armed. The name of his Śakti differs according to the number of his heads. Like Nairātmā, Vajrayoginī is another Śakti of Heruka. This goddess is shown as being red or yellow in colour, standing in *alīḍha*, carrying her own severed head in her upraised left hand and *kartari* in her right hand. One should not fail to recall in this connection the Śākta-Tantric conception of Chinnamastā. Sambara is not very different from Hevajra, since he is also Heruka in *yuganaddha*, i.e. in union with his Śakti Vajravārāhī. Yogāmbara also belongs to this class and is conceived of as embracing his Prajñā Jñānaḍākinī. Likewise Buddhakapāla, another emanation of Akṣobhya, is another form of Heruka. The *Sādhanamālā* says that when Heruka is embraced by Citrasenā he gets the name Buddhakapāla.[53] Saptākṣara is also a variety of Heruka-Hevajra, embraced by Vajravārāhī. Like Sambara this god also tramples upon Kālarātri and holds the *viśvavajra* on the crown. His name is Saptākṣara because his *mantra* consists of seven syllables. Heruka-Hevajra takes the name of Mahāmāyā when he is embraced by his Śakti Buddhaḍākinī and remains with her in *yuganaddha*.

Of the other male emanations of Akṣobhya, Hayagrīva is an adaptation from the Hindu pantheon. We have already come across Saptaśatika Hayagrīva as an emanation of Amitābha. This Hayagrīva has a terrible appearance; he is red and has three faces and eight arms. A god of similar character is Paramāśva or the 'great horse' who has four faces, eight arms, four legs and four gods as his vehicle. He tramples with his right legs Indrāṇī, Śrī, Rati and Prīti, and with his left legs Indra, Madhukara, Jayakara, and Vasanta. Yamāntaka has been conceived of by the Buddhists as the opponent and killer of Yama, the Hindu god of death. When Yamāntaka is red he is called Raktayamāri and when blue Kṛṣṇayamāri Jambhala is the Buddhist counterpart of the Hindu god Kubera. He has also another form known as Ucchuṣma. He is the god of wealth, three-faced and six-armed, embracing Prajñā with his first left hand. Ucchuṣma has a protruding belly. He is nude and his generative organ is pointed upwards. Vighnānta, who is represented in various forms, is conceived of as an opponent of Gaṇeśa whom he tramples under foot.

Vajrahuṅkāra in the same way tramples upon Bhairava or Śiva. Likewise Vajrajvālānalārka is conceived of as trampling Viṣṇu. Bhūtaḍāmara is probably an adaptation from the Hindu Tantric pantheon to whose name is attributed a Tantra. This god also tramples upon the prostrate form of Aparājita whose anti-Buddhist character is not very clear. The most interesting deity of this series is Trailokyavijaya who is depicted as blue in colour, four-faced and eight-armed. He stands in *Pratyālīḍha* attitude, tramples upon the head of Maheśvara with his left leg, while the right presses upon the bosom of Gaurī.

Thus in the case of the male emanations of Akṣobhya we have two sets of deities, one representing the god in union with his Śakti and the other in relation to rival Hindu divinities. Gods like Viṣṇu, Śiva, Gaṇeśa, Pārvatī, Indra and others are represented as being trampled upon by more powerful Buddhist deities. Of the other male emanations of Akṣobhya, the remaining one is Kālacakra with whom we shall deal later.

In the case of the goddesses emanating from Akṣobhya we have many interesting deities, terrible as well as benign. There are also a few goddesses who have been adopted from the Hindu pantheon. Of the goddesses emanating from Akṣobhya, Jāṅguli is worshipped as the goddess who cures snake-bite and even prevents it. She corresponds to the Hindu goddesss Manasā or Viṣahari. It is interesting to note that in Hindu Purāṇas and Tantras Jāṅguli is an epithet of Manasā. Parṇaśabarī is the goddess who prevents the outbreak of epidemics. She is closely akin to the Hindu goddess Śitalā. Often she is described as an emanation of Amoghasiddhi. In sculpture she is represented as trampling the Vighnas under her feet, sometimes symbolised by Gaṇeśa. Vasudhārā is the consort of Jambhala, the Buddhist counterpart of the Hindu Kubera, the god of wealth. She corresponds to the Hindu conception of the Earth and Corn Mother. She is conceived of as a young girl of sixteen years, exhibiting the *varada mudrā* in the right hand and carrying the ears of corn in the left. Often she is regarded as an emanation of Ratnasambhava.

The second set of the goddesses emanating from Akṣobhya consists of those belonging to the Tārā group. Foremost among these deities is Mahācīnatārā, who is also known in Buddhist Tantric literature as Ugratārā. She has been incorporated in the Hindu pantheon under the name of Tārā and is regarded as one of the ten Mahāvidyā goddesses. It is interesting to note that the *dhyāna* of

Tārā, as is found in the *Tantrasāra* of Kṛṣṇānanda Āgamavāgiṣa, is directly borrowed from the *Sādhanamālā*. It is remarkable that even the association of Akṣobhya with Tārā is maintained in the Śākta Tantras. Ekajaṭā is also a form of Tārā whose cult is reported to have been brought to India by Siddha Nāgārjuna from Bhoṭadeśa or Tibet. Minor goddesses belonging to this group are Vidyujjālā-karāli, Vajracarcikā, Mahāmantrānusāriṇī, Mahāpratyaṅgirā, Dhvajāgrakeyurā, Jñānaḍākinī and Vajravidāraṇī.

Two other female emanations of Akṣobhya, Nairātmā and Prajñāpāramitā, should be mentioned separately. The former, as we have seen, is the consort of Heruka. The word Nairātmā means 'no soul'. It is another name for Śūnya in which the Bodhicitta merges on the attainment of Nirvāṇa. The purely abstract conception of Śūnya crystallised into that of the goddess Nairātmā, having the colour of the voïd sky, in whose embrace the Bodhisattva is said to remain in eternal bliss and happiness. That is why she is represented in union with her consort. Individually she is represented as standing in a dancing attitude on a corpse. Her face looks terrible with bare and protruding tongue, and she carries a *kartari* in her right hand and *kapāla* in the left. Her form resembles that of Kālī. Prajñāpāramitā is the embodiment of scriptural knowledge, and is conceived of as a beautiful goddess sitting on a white lotus and carrying a red lotus in the right hand and a *Prajñāpāramitā* manuscript in the left. Unlike other emanations of Akṣobhya, she has a very beautiful face and a pleasant expression. Often she was worshipped in the form of a book. Of her many forms *sita* (white), *pīta* (yellow) and *kaṇaka* (golden) are widely known. According to the Buddhist tradition the *Prajñāpāramitā* texts were preserved in the nether region and it was Nāgārjuna who was responsible for their restoration. Ārya Asaṅga is credited with having composed one of the *sādhanas* for the worship of Prajñāpāramitā which is said to confer wisdom and erudition on her devotees.

Only one god emanated from Vairocana—Nāmasaṅgīti.[54] All the other deities emanating from him are females, the most important of them being Mārīcī who is sometimes regarded as the consort of Vairocana. Mārīcī is a sun-goddess whose chariot is drawn by seven pigs. Sixteen *sādhanas* in the *Sādhanamālā* describe her six different forms—Aśokakāntā, Ārya-Mārīcī, Mārīcīpicuvā, Ubhayavarāhananā, Daśabhūjasita and Vajradhātvīśvarī. She can be recognised by the sow-face (if she has many faces one must be of a sow) and the seven pigs that pull her chariot. The goddess Uṣṇīṣavijayā is a popular deity, white complexioned, three-faced, three-eyed, youthful and decked in beautiful ornaments. Her four right hands display double-thunder, Buddha on lotus, arrow and *varada* pose, and her four left hands show a bow, noose, the *abhyaya* pose and a water vessel. Sitātapatrā Aparājitā, and Mahāsāhasrapramardinī are minor goddesses. The same also holds good in the case of Grahamātṛkā. Of the important goddesses emanating from Vairocana, besides Mārīcī, mention should be made of Vajravārāhī and Cundā. The union of Vajravārāhī and Heruka is the theme of the celebrated *Cakrasaṃvara-tantra.* Having various forms, Vajravārāhī is also called Ḍakinī which implies any Śakti with whom the *yuganaddha* worship may be performed. The name Vajravārāhī has evidently something to do with the Mātṛkā known as Vārāhī in the Hindu Purāṇas and Tantras. Cundā is the conceptual embodiment of the Buddhist Dhāraṇi work called the *Cundādhāriṇī* to which a reference is made by Śāntideva. The name of this goddes occurs in the *Mañjuśrīmulakalpa* and in the *Śikṣāsamuccaya.* Cundā images are found illustrated in *Prajñāpāramitā* manuscripts. This goddess is conceptualised as being four-armed, one-faced and white complexioned in the *Sādhanamālā.* In the *Niṣpannayogāvalī* there are three descriptions of Cundā. There are several images of Cundā with sixteen arms. These have been identified with the help of a miniature painting of sixteen-armed Cundā available in a Cambridge Mss. of *Prajñāpāramitā* (Add. No. 1643). This miniature bears a label: *Paṭṭikere Cundāvarabhāvane Cundā.*

Of the emanations of Amoghasiddhi, Vajrāmṛta is the only god, the rest are all goddesses mostly belonging to the Tārā group. Of the goddesses outside the Tārā group, we have already had occasion to deal with Parṇaśabari who is also conceived of as an emanation of Akṣobhya, Vajraśṛmkhalā and Vajragandhārī are minor goddesses. Only Mahāmāyūrī has some importance to whose name a text is dedicated. She has a green complexion, six arms and three faces, each endowed with three eyes. She shows in her three right hands a peacock's feather, arrow, and *varada* pose and in three left hands jewel, bow and a water-vessel held on the lap. Goddesses of the Tārā group are Khadiravanī Tārā, Mahāśrī Tārā, Ṣaḍbhujā Sitatārā, Dhanda Tārā and Sitatārā. Tārā is the common name applied to a large number of goddesses such as Jāṅguli, Parṇaśabarī, Mahācinatārā, Ekajaṭā and others. Khadiravanī Tārā is also known as Śyāma Tārā because of her green colour. She is endowed with two hands and shows the *varada mudrā* with the right and *utpala* in the left. This is the most common and most popular iconographical trait of Tārā. Khadiravanī can be recognised by the figures of the two attendant deities, Aśokakāntā Mārīcī and Ekajaṭā. Mahāśrī Tārā has two more attendants, Jāṅguli and Mahāmāyūrī and she is also green. Vaśya Tārā, also known by the name of Ārya-Tārā, looks exactly like Khadiravanī Tārā with the exception that she sits in *bhadrāsana* with both legs dangling. Tārā also has many-handed forms. Sīta Tārā is a white variety of Tārā with one face and four arms. Ṣaḍbhūjā Sita Tārā, as her name implies, is a six-armed form of white Tārā. Dhanada Tārā is one of the four-armed varieties of Tārā. The special features of this goddess are that she rides an animal, and like Vajra Tārā is surrounded by eight goddesses. Other varieties of Tārā will be mentioned later.

Of the emanations of Ratnasambhava, Jambhala and Ucchuṣma Jambhala are sometimes also regarded as the emanations of Akṣobhya. Jambhala is connected with wealth and is said to distribute gems, jewels and riches to his devotees. His Hindu counterpart is Kubera and consort Vasudhārā with whom he is very often represented in *yab-yum*. When single, Jambhala is golden complexioned and carries a mongoose in the left hand and a citron in the right. His consort Vasudhārā, the corn goddess, is often also regarded as an emanation of Akṣobhya. Of other goddesses emanating from Ratnasambhava Aparājitā is conceived of as trampling upon Gaṇeśa and in *capeṭadāna* (as if slapping someone) pose. Mahāpratisarā is represented either singly or in a *maṇḍala* in the company of four other deities. Vajrayoginī is identical in appearance with the Śākta goddess Chinnamastā. She is generally represented as accompanied by two yoginīs, one on either side of her. Female emanations of Ratnasambhava also consist of two deities of the Tārā group, Vajra Tārā and Prasanna Tārā. The former is conceived of in the middle of the circle of eight mothers. She is eight-armed, four-faced and decked in all ornaments. She has numerous forms. Prasanna Tārā is of terrible appearance. She is yellow and has eight faces and sixteen arms.

Besides the emanations of the five Dhyānī Buddhas, there are many other deities in the Vajrayāna pantheon—ten gods and six goddesses of direction, eight Uṣṇīṣa gods, five protectresses, four door goddesses, four Ḍākiṇīs, twelve Pāramitās, twelve *vaśita* goddesses, twelve Dhāriṇīs, four Pratisaṃvits and Tārās of five colours. Some Hindu deities have been incorporated in the Vajrayāna pantheon such as Mahākala, Gaṇapati, Gaṇapatihṛdayā, Sarasvatī,

Indra, Yama, Varuṇa, Kubera, Īśāṇa, Agni, Nairṛti, Vāyu, Brahmā, Viṣṇu, Maheśvara, Kārttikeya, Vārāhī, Cāmuṇḍa, etc.

Of all the goddesses of the Vajrayāna pantheon Tārā became the most celebrated as the consort of Avalokiteśvara. In practice most of the Buddhist male deities of the later period came to be known as Avalokiteśvara or Lokeśvara, and all of the female deities came under the general name Tārā. Different forms of this goddess were classified from the viewpoint of her colour. To the red Tārā group belonged Kurukullā; to the blue group Ekajāṭā and Mahācinatārā; to the yellow group, Vajratārā, Jāṅguli, Parṇaśabarī and Bhṛkutī; to the white group Aṣṭamahābhayatārā, Mṛtyuvañcanatārā, Caturbhūja-tārā, Ṣaḍbhūja-Sitatārā, Viśvamātā, Kurukullā and Jāṅguli; and to the green group Khadiravanī-tārā, Vaśyatārā, Ārya-tārā, Mahattarī-tārā Varada-tārā, Durgottāriṇītārā, Dhanada-tārā, Jāṅguli and Parṇaśabarī. This shows that all the major goddesses of Vajrayāna came to be known as Tārā. In fact the cult of this goddess became so popular that in the Śākta Tantras also she has been given the position of the supreme being. The spread of the Tārā cult in Tibet and China has been described in the first part of this work.[55]

Kālacakrayāna

Kālacakrayāna is an offshoot of Vajrayāna. There is a Buddhist Tantra called *Kālacakratantra* which introduces the cult of Kālacakra. The cult of Kālacakra came into vogue in the 10th century and also became popular in Tibet and China.[56] He is considered as the principal deity in the Kālacakramaṇḍala of the *Nispannayogāvalī*. He is conceived of as dancing in *āḷīḍha* attitude on the bodies of Anaṅga and Rudra lying on the back. He is blue in colour, wears a tiger-skin and has twelve eyes, four faces and twelve principal hands on each side. His subsidiary hands, evidently symbolic, are twenty-four thousand. In the four blue right hands are held *vajra,* sword, *trisula* and *kartari,* in the four red hands are shown fire, arrow, *vajra* and *aṅkuśa,* and in the four white hands discus, knife, rod and axe. In the four blue left hands are shown *vajra*-marked bell, the plate, the *khaṭvāṅga* with the gaping mouth, and *kapāla* full of blood. In the four red hands can be seen bow, noose, jewel and lotus. The four white hands hold a mirror, *vajra,* chain, and the severed head of Brahmā.[57] However, the description of this god is insufficient to explain the creed. About Kālacakrayāna Waddell wrote:

In the tenth century A.D. the Tantric phase developed in Northern India, Kashmir and Nepal, into a monstrous and poly-demonist doctrine, the Kālacakra, with its demoniacal Buddhas, which incorporated the Mantrayāna practices, and called itself the Vajrayāna or the 'Thunderbolt vehicle', and its followers were named Vijrācāryā or followers of the thunderbolt.... The extreme development of the Tantric phase was reached with the Kālacakra which, although unworthy of being considered as a philosophy, must be referred to here as a doctrinal basis. It is merely a coarse Tantric development of the Ādi Buddha theory combined with the puerile mysticism of Mantrayāna, and it attempts to explain creation and the secret powers of nature, by the union of the terrible Kālī, not only with the Dhyānī Buddhas, but even with Buddha himself. In this way Ādi Buddha, by meditation evolves a procreative energy by which the aweful Sambharā and other dreadful Dākinī fiendesses, all of the Kālī type, obtain spouses as fearful as themselves, yet spouses who are regarded as reflexes of Ādi Buddha and the Dhyānī Buddhas. And these demoniacal 'Buddhas' under the name of Kālacakra, Heruka, Acala, Vajrabhairava, etc., are credited with powers not inferior to those of the celestial Buddhas themselves, and withal ferocious and blood-thirsty; and only to be conciliated by constant worship of themselves and their female energies, with offerings and sacrifices, magic circles, special *mantra*-charms, etc.[58]

On the basis of the Cambridge University Library manuscript of *Sri Kālacakratantra*[59] S.B. Dasgupta has rightly observed:

A study of the text does not confirm the statement that Kālacakrayāna is not that school of Tantric Buddhism which introduced the demoniacal Buddhas in its province—at least it is not the main characteristic through which the school should be recognised.... It is a system of Yoga which, with all its accessories of *maṇḍala* (magic circle) and consecration (*abhiṣeka*), is explanied within this very body... how all the universe with all its objects and localities are situated in the body and how time with all its varieties (viz. day, night, fortnight, month, year, etc.) are within the body in its process of the vital wind. In the body of the text Sahaja has been fully explained and the details of the sexo-yogic practices for the attainment of the Sahaja have also been described.[60]

The word Kālacakra means the wheel of time. Its Tibetan synonym dus-kyi-k'or-lo also means the circle of time. The theory of Kālacakra has also been explained by Abhinavagupta[61] in terms of the wheel of time and the process of keeping oneself above the influence of the whirl of time. The process of controlling time is possible, according to this authority, by controlling the vital winds in the nerves through yogic practices.[61] From the *Śekoddeśaṭikā*,[62] which is a commentary on the Śekoddeśa section of the *Kālacakra-tantra,* it is known that by *kāla* is denoted the ultimate immutable and unchanging reality remaining in all the elements and by *cakra* is meant the unity of the three kinds of existence, and as such Kālacakra is the same as the unity of Prajñā and Upāya.[62] In principle there is therefore no difference between Vajrayāna and Kālacakrayāna. Lord Śri Kālacakra is not basically different from Ādi Buddha or Vajrasattva or Vajradhara. In the *Laghu-Kālacakraṭīkā,* entitled the *Vimalaprabhā,*[63] Kālacakra is conceived of as the nature of Śūnyatā and Karuṇā. He is the source of the Buddhas, possessing the three *kāyas,* symbolical of the three times—past, present, and future. He is the Bodhicitta, the ultimate immutable substance, and is embraced by the goddess Prajñā in the absolute non-dual state.

Like other Anuttarayoga Tantras, the *Kālacakra* insists on Buddhahood, characterised by the four bodies (*kāyas*) of the Buddha. Besides the traditional three *kāyas* it refers to a fourth which is known as pure (*śuddhakāya*) or innately produced body (*sahajakāya*). The four letters of the word *kālacakra* symbolize the states of waking (*jāgrat*), dream (*svapna*), deep sleep (*suṣupti*) and the ultimate (*turīya* or *nīrāvaraṇa*). The state of Buddhahood is that of absolute bliss and knowledge, to be obtained by the practice of *mahāmudrā.* It is to be accomplished through practice (*sādhana*) which has two stages, that of generation (*utpattikrama*) and that of completion (*niṣpannakrama*). There are eleven initiations, the first ten of which are mundane (*laukika*) and the last one supramundane (*alaukika*), the former being obtained by the *maṇḍalas* and other practices and the latter by the practice of *mahāmudrā.*

The *Vimalaprabhā* on the *Kālacakra Tantra* is not restricted only to Tantric Buddhism, but includes matters related to the Vedas, Purāṇas, Dharmaśāstras, Yogaśāstras, Hindu Tantras, Āyurveda, alchemy, astronomy, philosphical systems, etc. According to this commentary the main thurst of the Kālacakra is the intutive wisdom or *prajñā* which is to be cultivated through the method of *vajrapada* by unifying the psychic nerves *lalanā* and *rasanā.* Both empiricism and transcendence are crystallised in *vajrapada.* All the *skandhas, dhātus* and *āyatanas* mark the *cakra* or wheel in the body. Just as the clockwise fragmentation of *kāla* or time, the vital breath (*prāṇa*) with its segments rests on the *cakras* and moves around them in the same way as the sun moves around the zodiac covering season and years. The *mahāmudrā* is conducive to the understanding of *sahaja* or the real nature of the things and as such it is called *sahajamudrā.* The aspirant should realise *advaya* or non-duality and have in himself the spark of Vajradhara or Vajrasattva through the four *yogas* of *mahāmudrāsiddhi* which are *śuddhajñanika* (pertaining to wisdom), *cittadharmika* (pertaining to mind), *vāksambhogaika* (pertaining to speech) and *kāyanirmāṇa* (pertaining to body). To quote Gagannatha Upadhyaya.

The text offers a conceptual image of *kāla* as being of the nature of a synthesis of phenomenal *karma* and *śūnyata* which truely symbolises *cakra,* what is great bliss, *kāla,* the seetheless (*paramākṣara*), weaves out the *skandhas* and *dhātus,* but is not of form but 'formless'. The body is like the wheel and thus the Kālacakra should be known 'Wisdom of the indestructible' to be as *prajñā,* and also *kāla* what is compassionate and wheel as the symbol of all the knowable world. Bliss is *Sūnyātmikā-prajñā* and the world is symbolised by the *cakra.* The abstruse nature of the Kālacakravajrayoga needs the grace of *yogini* to encounter the obstacles for which meditative practices are to be performed.This should be done with the help of a virtuous *guru* ... The Kālacakra, thus understood, is Bhagavān. He is Bhagavān for obliterating the evil and possesses all the qualities like *aiśvarya,* the great prosperity ... Literal and symbolic truths (*paramārthasamvṛti-satyobhyam*) have been drawn on the themes of Kālacakra. Thus the *prajñopāyātmakavajrayoga* is manifested in it that belongs to Lord Vajrasattva. The Vajrasattva possesses the natural body and has access to the moment of ultimate bliss. Contextually, *bhavanirvāṇa* in place of *apratiṣṭha-nirvāṇa* has been transcribed. The Kālacakra does not accept the *vīrakrama* and *svādhiṣṭhānakrama,* but only the *viśuddhakrama* for the inculcation of *mahāmudrā,* that which illumines the Paramādibuddha Tantra.[64]

Sahajayāna

Sahajayāna is also an offshoot of Vajrayāna. The word Sahaja means 'easy'. In philosophy the term *sahaja* denotes the ultimate inner nature of beings and elements; and in a religious sense it denotes the easiest or the most natural way by which human nature itself will lead the aspirant to realise the truth. Instead of suppressing, and thereby inflicting undue strain on human nature Sahajayāna holds that truth is something which can never be found through the prescribed codes of study, discipline, conduct, worship, and ritual. What is natural is the easiest, and hence there is no need for religious formalities, austere practices of discipline, reading and philosophising, fasting, constructing temples and images, and so on. This distinguishes Sahajayāna from Vajrayāna, although the exponents of the former recognise the well-known texts of the latter as their authority.

There is no exclusive literature belonging to Sahajayāna except the *dohās* and songs which have been the main source of inspiration of the regional literature of eastern India. In 1907 M.M. Haraprasad Sastri discovered as many as fifty songs composed by different Siddhācāryās belonging to Sahajayāna and these were published in 1917 under the caption *Bauddha Gān O Dohā*. Subsequently P.C. Bagchi was able to discover in the Tanjur collection the Tibetan translation of all these songs. Later investigations in this field show that these Buddhist Sahajiyā *dohā* and *caryā* songs were popular in a very wide area during a period roughly from the 8th to the 12th century A.D. P.C. Bagchi dicovered and published more *dohās* composed by Sarahapāda and Kānhapāda and also a number of *dohās* composed by Tillopāda. Rahula Samkrityayana too had discovered and published many more *dohās* of Sarahapāda and also published the Tibetan translation of many *dohās* of Saraha the originals of which are still missing. A number of important books have been written since the discovery of these *dohās* by eminent scholars in this field. In particular, light has been thrown on the Buddhist Sahajiyā cult and its various ramifications by S.B. Dasgupta in his *Obscure Religious Cults* and on the Vaiṣṇava Sahajiyā movement of Bengal by M.M. Bose in his *Post-Caitanya Sahajiyā Cult*.

The Sahajayāna considers the human body itself as the seat of all human experience including that of *sahaja-mahāsukha* which is the peaceful, blissful, radiant and waveless experience of *sahaja*. According to them everything lies within the human frame; the human body is the microcosm of the universe. In the matter of sexo-yogic practices, the Sahajiyā Buddhists go further than the Vajrayānists by laying greater emphasis on two points: the imperative necessity of making the body sufficiently strong and fit before starting with yogic processes, and the conception of an internal female force in the *nirmāṇacakra* (the navel region) corresponding to that of the *kula-kuṇḍalinī śakti* of the non-Buddhist Tantras. In this system, the identification of Upāya with the Male and Prajñā with the Female Principle has caused the transformation of the character of physical discipline into a kind of sexo-yogic practice, thus introducing an external element into it in the shape and form of a woman.

The Sahajayāna may rightly be regarded as the precursor of the medieval religious reform movements. Many elements in the Sant tradition and other protestant and non-conformist sects have been directly influenced by its theories and practices. That is why Sahajayāna requires elaborate treatment which we propose to do in a subsequent chapter.

NOTES

1. Th. Stcherbatsky, The *Central Conception of Buddhism*, rpt., New Delhim, 1970, pp. 65ff.
2. G.N. Roerich, *The Blue Annals* (tr. of *Deb-ther sṅon-po*, 2 parts, Calcutta, 1949, 1953), II, p. 102
3. Cf. *Lalitavistara*, BST, I, p. 1; *Samādhirāja*, BST, II, p. 250; *Saddharmapuṇḍarīka*, BST, IV; pp. 234-5; *Lankāvatāra*, BST, III, Ch. IX; *Kāraṇḍavyūha*, BST, XVII, p. 301, etc.
4. Ed. C. Bendall, pp. 142ff.
5. Ed. Cowell and Neil, p. 218.
6. Ed. U. Wogihara, pp. 273-4.
7. XXIII. 219.
8. BST, XVII, pp. 262-3, 292-304.
9. R.L. Mitra, *Sanskrit Buddhist Literature of Nepal*, Calcutta, 1888, pp. 241ff.
10. *Gilgit Mss.*, I, pp. 13-24; BST, XVII, pp. 168-9.
11. BST, XVII, p. 329.
12. IX. 77.
13. Cf. *Prajñopāya*, V. 25; *Jñānasiddhi*, I. 80-2; *Guhyasamāja*, pp. 20, 120.
14. Ed. G. Sastri, pp. 504, 647-8.
15. Ed. B.T. Bhattacharyya, p. 2.
16. For details see S.B. Dasgupta, *An Introduction to Tantric Buddhism*, Calcutta University, 1974, pp. 77ff.
17. *Advayavajrasaṃgraha* (GOS), p. 37
18. Ibid., p. 24.
19. *Prajñopāya*, III. 9; V. 45.
20. *Jñānasiddhi* (GOS), pp. 72-3.
21. *Kṛpo-pāyo bhaved yogī mudrā hetu-viyogataḥ śūnyatā karuṇā-bhinnaṃ bodhicittam iti smṛtam* Paṭala X.
22. *Prajñopāya*, p. 5; cf. *Advayavajrasaṃgraha*, pp. 2, 26, 55.
23. *Advayavajrasaṃgraha*, p. 62; *Sādhanamālā*, pp. 321, 329; etc.
24. *Guhyasamāja*, p. 19; *Śrīcakrasambhāra*, p. 28; *Ḍākārṇava*, Sahitya Parisad edn., p. 157, etc.
25. *Guhyasamāja*, p. 153; *Prajñopāya*, p. 42; *Jñānasiddhi*, II, 11; *Herukatantra Mss.*, ASB, p. 23, etc.
26. *Hevajra* (Snellgrove), Pt. I, pp. 90ff.
27. *Sādhanamālā*, p. 448.
28. *Dohākośa* of Kānhapāda, verse 5.

29. *Advayavajrasaṃgraha*, pp. 28ff.
30. *Pañcakrama*, Ch. V.
31. *Sādhanamālā*, p. 17.
32. Cf. *Śekoddeśa-ṭīkā* (GOS), p. 57.
33. *Śricakrasambhāra*, pp. 27, 29.
34. Vol. II, pp. 491ff.
35. ASB, Mss. p. 31.
36. *Advayavajrasaṃgraha*, p. 50.
37. *Guhyasamāja*, Ch. XVIII, pp. 16ff.
38. *Śekoddeśa-ṭīkā* , p. 24; *Guhyasamāja*, p. 20; *Sādhanamālā*, II, p. 586 *Jñānasiddhi*, pp. 12, 33, 71, 72.
39. *Hevajra*, I, p. 65.
40. *Śekoddeśa-ṭīkā* , pp. 2-5; *Advayavajrasaṃgraha*, p. 14.
41. *Sādhanamālā*, I, pp. 87, 270, 334; II, 575, 600; *Guhyasamāja*, pp. 27ff; *Hevajra*, I, pp. 50ff., etc.
42. *Hevajra*, I, p. 97.
43. *Advayavajrasaṃgraha*, p. 21.
44. *Guhyasamāja*, p. 154.
45. *Sādhanamālā*, I, p. 225; II. 421.
46. *Jñānasiddhi*, p. 31.
47. The conceptual descriptions of the Dhyānī Buddhas are to be found in the *Advayavajrasaṃgraha*, pp. 40-1.
48. *Niṣpannayogāvalī*, pp. 50ff.
49. A. Getty, *Gods of Northern Buddhism*, Oxford, 1928, p. 58.
50. 40-1, 61-4, 111, 304, 415, 317-19, 322, 447, 460.
51. *Niṣpannayagāvalī*, p. 50.
52. *Sādhanamālā*, pp. 507, 509.
53. *Sādhanamālā*, pp. 501-2.
54. His conceptual description is found in Amṛtānanda's *Dharmakośasaṃgraha* (ASB, Mss.) Fol. 91.
55. For the best classification of the deities of Vajrayāna, along with their conceptual and iconographical details, made on the basis of the *Sādhanamālā* and the *Niṣpannayogāvalī* readers are requested to see *Indian Buddhist Iconography* (rvd. edn. 1958) by Benoytosh Bhattacharyya. For their supplementation by extant sculptural specimens see my chapter in *East Indian Bronzes* (Calcutta University, 1978).
56. W.E. Clark, *Two Lamaistic Pantheon*, Harvard Yenching Institute Monograph Series, Cambridge, Mass. Vol. II, pp. 49, 233; A. Getty, op. cit., p. 146; A.K Gordon. *The Iconography of Tibetan Lamaism*, Columbia University Press, New York 1939, pp. 84-5.
57. *Niṣpannayogāvalī*, pp. 83-4.
58. L.A. Waddel, *Lamaism*, London, 1895, pp. 15, 31.
59. Cambridge MS, Add. No. 1364; critical edn. of the *Kālacakratantra* by B. Banerjee, Calcutta, 1985.

60. *An Introduction to Tantric Buddhism*, Calcutta, 1974, p. 66.
61. *Tantrāloka*, KSS, XVII, 1918, Ch. 6.
62. Ed. by Mario E. Carelli, GOS, Baroda, 1941.
63. Ed. in 3 vols. by Jagannath Upādhyaya, V.V. Dwivedi and J. Sastri Pande, Sarnath, 1986-95.
64. Ibid., I, preface.

7

Tantric Ideas and Practices in Medieval Religious Systems

Tantrism and Medieval Vaiṣṇavism

Rāmānuja (A.D. 1016-1137), the greatest exponent of the Śrīvaiṣṇava sect,[1] composed a commentary on the *Brahmasūtra* which came to be known as *Śrībhāṣya*[2] and tried to interpret the main tenets of Vaiṣṇavism in the Vedantic line. In *Mahābhārata* the Sāṅkhya theory is so modified as to make both Puruṣa and Prakṛti aspects of one *brahman* who is said to have produced from himself the *guṇas* of constituents of Prakrti.[3] The *brahman* of the Upaniṣads was invested with a distinct personality, and was called Īśvara, who appeared under different names and with whom the great gods of the sectarian religions were identified. The Purāṇas maintain this tradition. According to Śaṅkara, since *brahman* is one and without a second, there can be no reality apart from *brahman*, and hence the material world is actually non-existent, as false as a dream. He contends that the supposed existence of the world is a misconception which has developed out of a false sense of duality. A dualistic approach, on the other hand, is found in Bhāskara's commentary on the *Brahmasūtra* which emphasises the transformation (*pariṇāma*) of *brahman* and holds that the world of matter has real existence, though it is essentially of the same nature as *brahman*.[4]

Rāmānuja's interpretion is in between these two lines, and that is why it is known as Viśiṣṭādvaitavāda. According to Rāmānuja, the universe of *cit* (the sentient), *jīva* or *jīvtāmā*, individual soul, being endowed with life or consciousness and *acit* (the non-sentient, non-conscious elements, the material world) has its ultimate source in *brahman*, who is real (*satya*), conscious (*jñāna*), and infinite (*ananta*); it derives its essetial nature and function from *brahman*, who is known as the indwelling self (*antaryāmin*) of all beings. The entire creative process is the self-expression of *brahman* who reveals himself in creation. *Brahman* is *sat* (real) without a second and becomes the manifold of the sentient and non-sentient beings, the purpose of which is to give an opportunity for the finite beings to realise their divine destiny. He assumes three forms—*bhoktā* or the enjoyer manifested in *cit* or individual souls, *bhogya* or the enjoyable manifested in *acit* or the material world, and *preritā* manifested in Īśvara or Paramātman, the cause of creation, preservation and destruction.

According to Rāmānuja this *brahman* is no other than Viṣṇu who appears to his devotees in five forms: *parā, vyūha, vibhava, antaryāmin* and *arcā*, the well-known Pāñcarātra categories. The Śakti of Viṣṇu is Lakṣmī. According to the Pāñcarātra Āgamas, the Śakti or energy of Viṣṇu has the double aspect of *kriyā* and *bhūti*, answering to force and matter, and this effects the creation of the world. The Śrīvaiṣṇava school holds that the relation between Viṣṇu and his energy is one of inseparable connection like that of substance and quality. This Śakti element is probably due to some kind of Tantric influence.

After the death of Rāmānuja the Śrīvaiṣṇavas were subdivided into two groups, Vaḍakalai and Ṭenkalai, the former depending on Brahmanical tradition, Brahmanical social and legal system and Sanskrit language, and latter on non-Brahmanical and non-Sanskritic traditions. In the field of devotion the Vaḍakalai group believed in *markaṭa-mārga* (the devotee should cling to God just as a monkey-child clings to its mother) while the Ṭenkalai group believed in *mārjāra-mārga* (the devotee should remain effortless and surrender to God's will just as a kitten remains quite passive in its mother's mouth when she carries it from one place to another). The Ṭenkalai group did not believe in rituals, external formalities in regard to religious quest, caste-system, subordination of women, and social authoritarianism, all of which reminds us of the Sahajiyā tradition.[5]

Nimbārka (12th century) was another great exponent of Southern Vaiṣṇavism, though his disciples were mainly North Indians. His philosophy was known as Dvaitādvaitavāda and the sect which he founded was known as Sanaka-Sampradāya. Nimbārka composed a commentary on *Brahmasūtra*[6] and a small text called *Daśaślokī*.[7] According to him, *brahman* is both the material (*upādāna*) and instrumental (*nimitta*) cause of the world. *Brahman* is not the impersonal absolute, but a personal god—Kṛṣṇa or Hari. Like Bhāskara and Yādava he also believed in the theory of the transformation of *brahman.* He did not, however, explain how *brahman* might be regarded as the material and efficient cause of the world. This has been explained in Puruṣottama's *Vedāntaratnamañjuṣā* in which it is stated that during dissolution (*pralaya*) the entire universe returns to and remains in him in a subtle state as his natural powers. At the beginning of creation he manifests his *cit sakti* (power of sentience) and *acit sakti* (power of non-sentience) in the forms of soul and Prakṛti, and from the latter there is a gradual evolution of the material world. Since there is always a difference between the cause and the effect there must be some difference between *brahman* and the universe. Again the non-difference between them is no less true since in essence the effect is the cause itself. This cause-effect relation between *brahman* and the world is that of *identity-in-difference* (dvaitādvaita). Creation is due not to any need felt by God but merely for his sport. This god is Kṛṣṇa and his Śakti is Rādhā.[8]

Madhva, the expounder of the Dvaita or the dualistic school and the founder of the Brahma sect, flourised in Karnataka about the beginning of the 13th century. He was the celebraed author of thirty-seven works including a commentary on the *Brahmasūtra.* According to Madhva, *brahman* is *alaukika* (transcendent) and hence empirical knowledge will not help in determining his conception. The world of *cetana* (*cit*) and *acetana* (*acit*) is real, essentially *paratantra* or dependent having derived its reality from *brahman* who is no other than Viṣṇu whose Śakti is Lakṣmī. The sect founded by Madhva was later subdivided into two groups—Vyāsakūṭa and Dāsakūṭa. The former was conservative like the Vaḍakalai of the Śrīvaiṣṇavas while the latter was liberal.[9]

The Śuddhādvaita school of Vallabha, also known as *Rudra Sampradāya,* considers *brahman* as the embodiment of *sat* (existence), *cit* (consciouness), *ānanda* (bliss), and *rasa* (sentiment). For *līlā* (sport) he creates the world out of himself, and is thus both the efficient and material cause of the universe. He does not undergo any change even when he transforms himself into the world. This doctrine is known as *avikṛtapariṇāma.* This *brahman* is no other than Kṛṣṇa. He represents the principle of love by which his relation with the individual souls is determined. This love is of that type which takes place between a man and a woman. The Female Principle is idealised in Rādhā. Every individual should feel womanly passion for the beloved who is one and only one, the eternal lover Kṛṣṇa. The Rudra Sampradāya believed in *puṣṭimārga* or worldly enjoyment which was not considered as a bar to spiritual realisation.[10]

The Acintyabhedābheda school, also known as Gauḍīya or Bengal school, founded by Caitanya, holds that *brahman* is the material as well as the efficient cause of the universe and that he transforms himself into the universe remaining unaffected by the transformation.[11] There are three main *Śaktis* of *brahman*: *svarūpa* or *cit* (the sentient), *māyā* (non-sentient, material element same as *acit*) and *jīva* (intermediate). *Brahman* creates the universe with the help of his *māyā-śakti* which has two aspects, *guṇa-māyā* and *jīva māyā*, the former consisting of the three *guṇas* transforming at the time of creation into the constituents of the material world, and the latter with the power transmitted helps the creation by making individuals forget their selves and their relation with *brahman*. The universe is the *pariṇāma* (transformation) of *brahman* transfused with the *māyā*-śakti but still remaining untouched by *māyā*.[12] Here also *brahman* is identified with Kṛṣṇa who has a form resembling that of a human being but is really infinite and all pervading.

The concept of the *Śakti* of Viṣṇu or Kṛṣṇa has obviously been influenced by Tantric ideas. This *Śakti* was conceived by Rāmānuja and Madhva to be Lakṣmī and by Nimbārka, Vallabha and Caitanya as Rādhā. The doctrine of Rādhā found its first expression in the poems of the Āḷvar poetess Āṇḍal. Kṛṣṇa's sport with the Gopīs was foreshadowed in the *Bhāgavata-purāṇa* which was composed about 9-10th centuries A.D. The relation between Rādhā and Kṛṣṇa has been viewed from a special angle in Jayadeva's *Gītagovinda* (12th century), the *Brahmavivarta Purāṇa* (13th century), and in the poems of Vidyāpati and Caṇḍīdāsa. This special angle is the viewpoint of Sahajiyā which we have already mentioned in connection with Buddhism. The union of Kṛṣṇa and Rādhā, like that of the Buddhist Karuṇā and Śūnyatā or Upāya and Prajñā, symbolises the union of the Male and the Female Principles. Jayadeva's *Gītagovinda*, has been described by Nābhāji in his *Bhaktamāla* as *kokakāvya navarasa-śṛṅgāra-kau-āgāra*. In fact he wanted to put it in the same category as Kokkaka's *Ratirahasya*. Jayadeva described himself as a follower of the Sahajiyā tradition . The Parakiyā theory of Vaiṣṇavism evidently derived its main impulses from the Sahajayāna of the Buddhists. Jayadeva, Vidyāpati, Caṇḍīdāsa, Rūpa, Sanātana, Jiva Gosvāmin and others are reported to have followed the Sahajiyā way. Even Caitanya himself is said to have practised the Sahajiyā discipline with a female partner. In the *Vivartavilāsa* of Akiñcana Dāsa there is a list of female partners of the celebrated Vaiṣṇava aspirants.[13]

In Bengal and Orissa specially Tantrism exerted a tremendous influence on Vaiṣṇava ideas and practices. The Tantric goddess, Ekānaṃśā, was able to find her way into the Vaiṣṇava religion as the consort of Kṛṣṇa. Her image between Kṛṣṇa and Balarāma can be seen in the sanctum of the Ananta-Vāsudeva temple at Bhuvaneswar. In the Jagannātha temple at Purī she is placed between Jagannātha and Balarāma as their sister Subhadrā. Jagannātha was a tribal god worshipped with primitive Tantric rites. Subsequently he was taken into the fold of Vaiṣṇavism, but the Tantric rites associated with his cult continue to exist even today. According to the Sakta-Tantric tradition, the presiding deity of Śrīkṣetra is the goddess Vimalā and Jagannātha is her consort or Bhairava.

We have already had the occasion to refer to *Lakṣmītantra*, a Pāñcarātra text composed between the 9th-12th centuries A.D. in which the doctrine of Śakti is accorded such a high place that even the Śāktas regard this text as a scripture of their own. It appears that during this period Tantric elements began to act more effectively on the major existing religious systems. We have seen that in the philosophical speculations of the Southern Vaiṣṇavas, the doctrine of Śakti was able to find a place. Subsequently, it became so influential that a need was felt to bring the ten Avatāras of Viṣṇu into relation with the ten celebrated Tantric Mahāvidyās. The *Guhyātiguhya-tantra* explains it so:

Kṛṣṇamūrtiḥ Kālikā syād Rāmamūrtistu Tāriṇī/
Chinnamastā Nṛsiṃhaḥ syād Vāmano Bhūvaneśvarī/
Jāmadagnyaḥ Sundarī Syanmīno Dhūmāvatī bhavet/
Vagalā Kūrmamūrtiḥ syādbalabhadraśca Bhairavī//
Mahālakṣmīrbhavedbuddho Durgā syāt Kalkirūpiṇī/
Svayaṃ Bhagavatī Kālī Kṛṣṇastu Bhagavān svayam//

Tantrism and Southern Śaivism

Śaivism in South India received much inspiration from the Nāyanar saints who composed devotional verses in praise of Śiva. Of these saints Appar (A.D. 600-81), Sambandhar (A.D. 644-60), Māṇikyavācakar. (A.D. 660-92) and Sundarar (A.D. 710-35) were known as Samayācāryas. The devotional tradition created by them was later developed into a religio-philosophical system called Śaiva Siddhānta through the efforts of Myekaṇḍadeva (13th century) and his followers. Reference has already been made to Śaiva Siddhānta literature.

According to Śaiva Siddhānta, Prakṛti, the material cause of the universe, is unconscious like clay and so it cannot organise itself into the world. As the jar has the potter for its efficient cause, the staff and wheel for its instrumental cause, and clay for its material cause, so also the world has Śiva for its efficient cause, Śakti for its instrumental cause, and Māyā for its material cause. But the problem of the Śaiva Siddhānta doctrine and also of all other contemporary Vaiṣṇava and Śaiva schools was that since the material world as an effect has a material cause, and since that cause by its very nature cannot be different from the effect, *brahman* (Viṣṇu or Śiva or any supreme being of a sectarian religion) cannot be the material cause. So the cause has been ascribed to Māyā, the material principle. But here we are confronted with three problems. How was Māyā created? Is it eternal like God? If that is so, then God cannot be its creator. Secondly, even assuming that God is the creator of Māyā, he must have to create this material principle from his own entity which is pure consciousness. How can a material principle be originated from a non-material principle? Assuming this is possible, then God must have to become *pariṇāmī* or subject to transformation which goes against the very concept of *brahman*. Thirdly, since Māyā is material or *acit*, it cannot be self-working. It requires handling by an intelligent agent. But how can God be given this role? (cf. Guṇaratna's criticism of Nyāya-Vaiśeṣika theism).

Like all other systems, the Śaiva Siddhānta avoids these problems and explains the evolution of the world in terms of thirty-six principles as against the twenty-five principles of the Sāṅkhya. The material cause Māyā is divided into two categories—Śuddha (pure) and Aśuddha (impure). From Śuddha Māyā is produced Nāda (cognitive energy), from Nāda Vindu (conative energy) and from Vindu Sādākhya (cognitive and conative energies held in equipoise), from Sādākhya Maheśvari (cognitive energy subordinated to the conative), and from Maheśvari Śuddhavidyā (conative energy subordinated to cognitive). Likewise from Aśuddha Māyā is produced Kāla (time), Niyati (destiny) and Kalā (instrument), from Kalā, Vidyā (finite knowledge) and Prakṛti, and from Vidyā, Rāga (attachment). From Prakṛti is produced Citta (mind) and Buddhi (intellect) and from the later Ahaṃkāra (egoity). From Ahaṃkāra are produced Taijasa (sense organs), Vaikṛta (organs of action), and Tanmātra (five subtle elements) contained in the Mahābhūtas (five gross elements: earth, water, fire, air and space). Śiva or God does not directly act on Māyā. He does so through his Śakti. All the schools of Śaivism recognise these thirty-six principles or *tattvas*.[14]

In the practical aspects of religion the followers of the Śaiva Siddhānta school believe in absolute devotion to be achieved through *caryā, kriyā, yoga* and *jñāna.* In the first stage the devotee should feel like a servant of God, in the second stage as his son, in the third stage as his associate, and in the fourth stage as identical with him. These stages are known by the terms Sālokya, Sāmīpya, Sārūpya and Sāyujya.

The Śaiva Siddhānta had a Tantric branch which was known as Āgamānta Śaivism. This sect flourised from about the 11th century and had its original centre at Mantrakali on the Godavari. The Coḷa kings were patrons of Āgamānta Śaivism. The first authoritative digest of this sect is Aghora Śivācaryā's *Kriyākarmadyotinī,* composed about the 12th century A.D. Two later texts also deserve mention, Trilocana Sivācārya's *Siddhāntasāravalī* and Nigama Jñānadeva's *Jīrṇoddhāra-daśakam.* The Āgamānta Śaivas did not attach any importance to the Vedas. They believed in twenty-eight Āgamas which were said to have come out from the five mouths of Śiva. The Āgamānta Śaivas did not believe in the caste system and the Brahmanical tradition. That is why their opponents called them Apamārgīs, Nāstikas, Śūdras, etc.

A follower of this creed required initiation and guidance from a teacher. The qualification for initiation was the grace of the great goddess with which the novice was supposed to have been favoured. This grace was known as Śaktipāta. After initiation the candidate was given a new name. This initiation or *dīkṣā* was of three kinds—*samaya-dīkṣā, viśeṣa-dīkṣā* and *nirvāṇa-dīkṣā.* The first kind was for ordinary people, while the other two were for persons belonging to higher mental levels. Those who took *samaya-dīkṣā* had to worship the preceptor and Śivāgni (fire dedicated to Śiva), and had to consider themselves as the servants of God. This method was known as Dāsamārga. Those who were initiated into the special or *viśeṣa-dīkṣā* were known as Putrakas; they were entitled to follow the way of *kriyā* (rites) and *yoga* (concentration). The way of *jñāna* or knowledge was open only to those who had *nirvāṇa-dīkṣā.*

The Āgamānta Śaivas believed in the early Pāśupata doctrine of Pati (God), Paśu (*jīva,* individual soul) and Pāśa (worldy bondage). In their opinion God or Śiva proceeds to the work of creation being influenced by the *karma* of the individual souls. In Āgamānta Śaivism greater emphasis is laid upon the Pāśu or individual souls which are of three kinds—*vijñānākala, pralayākala* and *sakala.* The first one is the best. Worldly fetters are of four types—*mala, karma, māyā* and *roṣa. Mala* covers knowledge and action of the *jīva*; *karma* is that kind of action which comes from desire, *māyā* is gross matter, the material cause of the world, and the fourth is that power bestowed by Śiva on individual souls which helps them to become free from worldly fetters. The Āgamānta Śaivas believe in all Tantric rituals and ceremonies. Apart from *dīkṣā*, the cult of the *mantras*, different methods of achieving the eight *siddhis*—*prāṇayāma, dhyāna, samādhi, ṣaṭcakra*, etc.—form part of the practical aspects of their religion. They hold that God and individual souls are different entities and that the material cause of the world is Māyā. By means of *caryā, kriyā, yoga* and *jñāna* an individual becomes free from wordly bondage and subsequently identified with Śiva himself.

Tantrism and Vīraśaivism

Liṅgāyata or Vīraśaiva is a militant form of Śaivism which flourised in the Karnataka region about the 12th century A.D. The traditions of the ancient period were given a concrete shape of religion by Vasava, a Kannada Brāhmaṇa, whose purpose was to drive away the Jains from Karnataka and to establish an ideal society. The Vīraśaivas, irrespective of sex, carry a small Śivaliṅga on the body. This is the token of their upanayana or initiation which is known as *liṅga-sāyatta-dīkṣā*. Except Śivaliṅga they worship no other image. Their attitude towards the Vedas is that of indifference. They have a special tendency towards social reform. They do not believe in caste and are opposed to smoking and drinking. They believe in the equality of men and women. They support female education and widow-remarriage. Poor and oppressed peoples receive special attention from them. It is the compulsory duty of every Vīraśaiva to help the poor with food, water, medicine, and education.

The founder of this sect, Vasava, was a minister of Vijjala, the Cālukyan king of Kalyāṇa who reigned between A.D. 1157 and 1167. Vijjala had differences with Vasava at whose instigation he was eventually killed. Thereupon, taking advantage of political power, Vasava organised his sect wonderfully well. In 1160 he founded an assembly known as Śivānubhava Maṇḍapa, the purpose of which was to infuse new life in religious systems, to establish equal rights for men and women, to eradicate the caste system and to encourage trade and physical labour. Vasava did not compose any scriptural work, but his speeches were collected. These are known as *Vacanas* in Kannada literature. Of the authoritative Vīraśaiva texts written in Kannada the *Vasava Purāṇa* (13th century), *Channavasava Purāṇa* (16th century), and *Prabhuliṅgalīlā* are important. Sanskrit works of this sect comprise Mayideva's *Śivānubhava Sūtra*, Maridantācārya's *Vīraśaivāṇḍacandrikā*, Reṇukācārya's *Siddhāntaśikhāmaṇi*, etc. The Vīraśaiva doctrine rests on the following proposition:

> *Sarveṣāṃ sthāna bhūtatvāla laya bhūtattvatastathā*
> *Tattvānāṃ mahadādināṃ sthalamityabhidhīyate*[15]

It means that the source and support of all phenomenal existence is *Sthala*. *Stha* means *sthiti* or existence and *la* means *laya* or dissolution. The Vīraśaiva philosophers start with the notion that this Sthala represents the absolute and eternal self-consciousness, but they deny that in this condition the distinction of matter and form is abolished. The potential and material movement of the absolute is called Śiva, while its actual and formal movement is called Śakti. The Vīraśaiva philosophy summarily rejects Māyāvāda or the theory of illusion and holds that creation is the result of Śiva's Vimarśa Śakti that has power to do anything and everything. Śiva as *brahman* is both the material and the efficient cause of the world. Through his Śakti he is the material cause and in his own nature the efficient cause. The relation is relative and not indicative of a real difference for there is identity between Śakti and Śaktimat, as between attribute and substance.

Vīraśaiva philosophy is in fact a doctrine of Śakti and that is why it has been traditionally called Śakti-Viśiṣṭādvayavāda. Here greater importance is laid upon the concept of Śakti in its Vimarśa form. *Brahman* or Śiva is of eternal existence, consciousness and bliss and it is only due to his Vimarśa Śakti that he is aware of these. The real nature of Śiva is like the luminiscence of a gem which the gem itself cannot realise. This realisation is possible only by Śakti. That is why the relation between Śiva and Śakti is that of identity, *tādātmya* or *sāmarasya*, as that between heat and fire, light and sun. Here an objection may be raised by saying that there may be a subtle difference between Śakti and Śakta (the container of Śakti). The Vīraśaiva answer to this point is that in the case of the heat of fire, or the light of the sun, there is no difference of quality with the nature of the substance. Here quality and substance cannot be differentiated because of their identity. That is why Śakti is called Brahmaniṣṭhā Sanātanī.[16] Without Śakti Śiva has no meaning. This emphasis on

Śakti has brought Vīraśaivism very close to Śākta-Tantric ideas, and that is why in the texts and tradition of the latter the Śakti-Viśiṣṭādvaitavāda of Vīraśaivism is held in high esteem.

Tantrism and Kāśmīra Śaivism

A special form of Śaivism flourished in the Kashmir region from about the 9th century A.D. This was known as authoritative by the followers of Tantra. The exponents of Kāśmīra Śaivism such as Vasugupta, Somānanda, Abhinavagupta, Kṣemarāja, etc., were reputed names in the Tantric tradition.

A list of the texts belonging to this school is given in the second chapter. Kāśmīra Śaivism does not believe in the authority of the Vedas, nor does it believe in the caste system. There are three principles of Kāśmīra Śaivism—Trika, Spanda, and Pratyabhijñā. Trika is based on the three concepts known as Śiva-Śakti-Anu or Pati-Pāśa-Paśu. These three concepts also occur in other forms of Śaivism. In Kāśmīra Śaivism individual souls and the material world are identical with Śiva. The process through which Śiva is manifested in the form of the individual souls and the world is known as Spanda. Pratyabhijñā is the means of realising the experience Śiva's identity with the individual souls.

As in every school of Śaivism, the ultimate reality in Kāśmīra Śaivism is Śiva who is the self of all beings, immutable and ever perfect. He is both immanent and transcendent, material as well as the efficient cause of the world. The universe, though void of distinction, appears distinct from the perfectly pure vision of the supreme being. Diverse conditions are all of Śiva just as the diverse products of the sugar-cane belong to the sugar-cane itself.[17] The creation theory is known as Ābhāsavāda, a view which holds that the universe consists of appearances which are all real in the sense that they are aspects of the ultimate reality.

Śiva who is pure consciousness is the material and the efficient cause of the world. There is no difference between the effect and its cause. But the old question remains: How can the material world be produced from an immaterial entity? The Kāśmīra Śaiva standpoint is that God is an independent entity and the world is his reflection, the apparent difference being due to false knowledge. Just as the reflection of things in a mirror does not create any stain on the mirror itself, so also the universe as his reflection does not stain him.

The manifestation of the universe is effected through the Śakti of

Śiva which is not different from him. The important modes of this Śakti are *cit* (intelligence), *ānanda* (bliss), *icchā* (will), *jñāna* (knowledge) and *kriyā* (action). With the opening out of Śakti, the world appears, and with her closing, it disappears. This Śakti is conceived of as a Female Principle inseparable from Śiva like fire and heat.[18] When really transcendental Śiva is like a corpse, but there is an equilibrium between Śiva and Śakti, and the latter is conceived of as the essence of the former.[19] In Kāśmīra Śaivism Śakti is given a special distinction. Here Śakti is called Prakāśa-Vimarśamaya. Of the numerous meanings of Vimarśa one is vibration, and this term is used expressly in the case of Śakti. Śiva on the other hand is called Prakāśa. Prakāśa and Vimarśa are two aspects of one entity, but Vimarśa is characterised by the consciousness of the self. If the example of a man is used, Prakāśa is his mental and intellectual faculties and the awareness of those faculties is Vimarśa. According to Kāśmīra Śaivism the supreme being is at the same time static and dynamic, changeless and changing. The dynamic aspect is Śakti, that power which manifests itself in the world, as a banian tree manifests itself from a seed (*vaṭadhānikāvat*).[20]

According to Kāśmīra Śaivism, the realisation of indentity with Śiva is the way to become free from worldly fetters; no importance is attached to ceremonial worship, disciplinary practices and rituals. Regarding the Kāśmīra Śaivas Madhavācārya observed:

> *vāhyābhyantaracarya-prāṇāyāmādi kleśa prathāsakalāvaidhuryena*
> *sarvasulabhamabhinavam pratyābhijñāmātram*
> *parāparasiddhyupāyamabhyupagacchantaḥ pare*
> *māheśavarāpratyabhi jñāśāstramabhyasyanti.*[21]

According to this school *mokṣa* or liberation is the return to the original state, that is, to the Absolute. Abhinavagupta says that as soon as the dualistic ideas are removed, the *jīva* merges into *brahman* just as water into water or milk into milk. All the elements merge into Śiva. He who can realise himself along with the material world as identical with Śiva will be free from all sorts of sufferings and worldly fetters.[22]

Tantrism and Śāktism

In popular belief Tantrism is same as Śāktism; this belief is not without some historical foundation. Although Tantrism has a special position in Buddhism, Vaiṣṇavism and Śaivism, it is in the Śākta religion that the Tantric ideas and practices have found the most favourable ground for their meaningful survival and development. The most notable feature of the Śākta-Tantric ideas is that the supreme being is female and is worshipped under different names and forms. In other religious systems there is evidently a place for the goddess but the difference is that she is conceived of as the wife or consort of the male god, and where the Tantric influence is greater she is conceived of as his inherent Śakti, inseparable from his own entity or self. In Śāktism she is supreme, other gods having a subordinate position. According to the cosmogonical theories of the Śākta Purāṇas the great goddess, as Ādyā Śakti or primal energy, created from her own body Brahmā, Viṣṇu, and Śiva and then having divided her own self into three parts mated with them as a result of which life and the universe came into existence.

Although the present form of the Śākta religion is essentially medieval in character, its roots may be traced to the primitive cults and rituals of the Mother Goddess. We have already dealt with the evolution of the concept of the Female Principle with reference to the development of different goddesses. In reality, there were innumerable local goddesses, mainly agricultural in character, in different parts of India, and their cults survive even today. With the development of the idea of an all pervading Female Principle, a need was felt to equate these local goddesses with the supreme being of the Śāktas. For example, the presiding goddesses of the fifty-one Pīṭhas (in reality goddesses and Pīṭhas are many more) were basically local goddesses. For the sake of identifying them with the *Magna Mater* of the Śāktas the Sati legends were invented and fabricated according to which after the death of Satī (caused by the disrespect shown to her husband Śiva at Dakṣa's sacrifice) Śiva became mad with grief and began to roam over the world carrying her corpse. In order to save him from this infatuation, Viṣṇu, with the help of his *sudarśana-cakra,* cut the dead body of Satī into pieces. The places where the fragmented parts of her body fell came to be known as Pīṭhas or holy resorts of the goddess. The limbs of the goddess are represented by symbolical objects, each accompanied by a Śivaliṅga supposed to be the Bhairava of the goddess.[23] Apart from the Pīṭhas and their presiding goddesses we have in the Purāṇas 108 names and holy resorts of the great goddess.[24] The Lalitāsahasranāma section of the *Brahmāṇḍa Purāṇa* also mentions one thousand names and forms of the goddess.

In the *Devībhāgavata* we come across the process through which innumerable local goddesses were indentified with the supreme being of the Śāktas. In every creation of the universe, it is said, the Mūla-Prakṛti assumes the different gradations of *aṃśarūpiṇī, kalārūpiṇī,* and *kalāṃśarūpiṇī,* or manifests herself in parts, smaller parts, and further subdivisions. In the first grade, she is represented by Durgā, Lakṣmī, Sarasvatī, Sāvitrī and Rādhā; in the second by Gaṅgā, Tulasī, Manasā, Ṣaṣṭhi, Maṅgalacaṇḍikā and Kālī; and in the third by the Grāmadevatās or Village Mothers and by womenfolk in general.[25] This indicates that with the development of the concept of an all-pervading Female Principle when a need was felt for regrading the local goddesses as the mainfestations of the Śākta Devī, they were primarily given recognition to represent the fragments of Prakṛti, while the more important and popular goddesses were given relatively higher positions.

In the *Devībhāgavata,* the Śākta goddess is conceived of as the Ādyāśakti, or primordial energy, that resides in Brahmā as the creative principle, in Viṣṇu as the sustaining principle and in Śiva as the destructive principle. This Ādyāsakti pervades all space and animates everything of this phenomenal world.[26] In the *Devīgītā,* which forms a part of the *Devībhāgavata,* the Devī says:

> O king of the mountains, it was I who existed before the days of creation and there was nothing beyond me. Wise men think me in terms of *cit, śaṃvit, parabrahman,* etc. My original form is beyond inference, beyond end, beyond illustration and even beyond the concepts of life and death. I am identical with my energy called *māyā* which is neither *sat* (existent, real) nor *asat* (non-existent, unreal), nor a combination of both; it is beyond all these which exists until the final end. This *māyā* which is my inherent perpetual energy is like the heat of the fire, rays of the sun and light of the moon.... This *māyā* of mine is variously called *tapas, tamas, jaḍa, jñāna, pradhāna, prakṛti, śakti, aja,* etc. The Śaivas call it *vimarśa* while those well-versed in the Vedas call it *avidyā.*[27]

Details of Śākta-Tantric cults will be given later. Hence we shall confine ourselves only to what may be called the Śākta standpoint. In this connection we must bear in mind that, owing to Brahmanical handling, scholastic elements were superimposed on the Śākta-Tantric stream of thought as a result of which Śāktism and Tantrism lost some of their original features. The ever increasing influence of the Vedānta to a certain extent cornered the Sāṅkhya, though the Sāṅkhya concepts of Prakṛti, Buddhi, Ahamkāra, Tanmātra, Mahābhūta, etc., survived. The Puruṣa of the Sāṅkhya was transformed into the *brahman* of Vedānta with whom was Śiva equated. The original significance of Prakṛti was changed and interpreted in terms of the Vimarśa Śakti of *brahman*.

In the present position of Śākta philosophy both the dualist and the monist interpretation of Vedānta have their role. Of the various Tantric schools, Śrīkula and Kālikula are better known. The followers of Śrīkula depend on Śrīkaṇṭha's Śivādvaitavāda which has a leaning towards the Viśiṣṭādvaitavāda of Rāmānuja. According to this doctrine *brahman*, or Śiva, is the material and effcient cause of the world. The atomic elements by which the individual souls and the material world are composed are produced by his Śakti. The world is not different from *brahman*, just as a jar is not different from clay. But at the same time *brahman* is not completely identical with the world, because he is the intelligent or conscious cause while the world is partly non-conscious; and partly because in the world there are conscious beings as well as unconscious elements. The followers of Śrīkula believe in the *Brahmamīmāṃsā* of Śrīkaṇṭha[28] and *Śivārkamaṇidīpikā* of Appaya Dikṣita. They admit the *sat* (real) and *cit* (conscious) manifestation of Śiva, and regard Śakti as Vimarśinī or Śiva's natural vibrating power. The followers of Kālikula are exclusively monist. They hold that Śakti is same as *brahman* in its three aspects of *sat* (real), *cit* (consciousness), and *ānanda* (bliss), and not its Māyā-vivarta or transformatory aspect. According to them the theory of Śiva-Śakti is beyond all dualism and it can be understood only through experience.

The main contention of what we call the Śākta standpoint, which is now predominated by Vedāntic speculations, is that ultimate reality is the Prakāśa aspect of the supreme being, which is beyond time and space and of the nature of pure consciousness. What is known as Vimarśa is the independence of this Prakāśa in relation to action, but in reality the Vimarśa Śakti is the self of Prakāśa, standing in inseparable and completely identical relation. Śakti has two states, inactive and active; when it is in the inactive state it is said that Vimarśa is merged into Prakāśa. But when Śakti becomes active the supreme being becomes conscious. Its self-knowledge then manifests as Aham.[29] The whole universe is reflected in this Aham like objects reflected in a mirror. The supreme being, whose Prakāśa is Śiva and Vimarśa is Śakti, is at the same time transcendent and immanent.

With this supreme being, Śakti or Kalā is associated in eternal bond. Kalā means absolute transcendental power. The first transformation of this Śakti is *icchā* or will. Just as oil comes from oil-seed, so also Śakti emerges from the supreme being at the beginning of creation. This appearance of Śakti is like the reappearance of the memory of one who rises from deep sleep. The supreme being and Śakti are both of the nature of *cit* or pure consciousness, but since Śakti acts on everything it sometimes appears as knowledge and sometimes as action, according to the nature of the things themselves. According to the dualistic Śāktas, Vindu is material entity but dependent on the action of Śakti. Their main difference with the monist Śāktas is that although they consider Śiva as undifferentiated from Śakti and both as two aspects of the same supreme being, they make a difference between Śiva-Śakti equilibrium on the one hand and Vindu or material entities on the other. According to them matter or Vindu is eternal like Śiva and Śakti, and in the case of creation Śiva is the efficient cause, Śakti the instrumental cause and Vindu the material cause. Beacuse of its non-material nature, Śakti undergoes no transformation while it is on work, but it does when it is in relation with Vindu or matter.

The absolute monistic interpretation of Vedānta by Śaṅkara could not be accepted by the Vaiṣṇava, Śaiva, and Śākta schools because it was impossible from a religious viewpoint to deny the existence of the material world. Therefore, what they meant to say, in some form or other, was that the world was *somehow* either a transformation of *brahman* or a transformation of Śakti. But none could prove this point satisfactorily. The problem was greater in the case of Śāktism because here, apart from the problem of determining the relation between the sentient *brahman* and the non-sentient material world, there were other problems of synthesising various traditional elements and conflicting materials which came from a variety of primitive sources.

The Atimārgika Sects: Kāpālikas, Kālāmukhas, Mattamayūras

The Kāpālikas and Kālāmukhas were two Tantric offshoots of Pāśupata Śaivism. These sects represented a special ritualistic trend, a tradition of hoary antiquity, containing many obscure elements. These sects had no literature of their own; whatever is known about them comes from the writings of ancient authors belonging to the upper level of society who did not like their rituals and ceremonies and hence described them in a distorted and derogatory way. Even a mastermind like Śaṅkarācārya did not hesitate to resort to distortion and fabrication which is proved by the mode of his presentation of the views of his opponents. This held good in the case of other writers too. That is why the Atimārgika sects like the Kāpālikas, Kālāmukhas, Aghorapanthīs, etc., were treated with contempt and described in a disparaging manner. These sects were basically worshippers of the Female Principle. They had no faith in patriarchal and authoritarian social values, nor in the caste system. Conditioned by Smārta-Puranic tradition, these writers, whether ancient or modern, could not appreciate their views and practices.

The *Ṛgveda* contains a hymn known as Keśisūkta[30] in which mention is made of a class of ascetics who were half-naked, or had only short brown garments soiled with dust, kept long hair, were frenzied by the spirit of their cults and rituals. This peculiar attitude appears to bear some affinity with the practices of Rudra-Śiva and his worshippers, specially since the tradition of Rudra's drinking the poison is connected in this hymn with Keśi.[31] Patañjali's contemptuous attitude towards the *āyahśūlika* (one with an iron lance) and *dāṇḍājinika* (one with a club and hide-garment) seems to refer to the Atimārgika sects. His Śivabhāgavatas probably pertain to the Pāśupatas. Pāśupata practices like *krāthana* (feigning sleep when really awake), *spandana* (appearing to have no control over the limbs when walking), *śrṅgāraṇa* (expressing erotic gestures at the sight of women), *avitatkaraṇa* (indulging in apparently unsocial acts), *avitadbhāṣaṇa* (speaking absurd and senseless words), etc., have been condemned by Kauṇḍinya as anti-Brahmanical acts. In the *Rāmāyāna*[32] Śiva's and Umā's relation with the Yakṣas and Guhyakas has been mentioned. We have already referred to a passage of the *Bhāgavata Purāṇa*[33] which describes Śiva as *markaṭalocana* (monkey-eyed) roaming in the cremation grounds with Pretas and Bhūtas, *aśuci* (impure), *kriyāhīna* (bereft of any rites), *digambara* (naked), with matted locks on his head, walking here and there like a mad man, bathing in ashes, wearing bones and garlands of skulls as ornaments, mad himself and beloved of the insane, inauspicious (*aśiva*) though named Śiva, and so on. In reality, it was because of original relation with people belonging to the lower order of society, and to the inclusion of popular rites and customs in Śaivism, that writers belonging to the opposing group tried to depict Śiva in this way. Certain ceremonies, such as the *Caḍaka* or *Gājana* of Śiva are even today considered as barbarous because of their association with the people of the lower order.

In some of the earlier writings there are references to the Kāpālikas and Kāruṇikasiddhāntī. The latter is described by Rāmānuja and Keśava Kaśmīrī as the Kālāmukhas. According to Rāmānuja the Kāpālikas use six *mudrās* (*kaṇṭhahāra*, necklace, *alaṃkāra*; ornament; *kuṇḍala*, earring; *śiromaṇi*, jewel for head; *bhaṣma*, ashes, and *yajñopavīta*, sacred thread)—all made from human bones, and the attainment of highest happiness by concentrating on the supreme soul located in the female organ.[34] Kṛṣṇamiśra in his *Prabodhacandrodaya* has supplied the following data regarding the Kāpālikas: Their necklace and other ornaments are made of human bones; they break their ceremonial fast by drinking wine from the skull cup of a Brāhmaṇa corpse; their sacrificial fire is kept burning with the offering of human flesh, skull, lung, etc.; they propitiate the deity by offering human sacrifice and blood; their god is Śiva, the consort of the great goddess, who is conceived of as the creator, preserver and destroyer of the world; they live mainly in the Mālava region of Central India which is peopled mostly by the lower castes; they eat food in human skulls, smear their bodies with ashes, use clubs and offer the libation of wine to their deities; they do not belive in the caste system; their way of life is known as *mahāvrata*; there is no barrier for men of lower castes to be initiated in this *mahāvrata* and any such initiated person is regarded as belonging to the highest caste. Among the other references, Mādhava in *Śaṅkaradigvijaya*[35] relates an encounter between Śaṅkara and the Kāpālika teacher Krakacha. The Kāpālikas are also described in Bhavabhūti's *Mālatīmādhava*. Their important centre was at Śrīśalila in the Andhra country.

The Igatpuri copper plate of Nāgaravardhana, the nephew of the Cālukya ruler Pulakeśin II who ruled in the 7th century, records the grant of a village for the worship of the god Kapāleśvara and for the maintenance of the Mahāvratins who were no other than the Kāpālikas and Kālāmukhas. From another copper plate of the 7th century, found at a place called Nirmand in Kangra district, the existence of a temple of Kapāleśvara and that of the Brāhmaṇas who studied the *Atharvaveda* are known. A few medieval inscriptions from Arsikore in Karnataka record the existence of the Atimārgika sects that were regarded as branches of the Lākula-Pāśupatas. This is supported by two inscriptions from Arcot district in which it is stated that the Kālāmukhas of the villages Melpaḍi and Jambai were organised under the leadership respectively of Lakulīśvara Paṇḍita and Mahāvratin Lakulīśvara Paṇḍita.[36] An inscription of A.D. 1117 found from Karnataka describes a group of ascetics as Kālāmukhas and preachers of Lākulāgamasamaya.[37] Nilakantha Sastri has shown that in many parts of South India the Kālāmukha sect was very strong in 9-11th centuries.[38]

In Tripuri and its adjoining regions in Central India we come across, on the evidence of some inscriptions belonging to the 10th and 11th centuries, the existence of Śaiva sect called the Mattamayūras. This sect controlled a number of temples and monasteries; teachers belonging to this sect used the suffix Śiva or Śambhu, at the end of their names, e.g. Rudraśambhu, Dharmaśambhu, Mahāśiva, Cuḍāśiva, Kavacaśiva, Prabhavaśiva, Praṣāntāśiva, Prabodhaśiva, Aghoraśiva, etc.[39] A tribe known as Mattamāyūra is also mentioned in the *Mahābhārata*.[40] From the epigraphical evidence it is quite clear that the development of the sect had taken place between the 9th and 13th centuries of the Christian era. Elsewhere we have shown that in the Pāla period the Mattamāyūras flourished even in Bengal.[41] This sect held a liberal view regarding religious practices and insisted on Yoga and social work like feeding the poor, building hospitals, establishing schools and so on. Somaśambhu, a teacher of this sect, composed a treatise called *Somaśambhupaddhati* in which a comprehensive account of Śaiva Āgamas is given.[42] We have already referred to another text belonging to this sect—*Īśānaśivagurudevapaddhati*. H. Goetz suggests that the Mattamayūras were responsible for the sensual bas-reliefs of the Khajuraho temples.[43] The erotic depictions on the Khajuraho temples, however, have very little to do with Tantric sex practices.[44]

Tantrism and the Gāṇapatyas

Gaṇeśa or Gaṇapati is the god of *gaṇa* or tribe, as is evident from his name. In the *Ṛgveda*[45] a rudimentary conception of this god is presented thus: *gaṇānāṃ tva gaṇapatiṃ havāmahe*. As a symbol of the chief tribal deity of the past, even today Gaṇeśa is worshipped before the other gods are. His elephant head is probably a totemic symbol. His exclusively tribal character incorporates many features of primitive tribal life.

In his original character of the tribal chief, Gaṇeśa or Gaṇapati was an epithet applied to any leading god of the past. In this sense Indra was also Gaṇapati because he was basically the leader of a Vedic tribe who was raised to divinity. Therefore, very naturally, some of the attributes of Indra are found in the later conception of Gaṇeśa. But Indra did not function as a Gaṇapati or tribal leader for a long period. With the disintegration of tribal life and emergence of state power he became a king, and eventually the king of gods. Apart from Indra, the other deities of the *Ṛgveda*, Rudra and the Maruts were conceived of as the leader of the *gaṇas*. These deities had evidently something to do with the conception of Gaṇeśa. As *gaṇādhipati* the field of Rudra was greater, and as such his relation with Gaṇeśa was more intimate.

In the earlier concept of Gaṇeśa, like Rudra, he was a god to be feared. He was the creator of obstacles, an evil-doing god; his attention boded destruction, even if he looked at a woman she was bound to become barren. In the legends of later times we find that Gaṇeśa's head was lost owing to the evil glance of Śani and that it was replaced by the head of an elephant. The allegory is quite clear. It is the history of his transformation from Vighnarāja (the king of creating impediments) to Siddhidātā (bestower of success). As the god of creating obstacles, which was the original conception of Gaṇeśa, his evil-glance was as dangerous as that of Śani. He who was the victim of this glance was doomed. That is why when Gaṇeśa was transformed into Siddhidātā or bestower of success it was necessary to remove his ancient head. The evil-glance was really the fearfulness of his original entity.

As *gaṇādhipati* Gaṇeśa was more akin to Rudra, as we have seen, and this probably explains why in later tradition he was regarded as the son of Rudra, Śiva and Pārvatī. In the *Atharvaśiras Upaniṣad*, Rudra has been equated with Vināyaka, and Vināyaka is the other name of Gaṇeśa. The Amarakośa gives many names of Gaṇeśa:

> Vināyaka-Vighnarāja-Dvaimātura-Ganadhipāḥ /
> Apyekadanta-Heramba-Lambodara-Gajānanāḥ //

In the *Mahābhārata* Gaṇeśvaras and Vināyakas are described as the lords of the world.[46] If properly propitiated they remove all obstacles. In the *Mānava Gṛhyasūtra* four Vināyakas have been mentioned[47]—Sālakaṭaṅkaṭa, Kuṣmāṇḍarājaputra, Uṣmita, and Devayajana. In the

Purāṇas, such as the *Śiva, Liṅga, Varāha, Skanda, Brahmavaivarta,* etc., we have various conflicting ancedotes regarding the birth of Gaṇeśa. Iconological texts mention twenty-four forms of Gaṇeśa: Vināyaka, Ganādhīśa, Vighneśa, Pramathādhipa, Gaṇeśa, Vīja-gaṇapati, Heramba, Vakratuṇḍa, Bālagaṇapati, Bhaktavighneśa, Śaktigaṇeśa, Dhvajagaṇādhipa, Piṅgalagaṇapati, Ucchiṣṭagaṇa-pati, Lakṣmīgaṇeśa, Mahāgaṇeśa, Bhuvaneśa, Gaṇapati, Nṛtyagaṇa-pati, Ūrdhvagaṇeśa, Prasannagaṇeśa, Unmattavināyaka and Haridrāgaṇeśa.

There is no need here to go further into the history of the transformation of Gaṇeśa from Vighnarāja to Siddhidāta because we are mainly concerned with his association with Tantrism. It is very natural to expect that as a tribal god of antiquity Gaṇeśa had some connection with primitive Tantrism. This connection has been found even beyond the geographical borders of India. In a place called Bara in Java an early medieval image of Gaṇeśa has been found; the figure is seated on a row of skulls with more skulls embedded in his matted locks. In Indian sculptures Gaṇeśa is frequentily found with the Mātṛkās; and many images show Gaṇeśa in copulation with his Śakti.

In Ānandagiri's *Śaṅkaradigvijaya,*[48] and also in its *Diṇḍimākhya* commentary, six branches of the Gāṇapatyas or followers of the creed of Gaṇeśa (*Gāṇapatyamiti khyātaṃ ṣaḍbhirbhadaīḥ samanvitaṃ*) are known as Mahāgaṇapti, Haridrāgaṇapati, Ucchiṣṭagaṇapati, Navanītagaṇapati, Svarṇagaṇapati, and Santānagaṇapati. According to the worshippers of Mahāgaṇapati, Gajānana, also known as Ekadanta Gaṇapati, who is in eternal union with his Śakti, is the creator of the world and the ultimate reality. According to the worshippers of Haridrā Gaṇapati, Gaṇapati is the original cause of this phenomenal world and the other gods like Brahmā are his parts; they used to depict the head of Gaṇeśa on their hands.

The worshippers of Ucchiṣṭa Gaṇapati were undeniably followers of Tantrism. They visualised Gaṇeśa with four arms, three eyes, lasso (*pāśa*), goad (*aṅkuśa*), club (*gadā*) and in *abhaya mudrā.* His trunk is shown as drinking intoxicating liquor. Seated on a *Mahāpīṭha* he is engaged in kissing and embracing his Śakti who sits on his left lap:

Caturbhujaṃ trinayanaṃ pāśankuśa gadābhayaṃ/
Tuṇḍāgra tībramadhukaṃ gaṇanāthamahaṃ bhaje//
Mahāpīṭha niṣannaṃ taṃ vāmāṅga parisaṃsthitaṃ/
Devīmāliṅgya cumbantaṃ spṛśaṃastuṇḍena vaibhagam//

The Ucchiṣṭa Gāṇapatyas did not differentiate between merit and demerit. They did not find any fault in indiscriminate sexual intercourse among men and women. They did not obey caste distinctions nor observe various *saṃskāras* like marriage, etc. They drank wine. Their sect mark was a red circle on the forehead.

Tantrism and the Smārta Pañcopāsanā

The five major cults in India—Vaiṣṇava, Śaiva, Śākta, Gāṇapatya and Saura—came to some sort of an understanding among themeselves in the course of time, as a result of which a composite religious system came into existence known as Pañcopāsanā. It was settled that each sect should basically worship its own deity as the supreme being without disregarding the deities of others. This was also approved by the brahmanised Tantras. In the *Tantrasāra* it is said:

> *Bhavānīntu yadā madhye aiśānyamacyutaṃ yajet/*
> *Āgneyāṃ pārvatīnāthaṃ nairṛtyāṁ gaṇanāyakaḥ//*
> *Vāyavyāṃ tapanañcaiva pūjākramaḥ udāhṛtaḥ//*

It means that the goddess Bhavānī should be worshipped at the centre, Acyuta or Viṣṇu at the north-east corner, Pārvatīnātha or Śiva at the south-west, Gaṇapati at the south-east and Tapana or Sūrya at the north-west. Here the central deity is Śakti, but the others are not excluded.

The cause of the introduction of this Pañcopāsanā evidently lay in the conflict with anti-Brahmanical ideas. These five sects were originally anti-Brahmanical, but later they came under the total influence of Brahmanism and become zealous exponents of Brahmanical culture. In the *Prabodhacandrodaya* we have an interesting account of the united fight of the Vaiṣṇavas, Śaivas and Sauras under the leadership of the goddess Sarasvatī against the Buddhists, Jains, and the Cārvākas. Again whatever might have been the basic cause of the rise of these five major religious sects, at a certain stage of their development they were all influenced by the theistic interpretation of Vedānta. Their methods of argument followed the same line. Philosophical and doctrinal terminologies were common to all of them. As a result of all these a syncretistic outlook came into existence. Syncretistic icons, like those of Hari-Hara, Śiva-Śakti, Śiva-Sūrya, Viṣṇu-Sūrya, etc., were made and worshipped.

In the case of Pañcopāsanā the greatest inspiration was supplied by the Brāhmaṇa writers of the Smṛti texts. Persons belonging to the higher levels of society, despite their typical sectarian affiliations, followed the injunctions laid down by the Smṛti texts. The Smṛtis gave various directions to popularise Pañcopāsanā which still characterise modern Hinduism. It is, however, the Hinduism of the upper strata of society, and logically it should have very little to do with the greater section of the masses. But since persons belonging to the lower strata of society have a natural inclination to follow and imitate the culture of those belonging to the higher level, the religious beliefs and practices of the latter were able to influence those of the former. It should not also be forgotten that the five major deities of this Pañcopāsanā *originally* belonged to the lower strata, and despite the Brahmanical conversion of these deities, the simpler peoples did not sever their relation with them. This accounts for the wide popularity of Pañcopāsanā among all sections of peoples.

NOTES

1. This sect originally based itself on the teachings of the South Indian Āḷvars, and its earlier exponents were Nāthamuni, Puṇḍarīkākṣa, Rāmamiśra and Yāmunācarya.
2. Ed. by R. Tarkaratna, Calcutta, 1888-91; by V.S. Abhayankar, Bombay, 1914-16; by J.J. Johnson, Banaras, 1916; Eng. tr. by M. Rangacharya and M.B.V. Aiyangar, Madras, 1899; by G. Thibaut, in *SBE*, Vol. XLVIII, Oxford, 1904.
3. *Mahābhārata*, XII, 314, 12, etc.
4. Com. on *Brahmasūtra*, I. 4. 25, etc.
5. Important Vaḍakalai teachers were Kurukesa, Viṣṇucitta, Varadācārya, Ātreya Rāmānuja and Vedānta Deśika while those belonging to Ṭenkalai were Embār, Parāśarabhaṭṭa, Nāñjiyār, Nāmapillai, Kṛṣṇapāda and Pillai Lokācāryā. The most well-known exponent of the latter was Śrīmanabala Mahāmuni who flourished about the fourteenth-fifteenth century.
6. *Vedāntapārijātasaurabha*, ed. D.R. Sastri, 1932; V. Dvivedin, 1910; Eng. tr. by Roma Bose, Bibliotheca Indica, Calcutta, 1940.
7. Ed. with Puruṣottama's *Vedāntaratnamañjuṣā*, com. by R.G. Bhatta, 1907.
8. See Roma Chaudhuri, *Doctrine of Nimbārka and his Followers*, Asiatic Society, Calcutta.
9. Madhva's *Sūtrabhāṣya* on *Brahmasūtra* was ed. by Raghavendracharya, 4 vols., Mysore, 1911-12; Eng. tr. by S. Subba Rau, Madras, 1904.
10. Vallabha's commentary on the *Brahmasūtra* is known as *Anubhāṣya* which is available only up to III. 2. 33.

11. *Caitanyacaritāmṛta* I. 7. 117ff; see also I. 4; 1 5; II. 8.
12. *Caitanyabhāgavata,* I. 11. 39. X. 15. 35; 41, 31.
13. See Ch. VIII, 8; S.B. Dasgupta, *Obscure Religious Cults,* Calcutta, 1969, pp. 113ff.
14. *Mṛgendra Āgama,* II. 3-7; III. 1; VII. 11; VIII. 1-5; IX. 2-4; *Pauṣkara Āgama,* II. 17; III.4; V. 9; *Śivajñānabodham,* II. 5; XII. 3; *Śivaprakāśam,* I. 1., etc.
15. *Śivānubhava Sūtra,* II. 3.
16. *Siddhāntaśikhāmaṇi,* V. 39.
17. *Paramārthasāra,* 12 ff.
18. *Śivadṛṣṭi,* III. 7.
19. *Īśvara pratyabhijñā,* I. 5. 14.
20. *Pratyabhijñāhṛdaya,* 4 with com.
21. *Sarvadarśanasaṃgraha,* 90.
22. *Paramārthasāra,* 51-2.
23. For the *Pīṭhas* see D.C. Sircar, 'The Śākta Pīṭhas', in *JRASB,* Letters, XIV; 1948, pp. 1-108; rpt., New Delhi 1972.
24. *Matsya,* XIII. 26-53; *Padma, Sṛṣṭi* XVII, 184-211; *Skanda, Revā,* XCVIII. 66-92; *Devībhāgavata,* VII. 30. 55-83.
25. *Devībhāgavata,* XVIII. 42-51.
26. Ibid., I. 8.
27. Ibid., VII. 32.
28. His commentary on the *Brahmasūtra* is known as *Brahmamīmāṃsā,* ed. L. Śrīnivasacharya. For his doctrine see S.N. Dasgupta, *History of Indian Philosophy,* Vol. V, pp. 65-95.
29. *A* and *Ha,* the first and last letters of the alphabet, stand respectively for Prakāśa and Vimarśa. In between the unity of other letters is expressed by *M* or *anusvāra,* and these three letters constitute *Aham.* Here the alphabet has been used, symbolically because it contains all forms of knowledge and expression.
30. X. 136.
31. J.N. Banerjea, *Pauranic and Tantric Religion,* Calcutta, 1966, pp. 72-3.
32. V. 89.
33. IV. 2-7.
34. *Śrībhāṣya,* II. 2. 35-6.
35. XV. 1-8.
36. J.N. Banerjea, op. cit., pp. 96-8; R.G. Bhandarkar, op. cit., pp. 119-20.
37. *Epigraphia Carnatica,* Vol. V, pt. I. p. 135.
38. N. Sastri, *The Colas,* Madras, 1955, pp. 648-9.
39. R.D. Banerji, *The Haihayas of Tripuri* (MASI, 23), pp. 110ff.
40. II. 32. 4-5.
41. N.N Bhattacharyya, *Ancient Indian Rituals,* New Delhi, 1975, pp. 133-4.
42. *IHQ,* Vol. XXVI, 1950, pp. 15ff.
43. *Arts Asiatiques,* Tome V, 1958, Fasc. I, pp. 35ff.

44. For details about the Mattamayūras see V.V. Mirashi's introduction to *Corpus Inscriptionum Indicarum*, Vol. IV.
45. II. 23. 1; *Vājasaneyī Saṃhita*, XXIII. 19.
46. XIII. 150.25.
47. II. 14.
48. ANDS (Ed.) pp. 357ff.

8

Tantrism and the Religion of the Masses: The Lokāyata Tradition

The Siddhācāryas: Buddhist Tantric Influence

We have seen that within the fold of Buddhism there developed a special Tantric way, the aim of which was to attain *siddhi* or supernatural power.[1] In early Buddhism we have the concept of *ṛddhi* or *abhijñā* indicating supernatural power. The Hindu Tantras also mention eight *siddhis*—Animā, Laghimā, Mahimā, Prākāmya, Prāpti, Vaśitva, Īśitva, and Kāmāvasāyitva. In the Śakta-Tantric *Lalitāsahasranāma* three types of spiritual quest are mentioned—divya, mānava and siddha. In different Tantric texts mention is made of the Siddhas and sects like Siddhakula, etc.[2] According to this tradition there were 84 Siddhas who were endowed with supernatural power which they achieved through meditation and physical exercises. In Jyotirīśvara's *Varṇaratnākara* their names are mentioned. Their lives and works are preserved in the Tibetan canon[3] and in the histories of Bu-ston, Gos lo-tsa-ba, Tāranātha, Sumpa-khan-po and others. They are also known from medieval Nepalese traditions as also from their songs preserved in Apabhramśa such as *Caryāgītikośa* or *Caryāścaryaviniścaya.* These eighty-four Siddhas were well known in the literature of medieval Indian alchemy. The *Śabaratantra* gives a list of teachers of the Kāpālika sect in which are included such names as Nāgārjuna, Mīnanātha, Gorakṣa, Carpaṭa and Jālandhara, well known also in the Siddha traditions.[4] A few Siddhas are mentioned is some inscription also.[5] The list preserved in the Tibetan sources mentions

Luhi, Līlā, Vīru, Ḍombi, Śabara, Śaraha (Rāhulabhadra), Kaṅkāli, Mīna, Gorakṣa, Caurangī, Viṇā, Śānti, Tānti, Carmarī (Camarī), Khaḍga, Nāgārjuna, Kānha, Kānari, Thangana, Nāro, Śāli, Tilo, Chatra, Bhadra, Dvikhaṇḍī (Dokhaṇḍī), Ajogī, Kāḍa, Dhobi, Kaṅkana, Kampala (Kambala), Gingi (Tenki), Bhade, Taṇdhi, Kukkuri, Cujbi (Kusulī), Dharma, Mahī, Acinti,

Bhalaha, Nalina, Bhūsūku, Indrabhūti, Megha, Kuṭhāli (Kuṭhāri), Karmāra, Jālandhara, Rāhula, Garbharī, Ḍhākari, Jogī, Celuka. Gundari, Luñacka Nirguṇa, Jayānanda, Carpaṭi, Campaka, Bhikhana, Kumāri, Cavarī (Javari), Maṇibhadra (female), Mekhalā (female), Maṅkhalā (female), Kalakala, Kaṇṭhali, Dhahuli, Udhali, Kapāla, Kīla, Sāgara, Sarvabhakṣa, Nāgabodhi, Dārika, Putuli, Upānaha, Kokila, Anaṅga, Lakṣmīṇkārā (female), Samudra and Bhali.

According to Tāranātha the Siddhācāryas imparted Tantric knowledge during the Pāla period. They were Saraha or Rahulabhadra, author of *Buddhakapāla tantra*; Luipāda, author of *Yoginisaṃcaryā*; Kambala and Padmavajra, authors of *Hevajratantra*; Kṛṣṇa, author of *Sampuṭatilaka*; Līlāvajra, author of *Kṛṣṇayamāri-tantra*; Gambhīravajra, author of *Vajrāmṛta*; Kukkurī, author of *Mahāmāyā*; and Piṭo, author of *Kālacakra*.[6] In another work he gives a different list of succession in this order: Rāhulabhadra or Saraha, Nāgārjuna, Siddhaśabarī, Luipāda, Ḍombī, Tili, Nāro, Ḍombī junior, and Kuśalibhadra.[7] In the Tanjur the list is: Padmavajra, Anaṅgavajra, Indrabhūti, Bhagavatī Lakṣmī, Līlāvajra, Dārika-pa, Sahajáyoginī Cintā, and Ḍombī Heruka. Sumpa mentions Saraha, Nāgārjuna, Śabarī, Lui, Vajraghaṇṭā, Kacchapa, Jālandharī, Kṛṣṇācārya. Guhya, Vijya, Tailo, and Nāro.[8] In the *Blue Annals* a large number of Siddhācāryas are mentioned classified under several lines of teachers belonging to different Tantric disciplines.[9] However, there is no need to quote all the names here.

Many of the Siddhācāryas came from the lower ranks of society. As is apparent from names like Ḍombī, Śabarī, Tānti, Camari, Khaḍga, Tilo, Śāli, Dhobi, Kambala, Kuṭhāri, Karmāra, Jālandharī, Bāguri, Telī, Kumāri, etc., that they belonged to the caste of corpse-carriers, leather-workers, washermen, oilmen, tailors, fishermen, wood-cutters and the like. The Nātha Siddhas are also included in the lists and we find such names as Mīnanātha, Gorakṣanātha, Cauraṅgīnātha, Jālandhari and so on. These Siddhācāryas did not care for social distinction and the caste system. Saraha, who was a Brāhmaṇa, became a voluntary outcaste and ridiculed the Brāhmaṇas and the Brahmanical way openly. He married a woman of low caste. In his very first *dohā* he attacked Brahmanism. The followers of the Hevajrayoga regarded everyone as Buddha and did not differentiate between high and low. They used a special language and secret signs.[10]

The Siddhas believe in the divine power of the *guru* or preceptor who initiates the disciple according to his receptivity. There are five *kulas* or brands of the Siddha culture: Ḍombī, Naṭī, Rajakī, Caṇḍālī, and Brāhmaṇī. These are symbols of five female forms of Śakti. The way of the Siddhācāryas is basically that of *kāyasādhana* or the way of the body. According to the Siddha theory, there are thirty two nerves in the body through which Śakti flows from its main centre below the navel region. These nerves have different names: *lalanā*, *ramanā*, *rasanā avadhūtī*, *pravaṇā*, *kṛṣṇarūpiṇī*, *sāmānyā*, *pāvakī*, *sumanā*, *kāminī*, etc. The three most important are *lalanā*, *rasanā* and *avadhūtī* otherwise called *iḍā*, *piṅgalā*, and *suṣumnā*. The highest resort of Śakti is the cerebral region known as *mahāsukhasthāna*, or the place of greatest bliss, conceived of as a thousand-petalled lotus. Śakti reaches this point after crossing some important stations. These stations within the body are designated according to the names of the celebrated Tantric Pīṭhas such as Uḍḍīyāna, Jālandhara, Pūrṇagiri, Kāmarūpa, etc. The aim of the aspirant is the realisation of *sahaja*. *Sahaja* is the root of all existence, the source of eternal bliss and pleasure; when all the senses are merged in it the aspirant has the feeling of absolute non-dualism. He then sees everything as an integral part of his own self.

Liberation is not that of the soul. It is of the body which can be attained within the span of human life. The followers of the Siddha way use the turn *jīvanmukti*. It means the attainment of immortality which is possible by *kāyasādhana* or disciplining the body. Semen is the source of life and that is why it is *bodhicitta*. Immortality is possible by adopting the method of *parāvṛtti* or the opposite way. This means that instead of giving the semen the usual downward motion it should be given an upward motion which is possible by Yoga. This culture of Bodhicitta is connected with alchemy and that is why the use of chemical drugs is also desirable. The fluids flowing through the veins should be hardened because this enables the body and mind to be properly balanced. For this purpose mercurial drugs are required, because it is necessary to transform this ordinary mortal body into a divine one. From a theoretical viewpoint it is said that the *aśuddha-māyā* or impure elements of which the human body is made should be transformed into pure elements through certain processes. The physical body can assume three types of transformed body—*mantra-tanu*, *praṇava* or *vaindava-tanu*, and *divya-tanu*. This transformation is *jīvanmukti*, immortality or liberation within the span of life.

All believers in the Tantric *kāyasādhana*, including the Siddhas, believe that the body is the microcosm of the universe. Mountain, sea, moon, sun, river—all that of which the world is composed—are within the human body. It is by Haṭhayoga that one is able to have mastery over body and mind. Śiva and Śakti reside in the body, the former in the *mahāsukhasthāna* or the *sahasrāra*, that is, in the highest cerebral region, and the latter in *mūlādhāra*, the lowest extremity of the spinal cord. The right half of the body is Śiva and the left half Śakti. Through the nerve *piṅgalā* in the right flows the *apāna* wind which is the stream of Śiva. Likewise through the nerve *iḍā* flows the *prāṇa* wind which is the stream of Śakti. The aspirant, through yogic efforts, has to bring these two streams into the middle nerve which is *suṣumnā*. If this is achieved, there will be a perfect equilibrium of Śiva and Śakti within the body. Again, male is the symbol of Śiva and female that of Śakti, and their yogic union is supposed to be the cause of *mahāsukha*, or great bliss, arising out of the feeling of absolute non-duality.

Tantrism and the Nātha Siddha Tradition

Nāthism originated among persons belonging to the lower levels of society. There is no doubt that this system was profoundly influenced on the one hand by Jainism and Ājīvikism and on the other by Tantrism. All over North India, in the Maharashtra region of Western India and also in parts of South India the followers of Nāthism had their centres. We have already referred to the Maheśvara Siddha sect of the South which based their doctrines mainly on Nātha principles. Eighteen exponents of this sect are known, the chief of them being Mular or Śrīmūlanātha. He and his intimates (Kālaṅga, Aghora, Mālikadeva, Nādānta, Paramānanda, and Bhoga) were the founders of the seven subsects of the southern Śuddhamārga. Among these teachers Bhoga or Boger was a Chinese Taoist whose centre of activities was the Siddha mountain in Tinevelly district. In theoretical matters they depended on the Śaiva and Śākta Āgamas. In the practical field their aim was to attain *Siddhi* or miraculous power, and they characterised the method of attaining it as *rahasya* or esoteric.[11]

Initially Nāthism probably developed in the lower regions of the Himalayas. The Nātha Siddhas had a general predilection toward occult practices and acquisition of supernatural powers. The Nātha system had a great influence upon the Raseśvara Siddhas of the Antarvedi or Maharashtra region who believed that by the Yogic control of breath, disciplining of the body, and use of drugs made of mica and mercury it was possible to attain immortality. In a text called *Vīramāheśvara* it is said that about the middle of the 12th century, Gorakṣanātha, the celebrated Nātha teacher, came in touch with a Māheśvara Siddha somewhere on the Tuṅgabhadrā. This Siddha was a *jīvanmukta* or liberated soul who imparted secret knowledge to him. According to the South Indian tradition, nine Nātha Siddhas (*navanāthasiddha*) founded nine sects each of which numbered one crore members. In many places in North India the Nāthapanthīs are known as *kan-phaṭ-yogi* because they wear a peculiar earring known as *mudrā*, or *darśana*, or *kuṇḍala*. They use Śiva symbols and observe the Śivarātri festival. The Śākta Pīṭhas are their sacred places of pilgrimage, and their religious theories and practices contain many Śākta-Tantric elements. Their deities include Nirañjana, Śūnya, Anādi, and Ādinātha. This shows that in Nāthism there are diverse influences—Śaiva, Śākta, Buddhist and Jain. Ingredients of Islam and Vaiṣṇavism are also found in the Nātha way of life. Their religious discipline was that of Haṭhayoga. In North India there are many sanctuaries of different Nātha sects and subsects managed by sectarian Mahāntas. In Bengal and Assam the Nāthas are known as Jogī or Jugī and their main occupation is weaving.

According to the Nātha cosmology, before creation everything was dark and void. In that vacuity came into being a bubble from which an egg was formed. The yellow portion of the egg was the earth and the white portion the sky. From the sweat of the primal god, Ādinātha, was born his lover Ketakī or Manasā, and from their union sprung Brahmā, Viṣṇu and Śiva. In order to test them Ādinātha assumed the form of a mutilated corpse. Having seen the corpse Brahmā and Viṣṇu avoided it, but Śiva recognised it as the body of his father and took it to the cremation ground. When the body was in flames, Mīnanātha sprang from its navel, Gorakṣa from its head, Hāḍi-pa from its bones, Kānu-pa from its ear, and Cauraṅgī from its legs. They are the five original Nātha Siddhas.

Because Śiva was the most competent son of Ādinātha, the latter was married to Ketakī who came to be known as Gaurī or Caṇḍī. Śiva possessed *mahājñāna*, the knowledge which could make a man immortal. Śiva determined to impart this knowledge to Gaurī and took her to the middle of a sea to do so. Mīnanātha guessed Śiva's intention. Assuming the form of a fish he was able to learn this knowledge. When Śiva came to know this he cursed Mīnanātha that he would forget the knowledge. Meanwhile, Gaurī desired to make the five Siddhas worldly-minded. She used her erotic tricks so that they might be attracted to women. Except for Gorakṣanātha, the passions of other four Siddhas were aroused by her gestures, as a result of which Mīnanātha was snared to become the ruler of women in a country called Kadalīdeśa, Hāḍi-pā to become the stable sweep of queen Mainamatī, Kānu-pā was banished into Dahukā country, and Cauraṅgī cohabited with his stepmother. Gorakṣa, however, was married to a princess and had a son by her known as Karpaṭinātha.

According to the legend described in the *Gorakṣavijaya,* also known as *Mīnacaitanya,* Gorakṣanātha rescued his teacher Mīnanātha from the influence of the women of Kadalī. There are many contradictory accounts relating to Mīnanātha or Matsyendranātha. In a Tantric text called *Kaulajñānanirṇaya* he is described as the founder of the Yoginī-kaula. In the Buddhist tradition he is identified with Luipāda.[12] Mīna or Matsyendra is also mentioned in the Tibetan Buddhist lists of Siddhas. In Nepal he is identified with Bodhisattva Avalokiteśvara. Even today a cart festival is celebrated in his honour. Among the Muslims of Bengal he is known as Machandalī or Mochrā Pir. In Muṇidatta's *Caryāgītikośa* a few verses have been ascribed to him. In the texts of Vajrāyana Matsyendra and Gorakṣa are regarded as Siddhas. In the North Indian tradition Gorakṣa was a fisherman by caste while in the Bengal tradition he was a cowherd. A few Tantric texts such as the *Gorakṣasaṃhitā*[13] have been associated with his name. In North India Gorakṣa-panthā is regarded as an esoteric system connected with Tantra and Yoga.

Hāḍi-pa, as we have seen, became a stable-sweep of the queen Mainamatī. This queen was a Siddha Ḍākinī who easily recognised his supernatural powers. After the death of her husband Māṇikacandra, her son Gopīcandra, began to rule under her guardianship. Fearing his premature death Maināmati forced Gopīcandra to receive initiation from Hāḍi-pā. The king was reluctant because Hāḍi-pā belonged to a low caste and low profession. Later when he realised his greatness he became a recluse. Hāḍi-pā is also known by the name Jālandharī. In the Tibetan lists a few Tantric texts are ascribed to his name—*Vajrāyoginīsādhana, Śuddhivajradīpa, Śrīcakrasaṃvaragarbhatattavavidhi* and *Huṃkāracittavindubhāvanākrāma.* There are also a few *dohās* in Apabhraṃśa composed by Kānu-pā or Kṛṣṇapāda. Probably he began his spiritual career with Nāthism but later was converted to pure Tantrism. In the Tibetan lists we have references to *Vayutattvopadeśā* ascribed to Cauraṅgīnātha. Outside Bengal Siddha Kānari or Kaneri was popular; his works are mentioned in the Tanjur catalogue.

Nāthism is a composite system consisting of numerous tradition coming from a variety of sources. A historical study of this system should bring to light many hitherto unknown facts and explain many obscure problems.[14] The most interesting feature of Nāthism is that for a long time it was able to keep itself away from the influence of Brāhmanical culture. Recently, however, there is a trend among a section of Nāthas to come under the Brāhmanical fold, and some of them want to consider themselves as Rudraja Brāhmaṇas. But Nāthism was basically a religion of the down-trodden, and to its credit can be attributed the sanction of a new way of life for the masses. It denounced the caste system and formulated the doctrinal points mainly on the understanding of the popular and liberal tradition of Śaiva, Vaiṣṇava, Śākta, and Buddhist Tantras. Nāthism laid much emphasis upon the humanitarian aspects of all these systems.

According to Nāthism, the ultimate reality has two aspects symbolised by the sun and the moon. The sun is *kālāgni*, the ideal of death and destruction. On the other hand the moon is the symbol of unchangeability. The aim of a Nātha aspirant is to feel within his own self the ideal of non-duality which is possible by the attainment of immortality and the renovation of the body. Generally, Śiva represents this non-dual state, the attainment of which is possible by connecting the forces of the sun and the moon within the body. The moon is Soma, the source of the drug of immortality (*amṛta*), which resides in the *sahasrāra* or cerebral region of the body. The essence which helps the human body to survive is produced from this Soma. If it is properly utilised one can attain immortality. But there is a great difficulty. The *amṛta*, dropped from Soma or the moon, is consumed by the sun which resides in the navel region. However, there is a serpent-like channel within the body having two faces known as Baṅka-nāla or Śaṅkhinī, and the face from which the *amṛta* drops is known as the tenth door. If this door can be closed it is possible to save the *amṛta*. This can only be achieved by *kāyasādhana* or disciplining of the body.[15]

The Nātha Siddhas believe that Ādinātha is the first Nātha, the founder of all esoteric sciences. He is very often equated with Śiva and Vajrasattva. The Hara-Gaurī conception of Nāthism is an adaptation of both the Mahāyanic Karuṇā and Śūnyatā and the Vajrāyanic Upāya and Prajñā. The Śūnyavāda of the Mādhyamika system is also accepted in Nāthism. According to Nāgārjuna Śūnya or vacuity is of four kinds—Śūnya, Atiśūnya, Mahāśūnya and Sarvaśūnya. The followers of Nāthism believe in three kinds of Śūnya—Ādiśūnya, Madhyaśūnya and Antaḥśūnya. This Śūnya is to be realised through Yoga. The process has been described in a text called *Hāḍamāla*[16] which says that by the Yogic control of breath the thirty knots in the spinal cord can be loosened, as a result of which the two vital winds, *prāṇa* and *apāna*, can enter the spinal cord and move upwards as Haṃsa through the six nerve plexuses—*mūlādhāra, svadhiṣṭhāna, maṇipura, anāhara, viśuddha (vaisandharī),* and *ajñā (ādya)*—and on reaching the *sahasrāra* region assume the nature of Śūnya. There are 72,000 nerves within the body of which 64 can be distinctly located and 15 utilised for Yogic purposes. In the *Yogacintāmaṇī* section of the *Gorkh-Vijaya*[17] we have the concept of *navacakra* which is the addition of three extra stages to the Tantric *ṣaṭcakra*. These extra stages are the three forms of Śūnya—Ādi, Madhya and Antyaḥ. It also deals with *ultā-sādhana* which is a Yogic method of making the vital fluid upward.[18]

It has already been stated that the *amṛta* or nectar-essence which flows from the moon within the body is consumed by the sun. The former is the creative principle and the latter the destructive. These two principles are understood to stand for the right and left nerve channels respectively. According to another conception the moon is Śiva and the sun Śakti, representing man and woman respectively. The moon, being the source of creation and preservation, is supposed to hold in its bosom *amṛta* which the sun (Śakti or Woman) is eager to consume, and that is why women should be avoided. This aversion to women is traditionally attributed to Gorakṣanātha and his disciple Carpaṭinātha. In the legends of Gopicandra we find that he left his two wives, Adunā and Padunā, to adopt a life of celibacy. His teacher, Hāḍi-pā, sold him to a prostitute called Hīrānaṭī who tried to attract him sexually but failed.[19] The Nātha-yogīs tried to keep away from women as far as possible, indeed to shun them altogether, though in some of their yogic practices they had to use women as mere instruments.

Sahajayāna in the Caryā Poems

We have seen that in theory and practice the Tantric Buddhist Siddhācāryas and Nātha Yogīs had something in common with the Sahajayāna discussed earlier. The Sahajiyā Buddhists had no special religious texts of their own. They depended mainly on the texts of Vajrāyāna. Their way of life and approach to religion are reflected in a class of poems called *caryās* and *dohās* which are the earliest specimens of the regional literature of Eastern India. The *caryā* poems deal with subtle philosophical questions from the viewpoint of Sahajayāna under the garb of the facts of real life; the pursuits, hopes, and aspirations of common persons; love, hatred, and emotion, the beauty of nature and of women; the social classes, conflicts, and amalgamations; technical and manual labour; and a variety of other things.[20]

The philosophical standpoint of the Sahajiyā Buddhists is revealed in the verses of Sarahapāda:

Do not meditate on the inanimate. Do not wish selfhood. The illusory phenomena enter into (i.e. disappear in) the great bliss (*mahāsukha*) as salt disappears in water. Saraha says: So many are the mertis of the Jina. Such is the way, such is verily the ultimate reality. The immovable circle is without success (i.e. fails). The (rush of) wind breaks down in the grasp of one's own mind. Even the *citta* disappears, the *acitta* comes into existence. (The real state) dawns clear through the instruction of the excellent teacher. There is no peace in muttering *mantras*. Can the fallen wall rise up? Looking at the fruit the tree is not smelling it. Does the disease run away at the sight of the physician?[21]

Tillopāda says in a more categorical way:

The aggregates, elements, sense organs and senses are all bound by (i.e. merge in) the Sahaja nature. Do not think that there are existence and non-existence in Sahaja (i.e. do not attribute positive and negative character to Sahaja). There is in it the vacuity, compassion and *samarasa*. Kill the mind completely through Nirvāṇa (and) enter into vacuity of the three worlds. Do not erroneously decry non-cognition. Do not wish bondage for the self. When the mind united with vacuity enters into the (state of) joy which arises out of that communion, the object of the senses are not at all perceived. It is without beginning, without end—such non-dual (joy) has been communicated by best of Gurus. Where the mind dies the (vital) wind is dissolved completely. Such an essence of truth, which can be realised by self—how can that be told? The truth is unattainable by the fools, by other peoples as well as by the learned world. Can the mind remain inaccesssible to him who is blessed by the Guru? Tillopāda speaks of that essential truth which is to be fully known by the self. That reaches the mind is not the absolute truth. Purify the mind well through Sahaja. There will be manifestation of succcess and liberation in this very life. Where the positive aspect of the mind merges into, the negative aspect of the mind too merges. The state of communion (of the mind with vacuity) is pure and without any positive and negative character. The tree of non-dual mind has attained vastness in the three worlds. It contains the fruit and flower of compassion. There are no 'mine' and 'thine'. Do not falsely distinguish between self and nonself. All are ever Buddha. The three worlds are the best and sublime stations: mind is by its nature pure. Those which are the customs of all are (either) moving or non-moving. (But) the vacuity is free from impurity. Do not judge (it). He who thinks 'this is self', 'this is the world'—can he understand the nature of pure *citta*. I am the universe, I am the Buddha, I am (he who is) free from impurity—I am the mental inaction (in person) and I am the killer of the cycle of existence. Mind is the Bhagavān; the vacuity is the Bhagavatī. It (mind) should be fixed in the Sahaja day and night. Do not entertain illusion about birth and death. Then one's own mind will stay in a state devoid of duality. Do not attach yourself to sacred places and hermitages. You will not attain peace through prints of body. Brahmā, Viṣṇu, Maheśvara—do not worship (these) gods, O Bodhisattva. Do not worship the god; you should not go to holy places. You shall not attain salvation through devotion to gods. Worship the Buddha with unfalling mind. Do not stay in the (world of) being and the (world of) annihilation. Attach yourself to the union of sapience and means. When one is fixed in that, the supreme (knowledge) is attained. As (one) engaged in (the science of) poison swallows the poison, so does one enjoy the world (of existence), not being attached to the world. Do not slight the *karmamudrā*. (Through it) the different kinds of moments and pleasure may be known. Learn to differentiate between *parama* and *virama* by adoring well the feet of the worthy *guru*. He who knows the highest kind of spiritual bliss knows the Sahaja in a moment. He who knows the difference between the moments and joys comes to be called the Yogi in this life. It is the ultimate truth, free from merit and demerit. There is nothing (i.e. no merit and demerit) in what is realised by the self. Abandon always the mind and non-mind. Fix yourself in the very nature of Sahaja. (It) does neither come nor go; (it) is not anywhere; (it) enters the soul through the instruction of the Guru. Colour is also abandoned by (it). It is devoid of form; (but still) it is complete in all forms. Kill this mind in the *citta* completely without delay. In that the *mahāmudrā* is pure in the three worlds. Myself is vacuity, all that moves is vacuity, the three worlds are vacuity. There is no sin and merit in the pure Sahaja. Let the mind go wherever it likes (to go). Errors should not be made in this place. By opening the below with (spiritual) eyes I became fixed through Dhyāna.[22]

Thus, it may be said that the followers of Sahajayāna do not insist on external formalities so far as the spiritual question was concerned, nor believe in any god apart from the self which is regarded as the Buddha or Bodhisattva. Their aim is to realise the Sahaja, the ultimate nature of beings, with the help of *guru* or preceptor. The realisation of Sahaja, which is in fact the realisation of Śūnyatā or vacuity, as the only reality leading one to Mahāsukha or great bliss. Thus there is an inherent idealistic approach in the Sahajayāna viewpoint which seeks to explain everything in terms of illusion. It is stated that the mind is solely responsible for the creation of the illusory world. The notion of difference or duality proceeds from the notion of existence. Bhusukupāda, in a song, compared the mind to fickle rat:

Dark is the night and the play of the rat begins. Kill, O Yogin, this rat of the vital wind, whereby you will escape coming and going. The rat causes existence and makes holes; this fickle rat remains inactive only when skilful devices are employed. This rat is time or death itself (i.e. the fickle mind constructs all temporal existence), but in it there is no colour. When it rises to the void it moves there and drinks nectar. The rat remains restless; pacify it through the instructions of the wise preceptor. Bhusuku says: when the activities of the rat will be destroyed, all bondage will also be destroyed.[23]

Due to *vāsanā* or root-instincts man falsely conceives the notion of existence and gets fettered. When mind is conditioned by the realisation of Śūnyatā, the questions of birth and death, suffering and non-suffering, of bondage and liberation, cease to exist. Luipāda says:

Existence does not come, neihter is there non-existence. Who does understand the truth in this way? Incomprehensible indeed is the nature of pure consciousness, says Lui. In the three elements it sports but it itself is not known. How can the Āgamas and the Vedas explain that whose colour, sign and form are not known? By speaking of what, should I give an exposition of truth? Just like the moon in water it is neither real nor unreal. How should it be thought of ? says Lui. I do not see any magnitude or locality of what I am now.[24]

Although emphasis is laid on the illusory nature of the world, the Sahajayāna insists on the *pravṛtti mārga* or following the path along which the human nature itself leads the individual. Sarahapāda says in a song:

O Yogins, do not leave off this straight and easy path and follow the crooked and curved path. *Bodhi* lies near you. Do not go to Laṅkā in search of it. Do not take the glass to see the bracelets in your hands. Realise your own pure *citta* within yourself.[25]

Not only are worship, muttering of *mantras* and performing penances and rituals worthless, so also is that found in the scriptures and in the saying and interpretations of the so-called learned persons. Saraha says:

The Paṇḍitas pose to interpret the scriptures. But they do not know that Buddha is residing in their own body. By such scholarship they can never escape the cycle of birth and death. Yet these shameless creatures call themselves learned.[26]

The followers of Sahajayāna are also against caste system, social difference and all sorts of external formalities. The most penetrating, scathing criticism is made by Sarahapāda in his *Dohākoṣa*.[27] His arguments, as translated by S.B. Dasgupta, are:

Saraha says that the Brahmins as a caste cannot reasonably be recognised to be the highest of men—for the saying that they dropped from the mouth of Brahmā is a myth invented by a section of clever and cunning people; if, on the other hand, a man becomes Brahmin by religious initiations (*saṃskāra*), then even the lowest of men may be a Brahmin. If a man becomes a Brahmin by reciting the Vedas, let the people of the lower classes also recite the Vedas and they will also become Brahmins; and they also do read the Vedas, for they read grammar which contains many words of the Vedas.... In vain do they offer *ghee* to the fire, for thereby their eyes will only be affected with intense smoke.... The devotees of the Lord (Īśvara), again, anoint the whole body with ashes.... they whisper (religious doctrines) into the ears (of credulous people) and deceive them thereby. The widows, the Muṇḍīs (women taking the vow of fasting for the whole month) and others taking different vows, get themselves initiated by these devotees who do it only in greed of money.... [Against the Jaina Kṣapaṇaka Yogīs it is said] if only the naked attain liberation, the dog and the fox would also attain it; if liberation is attained by tearing off hairs, the hips of young women would also attain it.... The Celas, the Bhikṣus and the Sthaviras take the *vow* of *pravrajyā*; some of them are lost in explaining the Sūtras, some again in strenuous thinking and reading. Others rush into the Mahāyāna fold, but none of them get the ultimate truth.... What will one do with lamps, offerings, *mantras* and services? What is the good in going to holy places or to the hermitage? Can liberation be attained only by bathing in holy waters?[28]

Sahajayāna and the Female Principle

In the *caryās* and *dohās* we come across a goddess variously known as Nairātmā, Ḍombī, Caṇḍālī, Śabarī, etc. This Female Principle is same as Śūnyatā or Prajñā of the earlier Tantric Buddhist tradition, conceived of in other religious systems as Śakti. According to Sahajayāna, this Female Principle is not outside the human body. Kānhapāda says that *citta* or mind is god, Nairātmā his consort. Just as salt merges into water so also the mind of the aspirant becomes totally absorbed in Nairātmā. Tillopāda observes:

> *Citta khasama jahi samasuha palaṭṭhai*
> *India-visaa tahi matta ṇa dīsai*

> When *citta* (mind) and the one that is the same as space (Śūnyatā or Prajñā) are united in absolute equilibrium, no sense-matter can be perceived in it.

In the *caryā* songs we find the goddess singing and dancing with the aspirant;[29] sometimes she is conceived of as a Ḍombī or Ḍoma girl who is married to him and is constantly engaged in sexual union;[30] sometimes she is rebuked by the aspirant as *kāmacaṇḍāli* for her excessive sexual passion and harlot-like gestures;[31] sometimes she is Caṇḍāli, a girl belonging to Caṇḍāla caste, who has become a typical housewife and also a Bengali (Baṅgālī);[32] sometimes she is Mātaṅgī, a boat-woman, helping the Yogi to cross the river,[33] sometimes she is a Bediyā girl selling bamboo products with coquettish gestures;[34] sometimes she is Śabarī decked with peacock's tail and a garland of *guñja* having a domesticated life with a hunter.[35] She is addressed by the aspirant thus:

> *Joini tai vinu khaṇahi na jīvami/*
> *To muha cumbi kamalarasa pībami//*[36]

> Yoginī, without your company I will not be able to live for a moment. Having kissed your lips I will drink the essence of lotus.

The names Caṇḍālī, Ḍombī, etc., are also used symbolically to denote the different stages in the course of the upward march of Śakti—the fire-force in the Tantric Buddhist tradition. Like the *kulakuṇḍalinī* of the Śākta Tantras, this Śakti is conceived of in the Sahajayāna as Sahajasvarūpā or Nairāmaṇī. She resides in the *nirmāṇacakra* which, in the form of a sixty-four-petalled lotus is situated in the navel region of the individual. In this state she is known as Caṇḍālī. When roused by Yogic practice she blazes to create in the mind of the aspirant a feeling of vibratory joy which is known as *viṣayānanda*, rather material in character. Then she moves upward and as Dombī burns the *dharmacakra* which is situated in the heart. The kind of joy produced from this explosion is known as *paramānanda* which has also a tinge of materiality and hence is not perfect. The next higher stage is attained when the Śakti in her upward march reaches the *sambhoghacakra* which is situated just below the neck. When this is burnt the joy ensuing is known as *virāmānanda* which is of transcendental nature. In this state Śakti is known as Nairāmaṇi. But the highest pleasure is obtained when she reaches the *uṣṇīṣa-kamala* or the cerebral region in which is situated the *mahāsukhacakra*. Here she is known as Sahajasundarī or the Sahaja damsel and the pleasure obtained is known as *sahajānanda* or *sahajamahāsukha* which is of the nature of perfect and eternal bliss. The complete merger of mind into this perfect bliss is the aim of the aspirant.

The names Caṇḍālī, Ḍombī, Śabarī, etc., are suggestive of untouchable castes and the lower professions. Since Śakti or the goddess transcends all sense perception, she is Ḍombī, i.e. a woman of the Ḍoma caste, who cannot be touched by a Brāhmaṇa. Her hut is outside the city, i.e. outside the world of the senses. Men of sophistication pass by the hut but they cannot enter it and enjoy her company. She is available only to the unprejudiced, to one who can give up all feelings of egoism, disobey scriptural injunctions, and disregard public scandal. Kānhapāda says:

Outside the city, O Ḍombī, is thy cottage; thou goest just touching the Brāhmaṇas and the shaven-headed (and never reveal thyself to them). O Ḍombī, I shall keep company with thee and it is for the purpose that I have become a naked Kāpālī without aversions. There is one lotus and sixty-four are the petals—the dear Ḍombī climbs on it and dances there. Honestly do I ask thee, on whose boat dost thou come and go ? The Ḍombī sells the loom and also the flat basket (made of bamboo). For thee have I done away with the drama of life. Thou art the Ḍombī and I am the Kāpālī, for thee I have put on a garland of bones. The Ḍombī destroys the lake and eats up the lotus stalk. I shall kill thee, Ḍombī, and take thy life.

Of what nature, O Ḍombī, is thy cleverness? The aristocrats are outside thee and the Kāpālīs are within.[37] Thou hast spoiled everything, through the law of cause and effect, thou hast destroyed the moon. Some speak ill of thee, but the learned never cast thee off from the neck. Thou art Kāmacaṇḍālī—there is no woman more cunning and unfaithful than the Ḍombī.[38]

The Sahajiyās maintain the earlier Tantric Buddhist approach towards women—they also believe that woman is at the same time a material object and a goddess. In the texts of Tantric Buddhism it is said that the goddess Prajñāpāramitā is a pure transcendental entity, but in the disguise of a woman she is present everywhere.[39] That is why sexual union with a female partner or *mudrā* is necessary as a means to realise the great bliss of non-duality.[40] At the first stage when spiritual attainment is yet to be achieved, the *mudrā* is used simply as *karma*, i.e. plain sexual union yielding only transient pleasure, and the word *karmamudrā* may be applied to any woman. The next higher grades are denoted by the terms *jñānamudrā*, *mahāmudrā* and *phalamudrā*.[41] The experiences of *karmamudrā* and *jñānamudrā* are fleeting in nature; they do not produce any permanent effect. But *mahāmudrā* and *phalamudrā* are subtle principles personfied in the forms of women. It is only through union with them that an individual can realise the true nature of his self and have what is known as Sahajamahāsukha.

The Sahajiyā Spirit in Jain Dohās

The main principles of Sahajayāna have been summarised by N.R. Ray:

> Negatively speaking, these were (a) sharp criticism and rejection of all external formalities in regard to religious practices and spiritual quests; and (b) protest against and rejection of priestly and scriptural authority, celebacy, penances, austerities, and the like. Positively, the most important elements were (a) recognition of the *guru* as essential for any spiritual exercise and quest, (b) recognition of the human body as the seat and habitat of all religious and spiritual experience, indeed, of the Truth or Ultimate Reality and rejection of any transcendental reality external to man, and finally (c) recognition of the experience of the Ultimate Reality as one of inexpressible happiness and ineffable radiance, waveless equipoise, absolute peace and tranquillity, and of a absolute non-duality or complete unity.[42]

This spirit of heterodoxy and protestantism is also found in Jain songs and *dohās*. S.B. Dasgupta has drawn our attention to a collection of Jain *dohās* composed in Western Apabhraṃśa which is known as *Pāhuḍadohā*.[43] Its author Muni Rāmasiṃha, flourished about A.D. 1000. In this collection we come across a sharp protest against external formalities in religious life, the barrenness of scriptural study and dry scholasticism, the practice of pilgrimage or wandering in forests, the use of religious garments, and so on. It is said:

O the Puṇḍit of Puṇḍits, you are leaving aside the grains of corn and gathering husk instead. You are satisfied with the scriptures and their meaning, but O ye foolish people—you know nothing about the ultimate meaning of the world.... Much has been read, but foolishness has not been removed—only the throat has been parched into the bargain.... Prevent this elephant of the mind from going to the mountain of Vindhya—for it will trample under feet the forest of Śila and once more fall into the pitfall of the world.... Of no avail is travelling from one sacred place to another; for the body may be cleansed with water, but what about the mind?.... What may penances do when there is impurity within?.... Liberation can be attained only if the mind, stained with worldliness, be fixed on Nirañjana. The Jinas say: worship and worship. But if the self residing within one's body be once realised in its ultimate nature, who else remains to be worshipped?.... The snake shakes off its slough, but its poison is not destroyed thereby. Putting on of religious dress can never remove the internal desire for worldly enjoyment. O you, the head of all shaven-headed—you have indeed got your head shaven—but you have not got your heart free from worldly desires.[44]

The Vaiṣṇava Sahajiyās

The ideals of Buddhist Sahajayāna, which derived its main impulses from the Laukika-Tantras or the Tantric approach to life as found among the masses, deeply influenced all forms of medieval religious systems. Vaiṣṇavism, especially in Bengal, was no exception. The Vaiṣṇava Sahajiyā cult has a considerable literature to its credit. The followers of Vaiṣṇava Sahajiyā tradition considered all the major Vaiṣṇava poets and apostles to be exponents of Sahajiyā practice. Even Śrī-Caitanya himself is said to have practised Sahaja-*sādhanā* with female companions. In the *Caitanyacāritamṛta*[45] we find that his female partner was Sāthī, daughter of Sārvabhauma. In the *Vivartavilāsa* of Akiñcana-dāsa[46] it is said that the female partner of Śrī-Rūpa was Mīrā, of Bhaṭṭa Raghunātha Karṇabai, of Sanātana Lakṣmī-hīrā, of Lokanātha a Caṇḍāla girl, of Kṛṣṇadāsa Piṅgalā, a milkmaid, of Śrījiva Śyāmā Nāpitānī, of Raghunātha Mīrabaī and of Gopālabhaṭṭa Gaurapriyā. At least three of these female partners belonged to the lower castes. In the literature of the Vaiṣṇava Sahajiyās we find references not only to the sexo-yogic practices of the Tantras, but also to the Nātha practice of drinking nectar oozing from the moon situated beneath the lotus of Sahasrāra.[47]

M.M. Bose in his work *Post-Caitanya Sahajiyā Cult* has supplied us with valuable information regarding the literature of the Vaiṣṇava Sahajiyās and the doctrines and practices found therein. Some of the Post-Caitanya Vaiṣṇava Sahajiyā texts are introduced in the form of a dialogue between Śiva and Śakti, as is done in the case of Tantric texts, the former instructing the latter of the secrets of Vaiṣṇava Sahaja-sādhanā. In the *Ānandabhairāva* Śiva himself is said to have practised Sahaja-sādhanā in the company of Koch girls impersonating Śakti. The tradition of Śiva's dalliance with the Koch girls is much fabricated in the later *Śivāyanas*. Although most of the Sahajiyā Vaiṣṇava texts belong to the post-Caitanya period, their contents are derived from the ideology and methodology of the earlier Tantric and Buddhist sects. The recognition of the human body as the microcosm of the universe and as the seat of all spiritual experience, by which the Tantric and Sahajiyā Buddhist standpoint is characterised, and also that of the *guru* as the conductor of all spiritual exercise and quest, are asserted in Vaiṣṇava Sahajiyā tradition in which greatest emphasis is laid upon man: *Śuna he māṇuṣ bhāi, sabār upar mānuṣ satya, tāhār upar ñai* (Listen, men, my brethren; man is the truth above all truths; and there is nothing above that).[48]

In the Hindu Tantras the ultimate reality is the non-dual state of unity of Śiva and Śakti. In Buddhist Tantras it is the unity of Prajñā and Upāya. The realisation of this unity in one's own self is the state of *mahāsukha*, as is held by the followers of Sahajayāna. These two principles are represented by man and woman, supreme bliss arising out of the union of the two. The Vaiṣṇava conception of Kṛṣṇa and Rādhā is interpreted by the Sahajiyās in the same sense as that of Śiva and Śakti or Upāya and Prajñā. All men and women are thought of as physical manifestations of Kṛṣṇa and Rādhā. The highest state of the union of the two is that of supreme love and it is the real *sahaja-mahāsukha*. This love between man and woman may be conjugal (*svakīyā*) but preferably it should be unconventional (*parakīyā*). *Parakīyā* love literally means the love of a man for a woman who is the wife of another man. In Sahajiyā Vaiṣṇava texts such as *Dvīpakojjvala*, *Ratvilāsa-paddhati*, etc., the union of man and woman is conceived of as having two forms—*prākṛta* and *aprākṛta*, the former denoting union on a natural plane and the latter on the supernatural.

The Sahajiyā Vaiṣṇavas also insist on the Tantric mode of

kāyasādhana and the upward march of Śakti through the nerve channels. A thousand-petalled lotus in the cerebral region is conceived of as Gokula, the abode of Kṛṣṇa. The concepts of *liṅga* and *yoni* have become the symbols of Nārāyāṇa and Ramādevī, the Male and Female Principles of creation.[49] The body itself is conceived of as Vṛndāvana, the site of Kṛṣṇa's sport, where resides Sahaja in the nature of pure love which flows between Rādhā and Kṛṣṇa. In texts such as *Ratīvilāsapaddhati*,[50] *Rāgamayi-kanyā*,[51] *Sahaja-upāsanā-tattva*,[52] etc., man and woman as the representatives of the two streams of love are described respectively as *rasa* and *rati*, or as *kāma* and *madana*. The realisation of the true nature of man as Kṛṣṇa and that of woman as Rādhā is known as the principle of Āropa. In the *Ratnasāra*[53] it is stated that *prema* or pure love is a purified form of *kāma* (sensual love), the former not being possible in the absence of the latter. If one can realise the truth of the body (*bhāṇḍa*) one is able to realise the truth of the universe (*brahmāṇḍa*). All beings are born in Sahaja, they live in Sahaja, and again return to Sahaja.

Tantric and Sahajiyā Ideals in Medieval Religious Reform Movements and in the Teachings of the Saints

The concept of Sahaja was a characteristic common to all the religious systems of the medieval age. Etymologically it is *sahajāta* (*sahajāyate iti sahaja*), that which is the same as human instinct itself. God, by whatever name or attribute he may be characterised, resides in the heart of man. The realisation of god as identical with one's own self is the basis of all forms of Sahajiyā cult. This realisation is called by the Sahajayānī Buddhists as *mahāsukha* which is possible through the union of Śūnyatā and Karuṇā, or Prajñā and Upāya. The Nāthapanthīs understand *mahāsukha* in terms of immortality which is possible through *kāyasādhana*. All forms of Tantric teaching insist on the symbolical union of the Male and Female Principle—the efficient and material causes of creation—within the body and this concept has influenced all types of medieval religious ideas.

The idea of Sahaja also has a place in the Sikh religion. Like Nāthism Sikhism is anti-Brahmānical. Like the Sahajiyās and followers of the Tantric way the Sikhs also believe in the absolute authority of the Gurus. The *Granth Sahib* contains not only the writings of Sikh Gurus but those of the teachers of other sects as well. The medieval saints committed to liberal ideas such as Kabir, Ramdās, and others, have a place of great honour in Sikhism. In the *Ādi-Granth* five categories of the Sikh way of life are described. These are Dharam-khaṇḍ, Gian-khaṇḍ, Saram-khaṇḍ, Karam-khaṇḍ and Sach-khaṇḍ. The fifth one, Sach, is the same as Sahaja. According to Sikhism the realisation of this Sach or Sahaja is that of the personal god in the individual self and cannot be described in words. In the *Ādi-granth* it is said that this state is the fourth state (*cauṭhā-pad*) beyond the three qualities of *sattva, rajas* and *tamas,* and is known as *param-pad* or *turīyā-pad* or *sahaj-pād.* It is also called *amar-pad,* that which is of eternal peace and contentment. It is unchangeable because it is beyond the cycle of birth and death and beyond the tenth door (cf. the Nātha conception of the tenth door). It is the source of eternal light which causes the light of the individual soul to merge into that of god in the same way as a drop of water merges into the sea. It is that state in which the individual soul merges into the universal soul where there is an end to all sorts of dualism.[54] Nanak called this state *jīvanmukti* or *śuni* (*śūnya*)*-samādhi, sahaj-samādhi,* and *sahaj-yog* and its experience as *mahā-sukh, param-sukh* or *param-ānand.* In fact, Sahaja is not only the ultimate reality, it is Īśvara or Lord, the last resort, full of love, into which the self merges completely: *jākai antar vasai prabhu api nānak le jan sahajī samāti.*

In the medieval age many Vaiṣṇava, Śaiva, and Tantric sects launched religious reform movements. They fought for the religious rights of the down-trodden and women, preached their doctrines among the hill tribes and tried to bring back the converted Muslims into the fold of Hinduism. The Nibandhakāras, or law-makers on the other hand tried to maintain the purity of Hinduism by enforcing the Smṛti laws with maximum strictness and rigidity. These Nibandhakāras were closely counected with the rruling class. Lakṣmīdhara of the 12th century, Hemādri of the 13th and Caṇḍeśvara of the 14th were ministers of Govindacandra Gāhaḍavāla, Mahādeva Yādava, and Harisiṃha respectively. In the 16th century queen Durgāvatī had a seven-volume law-manual composed by Padmanābha Misra which was known as *Durgāvatī-prakāśa.* Akbar's revenue minister, Todaramalla, patronised the compilation of *Toḍarānanda.* In the 17th century Mitramiśra composed *Vīramitrodaya.* His patron was Vīrasiṃha, the feudal chief of Orcha. The Bundel king Bhagavant was the patron of Nīlakaṇṭha. Anantadeva's *Smṛtikaustubha* was composed owing to the munificence of Bajbahadur of Almora. Śivājī financed Keśava Paṇḍita. Of the other important Nibandhakāras mention should be made of Raghunandana, Pītāmbara Siddhāntavāgiśa and Kamalākarabhaṭṭa. Subsequently, the views of Raghunandana came to be regarded as the most authoritative. They brought significant changes in the caste-structure, because the traditional *varṇa* division could not be maintained. The position and hierarchy of the Śūdras had to be redefined under two broad categories, *sat* and *asat*, the former receiving higher social status owing to their holding of important Gubernatorial offices, feifs and lucrative professions and also to their adherence to the Brahmanical way of life and patronage to Brahmanical culture. Those who did not follow the Brahmanical norms of pure living and had lower occupations were relegated to the *asat* category.

The poet Tulsīdāsa was a champion of Brahmānism. In his celebrated *Rāmacaritamānasa*, while describing the customs of Kaliyuga, he refers to the Śūdras proclaiming their superiority and appearing in the role of teachers and to the Brāhmaṇas serving as their disciples. He notes with contempt that the Telīs, Kumārs, Caṇḍālas, Kirātas, Kols, Kalwārs and other persons belonging to the despised castes have become *gurus* by shaving their heads, that they are meditating, observing vows, and reading the Purāṇas and that the Brāhmaṇas are subservient to them (taking the dust of their feet).[55] This is simply a reflection upon the popularity of teachers like Rabidās, Dhannā, Senā, and others who belonged to the so-called lower castes and professions. In South India, as we have seen, the Śrī-Vaiṣṇavas were divided into two groups in relation to the caste status.[56] From a Tamil copper plate grant of 1596, it is known that during the reign of Venkaṭapatideva one Śūdra priest, on the strength of his numerous disciples, made Kaṇḍiya Devara the ruler of Vṛddhācalam in the presence of Mutta Kṛṣṇappa Nāyaka.[57] The social movement launched by the Ṭenkalais of the South spread to North India through the followers of Śrī-Caitanya and other apostles of the *bhakti* movement. Gopālabhaṭṭa's *Haribhaktivilāsa* is a protest against social discrimination, in the commentary on which Sanātana Gosvāmī strongly defends the right of the Śūdras.[58] Many of the non-Brāhmaṇa disciples of Śrī-Caitanya, like Narahari Sarkar, Narottam Thakur, etc., worked as *gurus* of the Brāhmaṇas. Tukāram of Mahārashtra, though himself a Śūdra, had numerous Brāhmaṇa disciples. Śaṅkaradeva of Assam and his chief disciple Mādhavadeva were Kāyasthas but they had a large following of Brāhmaṇas.

Of the North Indian leaders of the reform movement, Rāmānanda of the 14th-15th century belonged to the Śrī-Vaiṣṇava sect. In the *Granth Sahib* we have a song attributed to him in which he says that God (Rāma) cannot be found in any external object; he is not in the the Vedas; one should seek him in one's heart. Among his disciples, Rabidās was a *cāmār* (cobbler) by caste and profession who attracted numerous disciples owing to his liberal religious ideas. Kabīr himself held Rabidās in high esteem. The *Granth Sahib* contains more than thirty songs composed by him. Jhāli, queen of Chittor, was his follower, and the celebrated Mīrābāī his disciple. Most of the Indian cobblers belong to the sect of Rabidās and use his name as a surname. Senā was another disciple of Rāmānanda, a barber by caste. The ruler of Bandhogarh became his disciple. Dhannā was a Jat and a farmer by profession. He was born in 1415. Pīpā was born in Rajasthan in 1425. His stronghold was Pipavat in Dvārakā. Bhavānanda, Sukhānanda, Āsānanda, Surāsurānanda, Paramānanda, Mahānanda, and Śrī Ānanda belonged to the orthodox group of Śrī Vaiṣṇavas. Later they changed their views and became staunch followers of Rāmānanda.

Apart from Rabidās, the most celebrated disciple of Rāmānanda was Kabīr who was born in a Muslim family probably in 1398. He learnt from Rāmānanda the futility of the caste system, idolatry, pilgrimage, vows, fasts and all external formalities of religion. He made no distinction between man and woman. Among his followers were Hindus as well as Muslims. Many of his songs are quoted in the *Granth Sahib.* His *dohās* are treasured in North Indian literature. He earned his livelihood by weaving. His teachings are: Every man must work; he must earn to help others. but he should not accumulate wealth for his own interest; he should be truthful and accessible to all; he should realise the truth within himself; truth is in the form of love, compassion, and greatness; one religious system is different from another only in name; God may be called by any name; and external formalities in spiritual quest are meaningless. After the death of Kabīr his Muslim disciples established a separate sect in Maghar. His Hindu disciples, under the leadership of Surat Gopāl, founded another sect at Vārāṇasī. Their scripture was known as *Vijaka.*

Anatānanda, although a follower of Rāmānanda, did not belong to his intimate circle. His centre of spiritual activity still survives at Galta near Jaipur. His chief disciple was Kṛṣṇadāsa Pahārī. Among the disciples of the latter Kīlha founded a sect called Khākī in North-

Western India. The other one was Agradās whose disciple was Nābhā the celebrated writer of *Bhaktamāla*. Nābhā belonged to the untouchable caste. His disciple Priyadās composed a commentary on his master's work. Among those who were outside the circle of Rāmānanda, Sadnā was a butcher whose devoted career and noble ideals are recorded in the *Bhaktamāla*. Two of his songs are also quoted in the *Granth Sahib*. Nāmadeva of Gurudaspur, different from his celebrated Maharashtrian namesake, was a saint with liberal ideas. Ālam Shah, the last king of the Saiyad dynasty, established a monastery in his honour in 1446. A second Nāmadeva flourished in Bulandshar, and a third in Marwar. Poet Surdās flourished between 1483 and 1563. Dharmadāsa, a disciple of Kabīr and a Bania by caste, founded a sect with liberal ideas at Chattisgarh. Another disciple of Kabīr was Malukdās (1574-1682) whose centre was at Allahabad. His sect enjoyed great popularity in North India.

One of the best exponents of the way of Kabīr was Dādū (1544-1603) who was born in Rajasthan. His purpose was to synthesize all forms of religion; the sect founded by him was known as Parabrahma-Sampradāya. He made a selection of devotional writings from all forms of religion about A.D. 1600 and this was the first of its kind in the world. Dādū did not believe in any scripture. According to him the realisation of the self should be the aim of human life. His sons Garibdās, and Maskīndās, and daughters, Nānībāi and Mātābāi, composed many devotional poems. Of his disciples Sundardās and Rajjab deserve mention. The latter founded a sect, the teachers of which could be Hindus or Muslims. Of other medieval saints who thought and worked in the line of Kabīr and Dādū, mention should be made of Dharanīdās who was born in Chapra in 1556, Lāldās who belonged to the Meo tribe of Rajasthan, Puran Bhakat, Cajju Bhakat and Bābālāl of Punjab, and Narasimha Mehta of Gujarat.

Among the liberal religious leaders who flourished in North India in the first half of the 18th century, Bhān Saheb, a follower of Kabīr, formed a salvation army. His important disciples were Jīvandās and Rabi Saheb. Carandās, who was born at Dehar near Alwar in 1703, formed a sect of his own which was against caste system and all forms of superstitions. Śivanārāyāṇa, who was born in 1710 in Balia district, tried to synthesize Hindu and Muslim religious ideals. It is said that the Mughal emperor Muhammed Shah was his disciple. Prāṇa Nātha of Bundelkhand and Garibdās of Rotan followed the line of Śivanārāyāṇa. Rāmacandra or Sant Rām of Jeypore was the founder of a liberal sect called Ramasanehī. Jagjivan, who flourished in the last quarter of the 17th century, founded the Satyanāmi or Satnami sect. He and Gulal Saheb were disciples of the celebrated Sufi teacher Yari Saheb. They believed in the oneness of God and in the synthesis of Hindu and Muslim religious ideals. Gulāl Saheb's disciples were Bhikha to whose spiritual succession belonged Govinda Saheb and the famous devotional poet Paltu Saheb. One of the Satnami leaders was Ghāsidās who belonged to the caste of leather-workers. The Satnamis were against idolatry, untouchability and the caste system. Similar ideals were held by the Alakhnāmis, a sect which flourished in the Bikaner region under the leadership of Lalgir or Lalbeg.[59]

Although historically the sparks of protestantism came from South India, there was no important reform movement in that region in subsequent times. We may, however, refer to the Dāsakuṭa movement in Karnataka which rejected the caste system and external formalities. The Maharashtrian saints like Nivṛttinātha, Jñānadeva, Nāmadeva, Ekanātha, Tukāram, Rāmdās, etc., believed in absolute devotion and simplicity in religious life. Personally many of these teachers were free from caste prejudices and superstitious beliefs and practices, but they did not launch any socio- religious movement as did their counterparts in North India. The only exception was the Mahānubhava sect which was vehemently opposed to Brahmānism. The exponents of this sect were Govindaprabhu, Nāgadeva, Cakradhara, Bhāskara, Keśavarāja, Dāmodara Paṇḍita, Nārāyāṇa Paṇḍita, and the poetess Mahadambā. The Mahānubhavapanthīs composed their scriptures in symbolical language. Their views were inspired by liberal Vaiṣṇavism and Nāthism.

The Neo-Vaiṣṇavism preached by Śrī-Caitanya had a tremendons influence in Bengal and Orissa, and despite Brāhmanical handling it retained a popular character. After the death of Śrī-Caitanya it was divided into numerous subsects, and there was a great difference of opinion between the followers of Gaṅgādhara and those of Advaita.[60] In eastern Bengal the Caitanya movement was launched by Narottama Ṭhākur. It had a great influence upon persons belonging to the lower castes and also upon the trading class. In Assam, Śaṅkaradeva (1486-1568) launched a Bhakti movement. Himself a Kāyastha he was opposed to the caste system, image worship, and construction of temples. He had many Brāhmaṇa as well as Muslim followers. His views were also popular among the Nagas and the Maṇipuris. The sect founded by him was known as Mahāpuruṣīya. After the death of his successor Mādhavadeva in 1596, it was split into numerous subsects. One was known as Bāmunia and was led by Dāmodaradeva. Another sect was founded by Aniruddha which was known as Moamaria, because its followers came mostly from the fishermen community. This sect believed in the pure Tantric way. Śaṅkaradeva's grandson, Puruṣottama, was the founder of Ṭhākurīya sect. The views of Śrī-Caitanya were popularised in Orissa through the efforts of Syamānanda and his disciple Rasikānanda.

Bengal, Assam, and Orissa were basically the strongholds of Śaktism ahd Tantra. The goddess Kāmākhyā of Gauhati was really the Khasi tribal mother Ka-me-kha who latter came into the fold of Śakta-Tantric cults. Likewise, Jagannātha of Puri was originally a tribal god, and although he is now in Vaiṣṇava garb, his rituals speak of his Tantric character. Subhadrā, as we have already remarked, is the goddess Ekāṇaṃsā, symbolising the attributes of the local and tribal Mother Goddesses such as Sāmaleśvarī, Khichiṅgeśvari, etc. In the Śakta tradition Vimalā is the presiding goddess of Śrīkṣetra and Jagannātha her Bhairava. In Bengal, the Śakta ideals and the cult of Kālī were popularised by Kṛṣṇānanda Āgamavāgiśa, the celebrated compiler of *Tantrasāra*, Brahmānanda, author of *Śāktānandataraṅgiṇī*, and his disciple, Pūrṇānanda, author of *Śyāmārahasya*, hailed from Bengal. In public life Śakta Tantric ideals were also popularised by Sarvānanda (16th century), Ratnagarbha or Gosāin Bhattācārya (16th century), Jayadurgā (17th century), and others. The writers of the Śakta lyrics also deserve special mention in this connection. In Bengal, although Brāhmanical ideas were superimposed on Tantric texts, the basic liberalism of the Tantric way of life could not be suppressed. That is why it was able to attract millions of the masses, especially those belonging to the downtrodden classes.[61]

In Bengal, Assam, and Orissa, Nāthism is also known as Yogīpanthā. The songs of Gopīcandra are popular not only in Bengal but also over Northern India. Among their composers, many are Muslims, and they are known in North India as Bharthari. Although Muslims, they use ochre robes. In Orissa two other sects later came into prominence. These were known as Mahimā-panthā and Kumbhipanthā. Owing to the influence of the medieval reform movements, a lot of liberal sects flourished in Bengal like Khusi-visvāsī, Sahebdhanī, Rāma-ballabhī, Jagamohinī, Balarāmī, Neḍā, Āul, Bāul, Darbeś-Sāin, Saṃyogi, Kartābhaja, etc. These sects were influenced by the Nātha and Sahajiyā ideals and also to some extent by Islam.[62] There is reason to believe that the cult of Pirs and tombs, which is so popular among the Muslims of Bengal, was due to the influence of the converted Buddhists.[63]

Sufism and Tantric-Sahajiyā Tradition

Sufism was popular among a considerable section of the Muslim population of India during the medieval period. The origin of Sufism may be traced to a few verses of the *Koran*. The Sufis were unorthodox in religious beliefs and practices, indifferent to external happiness or sorrow, and guided by spiritual emotion. They depended more on the reason of the heart than on the injunctions of the scriptures. Islamic Sufism originated in Arabia but it was more popular in Iran.

There is a variety of views regarding the genesis of Sufism. Some scholars find in it the influence of Vedānta. Others ascribe to it the influence of Buddhism. Again a group of scholars ascribe its origin to neo-Platonism. Historically, however, it may be said that in all places and at all times are found spiritual aspirants who are not satisfied with the existing religious norms, who are free from all sorts of orthodoxy and parochialism, who believe that the human heart is the seat of God, that his relation with man is essentially personal and that for this reason scriptural injunctions are redundant and useless. who believe in the most easy (*sahaja*) method, and who believe that the human body is the microcosm of the universe. Like the unsophisticated Tantrics or the Sahajiyās, the followers of Sufism were also inclined towards this stream of thought.

In Sufism the greatest emphasis is laid upon the mental entity of man. There is no God outside the human mind. How should man realise God within his own self? What is the relation of God with the individual and with the material world? The answer is presented in two categories—*tariqat*, or way, and *marifat*, or knowledge. The way consists of seven stages—service, love, sacrifice, meditation, concentration, union, and equation. Knowledge is that which helps the realisation of God. Like the Tantrics and Sahajiyās the Sufis believe in a *guru*, or preceptor, known as *Pīr* or *Mursid*. Knowledge is of two kinds—*ilm* or that which is received through known sources like perception, inference, etc., and *marifat* or that which is obtained through the grace of God.

Sufism came to India with the Muslims; its earliest stronghold was Sind. The Sufi teachers had a great mass-contact, and that is why it was not difficult for them to find like-minded sects in the indigenous Hindu population. They, in their turn, also exerted great influence upon the medieval religious reform movements. Of the existing Sufi sects in India, at least four came into much prominence in later times: Chistiya, Kadiriya, Suhrabardiya, and Naqsbandi. Each of these sects produced many qualified teachers. It is interesting to note that just as in Tantrism Brahmānical elements were superimposed by a class of teachers, so also in Sufism there was a consistent attempt to graft orthodox ideas and practices. Theoretically Indian Sufis were divided into two broad categories—those who believed in absolute non-dualism (*yujudiya*) and those who had some reservation (*suhudiya*). The former held everything to be a manifestation of God while the latter considered everything as produced from God. The Sufis placed spiritual knowledge (*marifat*) above the scriptural injunctions (*shariat*). They built numerous monasteries and institutions where, under the guidance of *Pirs, Mursids* or *Saikhs*, the aspirants were led to self-realisation (*tarika*).

By the 14th century of the Christian era Sufism was completely absorbed in Indian soil. It was assimilated with the prevalent Tantric-Sahajiyā ideas. How smoothly the Sufi ideas could work in the Indian mind may be exemplified with reference to the Bāuls of Bengal. Outpourings from the heart as songs constitute an important religious mode with the Bāuls. In this we find on the one hand the influence of Bengal Vaiṣṇavism and on the other that of Sufi *sama*. The Sufi insistence on *guru-vāda*—the essentiality of preceptor in spiritual exercise—and on the human body as the microcosm of the universe is shared alike by the Tantrics, Sahajiyās, Āuls, Bāuls and most of the medieval religious sects which based their creeds on liberalism. The conception of the *man of heart* which is found in the Bāul songs really represents a mixture of the conceptions of the ultimate truth in the Tantric-Sahajiyā schools and in Sufism. The Sufi concepts of divination, of creation proceeding from love, of the cosmos supported by love, of the dual nature of man as finite and infinite, human and divine, of the imagery of the lover and the beloved in God's relation with man, etc., have a close affinity with medieval Indian religious ideas.

Among one section of Indian Muslims there was a tendency to follow the Tantric rahasya-sādhanā. In this connection we may refer to Gazi Mian or Sipah-Salar Masud Gazi who was the founder of a religious sect which in theory and practice resembled Sahajayāna Buddhism. He was a contemporary of Sultan Mahmud, and the sect founded by him was banned by Sikandar Lodi. During the reign of Akbar this sect was again allowed to function. Another similar sect was founded by Shah Mardan.[64] Apart from the celebrated Yavana Haridāsa, Śrī-Caitanya had a few Pathan followers whose leader was Bijuli Khan.[65] That the Muslims were easily accepted in northern Vaiṣṇavism has been mentioned by Mohsin Fani in his *Dabistan.* He himself had the blessings of a Hindu saint known by the name Caturvāpa. In 1642, at Lahore he met a saint called Nārāyaṇa Dāsa who had many Muslim disciples. Among them Mirza Saleh and Mirza Haider later became celebrated Sufi teachers. The Parabrahma sect founded by Dādū (1544-1603) tried to synthesize Hindu and Muslim liberal ideas. Prāṇa Nātha, a Hindu saint, composed a book called *Mahitariyal* in which he tried to show the similarities between the Veda and the Koran. He used to initiate disciples on the condition that the initiated ones, Hindus and Muslims, should dine together.[66]

Of the celebrated Sufi saints, Shah Karim of Sind, who flourished about the beginning of the 17th century, deserves special mention. His source of inspiration was a Vaiṣṇava *guru.* He and his followers used the Om symbol of the Hindus. Another Sufi saint of the same region was Shah Inayat who was greatly respected by the Muslims as well as the Hindus. But the most popular was Shah Latif, whose shrine at Bhit is still thronged by both Hindu and Muslim pilgrims. In Sind it was a very common practice for the Hindus to have Muslim teachers and for the Muslims to have Hindu teachers. The Sufi tradition produced a number of great poets in the Sind region like Bedil, Bekosh (Muhamad Hossain), Rohan, Kutub, etc., whose devotional songs are popular even today. Baori Saheb of Delhi was the founder of a Sufi spiritual lineage to which Biru Saheb, Yari Saheb, Gulal Saheb, and Jagjivan belonged. In the writings of Yari Saheb, Allah is equated with Rāma and Hari. Darya Saheb was a follower of the Kabīr-mārg. His followers did not believe in scriptures, hymns, pilrimage, image worship, and caste. There was a second Darya Saheb who flourished in Marwar about the middle of the 17th century. His views were similar to those of Dādū. His God was Rāma Parabrahman. He believed in Yoga as well. His songs were very popular in North India. Bulle Shah, who came from Istambul and made Kasur in Punjab the centre of his activities was a critic of the Koran and all other scriptures. The Rasul-sahis of Agra practised Tantric rituals.

Therefore, it appears that the medieval saints of North India were able to achieve a kind of synthesis between the Tantric Sahajiyā and Sufi ideas. In tune with the spirit of the Tantric, Sant, Sahajiyā and other non-conformist and protestant sects, the Sufis also came to commit themselves to what is commonly known as the Lokāyata tradition. Votaries of these cults very often came from the lower grades of society where the hold of Brahmānical Hindu codes and orthodox Islamic religious injunctions were rather loose. This Lokāyata or popular tradition had some important tenets and principles that provided the ideological base on which the ordinary Hindus and Muslims found a common platform.[67]

NOTES

1. See Ch. 7.
2. P.C. Bagchi, *Kaulajñānanirṇaya*, Calcutta Sanskrit Series No. III, pp. 33-4.
3. See Alaka Chattopadhyaya, *Catalogue of the Tanjur and Kanjur*, Calcutta, 1972.
4. *JASB*. Vol. XXVI, 1930, p. 132.
5. *IHQ*, 1929, pp. 14-30; *EI*, Vol. XXVI, pp. 247-8.
6. *Tāranātha's History of Buddhism*, ed. D.P. Chattopadhyaya, Simla, 1970.
7. B.N. Dutt, *Mystic Tales of Lama Tāranātha*, Calcutta, 1944, pp. 8-11.
8. *Śrīcakrasambhāra*, ed. Kazi Dawa Samdup, intro, p. XXXV.
9. Roerich, op. cit., Vol. II, pp. 753-5, 867-9.
10. Snellgrove, op. cit., Pt I, pp. 54ff.
11. Their theoretical standpoint is to be found in *Kāladahanatantra* which is a part of *Kāmikāgama*, *Mṛtyunāśakatantra* which is a part of *Vijayāgama*, Kumāradeva's *Śuddhasādhaka* and Rāvaṇārādhya's *Śivajñānadīpa*.
12. P.C. Bagchi, *Kaulajñānanirṇaya*, intro. XXXIII.
13. G.W. Briggs, *Gorakhnāth and the Kanphaṭa Yogis*, Calcutta, 1938, passim.
14. For a better understanding of Nāthism see Kalyani Mallik, *Nātha Sampradāyer Itihās*, in Bengali, Calcutta 1950; Hazari Prasad Dvivedi *Nātha Sampradāya*, in Hindi, 1966.
15. S.B. Dasgupta, *Obscure Religious Cults*, pp. 211-55.
16. Ed. Rajmohan Nāth, verses 153ff.
17. Ed. Panchanon Mandal, pp. 218ff.
18. Ibid., pp. 72ff.
19. *Gopīcandrer Gān*, ed. Asutosh Bhattacharyya, *passim*.
20. The songs used here are adopted from P.C. Bagchi's *Dohākoṣa* published

in the *Journal of the Department of Letters*, Calcutta University, Vol. XXVII, 1936, pp. 1-180. (Tillopāda, pp. 1-4. 41-5, 139-75; Sarahapāda, pp. 5-23, 28-31, 52-120; 176-80; Kānhapāda, pp. 24-7, 121-38.) and Vol. XXX, 1938, 'Materials for a critial edition of old Bengali Caryāpāda', pp. 1-106 (Tibetan), pp. 107-56 (Bengali). The Songs Nos. are taken from the latter. Besides Bagchi's notes and translations, S.B. Dasgupta's renderings in *Obscure Religious Cults*, pp. 35-122 have also been used.

21. P.C. Bagchi, op. cit., pp. 175-80.
22. Ibid., pp. 139-75.
23. Song No. 21; Dasgupta, op. cit., pp. 37-8.
24. Song No. 29; Ibid., pp. 39-40.
25. Song No. 32; Ibid., p. 52.
26. Bagchi, op. cit., p. 27.
27. Ibid., pp. 5-23, 28-31, 52-120.
28. Dasgupta, op. cit., pp. 55-6.
29. Song No. 17.
30. Song No. 19.
31. Song No. 18.
32. Song No. 49.
33. Song No. 14.
34. Song No. 10.
35. Song No. 28.
36. Song No. 4.
37. Song No. 10; Dasgupta., op. cit., pp. 103-4.
38. Song No. 18.
39. *Prajñopāya*, V. 22-3.
40. Ibid., III. 20
41. *Sekoddeśaṭīkā*, pp. 56ff.
42. N.R. Ray, *The Sikh Guru and the Sikh Society*, Patiala, 1970, p. 126.
43. Ed. H.L. Jain, *Ambadāsa Gavare Digambara Jaina Granthamālā*, No. 3.
44. Dasgupta, op. cit., pp. 59-60.
45. *Madhyalīlā*, Ch. X.V.
46. *Vaṅga Sāhitya Paricaya*, Vol. II, p. 1650.
47. See *Ānandabhairava*, in M.M. Bose's *Sahajiyā Sāhitya*, pp. 132-3.
48. Song ascribed to Caṇḍīdāsa.
49. *Brahmosaṃhitā*, V. 2-20. Also see *Hayaśirṣapāñcarātra* verses quoted in the *Bhāgavatsandarbha* of the *Ṣaṭ-sandarbha* of Jīva Gosvāmī.
50. Calcutta University Mss. No. 572.
51. Ibid., No. 581.
52. *Vaṅgīya Sāhitya Pariṣat Patrika*, 1355. B.S., No. 4.
53. Calcutta University Mss. No. 1111.
54. *Adi-granth, Sabdārth Śrīguru Granth Sahib jī*, 7-8, 22, 154, 227, 661, 688, 725, 940, 1110, 1112.
55. *Rāmacaritamānasa*, Nāgārī Pracāriṇī Sabhā edn., Uttarakāṇḍa, 483.

56. See A. Govindācārya in *JRAS*, 1910, pp. 1103ff; also *JBBRAS*, Vol. XXIV, pp. 126ff; *Ind. Ant.*, Vol. XIII, pp. 252ff.
57. Copper plate No. 75 of R. Sewell's List.
58. *Haribhaktivilāsa*, Bahrampur edn., V. 491-3.
59. K.M. Sen, *Medieval Mysticism in India*, Eng, tr. from Bengali by M.M. Ghose, 1929; G.H. Westcott, *Kabīr and the Kabīr Panth*, London, 1907; A.K. Datta, *Bhāratavarṣīya Upāsaka Sampradāya*, in Bengali, Calcutta, 1888, Vol. I, pp. 19-112; K.M. Sen, *Dādū*, in Bengali, 1935; H.P. Dvivedi, *Kabīr*, in Hindi, 1950; P.R. Caturvedi, *Uttarī Bhārat kī Sant Paramparā*, in Hindi, 1951.
60. *Caitanyabhāgavata* (ed. Atulkrishna Gosvāmī), II. 24.
61. N.N. Bhattacharyya, *History of the Śakta Religion*, New Delhi, 1974, passim.
62. A.K. Datta, op. cit., pp. 171-291.
63. N.N. Bhattacharyya, *Ancient Indian Rituals*, pp. 115-18.
64. N.R. Ray, op. cit.. pp. 17-18.
65. *Caitanyacaritāmṛta*, II. 18.
66. H.H. Wilson, *Religious Sects of the Hindus*, rpt., New Delhi, 1958, p. 186.
67. For Sufism see J.A. Subhan, *Sufism: Its Saints and Shrines*, Lucknow, 1960; J. Arberry, *Doctrine of the Sufis*, Cambridge, 1935; M. Anamul Huq, *Vaṅge Sufi Prabhāva*, in Bengali; *The Dubistan, or School of Manners*. Translated by D. Shea and A. Troyer. For medieval *bhakti* movements in general see N.N. Bhattacharyya (ed.), *Medieval Bhakti Movements in India*, New Delhi, 1989.

9

The Sophisticated Tantras with Śākta Orientation

Tantric Substratum of Śāktism

We have seen that Tantrism as a heterogenous set of ideas and practices characterised the religious fabic of India—ancient, medieval, and even modern—but although it was able to make its way into all forms of Indian religious systems, orthodox and popular, its influence was not uniform in all the cases.

The present form of Tantrism, as may be gleaned from a variety of sources, reveals a combination of two aspects—popular, or *laukika*, and the sophisticated, or that which is burdened with Brahmanical superimpositions. The category of *laukika* Tantra reflects the liberal attitude of the simpler peoples towards religion and society. In religion this attitude is marked by the negation of all external formalities and doctrinal intricacies in regard to spiritual quest and by the affirmation of the beliefs and practices which are regarded as the heritage of the primitive and unsophisticated, undifferentiated way of life. In the case of society this attitude is marked by the rejection of the caste system and patriarchy upheld in the Brahmanical Smārta-Paurāṇic tradition, and by its insistence on regulating the practical aspects of life like manual and technical labour, chemical sciences, medicine, metallurgy, and so on. This *laukika* Tantra was accepted in principle by the Atimārgika (those who do not believe in the codified norms of spiritual realisation) and the Vedabāhya (those who prefer to base their doctrines on anti-Vedic and anti-Brahmanical ideas) sects, the radicals and reformists belonging to the major religious systems of India, as well as by the followers both of the non-conformist and popular religious ideas and practices and of the medieval saints and their teachings.

The sophisticated Tantras, on the other hand, are full of

Brahmanical elements since their composers consistently attempted to interpret the teachings of Tantra in terms of Smārta-Paurāṇic ideals. The philosophical aspects of Tantrism were brought in line with Vedānta, as we have seen. Its social teachings were given a Smārta colour. But despite all these, the concept of Śakti in various forms and of its residence in the human body as the serpent-power (*kulakuṇḍalinī*) to be awakened and stimulated by yogic exercises, the efficacy of *mantras* and rituals, the symbolism of letters and syllables, the feeling of the presence of deities in different parts of the body and their symbolic representation in mystic diagrams, the typical Tantric mode of worship including the Vāmācāra and kindred rituals, the essentiality of women in *sādhanā* or the way of the realisation of truth, the special forms of *dīkṣā* or initiation, and the prominent role of the *guru* or preceptor as the spiritual guide, the idea of rejuvenating the body, the use of drugs prepared from mercury and mica, and many other features of the earlier systems were all retained in the sophisticated Tantras.

As we have seen, almost all forms of Indian religious systems were greatly influenced by Tantric ideas and practices. But Tantric ideas and practices, in their turn, could not find suitable ground for their own development and fruition specially in those systems which were completely under the grip of the Brāhmaṇas and other orthodox sections of the population. They survived, but as spent forces, like plants uprooted from their natural environment, and they were destined to become dry, mechanical, and lifeless. It was only in Śāktism that the earlier Tantric ideas and practices were able to flourish. Śāktism was basically a religion of the masses; it had a heterodox, receptive, and flexible character—and despite the fact that its theoretical standpoint was modified by Brahmanical handling, the practical and functional aspects of Śāktism were controlled by persons belonging to the lower order of society.

From the Śākta point of view, Tantric aspirants belong to three categories—Paśu, Vīra, and Divya—each representing a stage of *sādhanā*. Paśu denotes individual soul (*jīva* and *jīvātmā*), i.e. human beings in general. By the culture of good qualities a Paśu is transformed into a Vīra. An individual aspiring for upliftment in the Vīra stage should follow the way of justice and truth, work for social welfare, control his senses, feel equality and respect towards women, and fight for the cause of the oppressed. In other words he must become a perfect man. For this he does not need to become a Śākta or to have initiation into the Śākta creed; he may continue to be a Vedist, or a Vaiṣṇava, or a Śaiva.

Thus, by moral efforts Paśu is transformed into Vīra. The characteristics of a Vīra, as enumerated in the *Kāmākhyātantra*, are that he should be fearless, of inspiring personality, and be resolute to achieve his purpose. He should be polite in language, attentive, yet bold, courageous, intelligent and active. He should know social manners and be considerate of the welfare of others. Only men already at the Vīra stage are eligible for initiation to Dakṣiṇācāra and Vāmācāra. When initiated into Dakṣiṇācāra, an individual must follow the path of devotion (*bhakti*) and knowledge (*jñāna*). He must live a healthy social and moral life. If he takes up Vāmācāra he has to be initiated in *śakti-mantra* and *pañcatattva*. In this state he has the right to disregard social injunctions because his aim is to free himself from all fetters.

Divya is a still higher state which is achieved by an individual only when his acquired qualities become part and parcel of himself, when they cannot be dissociated from his own entity. It is in this state of existence that he can be initiated into Siddhantācāra and Kaulācāra. In the Vīra state a man has some feeling of egoity. He is a perfect man. Though soft in heart he maintains a strong personality outwardly. But in the Divya state he is as simple as a child. This transformation from the state of Paśu to that of Divya is the aim of all Śākta-Tantric aspirants.

The Functional Aspects of the Śākta Tantras

According to the Śākta-Tantric viewpoint the inner transformation of man is possible. It can be achieved through seven recognised religious methods. According to the *Kulārṇava* these are Vedic, Vaiṣṇava, Śaiva, Dakṣiṇa, Vāma, Siddhānta, and Kaula. The first three are intended for persons belonging to the Paśu or ordinary category. The fourth and the fifth are for persons who have reached the Vīra state. The last two are for persons of the Divya rank. The first is meant for purity of body and mind, the second for devotion, the third for knowledge, the fourth for coordination of the first three, the fifth for non-attachment, the sixth for the realisation of non-attachment, and the seventh for liberation. According to the *Paraśurāmakalpa* the first five of these methods require the aid of a preceptor, while in the case of the last two the aspirant is free. These seven methods are also described as Ārambha, Taruṇa, Yauvana, Prauḍha, Prauḍhānta, Unmanī, and Anavasthā. Lakṣmīdhara, the commentator on the *Saundaryalaharī*, makes a threefold classification of methods—Samayācāra, Miśrācāra and Kaulācāra.

The aspirant must always keep in mind that the *guru* is no other than god. If a male he is Śiva, if female Śakti. The preceptor will guide him completely. *Dīkṣā* or initiation means rebirth. It is of many kinds depending on the calibre of the aspirant. Ordinary *dīkṣā* is called *kriyā-dīkṣā* and the extra-ordinary variety is called *vedha-dīkṣā*. It is necessary for the aspirant to believe in the identity of *guru*, *mantra*, and the deity. Other types of *dīkṣā* include *tattva, bhuvana, pāda, varṇa, yantra, śakti, nāda, prāṇa, jīva, cora, sparśa, vastra, ghaṭa, nirvāṇa, sadyonirvāṇa, āloka, jñāna*, etc. Qualitatively *dīkṣā* is of three types—*Śāmbhavī*, *Śāktī*, and *Māntrī*. *Śāmbhavī-dīkṣā* is not for ordinary persons. It is also beyond the jurisdiction of ordinary preceptors. It is the initiation into Śrīvidyā or Lalitā or Kāmeśvarī doctrine. The Male Principle or Bhairava of Śrīvidyā is known as Kāmeśvara. In this system the person initiated has to perform secret rites for the realisation of the *sāmarasya* or equilibrium of Śiva-Śakti within his own self. In the *Śākti-dīkṣā* the preceptor infuses his own energy into the heart of his disciple. The *Māntri-dīkṣā* is of general type according to which the novice is taught to erect *ghaṭa* and *maṇḍapa*, utter *mantras*, and perform *homa*. He has to recite the *vījamantra* imparted to him by his teacher.

Mantras have a very important place in the Tantric system. The power of *mantra* is twofold—*vācaka* and *vācya*, the first revealing the nature of the second. The second is what is to be known, while the first is the method of knowing. The *vācaka* entity of a *mantra* is composed of sentence, which itself is made of words as the words are of sound. There are two grades of sound, the more subtle state is known as *vindu* and the most subtle as *nāda*. The expression of sound is possible through letters, and hence the letter is the *vīja* or seed of *mantra*. Hṛm, Kṛm, Aim, Śrīm, Klīm, etc., are thus *vījas*. Just as a big banyan tree remains in subtle form in the banyan seed, so also all the doctrines remain subtle in a single letter conceived of as *vīja* or seed. That is why the alphabet is thought of as Māṭṛkā or divine mother. The fifty letters of the alphabet are regarded as *mātṛkāvarṇa*; they are equated with the rosary of Sarasvatī and the garland of skulls of the goddess Kālī. The expressed aspect of the *vindu* and *nāda* constituting sound is *vīja*, and these three in conjunction constitute

Śabdabrahma, which is consciousness inherent in matter; in special Tantric language it is the all-pervading serpent power or serpent-like *kāmakalā*. *Vindu* is the symbol of Śiva, *vīja* of Śakti and *nāda* of their union.[1]

This mystery of *mantra* is equated with the principle of creation. In the earlier chapters we have dealt with the two forms of Śakti—Prakāśa and Vimarśa—as inseparable from Śiva. *Nāda* or subtle sound is produced when Śiva assumes the form of *vindu* while entering as Jyoti (illumination) or Prakāśa into Śakti existing in the form of Vimarśa. *Vindu* is conceived of as semen, the male seed (*śukra*) and *nāda* the female (*rajas*). Their union is *kāmākalā*. Thus *vindu* is the efficient cause of creation, while *nāda* and *kāmakalā* are the material and instrumental causes respectively.

Underlying Tantric cosmogony is the ancient belief that the body is the micorcosm of the universe, therefore *kāmakalā* or sexual process is responsible for the creation of the world. Although theoretically Śiva and Śakti are inseparable like fire and its buring power, still in the case of creation they have a dual role. Śiva is the Male Principle of creation and Śakti the Female, and their *kāmakalā* or union is the process of creation by Śiva and Śakti, the former is passive and the latter active. This reminds us of the Prakṛti-Puruṣa doctrine of the Sāṅkhya. Without Vimarśa Prakāśa has no practical value, just as without Prakṛti Puruṣa is quite inactive; and that is why it is stated that without Śakti Śiva is no better than a corpse (*śava*). The nature of creation is like a wheel continually revolving. Śakti, having issued from its source, completes a cycle of creation, preservation, and destruction and then returns to its source again. This process is in motion throughout the ages. The Tantrics imitate this process through symbolical union with their female partners. Śakti's return to its source is imitated by the rite of *ṣaṭcakrabheda*. Śakti resides at the same time in the microcosm and the macrocosm; it remains latent as the serpent-power in the *mūlādhāra-cakra* of the human body. This is to be awakened and sent to the *sahasrāra* or the highest cerebal region through different nerve-cycles situated within the body. This is how Śakti will meet its source. Details of this process will be treated in a subsequent section.

Only the followers of the Vāmācāra, Siddhāntācāra, and Kaulācāra are entitled to the rites of *pañca-makāra* or the Five Ms and *ṣaṭcakrabheda*. These three systems are more or less the same but the Kaulācāra is considered to be the best. The followers of Vāmācāra worship Kulastrī in different ways. Kulastrī does not mean any housewife; she is a woman specially chosen who functions as the Female Principle in whose worship the rites of the Five Ms and the use of *khapuṣpa* or menstrual blood are essential. All women symbolise Śakti, but since their *kumārī* (virgin) form is the most attractive, the great goddess is always pleased with the Virgin-worship. The followers of the Vāmācāra-Siddhāntācāra-Kaulācāra worship the goddess with wine and meat. In the *Kulārṇava* it is stated that wine and meat are the symbols of Śakti and Śiva respectively and their consumer is Bhairava. When these three are united salvation in the form of bliss is produced.[2] The drinking of wine is the symbol of drinking the essence derived from the Śiva-Śakti *sāmarasya* (equilibrium) in the *sahasrāra* (highest cerebral region). Sexual union is the symbol of the connection of Śiva and Śakti. How this connection takes place is narrated in a verse which states that the goddess having pierced all the *kulapathas* (ways of a Kaula)—in the *mūlādhara* (earth), *maṇipura* (water), *svādhiṣṭhāna* (fire), *anāhata* (air), *viśuddhi* (space) and *ajñā* (mind)—enjoys the company of her consort in the *sahasrāra.*

Mahīṃ mūlādhāre kamapi maṇipure hutavaham/
Sthitaṃ svādhiṣṭhāne hṛdi marutamākāśamupari//
Manopi bhrūmadhye sakalamapi bhitvā kulapatham/
Sahasrāre padame saha rahasi patyā viharase//[3]

The Kaula way is the best—and also the most difficult. In the *Śyāmārahasya* it is stated that a Kaula in order to hide his own self is a Śākta at heart, a Śaiva outwardly, and a Vaiṣṇava in the midst of an assembly.[4] For the Kaula *sādhanā* there is no law of time or space; somewhere gentle, somewhere depraved, he moves often attired like a ghost or *piśāca.* He is the real Kaula who makes no difference between clay and sandalwood paste, son and enemy, cremation-ground and home, gold and grass.[5]

Dikkālaniyamo nāsti tithyādiniyamo na ca/
Niyamo nāsti devesi mahāmantrasya sādhane//
Kacit śiṣṭaḥ kacit bhraṣṭaḥ kacit bhūtapiśācavat/
Nānāveśadharā kaulāḥ vicaranti mahītale//
Kardame candane ' bhinnam putre śatrau tathā priye/
Śmaśāne bhavane devi tathaiva kāñcane tṛne//
Na bhedo yasya deveśi sa kaulaḥ parikīrtitaḥ//

The Ṣaṭcakra: Conceptual Transformations

We have referred frequently to the Tantric concept of nerve-plexuses situated in different parts of the body and that of Śakti lying latent as serpent-power to be awakened and sent to its source through these areas by yogic practices. These concepts were accepted in theory by a number of Indian religious sects, including the Buddhists of the later period, and had wider implications at a cosmic level.

In the Tantric dogma, the body is divided into two main parts: the head and the trunk as one unit and the lower body as the other. The centre of the body is in between these two, at the base of the spine. The spinal cord is the axis of the body just as Mount Meru is that of the earth. The body below this centre is conceived of as being comprised of the seven lower or nether worlds and the centre upwards constitutes the seven upper regions marked by six nerve plexuses and the highest cerebral region. In a general way it may be said that these nerve plexuses (*cakra* or *padma*) are related in a particular way to a special mechanism of the body through intermediate conductor-nerves (*nāḍis*). There are fourteen principal *nāḍis.*

Mūlādharā-cakra, or the first nerve-plexus, which is so called for being the root of *suṣumnā* nerve where *kuṇḍalinī* Śakti rests, is in the region midway between the genitals and anus. Whatever its position inside the body may be, it is symbolically viewed as a crimson lotus with four petals representing four forms of bliss—*parama, sahaja, yoga,* and *vīra,* and four letters—Va, Śa, Ṣa and Sa. Each letter is a particular *śabda* (sound) or Śakti, and as such they are manifestations of the *kuṇḍalinī.* In the pericarp is the square *dharā-maṇḍala* (the supposed earth) surrounded by eight spears and within it the *dharā-vīja* (the seed of the earth symbolised by the letter La). Inside the *vindu* of the *dharā-vīja* is the child Brahmā. The presiding deity of this *cakra* is the Śakti Ḍākinī—red in colour, and holding in her four hands *śūla* (spear), *khaṭvāṅga* (skull-mounted staff), *khaḍga* (sword) and *caṣaka* (drinking cup). In the pericarp there is also the lightning-like tringle (*yoni,* female organ) inside which are *kāma-vāyu* (the vital wind of passion) and the *kāma-vīja* (vital fluid symbolised by the letter *klim*). Above this is the *svayambhū-liṅga* round which *kuṇḍalinī* is coiled.[6]

Svādhiṣṭhana-cakra is the second lotus of vermilion colour with six petals which is situated on the spinal centre of the region at the root of the genitals. On these six petals are the letters Ba, Bha, Ma, Ya, Ra, and La. Just as the *mūlādhāra* is associated with earth so *svādhiṣṭhāna* is with water which is indicated by the octagonal pericarp with a half-moon in the centre. Inside the *vindu* is Viṣṇu seated on Garuḍa with his usual symbols. The presiding deity of this *cakra* is the Śakti Rākinī. She is of *śyāma* colour and in her four hands she holds the *śūla* (trident or spear), *abja* (lotus), *ḍamaru* (drum), and *ṭanka* (battle axe). She is three-eyed and has fierce projecting fangs, and is too terrible to behold. She is fond of white rice and a stream of blood runs down from her nostril.[7]

Maṇipura-cakra is at the centre of the navel region. It is a lotus of ten petals on which are the Ḍa, Ḍha, Ṇa, Ta, Tha, Da, Dha, Na, Pa and Pha. In the pericarp of the lotus is the red region of fire, which is triangular in shape. Outside it, on its three sides are three Svastika signs. Within the trangle is the *vīja* of fire symbolised in the letter Ra. On the *vīja* is Rudra, seated on the bull. The presiding deity of the *cakra* is the Śakti Lākinī. She is blue, has three faces with three eyes in each, four-armed, one set of hands holds *vajra* and *śakti* weapons and other set shows *varada* and *abhaya* postures. She has fierce projecting teeth. She is fond of meat and wine.[8]

Anāhata-cakra is in the region of heart. It is a lotus of twelve petals on which are the letters from Ka to Ṭha, with the *vindu* above them, vermilion in colour. Its pericarp is the hexagonal *vāyu-maṇḍala*, for it is connected with the element of air. On the *vīja* of air is the three-eyed god Īśā who, like Haṃsa, extends two arms in the gesture of granting boons and dispelling fear. This *cakra* is presided over by the Śakti Kākinī. She is four-armed and carries a noose and skull in two hands while the other two are in *varda* and *abhaya* postures. She is of golden hue, is dressed in yellow raiment, and wears every variety of jewel along with a garland of bones. Her heart is softened by nectar.[9]

Viśuddha-cakra is at the base of the throat with sixteen petals of a smoky purple hue. Its filaments are ruddy, and the sixteen vowels *vindu* above them are on the petals. It is connected with the element of space. Inside it is the *candramaṇḍala* and above it is the *vīja* Ha. On the *vīja* is Sadāśiva in his Ardhanārīśvara aspect. The presiding deity of the *cakra* is the Śakti Śākinī, white in colour, four-armed, five-faced and three-eyed, clothed in yellow and carrying in her hands a bow, an arrow, a noose, and goad.[10]

Ājñā-cakra is situated in the forehead between the two eyes. It is white and has two petals on which are the letters Ha and Kṣa. It contains within a triangle, the inner *ātmā (antarātmā)*, lustrous like flame. On its four sides, floating in air, are sparks surrounding a light which by its own lusture makes everything visible between the Mūla and the Brahmarandhra. Above this, again, is Manas, above which is Haṃsa within whom Parama-Śiva stays with Śakti. The presiding deity of this *cakra* is the Śakti Hākinī. She is white, has six red faces each with three eyes, six arms, and is seated on a white lotus. Her hands depict *varada* and *abhaya* mudrās, and hold a rosary, a human skull, a drum, and a book.[11]

The highest cerebral region, above the end of the *suṣumnā-nāḍi*, is known as *sahasrāra*. It is conceived of as a lotus of a thousand petals. It is white with the filaments red. The fifty letters of the alphabet from A to La are repeated twenty times around its thousand petals. On its pericarp is Haṃsa and above it is Parama-Śiva himself. Above these are the *sūrya* and *candra-maṇḍalas*. In the latter (*candra-maṇḍala*) is a lightning-like triangle within which is the sixteenth *kalā* of the moon. Its subtle aspect is known as *nirvāṇa-kalā* which is *para-vindu* symbolising Śiva and Śakti. The Śakti of this *para-vindu* is known as Nirvāṇa-Śakti, which is light and exists in the form of Haṃsa.[12]

These descriptions of the *cakras* offer a bewildering variety of ideas; at the present state of our knowledge it is impossible to understand their original significance despite earlier attempts of writers and commentators to devise imaginary interpretations for them. From a historical point of view it may be suggested that the *padmas* or *cakras* were originally conceived of in terms of human anatomy for the purpose of physiological study. Accordingly the *cakras*, commencing with the *mūlādharā* and going upwards, were identified with the sacral, prostatic, epigastric, cardiac, laryngeal and cavernous plexuses, and the *sahasrāra* with the Medulla. At a subsequent stage in conformity with the Tantric idea that the human body is the microcosm of the universe, worldly objects such as the sun, moon, mountains, rivers, etc., were connected with these *cakras*. Each *cakra* was again thought to represent the gross and subtle elements: *mūlādhara*, the gross element of earth and the subtle elements arising therefrom like cohesion and stimulation of the sense of smell; *svādhiṣṭhāna*, the gross element of water and the subtle elements of contraction and stimulation of the sense of taste; *maṇipura*, the gross element of fire and the subtle elements of expansion, production of heat and stimulation of sight sense of colour and form: *anāhata*, the gross element of air and the subtle elements of general movement and stimulation of the sense of touch; *viśuddha*, the gross element of space and the subtle element of stimulating sense of hearing; and *ājñā*, gross element of mind and subtle elements of mental faculties. These subtle elements again as *tattvas* are connected with different organs, main and subsidiary; *gandha* or smell with nose and feet, *rasa* or taste with tongue and hand *rūpa* or form and colour with eyes and anus, *sparśa* or touch with skin and penis, and *śabda* or sound with ear and mouth.

Quite in accordance with the Tantric idea that the deities reside within the human body and that the aspirant has to feel the deity within the body itself, these *cakras* came to be conceived of the seat of the Male and Female Principles, symbolised by the male and female organs, *liṅga* and *yoni* or *trikoṇa*. The presiding deities of the *cakras* were originally special Tantric goddesses without any Vedic affiliation such as Ḍākinī, Rākinī, Lākinī, Kākinī, Śākinī and Hākinī. Subsequently, however, owing to Brahmānical influence, Brahmā, Viṣṇu, Rudra, Īśā, Sadāśiva and others were able to make their way, each into one *cakra*. The theory of letters, of the alphabet symbolising different *tattvas*, was also grafted, and in this way we come across the functioning of a very elaborate and complicated process which the *cakras* are supposed to represent in their qualitatively transformed capactiy.

Deities, Mantras *and Letters: Their Position in the* Cakras

It has been said that the letters (*varṇa*) of the alphabet are distributed in the *cakras*. In each of the lotuses there is also a seed (*vīja*)-*mantra*. Although commonly understood as prayer or formula of worship, in Tantrism *mantra* denotes a power (*śakti*) in the form of sound. In Indian philosophical tradition sound or *śabda* is the quality (*guṇa*) of *ākāśa* (space). This sound, when unlettered is known as *dhvani* or *dhvanyātmaka-śabda* and when lettered, as *varṇātmaka-śabda*. By mental actions such sounds are co-ordinated into words (*pada*) and sentences (*vākya*) from which a meaning (*artha*) transpires. The mind is thus both cogniser (*grāhaka*) and cognised (*grāhya*), revealer (*prakāśaka*), and revealed (*prakāśya*), denoter (*vācaka*) and denoted (*vācya*). The term *mantra* is derived from the root *man* 'to think'. The mind that thinks of itself as the object of cognition in the form of a deity is transformed ultimately into the likeness of that deity. This is a fundamental principle of Tantric *sādhanā*.

Śabda has four states or *bhāva* called Parā, Paśyantī, Madhyamā and Vaikharī. Parā is the motionless causal sound conceived as existing in the *kuṇḍalinī* in the *mūlādharā-cakra* in a dreamless state of deep sleep (*suṣupti*). Vaikharī is the gross sound, the uttered speech by which the ideas are expressed. Paśyantī and Madhyamā are in between these two, the former representing a non-particularised motion (*sāmānya-spanda*) and the latter a cognitive aspect of mental movement. Letters as symbols of these forms of sound are therefore supposed to exist within the *cakras*. This subtle aspect of the letters is called Mātṛkā. It is said that consciousness moves as Śakti, at first in the subtle form of mind which is in itself the motionless causal sound (*para-śabda*), then assumes a general undifferentiated movement (*paśyantī: sāmānya-spanda*), then a differentiated movement (*madhyamā: viśeṣa-spanda*) and finally in a clearly articulated speech (*vaikharī: spaṣṭatara-spanda*) in the gross form of language as the expression of ideas and of physical objects (*artha*).

Mantras are not meant for propitiating gods. Rather gods are produced from *mantras* according to the requirement of the aspirant. Utterance of *mantra* is a preliminary process, not the end. The *mantra* should be awakened. When this is done there is *mantra-caitanya*, the state where the *sādhaka* can make the *mantra* work. All *mantras* are in the body as unmanifest (*avyakta*) power of *śabda*. These are to be awakened and perceived through a determined variety of practices. The unmanifested power of *śabda* (*avyakta-rava*) is the cause of manifested *śabda* (specialised in the forms of letters, words and sentences) and *artha* (meaning, object). It becomes manifest when through the functioning of *kriyā-śakti* a differentiation of the Supreme *vindu* from Prakṛti is possible.[13] The former is the principle of consciousness and the latter that of material entities. In the above sense the universe is said to have been composed of letters. It is the fifty letters of the Sanskrit alphabet which are denoted by the garland of severed human heads which the goddess Kālī wears. The *kuṇḍalinī* as Mahāmātṛkā-sundarī also has fifty-one coils which are known as Mātṛkās or subtle forms of the gross letters or *varṇa*. Again, the total number of petals of all the lotuses from *mūlādhāra* to *ājñā* are fifty in number and they are identified with the fifty letters or *mātṛkās* of the Sanskrit alphabet.

Every *mantra* is a particular sound form. In Tantrism there are a very large number of short unetymological vocables or *vījas* such as *hrim, śrīm, krīm, hum, phaṭ*, etc. These are in fact abbreviations of the names of the deities and their functions, and are of three kinds—masculine, feminine and neuter. Commonly however the term *vīja* is applied to monosyllabic *mantras.* The connection between the particular letters and the *cakras* in which they are placed is said to be due to the fact that in uttering any particular letter, the *cakra* in which it is placed and its surroundings are brought in to play. The sounds of the Sanskrit alphabet are classified according to the organs used in their articulation—gutteral, palatal, cerebral, dental and labial. When so articulated each letter is said to touch *cakra* in which it is. In uttering them the *cakras* are supposed to react and function. This is the theory put forth in accounting for the position of letters in the *cakras.*

The *mantras,* because they are lettered and hence constituted by the *mātṛkās,* are eternal and ever effective. Their efficacy does not rest on argument or judgement. It is achieved through the realisation of supreme bliss when the equation of *mantra,* its deity and the teaching of the preceptor takes place in the mind.[14] The role of sound in the formation of *mantra* has been discussed above. We have seen that Parā is the motionless causal sound which produces on the one hand *nāda* or articulated sound-particle and *vāk,* the uttered speech. The subtle forms of these two are therefore known as *parā-nāda* and *parā-vāk* and their combination is supposed to be *parā-sakti,* the source of everything. This *parā-śakti* is same as the *kuṇḍalinī* residing in the *mūlādhāra.* The Śakti of *mūlādhāra* and that of *sahasrāra* are the same in nature, the only difference being that in the former Śakti is latent and in the latter it is active in the form of consciousness.

According to Rāghavabhaṭṭa, the commentator on the *Śaradātilaka,* this sound-element is the nature of consciousness of all beings, known as *vyāpakaśakti-kuṇḍalinī* or *kuṇḍalarūpa kāmakalā. Nāda,* the articulated sound-particle in the form of *vindu* or point without space, is eventually expressed as Śiva-Śakti equilibrium endowed with all consciousness. In the theory of *mantra, nāda* appears in the first stage as a developing, not yet completely expressed, Śakti, and in the second stage as *vindu* and *vīja,* the essential pre-conditions for the complete manifestation of Śakti. These three, *nāda, vindu* and *vīja* are the three angles forming a triangle, in Tantric symbolism, the *yoni* or *trikoṇa,* the female generative organ, the seat of *kāmakalā.* With the help of *mantra,* the Kuṇḍalinī-Śakti may thus be awakened and made to pass through the states of sound-mechanism like Parā, Paśyantī, Madhyamā and Vaikhari.[15]

The letters, as we have seen, are conceived as Mātṛkās and also equated with Sarasvatī. The letters are the makers of ideas and images, and from them the knowledge of the *vījamantras* (*mantras* in the form of seed) are derived. *Hrīm, krīm, aim, śrīm, klīm,* etc., are *vījas,* proper intonation in the recitation of which makes the meditation perfect and the deities are forced to appear before the eyes of the aspirant. In the first stage it is known as Devatāsiddhi or god-attainment. But the second stage is more important which is known as Jīvanasiddhi or the fulfilment of life which opens the door of direct knowledge. Just as a tree with its trunk, branches, leaves, flowers and fruits is basically the development of a seed, so also the entrie superstructure of Tantrism is based on the *vījas.*

The analysis of *vīja-mantra* reveals the knowledge of letters. Every letter is denotative of a deity in all his or her aspects. To take the example of the *vīja hrīm,* we find that it is composed of *Ha* (Śiva), *Ra* (Śakti), *I* (Māyā, the material aspect of Śakti) and *M* (Nāda and Vindu). In Tantric terminology every *vīja* consists of two causal elements—gross and subtle—and a third element which is beyond the law of causation. The *mantras* are Mātṛkā letters; Mātṛkā letters are Mātṛkā-śakti; Mātṛkā-śakti is Maha-śakti the great Mother. Śakti is inherent in every *mātṛkā-varṇa* (letter). The *mātṛkā-varṇas* are of two types—those having *vindu* or anusvāra (ṃ) and visarga (ḥ) suffixes, and those without them. Letters of the former category are generally used for the *mantras.*[16] The *mātṛkā-varṇas* are felt in different parts of the body through the process of *nyāsa.* The traditional seven or eight Mātṛkās, worshipped in all major forms of Hindu religion in temples and icons, are conceived in Tantra as presiding deities of different groups of *mātṛkā-varṇas.* In the *Svacchandatantra* it is stated:

A-varge tu Mahālakṣmī Ka-varge Kamalodbhavā/
Ca-varge to Maheśānī Ṭa-varge to Kumārikā//
Nārāyaṇī Ta-varge tu Vārāhī tu Pavanikā/
Aindrī-caiva Ya-vargasthā Camunda tu Śa-vargikā//
Etāḥ saptamahāmātaḥ saptalokavyavasthitāḥ//

Here we find that the letters of *A-varga* (the vowels beginning with A) are presided over by Mahālakṣmī, of *Ka-varga* (consonants beginning with *Ka*) by Brāhmī, of *Ca-varga* (beginning with *Ca*) by Māheśvarī, of *Ṭa-varga* (beginning with *Ṭa*) by Kaumārī, of *Ṭa-varga* (beginning with *Ta,* by Vaiṣṇavi, of *Pa-varga* (beginning with *pa*) by

Vārāhi, of *Ya-varga* (beginning with *Ya*) by Aindrī and of *Sa-Varga* (beginning with *Sa*) by Cāmuṇḍā. According to the *Vāmakeśvaratantra* these groups of letters are presided over by eight Vaśinī Kāmeśvarī, Modinī, Vimalā, Aruṇā, Jayinī, Sarveśvari and Kālinī. These *mātṛkā* letters are also known as Mālinī.

Employment of the Mantras *and Allied Methods*

We have seen that in Tantrism *mantras* are not merely a combination of letters or words. The *vīja mantras* like Hrīm (symbol of Tribhuvaneśvarī), Śrīm (symbol of Lakṣmī), Krīm (symbol of Kālī), etc., are really the Īṣṭadevatā (the core deity) of the aspirant, to be visualised and retained by him through spiritual efforts. Thus they have a deeper spiritual significance and historically they are a continuation of the archaic magical belief in the efficacy of sound. The *mantras* are supposed to possess wonderful and inconceivable powers. They are the means of securing the fruits desired.[17] According to *Jñānarṇava* millions of Vājapeyas and thousands of Aśvamedhas, and even gifts of crores of Kapilā cows are not equal in merit to the Śrīvidyā *mantra*.[18] The *Kulārṇava*[19] says that *mantra* saves aspirant from all storts of danger. There are varieties of *mantras* like *kavaca, hṛdaya, upahṛdaya, netra, astra, rakṣā* etc. Owing to Brahmānical influence a good number of Vedic *mantras*[20] have made their way into the Tantras. The *Prapañcasāra* devotes a complete chapter to the explanation of the words of the Gāyatrī and other similar Vedic terms. The *Mahānirvāṇa* even goes so far as to prescribe the performance of Vaidikī Sandhyā to be followed by Tāntrikī Sandhyā. The Tantrikī Gāyatrī is: *Ādyāyai vidmahe parameśvari dhīmahi, tan naḥ kālī pracodayāt.*[21]

It is interesting to note that some *mantras* of Tantric type have made their way into the Purāṇas. The *Garuḍapurāṇa*,[22] for example, prescribes monosyllabic *mantras* like *hrām, kṣaum, hrīm, hum, śrīm,* etc. It also contains a long prose *mantra* of Cāmuṇḍā.[23] The *Agnipurāṇa*[24] contains *mantras* for killing and subduing enemies, for bringing things under control and for *vidyās* of various types. Late Purāṇas like the Bhaviṣya have Tantric *mantras* such as hṛdaya, śikhā, kavaca, and so on. The medieval digests on Dharmaśāstras also prescribe some Tantric *mantras.*

The repetition of *mantras* is called *puraścaraṇa* in Tantric language. The term literally means 'performing or carrying out before'.

It consists of *dhyāna* (meditation on the form of the deity) worship, *japa* of the *mantra, homa, tarpana,* etc., in a broader sense. All the Tantric texts and digests have a chapter or section on this subject. Of the various methods of *puraścaraṇa,* a popular one is to concentrate on the Pañcatattva on some appointed days, especially of *mahāniśā* or midnight on the fourteenth new-moon day. The usual process is to muttering the *mantras* as many times as possible. Rāghavabhaṭṭa in his commentary on the *Śāradātilaka* has treated *puraścaraṇa* exhaustively. One of its effective methods, as prescribed by him, is that the aspirant, being sure of his physical and mental purity, should observe a fast, and then during an eclipse of the sun or the moon should stand in a river and recite the relevant *mantra* from the time the eclipse begins till it ends. The places for performing *puraścaraṇa* are generally holy places, riverbanks, caves, mountaintops, in the vicinity of a Tīrtha, holy forests, parks, and the like. During the days of *puraścaraṇa* the aspirant should obtain food by begging. He should aviod sexual intercourse, eating flesh, drinking wine, speaking untruth, and should repeat the *mantra* heart and soul. While performing *puraścaraṇa* seriously the aspirant may face various obstacles and disturbances, and often temptations, but he should not allow his mind to be affected by them.[25]

Another important method of Tantric worship is *nyāsa* which consists of feeling the god in different parts of the body. Actually, by performing *nyāsa* the aspirant invokes the god to come and occupy certain parts of his body. It is done by touching the chest and limbs with the tips of the fingers and the palm of the right hand accompanied by *mantras.* The prefix *ni* of the word *nyāsa* literally means 'placing or depositing in' and the root as 'to cast'. There are several kinds of *nyāsa* such as *haṃsa, praṇava, mātṛkā, mantra, kara, aṅga, piṭha,* etc.[26] The Tantric concept of *nyāsa* became popular in other forms of Indian religious systems as well, and we have Puranic references to this practice.[27] The medieval digests on the Dharmaśāstras also show that *nyāsa* was taken over from Tantric works in the Purāṇas and other texts for the rites of the orthodox peoples.

Much has already been said about the Tantric concept of *mudrā,* its various connotations and denotations. As a method of worship, it is rather simple—merely a hand pose useful for the purpose of *japa* (counting name of the deity) and concentration. Rāghavabhaṭṭa says that the five fingers represent the five elements, that their contact with each other induces the deity to be present at the worship; various appropriate *mudrās* help to secure some desired object or benefit. There is a great divergence in the Tantras regarding the number and names of the *mudrās*.[28] The common Tantric *mudrās* are: *āvāhanī* (folding both hands to make a hollow which can contain flower, etc.); *sthāpanī* (in which the folded hands are held upside down); *sannidhāpana* (two hands forming closed fist with the thumbs raised up); *sunnirodhanī* (same as the preceding one but with the thumbs closed inside the fist); *sammukhikaraṇī* (when the closed fist is held upwards); *sakalikṛti* (bodily positions while doing *nyāsas*); *avaguṇṭhaṇa* (closing the fingers and waving the hand round the cult object); *dhenumudrā* (a complicated hand posture made by intertwining the fingers of both hands in a peculiar way); and *mahāmudrā* (made by intertwining the thumbs of both hands and holding the other fingers straight). Besides there are *mudrās* like *khecarī, vajroli,* etc.,of esoteric significance used in connection with *laya-krama* or the awakening of *kuṇḍalinī*.[29] These will be dealt with in a subsequent section. The Śākta Purāṇas also mention many varieties of Tantric *mudrās*.[30]

Two other items of Tantric worship are *maṇḍala* and *yantra*. These two also have a variety of connotations and denotations as we have seen earlier. Maṇḍalas for ordinary Tantric worships are like geometrical diagrams to be drawn on the ground with powder of five colours.[31] The *Jñānārṇava*[32] equates *maṇḍala* and *cakra* and emphasises on the nine angles, as abodes of the deities, to be drawn on an altar. The *Śāradātilaka*[33] deals at length with the constructions of *sarvatobhadramaṇḍala* which is regarded as common to all forms of worship. *Yantra* or *cakra* is also a geometrical diagram engraved, drawn, or painted on objects. It is also of the nature of *maṇḍala*, the only difference being that while the former is employed in worship of deities in general, the latter is for a particular diety and for a special purpose.[34] *Yantra* is often considered as the deity itself; the *yantra-*gāyatri is: *yantrarājāya vidmahe, varapradāya dhīmahi, tanno yantraṃ pracodayāt.* One of the most popular forms of the *yantras* is *śrīcakra*.[35] There are nine *yonis* or female organs. Five of which have their apex pointing downwards, and these represents Śakti. The remaining four with apex pointing upwards represents Śiva. The *vindu* is situated in the smallest triangle pointing downwards. Then there are two sets of ten triangles, another set of fourteen triangles, two lotuses—eight and sixteen-petalled—three circles, and three boundary lines with four gates. The worship of *yantra* is called *bahiryāga* or the external worship of Śakti, while in her internal worship (*antaryāga*), the purpose of which is the awakening of *kuṇḍalinī* through the nerve-plexuses from *mūlādhāra* to *sahasrāra*, the *yantra* becomes a symbolical functionary. In the *Setubandha* commentary of the *Nityaṣoḍaśīkārṇava* it is categorically stated that the worship of Tripurasundarī is not devotional but ritualistic, to be performed either by recitation of *mantras* or by the worship of *yantra*.[36]

Yogic Exercise: Awakening of Kuṇḍalinī

The Tantras while prescribing ways and means for the awakening of the *kuṇḍalinī-śakti* insist on the existihg Yogic tradition of India. Yoga is a term for those physical and psychical processes which are used to discover man's inner essence.[37] It is the method by which the mental and intellectual feelings (*cittavṛtti*) are controlled and conditioned so that the aspirant is able to dissolve his own self into the absolute, the supreme reality as conceived by him. This state is called *samādhi*; it is like a grain of salt which when mingled in water becomes one with it. The *Māyātantra*[38] defines Yoga as the unity of the individual soul and the universal soul, that by which the sense of oneness or non-duality is attained. This sense is described in the *Kulārṇava*[39] as water poured into water.

Yoga is generally classified into four categories—Mantrayoga, Haṭha-yoga, Laya-yoga and Rāja-yoga. Each of these forms has eight subservients, called eight limbs or *aṣṭāṅga*, which are *yama, niyama, āsana, prāṇayāma, pratihārya, dhāraṇa, dhyāna* and *samādhi*. The first five are known as exterior methods (*bahiraṅga*)—chiefly concerned with the body—and the last three are inner methods (*antaraṅga*) employed for the development of mind. *Yama* is abstinence from evil propensities by which the mind is disturbed while *niyama* is commitment to certain moral values by which the mind is elevated and conditioned for some higher attainment. *Āsana* is posture of body, a physical disciplinary method to make the body fit for controlling senses, while *prāṇayāma* is breath-control needed for the same purpose. *Pratihārya* is the restraint and subjection of the senses to the mind. *Dhāraṇa* is the 'holding by', i.e. fixing the mind on a particular object of thought. *Dhyāna* is concentration of mind through which it acquires the quality of mental realisation. It is of two kinds: *saguṇa* or meditation on a form, and *nirguṇa*, in which the self is its own object. *Samādhi* is the ecstasy resulting from the equation of the individual soul with the ultimate reality. The state of complete *samādhi* is called Parā-saṃvīt or pure-consciousness. There are two degrees of *samādhi—savikalapa* in which the mind is yet to transgress the limit of wordly existence, and *nirvikalpa* in which this has been achieved with the effect that it becomes one with the subject of its contemplation.

Mantra-yoga comprises all those forms of *sādhanā* in which the mind is controlled by means of its own object. The universe is Nāmarūpātmaka made up of objects in name and form, and the nature of the mind is to adjust or modify itself into the form it perceives. In Mantra-yoga the aspirant is selective about the object of his contemplation. This is called *sthūla* or *sagūna dhyāna* of the gods in images, emblems, pictures, markings, *maṇḍalas, yantras, mudrās,* etc. It is the simplest form of Yoga. Haṭha yoga comprises those *sādhanās* which are concerned primarily with the control of gross or physical body for conditioning the subtle body. It requires a lot of physical practice which will be described later in details. The *Haṭhayogapradīpikā*[40] says that by Haṭha-yoga the body becomes healthy, the eyes bright, the semen hardened, the *nāḍis* purified, the internal fire increased and the *nāda* sound heard. Laya-yoga is also a physical process—an exercise of supersensible forces and functions of the inner body. Just as Haṭha-yoga is specially concerned with the physical body, Laya-yoga is concerned with the nerve-plexuses, and it is thus used as a means to stimulate the *kuṇḍalinī śakti.* This form of Yoga, as we shall see later, belongs exclusively to Tantric aspirants. The highest form of Yoga is, however, Rāja-yoga through which *nirvikalpa-samādhi* is attained. By means of *mantra,* Haṭha and Laya-yoga the aspirant steps to perfection in the form of Rāja-yoga which is complete and final liberation. It is a purely mental exercise in which discrimination between the real and unreal is possible.

The word Haṭha is composed of the syllables *ha* and *ṭha* symbolising the sun and the moon, the Prāṇa and Apāna *vāyus* respectively. The union of these two vital airs in the *suṣumnā* is called *prāṇāyāma.* The practice and exercise of Haṭha-yoga are divided into seven parts: cleansing (*śodhana*) by six processes (*ṣaṭkarma*), the attainment of strength (*dṛḍhana*) by bodily postures (*āsana*) of fortitude (*sthiratā*) by bodily position, (*mudrā*), of steadiness of mind (*dhairya*) by restraint of senses (*pratihārya*), of lightness by breath-control (*prāṇāyāma*), of realisation (*pratyakṣa*) by meditation (*dhyāna*), and of detachment (*nirliptatva*) in *samādhi*.

Cleansing (*śodhana*) is effected by six processes known as *ṣaṭkarma* which are (1) *dhauti* or inner-washing—the clearance of wind, phlegm, and bile, in a variety of ways the most important being filling the stomach with sufficient water and evacuating it by vomiting; (2) *vasti* or contraction and expansion of the anus in water; (3) *neti* or cleaning the nostrils; (4) *laulikī* or whirling of the belly from side to side; (5) *trāṭaka* or clearing the eyes; and (6) *vyutkrama* or removal of phlegm by inhalation and exhalation or by water drawn through the nostrils and ejected through the mouth or the reverse.[41]

Āsanas or bodily postures are required for strength or firmness. The *āsanas* are numerous, of which eighty-four are common.[42] The commonest are *muktapadmāsana* and *baddhapadmāsana*. In the case of the former the right foot is placed on the left thigh, the left foot on the right thigh, the hands crossed and placed similarly on the thighs. The latter is the same, except that the hands are crossed behind the back, the right hand holding the right toe and the left the left. There are certain other *āsanas*, peculiar to the Tantras such as *muṇḍāsana, citāsana, śavāsana, siddhāsana, ugrāsana, svastikāsana, trikoṇāsana* and *bhujaṅgāsana*.

Mudrās are for *sthiratā* or fortitude. According to the commentary on the *Haṭhayogapradīpikā*[43] *mudrā* is so called because it removes pain and sorrow (*mudrayati kleśam itī mudrā*). *Mudrā* is also described as the key for opening the door of *kuṇḍalinī śakti*. Several *mudrās* have already been mentioned. One of the most important *mudrās* is the *khecārīmudrā* which is the lengthening of the tongue until it reaches the space between the eyebrows. It is then turned back in the throat for closing the exit of breath previously inspired. In *yoni-mudrā*, the aspirant in *siddhāsana* (pressing with his heel the centre of the perineum thus closing the anal aperture and withdrawing the penis into the pubic arch) stops with his fingers the ears, eyes, nostrils and mouth, so as to shut out all external impressions. By *kākinī-mudrā* he inhales *prāṇa-vāyu* and unites it with *apāna-vāyu*, the lips forming a share to resemble the back of a crow.[44] There are other forms of *mudrās* used for arousing the sleeping *kuṇḍalinī* like *aśvinī mudrā, śakti-cālana-mudrā*, etc.

When the physical body is purified and controlled, there follows *pratihārya* to secure steadiness. The next important practice is *prāṇāyāma* meant for the lightening of the body. The aspirant, assuming the *padmāsana* posture inhales (*puraka*) and exhales (*recaka*) alternately through the left and right nostrils, retaining the breath meanwhile (*kumbhaka*) for gradually increasing periods. The theory is that the vital air (*prāṇa*) should enter the *suṣumnā* and stay there until it gathers sufficient momentum to pierce the *cakras* and reach the *brahmarandhra*. The Yoga manuals speak of various forms of *prāṇāyāma* and also of *kumbhaka*. *Prāṇayāmā* becomes successful only when *nāḍis* are purified, for unless this is so that *prāṇa* cannot enter the *suṣumnā*.[45]

The *Kulārṇava-tantra*[46] divides *dhyāna* into *sthula* (gross) and *sukṣma* (subtle) beyond which, it says, is *samādhi*. Bhāskararāya says that there are three forms of the Devī which equally partake of both the *prakāśa* and *vimarśa* aspects of Śakti and the Supreme (Para).[47] In *sthūla* or gross meditation the practitioner conceives a from of his Iṣṭadevatā. The next stage, known as *jyotir-dhyāna* is a conception in the abstract, not of the deity but its energy. The *sukṣma* or subtle meditation is possible when the *kuṇḍalinī* is roused.[48] Lastly, through *samādhi* the quality of *nirliptattva* (detachment), and thereafter *mukti* (liberation) is attained.

Laya-yoga is a higher form of Haṭha-yoga. It is specially connected with the functioning of *kuṇḍalinī*, and that is why the Tantras lay greatest emphasis on this form of Yoga. The *āsanas, kumbhakas, mudrās*, etc, are used to rouse *kuṇḍalinī* so that the life-force, withdrawn from the *iḍā* and *piṅgalā*, may enter into the *suṣumnā* and then go upwards towards the *brahmarandhra*.[49] The body on each side of the spinal column is devitalised, and the whole current of *prāṇa* (life-force) is infused into it. It generally takes years from the commencement of the practice of Laya-yoga to lead the Śakti to the *sahasrāra*. *Prāṇa* which exists in the form of vital air, generates heat which causes *kuṇḍalinī* to be aroused which then hisses and straightens itself and pierces the *Cakras*. This is possible through repeated efforts and by a gradual process. The Sādhaka sits in the prescribed *āsana* and steadies his mind by the *khecarimudrā*. The upper part of the body is then contracted so that the upwards breath is checked. By this contraction the air so inhaled is prevented from escaping. The air so checked tends downwards. This motion is again checked by the contraction of the anal muscle. The air thus stored becomes an instrument to animate the *kuṇḍalinī*.

The uncoiled *kuṇḍalinī* at first enters the *citriṇīnāḍī* and then pierces, in that *nāḍī*, each of the lotuses, and thereby absorbes into itself the regnant *tattvas* contained in each of them. As the ascent is made, each of the grosser *tattvas* enters ino the Laya state, i.e. the state of dissolution. By these *tattvas* are meant the five elements and their modifications. In the Laya-yoga there is a gradual process of involution of the gross world with its elements into its cause. Each gross element (*mahābhūta*) together with the subtle (*tanmātra*) from which it proceeds and the connected organ of sense (*indriya*), is dissolved into the next above it until the last element, space, with the *tanmātra*, sound, and *manas*, are dissolevd in egosim (*ahaṃkāra*), of which they are *vikṛtis*. *Ahaṃkāra* is merged in first manifestation of creative ideation, and the latter into *vindu* which is the Supreme Being. This is the Tantric adaptation of the Sāṅkhya categories. However, in her upward progress the *kuṇḍalinī* thus absorbs twenty-three *tattvas*, commencing from the gross elements, and then unites with Parāmaśiva whose nature is one with hers. This union is known as Sāmarasya. The *sādhaka* in Laya-yoga, thinking of himself as Śakti or the Female Principle of creation, feels himself in union (*saṅgama*) with Śiva and enjoys infinite pleasure. This union of the Śakti-kuṇḍalinī with Śiva in the body of the *sādhaka* is that coition of the *pañca-tattva* (Five Ms.) which is regarded in the Tantras as the best of all unions for those who have already controlled their passions through yogic exercises. On their union nectar flows, which runs from *brahmarandhra* to *mūlādhāra*, flooding the *kṣudra-brahmāṇḍa* or microcosm, i.e. the body of the *sādhaka*, who becomes forgetful of all in this world and immersed in ineffable bliss.

Kuṇḍalinī does not stay long in *sahasrāra*. She has an inherent tendency to return to her original place. Therefore the aspirant has to make continuous efforts to retain her in *sahasrāra*, because liberation is not gained by merely awakening *kuṇḍalinī*. It is possible only when she takes up her permanent abode in the *sahasrāra*. When, by preliminary *sādhanā*. purity of physical and mental function is gained, the aspirant learns how to open the entrance of the *suṣumnā*, which is ordinarily closed at the base. This is the meaning of the statement that the serpent with its coil closes the gate.

Use of Chemical Drugs: Raseśvara Darśana

In view of what has been said it is clear that *kuṇḍalinī* is the individual bodily representation of the great cosmic power. When this individual Śakti manifested as the individual consciousness (*jīva*) is merged in the universal consciousness, conceived as the Supreme

Being and the source of the former, the world for such *jīva* dissolves, and liberation (*mukti*) is attained. The rousing and stirring up of *kuṇḍalinī* is thus a form of merger of the individual into the universal consciousness. The whole process is very complex and depends entirely on the mental and intellectual faculties of the aspirant. The awakening of *kuṇḍalinī* and her upward march are not solely the domain of yogic practices. Yoga only gives aid to it. It makes the practitioner physically and mentally fit for higher physical training. Its purpose is to renovate the physical body.

The same purpose is also served by the use of drugs. In the introductory portion of the book we have elaborately dealt with the Tantric contribution to the sciences of alchemy and medicine. Here we shall see how the use of drugs is connnected with the Yogic system. One of the basic postulates of the Yoga doctrine is the insistence on transubstantiation and transfiguration. In a Yogic text it is stated that the perfect body of the Yogī is subtler than the subtlest, yet grosser than the grossest. He can transform his body according to his will. His form is above all disease and death. He can play in the three worlds according to his own desire. He can assume any form by his incomprehensible power.[50] The same belief is also found in the Rasāyana school which is fundamentally based on the ideal of *jīvanmūkti* (liberation within the span of life) and the method advocated is that of transubstantiation with the help of *rasa* or chemical preparations, generally of mercury, thus making the body immutable.[51]

Patañjali in the Kaivalya-pāda of his *Yogasūtra* says that *siddhi* can be attained even by the application of herbs or medicines (*janmauṣadhi-mantra-tapaḥ-samādhijāḥ siddhayaḥ*). In the commentary on this Sūtra, Vyāsa and Vācaspati say that *siddhi* by *auṣadhi* refers to the schools of Yogis who attained perfection with the help of Rasāyana. We have seen that the *rasa* of the Rāsayana school was replaced, in the cult of the Nātha Siddhas, by the nectar oozing from the moon situated in the *sahasrāra*, and the chemical process, though continued by them especially by the Southern Nāthas, was changed into the somewhat physico-chemical process of Haṭha-yoga. In Tibet among the Tantric Buddhists the use of Rasāyana is very much in vogue.[52]

In the first chapter of the *Rasārṇava* the aim of Rasāyaṇa is explained by Śiva to the goddess in terms of the concept of *jīvanmukti*. The same is also said in Mādhava's *Sarvadarśanasaṃgraha*[53] in which the Rasāyana school has been accepted as a school of Indian philosophy. The school is styled here as the *Raseśvara Darśana* and the doctrines of this school are explanied with reference to well-known texts on alchemy. In Mādhava's compendium it is stated:

> Other Māheśvaras there are who, while they hold the identity of the self with God, insist upon the tenet that the liberation in this life taught in all the systems depends upon the stability of the bodily frame, and therefore celebrate the virtues of mercury or quicksilver as a means of strengthening the system. Mercury is called *pārada,* because it is a means of conveyance beyond the series of transmigratory states.... It may be urged that literal interpretation of these words is incorrect, the liberation in this life being explicable in another manner. This objection is not allowable, liberation being set out in the six systems as subsequent to the death of the body, and upon this there can be no reliance, and consequently no activity to attain it is free from misgivings....
>
> The body, some one may say, is seen to be perishable; how can its permanency be effected? Think not so, it is replied, for though the body, as complex of six sheaths or wrappers of the soul, is dissoluble, yet the body, as created by Hara and Gaurī[54] under the names of mercury and mica, may be perdurable.... The ascetic, therefore, who aspires to liberation in his life should first make to himself a glorified body. And inasmuch as mercury is produced by the creative conjunction of Hara and Gaurī, and mica is produced from Gaurī mercury and mica are severally identified with Hara and Gaurī..... Some one may urge: If the creation of mercury by Hara and Gaurī were proved, it might be allowed that the body could be made permanent; but how can that be proved? This objection is not allowable inasmuch as that *can* be proved by eighteen modes of elaboration.... And these eighteen modes of elaboration are enumerated thus—sweating, rubbing, swooning, fixing, dropping, coercion, restraining, kindling, going, falling into globules, pulverising, covering, internal flux, external flux, burning, colouring and pouring, and eating it by parting and piercing.... The mercurial system is not to be looked upon as merely eulogistic of the metal, it being immediately, through the conservation of the body, a means to the highest end, liberation....

The *Sarvadarśanasaṃgraha* presents the arguments of the advocates of the Raseśvara school against those of their opponents and cites passages from the works of Govinda-bhagavat, Sarvājñarāmeśvara, and others and also from the celebrated chemical texts like the *Rasārṇava, Rasasiddhānta, Śākārasiddhi, Rasahṛdaya,* etc. According to the Reseśvara philosophy, as enumerated in this work, the attainment of liberation is the highest aim of life. It is possible even in lifetime if one is able to acquire a divine body with the help of mercurial drugs. It is only in this divine body that the union of the individual soul and the highest principle is possible.

Vāmācāra: Its Professed Anti-Brāhmanism

We have already had occasion to deal with Vāmācāra and its primitive social basis. In the Śākta Tantras the Vāmācāra rites predominate, and it is interesting to note that despite Brāhmanical superimpositions the anti-Brāhmanical character of Tantrism in general and Vāmācāra in particular could not be suppressed.

According to some Tantric texts there are seven Ācāras (ways)—Vedācāra, Vaiṣṇavācāra, Śaivācāra, Dakṣiṇācāra, Vāmācāra, Siddhantācāra, and Kaulācāra—belonging to three grades of aspirants—Paśu, Vīra and Divya. These seven ācāras are again divided into two broad categories—Dakṣiṇācāra and Vāmācāra. It is said that the rites containing five *mudrās*, etc., belong to Vāmācāra while those without them are known as Dakṣiṇācāra. It is also said that there are only two *ācāras*—Dakṣiṇa and Vāma. A man belongs to the former by virtue of his birth and to the latter only by initiation. Again it is said that Vedācāra, Vaiṣṇavācāra, Śaivācāra, and Dakṣiṇācāra belong to the broad category of Dakṣiṇācāra, and that Vāmācāra, Siddhantācāra, and Kaulācāra to the broad category of Vāmācāra.[55]

A few words about the ways supposed to belong to Dakṣiṇācāra are to be said before dealing with Vāmācāra. Vedācāra is for ordinary persons belonging to Paśu grade and that is why it is also called Paśvācāra.[56] The *sādhaka* may be a traditional Hindu who believes in the Vedic and Smārta-Paurāṇic norms He should rise early in the morning, worship his *guru* and Īṣṭadevatā (personal god) and meditate on the *vijamantra aiṃ*. He should develop clean habits. In Vaiṣṇavācāra all these should be maintained. In addition, the *sādhaka* should give up sex life, eating meat and malpractices. He should worship Viṣṇu and feel that his God is immanent. He should follow the advice of his *guru* unquestioningly. The follower of Śaivācāra should also follow the code of Vedācāra. In addition he should worship Śiva and Śakti with animal sacrifice. He should depend on the eight yogic exercises as prescribed by the yogic texts and go up to the extent of *dhyāna* and *samādhi*. He should think about the world in terms of the immanence of Śiva. He may resort to the path of knowledge. However, in Dakṣiṇācāra proper the goddesss comes to the forefront. She should be worshipped in the Vedic way, with the exception that the *sadhaka* should also recite her *mantras* at night being intoxicated by liquor and smoke. The Śakti should be worshipped in her three forms—Icchā, Jñāna and Kriyā—symbolised by the goddess Dakṣiṇakālikā conceived of as the primordial energy. The sādhaka should believe in *varṇaśrama* and be clean internally and externally.[57]

The Vedic influence or Brahmanical superimposition is clearly revealed in the four *ācāras* belonging to the broad general category of Dakṣiṇācāra. However, these ways are severely condemned by the Vāmācāra schools. For example, in some Tantras it is stated that the efficacy of Dakṣiṇācāra is limited and painful. It is like crossing a river with the help of a jar, while the Kaula system is like crossing a river on a nice, comfortable boat.[58] Vāmācāra is of various kinds. The *Merutantra* describes five types of Vāmācāra known as Śābara, Siddhānta, Cīna, Vāma and Kaulika.[59] The *Śaktisaṅgamatantra*[60] refers to the Vāmācāra system as current among the worshippers of Gaṇeśa, Rudra, Viṣṇu, Śiva, Svayambhū, Veda, Bhairava, Kṣetrapāla, Cīna, Kāpālika, Pāśupata, Bauddha, Kerala, Vīra-Vaiṣṇava, Śāmbhava, Cāndra, Aghora. etc.

The followers of Vāmācāra are expected to worship the goddess in the traditional way during the daytime, and at night in the special Tantric way with the help of Five Ms. They must give up Vedic rituals, and must not utter the name of Viṣṇu or touch a *tulasī* leaf.[61] The *Śaktisaṅgamatantra* says that among the Mahāvidyā goddesses Kālī, Tārā, Sundarī, Bhairavī, Chinnamastā, Mātaṅgī, and Vagalā are fond of Vāmācāra, while Kamalā, Bhuvaneśvarī, Vālā and Dhūmāvatī may be appeased by Dakṣiṇācāra. According to the *Rudrayāmala*, a Vāmācāra aspirant should keep a woman, expert in sexual arts, on his left side and a pot of wine on the right and should have a musical environment for his training under a *guru*.[63] According to one interpretation such sensual objects are required so that he may concentrate his mind on the meditation of the goddess by ignoring all worldly temptations.

It is emphatically stated that the Brāhmaṇas are not entitled to be initated in Vāmācāra but it is open to all other castes. Only those Brāhmaṇas can be accepted who are known to have fallen from Śrautācāra or the Vedic way, or to have denounced it openly. Tantras like *Vāḍavānalīya* categorically say that Dakṣiṇācāra is meant for the Dvijas, and Vāmācāra for the lower Varṇas. The same also is stated in texts like *Mahākālasaṃhitā* in which Vāmācāra and Kaulācāra are prescribed exclusively for the Śūdras and persons belonging to the lower order. In the *Siddhāntasāra* it is stated that a Brāhmaṇa ceases to be a Brāhmaṇa if he accepts Kaulācāra (*brāhmaṇyahānihetutvāt kulācāraṃ na cācaret*). In the *Merutantra* it is stated that liberation of the Śūdras and Yavanas can be achieved through Vāmācāra (*śūdrādiyavanāntānām siddhir vāmapathe sthitā*). If a Brāhmaṇa really feels the urge of accepting Vāmācāra, he may be admitted to it, provided that he denounces his Brahmanical heritage and clings to his new faith, notwithstanding slander from his friends, separation from his family, apathy from peoples, punishment from the king, or because of disease or proverty.[64]

Some of the fundamentals of Vāmācāra, Siddhāntācāra and Kaulācāra have already been discussed. Siddhāntācāra is a form of Vāmācāra in which the external rites of the Five Ms are regarded as subsidiary, the more important ones being *antaryāga* or the rites of inner purification.[65] Another form of Vāmācāra is known as Samayācāra. According to Bhāskararāya, there are three schools in the cult of Śrīvidyā—Samaya, Kaula and Miśra (*samayamataṃ kaulamataṃ miśramataṃ ceti vidyopastau matatrayam*).[66] Lakṣmīdhara says that the Supreme Lord composed a variety of Tantras for the four varṇas and other mixed castes. Of all these Tantras sixty four—such as *Māhāmāyā, Sambara,* etc.—belong exclusivey to the Śūdras; these are outside the pale of the Vedas and hence are not meant for the Brāhmaṇas. A section of the Brahmaṇas, however, follows the Samaya-mārga by using the five texts known as *Subhāgama-pañcaka.* The Samayācārīs worship the goddess Samayā as Śakti and the god Samaya as Śiva, and their relation is conceived as that of perfect equilibrium. They lay special emphasis on the cult of Sahasradalakamala and on *antaryāga.* They have nothing like *japa, puraścaraṇa,* and other external rites.[67] But in other Tantric texts Samayācāra is viewed in a different light. Rāmeśvara in his commentary on the *Paraśurāmakalpasūtra* defines Samaya as the creed established by the Kulaśāstras (*sāmayikāḥ samaye kulaśāstra maryādāyām vartamānāh te kulaśāstrapratipāditā upāsakadharmā iti*) and as a secret system (*samayo guptaḥ saṃketaḥ śāstrapaddhati*). Seven states of *sādhanā* are also mentioned in the same text known as Ārambha, Taruṇa, Yauvana, Prauḍha Tadanta, Unmana, and Anavasthā, of which the first four are described as Samayācāra and the last three as Svairācāra. In the first stage the aspirant has only the desire for Tantric lessons; in the second he is initiated under a *guru;* in the third he reads the texts; in the fourth he learns the essentials; in the fifth he tries to concentrate his mind; in the sixth he is able to meditate successfully; and in the seventh he achieves perfection.[68]

Kaulācāra is the most important form of Vāmācāra, and we have already referred to the characteristics of a Kaula *sādhaka*. In the Śākta Tantras the term Kula denotes Śakti and Akula Śiva (*kulaṃ śaktīriti proktamakulaṃ śiva ucyate*); the realisation of their equilibrium is the aim of a Kaula worshipper (*Śivaśaktisāmarasyaṃ vā kaulam tadvatī kaulinī*). In the *Tantrāloka* it is stated: *akulasyāsya devasya kulaprathanaśālinī.*[69]

According to Abhinavagupta this signifies that Kula is the penultimate state of *purṇa-saṃvit* (realisation of the ultimate reality). The term Kula also denotes the *mūlādhāra-cakra* and also the *suṣumṇā-nāḍi*. The *kuṇḍalinī śakti* in the *mūlādhāra* is called Kaulinī, also known by the name Kulayoṣit.[70] When the *kuṇḍalinī śakti* pierces the *candramaṇḍala* or lunar-circle of the *sahasrāra* and unites with Śiva the nectar which flows down and anoints the body of the *sādhaka* is called *kulāmṛta*. It is also said that Kula denotes the material elements and Kaulācāra the understanding of their functions in terms of the knowledge of *brahman*.[71]

According to the *Rudrayāmala* Kaulācāra is that form of the Tantric cult in which the worship of Kula-strī, Kula-guru and Kula-devī is essential. The text traces the origin of Kaulācāra to Vaṣiṣṭha's visit to China, which has been described in detail earlier. According to the evidence of the Vaśiṣṭha-legend, Kaulācāra is outside the pale of the Vedas; as a system it is better than the Vedic way. In the *Saundaryalaharī* it is categorically stated to belong to those sixty-four Tantras which are intended only for those expelled from the Vedic system. In the *Devībhāgavata*[72] Kaulācāra is called an uncouth way which is followed only by those who have no faith in the Vedas, Agnihotras, and pious deeds, and those who are Pāṣaṇḍas, Kāpālikas, Buddhists, and Jains. In a subsequent period, however, attempts were made to obtain Vedic sanction for Kaulācāra. In the *Kulārṇava*, for example, Śiva is made to describe the Kaula-worshippers who follow Vedic rites, as being nearer to him and the goddess (*vedaśāstrokta-mārgeṇa kulapūjāṃ karoti yaḥ, tatsamīpasthitaṃ māṃ tvāṃ viddhi nānyatra bhāvini*). We have already referred to the fact that in the *Siddhāntasāra* Kaulācāra is totally prohibited for the Brāhmaṇas.

There are two types of Kaulācāra, wet and dry. The former

includes the Five Ms and the latter excludes them.[73] According to Lakṣmīdharā, there are two sects of Kaulas, Pūrva and Uttara. The Pūrvakaulas belive in Śiva-Śakti equilibrium while the Uttarakaulas insist solely on Śakti. The Kaula worshippers consider the triangle of the *ādhāracakra* as the seat of the *vindu.* The triangle or *yoni* is of two kinds, the symbolic triangle of the *śrīcakra* and the actual female organ. The former is worshipped by the Pūrvakaulas and the latter by the Uttarakaulas.[74] The *Mahānirvāṇa-tantra* prescribes Kaulācāra for all castes and sects, including the lowest castes, and says that even Caṇḍālas and Yavanas are entitled to follow the Kaula way.[75] In the *Muṇḍamālā-tantra* it is stated that by becoming a Kaula caste-identity is lost.[76] The Kaula should regard every woman as his mother. A woman can never be bad. No deed should be performed by a Kaula which offends a woman. The Kaula attitude towards women is thus described in the *Śaktisaṅgama-tantra:*[77]

> Woman is the mother of the three worlds, the representative of the worlds, the container of the three worlds and body of the three worlds. Whether the form is male or female, all the best forms are those of woman. All the beauty the world contains is created by woman. There is no friend better than a woman, no way better than a woman, no luck better than a woman, no kingdom better than a woman, no *tapas* better than a woman, no *tīrtha* better than a woman, no Yoga better than a woman and no *japa* better than a woman.[78]

In the *Nityotsava* it is stated that the Kaula system should be accepted only by those who are fit in body and mind, who are selfless and bold, who have controlled their senses, and who have firm faith in the creed.[79] The aspirant must have the indicatory knowledge (*saṅketajñāna*) from his teacher before he takes up the regular course.[80] There are half crores of *tīrthas* and all the gods are within the body of a Kaula. The one who has the highest knowledge is known as Siddhakaula.[81] The Kaula should realise that everything is the manifestation of Śakti, even his words and deeds. He must keep his knowledge, also the ways and means, secret from the uninitiated. Even in the time of disaster he will speak the truth. He will earn not for himself but for others. He will not expose the weakness of other persons. In brief, the Kaula should be an ideal person in all spheres of life.[82]

From the conflicting accounts of the various Vāmācāra sects in the sophisticated Tantras, it appears that these sects, although to a great extent influenced by Vedic and Brahmanical ideas, maintained their non-Brahmanical identity and also the primitive rites and customs such as Pañcatattva (the Five Ms), *Cakra*-sitting, etc. They maintained a typical ethic of their own, a different attitude towards wine, women, and other sensual objects. Although followers of Vāmācāra were surrounded by the objects of physical pleasure and there was no restriction in enjoying such objects—rather enjoyment was considered an important means to achieve salvation—these were employed for the attainment of a higher end, the mysteries of which were not disclosed to the uninitiated.

The Śākta-Tantric Deities

One aspect of the Śākta-Tantric cult which should be mentioned at the outset is that, like the deities of Tantric Buddhism, all the Śākta-Tantric deities are creations of the mind created according to the desire and mental inclination of the *sādhaka*. These deities have no anthropomorphic background and no mythology. Although some of the Puranic deities have a place in the Tantric pantheon, their character and conception are totally different. The Puranic stories of the exploits of Kālī have nothing to do with the Tantric concept of the goddess. According to the Tantras, because the deities reside within the human body and they are worshipped symbolically in *yantras* or diagrams they cannot have any outer existence. The only exception is the case of the ten Mahāvidyā goddesses who were brought in relation to the Dakṣayajña legend as a concession to the followers of the Purāṇas. The Tantric cults themselves have nothing to do with such legends.

According to the Tantras, the great goddess has innumerable forms, some of which are distributed in different *āmnāyas* or regions.[83] The better known are the Mahāvidyā goddesses: Kālī, Tārā, Chinnā, Sundarī, Vagalā, Mātaṅgī, Lakṣmī, Śyāmalā, Siddhavidyā-Bhairavī, and Dhūmavatī.[84] Another list gives them as Kālī, Tārā, Mahādurgā, Tvaritā, Chinnamastā, Vāgvādinī, Annapūrṇā, Pratyaṅgirā, Kāmākhyāvāsinī, Vālā, and Śailavāsinī Mātaṅgī.[85] Sometimes thirteen, or more often eighteen, Mahāvidyā goddesses are also mentioned. They are Kālī, Tārā, Chinnā, Mātaṅgī, Bhuvaneśvarī, Annapūrṇā, Nityā, Mahiṣamardinī Durgā, Tvaritā, Tripurā, Puṭā, Bhairavī, Vagalā, Dhūmāvati, Kamalā, Sarasvatī, Jayadurgā and Tripurasundarī.[86] In the *Nāradapāñcarātra* it is stated that there are seven crore Mahavidyās and seven crore Upavidyās (junior goddesses). Their nimber cannot be settled (*saptakoṭirmahāvidyā upavidyāśca tādṛśā*) conclusively.[87]

In the *Mahanirvaṇa-tantra*[88] it is stated that the great goddess is of the nature of the infinite, and it is only for the sake of her devotees that she connects herself with Prakṛti (material world), characterised by three qualities—sattva, rajas and tamas—which is an integral part of her own self and assumes the forms of the Mahāvidyās. The primal (*ādyā*) *vidyā* is Kālī who is the bestower of direct liberation (*śūnyagarbhe sthitā Kālī kaivalaya padadāyinī*). The goddess Tārā is of *sattva* quality and she is the bestower of knowledge. Ṣoḍaṣī, Bhuvaneśvari, and Chinnamastā are of *rajas* quality and they bestow minor liberations like wealth, heaven, etc. Dhūmāvatī, Vagalā, Mātaṅgī, and Kamalā are of *tamas* quality. They are invoked especially in connection with *ṣaṭkarma* and allied purposes. Of all these deities specially important are Kālī, Tārā and Tripurasundarī.

Kālī is the abstraction of primal energy. In the *Śaktisangama-tantra*[89] it is said that according to the Hādimata Mahāśakti is called Kālī in Kerala, Tripurā in Kāśmīra, and Tārā in Gauḍa; and according to the Kādimata she is called Tripurā in Kerala, Tāriṇī in Kāśmīra and Kālī in Gauḍa. *Kāla* or time devours the world during its dissolution. She even devours Kāla and that is why she is called *Kālī* and is conceived of as the primal cause of creation and destruction.[90] She is *brahman* representing existence and consciousness and conceived of as with or without attributes. Just as a tree grows and merges with the ground, or a bubble in water or lightning in the cloud, so also all the gods have their origin and dissolution in Kālī.[91] The *vījamantra* of *Kālī* is *krīm,* the letters K, R, I, M. being suggestive of *dharma, artha, kāma* and *mokṣa* respectively. According to another interpretation *K* denotes the creative aspect of the goddess, *Ṛ* the destructive, *I* the sustaining, and *M* the equilibrium of Śiva-Śakti.[92]

In principle Kālī is one, and there can be nothing apart from her. But, according to the capability and desire of the worshipper, she may be conceived of in innumerable forms. According to the *Toḍalatantra* her well-known forms are eight—Dākṣiṇa, Siddha, Guhya, Śrī, Bhadra, Cāmuṇḍā, Smāśāna and Mahā. The *Mahākālasaṃhitā* gives nine names Dākṣiṇa, Bhadra, Smāśāna, Kāla, Guhya, Kāmakalā, Dhana, Siddhi and Caṇḍikā. The *Jayadrathayāmala* mention Kālīkā Ḍambara, Rakṣā, Indīvara, Dhanada, Ramaṇi, Īśāna, Jīva, Vīrya, Prājñā and Saptārṇa. The *Śaktisaṅgaṃa* mentions Haṃsa and Vāśikaraṇa.

Of all these forms, Dakṣiṇākālī or Syāmā is the most important. In her *dhyāna*, quoted in the *Tantrasāra*, she is described as having a terrible appearance—a fierce face, four hands, untied hair, and a garland of severed heads around the neck. In her lower and upper left hands she holds a freshly severed head and a sword, and in the lower and upper right hands she exhibits *abhaya* and *varada* poses. Naked, dark as dense cloud in complexion, her body is streamed with blood which oozes from the garland of severed heads that she wears. Two corpses serve as her ear-rings. Terrible in face and teeth, she has well developed breasts; her girdle is made of hands cut off from the bodies of corpses. Her face is smiling, but it is stained with blood falling from both corners of her mouth. She screams terribly. She lives at the cremation ground. She has three eyes resembling the orb of the rising sun. Her untied hair hang to the right. She stands on the chest of Śiva lying as a corpse. She is engaged in *viparītarati* (inverted sexual intercourse also called *puruṣāyita*) with Mahākāla (Śiva).[93]

Śmaśānakālī or Śivā resembles Dakṣiṇakālī. She is also engaged in *viparīta-rati* with Mahākāla. According to the description in *Tantrasāra*, her sacred thread is a snake, and physical features being more or less the same as those of Dakṣiṇakālī. She, however, is surrounded by jackals and Yoginīs and is intoxicated as a result of drinking wine.[94] Siddhakālī is also a form of Dakṣiṇakālī. She is three-eyed and also has untied hair. She drinks *amṛta* from a skull held in her left hand. She wears a girdle and a jewelled crown. Her complexion is the colour of a deep blue lotus. She has a flaming tongue. The sun and moon are her ear-rings. She stands in *ālīḍha* posture, i.e. with the left leg in an advancing position.[95]

Guhyakālī is of the colour of clouds. According to the *Tantrasāra* she wears black graments, has a rolling tongue, terrible looking teeth, sunken eyes, smiling face, necklaces made of serpents, and has a crescent on the head. She frequently licks a corpse. Her sacred thread is a snake and she has the thousand hooded Ananta on her head. Śiva stands as a child to her left. According to the *Mahākālasaṃhitā* Guhyakālī has ten faces.[96] It also refers to different forms of this goddess characterised by the number of faces—100, 80, 60, 36, 30, 20, 10, 5, 3, 2, and 1. Bhadrakālī is described in the *Tantrasāra* as a hungry goddess ready to devour everything. Her eyes are sunken, face black as ink, hair untied and teeth blue-black like the *jambu* fruit. She holds a terrible and flame-like noose in both hands. In another description, her colour is like the clouds. Her teeth are white and terrible. She is three-eyed and has four arms, which hold a *kapāla, paraśu, damaru and triśūla.*[97] In some Tantras Bhadrakālī is conceived of as Mahiṣamardinī.[98]

Mahākālī, also known as Mahāraudrī and Kātyāyanī, is described in the *Tantrasāra* as having five faces, each containing three eyes, and in her left and right hands she holds a spear and trident, a bow and arrow, a sword and shield, and exhibits the *vara* and *abhaya* pose. This description is also given in the *Merutantra.* She also has a ten-faced form.[99] Rakṣākālī is variously depicted in Tantric literature. She has a white complexion, three faces, six arms, nine eyes, and matted locks of hair. Her garment is red. She is generally invoked as a protectress from calamities. Cāmuṇḍākālī is described in the *Tantrasāra* as having a pleasant face but a terrible appearance because of her fearful teeth. She has a *khatvāṅga* (a long bone with a skull at the top) and a sword in her two right hands and a noose and a human head in the two left hands. She wears a tiger skin and sits on a corpse. She lives in dense darkness.

Tārā, the Buddhist Tantric goddess, has been equated with Kālī. According to the *Śaktisaṅgama-tantra,*[100] Kālī, Tārā, Tripurasundarī and Chinnamastā are one and the same. The Buddhist character of Tārā is clearly observed in the *Tantrasāra* description of the goddess which characterises her as a youthful, fierce, short-statured and big-bellied goddess; she stands in *pratyālīḍha* pose and wears a garland of skulls; has a rolling tongue; in her right arms she holds a sword and knife and a skull and lotus in the left, her head adorned by the Dhyānī Buddha, Akṣobhya.[101] Also known as Tārinī, her *dhyāna* occurs in a good number of Tantric texts.[102] According to the *Matsyasukta,* as quoted in the *Tantrasāra,* the cult of Tārā is not only conducive to liberation but it also bestows knowledge, poetic ability, wealth, success in business, and position in the royal court. Various are the *mantras* and *kavacas* of Tārā.[103]

Of the different forms of Tārā, Ekajaṭā is important. She is so called because her matted locks are considered to be formed out of Rudra himself.[104] Ugratārā, another variety of the goddess, is described in the *Tantrasāra* as standing in *pratyālīḍha* pose with her right foot on a corpse; she holds a sword, blue lotus, knife and vessel in her hands. She is short-statured with brown matted locks and fierce snakes on her body. She destroys the inactivity of the whole world having put it in a skull-cup.[105] The third form of Tārā is known as Nīlasarasvatī. This goddess is said to have originated in a lake called Cola to the west of Mount Meru. While she was performing austerities her energy fell into the lake that had caused her complexion to become blue. There are other forms of Tārā collectively known as Aṣṭa-tārā or Aṣṭa-tāriṇī (cf. Buddhist concept of the Aṣṭamāhābhaya -tārā). They are known as Tārā, Ugrā, Vajrā, Mahogrā, Kālī, Sarasvatī, Kāmeśvarī and Bhadrakālī.

Ṣoḍaśī is a goddess of the Mahāvidyā category who is also known by the name Śrīvidyā-tripurā or Tripurasundarī. The name Tripurā has been used to explain all the threefold Tantric abstractions like *trikoṇa* (triangle), *triśakti* (three forms of Śakti—*icchā, jñānā, kriyā*), *trivindu* (three *vindus—rakta, śukla* and *miśra*), *tripīṭha* (Kāmarūpa, Pūrṇagiri and Jālandharā), *triliṅga* (three *liṅgas—vāna, itara, para*), etc.[106] This goddess is also known by the name of Lalitā. The *Tantrasāra* quotes the *dhyāna* of Ṣoḍaśī from the *Yoginīhṛdaya* according to which she is conceived of as a very beautiful and youthful damsel. Her nature is benign. She is installed on a red lotus, her garment is also red. She has four hands and three eyes. Her *dhyāna* also occurs in the *Mahākālasaṃhitā.*[107] Bhuvaneśī or Bhuvaneśvarī is conceived of as the protectress of the world. She is lustrous like the rising sun and has the moon on her crest. She has three eyes, highly developed breasts and a similing face. She holds a goad and noose in two hands and shows *varada* and *abhaya* poses with the other two.[108]

Bhairavī relieves her worshippers from all types of distress. Rāmeśvara in his commentary on the *Parāśurāmakalpasūtra*[109] says that her name is formed by the letters *bha* (symbolising *bharaṇa* or maintenance), *ra* (symbolising *ramaṇa* or sport like creation) and *va* (symbolising *vamana* or release). She has many forms and of them the lustre of Tripurabhairavī resembles that of a thousand rising suns. Her three eyes resemble red lotuses and the moon is fixed on her bejewelled crown. Her garment is red. She has a garland round her neck. Her breasts are covered with blood. She holds a rosary and manuscript in two hands and shows *varda* and *abhaya* poses with other two.[110] The conception of Caitanyabhairavī is also the same with the exception that she holds a noose, a goad and also a skull in her left hands. Bhuvaneśvaribhairavī is benign, clad in red garments and decked with a variety of ornaments. She has three eyes, highly developed breasts, four hands holding a noose and goad, showing *varada* and *abhaya* postures. Sampatpradābhairavī is a youthful goddess of the type of Ṣoḍaśī; she has an erotic figure. She shows *varada* and *abhaya* poses and carries a rosary and a manuscript.

Ṣaṭkuṭabhairavī has the complexion of the rising sun. She is adorned with necklaces made of severed human heads. Her breasts are developed and look like golden jars. She holds in her four hands noose, goad, manuscript, and rosary. Rudrabhairavī wears a garland of severed heads from which blood oozes. She uses Śiva as her throne and holds in her ten hands the trident, kettle drum, sword, shield, bow, arrow, noose, goad, manuscript, and rosary. Annapūrṇā-bhairavī, also known as Nityā, is the distributor of food. She has Bhūmi and Śrī beside her. She wears a crescent on the head, a crown sparkling with the lusture of nine kinds of gems, and a waist-band.[111]

Chinnamastā or Pracaṇḍacaṇḍikā bestows on her worshipper anything he wants. Her grace at once makes a man Śiva. Of her numerous *dhyānas* the one quoted in the *Tantrasāra* and other digests is the most widely known.[112] The worshipper should imagine a half-open white lotus on his own navel with the red orb of the sun in its pericarp. This orb is identified with the *yoni* triangle. Here resides Chinnamastā holding her own severed head in her left hand and drinking the blood flowing from her severed throat with her dreadful tongue. Her hair is dishevelled. She holds a skull-vessel in the left hand and a knife in the right. Fierce and naked, she stands in *pratyālīḍha* attitude. She stands on Rati and Kāma who are engaged in *viparīta-rati* (inverted sexual intercourse). She looks like a girl of sixteen and has highly developed breasts. Ḍākinī stands to her left and Varṇinī to her right, both of them drinking the blood which flows from her severed throat. Ḍākinī is full of effulgence having matted locks, three eyes, white teeth, developed breasts, dishevelled hair, skull-vessel in her left hand and knife in the right. Varṇinī is red-complexioned and has most of the emblems of the former. The conception of Chinnamastā recalls that of the Buddhist Vajrayoginī.

The goddess Dhūmāvatī is invoked for the purpose of destroying enemies: *Dhūmāvatīmanuh proktaḥ śatrunigraha-kārakaḥ*. She is conceived of as being pale (*vivarṇā*), tremulous (*cañcalā*), and angry (*ruṣṭā*). She is coarse, her robes are unclean, and her hair is untied. She is a widow and has only a few teeth. She rides a chariot on which the banner depicts a crow. She is tall and has hanging breasts, harsh-looking eyes, big nose, and generally asymmetrical features. She holds a winnowing fan in one hand and shows *varada* pose in the other which is trembling. She is always hungry and thirsty, terrorising and quarrelsome.[113] The *Nāradapāñcaratra* equates Dhūmāvatī with Vagalāmukhī but the former is an old widow while the latter is youthful and has a golden complexion. Moreover where the former is querulous and insatiable the latter is grave and drunk. According to the *Tantrasāra* descriptions Vagalā has three eyes and four hands, in which she holds a club, a noose, a thunderbolt and an enemy's tongue. She is clad in yellow clothes and has developed breasts.[114]

Mātaṅgī is three-eyed, dark-complexioned and seated on a bejewelled throne. In her four hands she holds a sword, shield, noose and goad. Her head is adorned by the moon.[115] Various forms of Mātaṅgī are known such as Ucchiṣṭamātaṅgī, Rājamātaṅgī, Sumukhī-mātaṅgī, Vaśya-mātaṅgī, and Karṇa-mātaṅgī. Ucchiṣṭa-mātaṅgī, also known as Ucchiṣṭa-Caṇḍālinī is conceived of as wearing black robes. Her feet are graced with red slip or wash. She has developed breasts, garlands of pearls and corals around her neck and ear-rings made of conch. Sumukhīmātaṅgī sits on a corpse. She has red robes and ornaments and is a youthful maiden of sixteen with highly developed breasts. Her left hand holds a skull and the right hand a chopper. Rāja-mātaṅgī is conceived of as residing within a triangle inside the pericarp of a lotus. She has long hair, a garland of *kadamba* around the neck, the moon on her head and a *tilaka* mark on her forehead. She has a smiling face which is bright because of mild perspiration. The region below her navel is marked by *trivali* or three lines under which is the pubic hair. She is clad in beautiful robes and decked with ornaments of pearls. She is two-armed and fickle-eyed owing to her drunken condition. She is a maiden of sixteen with big, round, firm breasts. Śuka and Sārī are her companions. She seems to be the embodiment of the sixty-four arts.[116]

The goddess Kamalā, also known as Lakṣmī and Śrī, has the complexion of gold. She is bathed by four white elephants which hold golden jars of nectar in their upraised trunks. She herself holds two lotuses in her two upper hands and shows *varada* and *abhaya* poses with her two lower hands. She is seated or standing on a lotus. She wears a crown sparkling with gems and silken clothes.[117] One of her forms is Mahālakṣmī who is a very youthful goddess, bedecked with all sorts of ornaments and select flowers and clad in the best of robes. Her physical features and figure are perfect; they radiate the highest degree of eroticism.[118] Sāmrājya-lakṣmī is also a form of Kamalā. Her complexion is like that of the *atasī* flower. She is adorned with ornaments made of pearls. She has eight hands holding a conch, wheel, club, lotus, bow, and arrow, and showing *varada* and *abhaya* poses.[119]

The *Tantrasāra* describes eight Yoginīs and quotes their *dhyānas* from the *Bhūtaḍāmara-tantra.* Of these Yoginīs, Kaṇakāvatī is conceived of as a fierce-faced but a youthful goddess having *bimba*-like red lips and wearing red clothes. Kāmeśvari is described as having a moon-like face, eyes as fickle as those of the Khañjana bird, agitated movements and weapons and arrows made of flowers. Nalinī charms the three worlds; she is fair-complexioned, wears beautiful clothes and ornaments, and has the appearance of a pleasant dancing girl. Padminī is dark complexioned, she has exaggerated breasts, soft limbs, a smiling face and eyes like the petals of a red lotus. The Yoginī Madhumatī has the colour of white crystal. She is decked with various jewels and such ornaments as anklets, necklace, armlets and earrings. Manoharā, as her name implies, has deer-eyes, an autumnal moon-like face, red lips like the *bimba* fruit and her body is rubbed with sandal paste. Though dark-complexioned, she has a pleasing appearance and full breasts. She wears *cīnāṃśuka* (dress made of China-silk). Ratisundarī is also of pleasing appearance with a complexion like that of gold. Her eyes resemble the lotus. She is adorned with all kinds of ornaments like anklets, armlets and necklace. Sura-sundarī is also fair-complexioned having a charming face resembling the full moon and highly developed breasts. She wears beautiful clothes.

Of the other Tantric goddesses, Ādyaśakti, also known as Tripuṭā, is conceived of as the embodiment of primordial energy. She is described as seated under a Kalpa tree, holding a bow, a noose, two lotuses, a goad and arrow made of flowers. She has three eyes, a golden-lotus-like complexion, highly developed breasts and a variety of ornaments. She is worshipped along with six companion deities—Lakṣmī, Hari, Gaurī, Hara, Rati and Smara or Madana. Gāyātri is conceived of as the goddess of knowledge and speech; she is also known as Brāhmī, the Śakti of Brahmā. In one of her *dhyānas* she is described as resembling the rising sun, wearing skin of a black antelope and holding a manuscript and the rosary in her hands. Dhanadā or Dhanadāyikā, the goddess who gives wealth is conceived of as a youthful maiden wearing costly ornaments. Dhavalāmukhī is described as smoke coloured, with three eyes and matted locks. She wears a tiger skin and holds a rosary of bones in one hand and a knife in the other. Besides these abstract deities, a good number of Purāṇic goddesses have made their way into the Tantric pantheon. Among these deities the important ones are Ambikā and Kātyāyanī also known as Mahiṣamardinī, Durgā, Pārvatī, etc., of Śaivite affiliation; and Śrī, Indirā, Kamalā, Kamalajā, Jaladhisutā, Lakṣmī, etc., of Vaiṣṇavite affiliation. Goddesses of knowledge such as Sarasvatī and her various forms—Vāgdevatā, Vāgdevī, Vagīśvarī, Bhāratī and Vānī; popular deities like Gaṅgā, Manasā, Ṣaṣṭhī, etc; and a host of other female deities are also described in the Tantric texts.

So far as the male deities are concerned, the Bhairava has a unique place in the Tantric cults. Although in the Śākta shrines Bhairava is symbolised by a Śiva-phallus—in popular imagination he is no other than Śiva—in the original conception he is the deified priest as well as the lover of the goddess. Each goddess has a Bhairava of her own. The Bhairava of Kālī is Mahākāla, of Tripurasundarī Laliteśvara, of Tārā Akṣobhya, of Chinnamastā Vikarālaka, of Bhuvaneśvarī Mahādeva, of Dhūmāvatī Kālabhairava, of Kamalā Nārayaṇa, of Bhairavī Vaṭuka, of Mātaṅgī Sadāśiva and of Vagalā Mṛtyuñjaya. There is, however, no uniformity in the Tantras regarding the names of the Bhairavas and their relation to the goddesses. Sectarian and Puranic gods like Acyuta, Viṣṇu, Kṛṣṇa, Ādivarāha, Garuḍa, Vāsudeva, Govinda, Hari, Mukunda, Hayagrīva, etc., have Vaisnavite character; Hara, Śiva, Śambhu, Īśā, Tryambaka, Rudra, Natārāja, Paśupati, Caṇḍeśvara, Dakṣiṇamūrti, Nilakaṇṭha, Mṛtyuñjaya, etc., belong to Śaivism; Gaṇapati or Gaṇeśa with his various forms like Mahā, Ucchiṣṭa, Hastimukha, Śakti, Heramba, etc. and Indra, Kandarpa (Kāma and Madana), Kārttikeya, Kṣeterapāla, Jagannātha, Ramā, Hanumāna, Laksmaṇa, Brahmā, Śūrya, etc., also figure in the Tantras. It should be noted, however, that these deities have only a symbolical significance in Tantric cults—their names are used to define some special positions in the *cakras* and *yantras*, each of them representing a typical attribute, or quality, or element and not the concrete person of the sectarian god.

Philosophy of the Śākta Tantras

Notwithstanding the antiquity of the Śākta-Tantric cults and rituals and their theoretical aspects, there has been no consistent attempt in the past to give them a complete philosophical shape. This can be attributed to the fact that the Śākta-Tantric teachings were transmitted from teacher to pupil as a secret and mysterious knowledge to be understood and retained only by those considered competent. That is why in the philosophical compendiums—the *Sarvadarśanasaṃgraha,*

Saddarśanasamuccaya, Sarvasiddhāntasamgraha, Vivekavilāsa, etc.—Śākta philosophy as a whole has no place, although some of its aspects have been referred to in connection with other philosophical systems.

The need for reconstructing the Śākta viewpoint on the basis of the available Tantric texts felt in the last quarter of the 19th century by the advocates of the Neo-Tantric movement who wanted to identify Tantrism with the totality of Hinduism and regard it as the essence of the Vedas. The greatest exponents of this line were Sir John Woodroffe and his associates who composed numerous interpretative works on Tantrism during the first three decades of the 20th century. In 1937 Panchanan Tarkaratna published his Śākta commentaries on *Brahmasūtra* and *Iśopaniṣad* in which he made a laudable attempt to put forward what is known as the Śākta viewpoint in Indian philosophical tradition. This branch of study was further developed by MM. Gopinath Kaviraj.

It is worth remembering that all these great scholars while interpreting the essentials of Śāktism depended on the sophisticated Tantric tradition which was burdened with Brāhmanical superimpositions and Vedantic elements. We have repeatedly said that the logic and the doctrines of the Tantras were given a very sophisticated tone and colour; a philosophy of extreme idealism was grafted onto them as opposed to the original materialistic outlook which Tantrism basically upheld. Since these accretions have now become an integral part of Tantrism, they should also be properly studied in the light of what has been understood by these great Tantric scholars.

We have seen that most of the Tantric works are medieval efficient and inefficient renderings or rewritings or the teachings of the earlier lost texts. It is said that the traditional sixty-four Bhairava-Āgamas were monistic, ten Śaivāgamas were dualistic and eighteen Raurdrāgamas were of diverse views.[120] Most of the original texts are lost. Generally, the Jñāna-pāda sections of the Āgamas contain some philosophical speculations. Among the Tantric texts of philosophical significance mention may be made of *Svacchanda, Mālinivijaya, Vijñānabhairava, Triśirobhairava, Kulagahvara, Paramānanda tantra, Āgamarahasya*, etc. The Śrīvidyā school has an extensive literature of its own. This school claims Agastya, Durvāsā and Dattātreya as its earlier exponents. References to a lost *Dattātreya-samhitā* are found. Some of its contents are said to have formed part of the *Tripurārahasya*, the *jñānā* section of which throws much light on Śākta philosophy.

Gauḍapāda's *Śrīvidyāratnasūtra,*[121] which is said to have been commented upon by Śaṅkarācārya himself, is a useful Śākta text. Philosophically important are *Prapañcasāra,* attributed to Śaṅkara and commented upon by Padmapāda, *Prayogakramadīpikā,* Lakṣmaṇa Deśika's *Śāradātilaka,* and the texts of the Kāśmira Śaiva school. Abhinavagupta in his numerous works has successfully established the foundation of Śākta philosophy. Among his successors, Gorakṣa or Maheśvarānanda composed an original work called *Mahārghamañjarī* and commentaries like *Parimala, Saṃvidullāsa,* etc. Puṇyānanda's *Kāmakalāvilāsa* is an authoritative work on Śākta philosophy. Its commentary, known as *Cidvallī* was composed by Nathanānanda. Amṛtānanda, a disciple of Puṇyānanda, wrote an important commentary known as *Yoginīhṛdayadīpikā* which was made on the Yoginīhṛdaya section of the *Nityaṣoḍaśikārṇava* of the *Vāmakeśvara-tantra.* He was also the writer of *Saubhāgyaśubhagodya* another text of great philosophical significance. Svatantrānanda's *Mātṛkācakraviveka* is an exceptional work in five parts in which the aspects of Tantric secret knowledge have been explained. The best exponent of Śākta philosophy is Bhaskāra-rāya who flourished in the 18th century. His most celebrated work is *Setubandha* which is a commentary on *Nityaṣoḍaśikārṇāva.* His other works include *Kaula-tripurā, Saubhāgyabhāskara* (commentary on the *Lalitāsahasranāma*), *Guptavatī* (commentary on the *Devīmāhātmyā*), *Śāmbhavānanda-Kalpalatā, Varivasyā-rahasya,* etc.

Śākta philosophy, as we have noted, was deeply influenced by the non-dualistic and dualistic interpretations of the Vedānta, though other systems like the Sāṅkhya, etc., formed its original basis. The Śākta philosophical terminologies are not different from those used in the Indian philosophical tradition in general. As in all idealistic systems, the ultimate reality in Śāktism is pure consciousness. It is known as *saṃvit.* In the Vedānta, specially according to its non-dualist interpretation, *saṃvit* is not limited by time, space and cause. In it the world is reflected just as an object is reflected in a clear mirror. From this analogy of the mirror we have three probabilities: The mirror (*saṃvit*) is, but there is nothing (world) reflected in ; the mirror is, and the thing (world) is inside it; and the mirror is, and the thing (world) reflected in it belongs to the outside. In all the three cases, the mirror (*saṃvit* or pure-consciousness) is one and only one without any change. That is why it is called *nirvikalpa* which literally means without any transformation. The first probability shows that there is nothing inside nor outside the ultimate reality; the second probability shows that the ultimate reality may be self-expressive inwardly but not outwardly; and the third probability shows that its inwardly self-expression may have outwardly contents. But the problem is in regard to the relation between the pure and unattached *saṃvit* and the worldly objects which are reflected in it. According to the Vedānta, specially to its extreme non-dualistic brand, creation does not proceed from *saṃvit* or *brahman*; the so-called world of existence is false and illusory.

But the Śākta Āgamas hold a different view. They recognise the independence of *saṃvit* and its power to create motion, although owing to the influence of Vedānta some of the texts hold that the world is an appearance. In Śāktism *saṃvit* is conceived of in terms of the functioning of Śakti in *parkāśa* and *vimarśa* aspects, the static and dynamic condition. *Saṃvit* is both immanent and transcendent, the former condition prevails when Śakti in its static state assumes the form of matter and the latter condition prevails when Śakti in its dynamic state assumes the form of consciousness. The first category is known as *anaham* and the second category as *aham*. In the sophisticated Tantras it is categorically stated that *anaham* is the so called unmanifested material entity and it is caused by the conscious principle by the concept *aham*. In other words, it is stated that matter is produced from consciousness. In modern philosophical terms this standpoint is known as idealism. This approach (in Indian philosophical tradition known as *cetana-kāraṇa-vāda*) is opposed to the earlier Tantric materialistic—approach to life and universe. It is obviously due to the Vedāntic influence. But like the Vedānta, the sophisticated Tantras also fail to explain conclusively how matter can be produced from consciousness.

We are not concerned with the fallacies of Tantric or Vedantic thinking. Here we shall see how the Śākta-Tantrics put forward their premises. They say that at the time of the dissolution of the universe pure consciousness or *saṃvit* remains absolutely free from material contaminations—it remains as pure *cit-śakti or parā-prakṛti*. But when the alternatives or material entities develop (they develop owing to the self-contraction of *saṃvit*, but the Tantras do not explain with any amount of reason how the contraction of pure consciousness can yield gross things), then Śakti manifests itself as *avidyā* or material Prakṛti. Thus the ultimate reality functions in its two aspects, as subject and also as object. It is stated that pure consciousness is universal in nature, that there is nothing to limit or cover it and that the material world is contained in it. The evolution of the material world from pure consciousness has been conceived of in three stages. The first is the seed stage in which matter does not express its existence and appear as an entity different from consciousness. This stage is regarded as pure. In the second stage there is a marked difference between consciousness and matter, both of which are subject to subtle manifestations. This is regarded as the mixed state. In the third stage the categories of the mixed state have gross manifestations. In this stage we have the evolution of Prakṛti, the primordial matter, in the shaping of the material world.[122]

The evolution of the material world has been traced to the following categories: Parameśvara, Śakti, Para-Nāda, Para-Vindu—subdivided into Apara-Vindu and Vīja, and Apara-Nāda.[123] Parameśvara is the supreme being with whom Śakti or Kalā is in inseparable relation. Just as oil issues from oil-seed so also in the beginning of creation Śakti appears. This appearance of Śakti is like the reappearance of the memory of a person who rise from deep sleep. The appearance of Śakti causes an unmanifested sound called Para-Nāda that fills up the vacuum and eventually concentrates itself on a point or centre which is called Para-Vindu. This Para-Vindu is again subdivided into three parts known respectively as Apara-Vindu, Vīja and Apara-Nāda. In this Apara-Vindu the Śiva element dominates and in the Vīja the Śakti element. In Apara-Nāda, there is Śiva-Śakti equilibrium. The sound caused by the subdivision of Para-Vindu is often called Śabdabrahma.[124] These transformations are due to the inseperable Śakti of the supreme being in the form of *icchā* (will) and *kriyā* (functioning).

In the Tantras the whole process is explained with reference to the human body. The space holding the thousand-petalled lotus in the cerebral region is called *brahmarandhra* or *śūnya.* It is the breeding spot of Icchā-Śakti and Para-Nāda. It is a part of the *visarga-maṇḍala* which is great causal state of *brahman* or *saṃvit* symbolised by Śabdabrahma or Kulakuṇḍalinī. The three subdivisions of Para-Vindu, namely Vindu (Apara), Vīja and Nāda (Apara), constitute the Kuṇḍalinī triangle. The subtle elements of matter differs from Kuṇḍalinī and they reside in different centres of the forehead and nerves. The aforesaid triangle symbolized by Śiva (Apara-Vindu), Śakti (Vīja) and their equilibrium (Apara-Nāda), is called A-Ka-Tha triangle, each of its lines being consisted of sixteen letters. Apart from the Para and Apara Nādas, there is a third Nāda, known as Mahā-Nāda, caused by the unmanifested sound of the letters which is conveyed by the Kuṇḍalinī. It serves as a link between the Para and Apara Nādas, between conscious and non-conscious elements. The upward and downward motions of the Nādas are carried through the main nerves.

To put the whole thing in a more intelligible way, it may be said that *saṃvit* or pure consciousness exists. In the Śākta Tantras it is conceived of as the non-dual existence of static Śiva and kinetic Śakti—two positions of the same thing. But, side by side, there is the existence of an unconsciousness, the material world. How can this be explained? According to the non-dualist Tantras it is said that the material world is caused by the self-expression or manifestation of pure consciousness. How can that be possible? The Tantras say that pure consciousness works through its Śakti or inherent power. This Śakti at first appears as Icchā-Śakti or will-power, the desire to be manifested. Subsequently it works in its two aspects—Vidyā-Śakti and Avidyā-Śakti or Māyā-Śakti. Both of these are conscious principles with the difference that while the former is illuminating consciousness, the latter is veiled consciousness, i.e. consciousness appearing as unconsciousness. This Māyā-Śakti is composed of three *guṇas*—Sattva, Rajas, Tamas—and known as Triguṇa-Śakti or Kāmakalā symbolised by the triangle. Hence this Māyā-Śakti is not unreal (this is a departure from the Vedāntic line), and it is the cause of the material world.

Śakti, operating as Cit and Māyā, is real. It is that aspect of the Supreme Being which is in fact, both the efficient and material cause of the world. Owing to the *vṛtti* of Māyā, or Śakti in the form of desire for creation in Parama-Śiva or the Supreme Being, there takes place what is known as *sadṛśapariṇāma* in which the Supreme Vindu appears. This, in its triple aspect is also known as Kāmakalā, the process of the manifestation of Śakti. Śakti as identical with the Supreme Being is immutable and without any transformation, but in its functional aspect it is *pariṇāmī* (subject to transformation). When Śakti passes from a potential state to one of actuality it produces Nāda or cosmic sound from which issues Vindu or Para-Vindu. The *Prapañcasāra* says that Śakti longs to create (*vicikirṣu*) and becomes massive or crystallised (*ghanibhūta*) and appears as Vindu. This Vindu or Para-Vindu divides or differentiates itself in the threefold aspects of Apara-Vindu, Vīja and Apara-Nāda, as we have already noted with reference to the *Śaradātilaka.* The first category is Śivamaya or Śiva-oriented, the second Śaktimaya or Śakti-oriented, the third Śivaśaktimaya in which Śiva and Śakti operate equally. These three categories are equated with all the tripartite concepts of Tantra-like Para-Sukṣma-Sthula, Icchā-Jñāna-Karma, Tamas-Rājas-Sattva, Moon-Fire-Sun and so on. These are all different phases of Śakti.

Creation is thus the self-expression of Supreme Being, the subject viewing itself as object, I (Aham) as it (Idam). In the dualistic Tantras, however, the whole process has been viewed from a different angle. Here both Śiva and Śakti, the static (*prakāśa*) and kinetic (*vimarśa*) aspect of the same reality, are treated as individual conscious principles. Śiva is unity behind all diversity. Śakti is the same but, since it acts on different things, it is expressed as the inherent nature of the things themselves on and through which it works. Still Śakti is not different from Śiva. Vindu is an eternal material entity outside the realm of Śakti, but it is dependent on the functioning of Śakti. Thus, these three separate entities are the three permanent categories described as three Ratnas. In the matter of creation Śiva is the efficient cause, Śakti is the instrumental cause, and Vindu is the material cause. Because Śakti is not material in nature; at the time of its activity it undergoes no change, but it may have transformation in Vindu.

In view of the foregoing we find that in the Śākta scheme *māyā* is not an unconscious principle but it is consciousness veiling itself as a Śakti of the Supreme Being. Śakti and Śaktimān (possessor of Śakti) are one and the same. Māyā-Śakti is therefore that particular aspect of *cit* or consciousness which it assumes as the material cause (*upādāna-kāraṇa*) in creation. Śiva as Śakti is the cause of the universe and as Śakti in the form of Jīva (all manifested forms) appears in them. There are two principles or aspects in the *brahman* or *saṃvit*—Prakāśa (static aspect) and Vimarśa (the kinetic and vibrating aspect), which in creation explicate into the universe. Vimarśa Śakti again has two forms. In the subtle state it is in the form of consciousness (*cidrūpiṇī*) and in the gross state it is in the form of the universe (*viśvarūpiṇī*). The ultimate reality is therefore Śiva in indistinguishable union with Śakti. This Śakti, conceived of as a Female Principle, when in non-dual state with Śiva is unmanifested *cit* or consciousness. The relation between Śiva and Śakti is one of inseparable connection or inherence such as that between—I-ness (*ahanta*) and I (*aham*), existence (*bhava*) and existent (*bhavat*), attribute (*dharma*) and attributed (*dharmī*), and so forth.

The evolution of the Supreme Being or supreme consciousness into the universe is described in a scheme of thirty-six *tattvas*, divided into *three* groups named Śiva-tattva, Vidyā-tattva, Ātma-tattva and Śuddha, Śuddhāśuddha and Aśuddha *tattvas*. Without going into the details of these thirty-six *tattvas*, it may be said that they are accepted both by the Śaivas and the Śāktas; they are taken from the northern Kāsmīra Śaiva philosophical school, which itself was based upon the older Āgamas like the *Mālinīvījaya* and others. The point which needs to be discussed is the nature of the evolution of the Supreme Being. It is not a case of complete transformation as we find in the case of milk transforming into curd. The Supreme Being is not exhausted by the transformation. The change is not qualitative. As already stated *Aham* (I-ness, the subject) and *Idam* (It-ness, the object) exist in an unitary state in Para-saṃvit, in which Śiva represents the Prakāśa and Śakti the Vimarśa aspect. The latter contains the potentialities of the universe within it. It begins to function leaving the Prakāśa standing alone as an 'I' without a 'This'. The purpose of this functioning is to make the subject experience itself as object. Then stage by stage the Māyā-Śakti or 'consciousness veiling itself' unfolds itself, and in this process we come across the emergence of multiple selves and objects forming the universe. At every stage of this evolution the Vimarśa-Śakti contracts itself into gross and more gross entities until it assumes physical forms and works as the life-principle of all things. At the end of this process, in dissolution, it again returns to its source and remains there in undifferentiated state with her other part, the Prakāśa aspect of the Supreme Being.

The process has also been described using the analogy of a *canaka* or grain by which the cosmic evolution is conceived of as a process polarizing the supreme being into static and kinetic aspects. A *canaka* has two seeds which are so close to each other that they seem one; they are surrounded by a single sheath. The seeds are Śiva and Śakti and the sheath is Maya. When the sheath is unpeeled, Māyā-Śakti operates, and the two seeds come apart. The sheath unrolls when the seeds begin to germinate. It is like reawakening from a dreamless slumber. As the universe in dissolution sinks into a memory which is lost, so it is born again from the germ of recalled memory or Śakti. After the dreamless slumber (*suṣupti*) of the *saṃvit* or the world-consciousness the remembrance of the past gives rise in it to creative thinking or the will to create (*sṛṣṭikalpanā*). It is thus that the indistinguishable unity of Śiva-Śakti or subject and object of the Supreme Being, is broken. It does not, however, take place all at once. There is an intermediate stage of transition, in which there is a subject and an object, but both are part of the Supreme Being which knows its objective form. Their separation becomes a reality when the object manifests itself apart from the subject. The process and the result are the work of Śakti whose special function is to negate, that is to negate its own fullness, so that it becomes the finite centre contracted as a limited subject perceiving a limited object, both being aspects of one ultimate reality. The principle of negation is a feature of *Śaktitattva* (*niṣedha-vyāparā-rūpa-śaktiḥ*). Where there is pure experience there is no manifested universe. Śakti negates the pure experience of consciousness because it disengages the unified elements, subject and object, which are latent in the pure *saṃvit* in absolute non-dual relation.

The Supreme Being of Śāktism is not a personal God. In its own nature it is more than that. The Śākta standpoint posits the reality of God as the cause of the universe. But it holds that while the effect is the cause modified, the cause as cause remains what it was, what it is, and what it will be. It holds that the supreme being is manifested in one of its aspects in an infinity of relations; and though involving all relations within itself, is neither their sum total nor exhausted by them. Śakti, which is its functional aspect, works by negation, contraction, and finitisation. As a Mother power she unfolds herself into the world and again withdraws the world into herself. The purpose of her worship is to attain unity with her forms, and this is the experience of liberation—a state of great bliss (*ānandaghaṇa*). In the natural order of development, Śakti is developed in worldly things but it is controlled by a religious *sādhanā*, which both prevents an excess of worldliness and moulds the mind and disposition (*bhāva*) into a from which develops the knowledge of dispassion and non-attachment. *Sādhanā* is a means whereby bondage becomes liberation.[125]

NOTES

1. *Śāradātilaka*, II. 108-11.
2. Surāśaktiḥ śivomāṃsaṃ tadbhoktā bhairavaḥ svayam/
   Tayoraikye samutpanne ānando mokṣa ucyate//

3. *Saundaryalaharī*, 9.
4. Antaḥśāktā bahiḥśaiva sabhāyāṃ vaiṣṇava mataḥ/
Nānārūpadharāḥ Kaulāḥ vicaranti mahītale//
5. *Nityatantra*, Paṭala 3.
6. *Ṣacakranirūpaṇa*, V.2-13; also see *Devībhāgavata*, XI.1.43; *Mantramahodadhi*, IV. 19-25; *Jñānārṇava*, XXIV, 45-54; *Mahānirvāṇa*, V. 113 ff. The *Rudrayāmala*, XXXVI. 6-168 sets out 1008 names of *Kuṇḍalinī* all of which begin with the letter *Ka*.
7. Ibid., vv. 14-18.
8. Ibid., vv. 19-21.
9. Ibid., vv. 22-7.
10. Ibid., vv. 28-31.
11. Ibid., vv. 32-8.
12. Ibid., vv. 41-9.
13. Cf. *Śāradātilaka*, I. 12.
14. *Paraśurāmakalpasūtra*, I. 11-12; *Śāradātilaka*, I. 55ff; *Prapañcasāra*, I. 41ff; *Mahānirvāṇa*, V. 18ff. etc.
15. *Śaradātilaka*, I. 108-11. For the understanding of the intricacies of Nāda, Vindu, Kalā, etc. see Gopinath Kaviraj in *Journal of the Ganganath Jha Research Institute*, Vol. III, pp. 97-108.
16. For details see S.S. Awasthi's *Mātṛkā aur Mātṛkāyo kā Rahasya* (in Hindi)
17. *Paraśurāmakalpasūtra*, I. 7.11; *Śāradātilaka*, II. 57ff.
18. *Jñānārṇava*, XXIV.74-6.
19. XVII. 54; *Prapañcasāra*, V.2.
20. Like *RV*, I. 55. 12; I. 99. 1; III.62.10; VIII.59.12, etc.
21. *Mahānirvāṇa*, V. 62-63; cf. *Taittirīya Āraṇyaka*, X. 1.
22. I. 7; I. 10.
23. I. 38.
24. .Chs. 121, 125, 133-5, 307, etc.
25. Rāghavabhaṭṭa on *Śāradātilaka*, XVI, 56; *Mahānirvāṇa*, VII. 76-85; *Kulārṇava*, XV; *Mantramahodadhi*, XXV. 66ff; *Jayākhyasaṃhitā*, XIX. 13-37, etc. For brief but useful details see the Puraśacarṇa sections in the *Tantrasāra* and the *Śāktānandataraṅgiṇī*.
26. Different forms of Nyāsas are described in most of the Tantric texts and digests. See especially *Jayākhya*, XI; *Prapañcasāra*, VI; *Kulārṇava*, IV. 18ff; *Śāradātilaka*, IV. 29-41; V. 5-7, etc.
27. Cf. *Garuḍa*, I. Chs. 26, 31, 32; *Brahma*, LX. 35-40; *Kālikā*, Ch. 77, *Padma* VI. 79. 17-36; *Devi Bh.* XI. 16.76-91, etc.
28. Thus *Śaradātilaha* (XXIII 106-14) mentions only nine *mudrās*, *Jayākhya* (VIII) fifty-eight, *Jñānārṇava* (IV. 31-47, 51-6, XV. 47-68) over thirty, *Haṭhayogapradīpikā* (III. 6-23) ten, *Gheraṇḍasaṃhitā* (III. 1.3) twenty-five and so on. The Buddhist *Mañjuśrīmūlakalpa* (XXXV, pp. 355-81) mentions 108 Mudrās. Two Jain texts *Mudrāvicāra* and *Mudrāvidhi* mention 73 and 114 Mudrās respectively. See U. P. Shah in *Journal of the*

Oriental Institute, Vol. VI, pp. 1-35.

29. See *Jñānārṇava* XV. 61-3, *Nityaṣoḍaśīkārṇava*, III. 15-23; *Haṭhayogapradīpikā*, III. 32-53, 82-96; *Śivasaṃhitā*, IV. 31-3; *Gheraṇḍasaṃhitā*, III. 25-7.
30. *Devībhāgavata*, XI. 16, 98-102; XI. 66. 62-5; *Kālikā*, LXX. 32-56; LXXVIII.3-6; *Agni*, XXVI; *Brahmāṇḍa* (in Lalitopākhyāna, Ch. XLVI).
31. Several Maṇḍalas are described in *Śāradātilaka*, III. 106-39; *Jñanārṇava*, XXV. 15-17.
32. XXIV. 8-10, XXVI. 15-17.
33. III. 106-30.
34. See *Kulārṇava*, VI. 85-6.
35. *Merutantra*, XXXIII. 13.
36. *Nityaṣoḍaśīkārṇava*, VV. 126-204 gives details of different items in the worship of *Śrīcakra*. For *Yantras* in general see *Prapañcasāra* XXI, XXXIV; *Śāradātilaka*, VII. 53-63, XXIV; *Kāmakalāvilāsa*, 22ff; *Tantrarāja*, II. 44-51, VIII. 30ff; *Mantramahodahi*, XX; *Kaulajñānanirṇaya*, X; *Kaulāvalinirṇaya*, III. 105-35, etc.
37. *Haṭhayogapradīpikā*, IV. 5-7.
38. vv. 51ff.
39. IX. 15.
40. V. 82.
41. *Gheraṇḍasaṃhitā*, III. 8ff.; *Haṭhayogapradipikā*, II. 21ff.
42. *Śivasaṃhita*, III. 84-91; *Haṭhayoga*, I. 19.35.
43. IV. 37.
44. *Gheraṇḍa*, III. 86-7.
45. *Haṭhayogapradīpikā*, II. 1-6.
46. IX. 3.
47. Com. on *Lalitāsahasranāma*, 53.
48. *Gheraṇḍa*, VI.
49. *Haṭhayogapradīpikā*, IV. 10ff.
50. *Yogavīja*, vv. 51-2.
51. *Rasahṛdaya-tantra*, Āyurveda Granthamālā, Vol. I, XIX. 63-4.
52. A. Gettey, *Gods of Northern Buddhism*, intro. XI.
53. Ch. IX.
54. *Sarvadarśansaṃgraha*, Eng. tr. by E.B. Cowell and A.E. Gough, rpt., Banaras, 1961, pp. 137-44.
55. *Prāṇatoṣaṇi*, VII. 4, Vasumati edn., p. 532; *Kaulamārgarahasya*, ed. S.C. Vidyabhusana, Sahitya Parisat Granthavali No. 76, p. 11.
56. *Kaulamārgarahasya*, p. 9.
57. *Prāṇatoṣaṇi*, III. 1; VII. 1, pp. 149, 499.
58. Cf. *Gandharva-tantra*, ed. R.C. Kak and H.B.Sastri, Śrīnagar, 1934, XXXVII. 33-4.
59. *Puraścaryārṇava*, by Pratapsimha Shah Bahadur Varma of Nepal in three parts, Calcutta, 1901, 1902, 1904, I, p. 22.

60. *Tārākhaṇḍa*, I.92-4.
61. *Prāṇatoṣani*, VII.1; p. 499; *Kaulamārgarahasya*, p. 10.
62. *Tārākhaṇḍa*, I. 84-90.
63. *Puraścaryārṇava*, I, pp. 26-7.
64. Ibid., pp. 24-7.
65. *Kaulamārgarahasya*, p. 10.
66. *Saubhāgyabhāskara* Com. on *Lalitāsahasranāma*, 144.
67. Lakṣmīdhara on *Saundaryalaharī*, vv. 8,33, 41.
68. *Vṛtti* on *Paraśurāmakalpasūtra*, VII. 1; X. 68; X. 80.
69. III. 67.
70. Lakṣmīdhara on *Saundaryalaharī*, vv. 8, 10, 41.
71. *Mahānirvāṇa-tantra*, VII. 97-8.
72. XII. 9. 96.
73. *Prāṇatoṣani*, VII. 4; p. 531.
74. Com. on *Saundaryalaharī*, vv. 23, 33, 34, 41.
75. XIV. 184, 187.
76. *Prāṇatoṣani*, VII. 4; p. 531.
77. *Gandharvatantra*, XXXIV. 9.
78. *Tārākhaṇḍa*, XXII. 43-7.
79. *Nityotsava*, GOS, Vol. XXIII, pp. 6-7.
80. *Vṛitti* on *Paraśurāmakalpasūtra*, VII. 1.
81. *Mahānirvaṇa*, X. 105-6.
82. *Paraśurāmakalpasūtra*, X. 77-9; *Nityotsava*, p. 9.
83. *Puraścaryārṇava*, I. pp. 11-13.
84. *Śaktisaṅgama-tantra*, *Tārākhaṇḍa*, VI. 16-17.
85. *Mālinīvijaya* quoted in *Śāktānandatarāngiṇī*, III.
86. *Niruttārā-tantra*, Paṭala XV.
87. *Prāṇatoṣani*, V. 6, p. 376.
88. XIII. 4.
89. *Kālīkhaṇḍa*, V. 24-6.
90. *Mahānirvāṇa*, IV. 30-2.
91. *Nirvāṇatantra*, Paṭala X.
92. *Toḍalatantra*, *Ullāsa* 6; *Puraścaryārṇava*, IX, p. 724.
93. The *Niruttara-tantra*, Paṭala II, gives a slightly different version of this *dhyāna*.
94. Other forms of her *dhyāna* is quoted in the *Śyāmārahasya*, Ch. VI, and *Prāṇatoṣani*, V. 6, p. 389.
95. *Kālītantra*, X. 33.
96. *Puraścaryārṇava*, IX, p. 764
97. *Prapañcasāra*, XXXII. 9.
98. *Yoginītantra*, Pūrva, Paṭala IX.
99. *Puraścaryārṇava*, IX, p. 754; XI, p. 956.
100. *Sundarīkhaṇḍa*, IV. 51.
101. Cf. *Nīlatantra*, Paṭala III.

102. *Puraścaryārṇava*, IX, pp. 794-5.
103. Cf. *Tārātantra*, VI. 3-4.
104. *Tārārahasya*, Paṭala I.
105. *Setubandha* com. on *Nityaṣoḍaśikārṇava*, p. 141.
106. *Kāmakalāvilāsa*, 13-14.
107. *Puraścaryārṇava*, IX, p. 799.
108. *Śāradātilaka*, IX. 14.
109. I. 12.
110. *Śāradātilaka*, XII. 31.
111. These conceptions are from the *Tantrasāra*; see also *Puraścaryārṇava*, IX, pp. 809-13.
112. Ibid., pp. 816-17.
113. *Phetkāriṇī*, Paṭala 7.
114. *Puraścaryārṇava*, IX, p. 825.
115. Ibid., p. 827.
116. Ibid., pp. 828-32.
117. *Śāradātilaka*. VIII. 5.
118. Ibid., VIII. 74-8.
119. *Puraścaryārṇava*, IX, p. 840.
120. *Jayāratha-Tantrāloka*, I, 18.
121. Ed. N. Sastri Khiste, Sarasvati Bhavana Series.
122. *Tripurārahasya*, Jñānakhaṇḍa, ed. Gopinath Kaviraj, Ch. XIVff.
123. *Śāradātilaka*, I.7-8.
124. Ibid., I. 11-12; *Prapañcasāra*, I. 44.
125. This section is based mainly upon the monistic interpretation of the sophisticated Śākta Tantras made by Sibchandra Vidyārṇava, MM. Gopinath Kaviraj and Sir John Woodroffe.

10

Tantric Art: A Review

The Problem

Books flaunting Tantric labels and containing colourful pictures of male-female union are being publised in abundance nowadays. Their writers depend solely on the copulative aspects of the male-female union as found in the Indian art tradition and preserved in numerous printed art-albums. These are popularly regarded as specimens of Tantric art. Some recent writers even go so far as to state that the conception of art originally developed among the followers of Tantrism and that Tantric art was the precursor of modern abstract art. The term Tantric art is evidently a misnomer. There can be no invariable and inevitable concomitance between erotic depictions and Tantrism, or that between the earlier Tantric symbols and the intricacies of modern art. But there are some questions which cannot be avoided. What is the rationale of erotic depictions on religious objects? What are their thematic contents? To what extent are they connected with Tantrism?

A consistent explanation relating to all these questions has been offered by Devangana Desai in her work on the erotic sculptures of India.[1] Her enquiry is concerned as much with the question of religious sanction as with the sociological factors generating the permissive atmosphere and mood for the depiction of sexual motifs. The presence of erotic themes in temples has so long been explained according to the personal whims of the viewer. Imaginary interpretations have been devised by the guides or *pāṇḍās* so as to convey the idea to the inquisitive tourist that these erotic depictions are really meant for mental purification. The merit of seeing the idol enshrined in the temple can only be acquired if the individual is able to control his mind after experiencing visually the objects of excitement.[2] This explanation was popular among laymen and devotees but it could not satisfy the serious scholar and student. Some art-historians tried to explain these erotic elements in terms of Tantric ideas and practices. Thus, they were interpreted to be symbolic representations of eternal bliss, or of the creative process, or of the principle of *yuganaddha* suggestive of non-duality, and so forth. Heinrich Zimmer observed:

Such living forms are suggested to the Indian artist by a dynamic philosophy that is intrinsic to his religious and philosophical tradition, for the worship of the life force pouring into universe and maintaining it, manifesting itself no less in the gross matter of daily experience than in the divine beings of religious vision constitutes the very foundation of Indian religious life. According to this doctrine which was particularly influential in the great periods of Indian art, release from the bondage of our normal human imperfection can be gained not only through the world-negating methods of asceticism (*yoga*) but equally through a perfect realization of love and sexual enjoyment (*bhoga*). According to this view which has been eloquently expressed in the so-called Tantric symbols and rituals of both the Hindu and the Buddhist traditions, there is intrinsically no antagonism between *yoga* and *bhoga*. The role played by the *guru*, the spiritual guide and teacher in the stern masculine discipline of *yoga* is taken over in the initiations of *bhoga* by the devout and sensual female helpmate. The initiating woman plays the part of Śakti while the male initiate assumes that of Śiva, and both attain together a realization of the immanence within themselves of the consubstantiality of the Goddess and the God.[3]

This is also an one-sided interpretation, because the sexual depictions on temples accord more with the *Kāmaśāstra* descriptions of sexual acrobatics than with Tantric principles. The interpretation of every sexual motif in terms of Tantric ideas evidently leads to the fallacy of over-simplification. Again we cannot absolutely deny Tantric influence. Hence the question needs to be answered with much care and caution.

The evolution of art in India and elsewhere, from the primitive stage to its more advanced forms, depends on a parallel evolution of man's emotional attitude towards the world. But the evolution of this attitude differs very naturally from one section of people to another. The outlook of the sophisticated class and that of the simpler peoples cannot be the same in this respect in all cases. We have seen that two sets of beliefs and ideals simultaneously worked in the field of Indian history, one represented by the simpler peoples and the other by the dominant section. Sometimes some of the beliefs and rituals of the former were adopted by the latter, but with a totally different purpose. Among the simpler peoples art is not a product of leisure;

it is a guide to action, an illusory technique complementary to the deficiencies of the real techniques. By the symbolical representation of an event, primitive man thought that he could secure the actual occurrence of that event.

There are two distinct methods of securing this desired result—the organic and the geometrical. These two types persist all through the history of art. Ritual drawings, very often with pronounced erotic motifs, are quite common in different parts of India. The purpose of this ritual art is entirely different from that of the so-called civilized art although the subject matter may be same in both cases. For example, a few terracotta specimens from Lower Bengal, emphasising exclusively the copulative aspect of the male-female union, exhibit identity in form and content with some Khajuraho reliefs.[4] But the source of inspiration in both cases is quite different. While the former can be explained in terms of magical fertility rites and also connected with existing Tantric cults, the latter admits of a quite different explanation.

It is tempting to connect the sexual depictions on the temples of Khajuraho, Konarak, Ellora, Halebid, etc., with primitive sex rites and Tantrism, but before we do so we must be sure about the real extent of the influence which is supposed to have been exerted on the former by the latter. There was obviously a link between the two, since some of the popular sexual themes first presented in terracotta were executed later in stone under certain historical conditions. But when these came to reflect the art of the dominant class they served a totally different purpose. From this point of view, the sculptural extravagance of Khajuraho, Konarak and other temples was mainly the reflection of the abnormal desires of the wealthy Nāgarakas whose munificence was responsible for their construction. The themes were selected from the *Kāmaśāstras*. The impossible copulative poses and techniques of these sexual acts were meant to excite perverse imaginations. A few examples from Khajuraho will make the point clear. A man standing on his head, with legs folded, has a woman sitting in the fold of his legs on his visible organ. The woman's hands rest on the necks of two females standing on either sides of her while the man titillates with his hands the sex organs of the two standing nudes. Another group depicts a standing woman who is copulated by one man in the front, face to face, and at the same time she has anal intercourse with another man from behind. Another woman is uplifted with bent knees and in that position locked in copulation. Yet another shows a woman astride the shoulder of a standing man who with bent head licks her cunnus while she, bending downwards, holds his erect penis in one hand and licks it. These are clear reflections of the perversion of the aristocratic class and have no bearing on the purpose of primitive sex rites of fertility or Tantrism.

But why were temples selected for this? It appears that the ancient idea of the holiness of temples differed significantly from the modern. It is impossible to say what exactly the temples meant for the worshippers at different ages. The Cola kings destroyed many temples in the land of their enemies while they built magnificent temples in their own land which shows that the idea of 'sacredness' was not inherent in the temples themselves. Temple spoilation was a part of state policy of some of the kings of Kashmir. There are also some reasons to believe that the vivid portrayal of sexual intercourse could be made only on the temple walls and this was somehow related to the very structure of the temple itself. Functionally, also, the temples provided a logical and appropriate place for them. We have already referred to an inscription of the Gupta period which describes a temple as a terrible abode of Ḍākinis uttering loud and tremendous shouts of joy in wild ecstacy. Actual sexual acts were not rare in the temples. The custom of prostitution was prevalent in many Indian temples; it was abolished only a few years ago by the Government of India. The women attached to the temples were called Devadāsīs. In the great temple of Tanjore once four hundred Devadāsīs were employed. The girls were formally married to the idol and regarded as the wives of the god. The god, impersonated by the priests, would have sexual intercourse with them. Their children by the priests often constituted a special caste.

Thus things sexual were not really inconsistent with the supposed holiness of temples, and this alone explains why the sexual depictions on the temple walls revealing the lusts of the aristocratic class were tolerated and given some sort of social sanction by the simpler peoples. This they did partly because they found in those depictions the illusion of a lost reality—the reality of their traditional beliefs and rituals, and partly because they were compelled to do so by the pressure of the dominant class. Artists and craftsmen had no freedom of their own; in India, a Phoedius or a Praxitiles had no social status. They always came from the lower castes, and for their livelihood they had to meet the demands of their employers and customers; their art, thus, had nothing to do with artistic inspiration. This holds good also in the case of terracotta productions. Although a few of them, evidently the earlier ones, were meant to serve ritualistic purposes, most of them, however, specially those with very pronounced sexual characteristics, were evidently intended for wealthy customers. Such things are produced and sold even today.[5]

Tantric Architecture: Some Aspects

In the preceding section we have remarked that there are reasons to believe that the vivid portrayal of sexual themes could be made only on temple walls, and that this was somehow related to the very structure of the temple itself. In other words, structurally the temples bore a special tradition with which the portrayal of erotic elements was not inconsistent, and that is why temples were specially selected for this purpose. This tradition was very ancient and may be connected with the primitive fertility concepts with which it started; however, in course of time it lost its original significance.

A conceptualisation of the temples in sexual terms is met with in the canons of Orissan temple architecture. Orissa was always a strong seat of Tantric cults and rituals. Purī which is the celebrated seat of Lord Jagannātha is also mentioned in the Tantras as a place where Jagannātha is the subordinate male consort (Bhairava) of the goddess Vimalā. This consort of the goddess was regarded as the king of the land (the actual rulers considered themselves as vassals of Jagannātha), just as Virbius, the consort of the goddess Diana, impersonated by the priest, was the king of Nemi. The influence of Tantric rites is clearly visible in the mode of daily worship of Jagannātha. Behera tells us:

> It is equally interesting to notice the *pañcatattva* of Tantricism in the ritualistic worship of the deity wherein fish is substituted by green vegetables mixed with *hiṅgu,* meat by *ādāpacedi* (ginger), wine by green cocount water offered in bellmetal pots, grain by *kānti* (preparation of flour and sugar) and *mithuna* by the dance of Devadāsīs and the offering of *aparājitā* flowers.[6]

There are two major types of temple buildings in Orissa, the Rekha and the Bhadra, which are joined to each other in a very intimate manner. Their junction is expressed by a term which literally means a ceremonial knot tied between the garments of the bride and the bridegroom. The Rekha is male and Bhadra female;

they are attached to one another in a state of union.[7] The architecture of temples varies from region to region but temples themselves do not differ basically. As a rule, they are similar in construction and the various parts are given the same name all over. The most important part of the temple is called the *garbha* (womb). The name describes it perfectly. The god, in the form of the chief idol, is placed in the womb. Leading up to the *garbha* from the porch is a kind of corridor through which one enters. This sexual design pertains to West Asian temples also—they were divided into three parts—porch representing the lower end of the vagina up to the hymen, the hall or the vagina itself, and the inner sanctum or the uterus.

Some recent scholars assert a relational correspondence betwen the Tantric *maṇḍalas* and religious monuments such as structural temples, cave temples, stūpas, etc., viewed as that existing bewteen a site-plan and a building. Prabhakar Apte and V.S. Moorti[8] refer to the *maṇḍala* designs presented in the *Pauṣkara Saṃhitā* which are suggestive of a three dimensional architectural potential.[9] According to S.K. Rāmachandra Rao, 'the plan of a temple is essentially a *maṇḍala*; and its functions are spiritual and deal with several aspects of individual and collective worship. The study of Indian temple architecture would thus be the most appropriate while considering the nature of *maṇḍalas*'.[10] Bettina Baumer has described the Rajarani temple at Bhuvaneswar as a Mañjuśrī type of temple based on Śrīcakra or Śrīyantra.[11] In this connection Apte and Moorti write:

> The temple in its solid mountain-like elevation represents the *ādhibhautika* aspect, the external manifestations of the Śrīyantra as Meruprastara. The Śrīyantra underlying it is *ādhidaivika* aspect, the microcosm containing the deities and Śaktis. Human body is the *ādhyātmika* aspect, in which all this symbolism is experienced and internalised. Thus the three levels can be identified according to different equations. The human body is the temple of Divine Energy, and vice versa the temple is the body of Śakti. The Śrīyantra is the temple and vice versa the temple is the solid Śrīyantra. The Śrīyantra is internalised in worshipper's body, and thus as integration of the three levels is operated. The external, the internal and the symbolic dimensions of worship are combined and bestow meaning to each other."[12]

Geri H. Malendra has sought to prove that the Ellora caves are designed panel by panel on the *maṇḍala* plans and the Bodhisattva images carved thereon are the three dimensional representation of the total *maṇḍala* iconography.[13] She holds that the presence of an extended list of Bodhisattva and female images would suggest that

Ellora was influenced by nascent Tantric teachings and tries to demonstrate that a *maṇḍala,* a scehmatic diagram portraying deities in a set order, provides a guide to the organisational scheme of Ellora's Buddhist caves from earliest to latest.

In addition to what has been stated above we may refer to a rather modern Tantric temple of eastern India. It is the Haṃseśvarī temple situated at Bansberia in Hooghly district of West Bengal, about fifty km to the north of Calcutta on the western bank of the Ganges. Its construction was begun by Raja Nrisimha Devaraya in 1799 and was completed by his widowed queen Śaṇkarī Devī in 1814. In this six-storeyed temple the *maṇḍala* pattern is unfolded. The plan of the temple was entirely the conception of Nrisimha Devarāya who was a Tantric *sādhaka* and the Bengali translator of *Uḍḍīśatantra,* and his purpose was to demonstrate through this temple the essentials of Tantrism, especially those of the *ṣaṭ-cakra-bheda.* His achievement as its maker and the spiritual significance of this temple are recorded by Alexander Chapman in a poem, the last eight lines of which are:

What did he do? He built a temple. Still
It stands, and I have seen it, but too ill
Would words of mine describe it, Inside, out.
Silent on earth, in pinnacled air a shout,
It doth reveal what to the initiate
Figures pure thought. So unto them a gate
It opened to deliverance. I outside,
Alien but not unmoved, untouched, abide.

The Haṃseśvarī is one of the finest temples of India. In height it is seventy feet and has six storeys. There are thirteen cupolas of *śikhara* type in this temple, eight placed on the corners of the balcony of the third storey, four placed on the corners of the fifth storey and one on the top of the sixth storey. The minerats are arranged in the form of a lotus, and the rooms and channels inside the temple constitute a labyrinth from which it is impossible to emerge without a guide. The interior of the temple is made in accordance with the six *cakras* of the human body through which the Kuṇḍalinī Śakti, symbolised as the goddess Haṃseśvarī, marches upward. The Śakti is coiled in the *mūlādhāra,* the awakening of which is not possible for an ordinary person who will inevitably stumble into the labyrinth. But one who knows the secrets of *sādhanā* can send the *kuṇḍalinī* to the highest cerebral region by Yogic exercise and by the proper utilisation of the functioning of the nerves. Five such nerves are thus indicated inside the temple by peculiar and complicated ladders; these are *iḍā, piṅgalā, suṣumnā, vajrākṣa* and *citrinī*. An ordinary person cannot reach the top through these ladders unless he knows the right way. In the sanctum of the temple is the image of the goddess Haṃseśvarī made of *neem* wood. The iconic composition of the goddess is very interesting. Śiva is shown as lying down on a *trikoṇa-yantra* (a Tantric composition of a triangular shape), and from his navel a slender and long stem ending in a lotus rises on which the goddess is seated with her left foot on the knee of the pendant right leg. The goddess is four-armed and blue in complexion. Her upper left hand carries a sword and the lower left a human head. Her upper right hand shows the *abhaya-mudrā* while the lower right holds a conch. There are fourteen *Śiva liṅgas*, one at each *cakra*-point from the base to the top, marking the different states in the upward march of *kuṇḍalinī*. Haṃseśvarī is a symbolical conception. *Haṃ* denotes Vīja connected with the concept of Ahaṃ (the self-expression of the Supreme Being as the subject viewing itself as object) and *saḥ* denotes Śakti, especially its Vimarśa or kinetic aspect manifested in the universe. The two letters are locked, and this locking (*kīlaka*) is regarded as the means of the highest realisation. He who concentrates his mind on *haṃsa* can find what is known as *haṃsa-ātman*, i.e. the self-manifested as subject and object, within the eight-petalled lotus of his heart. The goddess represent these principles.

Referring to the temple of Haṃseśvarī Sambhu Chunder Dey in his *Bansberia Rāj* (Calcutta, 1890) oberved:

> The temple of Haṃseśvarī is one of the most noted in India, and stands almost unparalleled in Bengal. Not to speak of the plan in which it is built and which none but the initiated are in a position to understand fully, it has a beauty of its own which is not to be found in any other shrine. It is in reality a glorious specimen of the wonderous achievement of the architectural art. The temple of Bhuvaneswar with all its vaunted wealth of architecture seems to fall short of it.[14]

Sexual Depictions: Their Tantric Probabilities

The earliest depiction of the sexual act through linear rendering is found on a pot of the Chalcolithic period, phase III, at Daimabad in Ahmadnagar district of Maharashtra.[15] Another early representation of sex is seen in the Kupgallu cave in Mysore.[16] Figures of terracotta and other objects representing nude goddesses or females with legs wide apart and sex organ grossly indicated, belonging to the early Christian era have been found from Bhita, Jhusi and Kausambi in Uttar Pradesh; Ter and Nevasa in Maharashtra; and Nagarjunikonda in Andhra Pradesh. These must have some connection with primitive fertility concepts. One interesting terracotta plaque from Awra in Mandasaur district of Madhya Pradesh, belonging to *c.* 100 B.C.-A.D. 300, depicts the goddess Śrī flanked by couples engaged in sexual union and pitchers, probably containing wine, in the foreground. 'The ritual coitus in which her devotees indulge, and the presence of wine in the pitchers draw our attention to the sacred orgies of the later Tantras'.[17] The depiction of coital couples and orgies is seen in the terracottas of Candraketugarh and Tamluk from *c.* 2nd century B.C. onwards and in those of Kausambi and Bhita of the 2nd-1st century B.C. According to Desai, terracottas and objects of the ancient period offer two types of representations:

> Cultic and ritual, as in the examples of the female divinity and her male partner and crudely carved plaques bearing sexual and orgistic themes; and
>
> Secular, with poetic and *nāgaraka* touches, fulfilling the demands of the sensuous public, as in the example of terracottas with secular subjects from Mathura, Rajghat, Ahicchatra, Candraketugarh and numerous excavated sites of the historical period.[18]

The earliest depictions of *mithunas* (couples) associated with Śrī, the goddess of abundance, in stone art is found on the 2nd century B.C. monuments of Sanchi and Bharhut, and also in Bodhgaya. In the Western Deccan also we come across *mithuna* depictions in the Buddhist caves of Kondane and Pitalkhora, belonging to c. 2nd-1st century B.C.[19] A few of these contain some erotic features. Between the 1st and 3rd centuries A.D. the *mithuna* theme became very popular and found a varied expression in the arts of Gandhara, Mathura, Western Deccan and the Andhra region. There is a gradual sensualisation of the motif and an increasing use of secular themes. Instead of simple portrayals of couples holding hands or with offerings for worship which we find in the early monuments, we come across varieties of *mithuna* motifs including kissing, embracing, and other precoital activities at Mathura, Nagarjunikonda, and other places.[20]

The period between A.D. 400 and 900 marks a qualitative change in the art tradition owing to the increasing feudalisation of society

Besides the abundance of the *mithuna* motifs and cultic figures, we come across numerous specimens depicting sexual activities, a few of which may vaguely have someting to do with Tantric rituals. It is, however, interesting to note that from the 5th century onwards we get inscriptional evidence of patronage by ministers and feudal chiefs towards Tantric worshippers. In the temple art of Aihole, Badami and Mahākuṭeśvara we come across an increasing presence of the Kāmṣāstrīya poses of love-making. The lintel of Cave I of Badami depicts a man and woman in copulation in the frontal pose.[21] That the depiction of erotic motifs was a convention independent of sectarian influences in this period is proved by their corresponding and contemporaneous appearance in the Buddhist caves at Ajanta, Ellora, and Aurangabad. Coital scenes also occur on the temples of Pattadakal, the alternate capital of the Cālukyas. But it should be noted in this connection that the depiction of sexual intercourse had not yet been accepted at all sites of the period, not even in the shrines associated with Tantrism like Pāśupata caves of Elephanta, Maṇḍapeśvara, and Jogeśvarī in Bombay; the Śākta temple of Chauṣaṭh Yoginīs at Khajuraho; and the Buddhist Tantric caves of Ellora and Kanheri.

In the subsequent epoch from *c.* A.D. 900 onwards, there was really an outburst of erotic expression—bold, frank, and gross, with countless varities of copulative acrobatics—on the exteriors and interiors of religious buildings. Besides the well-known temples of Puri and Konarak in Orissa and the Khajuraho groups, we have numerous temples in Madhya Pradesh (Sohagpur, Gurgi, and Baijnatha in Jubbalpur area; Padhavli and Kadwaha in the Gwalior region; Sanchi, temple No. 15, Kakpur, Badoh, Udayapur, and Oṃkāreśvara in the Malwa region), Gujarat (Modhera, Sunak, Roda, Motap, Siddhapur, Kheda-Brahma, Galteśvara, Sejakpur, Ghumli, Bavka, and Dabhoi), Maharashtra (Ambernath, Lonad, Sinnar, Balsane, Devlana, Patna, Pedgaon, Karjat, Katarkhatav and Gursala), and Mysore (Belur, Halebid, Somanāthapur, Bagali, Belgamve, and Hangal) where erotic scenes are abundantly exhibited.[22]

The erotic depictions can roughly be divided into two categories—non-orgiastic and orgiastic. Both these categories include many types and they correspond closely to the descriptions of sexual acts found in the Kāmaśāstras. Desai classifies the types as:

- I-A A man with two partners
- I-B Two men with one woman in subdued relationship
- II-A A man with two women in sexual relationship
- II-B Two men having sexual relation with one woman
- III-A Attendants present near an amorous non-coital couple
- III-B Attendants present near a copulating couple
- III-C Attendants helping the copulating couple
- III-D One of the partners while copulating touching the sexual parts of the attendants—who are also shown in excited conditions—with their own hands on the sexual parts
- IV-A A man in company of many women
- IV-B Many men in sexual relationship with one woman
- V Many men and women in a promiscuous orgy
- VI A number of couples simultaneously involved in sexual relations

Central India represents all the types; Gujarat I-A, I-B, II-A, II-B, III-B, IV-B, V and VI; Karnataka II-B in general and also III-B, III-C and V; and Orissa specially III-C. Type IV-B is peculiar to Gujarat and Rajasthan. Type V is mainly restricted to Gujarat, Maharashtra and central India, except for rare depictions at Konarak, Khiching, and Belgamve. Type VI is represented mainly in western Deccan, Gujarat and central India. Type III-D is depicted at Khajuraho. Type IV-A is very rare.[23]

But how far are all related to Tantrism? There are some writers who hold that the coital postures in which the lovers are shown on the medieval temples are sexo-yogic.[24] Of course there are some postures which appears to involve Haṭhayoga techniques as are seen in the head down poses of Khajuraho, Padhavli, Belur, and other places. But these are imaginative techniques, having nothing to do with Haṭhayoga proper. The gymnastic poses representing mutual mouth-congress on the temples of Khajuraho, Galteśvara, Puri, and Konarak involve women in considerable athletic feats. Again most of the postures in which sexual intercourse is depicted represent frontal standing poses, and also copulation from the rear (*vyānata* pose) and other varieties which are not associated with yogic techniques or aims. Even ascetics who are depicted in the sexual scene are not shown in yogic poses. The inspiration behind all these depictions is the *Kāmaśāstra* literature meant for the titillation and pleasure of the aristocratic class and the *nāgarakas* or wealthy city dwellers.

Some traces of Tantric influence are however found in some erotic sculptures. For instance in the depiction of the sexual act near the deity (as at Padhavli in central India), or representation of sexual couples flanking the deities on the *kumbha* (as in some temples of Gujarat and Rajasthan), or nude goddess flanked on one side by an orgiastic scene and on the other by musicians and dancers (at Bavka and Ambernath), during haircutting ritual in association with copulation (at Bhuvaneswar, Puri, Konarak, and Ratnagiri in Orissa and in Bagali in Karnataka) and so on. But these Tantric glimpses do not prove an obvious link between the erotic depictions on temples and Tantrism. If there be any true Tantric art it should be functionally related to *upāsanā* and *sādhanā* to attain the bliss of non-duality. Unfortunately the temple depictions do not give us such an idea. The original Śākta-piṭhas are not associated with any sexual display. It is significant that in the Causaṭh Yoginī temple of Bheraghat there are representations on the pedestals, on which the images of goddesses are carved, of a *yantra* but not of erotic figures. Moreover, since it is a basic tenet of Tantra that the followers of Tantrism cannot expose their practices to the uninitiated, everything is conducted by them in secrecy. Only this much can be said that the apparently Trantric elements as may be gleaned from the erotic depictions on temples are in reality specimens of art influenced by some Tantric ideas but not functionally related to them.

Tantric Icons

We have seen that the followers of Tantrism believe in the state of non-duality which can be attained through the union of the Male and Female Principles represented either within one's body as Śiva in the *sahasrāra* and Śakti in the *mūlādhāra* or in the external world as the man and the woman. The *kuṇḍalinī śakti,* coiled like a snake, traversing through six *cakras* to the *sahasrāra* of the Yogin's body, is often represented in the symbolic form of *yantra.* If someone calls this and allied pictorial representation as Tantric art, it should also be admitted that such art is not essentially expressive or decorative. It is purely cultic. So also are the icons. Although Indian figures of deities are regarded as specimens of art, because they have artistic qualities, by the art-historians, they are nothing but cult-images or icons in the eyes of the people at large.

Tantric deities, mainly the Mahāvidyā goddesses, are very often worshipped in images. The most popular image is that of Dakṣiṇa-Kālī which is worshipped all over Bengal and also in different parts of India in shrines dedicated to the goddess. The iconic cult of Kālī is a recent development; it became popular only from the 17th century onwards. It is also interesting to note that the form in which the goddess is worshipped now does not strictly follow her textual iconological description. She stands on the chest of Śiva lying as a corpse. She has four hands, in two of which she holds a skull and a sword and the other two exhibit *vara* and *abhaya* poses. She has untied hair and a lolling tongue pressed by her teeth. There are many legends regarding the genesis of this form. According to one version, Kṛṣṇānanda Āgamavāgīśa (or some other saint, the names differ) wanted to introduce a popular image of Dakṣiṇa-Kālī, and while he was contemplating on it, the goddess came and asked him to make the image according to the pose and position of the first person he would come across the next morning. The following morning when he came out of his house he saw a milkmaid sticking cow-dung cakes for fuel on the wall of her house. She had one leg on the ground, the other one was on the heap of cow -dung; her right hand containing a lump of dung was raised. Seeing him she became very embarrassed and opened her mouth and pressed her tongue between her teeth—a typical Bengali mannerism expressing the sense of being ashamed. This became the model of popular Kālī imges. But the image of Dakṣiṇā-Kālī worshipped by the Tantrics themselves is different. Here Śiva lies on the ground with his penis erected and the goddess is seated naked on him having taken his penis into her sex organ in *viparita-rati*.

There is no need, nor room, to give the details of all the Devi-icons from the earliest period.[25] We shall refer only to those which have some pronounced Tantric character. Self-mutilation was probably a feature of the worship of the goddess during the early Pallava and Cola period, as is evident from several Pallava panels where the devotee is shown as offering his own head. This custom might have some bearing on the Tantric conception of Chinnamastā. A late Pallava inscription upon a slab refers to a warrior who had offfered his own head to the goddess and the slab itself contains a relief of that act.[26] Tantric Mahālakṣmī is represented in an eighteen-armed image at Jajpur in the front facade of the Trilocana temple. Also a twenty-armed goddess, identified with Mahālakṣmī, belonging to the 10th century, is found at Simla in Rajsahi district. The Tantric goddess Ekānaṃśā, who in the course of time assumed a Vaiṣṇavite character, is worshipped as the principal deity in the Ananta-Vāsudeva temple at Bhuvaneswar with Kṛṣṇa and Balarāma on either side of her. Several medieval eastern Indian stone and bronze reliefs of Ekānaṃśā have been discovered, of which reference may be made to an inscribed bronze image recovered from Imadpur in Bihar, and now in the British Museum, which shows the two-armed goddess standing erect on a lotus with her right hand stretched down in *varada* pose and her left hand holding a mirror.[27]

The Jain representation of the Seven Divine Mothers (Sapta-Mātṛkā) at Khandagiri is well-known. The Sapta-Mātṛkās are often carved in relief on a regular stone slab with the figures of Vīrabhadra and Gaṇeśa on either side. A bronze composition, originally found at Imadpur, and now in the British Museum, shows three Mātṛkās—Brahmāṇī, Kaumārī and Vaiṣṇavī—seated between Vīrabhadra and Gaṇeśa. Separate reliefs of Mātṛkās are also common, such as those found on the bank of the Mārkaṇḍeya Sarovara at Purī. The Patna Museum contains a complete set of individual Sapta-Mātṛkā sculpture from Seraikela in the Singhbhum district.[28] The colossi of the Eight Mothers (Aṣṭa-Mātṛkā) from Muktimaṇḍapa near Jajpur and the Eight Mothers with Śivadūtī on the bank of the Vaitarani indicate their popularity in Orissa. We have two sets of Mātṛkās at Jajpur. Besides the one referred to above we have another of which two colossal figures of Vārāhi and Indrāṇī survive. The Paraśurāmeśvara temple, the Vaitala temple and the Mukteśvara temple of Bhuvaneswar contain Sapta-Mātṛkā images carved in relief. Individual and collective images of the Mātṛkās are found at Jodhpur, Jaswantpur, Bhinmal, Ajmer, Mandor, Nagda, Chitorgarh, Ramgarh, Kekinda, Phelodi, Osian, and other places of Rajasthan. Specially important is the group of Eight Mātṛkās at Mandor and Kekinda. The goddesses belonging to the Sapta- Mātṛkā panel of Ellora are shown as carrying babies on their laps. In the south sculptural representations of the Mātṛkās are found in the Kailāsanātha temple at Kanchipuram and in the Pāṇḍya and Muttaraiya cave temples at Tirugokarnam, Malayadippati, Kunnatur, and Tirukkalakkudi. From the 9th century onwards, it became an established fashion to construct small shrines of the Mātṛkās in the temple enclosures.

Of the individual Mātṛkā images, an inscribed one of Cāmuṇḍā comes from Jajpur which was installed by queen Vatsadevī, probably of the Bhumakara dynasty.[29] The Vaitala temple of Bhuvaneswar contains a terrific figure of Cāmuṇḍā. In Bengal some of her forms such as Rūpavidyā, Siddhayogeśvarī and Dantūrā have found independent representation. An image of the last-mentioned aspect of Cāmuṇḍā, now in the Vaṅgīya Sāhitya Pariṣat Museum, Calcutta (found originally in a Burdwan village), shows a two-armed deity sitting on her haunches, strikingly Tantric features. Several other images of Dantūrā have been found in North Bengal. Cāmuṇḍā images have also been found from Betna, the ruins of Rampal and Attahāsa. A relief originally hailing from Sutna in Madhya Pradesh and now in the collection of the Indian Museum, Calcutta, depicts an eight-armed image of Nārasiṃhī seated in the *ardhaparyaṅka* pose on the back of a stylised lion. The Asutosh Museum of the Calcutta University preserves a figure of Vārāhī which shows the four-armed form of the goddess in question, with a fish in one of her right hands. The figure of a four-armed Vaiṣṇavī with Garuḍa beneath her seat, hailing from Khiching, deserves special mention. This goddess is sometimes replaced by the Tantric Vāgīśvarī whose figure in octoalloy, with eight hands, is now in the Rajsahi Museum. Another inscribed four-armed image of Vāgīśvarī of A.D. 940 comes from Nalanda.

A remarkable sculpture from Kagajipara at Vikrampur in East Bengal, four feet in height, shows in its lower part a well carved Śivaliṅga from the top of which emerges the half-length figure of a four-armed goddess, profusely ornamented, her first pair of hands in *dhayānamudrā*, the second pair carrying a rosary and a manuscript. It may stand for Mahāmāyā or Tripurabhairavī.[30] A Caṇḍī image from Dalbazar in Dacca (third year of Lakṣmaṇasena) is often identifed with Tantric Bhuvaneśvarī. A six-armed goddess, also indentified with Bhuvaneśvarī, is found at Shekati in Jessore district, while another, a twenty-armed goddess, identified with Mahālakṣmī is found at Simla in Rajsahi district. Two images of Śarvāṇī are found, one from Mangalbari in Dinajpur and another from Chauddagram near Tippera. A seated image from Nowgong is identified with Sarvamaṅgalā while another in sandstone from Niamatpur with Aparājitā. These imges belong to the Pāla-Sena period.

The Yoginīs occupy an important place in the Tantric cults. The term Yoginī denotes female Tantric aspirants, a class of goddesses, and also different aspects of the Female Principle residing within the human body. The earlier Yoginīs were women of flesh and blood, priestesses supposed to be possessed by the goddess. Later they were raised to the status of divinity. Each of the eight Mātṛkās is again said to have manifested herself in eight forms, thus, making a total of sixty-four Yoginīs. Village Hirapur in Orissa contains a temple of sixty-four Yoginīs. In the inner face of the circular wall of the enclosure there are sixty niches, each containing an image of a Yoginī. All of them are in standing posture. Circular Yoginī temples are also found at Ranpur Jharial, Dudhai, and Lalitpur in Orissia. Temples dedicated to the sixty-four Yoginīs are scattered all over central India. The Yoginī temple at Khajuraho deserves special mention for its architectural features. The sixty-four Yoginī temple at Mitauli near Padhauli (11th century) is marked by sixty-five principal chapels and a circular central shrine with a *maṇḍapa* in front. In the sixty-four Yoginī temple at Bheraghat near Jabalpur are found not only sixty-four Yoginīs but also eight Śaktis, three rivers, four other goddesses, Śiva and Gaṇeśa, thus making a total of eighty-one figures. The Bheraghat figures are damaged, but most of them fortunately retain their names inscribed in the peripheral chapels. The names are not canonical and are evidently adopted from popular cults.

Some of the Jain Yakṣiṇīs acquired a purely Tantric character. These goddesses are Jvālamālinī, Padmāvatī, and Ambikā whose temples and images are found in Karnataka.[31] In such works as *Jvālinīkalpa, Bhairavapadmāvatīkalpa,* etc., dedicated to these goddesses, we come across an increasing insistence on Tantric principles. Jvālamālinī is conceived of as a terrible deity having eight hands which hold deadly weapons like discus, arrow, shield, trident, bow, snake, etc. The use of *mantra, nyāsa, yantra* and *mudrā* form the essentials of her cult. The *Padmāvatīkalpa* devotes one chapter to the rites relating to *vaśīkaraṇa.*

But more numerous are the representations of the deities of Tantric Buddhism. The Rajsahi Museum contains an 11th century image of Ratnasambhava, hailing from Vikrampur, seated in *vajrāsana* on a lotus with his usual symbols and attendants.[32] The Orissa State Museum at Bhuvaneswar contains two images of Amoghasiddhi, one in *dhyānamudrā* against the background of a seven-hooded snake forming his umbrella, and the other, a life-size stone image, found from Udayagiri in Phulbani, with the same emblems. The National Museum at New Delhi contains a 10th century bronze image of Vajradhara from Nalanda seated in *vajrāsana* on a lotus supported by four lions. The Sukhabalpur (Dacca) image of Vajrasattva, now in the Dacca Museum, contains the Buddhist creed on its back written in the tenth century Bengali characters.[33] The Indian Museum of Calcutta has three Vajrasattva images in stone—one from Nalanda and two from Salimpur. The Nalanda Museum contains a stone image of this god along with his companions. The Banpur hoard, preserved in Bhuvaneswar Museum, contains five bronze images of Vajrasattva in *vajrāsana*, the right hand holding *vajra* against the chest and the *ghaṇṭā* resting on the thigh.

The Padmapāni brand of Avalokiteśvara images is very common. Generally one-faced and two-armed, and represented as displaying the *varada* pose with the right hand and holding a stem of lotus in the left, images of this god in stone and metal are preserved in all the important museum of India. Of other brands of Avalokiteśvara, images of the Ṣaḍakṣarī-Lokeśvara group are to be found in the Sarnath Museum, Indian Museum, Patna Museum, Rajsahi Museum, and Maldah Museum. The one in Maldah, hailing from Ranipur, is a four armed deity in *vajrāsana*, holding his usual symbols, to whose right and left are Maṇidhara and Ṣaḍakśarī Mahāvidyā.[34] Nice specimens of Siṃhanāda Lokeśvara from Mahoba and Magadha are now preserved in the Lucknow Museum. The Kurkihar hoard, preserved in the Patna Museum, contains a bronze image of Siṃhanāda, seated on a lion, left hand stretched downwards with lotus stalks while the right hand is pendant on the right leg. The Dacca Museum contains two stone images of Khaṣarpaṇa, a form of Avalokiteśvara, seated in *lalitāsana* on a lotus seat, right hand in *varada* and the left holding a stalk of lotus, with Tārā, Sudhanakumāra, Bhṛkutī, and Hayagrīva as companions.[35] The Rajsahi Museum contains a stone images of Khaṣarpaṇa, found at Mulchar in Vikrampur, the Indian Museum two stone images from Nalanda, the Patna Museum two images, one from Udayagiri in Cuttack and the other from somewhere in Bihar. A rock-cut standing and also a rock-cut seated image of the Lokanātha form of Avalokiteśvara are in the Ellora caves, which belong to 7th century A.D. Stone images of Lokanātha found from Mahoba, Sarnath, Nalanda, Bishenpur and other places and also metal images mainly from Nalanda and Kurkihar are common. Standing stone images of Jaṭamukuṭa Lokeśvara, belonging to 9-10th centuries have been found from Ratnagiri, Udayagiri, Kurkihar, and Nalanda. The National Museum contains a tenth-century bronze image of this god standing in *samapadasthānaka* with four hands, having *akṣamālā* in upper right, *varada* in upper left, lotus supporting *vajra* in lower right and water pot in lower left. The principal left hand of the Indian Museum bronze image of this god is broken. The Sugatisandarśana form of Avalokiteśvara is found in a tenth-century stone image from Gaya, now in the National Museum, a ninth-century stone from Kurkihar, now in the Patna Museum, and a tenth-century stone from Nalanda, now in the Indian Museum. A rare eleventh-century image of this god is in the Rajsahi Museum. It is six-armed, five of which show *pāśa, tridaṇḍī, akṣamālā, kamaṇḍalu* and *varada* pose. The Asutosh Museum of the Calcutta University has a tenth-century stone image of this god from Bihar Sarif. An image of Nilakaṇṭha Lokeśvara, hailing from Sarnath, now in the National Museum, shows two tiny figures carrying bowls instead of the usual serpent symbol. Another eleventh-century stone image of Nilakaṇṭha is in the Nalanda Museum; it is seated in *vajrāsana* on a lotus with two hands holding a vase near the breast. Two tenth-century stone images of the Vajradharma form of Avalokiteśvara from Nalanda, one in the Indian Museum and the other in the Nalanda Museum, show the distinguishing trait of the god—he is opening the blossom of a lotus with his right hand near the breast. A tenth-century stone image in the Rajsahi Museum, pot-bellied and dwarfish, standing on a lotus with three faces and fierce mien, six hands (one broken) containing different emblems, corresponds to the description of Hālahala Lokeśvara.[36] The Nalanda collection of the Patna Museum contains a bronze image of Trailokyavaśaṅkara or Uḍḍīyāna Lokeśvara seated in *vajrāsana* and holding indistinct objects. He has matted hair arranged like a crown.[37] A bronze image found at Baudh in Orissa and now in the Bhuvaneswar Museum, showing four-armed, one-faced deity sitting erect on a lotus throne with his right foot on a foot-stool, carrying in his upper right hand a conch-shell, has been identified with Śaṅkhanātha Lokeśvara. The Indian Museum contains a bronze image of Arogyaśālī Lokeśvara, having a *stūpa* on the crest and decorative herbal plants on two sides. In sculptural representations Avalokiteśvara is often flanked by goddesses, very often by the name Tārā.

Besides the very well-known gold-plated sixth-century bronze figure of Mañjuśrī found at Balaidhap in Mahasthan and now in the Rajsahi Museum,[38] we have several varieties of Mañjuśrī images. The Indian Museum contains a bronze image of Vāk or Vajrarāga Mañjuśrī in *vajrāsana* and *samādhi mudrā*. A nice bronze image of this god is in the Baroda Museum.[39] The National Museum has a stone image of

Vāk belonging to the 10th century. It has also two standing seventh -century stone images of the Siddhaikavīra form of Mañjuśrī, from Sarnath and Nalanda. The Indian Museum has two stone images, belonging to the 9-10th centuries, from Nalanda and Bihar Sarif, while the Asutosh Museum has an eleventh-century stone from Bhangur. Bronze images of this god are also very common. A confusion is likely to arise between the forms of Lokanātha and Siddhaikavīra, because both of them have the same symbol (lotus) and same *mudrā* (*varada*). The Arapacana form of Mañjuśrī is common[40] and a few of his images have been found even in Indonesia (cf. the Javanese Arapacana of the Leyden Museum). He is frequently represented in Nepalese bronzes in which his main symbol, a manuscript, is placed on a lotus. The National Museum has a bronze image of this god, seated in *vajrāsana*, right hand upraised and brandishing sword while the left holds a manuscript close to his breast. The Indian Museum also has a similar tenth-century image. The Banpur hoard contains two bronze images. The best image corresponding to all iconographical details and with attendant deities—Jālinī, Upakeśinī, Candraprabha and Sūryaprabha—is in the Dacca Museum. It was found at Jalakundi in Dacca.[41] The Vangīya Sahitya Pariṣat (Calcutta) sculpture of Mañjuśrī holding in his left hand a sword on a lotus and with his Śakti on his left side, probably corresponds to Sthiracakra Mañjuśrī, whose bronze images from Nalanda are in the National Museum and the Indian Museum. The latter contains a stone image of the Vāgiśvara form of Mañjuśrī carrying a bell in his right hand sitting on a lion throne. The bronze Vāgīśvara of the Kurkihar hoard is seated on a lion with *prajñāpāramitā* manuscript on a blue lotus in the left hand. The yellow variety of Vāgīśvara, which is known as Mahārajalilā Mañjuśrī, is nicely represented in a bronze image belonging to the Kurkihar hoard. A beautiful stone image of the Mañjuvara variety of Mañjuśrī, found at Nalanda and now in the Rajsahi Museum is shown seated on the back of a lion with hands resting in *dharmacakramudrā* and a book placed on a lotus. It belongs to 11-12th centuries A.D.[42] The Rajsahi Museum has three other Mañjuvara images in stone. From Nalanda four stone images of Mañjuvara have been recovered, three of which are in Nalanda Museum and the fourth in the Indian Museum. An image of this god has also been discovered from Birbhum district in West Bengal. In the Kurkihar hoard we come across five bronze images of Mañjuśrī-Kumārabhūta, pot-bellied, wearing the sacred thread, round ear-rings, jewels and *jaṭāmukuṭa*, seated in single or double-petalled lotus with left leg pendant and supported by a lion, the left hand holding a book. Attendant deities are also present.[43]

A rock-cut image of Bodhisattva Vajrapāni, belonging to the 7th century, is to be found in an Aurangabad cave. A ninth century stone image has been found at Ratnagiri in Orissa. From Nalanda a good number of stone and bronze images have been discovered. One of them shows Vajrapāni as surrounded by four seated female figures. His left hand is placed on the left thigh, while he holds a *vajra* in his right hand against his breast.[44] A few seated bronze images from Nalanda show him with a *cāmara* or fly-whisk in the right hand. He wears a crown, ear-rings, necklace, and bracelets.[45] In the Kurkihar hoard, a ninth-century bronze image of Vajarapāni is seen with left hand pendant grasping the stalk of a lotus on which is placed a *vajra*. The right hand is in *abhayamudrā*.[46] Minor Bodhisattvas are rarely represented in sculpture. The Patna Museum contains a bronze image of Bodhisattva Gaganagañja, recovered from Nalanda and belonging to the 9th century A.D., in *lalita* pose on a *triratha* pedestal. The right hand is in *varadamudrā* with jewel in it. In the left hand is the root of a *kalpavṛkṣa*. The halo is broken.[47]

Among the gods and goddesses of Tantric Buddhism Heruka is very popular. Nairātmā is the Śakti or Prajñā, i.e. the female consort of Heruka. When in embrace with this Śakti Heruka is known as Hevajra whose *yuganaddha* form is well-known in Tibet. Vajrayoginī is another Śakti of Heruka. The depiction of her recalls that of the Śākta-Tantric Chinnamastā. The Sarnath Museum contains a stone image of Heruka, found at the same place, dancing in *ardhaparyaṅka* on a human corpse. The upraised damaged right hand holds a *vajra*. The left forearm, presumably holding a *kapāla* is missing, though the portion having *khatvāṅga* may be seen. He has a grinning face and a garland of human heads. The Nalanda Museum contains a tenth-century stone image of Heruka; it is much mutilated—its hand and legs are missing. The Indian Museum has a unique image of Heruka in bronze. The Banpur hoard contains only one bronze image. A unique specimen of this deity in black chlorite, hailing from Badkamta in Tippera and belonging to the 11th century is now in the Dacca Museum.[48] A sixteen-armed image of Heruka in union with his Śakti is now in the Nahar family collection.

The Paharpur image of Hevajra has eight heads and sixteen arms. It is represented in *yuganaddha* with Śakti. Miniature dancing figure are carved round the main pair and beneath them are a number of corpses.[49] A smaller image, without the Śakti, has been found in Dharmanagar subdivision of Tripura. A stone image of Nairātmā from Nalanda, belonging to the 10th century is now in the Indian Museum. It is one-faced and two-armed, the right holding a *kartari* and the missing left apparently a *kapāla*. It is represented as dancing in *ardhaparyaṅka* on a corpse, with garland of skulls, fierce mien, upraised hair and Akṣobhya on the crest. A supposed eleventh-century stone image of Vajrayogīni is in Patna Museum standing in *ālīḍha*, hands holding *kartari* and *kapāla*, with a *khatvāṅga* slung between the forearm and upper arm, it has a fierce mien and a grinning face. Sambara is not very different from Hevajra, since he is Heruka in *yuganaddha* with his Śakti Vajarvarāhī. A ninth-century Nalanda stone image of this deity is in the Indian Museum. Three-headed and twelve armed, the god stands in *ālīḍha* posture, with hands holding magic wand, skull-cup, severed head of Brahmā, etc. Above his head, a four-armed goddess stands in the same pose, and this figure is repeated thrice below—between the legs of the central figure and at the sides. There is no doubt that she is Vajarvārāhī.[50] Yamāntaka or Yamāri is also represented as embracing his Śakti. The Nalanda Museum contains a tenth-century stone image of Yamāri, in *pratyālīḍha* on a buffalo, having six heads and hands holding various emblems, dwarfish and pot-bellied, and with three round, rolling eyes in the bearded and bewhiskered main face which is crowned with a garland of human heads. An interesting sculpture in the collection of the Rajsahi Museum, hailing from Vikrampur, represents Kṛṣṇā-Yamāri. A from of this god has been identified in a bronze image from Ratnagiri.

Images of Jambhala, the Buddhist counterpart of the Hindu Kubera, have been found in Gandhara, Mathura, Sarnath, Magadha, Bengal and Nepal. The image of Jambhala is common in Orissa where we come across his pot-bellied form at Ratnagiri, Ayodhya, and Prachi valley. A good number of stone and bronze images of Jambhala have been discovered from Nalanda. The pot-bellied god, often with and sometimes without his consort Vasudhārā, is shown seated in *lalitāsana* with feet resting on a lotus or on Kalasa, holding citron in his right hand and a mongoose in the left. Such images are very common and have been found in various parts of eastern India.[51] Vasudhārā images can be easily identified because of her corn symbol. A tenth-century Nalanda stone image shows the goddess, in her left hand a vase with sprouting foliage indicating plenty for which she stands. The Indian Museum contains several metal images of Vasudhārā, all seated in *lalitāsana* with right hand in *varada* and left holding stalks of corn. The latter is sometimes shown separately, rising from the pedestal itself. The Patna Museum contains a few bronzes of Vasudhārā from Nalanda and Kurkihar.[52]

A few Trailokyavijaya images have been found at Nalanda. One of them in stone is four-armed and is seen trampling on postrate figure of Śiva. In other images the god is shown trampling on both Śiva and Pārvati.[53] National Museum contains an eleventh-century stone image of this god. A seventh-century bronze image in the Nalanda collection of the Patna Museum shows the god trampling upon the head of Śiva with his left leg and the body of the Gaurī with his right. The most interesting is one from Banpur in bronze. Here the trampled Śiva image under his foot is eight-handed. Gaurī with four hands, lies flat on her back and the god's foot presses down on the bosom. The main figure is in *pratyālīḍha* attitude with two hands clasped against the chest. He wears a crown decked with five Dhyānī Buddha figures, *kuṇḍala* in looped ears, broad necklace, and ornaments all over the body.

The Banpur hoard contains two bronze images of Kurukullā. One is in sitting posture, six armed, three-faced, three-eyed and blooming with youth. The other one represents Uḍḍiyāna Kurukullā. It is fierce in form and has a garland of skulls, the four hands hold a bow, a stalk of lotus, an arrow of flowers, and goad. She is in *ardhaparyaṅka* pose dancing on a corpse. The Nalanda collection of the Patna Museum contains a bronze image of Bhṛkutī, four-armed, crowned, and standing. Her hands contain a rosary, a tree-branch, a *kamaṇḍalu* and an unknown object. The image belongs to 9th century A.D.[54] The Indian Museum has an image of Parṇaśabarī with three faces and six arms, represented as trampling upon Gaṇeśa. Two tenth-century stone images discovered in Nalanda and Vajrayoginī villages of Dacca district, now in the Dacca Museum, show them with prostrate figures of disease and pestilences in human shape under their feet.[55] The Kurkihar hoard contains seven bronze images of Paraṇaśabarī belonging to 10th-12th centuries A.D.[56]

One of the finest images of Prajñāpāramitā, originally from Java, is now in the Leyden Museum. This has only one lotus bearing the manuscript of her name in her left hand, but the Indian Museum image has two lotuses one on either side, each bearing a manuscript. The Maldah Museum contains a very nice stone image of this goddess, shown cross-legged and two-armed.[57] The Nalanda collection of the Patna Museum has four bronze images of Prajñāpāramitā, all four-handed and in *vajrāsana.* There are also two inscribed bronze images of the same type in the Kurkihar hoard.[58] The Nalanda Museum has five bronze images of Prajñāpāramitā. Stone images of Aparājitā trampling upon Gaṇeśa, with the right hand held in a slap-giving position, belonging to the 9-10 centuries, are in the collections of Indian Museum, Patna Museum, Nalanda Museum and National Museum. There is a bronze image of an eight-handed goddess, originally found in Tippera and now in the Dacca Museum, which has been wrongly identified with Sitātapatrā Aparājitā by Bhattasali.[59]

An eighth century stone image from Ratnagiri, seated in *lalitāsana*, right hand in *varada* and left holding an *aśoka*-twing, flanked by Vidyādharas on either side, shows Mārīci in her Aśokakāntā form. The eight-handed form is known as Sita-Mārīcī, corresponding images of which type have been found in Ujani and Panditsar, now in the Dacca Museum,[60] and from Vikrampur, now in the Rajsahi Museum. The Indian Museum contains a few eleventh-century stone images of Pīta-Mārīcī (same as Sita, difference being in colour), and the Rajsahi Museum has one secured from Narkelberia. The three-faced, eight-armed Picuva form of Mārīcī is represented in three Nalanda stone images, two belonging to the National Museum and one to the Indian Museum. The latter also contains a tenth-century stone image from Nalanda which shows the goddess, three-faced (the right one or left is of a sow) six-handed, standing on a chariot drawn by pigs. The Banpur hoard contains one image of Mārīcī in bronze. Mārīcī is usually represented with three faces, the left one being that of a sow.

A tenth-century stone image of Cundā from Nalanda, now in the National Museum, shows the goddess in *vajrāsana,* the main pair of hands rest on the crossed soles of the feet and hold a bowl. Metal images of Cundā represent a variety of forms. The Indian Museum has a few four armed images, the main pair of hands joined on crossed soles, the remaining right hand holding a rosary or in *varada* pose and the left one holding a manuscript-on-lotus. Similar images belonging to 9-10th centuries are in the Nalanda and Patna Museum.

A tenth-century twelve-armed bronze image of Cundā from Nalanda, now in the Indian Museum, deserves special mention. The Patna Museum contains a Nalanda bronze image of eighteen-armed Cundā in *vajrāsana* on a lotus throne.[61] Another eighteen-armed bronze image of this goddess from Nalanda is now in the National Museum. The eighteen-armed stone Cundā image from Niamatpur in Rajsahi, now in the Rajsahi Museum, is also of great importance.[62]

The goddess Tārā in her early and simple form is endowed with two hands and is generally found seated on a lotus, right hand exhibiting *varada* (rarely *abhaya*; cf. the Ellora specimen) and the left holding a stem of lotus. This form is found in numerous sculptural specimens. A form showing the goddess bearing a *cakra* of white lustre on her breast, known as Mṛtyuvañcana, is represented in a stone image of Rajsahi Museum and two tenth-century bronze images now in the Nalanda Museum. The well-known variety of Ārogya Tārā (*ardhaparyaṅka, varada* in right hand, *utpala* in the left) has numerous broze representations. Stone images of Aṣṭamahābhaya-Tārā, so named because she is invoked to dispel eight fears, represented amidst eight other goddesses, have been found at Ratnagiri in Orissa, now in the Patna Museum; at Nalanda, now in Nalanda Museum; and at Somapara in Bangladesh, now in the Dacca Museum. The one in Dacca has eight miniature figures of goddesses on the *prabhāvalī*, four on each side and the figure of Vajrasattva on the extreme right corner of the pedestal.[63] The Kurkihar hoard of the Patna Museum has as many as eight seated bronze images of the Śyāmatārā group.[64] There are twenty standing images in the Kurkihar hoard, nine bending forward slightly and eleven in *samapadasthānaka*. The Banpur hoard has eleven Tārā images in bronze all in *lalitāsana* carrying *utpala* in the left hand and exhibiting *varada* in the right. An eight-century standing bronze image of Dhanada Tārā exhibiting *abhaya*, rosary, lotus-stalk and manuscript is in the Nalanda Museum. A bronze image of Vajra Tārā in the Dacca Museum, originally hailing from Majvadi, Faridpur, is shown within an eight petalled lotus with the figures of eight attendants carved on the inside of the petals.[65] It reminds us of one of the same type of images found at Chandipur in Bhagalpur and now in the Indian Museum. This image is also in the form of a lotus and represents the complete *maṇḍala* with all the attendant deities. It is so constructed that it can be opened and closed at will. The petals are eight in number and each bears the image of an attendant deity.

NOTES

1. Devangana Desai, *Erotic Sculpture of India: A Socio-Cultural Study*, New Delhi, 1975, pp. 87-145.
2. F. Yeats-Brown, *Bengal Lancer*, London, 1930, pp. 236-7.
3. H. Zimmer, *Art of Indian Asia*, Bollingen Series XXXIX, New York, 1964 (rpt.), pp. 129-30.
4. D.K. Chakrabarti and K. Glantz in *Journal of Ancient Indian History*, Vol. V, pp. 149-54.
5. N.N Bhattacharyya, *History of Indian Erotic Literature*, New Delhi, 1975, pp. 26ff.
6. K.S. Behera in *Śakti Cult and Tārā*, Calcutta University, 1967, pp. 84-85.
7. N.K. Bose, *Canons of Orissan Architecture*, Calcutta, 1932, pp. 92, 154.
8. Paper presented in International Symposium of Indo-Tibetan Tantric Buddhism, Sarnath Institute, March, 1995.
9. Ed. and trans. by P. Apte, Tirupati, 1991.
10. *Evolution of Maṇḍala in Temple Architecture*, Bangalore, 1990, p. 1.
11. See her edn. and trans. of *Silparatnakośa* (by Sthāpaka Niranjan Mahāpatra), IGNCA, pp. 3-7.
12. Apte and Moorti *loc. cit.*
13. *Unfolding a Maṇḍala: The Buddhist Cave Temple at Ellora*, Albani, 1993.
14. See also L.S.S. O'Malley, *Hooghly District Gazetter*, p. 254.
15. *Indian Archaeology: A Review* (hereafter *IAR*), 1958-9, fig. 7.
16. D.H. Gordon, *The Prehistoric Background of Indian Culture*, Bombay, 1958, p. 115.
17. Moti Candra in *Bulletin of the Prince of Wales Museum*, Bombay, No. 9, p. 25, fig. 17.
18. Devangana Desai, op. cit., pp, 16-17.
19. M.N. Deshpande in *Ancient India*, No. XV, pp. 69ff., 81ff.
20. Desai, op.cit., p. 26.
21. R.D. Banerji, 'Bas-Reliefs from Badami' in *Memoirs of the Archaeo-logical Survey of India*, (hereafter *ASIAR*), No. XXV, 1928, pl. IVe.
22. For details see Desai, op. cit., pp. 40-70.
23. Ibid., pp. 71-3.
24. Mulk Raj Anand, *Kāmakalā*, 1958, p. 38; A. Danielon, 'An Approach to Hindu Erotic Sculpture' in *Marg*, Vol. II, p. 88; K. Lal, *The Cult of Desire*, Delhi, 1966, p. 95.
25. This is to be found in my *Indian Mother Goddess*, 2nd edn., New Delhi, 1977, pp. 145-93.
26. *South Indian Inscriptions*, XII, No. 106.
27. *JRASB*, Letters, Vol. XVI, pp. 247-51, pl. XII.
28. *Patna Museum Catalogue of Antiquities* (hereafter *PMCA*), Patna, 1964, pp. 94-5.

29. E.I., XXVIII, pp. 184-85.
30. N.K. Bhattasali, *Iconography of the Buddhist and Brahmanical Sculptures in the Dacca Museum*, Dacca, 1929, pp. 192-4; J.N. Banerjea, *Development of Hindu Iconography* (*DHI*), Calcutta, 1956, p. 509, see also R.D. Banerji in *ASIAR*, 1924-5, p. 155.
31. P.B. Desai, *Jainism in Karnataka*, pp. 143ff.
32. *History of Bengal*, Dacca University, 1943, Vol. I, p. 467n.
33. N.K. Bhattasali, op. cit., pp. 22-3, pl. IIIa.
34. *History of Bengal*, p. 468, pl. XXII, 56.
35. N.K. Bhattasali, op. cit., pp. 24f. pl. VII.
36. For iconological description see *Sādhanamālā*, 65-6.
37. *PMCA*, p. 121.
38. *History of Bengal*, p. 466, pl. XLVI, 111, 113.
39. *IBI*, p. 103, fig. 75.
40. A. Getty, *Gods of Northern Buddhism*, p. 111.
41. N.K. Bhattasali, op. cit., pp. 28-9, pl. VIIb.
42. *History of Bengal*, pp. 469-70, pl. XXII. 57.
43. *PMCA*, p. 143.
44. *ASIAR*, 1930-4. p. 278, pl. CXCLI. 9.
45. Ibid., 1927-8, p. 159; 1929-30, p. 201, pl. XXXIII d.
46. *PMCA*, p. 144.
47. Ibid., p. 120.
48. N.K. Bhattasali, op. cit., p. 37, Pl. XII.
49. *ASIAR*, 1927-28, p. 107, pl. XLIXa.
50. Ibid., 1934-5, p. 80, pl. XXIVc.
51. Ibid., 1920-1, pp. 42-6, 1927-8, p. 159, 4928-9, p. 146, 1933-4, p. 278; *History of Bengal*, p. 471, *PMCA*, pp. 123, 144, etc.
52. *PMCA*, pp. 125, 149-50.
53. *ASIAR*, 1934-5, p. 278, pl. CXLI. 15.
54. *PMCA*, p. 122.
55. N.K. Bhattasali, op. cit., pp. 58-61, pl. XXIIIa-b.
56. *PMCA*, pp. 150-1.
57. *History of Bengal*, p. 472, pl. XXVI. 62.
58. *PMCA*, pp. 122, 149.
59. N.K. Bhattasali, op. cit., pp. 53-4, pl. XVIII.
60. Ibid., pp. 43-4, pl. XIII.
61. *PMCA*, p. 123, pl. XXVI.
62. *History of Bengal*, p. 473.
63. N.K. Bhattasali, op, cit., pp. 56-67, pl. XXI.
64. *PMCA*, pp. 147-9.
65. N.K. Bhattasali op. cit., pp. 45-53, pl. XXV-XXVII.

11

A Glossary of Tantric Technical Terms

This glossary is based mainly on the following works: *Kālivilāsatantra* (Tantric Texts, Vol. VI, 1917), *Kulacuḍāmaṇitantra* (TT, Vol. IV, 1915), *Kulārṇavatantra* (TT, Vol. V, 1917), *Kaulāvalīnirṇaya* (TT, Vol. XIV). *Kaulamārgarahasya* (ed. S.C. Vidyābhuṣaṇa, Sāhitya Pariṣat, Calcutta Series, No. LXXVI), *Kramadīpikā* (Chowkhamba Sanskrit Series, No. CCXXXIII), *Gandharvatantra* (eds. R.C. Kak and H.B. Sastri, Śrīnagar, 1934), *Gāyatrītantra* (ed. and pub. R.M. Chatterjee), *Gorakṣasiddhāntasaṃgraha* (Sarasvati Bhavana Texts, No. XVIII, 1925), *Gheraṇḍa Saṃhitā* (Pāṇini Office pub. 1914), *Tantrarājatantra* (TT, Vols. VIII, XII), *Tantrasāra* (Vasumati edn. 1341 BS, 1934), *Tantrāloka* (Kashmir Series of Texts and Studies, 1918-36), *Tārābhaktisudhārṇava* (TT, Vol. XXI, 1940), *Tripurārahasya* (Sarasvati Bhavana Texts, No. 15, 1925), *Nirvāṇatantra* (ed. and pub. R.M. Chatterjee), *Parāśurāmakalpasūtra* (Gaekwad's Oriental Series, Vols. XXII-XXIII), *Pādukāpañcaka* (TT, Vol. II, 1913), *Puraścaryārṇava* (Pratāpasiṃha Shah Bahadur Varma, 3 pts., Calcutta, 1901, 1902, 1904), *Prapañcasāra* (TT, Vols, III, XIX, XX), *Prāṇatoṣanī* (Vasumati edn.), *Nityaṣodasikārṇava* (Ānandāśrama Sanskrit Series, Vol. LVI, 1948), *Mahānirvāṇatantra* (ed. A. Avalon, Calcutta, 1929), *Mātṛkābhedatantra* (ed. C. Bhattacharyya, Calcutta Sanskrit Series, Vol. VII), *Yoginītantra* (ed. and pub. R.M. Chatterjee), *Yoginīhṛdayadīpikā* (ed. Gopinath Kaviraj, Sararsvati Bhavana Texts, No. XV), *Rudrayāmala, Uttaratantra* (ed. Jivananda Vidyasāgara, Calcutta, 1937), *Śaktisaṅgamatantra* (GOS, Nos. LXI, XCI, CIV), *Śāradātilaka* (TT, Vols. XVI, XVII, 1933). *Guhyasamāja* (GOS, No. LIII), *Ṣaṭckranirūpaṇa, Ṣaṭcakravivṛti* (ed. T.N. Vidyaratna, TT, Vol. II, 1913). *Haṭhayogapradīpikā* (Veṅkateśvara Press, 1952) and *Kāmakalāvilāsa* (ed. A. Avalon, Madras, 1953).

Abhayamudrā

Gesture of protection. The hand showing this mudrā should be slightly elevated and bent with the palm turned outward, the fingers being outstretched and elevated.

Abhicāra

Rites for performing black deeds and causing harm to others like *māraṇa* or killing someone, *vaśīkaraṇa* or hypnotizing, *stambhana* or arresting, *ucāṭana* or driving away, *vidveṣaṇa* or creating bad blood and so on. *Śāradātilaka* XXIII. 123-5; *Śaktisaṅgama*, Kālī, VIII.102-5. Such acts should not be indiscriminate. *Tantrarāja*, XIII. 94-5.

Abhiṣecikī

A form of consecration in which the teacher worships Śiva and Śakti in a vessel and then anoints the disciple with its water. Rāghava on *Śāradātilaka* V. 127-40.

Abhiṣeka

Consecration of the aspirant to be performed before or after the initiation. Rāghavabhaṭṭa on *Śāradātilaka*, IV. 1; *Prāṇatoṣaṇī* II. 5, p. 142. It is of two kinds—Śāktābhiṣeka and Pūrṇābhiṣeka. It is done by sprikling holy water on the aspirant while chanting *mantras* to propitiate different deities specially those driving away evil spirits. *Puraścaryārṇava*, V, pp. 405ff. The candidate for Pūrṇābhiṣeka has to pass through severe ordeals. This special form of consecration bestows upon the aspirant a divine nature. *Śaktisaṅgama*, Kālī, XI. 29-37.

Ācamana

Symbolic purification of body by sipping water from the palm and sprinkling it on different parts of the body. Tantric Ācamana consists in the purification of the three forms of body,—gross, subtle and causal. *Mahānirvāṇa*, V. 39.

Ācāra

The means of spiritual attainment which varies from person to person according to competence. *Mahānirvāṇa* IV. 36-7. *Ācāras* are generally of seven kinds—Veda, Vaiṣṇava, Śaiva. Dakṣiṇa, Vāma, Siddhānta and Kaula, falling into two broad categories—

Dakṣiṇa and Vāma. Interpretations vary regarding the nature and grouping of the *ācāras*. It is generally held that those who participate in the rituals of Five Ms belong to the category of Vāmācāra. *Kaulamārgarahasya*, p. 11. According to a different tradition everyone is a follower of Dakṣiṇācāra by birth. It is only by initiation that one becomes a Vāmācārī. *Prāṇatoṣaṇī*, VII. 4, p. 532. Some authorities are inclined to exclude Veda and Vaiṣṇava from the category of Tantric *ācāras*. *Mātṛkābheda*, p. 6. In a few works we come across a two fold division of the *ācāras*.—Aghorācāra and Yogācāra.

Ācārya

The preceptor who has mastery over the scripture, who understands the real significance of the rites and who is disciplined physically and mentally is known as *ācārya*. *Kulārṇva*, XVII.

Acit-Śakti

One of the two forms of Śakti, the other being *cit* or consciousness. It is also known as Parigraha-Śakti and Upādāna-Śakti, i.e. material cause, of which the universe is a manifestation.

Adhaḥ-āmnāya

One of the six geographical regions of the Tantric cult, presiding over by goddesses such as Vāgiśvarī, Vajrayoginī, Paṇṇagī, Nairṭeśvari, etc., of Buddhist and Jain affiliation. *Śaktisaṅgama, Sundarī*, III. 182-8; *Prāṇatoṣaṇī*, I. 9, p. 64; *Puraścaryārṇava*, I. p. 13.

Adhikāra

Qualification and competence for Tantric worship. Only those who are free from all narrowness and are actively engaged in the work of human welfare have this competence. *Sarvahiṃsā-vinirmuktaḥ sarvaprāṇihite-rataḥ, so'asmin śāstre' adhikārī tadanyo bhramasādhaka*. *Gandharvatantra*, 11.19. There are various types of Tantric *sādhanā* with a variety of purposes, and hence the qualification for initiation vary from person to person according to the nature of *sādhanā* one undertakes. Those who do not believe in the Vedic way are specially entitled to have Tantric initiation. *Kaulamārgarahasya*, pp. 91, 105.

Advaya, Advaita

Non-dualism as opposed to dualism (*dvaita*) which is one of the main features of the idealistic philosophical systems of India. In all forms of Indian religious beliefs, Tantrism included, this philosophical concept plays a significant role.

Adhvaśodhana

The process of purifying the body which consists of six *adhvas* technically known as *varṇa, pada, mantra, kalā, tattva* and *bhuvana*. See Rāghavabhaṭṭa on *Śāradātilaka*, v. 77.

Adhyāsa

A form of symbol worship. The objective approach to the symbol is known as *sampad*, while the subjective is known as *adhyāsa*. The former is like the visualization of the deity or idea in a thing, may be an image or a symbol, while in the case of the latter, though the thing exists and is used as a means of concentration, the main emphasis is on the mind of the worshipper and on the deity or idea that is chiefly concerned. *Āropyapradhānā sampat adhiṣṭhāna-pradhāno 'adhyāsaḥ, Vedāntakalpataru*, 1.1.4.

Ādyā-Śakti

Premordial energy conceived as a goddess.

Aghamarṣaṇa

The way of driving away sins from the body conceived as *pāpa-puruṣa* (the sinful being) by sprinkling water on its different parts. *Mālinītantra* quoted in *Tantrasāra*, p. 79.

Aghora

One of the five forms of Śiva, black in colour, terrible in nature, the presiding deity of the southern region. *Nirvāṇatantra* quoted in *Prāṇatoṣaṇī*, I. 9, pp. 63-4. Name of a Śaiva sect following the Vāmācara way. *Śaktisaṅgama* (Tārā), I. 92-4. Name of one of the two general divisions of Tantric *ācāras*, the other being *yoga*. Aghorī means 'terrible', 'fearful'.

Āgneya-kalā

Aspects of a particular state in cosmic evolution. These are connected with the element of fire and symbolised, by ten goddesses—Dhūmrārci, Umā, Jvālinī, Visphuliṅginī, Suśrī, Surūpā, Kapilā, Havyavahā and Kavyavahā. *Prapañcasāra*, III. 18-19.

Āgneya-varṇa

Letters connected with the elements of fire. These are *ya, ra, la, ba, śa, ṣa, ṣa, ha* and *kṣa*. Rāghava's com. on *Śarādātilaka*, II. 1-3.

Ahamgrahopāsanā

The form of worship which, according to Appaya Dikṣita's commentary on the *Bhāvanopaniṣad*, is based upon the feeling of total identity of the worshipper and the deity.

Ahaṃkāra

An evolute of Prakṛti which, according to the Sāṅkhya, originates from *mahat* or *buddhi* and generates *manas* or mind. In Tantra this *Ahaṃkāra* or principle of egoity is brought in relation to *ājñācakra*, one of the six nerve-plexuses situated within the body.

Ajapā

A special form of effortless meditation. Rāghavabhaṭṭa of *Śāradātilaka*, XIV. 91. The sounds *haṃ* and *saḥ* processed by the movements of breath themselves constitute the *mantra* and henee there is no need of muttering anything. The automatic constitution of the *haṃsa-mantra* takes place simultaneously in *mūlādhāra, anāhata* and *ājñācakras. Gheraṇḍa*, V. 85. *Ajapā* is twofold—secret and expressed. The latter is again divided into two categories, sound and light. See under *Haṃsa.*

Ājñācakra

One of the six nerve-plexuses situated between the eyebrows. It looks like a two-petalled white lotus, symbolised by the letters *ha* and *kṣa*, and is regarded as the seat of mind. *Ṣaṭcakranirūpaṇa*, XXXII; *Ājñā* denotes command, evidently of the *guru* who is supposed to reside symbolically within this nerve-cycle. *Saubhāgyabhāskara* on *Lalitāsahasranāma* 90. Within the pericarp of the lotus resides the six-faced and white-complexioned goddess Hākinī.

Ajñāna

False knowledge, divided into two kinds, *pauruṣa*, which concerns human nature, and *bauddha*, which concerns intellect. The former is also known as *ānava-mala* which is the root of worldly existence. *Tantrāloka,* I, p. 55. It is uprootd by *dīkṣā* or initiation. The latter, for its eradication, requires, in addition, knowledge in scriptures. *Vṛtti* on *Paraśurāmakalpasūtra,* I.3.

Akṣamālā

String of beads for counting the name of deity or *mantra* made of a kind of dried fruit called Rudrākṣa. It may be made with other materials also, like crystals, etc.

Akula

The Śiva aspect of Śakti. *Akulasyāsya devasya kulaprathanaśālini, Tantrāloka,* III.67. According to Abhinavagupta that which is manifested from Kula or Śakti is *akula* and it is endowed with the elements of Śiva.

Ālambhana

A term for sacrifice.

Ālīḍha

A posture of legs, as if a bow is charged with an arrow. The right leg is outstretched while the left is slightly bent. *Pratyālīḍha* is the reverse posture in which the left leg is outstretched while the right is slightly bent.

Amākalā

A type of *kalā* or the active aspect of Śakti. It is equated with Ṣoḍaśikalā in *Ṣaṭcakravivṛti* and described as eternal and creative containing nectar flowing from the union of Śiva and Śakti. See *Tantric Texts,* Vol. II, p. 130. It has also been brought in relation to the phases of moon. It is said to reside within the triangle of the *sahasrāra* lotus. See under *kalā.*

Āmnāya

Zones of Tantric culture, five or six in number. *Kulārṇava,* III. 7; *Śaktisaṅgama, Sundarī,* V.182-7.

Amṛtīkaraṇa

Purification of the deity. The aspirant should recite three times the *mūla-mantra,* the *dīpanī-mantra* and the *mātṛkā* and then with letters and then with *dhenu-mudrā* he should sprinkle water on the head of the deity. *Puraścaryārṇava*, V, p. 343.

Anāhata

One of the six nerve-plexuses (*ṣaṭcakra*) situated in the heart-region. It is conceived as a twelve-petalled lotus and as the seat of the element of air. The goddess Kākinī is its presiding deity. *Anāhata* is also the name of a particular form of sound.

Anākhya-śakti

One of the five concepts of Śakti found in the Krama doctrine.

Āṇavī-dīkṣā

One of the three forms of *dīkṣā* or initiation mentioned in the *Rudrayāmala*, the other two forms being Śākti and Śāmbhavī. It is an elaborate system of initiation in which *mantra, arcanā, āsana, nyāsa, dhyāna* and different *upacāras* or articles are required. *Prāṇatoṣaṇī*, II. 4, p. 117. It is of various types like Smārtī, Mānasiki, Yaugī, Cākṣukī, Spārśanī, Vācikī, Māntrikī, Hotrī, Śāstrī and Abhiṣecikī. See Rāghava's com. on *Śāradātilaka*, V. 127-40.

Āṇavopāya

A means of spiritual attainment which is also known as *kriyā-upāya*. Though *kriyā* means action, it is used in the sense of knowledge. According to Abhinavagupta, when knowledge is derived after the control of desires it is known as *kriyā*. *Tantrāloka*, I. 151. The knowledge by which *āṇavopāya* or *kriyā-upāya* is characterised is, however, dualistic and to some extent dependent on external objects, ibid, I. 219-20.

Ānanda

Bliss.

Ānandabhairava, Bhairavī

The chief male and female deities of the *bhairavī-cakra*. Their meditation is necessary for the purfication of wine. *Prāṇatoṣaṇī*, VII. 2, p. 511. For the *mantras* of their meditation see *Mahānirvāṇa*, VIII. 166-7.

Ānandakanda

Name of the eight-petalled lotus which is situated in the *anāhata-cakra. Garland of Letters*, p. 119n.

Ānandanātha

A term generally prefixed before the term *guru. Śaktisaṅgama, Sundarī*, I. 139-40.

Anavasthollāsa

The last stage of spiritual progress according to some Tantric schools, the preceding ones being *ārambha, taruṇa, yauvana, prauḍha, tadanta* and *unmana*. According to the *Parasurāma-kalpasūtra*, X. 68 the first four stage belong to the Samayācāra and the last three, *anavasthā* included, to Svairācāra. At this stage the mind of the aspirant gets totally absorbed in the deity.

Aṅganyāsa

Feeling of the different parts of the body. It is five-fold (*pañcāṅga*) or six-fold (*ṣaḍaṅga*). The centres are heart, head, protective symbol, eyes and intestine. See under *Nyāsa*.

Aṇimā

A kind of *siddhi* or attainment of miraculous power.

Añjali Mudrā

Also known as *sarvarājendra* and *sampuṭāñjali* it is a gesture of veneration in which the two hands are clasped against the chest, palm to palm, both of which are extended upward with all fingers erect or slightly bent.

Āñji

Regarded as a *Kalā* or evolute of Śakti, often described as the *vyāpikā-śakti* or all-pervading energy. Kālīcaraṇa's com. on *Ṣaṭcakranirūpaṇa*, XL. It is often described as an alphabetical symbol..

Aṅkuśa

Elephant goad. When the goad is surmounted by a *vajra* it is called *vajrāṅkuśa*.

Antaḥkaraṇa

The collective name of intellect (*buddhi*), egoity (*ahaṃkāra*) and mind (*manas*). *Tantrāloka* IX. 236; *Śāradātilaka*, I. 36.

Antardaśāra

The internal body of the mystic diagrams. According to the *Kāmakalāvilāsa*, 30, it is the inner shade of the flames of the *cakras*, known as *vindu*, *trikoṇa* and *aṣṭakoṇa*, while the outer one is known as Bahirdaśāra. According to the *Nityaṣodaśikārṇava*, VI. 15 it is the expressed ray of the *navatrikoṇa* or *navayonicakra*, i.e. the *cakra* consisting of nine triangles.

Antarmātṛkānyāsa

Feeling of the deity in the region around the neck where the existence of *viśuddha-cakra* as a sixteen-petalled lotus is conceived. The letter or *mātṛkā* symbolizing the essence of the deity which is supposed to exist in each petal is to be felt and meditated. *Jñānārṇava* quoted in *Tantraśāra*, p. 88. See also *Puraścaryārṇava*, V, p. 330.

Antarpūjā

See under Antaryāga.

Antartīrtha

Tirthas or holy places supposed to exist within the human body. *Prāṇatoṣaṇī*, III. 3, p. 178. See under Mānasatīrtha.

Antaryāga

Internal worship meant for aspirants belonging to higher grades. It is mental worship in which external formalities are redundant. See *Mahānirvāṇatantra*, V. 143-9. According to the *Devībhāgavata* VII. 39.44. pure-consciousness is the absolute form of the goddess beyond all attributes, and the complete merger of the self of the aspirant in this stream of consciousness is *antaryāga*. The *Gautamīya-tantra*, Ch. IX. says that *antaryāga* leads to salvation within the span of one's life. Its virtues are elaborately stated in the *Gandharvatantra*, XII. 24-7.

Aṇu

The term for atom. Aṇu also denotes one of three categories of Trika philosophy indicating *jīva* or individual, also known as *paśu*. When Śiva owing to his own independence expresses himself in the contracted form of a fettered individual he comes to be called as Aṇu. *Sa eva svātantryāt ātmānāṃ saṃkucitaṃ avabhāsayan aṇuriti ucyate. Tantrasāra,* p. 6. The term Aṇu is also used to denote a means (*upāya*) for spiritual attainment which contains an element of dualistic sense. It leads to *vikalapa* knowledge, i.e. knowledge based on object, which is of course a means but not an end. See *Tantrāloka,* I. 150. 51; I. 219.21. According to Abhinavagupta that which is fettered by six false coverings in the body is called Aṇu and as such the term is a synonym of *paśu, puruṣa* or *jīva.* Every being is enveloped by *kañcuka* or coating of impurity. This coating is known as *Āṇavamala,* ibid., I. 74; IX. 113, 144, 205, 206. Aṇu is also a term for *mantra.* As the external form of an individual is fettered by the veil of impurity, but in reality the individual is pure, so also the material body of a *mantra* constituted by sound, appears to be a fettered entity, a mere combination of words and sound, although in reality it is a conscious principle. See Bhāskara's *Setubandha* com. on *Nityaṣoḍaśikārṇava,* VII. 43.

Anukalpa

Substitutes, especially of the Five Mṣ, like garlic for meat, coconut-water for wine, etc. This substitution holds good also in the case of sacrifices.

Anupāya

Knowledge resulting from *ānanda* or bliss which leads to the realisation of non-duality with Śiva. *Tantrāloka,* I. 242.

Anuttara

The manifested form of the Supreme Being. The term is used in a variety of senses. See *Parātriṃśikā,* pp. 19ff. Anuttara is the name of a form of Śakti according to Kāśmīra Śaivism. *Tantrāloka,* III. 186.

Ap

The element of water as one of the constituents of the universe. This is symbolically represented as belonging to *svādhiṣṭhāna-cakra* of the human body. *Ṣaṭcakranirūpaṇa,* vv. 15ff.

Aparā

The term for material or mundane. *Aparā vidyā* is material knowledge. Likewise *aparā* śakti is that aspect of Śakti which confers a variety of material attainments upon the worshipper. *Aparā* worship is also meant for practical purposes.

Apara-Nāda and Apara-Vindu

See under *Nāda* ane *Vindu.*

Āpyāyana

Processing of the *mantras* by various means. *Tantrasāra,* p. 54.

Ārambha-ullāsa

The first of the seven stages of spiritual attainment. Others being *taruṇa, yauvana, prauḍha, prauḍhānta, unmana* and *anavasthā. Parāśurāmakalpasūtra.* X. 68.

Ardhacandra-śakti

Symbolical half-moon as the repository of Śakti where the aspirant becomes all-knowing. It has five *kalā* or functional aspects known as Jyotsnā, Jyotsnāvati, Kānti, Suprabhā and Vimalā. *Garland of Letters,* 3rd. edn., p. 196.

Ardhaparyaṅka

Also called Mahārājalīlā, it is a peaculiar *āsana* of sitting. Both the legs are on the same pedestal. One of the knee is raised while the other is bent.

Artha

One of the four Puruṣarthas denoting wealth or material prosperity. The term is also used to denote 'meaning' and 'expression'.

Aruṇā

Name of the presiding Śakti of one of the eight corners of the *aṣṭakoṇacakra. Nityaṣoḍaśikārṇava,* I. 191-2.

Asamprajñāta samādhi

Name of Nirvikalpa Samādhi.

Āsana

Posture, seat, pedestal. The term denotes a mystic or any attitude exhibited in the lower limbs. *Āsana* is of various kinds, such as *paryaṅka, vajraparyaṅka, ardhaparyaṅka, lalita, bhadra, ālīḍha,* etc.

Āsava

A type of wine.

Aṣṭadalapadma

Eight-petalled lotus, actual or imaginary, used as universal Tantric symbol in the composition of the *cakras* within and without the human body and also in the diagrams. The petals are said to contain the letters *Ka, Ca, Ṭa, Ta, Pa, Ya, Śa* and *La, Kāmakalāvilāsa,* 33. Presiding goddesses Anaṅgakusumā, Anaṅgamekhalā, Anaṅgamadanā, Anaṅgamadanāutarā, Anaṅgarekhā Anaṅgaveginī, Anaṅgāṅkuśā and Anaṅgamalinī. *Nityaṣodaṣikārṇava,* I. 177-78. They are known as Guptatarayoginī. The attainment is known as Mahimāsiddhi; associated *mudrā, akarṣīnī. Gandharvatantra.* V. 96; XVII. 42.

Aṣṭakonacakra

Octagonal diagram said to be the extension of *trikoṇa-cakra* or triangular diagram. *Kāmakalāvilāsa,* 29. It is regarded both as the gross and as the subtle body of the goddess. *Cidvallī* com. on ibid. 40ff. Each of the eight corners of this *cakra* is presided over by a goddess or Śakti, known respectively as Vaśinī, Kāmeśī, Modinī, Vimalā, Aruṇā, Jayinī, Sarveśī and Kaulinī. *Nityaṣoḍśikārṇava,* I. 191-2. The attainment resulting out of this *cakra* worship is known as *bhuktisiddhi.* The presiding deties are known as Rahasyayoginī and they are propitiated by offerings in *khecarimudrā. Gandharvatantra,* XVII. 74-6.

Aṣṭamaithunāṅga

Eight techniques required for sexual union—*smaraṇa* (calling up), *kīrtana* (uttering sweet words), *keli* (sport), *prekṣaṇa* (special looks) *guhyabhāṣaṇa* (secret dialogue), *saṅkalpa* (determination), *adhyavasāya* (patience and perseverence)and *kriyāniṣpatti* (completion of the sexual commerce). *Dakṣasaṃhitā,* VII. 31-2.

Aṣṭamātṛkā

The eight Mātṛkā goddesses—Brahmāṇī, Māheśvarī, Kaumārī,

Vaiṣṇavi, Vārāhi, Aindrī, Cāmuṇḍā and Mahālakṣmī—supposed to reside in the Viṣṇurekhā of the *bhupurayantra. Nityaṣoḍaśikārṇava*, I. 169-71.

Aṣṭapāśa

Eight fetters leading to human bondage: *ghṛṇā* (hatred), *lajjā* (shame), *bhaya* (fear), *śaṇkā* (misgiving), *jugupsā* (upbraiding), *kula* (pedigree), *śīla* (manners) and *jāti* (birth or caste). *Paraśurāmakalpasūtra,* X. 70.

Aṣṭaprakṛti

Collective name of the first eight Sāṅkhya *tattvas*: Prakṛti, Mahat, Ahaṃkāra and the five Tanmātras.

Aṣṭasiddhi

Eight miraculous attainments.

Aṣṭa-Tārā

Eight forms of the goddess Tārā: Tārā, Ugrā, Mahogrā, Vajrā, Kālī, Sarasvatī, Kameśvarī and Bhadrakālī.

Aśvakrāntā

The region extending from the Vindhya hills to the great sea. In the *Mahāsiddhasāratantra* the western boundary of Aśvakrāntā has been located on the Karatoyā in the Dinajpur district and the eastern boundary in Javadvīpa or Java.

Atimārgī

Follower of an extreme path.

Ātmasamarpaṇa

Surrender of the self to the Sādhyadevatā or chosen deity. For the mantra see *Śāradātilaka,* VII; *Mahānirvāṇa,* VI. 178-91.

Ātmaśuddhi

Purification of the self by various processes. *Kulārṇava,* VI.

Ātmatattva

Doctrine of the self.

Ātmavali

Sacrifice of the self, i.e. complete surrender of one's mental faculties like thinking, feeling and willing to the supreme goddess. *Gāyatrītantra*, V.

Atinaya

An aspect of Krama doctrine. See under Krama.

Atirahasyayoginī

Collective name of the three presiding goddesses of three angles of the *trikoṇa* or mystic triangle. The goddess on the top angle is known as Kāmeśvarī, on the right angle as Vajreśvarī and on the left angle as Bhagamālinī. *Gandharvatantra*, V. 112-13.

Audaka Snāna

Bathing in a river. It is also known as Varuṇa-snāna.

Avadhūta

The aspirant who commands universal reverence, who is free from all prejudices and who has knowledge of his own self is known as Avadhūta. *Kulārṇava*, XVII. They are divided into two classes—householders and recluses. *Prāṇatoṣaṇī*, VII. 4, p. 532 Avadhūtas belonging to the highest grade are known as Kūlāvadhūtas. They have a divine character. *Mahānirvāṇa*, VII. 271-83. *Avadhūta* is also the name of a nerve.

Avaguṇṭhana-Mudrā

Name of a hand-pose which is formed by clasping the fingers of the left hand. Only the fore-finger is to remain open and pendant.

Āvāhanī-Mudrā

A hand pose made by joining two outstretched palms and holding the ring finger by the thumb. *Tantrasāra*, p. 567.

Āvaraṇa-Cakra

A different name of *navacakra, Tantrarāja*, V. 9-11.

Āvaraṇadevatā

Goddesses also known as Yoginīs presiding over the nine *cakras*. Their names are Prakaṭā, Guptā, Sampradāyā, Kulakaulyā,

Nigarbhā, Rahasyā, Atirahasyā and Parāpararahasyā. *Setubandha* com. on *Nityaṣoḍaśikārṇava*, I, 164-5.

Avidyā

False knowledge.

Avinābhava Sambandha

Relation of non-duality or identity which holds good in the case of Śiva and Śakti in the Tantras.

Avīra

Aspirants belonging to the probationary stages of *ārambha, taruṇa, yauvana* and *prauḍha*. Rameśvara's *Vṛtti* on *Paraśurāmakalpasūtra*, X.68. They are not so advanced in spiritual attainment as to teach the Vīra standard.

Avyakta

The unmanifested. A synonym of Prakṛti or primordial substance. In the *Saubhāgyabhāskara*, p. 99 the term *avyakta* has been used to denote *Kāraṇa*-Vindu or the root cause to be manifested in effect.

Āyudha

Weapon.

Bahiḥpūjā

See under Bahiryāga.

Bahirdaśāra

The external body of the mystic diagrams, meant for the expression of the five elements like space, etc., and five *tanmātras* like sound, etc., symbolised by ten letters beginning with Ka; *Nityaṣoḍaśikārṇava*, VI. 16. The ten triangles by which the theme is represented are presided over by ten goddesses. Ibid., I. 184-6. They belong to the clan of Āvaraṇadevatā and are styled Kulakaulayoginī. *Gandharvatantra*, V. 102. See *Antardaśāra*.

Bahirmātṛkānyāsa

Feeling of the deity in three forms—creative, sustaining and destructive—in the outer parts of the body in terms of the symbolism of prescibed letters known as Mātṛkās. It is to be done after performing the *antarmātṛkānyāsa*. *Tantrasāra*, p. 89.

Bahiryāga
External worship complementary to *antaryāga* or internal worship.

Bāhyapūjā
See under Bahiryāga.

Bali
Sacrifice, oblation, gift offering.

Baṇāliṅga
One of the three forms of Liṅga or phallus, symbol of Śiva, others being Itara and Svayambhū. In Tantric conception it is said to reside within the triangle of the *anāhata-cakra*. *Ṣaṭcakranirūpaṇa*, XXV.

Bhaga-liṅga-kriyā
Actions involving female and male genital organs in Devī worship.

Bhairavaikātmya
A term for *mokṣa* (liberation) or *jīvanmukti*. It is the unity of *jīva* (individual) with *bhairva*. Only those who are born of parents mentally impersonating Śiva and Śakti are entitled to this form of liberation. *Parātriṃśikā*, p. 234.

Bhairavīcakra
A *cakra* ritual in which Five Ms are used. The male and female aspirants sit collectively and perform the rites which include drinking of wine and sexual intercourse. For details see *Mahānirvāṇa*, VIII. 54-206; *Kaulāvalinirṇaya*, VII; *Kulārṇava*, VIII.

Bhakti
Devotion.

Bhāṇḍabrahmāṇḍatattva
The theory that the body is the microcosm of the universe.

Bhāṇḍikera
A Tantric sect mentioned in the *Śaktisaṅgama-tantra*

Bhāvanāsiddhi
A form of devotion and attainment in which the deity is conceived of in terms of certain characteristics.

Bhīma
Name of the six-petalled lotus of the *svādhiṣṭhāna-cakra*, *Nirvāṇatantra*, V.

Bhujaṅgama Mantra
A class of defective *mantras*. Rāghava on *Śāradātilaka*, II. 111.

Bhuktimukti
All- round success.

Bhuktisiddhi
Name of an attainment, consisting of material and spiritual success, to be achieved through the rituals of *aṣṭakoṇacakra*. *Gandharavatantra*, XVIII. 75.

Bhūmisparśa
A *mudrā* in which the right hand has the palm turned inward and the fingres outstretched, with the tips touching the ground.

Bhupura
A quadrangle with four doors and a triangle inside, the lines being known as Brahmā, Viṣṇu and Śiva. On the Brahmā line are situated ten Siddhis, on the Viṣṇu line eight Mātṛkās and on the Śiva line ten Mudrā-Śaktis. *Gandharvatantra*, V. 76; *Nityaṣoḍa-śikārṇava*, I. 166ff.

Bhūta
The material elements. The term also denotes a class of mis-chievous spirits or hobgoblins.

Bhūtāpasaraṇa
Chasing away evil spirits and disturbances with the help of *mantras*. Rāghava on *Śāradātilaka*, IV. 10; *Puraścaryārṇava*, III, p. 154.

During sacrifice it is done by sprinkling white mustard seeds. *Tantrasāra*, p. 616.

Bhūtaśuddhi

Purification of the five elements—earth, water, fire, air and space—of which the body is constituted. It is done with the help of *mantras* and magical rites and also with the help of yogic exercises. *Tantraśāra*, pp. 58-87 *Prāṇatoṣaṇī*, III.5, p. 202; *Puraś-caryārṇava*, III. 6, pp. 164-8; *Tārābhaktisudhārṇava*, V. pp. 153-7.

Bīja

Seed. In Tantra it signifies the germ-syllable which takes the form of a deity. It is also the term for semen.

Bodhana

Processing of *mantra*. *Tantrasāra*, p. 54.

Bodhinī

A form of Śakti situated on the second point above the *ājñācakra*, it is considered as a seed. Kālīcaraṇa on *Ṣaṭcakranirūpaṇa*, XL *Bodhinī* is also described as one of the five *kalās* or manifestations of Nirodhinī-Śakti (the Śakti which offers resistance to the up-ward march of *kuṇḍalinī*). *Garland of Letters*, p. 196.

Brahmacakra

Name of a *cakra* representing equilibrium of Śakti in the form of *vindu*. It has been equated with Uḍḍiyāna Pīṭha. *Gandharvatantra*, V. 123. *Nityaṣoḍaśikārṇava*, VIII. 171.

Brahmādvāra

The passage through which *kuṇḍalinī* moves. It is a hole within the Svayambū-liṅga. Viśvanātha's com. on *Ṣaṭcakranirūpaṇa*, III.

Brahmagranthi

One of the three knots situated in the *mūlādhāracakra*. Com. on *Brahmavidyopaniṣat*, 70.

Brahmajñāna

Knowledge of *brahman*.

Brahmakapāla

Severed head of Brahmā carried by Tantric Buddhist deities.

Brahmanāḍī

A nerve situated within the *citrinī* nerve, or it may be the inner side of *citrinī*. Kālīcaraṇa on *Ṣaṭcakranirūpaṇa*, II. Other authorities equate it with *suṣumnā*. *Yogaśikhopaniṣat*, V.17.

Brahmāṇī, Brāhmī

One of the seven or eight Mātṛkās.

Brahmapadma

Name of the four-petalled lotus of the *mūlādhāra*. *Nirvāṇatantra* IV.

Brahmarandhra

A passage in the cerebral region.

Brahmasvarūpiṇī

An attribute of the goddess.

Buddhi

One of the evolutes of Prakṛti, according to the Sāṅkhya, which has been accepted in Tantra as a category of quality. Rāghava on *Śāradātilaka*, I. 17. According to the *Kaṅkālamālinītantra*, II, it is a feature of that aspect of mind which is conditioned by the element of fire. It is situated in the *ājñācakra* and controlled by the goddess Hākinī.

Caitanya

Consciousness. In internal worship (*antaryāga*) the aspirant has to think that the goddess is enshrined within his body as pure-consciousness or the self. Again, *guru*, *mantra* and *devatā* are also conceived as three forms of *caitanya*. *Śaktisaṅgama*, *Sundarī*, III. 11-13.

Cakra

Circle, used in a variety of senses, symbolising endless rotation of Śakti. In rituals there are different *cakra-sādhanā* in which men and female aspirants assemble and perform the rites of Pañcamakāra. See under *bhairavi-cakra*. According to the *Niruttaratantra*, X, *cakras* are of five types—*rajā, mahā, deva, vīra* and *paśu*. The term *cakra* is also used to denote *yantras* or mystic diagrams and variously known as *trikoṇa-cakra, aṣṭakoṇa-cakra* and so forth. Again the term is used to denote different nerve-plexuses within the body.

Cākṣusī-dīkṣā

A form of initiation in which the *guru* having concentrated his mind on the Supreme Being converts the disciple with only a complete glance. It is otherwise called *dṛk-dīkṣā*. *Kulārṇava*, XIV; Rāghava on *Śāradātilaka* V. 127-40; *Merutantra* quoted in *Puraścaryārṇava*, V, p. 390.

Cañcālā

See Caramālā.

Cāndra

A Vāmācarī sect mentioned in *Śaktisaṅgama-tantra*, Tārā, I. 92-4.

Candrakalā

Symbol of crescent moon which exists on the crown of the goddess as the source of everflowing nectar. *Mahānirvāṇa*, XIII. 7.

Candranāḍī

Name of the nerve *idā* which is conceived as a feminine entity, white in colour and representing Śakti in the form of moon. *Ṣaṭcakranirūpaṇa*, I.

Candratattva

Name of introvert mind which develops with successful controlling of the functions of *iḍā* nerve.

Caramālā

Garland made of *rudṛākṣa*, conch, crystal and other objects meant for *japa* or recalling the name of the deity. *Tantraśāra*, p. 29.

Caṣaka

Wine-glass.

Catuḥṣaṣṭhi-Yoginī
The sixty-four Yoginīs.

Caturdasāra
A mystic diagram supposed to represent the combined effect of various *cakras*. It is made of fourteen triangles each being presided over by a goddess. These goddesses are collectively known as Sampradāyayoginī. The attainment derived from it is known as Īśitvasiddhi. *Nityaṣoḍāśikārṇava* IV. 149; VI. 17; XI. 179-83; *Gandharvatantra*, V. 99; XVII. 49.

Caturviṃśati-tattva
The twenty-four Sāṅkhya fundamenals very often used in Tantric formulation. These are five *bhūtas* or gross elements, five *tanmātras* or the subtle elements, five *jñānendriyas* or sense-organs, five *karmendriyas* or organs of action and *manas* (mind), *buddhi* (intellect), *ahaṃkāra* (egoity) and *prakṛti* (primordial substance).

Catuṣkuṭā
Arrangement of letters peculiar to the cult of Śrīvidyā. *Tantrasāra*, p. 244.

Chāyā
Śakti of sun.

Cīnācāra, Cīnakrama
A form of Kaulācāra. The aspirant who is free from dualistic knowledge, is engaged in the welfare of human beings, has given up caste-prejudices, is peaceful and unattached and is free from all sins is entitled for Cīna-*sādhanā*. *Tārātantra*, p. 20. A *cīnācārī* is a follower of Tārākrama and Chinnamastākrama. *Śaktisaṅgma, Sundarī*, I. 188ff. In the *Merutantra cīnācāra* is described as one of the five fingers of Vāmācāra. *Puraścaryārṇava*, I, p. 20.

Cintāmaṇi
The gem that satisfies all desires.

Citkalā
Name of *saṃvit* or pure-consciousness. It is that which from the vibration caused by the break of Prakāśa-Vimarśa equilibrium of the Supreme Being.

Citriṇī

A nerve, also known as *brahma-nāḍī*, which is like the fibre of a lotus stem. It is very often equated with *suṣumnā*. It is also said that the *suṣumnā* is constituted by three *nāḍīs*, *citriṇī* which is of Sattva quality, *vajrā* which is of Rajas quality and *brahma* which is of Tamas quality. *Prāṇatoṣaṇī*, I. 4, p. 32.

Citśakti

The principle of consciousness.

Cittaśuddhi

Purification of mind.

Cuḍācakra

A type of spiritual exercise meant only for those who have attained the status of Vīra. This exercise consists of *laya-yoga*. *Śaktisaṅgama, Sundarī*, I. 197-200.

Ḍākinī

Various types of deities. In Tantric Buddhism they are especially celebrated. In the *Nāradapāñcarātra* Ḍākinī is described as a companion of Pārvatī and connected with the emergence of Chinnamastā. *Prāṇatoṣaṇī*, V. 6, pp. 378-9. Regarded as special forms of Parāśakti, the existence of Ḍākinī is to be conceived in the *mūlādhāra*. *Tantrasāra*, p. 338. As the presiding deity of the *mūlādhāra-cakra* Ḍākinī imparts spiritual knowledge to the aspirant. *Ṣaṭcakranirūpaṇa*, VIII.

Dakṣiṇācāra

See under *ācāra*. It is the way of the spiritual attainment without the use of *pañca-makāra* and other extreme forms of rituals. Often Vedācāra Vaiṣṇvācāra, and Śaivācāra are included within this category. The followers of Dakṣinācāra worship the great goddess in the traditional way. They believe in *varṇāśrama* and in the existing Brahmānical methods.

Dakṣiṇa Mārga

See Dakṣiṇācāra.

Dakṣiṇasrotatantra

Tantric texts belonging to the southern current. These are

Yoginījāla, Yoginīhṛdaya, Mantramālinī Aghoreśī, Krīḍāghoreśvarī, Lākinīkalpa, Mārīcī and *Mahāmārīcī*.

Ḍāmara

A class of Tantric texts, traditionally six in number, *Yoga, Śiva, Durgā, Sarasvatī, Brahmā* and *Gandharva*.

Daśa Mahāvidyā

Ten Tantric goddesses—Kālī, Tārā, Ṣoḍaśī, Bhuvaneśvarī, Bhairavī, Chinnamastā, Dhūmāvatī, Vagalā, Mātaṅgī and Kamalā, *Prāṇatoṣaṇī*, V. 6, p. 374. The names vary in different Tantras.

Daśa Mudrāśakti

Ten goddesses, conceived as *mudra-śakti*, are supposed to reside in the *Śiva-rekhā* of the mystic triangle. Their names are Sarvasaṃkṣobhanī, Sarvavidrāviṇī, Sarvākarṣaṇī, Sarvāveśakarī, Sarvonmādinī, Mahāṅkuśā, Khecarī, Vījamudrā, Yonimudrā and Trikhaṇḍā. *Nityaṣoḍaśikārṇava*, I. 199-200.

Daśa Saṃskāra

The ten sacraments prescribed for the Hindus—*jīvaseka (garbhādhāna), puṃsavana, sīmantonnayana, jātakarma, nāmakaraṇa, niṣkramana, annaprāsana, cuḍākaraṇa, upanayana* and *udvāha (vivāha), Mahānirvāṇa*, IX. 4.

Daśāṅga Puraścaraṇa

Ten limbs of Purścaraṇa—*japa, homa, tarpaṇa, abhiṣeka, aghamarsaṇa, sūryārgha, jalpana, praṇāma, pūjā,* and *brāhmaṇabhojana. Kaulāvalinirṇaya*, XV.

Daśa Siddhi

Ten miraculous attainments—Animā, Laghimā, Mahimā, Īśitva, Vaśitva, Prakāmya, Bhuktisiddhi, Icchāsiddhi, Prāptisiddhi and Sarvakāmasiddhi. *Nityaṣoḍaśikārṇava*, I. 166-8.

Dasavatāra

The ten incarnations of Viṣṇu often brought in relation to the ten Mahāvīdyā goddesses.

Deha Sādhanā

See under *Kāyasādhanā*.

Devatāśuddhi

Purification of the image of a deity with *mantra* and water. *Puraścaryārṇava*, III, p. 153.

Devīcakra

General name of the nerve-plexuses.

Dhāraṇa Yantras

The *yantras* which are generally used as amulet or talisman. These are drawn on leaves and dedicated to the names of different deities. Their use is regarded as efficacious. *Tantrasāra*, p. 585; *Śaktisaṅgama*, Tārā, LI. 2.

Dhāraṇi

Conglomeration of syllables, containing esoteric terms, used as a charm or prayer among the Tantric Buddhists.

Dhātuśakti

Collective name of Ḍakinī, Rākinī, Lākinī, Kākinī, Sākinī and Hākinī, presiding goddesses of the *Cakras*.

Dhauti

One of the *ṣaṭkarmas* of the Yogic practices. It denotes washing, internal and external, for making the body pure. *Dhauti* is of four kinds—*antardhauti, dantadhauti, hṛddhauti* and *mūlaśodhana*. *Gheranda*, I. 13.

Dhyāna

Meditation, which is concentration of mind on the chosen deity by controlling all the sense organs. *Kulārṇava*, XVII.

Dhyānamudrā

Also known as *samādhimudrā*, it is the position of hands while in meditation. The hands with palm upwards lie one upon the other on the lap with fingers stretched.

Dhyānāsana

Also known as *vajraparyaṅka* or *vajrāsana* it is the meditative pose in which the two legs are firmly locked with both soles visible.

Dhyānayoga

Mental concentration on the process of the upward march of *kuṇḍalinī*. Kālīcaraṇa's com. on *Ṣaṭcakranirūpaṇa*, LI.

Digambara

A class of *avadhūtas* having the quality of Śiva. *Prāṇatoṣaṇī*, VII. 7, p. 532. The term also applies to a sect following Vāmācāra. Lakṣmīdhara's com. on *Saundaryalaharī*, 32.

Dīkṣā

Initiation as an essential precondition of Tantric Sādhanā. According to *Viśvasāra-tantra*, *dīkṣā* is of four types—*kriyāvatī*, *kalāvatī*, *varṇamayī* and *vedhamayī*. *Prāṇatoṣaṇī*, II. 4, p. 118. According to *Kulārṇava* XIV, it is of seven kinds—*kriyā*, *varṇa*, *kalā*, *sparśva*, *vāk*, *dṛk* and *mānasa*. These are again subdivided into different categories. According to the *Rudrayāmala*, *dīkṣā* is of three types—*āṇavi*, *śāktī* and *śāmbhavī*. *Prāṇatoṣaṇī*, II. 4. There are other types of *dīkṣā* like *krama*, *pañcāyatana*, *ekamantra*, etc.

Dīpana

Processing of *mantra*. *Tantrasāra*, p. 54.

Divya bhāva

The highest spiritual standard of the Tantric aspirant.

Divyacakra

Also known as *tattvacakra* it is also a *cakra* ritual meant only for those who have attained much spiritual progress. This *cakra* also requires the use of the Five Ms. *Mahānirvāṇa*, VIII. 204-19.

Divyadeha

Rejuvenated body. See under Raseśvara Darśana.

Divyapāna

One of the three forms of drinking wine before the goddess, others being Paśu and Vīra. *Kulārṇava*, VII; *Śaktisaṅgama*, Tārā, XXXIII. 6-8.

Divya sādhaka

The aspirant who makes spiritual exercise in the highest level.

Divyatattva

One of the three categories of *Pañcatattva,* others being *pratyakṣa* and *anukalpa.* See under Pañcatattva.

Divyaugha

One of the three lines of succession of the *gurus,* the others being *siddhaugha* and *mānavaugha. Bhāvacuḍāmaṇi* quoted in *Śyāmārahasya,* III.

Doṣa

Defects in regard to *mantras.* Defective *mantras* like *chinna, ruddha,* etc., do not produce any result. *Śāradātilaka,* II. 64-108.

Dravyaśuddhi

Purification of cultic materials with *mantras* and *dhenumudrā. Puraścaryārṇava,* III, p. 153.

Dṛk-Dīkṣā

See under *Cākṣuṣī dīkṣā.*

Dūtī, Dūtīyāga

Female partnerof the aspirant is known as *dūtī.* Ritual union with her is known as *dūtīyāga.* Her organ is conceived of as the sacrificial fire and the semen of the aspirant as the clarified butter which is to be offered in the fire. *Paraśurāmakalpasūtra,* X. 63.

Dvaitavāda

Dualism.

Gajakrāntā

Same as Aśvakrāntā, a geographical region of Tantric culture.

Gajalakṣmī

Lakṣmi anointed by a pair of elephants.

Gandhāṣṭaka

Eight smelling substances combined together and used as a substitute for wine. It is of three kinds—Śaktisamvandhī, Śivasamvandhī and Viṣṇusamvandhī, i.e. connected with Śakti, Śiva and Viṣṇu. *Śāradātilaka,* IV. 79-80.

Gāyatrī

The Gāyatrī *mantras* are used by the Tantrics in the name of their own deities, e.g. *Kālīkāyāi vidmahe śmasānavāsinyai dhīmahi, tanno ghore pracodayāt*, etc.

Gauḍa Sampradāya

A sect of Vāmācārī Tantrics belonging to eastern India. This sect depends solely on the rituals of the Five Ms and insists on the unity of *devatā, guru,* and *mantra* as manifestation of the energy of the great goddess. *Puraścryārṇava,* IX, p. 866; *Śaktisaṅgama, Sundarī,* III.15-18.

Gauṇī Bhakti

A form of devotion marked by meditation, worship, muttering of names of the deity and so on.

Gaurīpaṭṭa

The pedestal on which Śiva-liṅga is erected. It looks like the female organ which it symbolises. It is also known by the name *yoni* or female organ.

Gokula

The abode of Kṛṣṇa. In Vaiṣṇavite Tantras this place has been equated with *sahasrāra-padma. Brahmasaṃhitā,* 2-4.

Grahītrālambanā

Attitude of devotion marked by non-difference from the deity, just as a baby in the womb is inseparable from its mother.

Grāhaṇālambanā

Attitude of devotion marked by the feeling of a baby below two years who knows none but its mother.

Grahitralambana

Attitude of devotion marked by a non-difference from the deity, just as a baby in the womb is inseperable from its mother.

Grāhyālambanā

Attitude of devotion marked by the feeling of a baby between three and five years that demands everything of its mother.

Gṛhāvadhūta

Tantric *sādhaka* with house-holder's life. He who is with clothes and with wife, who is a thinker, an aspirant and a pure entity, who is devoted to his teacher, wise, internally and externally faithful, accustomed with Yogic practices, free from passions and is pure in soul by knowledge, is known as *Gṛhāvadhūta*. *Prāṇatoṣaṇī*, VII. 7, p. 532.

Guhyasādhanā

Observance of secret rituals, meant for the aspirants of the Vīra stage. The symbolic features are to be understood from the teacher. These rituals are performed in secret *cakra*-assembly. Uninitiated persons are not entitled to participate. *Niruttara tantra*, X.

Guptatarayoginī

Collective name of the goddesses serving as Āvaraṇadevatā of the mystic diagram known as *āṣṭadalapadma*. *Gandharvatantra*, V. 96.

Gupti

Term for keeping the *mantra* to be uttered in secret. *Tantrasāra*, p. 54.

Guru

The preceptor or teacher who is the pivot of Tantric Sādhanā. *Guru* is one who dispels darkness. *Kulārṇava*, XVII. The characteristics of *guru* are recorded in the *Rudrayāmala*, *Uttara*, II, *Prāṇatoṣaṇī*, II. 2; VI. 4; *Kulārṇava*, XIII; *Tantrarāja*, I; *Gandharvatantra*, XXVI; *Śāradātilaka*, II., etc. For female *guru* see *Rudrayāmala*, *Uttara*, II. Characteristics of false *guru* : *Prāṇatoṣaṇī*, II. 2; *Tantrasāra*, p. 2. Methods for recognising good teachers: *Mahānirvāṇa*, XV. 139. Rāghava on *Śāradātilaka*, II. 143-4; The teacher and the student should test each other mutually. *Kulārṇava*, XI, XIV. *Prapañcasāra*, XXXVI. 50; *Tantrasārā*, 3; Divinity of *guru*: *Prāṇatoṣaṇī* II. 22; *Kulārṇava*, XIII; *Kāmākhyātantra*, IV. To be propitiated, worshipped and served. *Prāṇatoṣaṇī*, II. 2; *Kaulāvalīnirṇaya*, X; Complete self-surrender to the *guru* is needed: *Paraśurāmakalpasūtra*, X. 74; *Śāktānandataraṅgiṇī*, II. His mere command leads to liberation: *Kaulāvalinirṇaya*, X. Even if he commands the perfomance of any low work it should be done. Rāmeśvara on *Paraśurāmakalpasūtra*, X. 75: Meditation of *guru* is also recommended. *Prāṇatoṣaṇī*, III.1; Hymns for worshipping *guru*; *Gandharvatantra*, VI. 19-25: *Śāradātilaka*, II; Duties of the student; *Kulārṇava*, XII; Gifts to be offered: *Śāradātilaka*, II; The best from of *guru* is Kaula-*guru* : *Mahānirvāṇa*, X. 200-1.

Guru-catuṣṭaya

Four classes of teachers—*guru, paramaguru, parāparaguru* and *parameṣṭhiguru*—conceived of as identical with Śiva. *Nirvāṇa-tantra*, III.

Gurudhyāna

Meditation of the *guru* who is to be conceived of as a god of white complexion with two hands in *varada* and *abhaya* posture and with Śakti on his left side. *Tantrasāra*, p. 78.

Guru Pātra

Pot of wine. *Kaulāvalinirṇaya*, III.

Hādividyā: Hādimata

Vidyā (knowledge, *mantra*, deity) emanating from Kāmarājavīja. *Ha* is the symbol of Śiva after which the school is designated. *Hakārāt Śivarūpatvaṃ tad-hādimatamīrtiam, Śaktisaṅgama*, Tārā, LVIII. 81. This school was influential in Kerala and Kāśmīra.

Hākinī

The presiding goddess (Śakti) of the *ajñā-cakra*. She is six-faced and white in complexion. *Ṣaṭcakranirūpaṇa.*

Haṃsa

A symbolic *mantra* in the form of inhaling (*haṃ*) and exhaling (*saḥ*) of breath. *Haṃ* is the symbol of Vindu (Puruṣa, Male Principle of creation) and *Saḥ* of Visarga (Prakṛti, the Female Principle of creation). Kālīcaraṇa on *Ṣaṭcakranirūpaṇa*, XLIII.

Haṃsamantra

Name of the *mantra*, based on *haṃ* and *saḥ* symbolism, for the awakening of *kuṇḍalinī*.

Haṃsapāda

See Hārdhakalā.

Haṃsapīṭha

The region of Haṃsa supposed to exist within the pericarp of the lotus of *sahasrāra* (the highest cerebral region). It is indicated by the *A- Ka-Tha* triangle and marked by the letters *Ha-La-Kṣa.* In this region the aspirant should meditate on the *guru* as the form of Śiva. Kālīcaraṇa on *Padukāpañcaka,* I.

Haragaurīsṛṣṭi

Chemical processing of mercury and mica for making drugs of immortality.

Hārdhakalā

Sex organ drawn on mystic diagrams. It is also known as *haṃsa-pāda* or *yoni.* Hārdhakalā is also the name of the wave of bliss arising out of Śiva-Śakti union.

Haṭhayoga

A form of physical exercise for making the body so disciplined as to serve all spiritual purposes. In the *Yogaśikhopaniṣat,* I. 133 it is described as the unity of the Sun (*Ha*) and Moon (*Ṭha*). In the *Haṭhayogapradīpikā,* I. 10 it is regarded as the source of all forms of Yoga.

Hlādinī

The blissful Śakti of the Supreme Being according to the Vaiṣṇavite Tantra. It is symbolised by Rādhā. *Caitanyacaritāmṛta,* I. 1. 5.

Homa

Offering oblations into the fire for the attainment of various purposes of different kinds like *sthūla* (gross), *sūkṣma* (subtle), and *parā* (transcendental) or *bāhya* (external) and *antara* (internal) or *nigraha* (black acts) and *saumya* (beneficial) and so on. *Mātṛkābheda,* XI. 8; *Puraścaryārṇava,* VI, p. 515; *Tantrarāja,* XXIX-XXXII; *Tantrasāra,* IV; *Śāradātilaka,* XVII-XVIII; *Tārābhakti-sudhārṇava,* pp. 247ff.

Hotrī Dīkṣā

A form of initiation in which the *guru* offers *homa* for purifying the six quarters. Rāghava on *Śāradātilaka,* V. 127-40.

Icchāsiddhi
The spiritual attainment from the rituals of *trikoṇacakra*. *Nitya-ṣoḍaśikārṇava*, VIII. 170.

Icchopāya
Otherwise known as Śāmbhavopāya it is the power of will which develops from pure knowledge. *Tantrāloka*, I. 146.

Iḍā
One of the fourteen principal nerves. As the symbol of moon it is situated on the left side of the spinal cord on the right of which is situated *piṅgalā* as the symbol of the sun. *Ṣaṭcakra-nirūpaṇa*, I. It is of white colour and representative of the *amṛta* (life-giving power) aspect of Śakti.

Iddhi
Iddhi or attainment of miraculous power mentioned in Buddhist texts like *Brahmājaḷa-sutta*, I. 26; *Mahāvagga*, VI. 24; *Cullavagga*, V. 8, etc.

Indrayoni
Name of a nerve-plexus situated between the *viśuddha* and *ājñā cakras*.

Iṣitvasiddhi
The spiritual attainment from the rituals of Caturdasāra. *Nityaṣoḍaśikārṇava*, VIII. 149.

Iṣṭadevatā
The personal deity.

Iṣṭamantra
The secret *mantra* imparted to the aspirant by the *guru*.

Itaraliṅga
One of the three forms of *liṅga* or phallus, symbol of Śiva, others being *bāṇa* and *svayambhū*. It is connected with *ajñā-cakra*. *Śāradātilaka*, IV.

Jaḍaśakti

The material cause of creation.

Jāgrata

The waking state.

Janana

Procreation. The term is also used in the sense of processing a *mantra*, its gradual recovery from the *mātṛkāyantra*. *Tantrasāra*, p. 54.

Jaṅgama

A Śaiva sect mentioned in Ānandagiri's *Śaṅkaravijaya*.

Japa

Taking within and muttering of the syllables in terms of the identity of *guru*, *mantra* and *devatā*. *Puraścaryārṇava*, VI, p. 541; *Yogasūtra*, I. 28; *Kulārṇava*, XVII. It is a must for the aspirant. *Śaktisaṅgama*, Tārā, XLVI. 2-3; *Gandharvatantra*, XVIII. 3-4. It is an easy process of spiritual attainment, *Gandharvatantra*, XXIX. 9; *Kulārṇava*, XV. It is of three kinds—*vyakta* (manifested), *avyakta* (unmanifested) and *sukṣma* (subtle), otherwise called *vācika*, *upāṃṣu* and *mānasa*. *Rudrayāmala*, *Uttara*, XXVI. The first is loud utterance to be heard by everyone; the second is whispering to be heard only by the practitioner himself; and the third is purely mental to be heard by none. *Puraścaryārṇava*, VI, p. 541. There are other three categories of *japa* —*nitya* (to be done everyday), *naimittika* (to be done occasionally) and *kāmya* (to be done for any special purpose). Rāghava on *Śāradātilaka*, IV. 55-6.

Japamālā

Necklace made of *rudrākṣa* and other articles for counting the number of recitation.

Japasamarpaṇa

The last feature of *japa* ritual. After the *japa* is complete, its result is to be surrendered to the deity. *Śyāmārahasya*, III.

Japayoga

Mental concentration with the help of *japa*.

Jātasūtaka

The born-child. Since *mantra* is a living entity it is conceived of as a new born child during initiation. *Śaktisaṅgama*, Tārā, XLV. 7.

Jīvacakra

A type of spiritual exercise meant only for those who have attained the status of Vīra. This exercise consists of Bhāvayoga. *Śaktisaṅgama, Sundarī*, I. 197-200.

Jīvana

Term for processing of *mantra*. *Tantrasāra*, p. 54.

Jīvanmukti

Liberation within the span of bodily existence, a very important Tantric concept. He who has a complete grasp of the knowledge of the self, has dispelled from within the darkness of false knowledge by constant practice and meditation and is reaping the fruits of his *karma*, may be called a *jīvanmukta*. The term is also used in the sense of immortality which is possible by transforming the material body through certain chemical processes into a divine one. *Sarvadarśanasaṃgraha*, Ch. IX.

Jīvaśakti

Name of *kuṇḍalinī* which works as the energising force within the human body. *Tantrarāja tantra*, XXX. 34.

Jīvātmā

Individual soul.

Jīvatattva

Also known as Puruṣatattva, it denotes *jiva* or individual fettered with *niyati* (destiny), *kāla* (time), *rāga* (dissatisfaction), *kalā* (conceit) and *avidyā* (ignorance). Rāmeśvara on *Paraśurāmakalpa-sūtra*, I. 4.

Jñāna

Knowledge which exterminates suffering resulting from *avidyā* or false notions. It is basically of two kinds—*Bauddha* (intellectual) and *Pauruṣa* (intuitive). By meritorious practices the latter is developed within the human being which is conducive to *mokṣa* or liberation, but it should be supplemented by some sort of intellectual attainment which is possible through study of scriptures, deep meditation and so on. *Tantrāloka,* I.41ff.

Jñānabhūmika

Seven stages of knowledge often identified with seven *ācāras.*

Jñānacatuṣka

Four means of knowledge—*anupāya, śāmbhavopāya, śāktopāya* and *āṇavopāya.*

Jñānahoma

The *homa* offered during internal worship (*antarapūjā*). *Nityātantra* quoted in the *Prāṇatoṣaṇī,* VII. 4, p. 535.

Jñānayoga

The form of Yoga which yields knowledge of the *tattvas.*

Jñānopāya

The means through which *nirvikalpa* (complete) knowledge is reached from *vikalpa* (lesser degree) knowledge. It is also known as *śāktopāya.*

Jyotirdhyāna

Meditation of the self supposed to reside on the *kuṇḍalinī* coil in the *mūlādhāra* in the form of light. It is also known as *tejodhyāna. Gheraṇḍa,* VI. 17.

Kahādimata

One of the three principal Tantric schools mentioned in the *Śaktisaṅgama,* Tārā, LVIII. 81-2. It is also known as Tāriṇīmata. Ibid., Kālī, VI. 125.

Kādimata

One of the principal Tantric schools mentioned in the *Śaktisaṅgama,* Tārā, LVIII, 81-2. Its theoretical doctrines make the letter *ka* their symbol. This school is also known as Vīrādanuttara and Kālīmata. It was popular in the Gauḍa region. Ibid., Kālī, V. 24-6.

Kādividyā

Special knowledge which derives its name from the first letter of Vāgbhava-vija (*Ka, Ē, Ī, La, Hrāñ*). Com. on *Sāradā*, I. 1.

Kākinī

The presiding goddess of the *anāhata-cakra*, three-eyed, yellow in colour, having her abode within the pericarp of a twelve-petalled red lotus. *Ṣaṭcakranirūpaṇa*, XXIV.

Kāla

Time and doctrine of time. According to Rāmeśvara's com. on *Paraśurāmakalpasūtra*, I. 4 it is said that the eternalism of Śiva, owing the influence of six *bhāvavikāras* or conditions, becomes contracted and is known as Kāla. The goddess Kālī is described as Kālagatā Śakti and it is in the sense of time. It is said that during dissolution Kāla or Mahākala devours the universe, but the goddess even devours *kāla*, and hence she is known as Kālī. *Mahānirvāṇa*, IV. 30-2.

Kalā

Evolutes of *varṇa*. In Tantra every letter or *varṇa* symbolically reflects an aspect of the Great Mother. From the three groups of letters—Saumya, Saura and Āgneya—thirty-eight *kalās* emanated, sixteen from Saumya, twelve from Saura and ten from Āgneya. *Prapañcasara*, III. 11-12. A *kalā* is identical with the *varṇa* from which it evolves. Rāghava on *Śāradātilaka* I.111. According to another tradition there are fifty *kalās* having emanated from the five parts of Praṇava- *A, U, Ma, Vindu* and *Nāda*. Ibid., II. 17. In the Tantras the term *kalā* has also been used in other senses. It denotes Prakṛti, Śakti and Māyā. Ibid., I. 6; I. 15; *Prapañcasāra*, I.26. In the commentary of the *Haṭhayogapradīpikā*, IV. 1 *kalā* is described as *nādaikadeśaḥ*, i.e. a portion of *nāda*.

Kālacakra

A minor nerve-cycle which is situated above the *viśuddha* and below the *ājñā*. It is also known as *lalanācakra*. *Kālacakra* denoting wheel of time is the principal god of the Tantric Buddhist Kālacakrayāna.

Kālāmukha

A Vāmācārī Śaiva sect, akin to the Kāpālikas, mentioned by Rāmānuja, Keśava Kaśmīrī, Haribhadra and others. Epigraphical evidences testify to their existence at Kanchi, Tiruvariyur, Melpadi, Kodumbalur and other places.

Kalāmūrti

Complete or fragmentary forms of the figure of the Śakti of the deity. In Tantra the Śakti of any deity is divided in sixteen *kalās*. When the figure is complete in sixteen *kalās* it is known as Pūrṇakalāmūrti, and the parts are known as *kalāmūrti*. Further subdivisions are known as *aṃśamūrti. Garland of Letters*, p. 194.

Kalānyāsa

Feeling the existence of deity in different parts of the body of the Śakti or female partner of the aspirant. *Tantrasāra*, p. 628.

Kalā(vatī) Dīkṣā

A form of initiation in which the *ācārya* locates the existence of five *kalās* known as *nivṛtti, pratiṣṭhā, vidyā, śānti* and *śāntyatīta* in different parts of the body of his disciple, and having meditated on them anoints him. *Śāradātilaka*, V. 121-6.

Kalātattva

The contracted manifestation of Śiva in individuals. *Tantrāloka*, IX. 155.

Kālīkula

A Tantric school which lays supreme importance on the cult of Kālī. The scriptures of this school are *Kālajñana, Kālottara, Mahākālasaṃhitā, Vyomakeśasaṃhitā, Jayadrathayāmala, Uttaratantra* and *Śaktisaṅgamatantra (Kālīkhaṇḍa)*.

Kālīnaya

A name of the Krama doctrine.

Kālīmata

See Kādimata.

Kalpataru

Wish-fulfilling tree. In the Tantras the term is used to denote the *anāhatacakra* which gives effect more than it is desired. *Ṣaṭcakranirūpaṇa*, XXII.

Kāmakalā

Sexual art. In sophisticated Tantric approach Kāma is the equilibrium of Prakāśa (static) and Vimarśa (dynamic) Śakti of Śiva. *Setubandha* com. on *Nityaṣoḍasikārṇava*, VI. 10-11. Technically *kāmakālā* is conceived of as the combination of the three *vindus* of Ravi, Agni and Soma. Conceived as Mahātripurasundarī it is of the nature of consciousness (*cit*), bliss (*ānanda*), will (*icchā*), knowledge (*jñāna*) and action (*kriyā*). *Cidvelli* com. on *Kāmakalāvilāsa*, VII. In human body *kāmakālā* is said to reside in the form of a triangle within the *candramaṇḍala* (lunar orb) of the pericarp of the down-faced white lotus known as *sahasrārapadma* situated in the cerebral region. Kālīcaraṇa on *Ṣaṭcakranirūpaṇa*, XL.

Kāmākhyāyoni

Name of the soft and bright triangle on the *mūlādhāra*-lotu Viśvanātha on *Ṣaṭcakranirūpaṇa*, VIII.

Kāmarājakūṭa

Totality of *Kāmarāja-vīja*. *Kūṭa* means total, and hence it is the total recitation of the letters belonging to the said category.

Kāmarājavīja

Name of the letters *Ha, Sa, Ka, Ha, La, Hrāñ*, each symbolising an aspect of Śakti or Vidyā. *Siddheśvarīmata* quoted in the com. of *Śāradātilaka*, I. 1.

Kāmatattva

Theoretical interpretation of sex symbolism. According to *Tantrāloka*, III. 150 the effect of sexual intercourse brings a mental detachment which is conducive to obtaining pure knowledge.

Kāmika

Name of the seat for *kāmya-japa*, i.e. recital of *mantra* to attain a certain purpose. It is variously made of the skin of deer, tiger and ram and also of cane. *Puraścaryārṇava*, VI. p. 420.

Kāmyapūjā

Worship for the attainment of certain purposes. *Gandharvatantra*, XXII. 12.

Kanda

Root of the *nāḍīs* or nerves. According to the *Śivasaṃhitā*, V. 79-80 it is situated near the *yoni* or the female sex organ. It looks like egg of a bird. Kālīcaraṇa on *Ṣaṭcakranirūpaṇa*, I.

Kanphat Yogi

A sect of ascetics believing in theories and practices of Haṭhayoga and Nāthasiddha tradition.

Kāpālī, Kāpālikā

Ramya-Sakti, which is personification of that aspect of Śakti which becomes sexually passionate on seeing the performance of her rites. *Niruttaratantra*, XV. In the *Uttaratantra* such aspects of Śakti are mentioned as Kulanāyikā. *Tantraśāra*, p. 627.

Kāpālikā

An extremist Śaiva sect, committed to the Tantric cult of Śakti, mentioned in Mahendravarman's *Mattavilāsa*, Bhavabhūti's *Mālatīmādhava*. Ānandagiri's Śaṅkaravijaya, Ramanuja's Śrībhāsyā, etc. According to the *Śaṅkaravijaya* they did not believe in the Vedas. They used to drink wine in human skulls which they considered as the elixir of life resulting out of the union of Śiva and Śakti. The *Gorakṣa-siddhāntasaṃgraha*, pp. 16ff connects Kāpālikism with Nathism. Reference to a Kāpālika text known as *Kāpāla-agama* is found in *Sutasaṃhita*, I.1.12. The Śakta conception of Kāpālika is recorded in the *Śaktisaṅgamatantra*, Kālī, VIII. 9-10.

Kāpālabhāti

One of the *ṣaṭkarmas* or six acts required for Yogic exercise, others being *dhauti, vasti, neti, laulika* and *trātaka*. Kāpālabhāti is of three kinds—Vāmakrama, Vyutkrama and Sitkrama. These practices prevent diseases arising out of cold and catarrh. *Gheraṇḍa*, I.13-60; *Haṭhayogapradīpikā*, II. 24-35.

Karamālā

Parts of fingers used for counting the number of the *mantra* during its recital. *Puraścaryārṇava*, VI, pp. 447-9. *Tantrasāra*, pp. 27ff.

Kāraṇa

Tantric term for wine. *Kāraṇa* means cause. In the *Kaivalyatantra* it is said that since wine is the cause of all knowledge of *dharma*, *artha*, *kāma* and *mokṣa*, it is known as *kāraṇa*. *Prāṇatoṣaṇī*, VII. 2. p. 510.

Karmayoga

A type of Yogic exercise.

Kāraṇadeha, -Śarīra

A form of subtle body capable of containing the doctrines of Śiva.

Karanyāsa

Feeling the deity in the palms. The fingers and the back of the palm are used to invoke deities in the forms of letters. *Tantrasāra*, pp. 88ff.

Kartari

Mantra consisting of two letters. *Tantrarāja*, XXXV. 28-9.

Kāruṇikasiddhānti

Name of a Śaiva-tantric sect which was theoretically akin to the Kāpālikas.

Kavaca

That which saves the body from the weapons of the enemy. *Kavaca* means armour. In Tantra the term is used to denote a special mantra which protects the body and soul of the aspirant. This *mantra* is to be recited during worship and its written version is to be carried on the body as a talisman. *Kavacas* are connected with the names of different Tantric deities and they are supposed to be more efficacious than worship, meditation, etc. *Syāmārahasya*, IV.

Kāryavindu

Vindu in effect. Of the various connotations of *vindu*, one is that which is the contracted form of the conscious Śakti when it desires to create. *Prapañcasāra*, I.41. This is casual or *kāranavindu* and when it manifests into effect it is known as *kāryavindu*.

Kāśmīra Sampradāya

Tantrics of the Kāśmīra region whose theories and practices are described in the *Śaktisaṅgamatantra, Sundarī*, III, 11ff. and *Puraścaryārṇava*, IX, p. 866. They depend also on the texts of Kashmir Śaivism.

Kaulamārga

The last of the seven Tantric *ācāras* or ways of spiritual exercise. It is so influential that it is often equated with Tantrism itself. It is same as Kulācāra or Kulamārga, Kaula being the derivative of Kula with *ṣna* suffix. For the definition of Kaula from a variety of view-points see *Saubhāgyabhāskara* on *Lalitāsahasranāma*, CXLIV; *Kaulamārgarahasya*, p. 5; *Nirvāṇa-tantra*, XI; *Kulārṇavatantra*, XVII. In practice it is the exclusive cult of Śakti as the Female Principle with the rituals of Five Ms, viz, *madya* or wine, *māṃsa* or flesh, *matsa* or fish, *mudrā* or cereals and *maithuna* or sexual union, the aim being the realisation of the *sāmarasya* of Śiva and Śakti within the self. In *Rudrayāmāla, Uttara*, XVII and other Tantras it is said to have been imported from China. In *Devībhāgavata*, XII. 9.96 and other texts it is regarded as anti-Vedic. Śrīvidyā and her forms are the principal objects of this cult. *Kaulamārgarahasya*, p. 250; *Kulacuḍāmaṇi*, I. 1-2. Of the two categories wet and dry, *Prāṇatoṣaṇi*, VII. 4, p. 531; for different Kaula sects see *Kaulajñānanirṇaya* (ed. Bagchi), XIV, XVI, XXI; for qualification and competence see *Mahānirvāṇa*, XIV. 184ff; for the nature of exercises see *Kaulāvalinirṇaya*, XXI. 189-90; physical and mental fitness required, *Gandharvatantra*, XXXIV. 14ff; about knowledge, *Kulārṇava*, II; *Niruttara*, XII; Rameśvara on *Paraśurāmakalpasūtra*, III, 31; VIII. *Mahānirvāṇa*, IV. 38; greatness of *Mahānirvāṇa*, X. 105-6; Ramésvara on *Parāśurāma-kalpasūtra*, V. 22; characteristics of a Kaula, *Kulārṇava*, IX; *Mahānirvāṇa*, VII. 94; X. 108; attitude towards women, *Kulārṇava*, XI; *Kaulāvalinirṇaya*, X; *Gandharva*, XXXVI. 9; *Śaktisaṅgama*, Tārā, XIII. 43-7; attitude of a Kaula, *Puraścaryārṇava*, IX, p. 861; *Prāṇatoṣaṇī*, VII.4, p. 532; praise of Kaulamārga, *Mahānirvāṇa*, IV. 43; XIV. 179; relation to Yoga, *Rudrayāmāla, Uttara* XIII, XXII; secrecy, *Prāṇatoṣaṇī*, VII. 4, p. 531; *Tantrasāra*, p. 623; warning against misuse of Kaulamārga, com. on *Parāśurāmakalpasūtra*, III. 31; X. 56; *Mahānirvāṇa*, I. 58-60.

Kaulika

Followers of Kula or Kaula school. For their characteristic see *Nirvāṇatantra*, XI; *Kulārṇava*, II. XVII.

Kaulikī Śakti

Same as Kulanāyikā, the Śakti within the heart which is stainless and independent. It is also known by the names *anuttarā, parā, pratibhā, khecarī*, etc. *Tantrāloka*, III. 67, 143, 187; *Parātriṃśikā*, p. 61.

Kaulikī Siddhi

Name of *mokṣa* according to the Kula-mata of Kashmir Śaivism. The experience of *kula* or the ultimate reality through body and soul brings this form of liberation. *Parātriṃśikā*, p. 36.

Kaulinī

See under *Kulayoṣit*.

Kerala Sampradāya

Name of a Tantric sect the followers of which are scattered in nineteen countries from Āryāvarta to the sea. *Śaktisaṅgama*, Kālī, IV. 3-6. Their theories and practices are described in the *Siddhāntasaṅgraha*. See *Puraścaryārṇava*, IX, p. 867.

Kha-Puṣpa

Menstrual blood.

Khecarī Mudrā

Name of Yogic posture which bestows spiritual attainment and enables one to overcome disease and death. *Gheraṇḍa*, III. 1-3; *Haṭhayogapradīpikā*, III. 67. It is required for the meditation of Tripurasundarī. *Mudrānighaṇṭu*, 14-16.

Khecarī Śakti

Same as Kauliki-Śakti. *Kha* denotes *brahman*, and that power which moves (*cara*) as the kinetic energy of *brahman* is known Khecarī. Though one and undifferentiated it is manifested in numerous forms. *Parātriṃśikā*, p. 30.

Khecarī Samatā

Identity with Khecarī-Śakti which is the cause of Jīvanmukti.

Kīlaka

Name of a Tantric *nyāsa.*

Kramadīkṣā

A form of Śākta *dīkṣā* in the *mantras* of Kālī, Tārā and Tripurasundarī. It is not for all. *Prāṇatoṣaṇī*, II. 5, p. 143.

Kramamata

A Kashmir Tantric system, the texts of which are mentioned in works like *Tantrāloka, Mahārthamañjarī*, etc. Abhinavagupta's *Kramakeli* and *Kramastotra* are expositions of this system. There are two streams of this system. One is Śaiva oriented and the other is Śākta-oriented. In this system Kālī is regarded as the ultimate reality. See *Tantrāloka*, IV, 157ff.

Kriyāśakti

Three forms of occult power—*manojavitva* (doing any act at any time), *kāmarūpitva* (assuming any form at will) and *vikaraṇadharmitva* (infinite mental power to consume and transmit). *Sarvadarśanasaṃgraha*, VI. 56-7.

Kriyāvatī Dīkṣā

One of the forms of Tantric *dīkṣā* in which many rituals are involved. The *guru* purifies the six *adhvas* of the disciple's body, infuses into him his own consciousness and anoints him with different rites. *Prāṇatoṣaṇī*, II. 5, pp. 140-2.

Kriyāyoga

A form of Yogic exercise prescribed for those who have attained the status of Puṣpacakra-vīra. *Śaktisaṅgama, Sundarī*, I. 197- 200.

Kriyopāya

Same as *Āṇavopāya.*

Kṣititattva

The conception of earth as one of the five traditional material elements. This element is said to reside in the *mūlādhāra* within the human body. *Ṣaṭcakranirūpaṇa*, XL.

Kula

Clan or family. In the *Saubhāgyabhāskara* com. on *Lalitā-sahasranāma,* I, the term is used in the sense of a spiritual lineage from Parāmaśiva to one's own *guru.* This lineage is equated with *gotra* in *Kulārṇava,* XVII. Kaulamārga or Kaulācāra is thus a way of *sādhanā* restricted within the spiritual lineage of a particular group of Tantric teachers.

Kulācāra

See under Kaulamārga.

Kuladravya

Same as Kulatattvs or Pañcatattva. *Kaulāvalinirṇaya,* VIII.

Kulajñāna

The knowledge in Kaulamārga, admission to which is highly restricted. Rāmeśvara on *Parāśurāmakalpasūtra,* III. 31.

Kulakaulayoginī

Presiding deities of *cakras* belonging to Bahirdasāra class. *Gandharvatantra,* V. 102.

Kulakuṇḍalinī

See under *Kuṇḍalinī.*

Kulamārga

See under Kaulamārga.

Kulamata

See under Kaulamārga. In Kashmir Saivism it is regarded as a left-handed way in which the rituals of Five Ms are excluded.

Kulāmṛta

The nectar which flows from the cerebral *candramaṇḍala* down the inner body of the aspirant when *kuṇḍalinī* pierces *ṣaṭcakra.*

Kulanāyikā

The Śakti within the heart. *Parātriṃśikā,* p. 61.

Kulapatha

The way through which *kuṇḍalinī* pierces the *ṣaṭcakra.* See *Saundaryalaharī,* X.

Kulapadma

A six-petalled lotus within the Sahasrāra.

Kulasaṅketa

Technical mysteries of Kaulamārga. These are Kramasaṅketa, Pūjāsaṅketa, Mantrasaṅketa, Tantrasaṅketa and Mantrayantralikhanasaṅketa. Without initiation into all these the practices of Kaulamārga are dangerous. *Niruttara*, XII; *Kulārṇava*, II; Rameśvara on *Parāśurāmakalpasūtra*, VII. 1.

Kulatattva

Another name of Pañcatattva or Pañcamakāra (Five Ms). *Yoginītantra*, Pūrva, VI.

Kulāvadhūta

See under Avadhūta.

Kulayoṣit

Also known as Kaulinī, it is the name of *Kuṇḍalinī* śakti situated in the *mūlādhāracakra*. Lakṣmīdhara on *Saundaryalaharī*, VIII, XLI.

Kumārīpūjā

Worship of a virgin as representative of the great goddess.

Kumbhaka

Breath-control. *Tantrasāra*, pp. 85ff. Eight types of *kumbhaka* are mentioned in the *Gherandasaṃhitā*, V. 46. These are *sahita, sūryabheda, śitalī, bhastrikā, bhrāmarī, murcchā* and *kevalı*. The *Hathayogapradīpikā*, II. 44 adds two more types, *sitkari* and *plāvinī*.

Kuṇḍa-Golodbhava

Menstrual blood sacred to the goddess. Kuṇḍodbhava is the blood of a married woman and Golodbhava that of a widow.

Kuṇḍalinī

The serpent power remaining latent in the Mūlādhāra. *Tantrarāja*, XXX. 65; *Gheraṇḍa*, III. 44. As the source of all energy *kuṇḍalinī* reveals itsself when roused by Yogic exercise. *Ṣaṭcakranirūpaṇa*, XI; *Śāradātilaka*, XXV. 27. It has two forms dynamic or kinetic and static or potential. For various interpretations of *kuṇḍalinī*, its awakening and function, see Lakṣmīdhara on *Saundarya-laharī*, X; *Rudrayāmala, uttara*, XXI; *Siddhasiddhāntasaṃgraha*, IV. 20ff; *Prāṇatoṣaṇī*, I. 6, pp. 41ff; *Tantrarāja*, XXX; *Mātṛkābheda*, XIV, etc.

Kūṭa
Collection, a collective entity. The term is applied as a suffix to denote utterances of *mantras* and letters.

Laghimā
One of the ten *siddhis* or miraculous attainments. *Nityaṣoḍaśikārṇava*, I. 166-8.

Lākinī
The presiding goddess of the *maṇipura-cakra*.

Lalanācakra
See *kālacakra, lambikāgra*.

Lambikāgra
A minor nerve-cycle situated above the *viśuddha* and below the *ājñā*. It is also known as *lalanā* and *kālacakra*.

Latā
The female partner of the aspirant, also known as *dūtī*.

Latāsādhanā
Pañcamakāra rituals with female partner.

Layasiddhiyogasamādhi
The state of absolute bliss. The aspirant through *yonimudrā* will acquire spiritual power and have pleasure of the coital type leading to a realisation of a sense of non-duality with the supreme being. *Gheraṇḍa*, VII. 12-13.

Layobhogāṅgavidhāna
The method of separating three fetters—*āṇava* (caused by material ingredients), *kārma* (caused by the effects of deeds) and *māyīya* (caused by false knowledge) from the body of an indi-

vidual. It is a part of Smārti dīkṣā. Rāghava on *Śāradātilaka*, V. 127-40; *Purāścaryārṇava*, V, p. 392.

Layayoga

The higher form of Haṭhayoga which destroys (*laya*) all forms of mundane desire. It is an experience of eternal bliss in which the mind totally merges in the Supreme Being. *Yogaśikhopaniṣat*, I. 134-6; *Haṭhayogapradīpikā*, IV. 31-4.

Liṅga

Male generative organ worshipped in phallic symbols. *Liṅga* is the symbol of Śiva while *yoni* or female organ is that of the Devī.

Liṅgapuṣpa

Name of Raktakaravī flower, used as a substitute for *maithuna*, the other item being *yonipuṣpa* which is blue Aparājitā flower. Com. on *Paraśurāmakalpasūtra*, X. 63.

Liṅgatraya

Three types of Śiva-phallus known as Itara, Svayambhū and Bāṇa which are symbolically connected with the nerve-plexuses within the human body.

Lipinyāsa

See Mātṛkānyāsa.

Lopāmudrā

The *mantras* of Śrīvidyā consisting of fifteen symbolic letters. *Tantrasāra*, pp. 242-3.

Madhyamā

Name of a special type of sound which is between Paśyantī and Vaikharī. Madhyamā is that which is within and connected with intellect. Com. on *Prapañcasāra*, II.43. It is also called as a state of equilibrium of Parā and Paśyantī. *Cidvallī* on *Kāmakalāvilāsa*, XXVI. According to Bhāskara-raya, *brahmān* as sound having manifested as Paśyantī becomes specially articulated with the help of wind in the heart region as *nāda*. This state is known as Madhyamā which is the third stage of sound. *Saubhāgyabhāskara* on *Lalitāsahasranāma*, 99.

Madhyamasrota Tantra

Tantric works belonging to the middle current. These are *Vijaya, Niśvāsa, Svāyambhūva, Vātula, Vīrabhadra, Raurava, Makuṭa* and *Vīreśa.*

Madya

The first of the Five Ms. It is wine, various types of which are described in the *Paraśurāmakalpasūtra,* X. 62. Paiṣṭī, Gauḍi and Mādhvī are the three best types as described in the *Kulārṇava,* V and *Mahānirvāṇa,* VI. 2-3. Thirteen types of wine used by the Gauḍa-sampradāya are mentioned in the *Śaktisaṅgamatantra,* Kālī, IX. 46. Any type of wine, purified by *mantra,* is fit for *sādhanā. Mahānirvāṇa,* IV. 4. Milk, honey and sugar-juice are regarded as substitutes for wine. Ibid., VIII. 170-1. Symbolically *madya* is described as the nectar-essence of the union of Śiva-Śakti flowing from the highest cerebral region. *Kulārṇava,* V.

Mahācakra

See under *cakra* and *bhairavī-cakra.* It is one of the five *cakra* rituals, others being Rāja, Devī, Vīra and Paśu. In *mahācakra* mother, sister, daughter, daughter-in-law, and wife of the aspirant are to be worshiped as *pañca-śakti,* or Śakti in her five forms. *Niruttara,* X.

Mahācīnācāra, Mahācīnakrama

See under Cīnācāra and Cīnakrama.

Mahākāraṇa Deha (Sarīra)

Subtle body an individual acquires by *sādhanā.*

Mahāmāṃsa

Flesh of eight animals—cow, man, ram, horse, buffalo, boar, goat and deer—regarded sacred to the deity. *Śyāmārahasya,* III; *Tantrasāra,* p. 630.

Mahāmudrā

A form of bodily posture. *Gheraṇḍa,* III. 1-3. Mahamudra also stands for women generally and also the female organ.

Mahānāda

Same as Śabdabrahma (*brahman* in the form of sound) and its constituent Anāhata-nāda (so called because this sound has a spontaneous origin having nothing to do with that resulting from the rubbing of one article with another). Mahānāda is also different from that form of Nāda which is produced from the union of *kāranavindu* and Vīja.

Mahāpaśu
The uninitiated individual. *Niruttara*, XII.

Mahāsāmrājya Dīkṣā
A form of initiation which is precondition of Kaula *sādhanā*.

Mahāsetu
Name of a *mantra*.

Mahat
The Sāṅkhya category of intelligence as evolute of Prakṛti, also known as *buddhi*. In the Tantras it is traced to Śabdabrahma. *Prapañcasāra*, I. 45; Rāghava on *Śāradātilaka*, I. 17.

Mahāvidyā
See under Daśa Mahāvidyā.

Mahāvīja
See under Vīja.

Mahāvindu
See under *Vindu*.

Mahāyantra
See under *Yantra*.

Mahāyoni
Female sex organ. It is the supposed triangle of the *sahasrāracakra*. *Kaulamārgarahasya*, p. 256.

Mahimāsiddhi
A kind of miraculous attainment acquired through the rituals of aṣṭadala padma. *Nityaṣoḍaśikārṇava*, VIII.143.

Maithuna

Sexual intercourse which is regarded as one of the Five Ms. For its procedure and reasons see *Mahānirvāṇa*, VI. 10ff; *Prāṇatoṣaṇī*, VII. 4, p. 548. For its substitutes see com. on *Paraśurāmakalpa-sūtra*, X. 63; *Mahānirvāṇa*, VIII. 172-3. For spiritual interpretation see *Kaulamārgarahasya*, pp. 255-6; *Yoginītantra*, Pūrva, VI; *Kulārṇava*, V.

Mala

Fetters, same as Pāśa, the cause of worldly existence and suffering. It is of three types—Āṇava, Kārma and Māyā.

Māṃsa

Flesh which is one of the Five Ms. See under Mahāmāṃsa. It is supposed to be the body of Śiva. Ginger, Garlic, etc., can be used as substitutes.

Mānasa Dīkṣā

See under *Manodīkṣā*

Maṇḍala

A gathering of aspirants for collective functioning of the ritual of the Five Ms. They sit in a circle (*cakra*) with their female partners with the *nāyaka* or *adhīśvara*, the central figure of the rituals and his consort, in the middle. *Kaulāvalinirṇaya*, VIII; *Mahānirvāṇa*, VIII. 154-6. Maṇḍala also denotes tantric diagrams, and there are varieties of such *maṇḍalas* like *Sarvatobhadra*, etc.

Maṇipura

A *cakra* or nerve plexus near the navel region. It is also called *nābhicakra*. It looks like a ten-petalled lotus of blue colour, each petal containing a letter. Within the lotus there is a triangle of the colour of rising sun. The outer sides of the triangle are represented by three svastika symbols. *Ṣaṭcakranirupaṇa*,XIX. This *cakra* is presided over by the goddess Lākinī. Ibid., XXI.

Manodīkṣā

Also known as *mānasa* or *vedhamayī-dīkṣā*, it is a form of initiation only by the *guru's* thought and mental action. *Kulārṇava*, XIV.

Manonmani

A state of transcendental bliss which comes out as a result of *bhaktiyogasamādhi*. *Gheraṇḍa*, VII. 14-15.

Mantra

Śakti or power in the form of sound, words and letters. It is that which is the culture (*man, manan*) of true knowledge for getting rid (*trai, trāṇa*) of wordly fetters. Rāghava on *Śāradātilaka*, VII. 1. *Mantra* is *brahman* or ultimate reality in the form of sound. Letters, words and sentences are its different forms through which Śakti appears in the individual. *Gandharvatantra*, XL. 10; com. on *Tantrarājatantra*, XXVI. 36-43; *Śāradātilaka*, I. 55; II. 57.

Mantra-Adhvā

Blood, to be purified for *sādhanā*. *Adhvā* means constituents of the body which is of six types—*bhuvana* (cerebral organs), *mantra* (blood and flesh), *pada* and *varṇa* (muscles and veins), *dhātu* and *reta* (bones and fluid substances). Rāghava on *Śāradātilaka*, V. 95-6.

Mantracaitanya

Consciousness latent in the *mantra* to be roused by efforts. *Prāṇatoṣaṇī*, IV. 1, p. 222; *Puraścaryārṇava*, VI, p. 528; *Gandharvatantra*, XXIX. 24-5.

Mantrārtha

Understanding of the significance of *mantra*, which is the sense of identity of preceptor, deity and *mantra*. The understanding is threefold—the simple meaning of *mantra*, the belief that every letter of it is the manifestation of the real nature of Śakti and merger of the aspirant in the essence of the object of his exercise. *Puraścaryārṇava*, VI, p. 526; *Tantrarāja*, XXXV. 64-6.

Mantraśakti

The power of *mantra* which is beyond thinking and reasoning. *Paraśurāmakalpasūtra*, I. 8. It is neither good nor bad. It is determined only by the purpose of its application.

Mantrasaṃskāra

Ten ways of purifying *mantras* which are *janana, jīvana, tāḍana, bodhana, abhiṣeka, vimalīkaraṇa, āpyāyana, tarapaṇa, dīpana* and *gupti*. *Tantrasāra*, p. 52.

Mantrasiddhi

Spiritual attainment through *mantras*. Those who have attained it acquire a special brightness of body and an ever-peaceful state of mind. *Puraścaryārṇava*, VI, pp. 557-8.

Mantraśikhā

A purificatory flame roused within the body during the march of *kuṇḍalinī*. *Puraścaryārṇava*, VI, pp. 527-8; *Haṭhayogapradīpikā*, IV. 10.

Mantraśodhana

Purification of *mantra* with *prāṇāyāma* (breath-control) according to the *yonimudrā* process and reciting it one thousand and eight times. Rāghava on *Śāradātilaka*, II.111.

Mantraśuddhi

Purification of *mantra* by reciting the letters from left to right and right to left. *Kulārṇava*, VI.

Mantratanu

Transformed state of body achieved either by Yogic exercise or by the use of drugs. The body of god is also called *mantratanu*.

Mantrayāna

A name of Tantric Buddhism.

Mantrayoga

The *haṃsa* practice of Yoga consisting of inhaling (*haṃ*) and exhaling (*saḥ*) of breath. *Yogaśikhopaniṣat*, I. 130-2.

Māntrīdīkṣā

Initiation in which the *guru*, by *mantras* and rituals, purifies himself and then consecrates the disciple. Rāghava on *Śāradātilaka*, V. 127-40. It requires *kumbha*, *maṇḍala*, and other objects. *Prāṇatoṣaṇī*, II. 4, p. 11.

Māraṇa

The act of killing.

Mātra

A means of *prāṇāyāma. Puraścaryārṇava,* III, p. 161.

Mātṛkā

Divine Mothers. It is also the name of mystic letters.

Mātṛkānyāsa

Feeling the Mātṛkā or Śakti manifested in the form of letters in different parts of the body. It is of two kinds—Antarmātṛkānyāsa and Bahirmātṛkānyāsa. *Tantrasāra,* pp. 88ff.

Mātṛkāvarṇa

The letters from *A* to *Kṣa,* each symbolising an aspect of Śakti or the Great Mother.

Matsya

Fish which is one of the Five Ms. Three types of fish—*uttama, madhyama* and *adhama. Śyāmārahāsya,* III; *Mahānirvāṇa,* VI. 8. Substitutes of *matsya* are cakes made of pulse and other articles. Com. on *Paraśurāmakalpasūtra,* X. 63. Symbolically *matsya* is described as that which destroys the fetters and leads to the way of salvation. *Prāṇatoṣaṇi,* VII. 2, p. 508.

Māyā

Illusion; false knowledge; matter; material cause of creation; etc.

Miśramata

One of the methods of Śrīvidyā cult. *Saubhāgyabhāskara* on *Lalitāsahasranāma,* 144.

Miśravindu

The Vindu produced from the equilibrium of Prakāśa (static) and Vimarśa (kinetic) aspects of Śakti. *Cidvalli* on *Kāmakalāvilāsa,* 6-7.

Mokṣa

Liberation.

Mudrā

Postures of the body, especially of hands, needed for yogic exercise and spiritual attainment. *Gherandasaṃhitā,* III. 1-3, records such *mudrās* as *mahā, nabho, uḍḍhiyāna, jālandhara, mūlabandha, mahābodha, khecarī viparītakārī, yoni, vajroli, śakticālanī, tāḍagī, manḍukī, śāmbhavi, pañcadhāriṇī, aśvinī, pāśini, kākī, mātaṅgī* and *bhujaṅginī.* See also *Haṭhayogapradīpikā,* III. 128. Mudrā is also the name of one of the Five Ms. It denotes fried cereals, geometrical diagrams and women. In Buddhist Tantras the terms *mudrā* and *mahāmudrā* are used exclusively in the sense of woman and of her generative organ.

Mukhaśodhana

Purification of the tongue by *mantras. Prāṇatoṣaṇī,* IV. 1, p. 215.

Mukti

Salvation.

Mūlādhāra

The first of the six nerve plexuses, situated in the lowest extremity of the spinal cord, where the *kuṇḍalinī* is coiled. *Ṣaṭcakranirupaṇa,* V.

Nābhipadma

Name of *maṇipura-cakra. Ṣaṭcakranirupaṇa,* XIX.

Nāda

A term used in Tantra in a variety of senses. Its simple meaning is sound. In Tantric concepts, the Supreme Being (Para Śiva or Pārā Śakti) is soundless and without any vibration. When this Parā Śakti goes to express itself in creation its first vibration is known as Nāda. It is the manifestation of the consciousness of the Supreme Being revealed as sound. This manifestation is thought of in terms of the copulation of Śiva and Śakti (the static and kinetic aspects, also known as Prakāśa and Vimarśa, of the same ultimate reality) and the thrill of the pleasure of this union (*maithuna*) is known as Nāda. The condensed form of Nāda is Vindu. *Śāradātilaka,* I. 6ff; Kālīcaraṇa on *Ṣaṭcakranirupaṇa,* XXXIX; *Prapañcasāra,* I. 41. For other aspects and interpretations see under *Vindu* and *Vīja.*

Nādabrahma

Nāda conceived as *brahman* in the form of primordial sound expressed in Parā, Paśyantī, Madhyamā and Vaikharī. *Cidvālli* on

Kāmakalāvilāsa, IX; Lakṣmīdhara on *Saundaryalaharī*, XLI.

Nāda-Udbhūta

Sixteen *kalās* or Śaktis are said to have been derived from Nāda. These are Nivṛtti, Pratiṣṭhā, Vidyā, Śānti, Indhikā, Dīpikā, Recikā, Mocikā, Parā, Parāparāyanā (Sūkṣmāmṛtā) Sūkṣmā, Amṛtā (Jñānāmṛtā), Āpyāyinī, Vyāpinī, Vyomarūpā and Anantā. *Prapañcasāra*, III. 25-7, *Śāradātilaka*, II. 26.

Nāḍī

Nerves of the human body supposed to be 72,000 in number. Of these seventy-two are major nerves, the most important ones being ten or fourteen: *iḍā, piṅgalā, suṣumnā, gāndhārī, hastijihvā, yaśavinī, alambuṣā, kuhū, śaṅkhinī, sarasvatī, vāruṇī, puṣā, viśvodarā* and *pāyasvinī*. *Prāṇatoṣaṇī*, I. 4, pp. 32-3.

Nāḍīśuddhi

Purification of the nerves. When done by *mantras* it is known as *samanu* and when done by physical exercise like *dhauti*, etc. it is known as *nirmanu*. *Gheraṇḍa*, V. 36.

Naimittika Pūjā

Occasional worship for the attainment of certain purpose.

Napuṃsaka Mantra

The *mantras* which are neither male nor female. The *mantras* for male deities are known as *puruṣa-mantra* and those intended for female deities are known as *strī-mantra* or *vidyā*. The rest belongs to *Napuṃsaka* category. Śāradā, II. 57-58.

Napuṃsaka Varṇa

The letters which are neither male nor female. To this category belong long ṛ and long ḷ. Rāghava on *Śāradā*, II. 5-7.

Naramedha

Human sacrifice.

Naṭī

Female dancer. The term applies to Śakti when the goddess dances out of delight at the performance of her rituals. *Niruttara*, XV.

Navacakra

Nine *cakras* or circles (actually these are triangular) by which Śrīyantra is constituted. According to the *Bhairavayāmala* five of these belong to Śakti and the remaining four to Śiva, and thus the Śrīyantra consisting of nine *cakras* is the combined body of Śiva and Śakti. The five Śakti triangles are pointed upward and the four Śiva triangles downwards. Lakṣmīdhara on *Saundaryalaharī*, IX. *Navacakra* has three parts, each symbolically dealing with creation, preservation and destruction. *Setubandha* com. on *Nityaṣoḍśikārṇava*, I. 47. It is also known as *āvaraṇacakra* and is said to exist even in the human body. Ibid on VI. 25-7

Navanāda

Nine Nādas or special forms of sound supposed to denote the nature of *kuṇḍalinī*. These are known as *cīni, ghaṇṭā, śaṅkha, tantrī, karatāla, venu, veru, mṛdaṅga* and *megha*. *Cidvalli* on *Kāmakalāvilāsa*, XXVII. The letters *A, Ka, Ca, Ṭa, Ta, Pa, Ya, Śa,* and *Kṣa* are also known as Navanāda. Lakṣmīdhara on *Saundaryalaharī*, XXXIV.

Navarasa

Nine *rasas* or mental feelings—Śṛṇgāra, Bhyānaka, Raudra, Vībhatsa, Hāsya, Vīra, Karuṇa, Adbhūta and Śānta.

Navavarga

Nine groups of letters beginning with *A, Ka, Ca, Ṭa, Ta, Pa, Ya, Sa* and *La*. *Cidvalli* on *Kāmakalāvilāsa*, XXVII.

Navayonicakra

Cakra or diagram consisting of nine triangles or *yonis*. It is also known as *navatrikoṇa*.

Nimeṣa Śakti

The power of will by which the concept of Sadāśiva is characterised in Kashmir Śaivism. *Īśvarapratyabhijñā*, III. 1.3. Nimeṣa technically means the latent condition of 'Itness' and 'I-ness'.

Nimitta Kāraṇa

Efficient cause.

Nirodhinī

One of the five aspects of Śakti. *Śāradātilaka*, V. 79.

Nirvāṇa

Same as *mukti* and *mokṣa,* i.e. liberation.

Nirvāṇa Kāla

An aspect of Śakti, said to be the essence of Amākalā and conceived as the seventeenth *kalā* and also as a goddess. *Ṣaṭcakranirūpaṇa,* XLVII; *Kaṅkālamālinī,* II.

Nirvikalpa Samādhi

The Samādhi or that blissful state of mind in which the distinction of the knower, knowledge and what is to be known vanishes absolutely.

Nityapūjā

Daily worship. *Gandharvatantra,* XXII. 10.

Nivṛttikalā

One of the five *kalās* or aspects of Śakti. *Śāradātilaka,* V. 79.

Nivṛttimārga

The *sādhanā* or spiritual exercise which insists on abstinence from all worldly pleasures.

Niyati

Fate or destiny. The term is also used to denote a category of *vidyā-tattva.*

Nyāsa

Feeling of the deity in different parts of the body. *Saubhāgyabhāskara* on *Lalitāsahasranāma,* I. 4. It is an exercise of the aspirant to become god. *Gandharva,* IX. 2. It also serves as a protection against evil. *Tantrasāra,* p. 93. Without proper *nyāsa* worship is meaningless. *Tārātantra,* II.3. There are many types of *nyāsas* like Mātṛkānyāsa, Ṣoḍanyāsa, Tārakānyāsa, Ṛṣyādinyāsa, Ṣaḍaṅganyāsa, Karāṅganyāsa, Vidyānyāsa, Tattvanyāsa, etc., each giving a special result. *Śāradātilaka,* VII. In Mātṛkānyāsa, which is divided into *antaḥ* and *vahiḥ,* the Śakti of letters or Mātṛkās is to be felt on the head (*Ṛṣi*), face (*Chandas*), rectum (*Vīja*), legs (*Śakti*) and the whole body (*Kīlaka*). *Tārābhaktisudhārṇava,* V. p. 169. In Ṣoḍanyāsa six kinds of *nyāsas* are used in regard to *vidyās* like Kālī, Tārā, etc.

Puraścaryārṇava, XII. p. 1165. There are other types of *nyāsas* besides those found in the classified lists. For example, in Pīṭhanyāsa, Pīṭhas or holy resorts of Śakti are to be felt in different parts of the body like Kāmarūpa in heart, Jālandhara on the forehead, and so on. *Tantrasāra*, p. 339.

Pada, Padādhvā

Words compared by letters regarded as the body of *mantra*. *Śāradā*, V. 91.

Padmāsana

A sitting posture for yogic practice in which the right foot should be placed on the left thigh and the left foot on the right thigh.

Pañca Bandhana

Five fetters resulting from *avidyā* or false knowledge.

Pañcabhūta

Five gross elements—earth, water, fire, air and space.

Pañca Kalā

Five aspects of Śakti—Nivṛtti, Pratiṣṭhā, Vidyā, Śānti and Śāntyātīta. *Śārada*, V. 79.

Pañca Kañcuka

Five evolutes of Aśuddha Māyā or impure material elements—*kāla, niyati, kalā, vidyā* and *rāga*—which cause different types of human bondage.

Pañca Kleśa

Five fetters in the forms of *avidyā* (false knowledge), *asmitā* (self-conceit), *rāga* (attachment), *dveṣa* (hatred) and *abhiniveśa* (adherence).

Pañca Kṛtya

Five active expressions of Śakti—Sṛṣti (creation), Sthiti (maintenance), Saṃhāra (destruction), Tirodhāna (disappearance) and Anugraha (favour). *Tantrāloka*, I.121.

Pañca-makāra

See under Pañcatattva.

Pañcāmnāya
Five *āmnāyas* or zones celebrated for Tantric culture.

Pañcamatattva
See under *maithuna.*

Pañcamudrā
See under Pañcatattva.

Pañcamuṇḍi
A seat for Tantric *sādhanā* prepared by the severed heads of two Caṇḍālas, one jackal, one monkey and a snake.

Pañcāṅga Nyāsa
Feeling of the deity in heart, head, central cerebral region, protective symbol and intestine.

Pañcāṅga Puraścaraṇa
Japa, homa, tarpaṇa, abhiṣeka and *viprabhojana* (feeding the Brāhmaṇas). *Tantrasārā*, p. 48.

Pañca Preta
Brahmā, Viṣṇu, Rudra, Īśā and Sadāśiva, forming the seat of Devī, are collectively known as Pañca Preta.

Pañca-Śakti
Mother, sister, daughter, daughter-in-law and preceptor's wife are collectively known and worshipped as five great Śaktis. *Niruttara*, X.

Pañca Śuddhi
Purification of the self, place, mantra, articles of worship and deity. *Kulārṇava*, VI.

Pañcatanmātra
Five subtle elements, the essence of sound, touch, colour, taste, and smell conceived as physical principles, corresponding to five sense organs.

Pañcatattva
Theories and practices regarding the Five Ms—*madya* (wine),

māṃsa (meat), *matsya* (fish), *mudrā* (cereal, diagram, woman) and *maithuna* (sexual intercourse). Also known as Pañcamakāra, Pañcamudrā, Kuladravya, Kulatattva, etc.

Pañcāyatanī Dīkṣā
Initiation into the cults of Śiva, Śakti, Viṣṇu, Sūrya and Gaṇeśa. *Tantrasāra*, pp. 70-2.

Pañcopacāra
Five articles for worship, viz., *gandha* (sweet smelling things), *puṣpa* (flowers), *dhūpa* (incense), *dīpa* (candle) and *naivedya* (food-offering). *Puraścaryārṇava*, III. 224.

Parabrahma
The supreme being, the absolute, the ultimate reality in the form of pure consciousness.

Pārada
Mercury which is regarded as the essence of Śiva's body. It is conducive ro *mokṣa*. *Sarvadarśanasaṃgraha*, IX. 5-9.

Parākīyā
Female partner of the aspirant who is not his own wife.

Parāliṅga
Imaginary phallus in terms of which the *vindu* or vacuity within the *sahasrāra* triangle is conceived.

Parama Haṃsa
The aspirant who has attained success in *haṃsa mantra*.

Parāmeṣṭhi Guru
The fourth spiritual ancestor of the *guru*. *Mahānirvāṇa*, VI.98.

Parameśvarī
Goddess conceived as Supreme Being.

Paramīkaraṇa
Anointation of the deity with the help of *mahāmudrā*. *Puraścaryārṇava*, V. 346.

Parāmudrā

Subtle form of *mudrā*. *Tantrarāja*, IV. 55.

Parāpara Guru

Third spiritual ancestor of the *guru*. *Mahānirvāṇa*, VI. 98.

Parā Pratibhā

Same as Kaulikī Śakti. *Parātriṃśikā*, p. 102; *Tantrāloka*, III. 74.

Parā Pūjā

Highest form of worship which can be performed only by those who have knowledge of the self.

Parā Rūpa

The original form of deity which is beyond the comprehension by the sense organs. Other forms are *sthula* (gross) and *sukṣma* (subtle).

Parā Śabda

One of the four constituents of the sound-producing energy conceived as identical with *kuṇḍalinī*.

Parā Śakti

A term for the female partner of the aspirant.

Parā Śakti

A term variously used to denote different aspects of Śakti. It is that power which denotes the Śivaness of Śiva. *Śivārkamaṇidīpikā* on *Brahmasūtra*, II. 2-38. Parā Śakti is therefore the energy of Śiva, often regarded as instrumental cause of creation. The term is also used to denote the power of independence of the Supreme Being. It is that power, undifferentiated from *saṃvit* or pure consciousness by which the Supreme Being expresses itself. *Pratyabhijñāhṛdaya*, p. 68. In *Tantrāloka*, III, 103-4 it is regarded as Visarga-*śakti* which is by nature extrovert. Ibid., III, 141-2. In Śāiva and Śākta outlook Parā Śakti is the Vimarśa, that is, vibrating or kinetic energy of the Supreme Being. Parā Śakti is conceived in diffferent names and forms. When it goes to manifest itself in creation the vibration caused thereby is called Nāda. Com. on *Śāradā*, I. 7. It is revealed in the form of Vāk, etc. *Nityaṣoḍaśikārṇava*, VI. 36. All the goddesses are its forms. *Mahānirvāṇa*, V. 2. Conceived as Female Principle Parā Śakti is said to be in union with the other part of her own self, that is Para Śiva, within the body of the aspirant, and this forms the *maithunatattva* of Tantra. *Kulārṇava*, V. Ḍakinī, Rākini, etc., are special forms of Parā Śakti. It is the force behind the formation of Parā-vāk, Paśyantī, Madhyamā and Vaikharī, the ingredients of Śabdabrahma. *Kāmakalāvilāsa*, XXII- XXIII. It is equated with *Kuṇḍalinī* and its functioning. *Śāradā*, I. 51-4; Kālīcaraṇa on *Ṣaṭcakranirūpaṇa*, LI.

Parā Vāk

See under Parā Śabda. It is the first stage of sounds expressing itself only at *mūlādhāra*. It is without any vibration. It is like a flame of light, unmanifested yet indestructible. *Cidvallī* on *Kāmakalāvilāsa*, XX. It is not only connected with *Kuṇḍalinī* but also serves as the middle point of the triangle representing *kāmakālā*. Ibid., XXIII.

Parāvindu

See under Vindu.

Parigraha Śakti

Material cause of creation, divided into two categories, pure and impure.

Pariṇāmavāda

Doctrine of transformation in cause-effect relation.

Pāśa

Fetters. These are generally considered to be eight in number. *Parāśurāmakalpasūtra*, X. 70. See under *aṣṭa-pāśa*. A list of sixty-two fetters is also found in different texts. See *Saubhāgyabhāskara* on *Lalitāsahasranāma*, 129.

Paścima Āmnāya

The Western Tantric Zone.

Paśu

Fettered individual. To this category belong men, animals and even gods. Kauṇḍinyabhāṣyā on *Pāśupatasūtra*, I. 1; V. 7. In Tantra,

Pasu is divided into two classes, *sabhāva* (when influenced by knowledge) and *vibhāva* (when knowledge leaves a mark on it) *Kaulavaliniranaya*, XI. 187. It is also divided into *dikṣita* (initiated) and *adīkṣīta* (uninitiated) categories. *Niruttara*, XII.

Paśu Bhāva

Ordinary human state. Certain spiritual exercises and cultivation of virtues are prescribed for individuals belonging to this state, by performance of which they are entitled to reach the higher level known as Vīra. *Rudrayāmala, Uttara*, VI. 50-1. XI. 28-9.

Paśu Cakra

One of the five *cakra* rituals, other being Rāja, Mahā, Deva and Vīra. *Niruttara*, X.

Paśu Śāstra

Name of Tantric texts belonging to the non-Kaula groups. *Kulārṇava*. II.

Paśvācāra

A term by which Vedācāra, Vaiṣṇavācāra, Śaivācāra and Dakṣiṇācāra are characterised.

Paśyantī

One of the constituents of sound, regarded as the second stage of its development. This form of sound belongs to the navel region. It has little vibration and is connected with Nādatattva. Com. on *Prapañcasāra*, II. 43.

Piṇḍabrahmāṇḍamārga

The route of the upward march of *kuṇḍalinī*. It is also known as *ṣaṭcakramārga*.

Pingalā

One of the major nerves. Together with its sister nerve *iḍā* it rises from *mūlādhāra* and ends in the right nostril. *Prāṇatoṣaṇī*, I. 4, p. 33. It is also known as *sūrya-nāḍi*, having the masculine characteristics of the sun. *Sanmohana* quoted by Kālīcaraṇa in the com. on *Ṣaṭcakranirūpaṇa*, I. It symbolizes waking state and leads individuals to violent actions. Rāghava on *Śāradā*, XXV. 38.

Pīṭha

Holy resorts of Śakti, traditionally fifty-one in number. Their origin is associated with the Puranic Dakṣayajña legend. Each Pīṭha is supposed to contain a limb of Sati, the Śakti of Śiva, a presiding goddess and her Bhairava. There are also minor Pīṭhas known as Upapīṭhas.

Pīṭhanyāsa

See under Nyāsa.

Pīṭha Śakti

Collective name of the goddesses Icchā, Jñāna, Kriyā, Ramadā, Kāmadāyinī, Rati, Ratipriyā, Nandā and Manonmanī, each representing an aspect of Śakti. *Śyāmārahasya*, III.

Pradakṣiṇa

Circumambulation.

Prakāmyasiddhi

A type of Siddhi or attainment of miraculous power which may be obtained through the rites of Antardaśāra. *Nityaṣoḍaśikārṇava*, VIII. 159.

Prakāśa

The static aspect of the ultimate reality.

Prakṛti

Female Principle of creation, variously conceived of as primordial matter or energy. Often identified with Śakti, the Supreme Being of the Śāktas.

Prāṇayāma

Breath-control with three processes—*puraka* (to take the breath inside), *kumbhaka* (to retain it), and *recaka* (to discharge it). *Prāṇatoṣaṇī*, VI. 1, p. 408. There are also other processes of *prāṇāyāma*.

Pratyālīḍha

See under Ālīḍha.

Pravṛttimārga

Spiritual exercise following the course of human nature.

Pūjā

Worship, the ultimate purpose of which is unification with the deity. *Mahānirvāṇa*, XIV. 123-4. It is of two kinds, *bāhya* (external) and *abhyantara* (internal). It may be *sādhārā* (with object) or *nirādhārā* (without object). It is often classified into Vedic, Tantric and Miśra. *Śrīmadbhāgavata*, XI. 57.7. Of other classifications we have Nitya, Naimittika and Kāmya, Sāttvika, Rājasika and Tāmasika; and Uttama, Madhyama and Adhama. *Gandharva*, XXII. 10-12; XXIV. 22-3; *Mahānirvāṇa*, XIV. 122.

Puraka

A form of Prāṇāyāma or breath-control.

Puraścaraṇa

Repeated recitation of *mantra* without which it cannot be effective. *Śaktisaṅgama*, Sundarī, III. 155-6; XIV. 45-6; *Gandharva*, XXVIII. 7-8. It is regarded as the first step of *sādhanā*. *Puraścaryārṇava*, VI. p. 413. It has five steps—*japa, homa, tarpaṇa ābhiṣeka* and *viprabhojana*. *Tantrasāra*, p. 48. In some texts five extra steps are added. There are different degrees of this rite pertaining to aspirants of Paśu, Vīra and Divya categories. In the Kali-age proper *Puraścaraṇa* is not possible. *Kālīvilāsatantra*, IV. 6-7. *Japa* or muttering the *mantra* is the main feature. *Kriyāsāra* quoted in *Tantrasāra*, p. 48. There are elaborate rules and tabus in relation to food habits, behaviour, time and space. The purpose of *Puraścaraṇa* is to attain *Mantrasiddhi*.

Pūrṇābhiṣeka

Highest form of initiation.

Puruṣa-Prakṛti

Male and Female Principles of creation, later equated with the principles of soul and matter.

Pūrva Kaula

A sect of the Kaulas mentioned by Lakṣmīdhara in his com. on *Saundaryalaharī*, XXXIII.

Puryaṣṭaka

Eight subtle and gross elements by which the body of the god-dess as represented in the *aṣṭakoṇa-cakra* is composed. *Kāmakalā-vilāsa*, XI.

Rādhākṛṣṇatattva

The Rāsa conception of Vaiṣṇavas in terms of intense emotional attachment between the Male and Female principles symbolised by Kṛṣṇa and Rādhā, two aspects of the same ultimate reality and impersonated by the aspirant and his female partner in Rāsalīlā or love-sport.

Rāga

Attachment.

Rahasyayoginī

Eight presiding goddesses of the *aṣṭakoṇā-cakra*. *Ghandharva*, XVII. 74.

Rājacakra

One of the five forms of *cakra*-worship in which mother, sister, daughter, daughter-in-law and preceptor's wife are regarded as Śaktis, *Niruttara*, X.

Rajakī

Woman belonging to washerman-caste and serving as the female partner of the aspirant. The term is also used to denote Śakti as Kulanāyikā. *Niruttara*, XV; *Tantrasāra*, p. 627.

Rājayoga

A form of Yoga in which the mind automatically merges in *brahman* just as air merges in the sky. *Prāṇatoṣaṇī*, VI. 3, p. 433. It is free from all dualism. *Śivasaṃhitā*, V. 17. It leads to *nirvikalpa samādhi* in which there is absolute unity of knower, knowledge and source of knowledge. This *samādhi* is known as *rājayoga samādhi* which is also possible by a special *kumbhaka* process of breath-control known as *manomurcha* which connects the mind with the Supreme Being. *Gheraṇḍa*, VII. 16.

Rasa

Sap, elixir, sentiment. According to *Raseśvara-darśana*, by the use of chemical drugs, especially those prepared from mercury, renovation of the body is possible which is conducive to *jīvanmukti* or liberation within the span of life. *Sarvadarśanasaṃgraha,* IX. 1ff. Besides chemical elixir, *Rasa* is also conceived in terms intense emotional attachment between the Male and Female Principles, symbolising two aspects of Śakti and impersonated by the aspirant and his partner. See *Lalitāsahasranāma,* 106. This conception is very popular also among the Vaiṣṇava Sahajiyās, the Bāuls and others.

Rāsalīlā

See under *Rādhākṛṣṇatattva.*

Rasānanda Yoga Samādhi

A state of Yogic bliss achieved by the control of breath. *Gheraṇḍa,* VII. 10-11.

Rasatattva Sādhana

See under *Rasa.*

Raseśvara-darśana

See under *Rasa.*

Rathakrāntā

A zone of tantric culture extending from the Vindhyas to Mahācīna.

Recaka

A form of *prāṇāyama* or breath-control. It is the exhaling of breath.

Ruddha Mantra

Defective *mantra* containing *laṃ* in the beginning, middle or end. *Śāradātilaka,* II. 72.

Rudragranthi

A knot in the *ājñācakra* obstructing the upward march of *kuṇḍalinī.* Com. on *Yogaśikhopaniṣat,* I. 87; *Saubhāgya-bhāskara* on *Lalitāsahasranāma,* 89.

Śabdabrahma

Brahman or Śakti conceived as the substratum of sound. See under Parā, Paśyantī, Madhyamā and Vaikharī.

Sādhaka
Spiritual aspirant.

Sādhanā
Term for spiritual exercise.

Sādhanadeha
Purified body fit for *sādhanā*.

Ṣaḍaṅganyāsa
Nyāsa or feeling of the deity in six parts of the body—heart, head, top of the head, protective amulet, eyes and intestine.

Sādhāraṇī
Female partner of the aspirant, drawn from public women.

Sādi Vidyā
A stream of knowledge designated after the symbolic first letter of the Śakti Vīja.

Sadyojāta
One of the five faces of Śiva from which a number of Tantras emanated.

Sahaja
The *mārga* or way of spiritual exercise which is the easiest and most natural. It is also the term for ultimate reality among the Sahajiyās, i.e. those who believe in this *mārga*.

Sahasrāra
The highest cerebral region above all the *cakras* or nerve-plexuses where *kuṇḍalinī* meets its source. For its description see *Ṣaṭcakranirūpaṇa*, XLI-XLIII.

Śaivācāra
A form of Dakṣiṇācāra which insists on the cult of Śiva-Śakti, Vedic way, eightfold Yogic practices and animal sacrifice. *Prāṇatoṣaṇī*, VII. 1. p. 499.

Śākinī
Presiding goddess of the *visuddha cakra*. Kālīcaraṇa on *Ṣaṭcakranirūpaṇa*, XXX.

Śakti

The basic conceptual foundation of Tantrism. It is the power of the Supreme Being conceived as a Female Principle through which the manifestation of the universe is effected. The important modes of this power are *cit* (intelligence), *ānanda* (bliss), *icchā* (will), *jñāna* (knowledge) and *kriyā* (action). See under entries prefixed and suffixed by Śakti.

Śakti

Female partner of the aspirant; of three kinds—*svakīyā* (the wife), *parakīyā* (wife of another) and *sādhāraṇī* (common women); for her qualifications see *Kulārṇava*, VII; women of the lower castes and despised professions are regarded as excellent partners. *Niruttara*, XIV; *Tantrasāra*, p. 627; *Gandharva*, XXIII. 19; *Prāṇatoṣaṇī*, VII. 4, p. 548.

Śakti

One of the six limbs of *mantra*, others being Ṛṣi, Chandas, Devatā, Vīja and Kalīka. Dīpikā on *Śrīvidyāratnasūtra*, I.

Śakticakra

The five Śakti triangles in Śrīyantra. *Bhairavayāmala* quoted by Lakṣmīdhara on *Saundaryalaharī*, IX.

Śakticālanī

A *mudrā* which bestows great success. *Haṭhayogapradīpikā*, III. 6-7; *Gheraṇḍa*, III.1-3. The process is as follows. The aspirant will have to sit in *siddhāsana* posture. With both his nostrils he will inhale air and send it to the spinal cord. Until it reaches there he will contract his anus and stop exhaling by *kumbhaka* process. The confined wind will then push the *kuṇḍalinī* and send it upwards.

Śakti Dīkṣā

Initation which does not require any external rite. It is connected with pure knowledge. Rāghava on *Śāradā*, IV. 1; *Prāṇatoṣaṇī*, II. 4, p. 118.

Śaktikāraṇavāda

The conception of Śakti as the material and efficient cause of the universe. *Nityaṣoḍaśikārṇava*, IV. 5; *Kaulamārgarahasya*, p. 196;

Lalitāsahasranāma, 112ff; *Saundaryalaharī,* I; *Śaktisaṅgama,* Tārā, VIII. 28; *Devībhāgavata,* I. 8.39; III. 6.19.

Śaktikūṭa

Technical name of Śakti-Vīja or symbolic letters. Com. on *Śāradā,* I. 1.

Śaktipīṭha

See under Pīṭha.

Śaktitrikoṇa

Śakti-triangles supposed to exist in different parts of the body, depicted on diagrams and erected as stone, wooden or other objects for cultic purposes. The three lines symbolise any set of threefold theories and the angles are said to be presided over by different goddesses.

Śakti Varṇa

The vowels. Com. on *Śāradā,* VI. 2.

Śaktiiśiṣṭādvaitavāda

A theory of the Vīraśaivas according to which the potential and material moment of the Absolute is called Śiva while the actual and formal moment is called Śakti. It holds that creation is the result of the Vimarśa-Śakti of Śiva. Śakti is the power which resides eternally in Śiva as his inseparable attribute.

Śaktyādvayavāda

A theory of the Kashmir Śaivas according to which Śakti is not different from Śiva and as such the material world is the Pariṇāma or consequence of Śakti.

Samādhi

State of perfect bliss in which the world of senses disappears from the mind of the aspirant. It is the aim of all Yogic exercises. Vyāsabhāśyā on *Yogasūtra,* I. 1; *Gheraṇḍa,* VII. 1ff; *Haṭhayoga-pradīpikā,* IV. 5; IV. 7; *Gandharva,* VI. 66ff; *Kulārṇava,* IX. 13-14; etc.

Sāmarasya

Equilibrium of Śiva and Śakti, Male and Female Principles. In

Buddhism it is that of Upāya and Prajñā. Very often this equilibrium is conceived in sexual terms. Its spirit is felt by the aspirant within his own self. Complete understanding of this equilibrium leads to the sense of non-duality.

Samayācāra

A mārga or way of the Śrīvidyā cult. For details see Lakṣmīdhara's com. On *Saundaryalaharī,* vv. 31ff; *Saubhāgyabhāskara* on *Lalitāsahasranāma,* 144; Rameśvara on *Paraśurāmakalpasūtra,* VII. 1; X. 68; X. 80.

Śāmbhavīdīkṣā

A form of higher initiation which is conducted by the mere touch or glance or will of the *guru.* It is connected with the secret cult of Kāmeśvarī. *Nityotsava,* p. 9.

Saṃhāracakra

One of the constituents of *navacakra. Nityaṣoḍaśikārṇava,* I. 47.

Saṃhārakramanyāsa

Feeling of the destructive aspect of the deity in the body. The symbolic letters are to be felt in inverse direction, from *Kṣa* to *A. Puraścaryārṇava,* V, p. 330.

Samprajñāta Samādhi

Same as Savikalpa *samādhi.*

Saṃvit

Pure consciousness which is the form of the Absolute.

Śankhinī

Name of a cerebral nerve. *Prāṇatoṣaṇī,* I. 4, p. 33.

Śānta Śakti

A form of Śakti containing the aspects of will (*icchā*), knowledge (*jñāna*) and action (*kriyā*).

Śānti, Śāntyatītā

Kalās generated from Nāda. *Śāradātilaka,* I. 26.

Ṣaṭcakra

The six nerve-plexuses. See under *mūlādhāra, svādhiṣṭhāna, maṇipura, anāhata, viśuddha* and *ajñā.*

Śaṭkañcuka

Six veils which are the causes of human bondage. *Tantrāloka,* IX, 164, 204.

Śavasādhanā

Ritual with the corpse. See *Kaulāvalinirṇaya,* XIV; *Śyāmārahasya,* XIV; *Tārābhaktisudhārṇava,* IX; *Puraścaryārṇava,* IX.

Savikalpa Samādhi

A state of bliss in which a sense of difference somehow survives between the knower and his object of knowledge.

Setu

Bridge made of knowledge to cross the ocean of suffering. Crystallised as a form of *mantra* it should be muttered. Its higher form is known as *Mahāsetu. Puraścaryārṇava,* VI, pp. 532-3.

Siddha, Siddhi

Siddhi is spiritual attainment. The term is also used to denote the attainment of miraculous power. He or she who has attained *siddhi* is known as Siddha.

Siddhamantra

The *mantra* which becomes at once effective. Very few are in possession of such *mantras.* If chance provides, such *mantras* may be accepted even by disregarding scriptural rules. *Rudrayāmala, Uttara,* II; *Tantrasāra,* p. 6.

Siddhantācāra

One of the seven Tantric *ācāras* or *mārgas* or ways. In particular it is described as a form of Vāmācāra. *Puraścaryārṇava,* I, p. 22. It is meant for the aspirants of the Vīra state. It insists more on *antaryāga* or internal worship than on external. *Kaulamārga-rahasya,* p. 10. One of the intersting characteristics of Siddhantācāra is that its followers worship Viṣṇu by the daytime while at night they practise the rites of pañcamakāra.

Śiṣya

Disciple. His method of selecting teacher is described in *Kulārṇava*, XI, XIV; *Rudrayāmala, Uttara*, II; *Prapañcasara*, XXXVI. 50. His test before initiation; *Tantrasāra*, p. 3; *Śāradātilaka*, II.153; characteristics of a good disciple; *Śāradā*, II. 145-50; *Tantrarāja*, I.23-4; of a bad disciple: *Rudrayāmala, Uttara*, II; his duties: *Kulārṇava*, XII; *Kaulāvalinirṇaya*, X; *Parāśurāmakalpasūtra*, X. 74.

Śītkrama

To inhale breath by mouth with a sound and to exhale it by the nose. This Yogic practice prevents diseases. *Gheraṇḍa*, I. 60-1.

Śiva Cakra

The four Śiva-triangle as constituents of Śrīyantra. *Vinducakra, aṣṭadalapadma, bhupura*, etc., are also known as *Śivacakra*. Lakṣmīdhara on *Saundaryalaharī*, IX.

Śivahasta

The hand of the preceptor which is purified by *mantras* when it is used to initiate someone in *sparśa dīkṣā*. Rāghava on *Śāradā*, V. 127-40.

Śivavīja

Name of Parāda or mercury.

Śiva Yogī

A term used to denote Jīvanmukta or liberated persons. *Bhāvanopaniṣat*, XXXV.

Śivayuvati

Name of Śakti-triangle. *Saundaryalaharī*, XI.

Smārti Dīkṣā

Initiation when the candidate is absent. The teacher by mental recall will free him from three fetters known as *āṇava, kārma* and *māyīya* and by his power elevate the soul of his disciple for union with Supreme Being. Rāghava on *Śāradā*, V. 127-40.

Ṣoḍaśadala Padma

Sixteen-petalled lotus, each petal having a vowel symbolising

Mātṛkā. *Kāmakalāvilāsa*, XXXIII. It is also conceived as existing in the *cakras*.

Ṣoḍaśādhāra

Sixteen containers known as Mūlādhāra, Svādhiṣṭhāna, Maṇipura, Anāhata, Viśuddha, Ajñā, Vindu, Kāla, Pāda, Nivodhikā, Ardhendu, Nāda, Nādānta, Unmanī, Viṣṇuvaktra and Dhruvamaṇḍalikā. *Prāṇatoṣaṇī*, II. 2, p. 93.

Ṣoḍaśopācāra

Sixteen articles required for worship: *āsana, svāgata, pādya, argha, ācamanīya, nyāsa, madhuparka, punarāeamanīya, snāniya, bhuṣana, gandha, puṣpa, dhūpa, dīpa, naivedya* and *vandanā*. *Mahānirvāṇa*, XIII. 203-4.

Śodhana

Purification. In Tantric language it is the establishment of a thing in its real form. It is done by *mantras* and rituals.

Ṣoḍhānyāsa

A form of *nyāsa* in which the deities are singly felt in the body. It has six processes. For details see *Tārābhakti-sudhārṇava*, V, p. 163; *Śāradātilaka*, VII; *Puraścaryārṇava*, XII, p. 1165; *Tantrasāra*, pp. 272, 309ff.

Somacakra

A mintor nerve-cycle within the body.

Sparśa (Spārśanī) Dīkṣā

Initiation by touch. *Kulārṇava*, XIV; *Puraścaryārṇava*, V, p. 391; Rāghava on *Śāradā*, V. 127-140.

Śrīcakra

See under Śrīyantra.

Śrīkaṇṭha

Name of Śiva-triangle of the Śrīyantra. *Saundaryalaharī*, XI.

Śrīkula

A major Tantric school. Texts like *Tripurārahasya, Subhagodayastuti,*

Prapañcasara, Saundaryalahari, Prayogakramadīpikā, Śāradātilaka, etc., belong to this school.

Śrīyantra

The most important Tantric diagram connected with the cult of Śrīvīdyā. It is also known as Śrīcakra and Tripuracakra. This diagram symbolises the body of the goddess. *Nityaṣoḍaśikārṇava,* VI.24; *Kāmakalāvilāsa,* XXXVI. It consists of nine triangles or *yonis,* five in the name of Śakti and four in that of Śiva. The Śakti-triangles are pointed upwards and the Śiva-triangles downwards. Lakṣmīdhara on *Saundaryalahari,* IX.

Śṛṣṭicakra

One-third of the triangles of the Śrīyanta representing the creative aspects of Śakti. *Setubandha* on *Nityaṣoḍaśikārṇava,* I. 47.

Śṛṣṭikramanyāsa

Nyāsa or feeling the deity in different parts of the body. The deity should be conceived in terms of letters from *A* to *Kṣa* and felt in different spots between the forehead and the heart. *Puraścaryārṇava,* V, pp. 328-9; *Tantrasāra,* p. 90.

Stambhana

One of the *ṣaṭkarmas* by which efforts of the opponents can be arrested. *Śāradātilaka,* XXIII. 124.

Sthāna Śuddhi

Purification of the place of worship. *Kulārṇava,* VI.

Sthiticakra

One-third of the triangle of Śrīyantra representing the preserving aspect of Śakti. *Setubandha* on *Nityaṣoḍaśikārṇava,* I. 42.

Sthitikalā

Power of preservation symbolised by the letter *U,* the sign of Viṣṇu. This is represented by ten goddesses: Jarā, Pālinī, Śānti, Aiśvarī, Rati, Kāmikā, Varadā, Hlādinī, Prīti and Dīrghā. *Prapañcasāra,* III. 21-2.

Sthitikramanyāsa

Nyāsa in which deities are to be conceived in terms of letters from

Da to *Kṣa* and felt in different spots from the heart to the knee. *Puraścaryārṇava*, V. p. 329.

Sthūla Deha (Śarīra)
Gross body.

Sthūla Dhyāna
Meditation on the basis of some objects like image of the deity, etc. It is regarded as being very helpful in spiritual quest. *Mahānirvāṇa*, V. 139; *Śaktisaṅgama, Sundarī*, II. 126.

Strī-Guru
Female preceptor. For her characteristics see Rudrayāmala, *Uttara* II. The *Yoginītantra* describes the efficacy of getting initiated under a female teacher. *Tantrasāra*, p. 3; see also *Śaktisaṅgama*, Tārā, LVIII. 7-8. The *Mātṛkābheda*, VII gives the verses of her worship. The process of the meditation of her form is given in *Prāṇatoṣaṇī*, III. 1, p. 155.

Strī Mantra
Mantras attributed to the female deities. Com. on *Śāradā*, II. 57ff.

Strī Varṇa
The long vowels are known by this name. Com. on *Śāradā*, II. 5-7.

Śubhāgamapañcaka
Five Tantric texts, each said to be propounded respectively by Vaśiṣṭha, Sanaka, Śuka, Sanandana and Sanat Kumāra, which were intended for the followers of the Vedic way.

Sūkṣma Deha (Śarīra)
Subtle body.

Śūnyatā
The Buddhist idea of vacuity conceived in terms of the Female Principle. It is also known as Prajñā and symbolised in the forms of different goddesses. The Male Principle is thought of as Karuṇā or Upāya.

Surāśodhana
Purification of wine. For the procedure see *Prāṇatoṣaṇī*, VII. 2,

Kulārṇava, VI; *Gandharva*, XXXIV. 86-9; *Mātṛkābheda*, III. 13; *Tārāhasya*, III; *Mahānirvāṇa*, V, etc.

Sūrya Nāḍī

Another name of *piṅgalā* nerve.

Suṣumnā

The most important nerve, also known as Brahmanāḍī. It is said that the universe itself is contained in this nerve. *Yogaśikhopaniṣat*, VI. 13. It extends from the *mūlādhāra* to *brahmarandhra*. It is the route by which *kuṇḍalinī* marches upwards. *Ṣaṭcakranirūpaṇa*, I ff. According to the *Śaṇḍilyopaniṣat*, I. 4.10 if the *prāṇa*-wind be pushed through this nerve by means of Yogic exercise the aspirant will be liberated. That is why it is also called *mokṣamārga*.

Svādhiṣṭhāna

The nerve-plexus situated above the *mūlādhāra*. It is like a six-petalled lotus. This *cakra* is presided over by the goddess Rākinī. *Ṣaṭcakranirūpaṇa*, XV-XVII; Lakṣmīdhara on *Saundaryalaharī*, IX.

Svakīyā

Female partner who is the valid wife of the aspirant.

Svakula Varṇa

Letters belonging to one's own group. There are three other categories of letters—*mitra* (friendly), *udāsīna* (neutral) and *śatru* (enemy). *Prapañcasāra*, III. 70-2.

Svapuṣpa

The first menstrual blood of a newly married woman sacred to the Devī.

Svayambhūkusuma

Menstrual blood of a maiden.

Svayambhūliṅga

One the three forms of Śiva-liṅga, others being Bāṇa and Itara.

Tāḍana

Processing of *mantras*. Each letter of the *mantra* concerned should be recited ten times or a hundred times. Tāḍana is also done by writing the letters and sprinkling sandalwood water on them. *Tantrasāra*, p. 54.

Taijasa Ahaṃkāra

Egoity arising from heat which is the cause of ten sense organs and mind. Com. on *Śāradā*, I. 19.

Taijasa Varṇa

Same as Āgneya-varṇa, i.e. *I, Ī, Ai, Kha, Cha, Ṭha, Tha, Pha, Ra,* and *Kṣa,* said to have sprung from heat or *tejas*. *Prapañcasāra*, III. 70-2; Com. on *Śāradā*, II. 10-11.

Tāriṇīmata

Same as Kahādimata. *Śaktisaṅgama*, Tārā, LVIII. 81.

Tarpaṇa

Remembrance of deities, sages and fathers after the recital of Gāyatrī hymn during worship. There are differences between Vedic and Tantric systems of *tarpaṇa*. *Puraścaryārṇava*, VI, p. 509. *Tarpaṇa* to Śakti is to be offered thrice, *Tantrasāra*, pp. 81-2; *Mahānirvāṇa*, V. 65. *Tarpaṇa* is also a term for processing *mantras*. *Tantrasāra*, p. 54.

Taruṇollāsa

The second of the seven *ullāsas* or stages of Tantric *sādhanā*. *Parāśurāmakalpasūtra*, I. 68; *Kulārṇava*, VIII; *Tārābhaktisudhārṇava*, VI, p. 255.

Tatpuruṣa

One of the five faces of Śiva from which texts like *Raurava*, etc., have been produced.

Tattvacakra

Also known as *Cakrarāja* and *Divyacakra*, the performance of this *cakra* is restricted only to those who have attained a certain stage of spiritual development. The performance needs no external rites. The aspirants sit together under the leadership of the *cakreśvara* and meditate with *haṃsa mantra*. *Mahānirvāṇa*, VIII. 204ff.

Tattvanyāsa

Feeling of the thirty-six *tattvas* (Knowledge: threefold—Ātma, Vidyā and Śiva) in different parts of the body. It has a variety of methods. *Tantrasāra,* pp. 271, 310.

Tejodhyāna

See under *Jyotirdhyāna.*

Traipura

A triangle within the quadrangular *pṛthivīmaṇḍala* which is situated within the pericarp of the container lotus near the mouth of *vajranāḍī.* It is also called Yoni or Kāmarūpa Pīṭha in human body. *Ṣaṭcakranirūpaṇa,* VIII.

Trāṭaka

A form of yogic *ṣaṭkarma.* The aspirant has to fix his sight on a point until his eyes water. This is called *trāṭaka* by which attainment of Śāmbhavī Śakti is possible. It is supposed to cure eye diseases and give divine eyesight. *Gheraṇḍa,* I. 54-5.

Tridhāma

Collective designation of Soma, Sūrya and Agni. *Kāmakalāvilāsa,* XIII, XIV.

Trikoṇa

Triangle, also known as *yoni.* It is said to be due to the elevation of *vindu. Kāmakalāvilāsa,* XXII. In the drawn triangle which is required for Tantric worship, Parā Śakti or Parā Vāk serves as the middle point while the three arms, constituting three angles symbolise the three other forms of sound (Paśyantī, Mahyamā, Vaikharī), three Vījas (Vāgbhava, Kāmāraja, Śakti), three Śaktis (Vāmā, Jyeṣṭhā, Raudrī or *icchā-jñāna-kriyā*), three goddesses (Kameśvarī, Vajreśvarī and Bhagamālinī), three tattvas (Prakṛti, Mahāt, Ahaṁkāra), three Pīṭhas (Kāmarūpa, Jālandhara, Pūrṇagiri), and all other threefold concepts. Ibid., XXIII; Setubandha on *Nityaṣoḍaśikārṇava,* VI. 36-40; Rāmeśvara on *Paraśurāma-kalpasūtra* V. 11; *Gandharvatantra,* V. 112-13; *Tantrarājatantra,* XXXV. 12-13.

Triliṅga

Bāṇa, Itara and Parā, three types of phallus. *Kāmakalāvilāsa,* XIII, XIV.

Trilokyamohanacakra
A form of Śrīcakra or Śrīyantra.

Tripīṭha
Collective name of Kāmarupa, Pūrṇagiri and Jālandhara Pīṭhas. *Kāmakalāvilāsa*, XII, XIV.

Tripuracakra
Same as Śrīcakra or Śrīyantra.

Tripurasundarī Mata
Name of Hādimata. *Śaktisaṅgama*, Kālī, VI. 125.

Triśakti
Jñāna (knowledge), *icchā* (will) and *kriyā* (action). *Kāmakalāvilāsa*. XIII, XIV.

Trivīja
The seeds of the *mantras* of Tripurasundarī which are known as Vāgbhava, Kāmarāja and Śakti. *Cidvalli* on *Kāmakalāvilāsa*, XXIII.

Turīya
A very high state. The *sahasrāra-cakra* is supposed to contain a field of knowledge which is also known as Turīya.

Uccāṭana
One of the *ṣaṭkarmas* or six black acts by which one can drive one's rival from the land. *Śāradā*, XXIII. 125.

Ugra
A Śaiva sect mentioned in Ānandagiri's *Śaṅkaravijaya*.

Ullāsa
Stages of Tantric sādhanā—*ārambha, taruṇa, yauvana, prauḍha, prauḍhānta, unmana* and *anavasthā*. *Paraśurāmakalpasūtra*, X. 68.

Unmana, Unmanī
The sixth stage in spiritual exercise. The aspirant in this stage has a feeling of great joy in which his sense organs cease to function. *Kulārṇava*, VIII; *Tārābhaktisudhārṇava*, VI, p. 255.

Upacāra

Articles for worship, consisting of five, seven, ten, twelve, sixteen, eighteen, thirty-six and even sixty-four items. *Puraścaryārṇava*, III, pp. 224-5; Rāghava on *Śāradā*, IV.92; *Tantrasāra*, pp. 551-2; *Mahānirvāna*, VI. 78-9; XIII. 203ff.

Upādāna Kāraṇa

Material cause of creation.

Upāsanā

Worship, the act by which one can stay near god. *Kaulamārgarahasya*, pp. 113-14. It is surrendering of one's own self to the supreme being. Rāmeśvara on *Paraśurāmakalpasūtra*, I. 1. It may be internal or external; see Antaryāga and Bahiryāga. It is of many types. For the mood of the worshipper see under *Grāhyālambanā*, *Grahaṇālambanā* and *Grahītrālambanā*.

Uttarakaula

A sect of the Kaula worshippers mentioned by Lakṣmīdhara in his com. on *Saundaryalaharī*. XXXIII according to which there is no Śiva-tattva apart from Śakti-tattva. Ibid., on XXIII.

Uttarāmnāya

The northern zone of Tantric culture.

Uttarasādhaka

Partner of the aspirant whose qualifications are mentioned in *Kaulāvalinirṇaya*, XIV.

Vācaka, Vācya

Śakti or power of *mantra*; the former is the denoting or signifying aspect, while the latter is the basic. *Vācya* is contained in the *vācakā* and formally there is no distinction between them. *Janyajanakayorbhedābhāvād vācyasya vācakenāpi*. *Varivasyārahasya*, II. 81.

Vācikā, Vāk Dīkṣā

The common form of initiation with *mantras*. Rāghava on *Śāradā*, V. 127-40; *Puraścaryārnava*, V, p. 391.

Vāgbhava

A term applied to Vījas. It is also the name of a triangle.

Vaikharī

One of the four ingredients of sound, others being Parā, Paśyantī and Madhamā. It is that sound which is carried by the wind inside the body and becomes articulated in the throat. It is the gross sound. According to Rāghavabhaṭṭa Parā is unmanifested sound; Paśyantī reveals letters, Madhyamā words and Vaikharī sentences. Com. on *Śāradā*, I. 1; see also *Setubandha* on *Nityaṣoḍaśikārṇava*, VI. 10-11.

Vajra

Thunderbolt, a weapon frequently found in the hands of the Tantric Buddhist icons.

Vajra

Name of a nerve situated within the *suṣumnā.*

Vajrayāna

A form of Tantric Buddhism.

Vāmācāra, Vāmamārga

See under *ācāra.* Different forms of Vāmācāra are described in *Puraścaryārṇava*, I, pp. 20ff., and *Śaktisaṅgama*, Tārā, I. 90ff.

Vara, Varada

Mudrā or hand pose in the form of granting boon, right hand raised upwards with palm bent downwards.

Varṇa

Letters, also called Mātṛkās, symbolising different manifestations of Śakti.

Varṇa (Mayī) Dīkṣā

Initiation by infusing the spirit of letters in different parts of the candidate's body. *Śāradā*, V. 116-21.

Vaśīkaraṇa

One of the six black acts which is to hypnotise someone. *Śāradā*, XXIII. 123.

Vedācāra

One of the sevenfold Tantric *ācāras.* Its followers insist on the Vedic way. *Prāṇatoṣaṇī,* III. 1, p. 149.

Vedha (Mayī) Dīkṣā

See under *manodīkṣā* and *mānaṣadīkṣā.* In this form of initiation the mental faculties of the candidate are determinted by the contemplation of the *guru. Kulārṇava,* XIV.

Vibhāva

A term, as opposed to *sabhāva,* used as an attribute of the aspirants belonging to Paśu and Vīra grades. The *vibhāvas* belong to the Rajas level, i.e. to the second grade of spiritual attainment.

Vidveṣaṇa

Rite for creating bad blood. *Śāradā,* XXIII. 124.

Vidyā

Vidyā denotes knowledge, female-deities and their *mantras,* female partner of the aspirant. certain forms of *tattvas* and *kalās,* Vimarśa Śakti expressed with the idea of I-ness, name of schools and sects, and so on.

Vighnāpasāraṇa

Also known as *bhūtāpasāraṇa,* it is the clearance of all evil elements with the help of *mantras. Puraścaryārṇava,* III, p. 154; Rāghava on *Śāradā,* IV.10.

Vīja

Seed. It is the microcosm of universe, deity, doctrine and *mantra.* For its formation and Śakti-orientation see under *nāda* and *vindu.* It is one of the seven limbs of *mantra,* others being *ṛṣi, chandas, kīlaka, śakti, nyāsa* and *dhyāna.* Dīpikā on *Śrīvidyāsūtra,* I. As a *mantra* it is single-lettered in which the deity is revealed in subtle form. See *Śāradā,* I. 57, *Tantraśāra,* pp. 182ff.

Vilāsa

One of the four principal Tantric schools, others being Kerala, Kāśmīra and Gauḍa.

Vimalīkaraṇa

Processing of *mantra. Tantrasāra*, p. 54.

Vimarśa

The vibrating, dynamic or kinetic aspect of the power (Śakti) of the Absolute, the static being known as Prakāśa. *Tantrāloka*, III. 2ff.

Vindu

A term used in a variety of senses. As a dot it denotes Śiva and as a double-dot (Visarga), Śakti, both being alphabetical signs. In Śaiva conception, *vindu* is an evolute of *nāda* which is produced owing to the *kriyāśakti* of Śiva. *Śivapurāṇa*, Vāyavīya, *Uttara*, V. 18ff. In Kashmir Śaivism *vindu* is one of the ten Vidyātattvas. *Tantrāloka*, I, 216. It is *anuttara* Śakti as also the *nāda*-oriented sound in every being. Ibid., 116ff. It is regarded as the condensed form of *nāda*. But according to *Prapañcasāra* I. 41, *vindu* is not preceded by *Nāda*. According to the *Śāradātilaka*, I. 7ff. *vindu*, by which Parāśakti is characterised, becomes divided into three parts: *vindu*, *nāda* and *vīja*. *Vindu* is Śiva-oriented, *vīja* Śakti-oriented and *nāda* their combination. *Nāda* and *vindu* of this second category are known as *apara-nāda* and *aparā-vindu*, while their primal forms are prefixed by the term Parā. *Vindu* has three forms—Prakāśa (static), Vimarśa (kinetic) and Prakāśa- Vimarśa (combination of both), *Cidvallī* on *Kāmakalāvilāsa*, V- VII. It is the cause of the origin of letters and elements. Com. on *Śāradā*, VII. 9. Four *Kalās*—Pītā, Śvetā, Aruṇā and Asitā—are emanated from it. *Prapañcasāra*, III. 20, 21. It also stands for male organ while its complementary principle Visarga for the females.

Vindu Cakra

Diagrams with *vindu* as the central point. The elevation of *vindu* is said to form the triangle or *trikoṇa*. *Kāmakalāvilāsa*, XXII. In the diagrams *vindu* represents the equilibrium of Kāmeśvara and Kāmeśvarī. The *vindu* diagrams are also known as Uḍḍiyānapīṭha and Brahmācakra. *Gandharva*, V. 123. The attainment of exercise in *vindu cakra* is known as *prāptisiddhi*. *Nityaṣoḍaśikārṇava*, VIII. 173.

Viniyoga

Application.

Vīra: Vīrācāra

Tantric aspirant of the second grade whose mental faculties are of advanced nature. For the interpretation of the word Vīra see *Kulārṇava*, XVII; *Rudrayāmāla*, Uttara, I. 136. Characteristics are mentioned in com. on *Paraśurāmakalpasūtra*, VI. 39; *Nirvāṇatantra*, XIV; *Kāmākhyātantra*, IV; *Niruttara*, XI; *Rudrayāmāla*, Uttara, LI. 20-1; Classifications; *Śaktisaṅgama, Sundarī*, I. 197-200, Tārā, XLIII, 204; *Puraścaryārṇava*, IX. p. 863; *Prāṇatoṣaṇī*, VII. 1, pp. 495ff. Spiritual exercises of a Vīra are known as Vīrācāra.

Vīracakra

One of the five *cakra* rituals mentioned in *Niruttaratantra*, X. In this *cakra* five Śaktis are to be worshipped in the forms of mother (Bhūmīndrakanyā), daughter (Rajakīsutā), sister (Svapacī), daughter-in-law (Kāpālī) and wife (Yoginī), Ibid., X.

Visarga

Alphabetical sign of double-dot which is symbolically regarded as the complementary Śakti of Vindu. It signifies both the *parā* and *aparā* aspects of Śakti. *Tantrāloka*, III. 120ff. It is also known as Kaulikī Śakti. Ibid., III. 143. It is Female Principle (*saḥ*) as complementary to the Male Principle (*haṃ*) *vindu*. *Prapañcasāra* quoted by Kālīcaraṇa in his com. on *Ṣaṭcakranirūpaṇa*, XLIII. See under *vindu*.

Viṣṇugranthi

A knot in the *anāhata-cakra* which the *kuṇḍalinī* has to pierce during its upward march.

Viṣṇukrāntā

A zone of Tantric culture extending from the Vindhyan range to Caṭṭala.

Viśuddha

The nerve-plexus above the *anāhata* in the neck region. It looks like a sixteen-petalled lotus. Its presiding deity is the goddess Śākinī. *Ṣaṭcakranirūpaṇa*, XXVIII-XXX.

Vyāpakanyāsa

A form of *Ṣoḍhānyāsa* in which the deity is to be felt over the whole body.

Yantra

Symbol of deity. It is generally in the form of diagram or geometrical pattern serving as chart for revealing the characteristics of the deity. For the efficacy of *yantra* in Tantric worship see *Gandharva*, V. 1; *Mātṛkābheda*, XII. 6ff. *Yantra* is variously interpreted as instrument, the body and abode of deity, amulet, mental faculties, pure consciousness, doctrinal intricacies, microcosm of the human body and so on. *Kulārṇava*, VI, XVII; *Gandharva*, V. 39-40; *Saundaryalaharī*, XI; *Śaktisaṅgama*, Tārā, XIII. 203; LI.2; *Puraścaryārṇava*, VI, pp. 518ff; *Tantrasāra*, pp. 312ff. *Yantras* are drawn or engraved on cloths, papers, leaves, stones and metals.

Yaugī Dīkṣā

Initiation in which the *guru* enters the body of his disciple in subtle form and imposes his own self on that of the latter. Rāghava on *Śāradā*, V. 127-40.

Yauvanollāsa

The third stage of spiritual exercise in which the aspirant becomes well-versed in the scriptures. Rāmeśvara's com. on *Parāśurāmakalpasūtra*, X. 68.

Yoga

Disciplining of the body for various purposes—physical, mental and spiritual.

Yoganāḍī

A nerve which carries the vital air.

Yoginī

A class of goddess, generally sixty-four in number, supposed to be the multiplication of the eight Mātṛkās. The term is also used to denote the female partner of the aspirant, the goddesses presiding over the nerve-plexuses from *mūlādhāra* to *sahasrāra*, different manifestations of Śakti, a Tantric school, a class of female ascetics imparting Tantric knowledge to the masses, medicine-women, women possessed by the goddess, and so on.

Yama

One of the eight limbs of Yoga.

Yoni

Female generative organ.

Yonimudrā

A posture of body in which the aspirant should fix his anus on the left heel, tongue on the palate and eyes on the tip of the nose. This posture helps to awaken the *kuṇḍalinī*. *Prāṇatoṣaṇī*, I. 10, pp. 70ff. For its symbolism see *Bhūtaśuddhitantravacana* quoted in *Śāradātilaka*, IX.

Yonipuṣpa

Black Aparājita flower as *maithuna* (sexual intercourse) symbol. *Paraśurāmakalpasūtra*, X. 63.

Yuganaddha

Male Principle in union with the Female Principle, a theme very often represented in Tantric Buddhist art. In Tibetan it is called *Yab-Yum*. It is the non-dual state of unity of Śūnyatā and Karuṇā. *Sādhanamālā*, II, p. 505.

Bibliography

Most of the works referred to in the notes are not quoted here. The original texts have been mentioned in the notes and in the glossary portion with reference to their respective editions. This bibligraphy is only a list of some secondary works on Tantra. For a detailed bibliography of the original texts and also of important secondary works readers are requested to see P.V. Kane's *History of Dharmaśāstra,* Vol. V. pt. II, Poona, 1962, App. to sec. VI, pp. 1140-51, M. Eliade's *Yoga, Immortality and Freedom,* New York, 1958, special notes, pp. 399-424, Bib. pp. 435-80 and A. Bharati's *The Tantric Tradition,* London, 1965, pp. 302-36. In case of abbreviations in regard to this section, the following may be noted:

ABORI	*Annals of the Bhandarkar Oriental Research Institute.*
IHQ	*Indian Historical Quarterly.*
JAOS	*Journal of American Oriental Society.*
JDL	*Journal of the Dept. of Letters.*
JASB	*Journal of the Asiatic Society of Bengal.*
JBORS	*Journal of Bihar and Orissa Research Society.*
JRAS	*Journal of the Royal Asiatic Society.*
MCB	*Melanges Chinois et Bouddhiques.*
ZDMG	*Zeitschrift der Deutschen Morgenlandischen Gesellschaft.*

Anand, M.R., *Kāmakālā: Some Notes on the Philosophical Basis of Hindu Erotic Sculpture,* New York, 1958; *Tantric Magic,* in Collaboration with A. Mookherjee, New Delhi, 1977.

Anuruddha, R.P., *Introduction to Lamaism,* Hoshiarpur, 1959.

Avalon, A. (J. Woodroffe), *Principles of Tantra,* rpt., Madras, 1955; *Hymns to Kālī,* 2nd. edn., Madras, 1953; *The Great Liberation,* 5th edn., Madras, 1952; *The Serpent Power,* rpt., Madras, 1958; *Shakti and Shakta,* rpt., Madras, 1956; *Tantrarāja Tantra,* Madras, 1952; *Garland of Letters,* 3rd edn., Madras, 1955.

Ayyangar, T.R.S., *Hathayogapradīpikā,* Eng. tr. Adyar, 1933.

Bagchi, P.C., *Studies in the Tantras,* Calcutta, 1939; *Kaulajñānanirṇaya,* Calcutta, 1934; Sandhyābhāṣā, *Visvabharati Quarterly,* 1924; 'Primitive Elements in Jainism', *JDL* V., 1921, 349-64; 'On some Tantric Texts studied in Ancient Kambuja', *IHQ*, V., 1928, 754-69; VI, 1930, 97-107,

Bagchi, S.G., *Eminent Śākta Centres in Eastern India*, Calcutta, 1980.

Balfour, H., 'The Life of an Aghorī Fakir', *Journal of the Anthropological Institute*, XXVI, 1897, 340-57.

Banerjee, J.N., *Development of Hindu Iconography*, Calcutta, 1956; *Pauranic and Tantric Religion*, Calcutta, 1966.

Banerjee, S.C., *Tantras in Bengal*, Calcutta, 1978; *A Brief History of Tantric Literature*, Calcutta, 1988.

Barrow, H.W., 'On Aghorīs and Aghorapanthīs', *Journal of the Anthropological Society of Bombay*, III, 1893, 197- 251.

Beane, W.C., *Myth, Cult and Symbols in Śākta Hinduism: A Study of the Indian Mother Goddess*, Leiden, 1977.

Bernard, T., *Haṭhayoga, Report of a Personal Experience*, New York, 1944, London, 1958.

Bayer, G., *The Cult of Tārā, Magic and Ritual in Tibet*, London, 1973.

Bharati, A., *The Ochre Robe*, London, 1961; *The Tantric Tradition*, London, 1965; 'Metaphysics of Tantrism' in *Quest*, XXV, 1962.

Bhattacharyya, B.T., *Introduction to Buddhist Esoterism*, London, 1932; *Indian Buddhist Iconography*, Calcutta, 1959; *Sādhanamālā*, GOS, CCVI, XLI, Baroda, 1925-8; *Niṣpannayogāvalī*, GOS, LXI, XCI, CIX, Baroda, 1949; *Śaktisaṅgama*, GOS, LXI, XCI, CIV, Baroda, 1932, 1941, 1947; *Two Vajrayāna Works*, GOS, XLIV, Baroda, 1929; *Guhyasamāja-tantra*, GOS, XLIV, Baroda, 1931; 'Glimpses of Vajrayāna', *Proc. and Trans. of the 3rd Oriental Conference*, 1924, Madras, 1925, 129-41; 'The Cult of Bhūtaḍāmara', *Proc. and Trans. of the 6th Oriental Conference*, 1930, Patna, 1933, 349-70; 'The date of Bauddha Gān O Dohā', *JBORS*, XIV, 1928, 341-57; 'A Peep into Vajrayāna', *ABORI*, X, 1930; 'The Home of Tantric Buddhism' in *B.C. Law Volume I*, Poona, 1945, 254-61; 'Origin and Development of Vajrayāna' in *IHQ*, III, 1927, 733-46.

Bhattacharyya, D., *The Mirror of the Sky: Songs from the Bauls of Bengal*, London, 1969.

Bhattacharyya, D.C., *Tantric Buddhist Iconographic Sources*, New Delhi, 1974; *Studies in Buddhist Iconography*, New Delhi, 1978.

Bhattacharyya, N.N., *History of Indian Cosmogonical Ideas*, New Delhi, 1971; *History of the Śākta Religion*, New Delhi, 1974; *History of Indian Erotic Literature*, New Delhi, 1975; *Ancient Indian Rituals and their Social Contents*, New Delhi, 1975; *The Indian Mother Goddess*, 2nd edn., New Delhi, 1977; *History of Researches on Indian Buddhism*, New Delhi, 1981.

Bhattacharyya, S., *Tantra Parichaya*, Santiniketan, B.S.1359.

Blofeld, J., *The Way of Power—A Practical Guide to the Tantric Mysticism of Tibet*, London, 1970.

Bose, D.N. and H.L. Haldar, *Tantras: Their Philosophy and Occult Secrets*, Calcutta, 1956.

Bose, M.M., 'An Introduction to the Study of the Post-Caitanya Sahajiya

Cult', *JDL*, XVI, 1927, 1-162; *Post-Caitanya Sahajiyā Cults of Bengal*, Calcutta, 1930.

Brauen, M., *Das Maṇḍala*, Köln, 1992.

Briggs, G.W., *Gorakhnath and the Kanphata Yogis*, Calcutta, 1938.

Bromage, B., *Tibetan Yoga*, London, 1959.

Brown, C.M., *God as Mother: A Feminine Theology in India—An Historical and Technological Study of the Brahmavaivarta Purāṇa*, Hertfort, 1974.

Brown, G.W., 'Prāṇa and Apāna' in *JAOS*, XXXIX, 1919, 104-12.

Careli, M.E., *Sekoddeśa-ṭīkā*, GOS, XC Baroda, 1941.

Chakravarti, C., *The Tantras: Studies on Their Religion and Literature*, Calcutta, 1963; 'Antiquity of Tantrism', *IHQ*, VI, 1930, 114-26; 'The Soma or Saumya Sect of the Saivas', *IHQ*, VIII, 1932, 221-3.

Chandra, L., *Maṇḍalas of the Tantrasamuccaya*, Delhi, 1969.

Chandra, P., 'The Kaula-Kāpālika Cult at Khajuraho', *Lalit Kalā*, 1-2, 1955-66, 98-107.

Chang, C.Y., 'An Introduction to Taoist Yoga', *Review of Religion*, XXI, New York, 1956, 131-48.

Chang, G.C.C., *Esoteric Teachings of the Tibetan Tantra*, New York, 1968.

Chatterjee, R.M., *Viviḍha Tantra Saṃgraha*, Calcutta, 1881-6.

Chattopadhyaya, D.P., *Lokāyata*, Delhi, 1950; ed. *Tārānatha's History of Buddhism* (trans. Lama Chima and Alaka Chattopadhyaya), Simla, 1970.

Chattopadhyaya, Alaka, *Atiśa and Tibet*, Calcutta, 1967; *Catalogue Of Tanjur and Kanjur*, Calcutta, 1972.

Chou-yi-liang, 'Tantrism in China', *Harvard Journal of Asiatic Studies*, VIII, 1945, 241-332.

Clark, W.E., *Two Lamaistic Pantheons*, 2 vols., Cambridge Mass., 1937.

Coburn, T., *The Devī Māhātmya: The Crystallization of the Goddess Tradition*, Delhi, 1985; *Encountering the Goddess: A Translation of the Devī Māhātmya and a Study of Its Interpretation*, Albeni, 1991.

Coomaraswamy, A.K., 'The Tantric Doctrine of Divine Biunity', *ABORI*, XIX, 1938, 173-83.

Cutnur, H., *A Short History of Sex Worship*, London, 1940.

Danielon, A., *Yoga: The Method of Reintegration*, London, 1949.

Das, H., *Tantrism: Cult of Yoginīs*, New Delhi, 1980.

Dasgupta, S.B., *An Introduction to Tantric Buddhism*, Calcutta, 1950; *Obscure Religions Cults*, Calcutta, 1946.

Dasgupta, S.N., 'A General Introduction to Tantric Philosophy', *Philosophical Essays*, Calcutta University, 1951; *Yoga as Philosophy in Relation to Other Systems of Indian Thought*, Calcutta, 1935; *Yoga as Philosophy and Religion*, London, 1924.

David-Neel, A., *With Mystics and Magicians in Tibet*, London, 1931.

De, S.K., 'The Buddhist Tantric Sanskrit Literature of Bengal', *New Indian Antiquary* I, 1938, 1-23.

Desai, D., *Erotic Sculptures of India: A Socio-Cultural Study*, New Delhi, 1975.

Diksitar, V.R.R., *The Lalitā Cult*, Madras University, 1942.

Douglas, N., *Tantrayoga*, New Delhi, 1975.

Dowman, K., *Masters of Mahāmudrā*, New York, 1985.

Durme, P.T. Van, 'Notes sur Lamaisme', *MCB*, I, 1931-2, 263-321.

Ehrenfels, O.R., *Mother-right in India*, Hyderabad, 1941.

Eliade, M., *Metallurgy, Magic and Alchemy*, Paris, 1938; *Le Yoga: Immortalite et Liberté*, Paris, 1954, Eng. trans, W.R. Trask. *Yoga: Immortality and Freedom*, Bollingen Series, New York, 1958; *Shamanism: Archaic Techniques on Ecstasy*, Princeton, 1968.

Evans-Wentz, W., *Tibet's Great Yogī Milerapa*, Oxford, 1928; *Tibetan Yoga and Secret Doctrines*, Oxford, 1935; *The Tibetan Book of the Dead*, London, 1935 (trans by Kazi Dawa Samdup).

Ewing, A.H., The Śāradatilaka Tantra, *JAOS*, VI, 23, 1902, 65-76.

Filliozat, J., *The Classical Doctrine of Indian Medicine* (trans. D.R. Chanana), Delhi, 1964; 'Les Origines d' une technique mystique indienna, Revue Philosophique', Paris, VI, 1946, 208-20.

Garrison, O.V., *Tantra: The Yoga of Sex*, New York, 1964

George, C.S., *The Caṇḍamahāroṣana Tantra*, New Heven, 1974.

Getty, A., *The Gods of Northern Buddhism*, Oxford, 1914.

Głasenapp, H.V., 'Tantrismus and Śaktismus', *Ostasiatesche Zeitschrift*, XII, N.S., Berlin, 1936, 120-33; 'Die Entestehung des Vajrayāna', *ZDMG* XC, 1936, 546-72.

Gordon, A.K., *The Iconography of Tibetan Lamaism*, New York, 1939.

Goudrian T. and S. Gupta, 'Hindu Tantric and Śākta Literature', Vol. II, fasc. 2 of *A History of Indian Literature*, ed. G. Gonda Wiesbaden, 1981.

Govinda, L.A., *Foundation of Tibetan Mysticism*, London, 1959.

Guenther, H.V., *The Jewel Ornament of Liberation*, London, 1959; *Yuganaddha: The Tantric View of Life*, 2nd edn., Varanasi, 1964; *The Life and Teachings of Naropa*, Oxford, 1963; 'The Concept of Mind in Buddhist Tantrism', *Journal of Oriental Studies*, Hongkong, July 1956.

Guha, A., 'Rasa Cult in the Caitanya Caritāmṛta', *Sir Asutosh Mukherjee Silver Jubilee Volume*, III, 1926-7, 368-88.

Hadamo, H., 'Human Existence in Tantric Buddhism', *Annual Reports of the Faculty of Arts and Letters*, Tohuku University, Sendai, 1958.

Hawley, J.S., and D. Wulf (eds), *The Divine Consort Rādhā and the Goddesses of India*, Berkeley, 1982.

Hazra, R.C., 'Influence of Tantra on the Tattvas of Raghunandana', *IHQ*, IX, 1933, 678-704.

Hopkins, E.W., 'Yoga Techniques in the Great Epic', *JAOS*, XXII, 1901, 333-79.

James, E.O., *The Cult of the Mother Goddess*, London, 1959.

Jhaveri, M.B., *Comparative and Critical Study of Mantrasastra*, Ahmedabad, 1944.

Jung, C.G., *Maṇḍala Symbolism*, trans. R.F.C. Hull, Princeton, 1972.

Kane, P.V., *History of Dharmaśāstra,* Vol. V, Poona, 1962.

Kaviraj, G.N., *Tantric Vāṅmaya men Śākta Dṛṣṭi,* Patna, 1963; *Tantra O Āgama Śastrer Digdarśan,* Calcutta, 1963.

Kinsley, D., *The Sword and the Flute: Dark Vision of the Terrible and Sublime in the Hindu Religious Tradition,* Berkeley, 1975; *Hindu Goddesses: Visions of the Divine Feminine,* Berkeley, 1986.

Leadbeath, C.W., *The Cakras,* Adyar, 1927, Madras, 1966, London, 1972.

Leonard, G.S., 'Notes on the Kanphata Yogis', *Ind. Ant.* VII, 298-300.

Levi, S., 'On a Tantric Fragment from Kucha', *IHQ,* XII, 1936, 197-214.

Li, An Che, 'Rñin-ma-pa: The Early form of Lamaism', *JRAS,* 1948, 143-63.

Lorenzen, D.N., *The Kāpālikas and Kālāmukhas,* New Delhi, 1972.

Mahendra, G.H., *Unfolding a Mandala: The Bhuddhist Cave Temple at Ellora,* Albeni, 1993.

Mallik, Kalyani, *Nath Sampradāyer Itihās,* Calcutta 1950.

Marr, G.S., *Sex in Religion: A Historical Survey,* London, 1936.

Mathan L. and C. Seely, *Grace and Mercy in Her Wild Hair: Selected Poems to the Mother Goddess* by Ramprasad Sen, Boulder, 1982.

Mitra, K.P., 'Magic and Miracle in Jaina Literature', *IHQ,* XV, 1939, 175-82.

Mitra, S.C., 'On the Cult of Gorakṣanātha in Eastern Bengal', *JDL,* XIV, 1927, 1-41; 'On the Cult of Gorakṣanātha in the District of Rangpur in Northern Bengal', *JASB,* XIV, 1927-8, 1-5.

Mookherjee, A., *Tantra Art,* Delhi, 1966; *Tantra Asana,* Basel, New York, 1971; *Yoga Art,* London, 1975; *The Tantric Way* (with M. Khanna), New York, 1977; *Kali, the Feminine Force,* London, 1988.

Mookherjee, R.K., *Rasajalanidhi or Ocean of Indian Chemistry and Alchemy,* 5 vols, Calcutta, 1926-38.

Nagaswami, R., *Tantric Cult of South India,* Delhi, 1982.

Needham, J., *Science and Civilization in China,* 2 vols., Cambridge, 1954-6.

Newmann, E., *The Great Mother,* New York, 1961

Olson, E. (ed), *The Book of the Goddess Past and Present: An Introduction to Her Religion,* New York, 1983.

Oman, J.C., *The Mystics, Ascetics and Saints of India,* London, 1913.

Pandit, M.P., *Light on the Tantra,* Madras, 1968; *Gems from the Tantra,* Madras, 1967; *Studies in the Tantra and the Veda,* Madras, 1963.

Panigrahi, K.C., 'Obscene Sculptures of Orissan Temples', *Proc. of the Indian Hist. Cong.,* VII, 94-7.

Patavardhan, R.V., 'Rasavidyā or Alchemy in Ancient India, *Proc. and Transc. of the 1st Oriental Conference 1919,* Poona, 1920.

Payne, E.A., *The Śāktas: An Introductionary and Comparative Study,* Calcutta, 1933.

Pott, P.H., *Yoga and Tantra,* Leiden, 1966.

Prester, J.J., *Cult of the Goddess: Social and Religious Change in a Hindu Temple,* New Delhi, 1980.

Preston J. (ed), *Mother Worship: Themes and Variations,* Chapel Hill, 1980.

Przylusky, J., 'Mudrā', Ind. Cult II, 1934, 715-19.
Rao, R.C., *Evolution of Maṇḍala in Temple Architecture,* Bangalore, 1900.
Rawson, P., *The Art of Tantra,* London, 1973.
Rele, V.G., *Mysterious Kulakuṇḍalinī,* Bombay, 1927.
Rendel, P., *Introduction to the Cakras,* Northern-ptonshire, 1974.
Rieker, H.U., *The Yoga of Light, Hathayogapradīpikā,* London, New York, 1972.
Roerich, G.N., *The Blue Annals,* 2 vols, Calcutta, 1949-53.
Sraswati, S.K., *Tantrayana Art Album,* Calcutta, 1979.
Sastri, D.R., 'The Lokāyatas and Kāpālikas', *IHQ,* VII, 1931, 152-7.
Sastri, H., *Origin and Cult of Tārā,* MASI, No. 20.
Sastri, H.P., *Advayavajrasaṃgraha,* GOS, XI, Baroda, 1927; *Bauddha Gān O Dohā,* Calcutta, 1916.
Sastri, M.R., *The Tantrasāra of Abhinavagupta,* Bombay, 1918.
Sastri, V.S., 'Sandhyābhāṣā', *IHQ,* IV, 1928, 287-96.
Saunders, E.D., *Mudrā,* London, 1966.
Shah, U.P., 'A Peep into the Early History of Tantra in Jaina Literature', *Bhāratakaumudī* II, Allahabad, 1947.
Sharma, S.R., *Tantric Mahāvijñāna,* Bareilly, 1970.
Tanaka, K., *Maṇḍala Iconology,* Tokyo, 1987.
Thomas, P., *Kāmakalā: Hindu Ritual of Love,* Bombay, 1960.
Tucci, G., 'Apropos the Legend of Naropa', *JRAS,* 1935, 677-88; 'Some Glosses upon the Guhyasamaja', *MCB,* III, 339-53, Brussels, 1934-5; *Tibetan Painted Scrolls,* Rome, 1949; *Theory and Practice of Mandala,* London, 1961; *Ratilīlā: An Interpretation of the Tantric Imagery of the Temples of Nepal,* Geneva, 1969.
Van, Kooij K.R., *Worship of the Goddess according to the Kālika Purāṇa,* Leiden, 1972.
Vira, R. and S. Taki, *A Dictionary of Secret Tantric Syllabic Code,* Lahore, 1938.
Waddell, L.A., 'Lamaism in Sikkim', in *Sikkim Gazetteer,* Calcutta, 1884, 241-392; *Buddhism of Tibet or Lamaism,* London, 1895; 'Dhāraṇī or Indian Buddhist Productive Spells', *Ind. Ant.* XLIII, 1914, 37ff; 'The Dhāraṇī Cult of Buddhism: Its Origin, Deified Literature and Images', *Ostasiatesche Zeitschrift* I, 1921, 155-95; 'The Indian Buddhist Cult of Avalokita and His Consort Tārā', *JRAS,* 1894, 51-89.
Wayman, A., *The Buddhist Tantras: Light on Indo-Tibetan Esotericism,* New York 1973; *Yoga of the Guhyasamāja Tantra,* New Delhi, 1977.
Zimmer, H., 'Zur Bedeutung des Indischen Tantra-yoga', *Eranos Jahrbuch* I, Zurich, 1933, 9-94.

Index